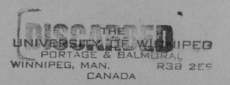

American Labor Policy

American Labor Policy

A Critical Appraisal of the National Labor Relations Act

Editor

CHARLES J. MORRIS

Professor of Law
Southern Methodist University

Based on the Proceedings of a Symposium:
The Labor Board At Mid-Century
Washington, D.C., October 2-5, 1985
presented by The School of Law,
Southern Methodist University

The Bureau of National Affairs, Inc., Washington, D.C.

Library of Congress Cataloging-in-Publication Data

American labor policy.

"Based on the proceedings of a symposium, 'The
Labor Board at mid-century,' October 2-5, 1985,
presented by the School of Law, Southern Methodist
University."
  Includes index.
  1. Labor laws and legislation — United States —
Congresses. 2. Trade-unions — Law and legislation —
United States — Congresses. 3. United States.
National Labor Relations Board — Congresses.
I. Morris, Charles J., 1923–   . II. Bureau of
National Affairs (Washington, D.C.)   III. Southern
Methodist University.   School of Law.
KF3369.A2A46   1987   344.73'01   86-32706
ISBN 0-87179-532-9   347.3041

Printed in the United States of America
International Standard Book Number: 0-87179-532-9

® GOU 302-1

FOR

Minnette,
Jeff, Jena,
Joe, Jack,
Jeremy, David,
Molly, Ilana,
Yussie, and Mandy

CONTRIBUTORS

INTRODUCTION BY:

John T. Dunlop. Lamont University Professor, Harvard University; author of many important works on labor economics and industrial relations, including the classic *Industrial Relations Systems* (1958); Secretary of Labor (1975-76); distinguished arbitrator and impartial chairman of numerous labor-management committees and governmental boards.

PRINCIPAL PAPERS BY:

F. Ray Marshall. Bernard Rapoport Centennial Professor of Economics and Public Affairs, LBJ School of Public Affairs, University of Texas; director, Center for the Study of Human Resources; author of many works in labor economics; distinguished arbitrator; Secretary of Labor (1977-80).

William P. Murphy. Paul B. Eaton Professor of Law, University of North Carolina; formerly professor at Universities of Mississippi and Missouri Schools of Law; author and editor of many works in labor law; well-known arbitrator; Southwestern Legal Foundation Distinguished Scholar in Residence; president, National Academy of Arbitrators.

Benjamin Aaron. Professor of Law, UCLA; author of numerous works on labor law and industrial relations, including many comparative studies; former Director, UCLA Institute of Industrial Relations; chairman and member of various Presidential boards and commissions; recipient of American Arbitration Association's Distinguished Service Award.

Theodore J. St. Antoine. James E. and Sarah A. Degan Professor of Law and former Dean, University of Michigan; author and editor of numerous articles and books on labor law; distinguished arbitrator and member of various boards and commissions; visiting professor at Duke and George Washington Universities.

Walter E. Oberer. Professor of Law and former Dean, University of Utah; formerly professor at University of Texas and Cornell University Schools of Law; author and editor of numerous articles and books on labor law; visiting professor at Columbia University and University of Arizona.

Charles J. Morris. Professor of Law, SMU; author and editor of many works on labor law, including *The Developing Labor Law* (1971, 1983); well-known arbitrator; served on various governmental boards and commissions, including Federal Service Impasses Panel; visiting professor, Monash University (Melbourne, Australia) and Cornell University.

RESPONSE PAPERS BY:

Howard Jenkins, Jr. Former Member, National Labor Relations Board; arbitrator and mediator; member Montgomery County, Maryland, Board of Appeals.

Peter G. Nash. Former General Counsel, National Labor Relations Board; senior partner, Ogletree, Deakins, Nash, Smoak & Stewart, Washington, D.C.; author and lecturer.

Elliot Bredhoff. General Counsel, Industrial Union Department, AFL-CIO; former Chairman, ABA Section of Labor and Employment Law; senior partner, Bredhoff & Kaiser, Washington, D.C.

Charles G. Bakaly, Jr. Former Chairman, ABA Section of Labor and Employment Law; senior partner, O'Melveny & Myers, Los Angeles, California; author and lecturer.

Edwin H. Benn. Arbitrator. Former partner, Asher, Pavalon, Gittler, Greenfield & Segall, Chicago, Illinois.

John H. Irving. Former General Counsel, National Labor Relations Board; partner, Kirkland & Ellis, Washington, D.C.; author and lecturer.

Kathy L. Krieger. Associate General Counsel, United Brotherhood of Carpenters, AFL-CIO.

William F. Joy. Former Chairman, ABA Section of Labor and Employment Law; senior partner, Morgan, Brown & Joy, Boston, Massachusetts.

Don A. Zimmerman. Former Member, National Labor Relations Board; Associate, Covington & Burling, Washington, D.C.

Eugene L. Hartwig. Former Chairman, ABA Section of Labor and Employment Law; Vice President and Associate General Counsel, General Motors Corporation.

Robert J. Connerton. Former Chairman, ABA Section of Labor and Employment Law; General Counsel, Laborers International Union, AFL-CIO; senior partner, Connerton, Bernstein & Katz, Washington, D.C.

Peter D. Walther. Former Member, National Labor Relations Board; partner, Drinker Biddle & Reath, Philadelphia, Pennsylvania.

Timothy P. O'Reilly. Partner, Morgan, Lewis & Bockius, Philadelphia, Pennsylvania.

Bruce H. Simon. General Counsel, National Association of Letter Carriers, AFL-CIO; senior partner, Cohen, Weiss & Simon, New York, New York.

John H. Fanning. Former Chairman and Member, National Labor Relations Board; of counsel, Hinckley, Allen, Tobin & Silverstein; Providence, Rhode Island.

Rosemary M. Collyer. General Counsel, National Labor Relations Board; former chairperson, National Mine Safety and Health Review Commission.

Laurence Gold. General Counsel, American Federation of Labor and Congress of Industrial Organizations.

Andrea S. Christensen. Partner, Kaye, Scholer, Fierman, Hays & Handler, New York, New York; author and lecturer.

COMMENTARY BY:

David Lewin. Professor, Graduate School of Business, Columbia University; author; mediator.

Reginald H. Alleyne, Jr. Professor, School of Law, UCLA; labor arbitrator.

Eleanor Holmes Norton. Professor, School of Law, Georgetown University; former chairperson, Equal Employment Opportunity Commission.

Carin A. Clauss. Assistant Professor, Law School, University of Wisconsin; former Solicitor of Labor.

Thomas C. Kohler. Assistant Professor, School of Law, Boston College.

Robert J. Rabin. Professor, School of Law, Syracuse University; author and labor arbitrator.

EPILOGUE BY:

Stephen I. Schlossberg. Deputy Under Secretary of Labor for Labor-Management Relations and Cooperative Programs; former General Counsel, United Automobile Workers; author and lecturer.

FOREWORD

This book represents more than a mere collection of papers on various aspects of the Wagner Act and its history since the early New Deal years. Although written by a variety of distinguished professionals, the book nevertheless makes a very important single contribution to the record of development of a critical period in the unfolding of the American experiment. The Wagner Act and the institutions it created can teach us a lot about the meaning of democracy in shifting economic and social conditions. And while the NLRB continues to be a controversial institution, its very controversy may well be its highest compliment. In drawing much of the fire and rhetoric of labor and management, the Board and its legal regime have allowed the American economy to mature relatively peacefully to the point that it has in this "post-industrial" era. At the same time, it is possible that the Board will not be the central feature of the next 50 years in American industrial relations. New trends in high technology and services industry suggest whole new approaches to the effective interaction of capital with labor in a productive economy. The recent settlement on a grand scale between the United Automobile Workers and General Motors which produced the Saturn Corporation may provide powerful incentives for new approaches. There are other features of today's industrial relations which the Wagner Act and its various amendments did not adequately foretell, for instance, the corporate provision of day care centers for employee's children and similar social innovations. This kind of trend suggests that labor and management have much more in common than they saw themselves as having in the formative years of the NLRB era. At the same time, as some of the papers demonstrate, attitudes of organizations on both sides die hard, and some of these become obstacles to further innovation and principled experimentation.

Even the nomenclature of "industrial relations" is no longer a very apt one for the 1980s in what seems to lie ahead for the American economy. Fewer individual employees think of themselves as part of a movement dominated by the term "labor." The gradual "gentrification" of workers is itself a significant social development with political and legal implications.

These and other themes are well developed, and opportunities for comparisons with other legal cultures are presented. The American experience with labor policy seems unique and if not emulated, at least worthy of examination by other countries' policy makers.

The collaboration of professionals in conceiving and producing this notable work is itself worthy of commendation. It represents the strongest tradition of academic scholarship blended with accounts of direct experience by those charged with active participation in the life of the institutions themselves under scrutiny. It is a work whose authority has been enhanced by careful editing and rigorous attention to details of structure, theme, and expression. The book will provide significant understanding as well as promote discussion of future possibilities to students and professionals of law, business, economics, management, and government for years to come.

KENNETH L. PENEGAR
Dean and Professor of Law
School of Law
Southern Methodist University

PREFACE

American industrial relations has entered a transitional stage, and coincidental with the economy's changing focus from heavy and labor intensive manufacturing to its present emphasis on high technology and service industry, the American labor movement has steadily declined both in members and influence. Enterprises have become sharply divided into union and nonunion sectors, with the nonunion sectors far outnumbering the remnant strongholds of collective bargaining. Thus, on the occasion of the completion of half a century of experience under the National Labor Relations Act, at a time when the National Labor Relations Board is the object of vigorous controversy—certainly not a novel condition for that Agency—and at a time when many unions have come to view the Board as either an obstacle to, or else irrelevant to, their normal objectives, it seemed appropriate to attempt an in-depth examination of the relationship between federal regulatory labor legislation and American labor policy. Because the NLRA and the NLRB represent the primary governmental expression of national labor policy, an examination of the NLRA and its enforcement becomes critical to any meaningful consideration of policy. Accordingly, answers were sought to the questions: What is the national labor policy? How successful have the NLRB and the courts been in the implementation of that policy? And what interpretive, administrative, or legislative changes in direction or means, if any, are needed?

Congress expressed the nation's labor policy in the enactment of the Wagner Act in 1935 and reaffirmed it, with limitations, in the Taft-Hartley amendments of 1949 and the Landrum-Griffin changes of 1959. Although there may be room for wide debate as to the extent of the influence which labor legislation has on shaping the contours of a nation's industrial relations system, it cannot be denied that the legislative impact in the United States has been substantial. Consequently, in view of the current state of the industrial nation, a reassessment of the role of the statutory centerpiece of the American labor relations system seemed to be in order.

Such was the impetus for the organization of the "Labor Board at Mid-Century" conference, which was held in Washington, D.C., in October of the 50th anniversary year of the passage of the National Labor Relations Act. The purpose of that conference was to gather a knowledgeable and representative group of labor relations scholars and practitioners, including two former Secretaries of Labor, several former NLRB Members and General Counsels and the present General Counsel, and several prominent union and management attorneys, and direct their attention to the critical issues posed by the Labor Board's decisional authority and its procedural and remedial practices. The resulting responses, comprising the contents of the Washington conference and this volume, shed considerable light on the subject of American labor law and the record of its enforcement. These consistently thoughtful descriptions of the general state of the law and the role of the Board and the courts in the administration of that law, with analyses of important substantive and procedural issues, provide a valuable portrayal of the problems that demand attention and suggest some of the means which might be utilized to achieve a more rational labor relations system.

The papers abound with questions and a variety of answers. It is not surprising that there is much diversity in the viewpoints and proposals expressed. But there is also much agreement as to the identification of many of the problems and suggested remedies. More significantly, however, the authors have pinpointed certain fundamental questions. And at this stage in time the questions may be more important than the answers, for if these papers become part of a continuing dialogue on the subject of what American labor policy ought to be and on what the most feasible means of achieving that policy should be, then, at least in the opinion of the conference organizer, the editor of this volume, these efforts will have achieved their intended purpose.

An Overview of the Papers

This book is a dialogue among 32 authors. It is divided into eight parts: An introduction, six chapters, and an epilogue. Each chapter contains a principal paper, which is followed by three response papers, representing a range of viewpoints, and then by a commentary. The introduction examines the legal framework of industrial relations and the economic future of the United States. Chapter 1 addresses the impact of the National Labor Relations Act on employment, society, and the national economy; Chapter 2 examines the subject of establishment and disestablishment of union representation; Chapter 3 treats the rights of individual employees under the Act; Chapter 4 examines the collective bargaining process; Chapter 5 discusses the regulation of union economic power; and Chapter 6 examines Board procedures, remedies, and the enforcement process. The dialogue concludes with an epilogue which comments on the balance in labor-management relations and how it might be tipped.

John Dunlop's Introduction, *The Legal Framework of Industrial Relations and the Economic Future of the United States*, begins the dialogue with a scathing indictment of the statute itself. He charges that we have inherited a legal framework for industrial relations that is destructive of our economic future. He views the system as excessively litigious and one that "creates endless delays and uncertainty, that makes it easier to withdraw from employer associations and unions, [it is a system] that changes the rules of industrial relations with shifting political weather rather than by consensus or objective developments in markets or technology." He concludes that such a framework is inadequate for the 1990s. But unlike many of the other contributors, Dunlop does not distinguish between the shortcomings of the statute itself and its administration. Nevertheless, his concentration on the results of the system serves to emphasize the end products of the statute's administration, leaving to others the refinement of specific legal means which might be employed to effect the change in direction which so many of the other authors also believe is needed.

Dunlop envisions a greater opportunity for industrial conflict and a lesser role for the Labor Board. But he argues that major elements of redesign of the system must come from discussion and consensus among labor and management, from the principals, not from their lawyers. And this process should be followed by public and legislative review. He thus urges labor and management to strive toward seeking a consensus as to the proper direction of the system. His own proposals for redesign include the following: (1) "Members of administrative agencies should only be appointed who command substantial support from a wide spectrum of labor and management organizations." (2) "Mediation should be introduced into the resolution of more issues, particularly such complex issues as work preservation, plant closures, and technological change." He specifically proposes a special mediation staff working at all levels of the Board's operations. (3) Enhance the "scope and role of arbitration, particularly during the life of a collective agreement." (4) "Provide more role for conflict, strikes, and lockouts." (5) Limit the level of judicial review to a single court beyond the Board, with only constitutional questions going to the Supreme Court. (6) Provide for "prompt determination" of representation questions and reduce the regulation of the election process. "The discharge for union activity should be dealt with by severe and effective penalties." (7) "Deregulate the collective bargaining process in subjects of bargaining and procedures where refusal to bargain is tantamount to nonrecognition." (8) "Recognize the realities of the characteristics of particular sectors such as maritime, construction, mining, and lumbering, and avoid the industrial plant stereotype."

Professor Dunlop says that we took the "wrong road in 1935," but he does not find it too late to take another road for the 1990s.

In *Chapter 1*, Ray Marshall discusses *The Act's Impact on Employment, Society, and the National Economy*. He finds essentially the same defects as Dunlop. He examines the American system of industrial relations within a comparative international framework and notes that the unique features of the American system are "exclusive representation," "decentralized bargaining," a condition in which "American employers are more hostile to unions than their counterparts in other major industrial nations," the existence of an "authoritarian management system," and the "nonsocialist political orientation" of our labor movement.

He attributes to collective bargaining the achievement of middle class income status for most union members; but the inflationary biases characteristic of United States labor relations have meant that when American industry was confronted by international competition, it became increasingly difficult to insulate wages from competition. He compares our labor relations to Japan's more flexible system with its consensus-based economic policy. He analyzes the economic facts which have shaped American industrial relations; and while deploring what has happened to the system, he concludes that the basic problem has been the implementation of national labor policy rather than its underlying philosophy.

Marshall is especially critical of the performance of the Reagan Board, documenting the substantially increased percentage of unfair labor practice cases which that Board has decided in favor of employers.

Like Dunlop, Marshall believes there should be a labor-management consensus. His specific recommendations for improving the present system are the following: (1) Attempt to build a new consensus about the desirability of collective bargaining and workers' rights to organize and bargain collectively. (2) Insulate the Board more effectively from the political process, or else establish new machinery to resolve representation issues and prevent prohibited conduct by unions and employers. (3) In order to achieve the necessary acceptance of a more effective national labor policy, one that would be compatible with the requirements of "an international information world," certain industrial relations professionals should take the lead. These would be professionals "who understand the value of the industrial relations system to a free society as well as the nature and importance of human resource management, dispute management, and consensus building."

Commenting on the Marshall paper, Howard Jenkins suggests some procedural changes which he feels would improve the Board's performance: Allow the Board to employ economists; provide that a member whose term has expired shall remain in office until a successor is appointed; permit the Board to hire a general staff of attorneys rather than require that each member maintain an independent legal staff; provide for greater finality of administrative law judges' decisions, with discretionary review by the Board; obtain congressional clarification of the relative roles of the General Counsel and the Board in the enforcement area.

Peter Nash also comments on the Marshall paper. He defends the record of the Reagan Board and particularly clarifies what the Board did in *Milwaukee Spring II*[1]. He agrees that the Board as an institution is equal to the task before it, but disagrees with the criticism which charges that Board remedies are ineffective

---

[1]Milwaukee Spring Div. of Ill. Coil Spring Co., 268 NLRB 601, 115 LRRM 1065 (1984).

and "not sufficiently tough or punitive" to require employers to obey the law, for he asserts that it is not the primary purpose and function of the Act to beat unions and employers over the head when they commit unfair labor practices but, rather, to guide the parties into a room where they may freely bargain to an agreement. "Congress structured the Act in a way best designed to make that bargaining work effectively."

Elliot Bredhoff also comments on the Marshall paper. Although he lists various Board activities which he finds defective, he generally agrees that the Act is satisfactory, though he feels it is presently administered unfairly toward unions. He suggests several amendments, however, which he believes would be in order.

David Lewin closes Chapter 1 with a review of Marshall's paper and the responses which it evoked. He notes an implicit assumption underlying the Act, "namely, that U.S. unionism is a narrow wage-oriented movement that eschews or at least should not be encouraged to pursue an enlarged role in enterprise management." He also stresses that economic forces are more fundamental than a regulatory statute, such as the NLRA, in the shaping of industrial relations. And he is not particularly disturbed by the Board's political swings, for in his view "the Board should be expected to be political."

In Chapter 2, William Murphy addresses the subject of *Establishment and Disestablishment of Union Representation*, i.e., the legal mechanisms whereby unions are certified or decertified and recognized or denied recognition as employee bargaining agents. He thoroughly reviews developments in the law and reaches some conclusions which he reports with sadness if not resignation.

First, he decries the Board's limited coverage over classifications of employees. And he finds the process of determining appropriate bargaining units to be basically "manipulative." His solution to the unit question is rule making, which he says could reduce delay in the election process as well as the frequency of post-election refusal-to-bargain violations by employers to obtain judicial review of the Board's unit determinations. He views the concept of "laboratory conditions [as] artificial, fictional, and inconsistent with the robust and free-wheeling rhetoric we have long expected and tolerated in labor disputes in this country." He would confine the extent of the Board's intrusion in the election campaign to the line drawn by Congress between coercive and noncoercive speech.

He then comments on a perceived unfairness in the campaign process whereby the law permits an employer to impose on its employees campaign limits by which the employer itself is not bound. He therefore recommends that unions be allowed "controlled access" to the employer's premises during the campaign, which "could be dealt with under the Board's Section 9 power to make time, place, and manner regulations."

Murphy believes that the problem of delay in the election process could be improved only modestly by the Board's tightening of procedures and that meaningful reform must come from legislative changes, especially those drawn from the Canadian experience, which would allow "instant elections" and certifications based on a sufficient showing of authorization cards.

Murphy opines that for many years there has been no labor policy of the United States. Rather, there have been many different policies dealing with discrete problem areas emanating from different sources—legislative, executive, judicial, and private as well as governmental. These policies are administered by a number of different departments, boards, commissions, and services, which are frequently inconsistent and in conflict with each other. He suggests that perhaps what we need is a Labor Code which "might give us more clarity of purpose and consistency of achievement than we now have. But only Congress can bring this to pass. Until it happens, the Board still has a function to perform."

Professor Murphy is essentially pessimistic. He says that it is "a sad irony that the statute which in its early years encouraged the growth of unionism has increasingly become a promise to the ear broken to the hope and is today viewed in many respects as a hollow mockery." Although his criticism of the administration of the Act spans the half century of the statute's history and is leveled at both the Board and the courts over those years, his expression of greatest despair is saved for the Reagan Board. He observes that "[i]t is a sad irony that the statute passed to promote unionism and collective bargaining is today consciously turned against itself to defeat the statutory objectives by the most blatantly antiunion Board in history."

Charles Bakaly, in his comments, objects to Professor Murphy's characterization of the current Board as "the most blatantly antiunion Board in history" and to his charge that it is failing to carry out its obligations under the Act. Although Bakaly does not suggest any other Board for that antiunion title, he does provide details regarding the Board's statutory mandate, asserting "that the current Board, within the bounds prescribed by Congress, has done as much or more than any of its predecessors to fulfill [that] mandate." He also discusses several cases to illustrate his thesis.

Bakaly views rule making as an unwise approach to unit determination, foreseeing that it would result in "an unfortunate standardization of management organization." He would leave the area of unit determination to ad hoc treatment but would temper it with the use of "certain guiding principles." It would seem that by another name these could be called "rules."

He would not attribute to the Board's rulings the responsibility for the decline in union membership or election victories. Rather, he sees that decline as caused by changes in the work force, the absence of depression or military experience, more affluence among workers and their more independent attitudes, and also changes affecting employers such as the offering of good wages and benefits.

Bakaly asserts that the Board's job is to protect the individual employee's right to engage in or refrain from engaging in collective action, and in his view the Board has done an admirable job of "returning the law to normalcy and away from the undisguised prounion position of the late 1970s." He says the Reagan Board is not "blatantly antiunion" but rather is "proemployee choice and noninterventionist." He says that so long as the Board continues in a moderate stance, it will continue to function as "an effective force in protecting employee rights and maintaining labor peace in the private sector. Nevertheless, as the proportion of union representation in the private sector continues to decline the Board will become less of a force in American society."

Notwithstanding his disagreement with much of Murphy's appraisal of the Board's performance, Bakaly joins with him and other contributors in hailing the benefits of a more cooperative approach between unions and employers. However, he views the prospect of a less adversarial relationship as one which will not necessarily include a union relationship. He states: "It is time for unions to stop attempting to make the Board the scapegoat for their own inadequacies and to concentrate on new methods of cooperation with industry for the good of all. The great challenge of future Boards will be to accommodate new concepts of industrial relations. We can only hope that Congress and the Board will encourage employers and unions to move beyond the mindset of the 1930s, that collective bargaining is the only solution to employee relations, and allow American business to develop new and less adversarial relationships that will result in a more productive and prosperous economy."

Edwin Benn also responds to the Murphy paper. He asks the tough question: Is the Board still a viable force after 50 years of regulating the representation process in the private sector? He demonstrates by statistical data gleaned from NLRB Annual Reports that a declining and now only a minuscule percentage of the private sector work force has actually been utilizing Board representing procedures, from which he concludes that the Board's processes may no longer be viable in a meaningful way. He asks these further questions concerning the Board's viability: Is an agency viable when throughout its history it has continually changed its doctrines? Is an agency viable when its procedures provide for immense delay? Is the Board viable after 50 years when its decisions have led unions to take action that will only lead to industrial strife?

Benn concludes that the Board's decisions against unions will inevitably lead to increased industrial strife, as unions seek to protect what they have and seek alternative means to achieve their objectives.

John Irving provides another opposing view to the Murphy paper. He treats Murphy's charge that the present Board is the "most blatantly antiunion Board in history" as a nonsequitur and faults Murphy for failing to document that charge. He generally disagrees with most of Murphy's conclusions. Although Irving staunchly defends the Reagan Board, he also asserts that "more attention should be devoted to making the present system work," thus implying that it may not be working, or at least that it may not be working well. He rejects as unbalanced or lacking in substance the various legislative proposals which Murphy suggests for improving the state of American industrial relations.

Reginald Alleyne closes Chapter 2 with a review of the papers and observes that the statute is "highly elastic," and that "the debate illustrates the wide range of respectable views the NLRA is able to absorb."

In Chapter 3, Benjamin Aaron considers the *Rights of Individual Employees Under the Act.* He presents a detailed exposition of the state of the law and a critical examination of how pertinent aspects of the law have developed. He identifies and discusses perceived defects in the interpretation and application of certain statutory provisions and doctrines and offers an insightful analysis of some of the Act's key features.

One such feature is the concept of majority rule. He tells us that the majority rule principle, embodied in Section 9(a), "was adopted primarily to prevent the continued efforts by employers or electoral minorities to fractionize workers within a plant or enterprise, thereby preventing them from creating, in a single, exclusive bargaining representative, an effective countervailing bargaining power to that of their employer." He explains that had employees been permitted to bargain individually or in groups over wages, hours, and working conditions, or to adjust grievances involving the interpretation or application of a collective agreement without the knowledge and consent of the exclusive bargaining representative, the venture as a whole would almost certainly have become clogged and frustrated. He notes that the same would have been true if minority unions had been allowed to bargain or adjust grievances for bargaining-unit employees.

On the subject of the union's duty of fair representation (DFR), he concludes that the duty has often proved illusory. He faults the courts for much confusion and disarray, charging that "some courts have broadened the unions' duty beyond reasonable or practicable limits; moreover, unions have been made increasingly vulnerable to substantial damages, while employers in some instances have been shielded from the normal consequences of their own wrongdoing." He cites the *Bowen*[2] case as an example of the Supreme Court apportioning the liability of the union and the employer in a "grotesque fashion."

Regarding the Board's *Rossmore House*[3] rule, which widely permits employer interrogation of employees about their union sentiments subject only to a case-by-case determination of whether coercion has in fact occurred, he raises a simple objection: "The trouble with *Rossmore* . . . is that the Board has failed to demonstrate why any interrogation is necessary."

---

[2]Bowen v. United States Postal Serv., 459 US 212, 112 LRRM 2281 (1983).
[3]269 NLRB 1176, 116 LRRM 1025 (1984), *enforced sub nom.* Hotel & Restaurant Employees Local 11 v. NLRB, 760 F2d 1006, 119 LRRM 2624 (CA 9, 1985).

Aaron sees the Supreme Court's *Pattern Makers*[4] decision, prohibiting union restrictions on withdrawal from union membership during a strike, as an impairment of the union's statutory right to strike. He finds the Court's emphasis on individual rights at the expense of group rights, which the Act was designed to protect, to be misplaced. He sharply distinguishes between rights of union members guaranteed by the Labor-Management Reporting and Disclosure Act (LMRDA), for which he advocates a liberal interpretation, and individual rights guaranteed by the NLRA; he emphasizes that the latter statute was primarily intended to protect group rights. He explains that when it comes to pursuing bargaining objectives and administering collective agreements, subject to principles of due process and fair representation, the claims of individuals must be subordinate to those of the group. He states: "Although we all know of some instances in which a tyranny of a union has proved to be as bad or worse than that of an employer, I still believe that the more enduring danger to individual employee rights lies in Board and court decisions in cases like *Pattern Makers* that seriously undermine a union's ability to maintain a united front against an employer during an industrial dispute."

Responding to Aaron's paper, Kathy Krieger indicates her agreement with his conclusion that the Board and the federal courts "have applied the Act inconsistently with respect to individual workers." It is her observation that "the Board vigorously defends the rights of individual employees against perceived infringement by labor organizations [but] displays little concern for shielding [them] from coercion and retaliation by their employers." She illustrates the point with this comment on the Board's *Meyers'*[5] decision: "The activist employee who successfully enforces legal rights in the workplace demonstrates how to stand up to management, raises fellow employees' consciousness of their own power, and enhances the climate for organizing; furthermore, she obviously makes a good prospect for leadership. *Meyers* permits the employer to weed out the employee 'troublemaker' and stifle potential organizing activity at its inception."

---

[4]Pattern Makers League v. NLRB (Rockford-Beloit Pattern Jobbers), 473 US__, 119 LRRM 2928 (1985).

[5]Meyers Indus., 268 NLRB 493, 115 LRRM 1025 (1984), *remanded sub nom.* Prill v. NLRB, 755 F2d 941, 118 LRRM 2649 (CA DC, 1985). On remand, the Board, as Professor Aaron had predicted, reaffirmed its rulings, this time with supporting rationale. 281 NLRB No. 118, 123 LRRM 1137 (1986).

Krieger sums up her reading of the target decisions with the conclusion that they reveal a profound hostility and distrust toward collective self-governance by workers. She finds such bias easily discernable in the union discipline cases, but less obvious though equally strong in the Section 8(a)(1) decisions: "Those cases, in effect tell us that employees need statutory protection and individual avenues for enforcing their interests only where they are already represented by a union."

William Joy also responds to Professor Aaron's paper, calling it "an incisive, in-depth review." He is not totally in agreement with Aaron's conclusions, however, particularly as to such cases as *Bowen* and *Pattern Makers*. He also disagrees on *Rossmore*, finding that the present state of the law on employer interrogation is appropriate and that it protects employee rights. However, he does not provide an answer to Aaron's implicit question: Why does the employer even need to inquire about an employee's union sentiments?

Don Zimmerman also responds to Aaron. He stresses that the original statute was modeled on a premise of conflict rather than cooperation. He is particularly critical of the Board's policy on deferral to arbitration, arguing that such policy "denies individuals the statutory forum for adjudication of unfair labor practice issues, and instead substitutes the almost unreviewable discretion of an arbitrator under private resolution procedures established pursuant to contract. [This] is another example [of how] the Board has focused on the statutory purpose of furthering collective bargaining in a way that derogates individual rights that would otherwise be protected and safeguarded by the Act."

Zimmerman finds neither the statute nor the Board adequate for the task assigned by Congress. He pessimistically reports: "The framers of the [Act] left it to the Board to interpret the statute, to fill in the many gaps, and to reconcile the competing rights and obligations that were established in conflict with each other. After 50 years, I believe most observers would have to concede that the task was more than the Board has been able to handle effectively. One might think that Congress would intervene to save the Board from any continuing misery. The political outlook for that prospect, however, remains as bleak as ever."

Eleanor Holmes Norton's commentary closes the chapter by contrasting the tension between the Act's protection of individual rights for workers and its support for collective prerogative of unions. She makes a reasoned plea for utilization of a different and more principled mode of legal analysis for the interpretation of the Act. She views such an approach as preferable to returning to Congress for legislative guidance. She cites Member Dennis' government deregulation philosophy as an example of a principled approach.

The approach which she finds most suitable, however, is one which she derives from an original theme of the Wagner Act, which was also reinforced by Taft-Hartley: to wit, the theme of labor peace. She finds this "peace principle" consistently dominant under both statutes.

Applying her analysis to the Supreme Court's *Bowen* decision, she concludes that the Court totally ignored the principled need to address the formation of the grievance process. In fact, she accuses the Court of "trivializing the process" by encouraging the filing and processing of marginal arbitration cases, thus putting the grievance and arbitration machinery at risk.

Norton says that she does not regret Board and judicial concern for individual rights, but she does regret the absence of a systematic search for a principled analysis. She observes: "Diverse trends outside of the law—including structural economic change that have encouraged management hostility to labor and a national climate that is particularly sensitive to individual rights—have raised questions about the accommodation between individual and group concerns in the Act." She would look to the Board and the courts, rather than to Congress, for the most likely actors to effect a change: "The most realistic approach appears to be a studied attempt by the interpreters of the Act to find the proper balance between individual and group rights. To do this," she says, "the strong and explicit statutory purposes, among them labor peace, should be plumbed. While underlying statutory policies do not guarantee that a more satisfactory balance will be found, they hold more promise than the uncharted present course of the courts and the Board."

In Chapter 4, Theodore St. Antoine addresses *The Collective Bargaining Process*. He asks these questions: Why has the collective bargaining process apparently lost so much appeal? And does it still hold hope for the future? He examines the "how" of bargaining—the "good faith" requirement, and the "what" of bargaining—the subjects of bargaining.

Notwithstanding a six-fold increase in illegal employer conduct during organizing drives since the mid-1950s, he says that he remains optimistic that "a properly constructed and properly enforced law can reclaim the salutary role it played in the balmier labor relations climate of the 1950s and 1960s."

Basic to St. Antoine's thesis is a conviction that the *Borg-Warner*[6] approach was wrong. He suggests two other approaches that might have made more sense: (1) "[T]he most straightforward solution would have been the obliteration of the whole mandatory-permissive distinction." (2) "A second, more modest approach would also have allowed the employer in *Borg-Warner* to prevail. That was the position adopted by Justice Harlan and three other Justices, who would have retained the mandatory-permissive distinction, but with a difference. Either party would still be required to bargain to impasse about mandatory subjects but not about permissive subjects, as is the case under existing law." St. Antoine notes that under the Harlan formulation, either party could persist in pursuing any lawful demand, regardless of how the Board might categorize it, and could refuse to contract absent agreement on that item. "Justice Harlan read Section 8(d) of the NLRA to mean exactly what it says, and only that: A party is obligated to bargain about wages, hours, and other employment terms, but an insistence on bargaining about more is not the equivalent of a refusal to bargain about a mandatory subject."

St. Antoine discusses the *First National Maintenance*[7] "balancing test" and the narrow construction which the Reagan Board gave that test in *Otis Elevator Co.*,[8] reminding us that the language of Section 8(d) contains the broad and infinitely expansible phrase "other terms and conditions of employment" rather than the narrower concept of "working conditions." He concedes that "[i]mposing a duty to bargain about managerial decisions such as plant removals, technological innovation, and subcontracting or 'outsourcing' would obviously delay transactions, reduce business adaptability, and perhaps interfere with the confidentiality of negotiations with third parties," and that in some instances bargaining would be doomed in advance as a futile exercise. Nonetheless, he contends, "the closer we move toward recognizing that employees may have something akin to a property interest in their jobs, the more evident it may become

---

[6]NLRB v. Wooster Div. of Borg-Warner Corp., 356 US 342, 42 LRRM 2034 (1958).
[7]First Nat'l Maintenance Corp. v. NLRB, 452 US 666, 107 LRRM 2705 (1981).
[8]269 NLRB 891, 115 LRRM 1281 (1984).

that not even the employer's legitimate regard for profit-making or the public's justified concern for a productive economy should totally override the workers' claim to a voice in the decisions of ongoing enterprises that will directly affect their future employment opportunities. A moral value is arguably at stake in determining whether employees may be treated as pawns in management decisions."

St. Antoine underscores the irony in the fact that the American labor movement is the most conservative and least ideological of Western labor movements. It is "traditionally committed to the capitalistic system and to the principle that management should have the primary responsibility for managing. Yet employers will pay millions of dollars to experts in 'union avoidance' in order to maintain their nonunion status." He observes "that such aversion to unionism can hardly be supported by a dispassionate analysis of the actual impact of collective bargaining in this country [for] collective bargaining has promoted both industrial peace and broader worker participation in the governance of the shop, while simultaneously stimulating higher productivity and causing only modest dislocations in the economy generally."

St. Antoine also believes that the full potential of collective bargaining has not yet been tapped. He states: "Because law serves such an important legitimating function in our society, collective bargaining may have been seriously undermined when the courts began to cut back the scope of mandatory bargaining to exclude managerial decisions even though they might have a substantial effect on employees' job security. Far better, it seems to me, would have been an open-ended mandate that lets the parties themselves decide what their vital interests are. The only exclusions from compulsory bargaining that I would readily admit are matters going to the very existence or identity of the negotiating parties, such as the membership of a corporation's board of directors, and perhaps the integrity of their internal structure and procedures." And he argues that participatory programs, which he deems to be the direction which industrial relations will take in the future, ought not to be classified as merely "permissive" subjects of bargaining.

St. Antoine sees the determination of such subject matter as being critical not only to the direction of the statute but also to the direction of our society: "As the underlying premise of the Wagner Act proclaims, that collective action on the part of the employees best ensures 'equality of bargaining power' with employers, then in setting the metes and bounds of mandatory negotiations we are engaged in far more than a pragmatic exercise in industrial relations policy. We are performing a task of profound moral consequence. We may be, in substantial effect, determining the capacity of American workers for fullest self-realization—for finding out, in this one life they have to live, who they really are."

Responding to Professor St. Antoine, Eugene Hartwig provides a prime illustration of that new direction which collective bargaining can take and has apparently already taken in the General Motors–United Automobile Workers Saturn Agreement. Hartwig pays his respects to the adversarial relationship which historically existed between labor and management, noting that such a relationship was reinforced by Board and Court decisions. But he concentrates his paper on the new relationship exemplified by the Saturn project. He first notes that "[t]he UAW's role in the development of Saturn is literally without precedent. Never before has a union been involved to this extent in designing work stations, business and people systems, and in the selection of the site where its members will be asked to work and relocate their families. Saturn would not and could not exist without the participation of the UAW." Here then is collective bargaining at its most sophisticated level: "It is a type of collective bargaining which results in employees, through the instrumentality of their union, becoming participants in the enterprise rather than simply contributing their labor to the production process.[9]

Robert Connerton also responds to Professor St. Antoine. In his view, recent Board cases bode ill for the very foundations of collective bargaining, and he questions whether the Board "continues to serve the purposes for which it was originally chartered." He says that "the picture at mid-century is that the NLRA is no longer a source of employee protection for many critical midcontract changes which go to the very existence of employment and job security." For example, *"Milwaukee Spring, Otis*

---

[9]On June 2, 1986, the Board's General Counsel issued an Advice Memorandum dismissing the charge which had alleged the Saturn agreement to be in violation of the Act. General Motors Corp., Saturn Corp., and Automobile Workers, 122 LRRM 1187 (1986).

Elevator, and their progeny do not simply permit midterm changes. They declare plant relocations, work transfers, and the like to be nonmandatory subjects of bargaining. If they are nonmandatory midterm, they are nonmandatory in contract negotiations. . . . In sum, the Board has removed the statutory prohibition against employer unilateral changes of core job security and job preservation issues while at the same time prohibiting unions from negotiating compensating contract protections."

Turning to the construction industry, Connerton asserts that Section 8(f) has been turned on its head—that the current decisions have had a destabilizing effect on the unionized construction industry. In fact, the Board has "made a joke of collective bargaining" in that industry.

Looking back on labor relations during the life of the NLRB, he wistfully observes that American unions have "passively and silently" accepted many types of managerial decisions, and they did so "on the basis of an implicit pact with management: A deal was a deal and so-called managerial decisions would not be employed to destroy the labor agreement. In substantial measure, management has now repudiated that basic premise and declared war on the trade union movement."

Connerton says that unions are discovering that the Board and the Act are "too frequently irrelevant" to their problems; therefore union action and reaction now often takes many innovative forms, for example, dealing with a chosen side in a corporate take-over campaign. Unions have thus shifted focus from the legal arena to other arenas, returning to the labor movement's motivating principle of "common good through solidarity."

In yet another response to Professor St. Antoine, Peter Walther analyzes and discusses the underlying purposes of the statute. He notes, citing Leon Keyserling, Senator Wagner's administrative assistant, that one of Wagner's objectives "was to bring about the redistribution of wealth and the raising of wages for employees, thereby increasing buying power. By increasing buying power, there would be a greater need for production, and therefore a creation of more jobs." Walther stresses that the underlying objectives of the Wagner Act were thus directed not just at employment relations, but were a major part of an economic program designed to alleviate the depressed state of the economy and reduce the possibilities of such conditions recurring in the future.[10]

He notes that the government in the United States is now substantially more involved in industrial relations. He reminds us that in both the areas of safety and pensions, OSHA and ERISA were enacted because collective bargaining was not able to successfully deal with those subjects and to bring about the proper and necessary protection of the rights of the employees. But notwithstanding such failures of collective bargaining, Walther views the Act as "unbelievably successful." He says that the "Act has worked so well that employers have struggled mightily to reach [collective bargaining] objectives through human resource programs without unionization and in the absence of collective bargaining." And in his opinion the Board is doing its job effectively. However, agreeing with much of St. Antoine, he states: "[T]he system fashioned by Congress is in jeopardy because, for collective bargaining to continue working, labor unions are essential. I frankly must admit that the majority of employers, as fair and wise as they may be, cannot be expected or trusted to maintain free workplaces, high wages, and fair distribution of wealth, absent the threat of viable union organizing." He thus considers labor unions essential to the American system; in fact, he says they are "our only bulwark against socialism in industrial relations."

He sees room for improvement nevertheless. Regarding bargaining about major business decisions affecting workers, he suggests that the concept of "consultative bargaining"[11] should be employed. And regarding the Board's failure to provide strong and effective remedies, he indicates his agreement[12] "that the Board presently has the power and capacity, with the exercise of some imagination and careful analysis and evaluation, to bring about changes and improvements in remedies and remedial procedures that are essential if we are to keep collective bargaining viable."

Carin Clauss concludes the chapter with a review of the papers and the observation that all four authors, notwithstanding their

---

[10]Eleanor Norton noted this same objective in her Commentary in Chapter 3.

[11]He refers to proposals in C. Morris, *A Fresh Look at Conventional Wisdom and Unconventional Remedies*, 30 VAND. L. REV. 661, 667–76 (1977).

[12]*Citing* Morris, *The NLRB at 50: Labor Board at the Crossroads*, 26 (BNA Special Report, 1985).

different perspectives, foresee the possibility of a healthy and vigorous industrial relations system.

In Chapter 5, Walter Oberer writes on *The Regulation of Union Economic Power*, which, he says, "is what our system of labor relations is all about." He sees the American system of collective bargaining now predicated on three elements: (1) economic warfare, (2) the role of the government as umpire, and (3) a desire to protect innocent bystanders from unnecessary involvement. Accordingly, "[t]hat which distinguishes labor relations from other relations is . . . the potential for lawful economic warfare." Thus, in our free society, the parties prefer "neutral conditions of warfare . . . to warfare with a governmental thumb on the grenade."

Noting the impact of foreign competition on American products, he says that "where our unions lack monopolistic power in the relevant market, economic warfare by those unions is a losing fight. The regulation of union economic power in such circumstances is not by law, but by life." And as to developments in the law which restrain unions' economic power, he asserts that "[l]egal realism proceeds on the premise that environment is more important than legal doctrine in deciding cases, particularly landmark cases."

Oberer presents a carefully crafted review of the legal history of the labor injunction. He then notes the shift in the government's role toward unions: from paternal protector before Taft-Hartley to that of umpire thereafter. He discusses secondary boycotts, hot-cargo clauses, and blackmail picketing, and the congressional responses to such activity. In addition, he notes the Landrum-Griffin restrictions on union power through imposition of "citizenship rights of members akin to those possessed by members of society at large" and also the "closely related right" contained in the duty-of-fair representation doctrine.

He then turns to the subject of federal preemption, attributing the "underlying purpose" of the doctrine to an intent "to protect a nascent labor movement from inexpert and unfriendly local tribunals." Calling attention to the erosion of that doctrine under recent decisions of the Supreme Court, he observes that what has evolved "is a new balancing test, less preemptive of state regulation and, conversely, more invasive of Board jurisdiction."

Turning attention to the law of secondary boycotts—mainly Sections 8(b)(4)(B) and 8(e)—he argues that "the primary-secondary dichotomy no longer provides an apt criterion for distinguishing proper combatants from proper noncombatants," illustrating the point with reference to the *Enterprise Association*[13] case. He concludes that "the present state of federal labor relations law is inadequate to cope with these sophisticated problems," and offers two solutions: (1) amendment of the Act to define the licit and the illicit in a more refined fashion; (2) consign the matter to antitrust law and allow "federal judges to 'enact' their own version of social justice as these questions of labor policy are litigated." He prefers the former to the latter.

Responding to the "maligning" of the present Board, he asserts that the Board, "for better or worse, is a political body . . . not a labor court. . . . It is simply a fact of governmental life that each new administration places its own political stamp on the Board, [and criticism] by the adversely affected interest group, be it labor or management, is itself part of the institutional plan." In Oberer's opinion, "the pillorying of the Board for current labor restrictions [is] essentially misguided," for he attributes much of the recent trauma to the labor movement to "deregulation," to "the removal of a regulatory wall which permitted employers and unions to inflate prices and wages artificially, in defiance of free-market concepts."

Regarding the failure of the labor movement to expand its membership—or to stem its decline—he observes that workers today do not sufficiently "feel the sense of grievance or truly enough trust unions to optimize union efforts to collectivize them."

It is Oberer's thesis that the ultimate regulation of American union economic power is not the Board or the reviewing courts administering the Act—which he perceives to be, "in core if not in every detail, a model labor code"—but rather "life."

Oberer adds a "postscript" on pension fund leverage which many unions seek to exercise. He finds the approach "laudable" but believes that almost none of the strategic legal questions have been authoratively answered. He closes his paper with a prediction that the North and American labor will not rise again. "At least not without Congressional imprimatur."

---

[13]NLRB v. Plumbers Local 638 (Enterprise Ass'n), 429 US 507, 94 LRRM 2828 (1977).

The first response to Oberer's paper comes from Timothy O'Reilly, who focuses on the decline of union power and appeal, underscoring the decline in the public's favorable attitude toward unions. He commends the unions, however, for such innovative approaches as the Saturn project, pointing out that "[s]olutions developed by the parties are far preferable to legislatively imposed restraints."

O'Reilly, a management attorney, provides a thoughtful prescription for revitalization of the American labor movement of which unions might wish to take notice. He says that "the most important factor in shaping U.S. labor policy is the attitude of employees themselves." In order to appeal to young workers "unions need to appoint and elect younger organizers and leaders, and include more women in the ranks. Several must clean their own houses of corrupt officials. Where they represent the employees, they need to continue to work with companies to develop innovative projects, such as Saturn and the refinancing solutions that assisted Chrysler, Eastern, and Pan Am. Unions must also focus on the needs of the young workers. These include day care centers, job training, quality of work and life programs, and cafeteria approaches toward benefits. Blind allegiance to the union health and welfare and pension plans will no longer suffice."

O'Reilly also presents a formula for union pension fund leverage, indicating that in his opinion "socially sensitive investment policy will be permitted by the [Department of Labor] and the courts[;] and this will have a substantial impact on the unions' economic power in the coming decades, as long as a few guidelines are met: (1) the rate of return is reasonable, (2) the risk of principal is not appreciably greater than any alternative investments available, (3) the diversification is maintained, and (4) the social benefit is the indirect result of the investment. A suggestion to accomplish this is to make the investment policy passive, not active. That is, do not direct the investment advisor to make an investment in a particular project, but direct him instead to avoid undesirable investments, however those are perceived, unless there is no comparable investment opportunity available."

Bruce Simon, in his response to Professor Oberer, expresses strong disagreement. He says that "Oberer leaves us with the conclusion that 'authorative inscrutability' is the best the labor movement can expect." And he differs sharply with Oberer's affirmation of the Board's subjectivity to political use as a means to implement a president's own political agenda, asserting that a system which uses a frankly political tribunal that is not expected to render principled decisions "is the very antithesis of what our system was designed to be."

He notes various appropriate labor union responses "to a philosophy that has rendered the Board virtually irrelevant, and certainly no longer a forum for the protection of union rights." Aside from Lane Kirkland's suggested return to the "law of the jungle," he points to, "on a more civilized note," other innovative developments such as "employee ownership," as at Wierton Steel. He also says that "[s]ince 'takeover' mania appears to be with us for a while, and leveraged buyouts seem to be the order of the day, labor should understand that it can leverage the labor costs and productivity components of its contracts into an equity bargaining kit and it can trade its affection to the corporate rival offering the best proposal." And he predicts that "corporate campaign" strategy, such as that which was used at J.P. Stevens, will be used with increasing frequency.

Simon closes on a somber note, remarking that in the last 50 years we have seen a "social compact," which traded union recognition and fostering of unionism for labor peace, "destroyed, chip by chip." The resulting despair of labor unions today "will manifest itself either in destructive activity or [it] will be met with constructive measures by a society that will recognize the value of labor and collective action." He says that although we are at a "crossroads," the next few years do not give him a great sense of optimism as to which path this country will take.

Further responding to the Oberer paper, John Fannin reminds us that "[i]n the year before enactment of the Wagner Act there were almost 3,000 work stoppages on the issue of representation alone," a situation which the Act corrected. And on the decline of union power, he observes that unions are "as strong or as weak as the economy," that "the 'economic power' of labor and management is largely determined by the needs of the marketplace." He foresees that the era of "economic warfare" may in time be replaced by an era of "accommodating survival." He cites as examples two unionized companies that traded wages for profit sharing, where the employees now "regard, the companies as 'their' companies, and their interest in and empathy to their companies in much higher."

Thomas Kohler closes the chapter with a review of Oberer's history of the recent labor movement and a critique of his general thesis. Kohler questions the "paternalistic" label which Oberer attaches to the triad of labor statutes—the Railway Labor, Norris-LaGuardia, and Wagner Acts, asserting that instead Congress made a choice for "a private ordering system in which workers and their employers jointly establish and adjust the terms governing their relationship through collective agreement." This was in lieu of "a system of public ordering of the type that exists in Western Europe, characterized by comprehensive regulation of and strong and pervasive state intervention in the employment relationship."

Reflecting on the historical nature of the process, he defines collective bargaining as "an institution in which state decisional authority is delegated to those directly affected to determine, within the range set by market forces, the law that will govern the employment relationship." He again rejects Oberer's paternalistic characterization, contending instead that "bargaining affords workers the means to participate in the framing and administration of the law that has the greatest impact on their daily lives." And he is troubled by Oberer's characterization of the Taft-Hartley amendments "as establishing a regimen of 'government as umpire,'" for he views Taft-Hartley as hardly impartial in its impact.

Kohler tells us that one perception of law is as narrative. He ponders the questions of "what kind of story the law may be telling us about the future of collective bargaining as a social institution, and what that may portend for democractic ordering more generally." His inquiry consists of three strands.

The first strand is "the impact the law regulating union activity has had on the institution of collective bargaining." He notes that as a society we have never been comfortable with truly free collective bargaining. For example, *Borg-Warner*[14] allows courts to shape views about the types of concerns about which unions may legitimately speak. And the habits of practice and mind encouraged by *Borg-Warner* and its progeny, such as *Fibreboard*[15] and *First National Maintenance*,[16] show an ever-narrowing vision

---

[14]NLRB v. Borg-Warner Corp., 356 US 342, 42 LRRM 2034 (1958).
[15]Fibreboard Paper Prods. Co. v. NLRB, 379 US 203, 57 LRRM 2609 (1964).
[16]First Nat'l Maintenance Corp. v. NLRB, 452 US 666, 107 LRRM 2705 (1981).

of the types of matters that are susceptible to collective bargaining. These cases also indicate a lack of confidence in the private ordering process. The result is the promotion of confusion and subterfuge in the bargaining system.

He also observes that as the trend toward public ordering of the employment relationship continues, "the American labor law scheme is tending to converge with those that obtain in Western European countries," i.e., pervasive state control of and interventions in the employment relationship. He finds this especially ironic because Western European nations are now moving closer to the American style of collective bargaining.

Kohler's second strand is in the "reentry of the common law courts into the regulation of the employment relationship"—the judicial modification of the employment-at-will doctrine by state courts. He suggests that this has occurred primarily because "[w]hen private governance through self-associated groups declines, direct state intervention is inevitable."

His third strand is the "emphasis on individualism" which is so characteristic of American society. Kohler is alarmed lest the pernicious effects of extreme individualism described by de Tocqueville become manifest in American society. According to de Tocqueville, "[t]he people in this regimen exist for and of themselves, each preoccupied by his own matters, unaware and unconcerned with the fate of others, save that of his children and nearest friends," but de Tocqueville also wrote that in the United States the pernicious effects of this individualism had been neutralized by the formation of all types of free associations. Kohler fears that as government assumes the major protective role, the pernicious effects of individualism described by de Tocqueville will loom as a real threat to democractic ordering.

Kohler sees law as a constitutive force in society that significantly influences what we are and will become: "Collective bargaining affords citizens the means to participate in the forming and administration of the law that determines the details of daily life. It thereby encourages the habits of self-governance and direct responsibility. It also affords individuals increased control over their personal circumstances." He suggests that "society may be best served by removing the obstructions and impediments to private ordering before that opportunity is completely foreclosed."

In Chapter 6, Charles Morris[17] considers *Board Procedures, Remedies, and the Enforcement Process*. He begins by asserting that notwithstanding some popular misconceptions to the contrary, the language of the statute and its legislative history make it clear that the Taft-Hartley Act did not change the basic national commitment to the encouragement of collective bargaining and the protection of the rights of employees under Section 7 to organize into labor unions. The Taft-Hartley amendment specifying that employees also have the right to refrain from such activity did not change the basic commitment.

He seeks to put the Taft-Hartley amendments into proper legal perspective. Most of those amendments were perceived as antiunion, but they "did not change the core objective of the statute." Primarily, the changes added substantial union unfair labor practices, for the 80th Congress was concerned with the power of "big labor." For the most part, these union unfair labor practices are "ancillary to the core provisions of Section 7 and 8(a) because, in the main, [they] depend on the existence of established unions." Thus, the secondary boycott and jurisdictional dispute provisions of Section 8(b)(4) assume the presence of unions which have bargaining rights with primary employers, and the recognitional and organizational picketing provisions of Section 8(b)(7), which were added by the Landrum-Griffin Act in 1959, merely emphasize the primacy of Section 9 procedures and requirements for the establishment of union recognition.

Morris observes that the employer unfair labor practices which are contained in the statute today are basically the same as they were 50 years ago. They were not changed by Taft-Hartley or Landrum-Griffin. But the Board's record of enforcement of those "core provisions," involving employer interference with organizational activity and discriminatory discharges under Section 8(a)(1) and 8(a)(3), has been "woefully inadequate." This is in marked contrast to the Board's record of effective enforcement of Sections 8(b)(4) and 8(b)(7) against unions, where stronger remedies are mandated directly by the Act.

His review of statistical data and empirical studies of the Board's enforcement record "reveals that notwithstanding the

---

[17]In the interest of consistency, I shall use the *third person* in referring to my own paper. This will also provide a more depersonalized, though not necessarily a more objective, review of this material.

substantial number of employers against whom meritorious unfair labor practice charges have been filed in recent years, the Board has not been able to protect employees by providing effective enforcement"; nor has it created a legal atmosphere conducive to widespread voluntary compliance. He makes this observation: "Although the statistical data do not indicate that all employers who are involved in organizational campaigns violate the Act, such evidence does suggest and tend to confirm the popular belief that nonunion employers are more concerned with avoidance of the Act's requirements than with compliance with the Act's objectives. In other words, the spirit of the Act is regularly violated even when no violations of specific provisions are found or even charged. The prevalence of such efforts at union avoidance, coupled with the Board's dismal record in failing to provide meaningful remedies in the cases where violations are found, support the conclusion that the Board has failed in its primary mission."

Morris makes the assumption that the policy contained in the present law is both valid and desirable, for there have been sufficient examples of healthy collective bargaining to indicate that "the NLRA system fits comfortably within the general democratic framework of American political and economic life. Furthermore, notwithstanding the Board's bleak record in protecting employee rights, the NLRA, with its emphasis on employee self-determination, offers a suitable framework for channeling workers' participation into new decisionmaking processes concerning matters that affect their legitimate employment-related interests." He argues that "[t]he Act was devised with remarkable foresight. Given the proper institutional will, that statute could furnish the Board with a flexible means to provide positive responses to the demands of the industrial relations community for innovative and improved techniques for the organization of work—some of which might emphasize cooperative rather than adversarial arrangements—in order to better cope with this nation's ongoing process of either deindustrialization or reindustrialization."

He explores various enforcement alternatives which might improve the Board's enforcement record. While not wholly rejecting the approach of change through legislation, he cautions against seeking a "quick fix" or "palliative" from Congress and notes the Pandora's Box syndrome which usually accompanies major efforts to amend this Act. He also outlines a proposal for establishment of a specialized Article III labor court which could enforce this and other major federal labor laws with efficiency and respect.

He contends, however, that the most suitable approach, or at least the one which should be tried before turning to other alternatives, is for the Board to use the clout it already has. And the labor court alternative should only be viewed as "a solution of last resort." The approach which he discusses in detail is a series of proposals designed to encourage the Board to use its existing authority more efficiently. He says that "[t]he most plausible antidote for the Board's malaise is to be found in the potential of the statute itself. But achieving that potential may never be possible. Because of the political nature of Board appointments, their short five-year terms of office, and the absence of a strong institutional committment to vigorous enforcement of the Act [he] has virtually no expectation that the Board will ever reform itself." Nevertheless, because "hope springs eternal," he proceeds to document certain specific means which, in his view, would allow the Board to better achieve its major statutory objectives. These means consist essentially of "the activation of several unused or underused procedural devices, a reorganization of certain agency functions, and the employment of more effective and more injury-specific remedies." He proposes the following explicit alterations in the Board's procedures and practices: "(1) substantive rule making [which he highlights]; (2) streamlining of "R" case procedures; (3) making discovery available; (4) increasing the use of Section 10(j) injunctions, especially in discharge cases; (5) reorganization of administrative law judge operations; (6) ordering damage-specific final remedies; and (7) increasing the use of Sections 10(e) and 10(f) injunctions."

Regarding the first proposal, *rule making*, he lists 11 reasons for the Board to convert from adjudicative rule making to Administrative.Procedure Act (APA) notice-and-comment substantive rule making: (1) The language of the statute is broad and generalized. (2) Rule making is a superior source of necessary data. (3) Adjudicative rule making emphasizes specific facts rather than broad legislative policy. (4) Rule making can reduce the volume of litigation. (5) Rule making uses agency resources more efficiently. (6) Rule making can have a positive effect on appellate review. (7) Rule making provides a more effective prevention factor than adjudication alone. (8) Rule making provides a more suitable medium for articulation of the Board's rationale for a rule. (9) Rule making assists Congress in its oversight responsibilities. (10) The General Counsel factor, i.e., the separation of Board and General Counsel and the General Counsel's unreviewable discretion to refuse to issue a complaint impedes rule making by adjudication. (11) The information factor, for which rule making is vastly superior to adjudication.

Here is a sampling of factors which make up some of these reasons: "Case-by-case adjudication does not provide the Board with the necessary factual data or the best available analyses of such data on which to premise rules of broad application. In adjudicated cases, even those in which the Board announces major policy changes, oral argument is rarely permitted and amici briefs are rarely invited. By contrast, the rule-making process invites a dialogue between the labor relations community and the Board, for the notice-and-comment procedure contemplated by the APA encourages the parties who are likely to be affected by the proposed rule to submit relevant data and argument which the Board must consider." Regarding the information factor, adequate dissemination of substantive rules to persons whose employment can be affected by the Board's rules—particularly rules relating to conduct by workers who are not currently represented by a certified or recognized labor union—is a critical but missing element in the Board's process.

Morris does not suggest that the Board should suddenly attempt to convert to an exclusive rule-making system. He says that "[t]o be administratively realistic, the conversion would have to be gradual. But a beginning should be made; and, in particular, future major doctrinal changes should receive priority treatment for promulgation in accordance with APA rule-making procedures."

He provides a number of illustrations of rules which would benefit from promulgation through APA notice-and-comment procedures, including (1) a rule requiring the posting of a general notice of the Act's basic requirements by all employers and unions subject to the Board's jurisdiction; (2) rules relating to organizational campaigns; (3) rules relating to employee rights to engage in concerted activity for "mutual aid or protection," (4) rules defining labor organizations and rules relating to employer domination, support, and assistance to labor organizations; (5) rules defining an employee's rights regarding union representation, including the duty of fair representation, union security, checkoff of union dues, hiring halls, and resignations from union membership in relation to strikes; and (6) rules defining appropriate bargaining units.

His proposal regarding the *streamlining of "R" case procedures* includes use of rule making and summary judgment hearings.

His proposal on *making discovery available* emphasizes both the utility of discovery for fact-finding and its utility in the encouragement of settlements. But he also recognizes that discovery can be abused; therefore, the process must be "regulated and protected by requiring a showing of 'reasonable need' . . . and administrative law judges are the logical persons to provide such oversight and protection."

He proposes *increasing the use of Section 10(j) injunctions, especially in discharge cases.* He notes the legislative intent and the excellent record of success with the device when it has been used. He recommends a procedure to expedite the process and concludes that the potential of Section 10(j) has hardly been touched. He asserts that it can and should be used extensively "whenever the Board's ordinary remedy is too late or otherwise inadequate."

His proposal on *reorganization of administrative law judge operations* is designed to allow the ALJs to function more like court judges. They would be geographically decentralized, be assigned immediately after a complaint issues, and would usually oversee the case through a motion practice prior to trial. ALJs would also make available pretrial conferences and discovery, and they would provide an additional conduit for recommending Section 10(j) injunctive relief.

Morris' proposal for the Board's *ordering of damage-specific final remedies* includes provision for Section 8(a)(5) orders that relate to every item of unilateral activity affecting mandatory subjects of bargaining occurring prior to agreement on a first collective bargaining contract; and more realistic interest on backpay awards; a redefinition of "frivolous defense" reimbursement; and various other orders.

He also proposes greater use of *Sections 10(e) and 10(f) injunctions*, particularly involvement of the ALJ before whom the case was originally heard.

Morris concludes that he is pessimistic about the Board's future; however, "the Board is too important to the American political and economic system to be jettisoned without every reasonable effort being made to save it and use it." He says that "[i]f a President had the desire and political courage, as well as either strong popular support or substantial consensus among leading figures in the industrial relations community, or if the majority of the Board and the General Counsel, acting with the independence which is supposed to characterize an independent federal agency, were similarly motivated to chart a new course, then perhaps—just perhaps—the Board might be steered in a new direction; and it might become sufficiently depoliticized to achieve most of its true potential, or at least to make a beginning move in that direction. But if this does not occur, then we should explore other alternatives, including a labor court. Regardless of the direction taken, the National Labor Relations Act itself can be of inestimable value to the American industrial relations system and the economy it was intended to serve. Long-range economic objectives, particularly those relating to more equitable income distribution domestically and more successful industrial competition internationally, can benefit from a smoothly functioning industrial relations system, especially a system such as the National Labor Relations Act, which is based on principles of democracy and freedom of choice. The normative patterns which that Act was intended to foster can and should serve a vital role in moving this nation's economy toward those long-range objectives."

Rosemary Collyer, in her response to Professor Morris, notes the Board's "fine record" of resolving over 90 percent of the cases within 45 days and without formal litigation, and that the "settlement record has been above 90 percent for four years." Comparing the present record with that of the Eisenhower Board, she points out that the General Counsel's office now finds "merit in over 60 percent more of our case load than we did in 1958, and we do it 150 percent more quickly than we did then."

She agrees with Morris that "the Board's authority under Section 10(j) to seek temporary injunctions . . . is among the most effective weapons available to the Board in the enforcement of the Act," and advises that she is "taking steps to assure that [the] policy of aggressive and imaginative utilization of Section 10(j) proceedings will continue."

She defends some aspects of rule making by the adjudicative process, asserting that "[a]djudication permits the testing of theories in relation to the actual facts of individual disputes." Although she concedes that APA rule making may result in more stability in the law, she warns "that stability can become rigidity. [But] [t]he solution . . . may lie with a careful use of rule making in limited areas." However, "wholesale rule making at this watershed time of changes in the industrialization of this country may be exactly the wrong thing to do."

She states that "[i]n the area of remedies and compliance, [she] agrees[s] with Professor Morris' basic thesis that we can do more to enforce the Act within the existing structure." But she says that she cannot accept what she believes is "overly broad criticism of the Agency . . . . [W]e cannot "let . . . criticism [of the Board] ignore the outstanding record this Agency has had over its first half century. Millions of working people are better off because this Agency has been there and because of the way the Act has been enforced."

Laurence Gold presents his response to the Morris paper with a note of pessimism. He states that at the present time he has "no faith in the efficacy of procedural change as the means to revitalizing the statute." And "insofar as the Act was designed to change the mute fact of the employer's dominance, in [the employment] situation, the Act has failed." In his view, "this situation has come about because there are no major shared objectives between management and labor." He says that "[t]here is no way that the Board or the courts in administering this Act can basically change the nature of American enterprise." He faults management's attitude "that the less organization there is the better and the less collective bargaining there is the better." He indicates that although he cannot say what will eventuate, "something extraordinarily different from what we have today" will be produced; and it will be one of two things, either a more militant labor movement or else the prelude to such a labor movement, "namely, a situation such as existed in the first 30 or 40 years of this century in which people who work for a living know that they are powerless, do not know what to do about it, but look for the opportunity to change."

In her response to Professor Morris, Andrea Christensen indicates her agreement that the "Board's pernicious problem of delay" is a significant problem. However, she is unpersuaded that either administrative changes or a labor court could eradicate the problem. In her view, "the only effective way to expedite the administrative timetable is to find ways to encourage the participants themselves to precipitate the changes." She cites grievance arbitration as an example of a meaningful model shaped by the parties themselves. It is her thesis that nothing significant can change unless the attitude of the parties changes.

She favors substantive rule making, although she recognizes certain limitations in the process: "Professor Morris has correctly pointed out that there are virtues to administrative rule making to the extent that it can reduce the volume of litigation over uncertain statutory interpretations. But, once again, rule making is an effective tool only if the parties whose conduct is to be governed by the rules are predisposed to cooperate with the system. Many of the evils attendant to case-by-case adjudication are equally applicable to administrative rule making. Thus, parties who are so inclined can seek to test the outer limits of the rule instead of the last case. Moreover, though the process is more leisurely, rules as well as administrative precedent will change as the political composition of the rule making body is changed." She says that "though rule making by the NLRB would help to clarify some of the Agency's current positions on the law, the process would have no significant impact on the problem of administrative delay unless the attitude of the parties were to change." One rule that she specifically favors is "Morris' suggestion that the Board should require employers and unions to post a general notice describing the Act's basic statutory provisions." She emphasizes that one of the many reasons to support rule making is the "likelihood that through this process the Board will come up with both factual and empirical support for its conclusions, and also will be able to articulate the reason for its decisions in a way that courts can understand." Her overall appraisal of rule making is that it is perhaps "the answer" to many of the Board's ills.

She strongly opposes Morris' recommendation on pretrial discovery, because "if there is a desire to cause delay—depositions and interrogatories provide a fertile field for the recalcitrant party."

She attributes some procedural delay to the Board's "failing to decide issues expeditiously, which is caused in part by its uncertainty as to how to interpret the Act in light of current political pressures."

She sees limited applicability for the Section 10(j) injunction "since reinstatement and back pay are normally available so that the element of irreparable harm is difficult to prove."

Robert Rabin concludes the final chapter with a review and commentary. He characterizes the Morris' paper as a "comprehensive blueprint for change," but one that does not call for radical surgery. Rabin defends the Board's doctrinal shifts to reflect the mandate of a new administration's constituency provided, he cautions, that the Board stay within its statutory command and follow the kinds of procedures Professor Morris recommends.

He discusses some of those procedures. He applauds General Counsel Collyer's endorsement of an aggressive use of the 10(j) injunction, and he refers to Morris' rule-making proposals as the heart of his paper. He adds his own endorsement of rule making to that of Board Members Zimmerman and Dennis and Respondent Christensen, and he welcomes Collyer's limited endorsement. He emphasizes that through the process of rule making the Board will be more likely to arrive at factual and empirical support for its conclusions and better able to articulate rationales which the courts can understand. He also postulates that "[p]erhaps rule making [will] allow unions to pool their resources and meet management on equal terms in advocating their positions before the Board."

The book's dialogue closes with an Epilogue by Stephen Schlossberg: *On Tipping the Balance in Labor Management Relations.* Schlossberg asks whether American industry will return to "open warfare" or move toward the "goal of cooperation." Although he provides no definitive answer, he points to certain factors which might tip the scale toward the cooperative mode.

His prescription for getting workers sufficiently committed to make them and their enterprise competitive with workers of any nation in the world is to convince them that they are not marginal, that they really matter. He sees a strong force in the American economy and society "that wants to do certain things because they are right and decent," for example, some of the companies that are leading the way in cooperative work programs. He sees attitudes changing, including union attitudes. Unions cannot insist on doing things the old way, for "the hate-the-boss-and-fight-syndrome" will not work in a cooperative movement.

He reminds us that employers in the past responded to union economic pressure by granting restrictive work rules and higher wages in order to retain their so-called management rights, their control over decisionmaking and the running of the business. "Employers wanted to keep the camel's nose out of the tent. But now that has changed. They have found that the camel has something to bring to the tent, that the worker on the shop floor and the union may have a good notion of what can help the enterprise succeed. There is not a single labor leader in America . . . who does not know that an enterprise has to make a profit to exist, so it is in the interest of the union and the employees to help provide a constructive, healthy, and profitable business. If we put this combination together we have a receipt for success."

Schlossberg asks whether we need to tinker with the legal system. His answer: "Yes, we do need to tinker. We need to examine existing laws and see how they affect labor-management cooperation. It may be necessary to change some laws, including the NLRA. If the laws are construed solely in the context of hostile, adversarial relations, either the constructions must change or the statutory language must change. If we are to progress along this leading edge type of society, the laws should not forbid the parties from blurring distinctions between management and labor. If we move from a hostile, adversarial society to a cooperative society, all of the old rules cannot apply. So what do we do with a statute that is not adjusted to the new world? We either adjust the statute or adjust the world. We must give serious thought to how the NLRA can be adjusted, either by interpretation or by amendment, so that it will help the parties rather than impede them in working cooperatively in the labor-management relations of the future."

Common Threads, Recurring Themes, and Random Conclusions

The pages of this book contain and also mirror the ongoing debate about the Labor Board, the future of collective bargaining, and the future of the American labor movement. Although there is much disagreement among the participants about the direction which the Board should take in specific cases, there is an underlying agreement among most of the authors—almost a consensus—that the basic approach of the National Labor Relations Act is sound.

Only a few of the contributors advocate major legislative changes. A few are content with the status quo. The overwhelming majority recognized the existence of serious problems and the need for certain fundamental changes; however, most of that group attribute the problems which they describe to what they perceive to be unfortunate interpretations of various statutory provisions. Both the Board and the Supreme Court are faulted for departing from the basic objectives of the Act. In addition, the Board is faulted for failure to utilize more fully the procedural and remedial devices which are available under the existing statute. In other words, there is wide support for the view that the Board and the courts, without major legislative amendments, could make substantial improvements in the interpretation and administration of the Act. The specifics of these criticisms and suggested corrective actions are detailed in the papers.

Many of the contributors are pessimistic, however, about the Board's ability to change its direction, primarily because of the politicization which has characterized appointments to that Agency. A number of contributors express the view that legislative changes are therefore needed. Several feel that only by legislative changes can the Act be strengthened.

As a result of this extended dialogue, certain conclusions emerge. They are not all based on consensus, but they are supported directly or indirectly by the findings and observations of most of the contributors: (1) Collective bargaining is a healthy process which should be nurtured. (2) The system fashioned by Congress is in jeopardy because for collective bargaining to continue working labor unions are essential.[18] (3) Better enforcement is required to make the core provisions of the statute, which relate primarily to organizational activity, function in accordance with the intent of the statute. (4) Because the direction which collective bargaining should take in the future is toward cooperation rather than industrial warfare, the statute should either be re-interpreted to achieve that end or it should be amended to make it possible.

As one of the contributors stated, law serves an important legitimating function in our society; another referred to law as a constitutive force in society that significantly influences what we are and will become. Such characterizations are particularly appropriate to describe the impact of the National Labor Rela-

---

[18]These are the words of a management attorney and former Board Member.

tions Act on the American industrial relations and economic systems. The conduct and principles which that Act was intended to encourage could significantly help to move the American economy forward in its march toward the goals of more equitable income distribution, due process in the workplace, and successful competition in the international marketplace.

I am grateful to all of my colleagues for their valuable and incisive contributions to this book. May the dialogue continue.

Charles J. Morris

November 1986

CONTENTS

THE LEGAL FRAMEWORK OF INDUSTRIAL RELATIONS AND THE ECONOMIC FUTURE OF THE UNITED STATES

JOHN T. DUNLOP*

These remarks are concerned with the grand design, the cathedrals of thought, of the governmental framework of industrial relations, past and future, rather than with the bricks and mortar of decisions that are more appropriately the concern of the authors of the separate chapters in this volume.

Looking Back

Collective bargaining was not invented nor its most fundamental features designed by legislation, administrative tribunals, or the courts in this country. The distinctive American features are the joint creation of labor and management over many years of responding by trial and error to the changing problems of our environment. Those basic features include exclusive representation, collective agreements with fixed durations, and the related grievance procedures with arbitration and no-strike–no-lockout provisions, relatively decentralized bargaining structures, and detailed collective agreements. Yet various agencies of government with shifting personnel and ideology, largely without practical experience in industrial relations, have sought constantly to reshape collective bargaining in their graven images.

Unlike the emergence of the Railway Labor Act (1926), the enactment of the Wagner Act (1935), the Taft-Hartley Act (1947), the Landrum-Griffin Act (1959), and the aborted labor law reform bills (1978) arose out of extremely bitter partisan political conflict. These statutes were coalesced from traumatic events: the abuses of the Great Depression, the LaFollette Com-

---

*Lamont University Professor, Harvard University, former Secretary of Labor.

1

mittee investigation, and the refusal of employers to comply with NIRA labor board orders; the wartime strikes of coal miners and the post-war inflation and conflicts associated with the decontrol of prices and wages; and the McClellan Committee investigation. Irving Bernstein's research told us the Wagner Act was presented at the "most favorable possible moment" at the apogee of the New Deal,[1] and Leon H. Kyserling said on the 10th anniversary that the Act could have been passed no other time.[2]

While such charged environments and special moments may have generated the political will or legislative majority to do something about industrial relations on three occasions in the past 50 years, they scarcely were conducive to wisdom or dispassion and responsible long-term policy making.

The legislative framework and the detailed specification of industrial relations law have never been supported by any significant degree of labor-management consensus. As I pointed out 25 years ago to the Industrial Relations Research Association,[3] in the absence of consensus there is no possibility for a viable or stable legal framework for collective bargaining. No battle is ever settled in the shifting passage of prosperity and depression, with differing administrations and changing personalities in administrative agencies and the courts; the role of partisan politics in the details of industrial relations is vastly exaggerated. The absence of stability, the uncertainty, and impetus to conflict is destructive of productive industrial relations, subject to the political zigs and zags of administrative agencies and the lag in reaction time of the courts. Moreover, the Board has eschewed any role to help fashion a degree of consensus.

Incidentally, the National Mediation Board has been subjected to many of the same environmental changes with relatively little of the political zigs and zags, reflecting both its origins and the informal cooperation between labor and management in the appointment of members of the board and the railroad retirement system.

---

[1] THE NEW DEAL COLLECTIVE BARGAINING POLICY 116, 120 (1950).

[2] Kyserling, THE WAGNER ACT: AFTER TEN YEARS 13 (L. Silverberg ed., 1945).

[3] Dunlop, *Consensus and National Labor Policy,* PROCEEDINGS OF THE 13TH ANNUAL MEETING OF THE INDUSTRIAL RELATIONS RESEARCH ASSOCIATION 2–15, December 28–29, 1960.

Western governments everywhere have come to be extensive regulators of labor markets, despite wide variations in political philosophies. My reading of this regulatory experience is that in the absence of substantial labor organization in labor markets, these declarations of public policy are not generally enforced, save in larger enterprises that are generally more sensitive to public policy for a variety of reasons. The Congress will never appropriate the money and staff requisite to orderly enforcement; substantial unemployment periodically undermines declared policies; the inevitable game between regulator and regulatee eventually goes to the persistent and the well-heeled; and there is "ongoing trivialization of the regulatory impact of the statute," to use Professor Howard Lesnick's phrase.[4]

In 1975 I emphasized this perspective on the limited usefulness of regulation in visits to all regional offices of the Labor Department with the paper, "The Limits of Legal Compulsion."[5] The subtitle might have been "What You Can Do and What You Cannot Do With a Piece of Paper." The statement concluded with the sentence: "Trust cannot grow in an atmosphere dominated by bureaucratic fiat and litigious controversy: it emerges through persuasion, mutual accommodation and problem solving." Public policies for labor markets expressed in statutes require a substantial degree of consensus and an appreciable degree of labor organization to be effective.

One of the major difficulties in the labor market with the regulatory approach of the past, beyond the obvious problems of delay and compliance, is the apparent necessity of administrative agencies and the courts to apply uniform concepts and rules across all sectors of the economy, with a few limited exceptions such as with provisions relating to apparel and clothing and pre-hire agreements in construction. We have exalted process over substance. The great virtue of collective bargaining is its capacity to write and enforce provisions appropriate to separate markets, technologies, and localities. The precedents and decisions of the Board and the courts are applied across a complex economy in different sectors and localities. The straightjacket of

---

[4] *Remarks of Howard Lesnick Reviewing Decisions of Supreme Court During 1984–85 Term Before ABA Section of Labor and Employment Law,* 1985 DAILY LAB. REP. (BNA), 132:D–1.
[5] 27 LAB. L.J. 67–74 (1976).

the legal framework does not fit public purposes well in many situations.

The unreflecting tendency by separate agencies and the courts to apply the concepts of the NLRA in the past several decades to the emerging public sector collective bargaining illustrates the limitations of monolithic concepts. It is understandable that practitioners would look to the private sector for precedents, but the issues of unit determination, the nature of supervision, the impasse concept and its consequences, and the separation of executive and legislative functions in government require different approaches. In dealing with public employees, state legislatures, state agencies, and their counselors should be less imitative and more creative in industrial relations.

Other sectors excluded from the NLRA, like growers and agricultural workers, should heed the concern with their special problems rather than adopt the precedents under the NLRA, as I can testify to in having to arrange in August 1985 a representation determination by voluntary means for migratory farm workers and growers in Ohio harvesting tomatoes and picking cucumbers for sale to the Campbell Soup Company.

Among the most serious problems to labor and management with the Labor Board over the years has been the creation and application of concepts and doctrines that have little or no reality or semblance of practicality. The need to rationalize and to explain in long opinions is often artificial and even dangerous. Arbitrators are saved much difficulty since there is little actual transfer of precedent outside of the particular parties or the particular collective agreement. A few illustrations will indicate some of the conceptual difficulties.

The concept of "impasse," for instance, is to my mind a most dubious notion, particularly when the Board or a court is to determine whether one existed long after the event. My experience teaches that a dispute may be settled at one time but not at another. Moreover, the legal rewards for an impasse that the Board and the courts hold out to the parties, which they alone invented, such as withdrawal from an employer association, or unilaterally imposing wages and conditions, or removal of union security, or a lockout, or precipitating a strike on a work force, are a mighty incentive to refuse to bargain realistically. From my experience as a mediator, I defy anyone, even one on the actual scene, to make a reliable determination with skilled actors as to the reality of an "impasse." There is only agreement or non-agreement in the real world at a given time, not impasse. The concept is a delusion and an invitation to fakery, that with its special license to strong measures should be abolished.

Or take the *Yeshiva*[6] doctrine, that some faculties are so arranged that every tenured faculty member so participates in some decisions of management that collective bargaining should be denied to all. The Supreme Court defined managerial employees as those who "formulate and effectuate management policies by expressing and making operative the decisions of their employer by taking or recommending discretionary actions that effectively control or implement employer policy." Gobbledegook! Such phrasing needs to confront the tests of reality with real persons in real time. The transfer to the academic or to the medical care worlds of the industrial plant model of supervision or hiring, promotion, and discharge yields results that defy practical experience. A unit conforming to colleagiality may defile legal dogma but not academic or professional reality and the need for forms of representation.

Or consider the creation by the Board and the courts of the double-breasted employer, particularly in construction. This hybrid was relatively unknown until legalisms precisely specified the degree of independence and the degree of control over two subsidiaries or entities, one union and the other nonunion, under a single span of real control. The result has been that every contractor under collective bargaining has the need for one. Jobs may be bid by one entity and performed by another. Reflect on the widespread advocacy of union-management cooperation in a situation when you never know with which entity you are cooperating. Legal fiction generates its own world otherwise unknown.

Or consider the determination of jurisdictional disputes by the Board and the courts in construction. It is hard to envisage a more dogmatic and unrealistic result than has been created. At the outset of the Taft-Hartley Act, the Board and the General Counsel actively encouraged private machinery, even helping to write the agreement of the private parties. After 15 years or so of collaboration, the agency began to rule routinely that any assignment of work made by a contractor was proper, all in the most sanctimonious language as to what was a proper work assignment. The Board never recognized the simple truth that a

---

6 NLRB v. Yeshiva Univ., 444 US 672, 103 LRRM 2526 (1980).

large fraction of jurisdictional disputes in that industry were also disputes among contractors. Little wonder that the Board and the courts effectively destroyed the private effort to resolve these disputes specifically encouraged by the law and the predecessor Boards.[7]

A fuller treatment would explore the reality and appropriateness of such legal fictions as "sanitized elections" or "independent operators" in referring to many truck operators and to migrants who are distinguished only by picking cucumbers under a share-cropping method of pay while migrants picking tomatoes paid by the hour are employees.

A word about the sensitive matter of appointments to the NLRB and to the General Counsel. My experience teaches that in federal and state government, as in arbitration and mediation, a Board cannot effectively administer labor relations legislation, or employment regulation, without enjoying a wide measure of acceptability and respect in both labor and management communities. There are a number of seasoned members of management, labor organizations, and in academia who meet that test. There are likewise lawyers in firms who practice predominately for one side or the other who also meet that test. In the past several administrations there has been little concern with this vital ingredient for labor policy, I regret to say. The test of whether a Board is comprised three to two or two to three of one political party or the other is irrelevant to the questions of acceptability, experience, and respect.

Moreover, I am deeply concerned by the tendency to hire relatively inexperienced lawyers in industrial relations and employment regulation posts who inevitably tend to look forward, after a few years in government, to making substantial money in the places that money exists in our society, in business or in firms catering to business. That is an inherently bad system: to recruit public officials for public service in sensitive labor-management relations.

Looking Ahead

Cyrus R. Vance, in the 1980 Harvard Commencement Exercises, expressed the thought I would apply to the future of

---

[7] J. Dunlop, Dispute Resolution, Negotiation and Consensus Building 194–204 (1984).

industrial relations and its legal framework: "We must have in our minds a conception of the world we want a decade hence. The 1990 we seek must shape our actions in 1980, or the decisions of 1980 could give us a 1990 we will regret."[8] I hope the deliberations in this volume will help create for our country the legal framework for industrial relations and collective bargaining it needs in the 1990s and begin to affect behavior now.

It is widely said by press, politicians, and pundits alike that the economic future of the country, even its competitive survival, mandates a higher degree of labor-management cooperation or even partnership; a greater attention to quality of product and services, a higher rate of increase in human resources productivity; a much greater emphasis on training and retraining to enhance flexibility and adaptability of the work force in a world of changing job requirements; a more dedicated common attention to the administration of health care benefits, wellness programs, and rehabilitation to constrain costs, and common efforts to reduce the use of alcohol and drugs. A Wall Street Journal article[9] is captioned, "Loyalty Ebbs at Many Companies as Employees Grow Disillusioned," reflecting the eternal concern of managements with attitudes and performance. A White House Conference champions labor-management cooperation to enhance productivity. The Saturn project with the Automobile Workers and General Motors is widely applauded as the approach the country needs, but characteristically even that effort is promptly challenged in court as a violation of right-to-work laws.

Many factors, of course, influence our economic performance, and as an economist I would place considerable emphasis upon inconsistent macro-economic policies, including trade policy, as the source of our recent problems. Nonetheless, with aggregate labor costs constituting two-thirds of the total, it is fully appropriate to look critically at performance at the workplace. A national industrial relations system that exalts the litigious, sues somebody in the attempt to solve every problem, that creates endless delay and uncertainty, that makes it easier to withdraw from employer associations and unions, that encourages unilateral changes in pension plans, that changes the rules of industrial relations with shifting political weather rather than

---

8 N.Y. Times, June 6, 1980, at A–12.
9 July 11, 1985.

by consensus or objective developments in markets or technology, in my view is not adequate or suitable, particularly in our time of competitive stress. It is rather a millstone around our economic neck. We have inherited a legal framework of industrial relations that is destructive to our economic future.

Our legal framework teaches that some functions exercised in the enterprise are management's exclusive rights and preogatives and other matters are within the realm of collective bargaining, at least until the creation of something called an impasse. A sharp line is drawn, and the Board and the courts police that line with ever more detailed and trivial refinements—for example, the price of coffee in a company cafeteria, on which side of the line shall it be?

The needs of the country rather require joint study, joint discussion, joint development of the facts, and joint problem solving (and sometimes tripartite consultations) over such questions as shutdown of operations or plants and adaptations to new markets, technologies, and locations; the aspirations and concerns of individuals and groups of workers as with health care, the problems of chemicals in the work environment, and the needs of women workers and minorities; and the expectations of local communities and the nation for the workplace.

There is no public policy that comports with the national necessity that parties, at the workplace, enterprise, sector, or nation, talk about or talk out these common concerns or interdependencies. We only have a legalistic boundary line, often drawn long after any practical reality, specifying whether management can act by fiat or must bargain, or create the semblance of bargaining. That a few pairs of parties, often in economic distress, rise above the wall is no justification for continuation of a policy ill adapted to the desperate needs of the country. A declared policy and encouragement that parties should talk about such issues in systematic fashion, unenforced by legal proceedings, alone would be helpful and affect attitudes.

The "findings and policies" expressed at the outset of the Wagner Act and the Taft-Hartley Act, in my view, constitute an inappropriate basis for the legal framework of collective bargaining and industrial relations for the 1990s and beyond. The Wagner Act, with an eye to the Supreme Court and its interpretation of the Commerce Clause, was concerned with the inequality of bargaining power between "employees who do not possess full freedom of association or actual liberty of contract and employers who are organized in the corporate or other forms of ownership association," and was further concerned to reduce industrial strife or unrest which has the effect of burdening or obstructing commerce. Indeed, the flow of commerce was promoted by "restoring equality of bargaining power between employers and employees." The Taft-Hartley Act added the view that certain practices of labor organizations also burdened commerce through strikes and other forms of unrest and concerted action that should be eliminated to assure the rights of individual workers and employers guaranteed by the statute.

These foci—constitutionality, equality of bargaining power, and industrial conflict—whatever their merits as the centerpiece for a "declaration of policy" for industrial relations and collective bargaining in the 1930s, are totally inadequate to the necessities of the country in the 1990s.

1. The test of the *constitutionality* of a statute, ruling, or policy is largely irrelevant to whether it is a sound industrial relations policy and whether it contributes to the economic needs of the country at this time. I am surely not advocating unconstitutional measures, but the eye on that test is an entirely inadequate and insufficient judgment of industrial relations law or rulings.

2. *Equality of bargaining power*, or restoring such equality, was surely always a mirage of policy. I am, of course, aware that Beatrice Webb invented the term "collective bargaining" in 1891, although the institution had long existed, and in their classic work the Webbs contrasted individual bargaining with collective bargaining. Inequality is reduced.

> In organized trades the individual workman, applying for a job, accepts or refuses the terms offered by the employer, without communication with his fellow workmen, and without any other consideration than the exigencies of his own position. For the sale of his labor he makes with his employer, a strictly individual bargain. But if a group of workmen concert together, and send representatives to conduct the bargaining on behalf of the whole body, the position is at once changed.[10]

But that is a far cry from the expressed policy of "restoring equality of bargaining power between employers and employees," an unmeasurable and nonoperational goal.

3. The *emphasis upon strikes and other forms of industrial strife* that burden commerce may have facilitated constitutionality, but it is

---

[10] INDUSTRIAL DEMOCRACY 173 (1914).

a very limited and inadequate focus for policy in the 1990s, save perhaps in the cases of battles to death or extinction that border on the question of recognition. The Board has far too often expressed the view that it is the arbiter of conflict and in the absence of its role there would be excessive conflict. In general I do not agree, and my vision of the 1990s would permit the opportunity for more conflict and a far lesser role for the Board.

My basic point is that the labor policy, or industrial relations and collective bargaining, of the 1990s needs "findings and policies" concerned with enhancing consultation, improved quality, productivity, competitiveness, and increased responsibility for the two sides that are quite different from those articulated in the 1930s.

Unless representation can be promptly determined without discriminatory discharge, and unless first contracts can be readily negotiated, no adequate cooperation can be achieved at vital levels of industry and the economy. Unless parties can count on relatively predicable policies, they can make few commitments for the future. Unless employer associations can be strengthened to compromise internal differences, the most extreme position is enunciated. Unless the limits of fair representation are constrained, labor organizations cannot act responsibly and settle issues against their members. Unless independent unions can affiliate to strengthen bargaining relationships without the egregious notion that nonunion employees have a say, the natural growth and development of bargaining is delayed and weakened. Unless labor and management have a far greater role in shaping the rules of the game, they are not likely to act responsibly; and no system of law can enforce productivity, competitiveness, and responsiveness.

In looking ahead to industrial relations of the 1990s, there are as many proposals for redesign of the framework as there are architects. I am willing to exhibit my sketches to anyone, but I fear that such showings alone will not advance this symposium or the course of events very far. Moreover, in my view, discussion among experts alone is not likely to produce many changes.

I am rather dedicated to the proposition that the major elements of redesign must come from discussion and consensus among labor and management, principals not lawyers, to be followed by public and legislative review.

The fact is that very little, if any, effort has ever been devoted to seeking such general consensus. The labor-management conferences after World Wars I and II were more specialized efforts that floundered on issues of union security. I believe we should try, even if it should take a very long time. A legislative resolution urging such an effort by private parties might even be helpful. Legislative leaders in the continuing forum might help with mutual education. Some neutrals might possibly have a limited role. To have management and labor leaders remain outside the process and criticize each proposal, or have their lawyers conduct campaigns against them, is irresponsible in the extreme and will prove unproductive.

The major challenge to such consultation is on the side of management, which is devoid of an encompassing organization of procedures to compromise extreme positions; and in the absence of bold leadership the least common denominator tends to prevail on every industrial relations issue. In the absence of such leadership no package of proposals is very likely beyond formal positions.

It may be appropriate to recall the key roles that Walter C. Teagle of Standard Oil Company of New Jersey, Gerard Swope of General Electric, and Marion Folsom of Eastman Kodak played in shaping and securing support for the 1935 Social Security Act,[11] despite the fact that the National Association of Manufacturers strongly opposed that Act and fought it to a Supreme Court decision. In more recent days, it is well to remember as well that health care was the sole concern in business of the benefit manager until the pressure of costs and the leadership of Walter Wriston helped to raise the issue to the preoccupation of top executives and line management.

I am reminded of the words of Stanley Marcus, a thoughtful business leader:

> Who among the business community today would seriously propose that Congress repeal our child labor laws—or the Sherman Anti-Trust Act? The Federal Reserve Act, the Security Exchange Act? Or Workman's Compensation; or Social Security? Or Minimum Wage? Or Medicare? Or that Civil Rights legislation is an integral part of our system; that it has made us a stronger, more prosperous nation—and, in the long run, has been good for business. But we can take precious little credit for any of the social legislation now on the books, for business vigorously opposed

---

[11] J. Brown, An American Philosophy of Social Security, Evolution and Issues 21–22 (1972).

most of this legislation—and we get precious little credit from the people. . . .[12]

The need of the 1990s is for the Teagles, Swopes, and Folsoms of our day to take the lead for a more appropriate legal framework for industrial relations of the 1990s; it will never come, as it never has, from the resolutions of the numerous employer associations and their lawyers.

In this setting, it is appropriate to consider briefly intellectual proposals urged by the current conservative right to deregulate labor markets and industrial relations. At the outset, as I have explained elsewhere,[13] labor markets have many special features; they have a social element which mainstream economists have always recognized. Moreover, markets only exist in an institutional setting with established rules of operation that are subject to review and amendment affecting their performance and outcomes. There are no disembodied markets. This truth applies even to the stock market and certainly to labor markets.

It is particularly appropriate to quote William M. Leiserson on this point in lectures given almost 50 years ago. (Billy Leiserson was the first chairman of the National Mediation Board and the only person I believe to serve on both that board and the NLRB.)

> So long as people believe that the price of labor was determined by "natural laws of supply and demand," employers could and did disclaim responsibility for conditions of work and wages which from any moral point of view were indefensible. . . .
>
> When, however, people perceived that labor relationships were not the inexorable determinants of economic law, but largely the considered policies of industrial managers, with or without the consent of employees, then what Woodrow Wilson called the judgment of society began to change.[14]

The old natural-law argument is revived in the contemporary adoration of the uninhibited labor market.

There is a strong case, nonetheless, to be explored by labor and management, for deregulation of a number of features of the present legal framework of industrial relations and collective

---

[12] CAN FREE ENTERPRISE SURVIVE SUCCESS? (1975).

[13] Dunlop, *Industrial Relations and Economics: The Common Frontier of Wage Determination*, PROCEEDINGS OF THE 37TH ANNUAL MEETING OF THE INDUSTRIAL RELATIONS RESEARCH ASSOCIATION 9–23, December 28–29, 1984.

[14] RIGHT AND WRONG IN LABOR RELATIONS 11–12 (1942).

bargaining, given the detailed penetrations of regulation and the needs of the economy in the era ahead. Paul C. Weiler, in his paper to the National Academy of Arbitrators, has outlined a number of these areas.[15] These areas of deregulation open up new possibilities of labor-management discourse.

Although I am steadfast in the view that our major source of difficulty has been the absence of a major role of labor and management in shaping the policy framework of industrial relations—and I do not wish to see any more changes by the partisan political processes of the past— this symposium volume compels me to specify the general directions I see possible and desirable and potential areas of mutual consensus, rather than simply to defer to a grand negotiation and mediation process.

1. *Procedural*

a. Members of administrative agencies should only be appointed who command substantial support from a wide spectrum of labor and management organizations. No legislation is required.

b. Introduce explicit mediation into the resolution of more cases and particularly complex issues such as work preservation, plant closures, and technological change. (It is not adequate mediation to say that 85 or 90 percent of initial charges are settled or withdrawn. I would propose a special mediation staff working at all levels of the Board's operations.)

c. Enhance significantly the scope and role of arbitration, particularly during the life of a collective agreement. Also support private jurisdictional machinery.

d. Provide more role for conflict, strikes, and lockouts.

e. Limit the levels, and time, of legal review to a single court beyond the Board, with only genuine constitutional questions to go to the highest court. We used this arrangement to good effect in administering wage and price controls in the period 1971–74.

2. *Substantive*

a. Concentrate the agency on the prompt determination of representation and the first collective agreement and major prohibited practices. Reduce the regulation of the election proc-

---

[15] *I. Milestone or Millstone: The Wagner Act at Fifty*, ARBITRATION 1985: LAW AND PRACTICE, PROCEEDINGS OF THE 38TH ANNUAL MEETING OF THE NATIONAL ACADEMY OF ARBITRATORS 37–67 (W. Gershenfeld ed., 1986). *See also* the general appraisal of regulations in T. McCraw, PROPHETS OF REGULATION 300–309 (1984).

ess; sanitized elections are an unrealistic objective that have no counterpart in the nation's political life, as ward politics in our major cities well illustrate. The discharge for union activity should be dealt with by severe and effective penalties.

b. Deregulate the collective bargaining process in subjects of bargaining and procedures save where refusal to bargain is tantamount to nonrecognition.

c. Recognize the realities of the characteristics of particular sectors such as maritime, construction, mining, and lumbering, and avoid the industrial plant stereotype.

A word ought to be said about the Railway Labor Act as it applies to railroads and airlines. There are plenty of problems and unrealities created by legal fiction there, too, as in the distinction between minor and major matters and as to the procedures required to make a proffer of arbitration. But much as any experienced mediator might suggest changes, the fact is the parties are the trustees of the statute, and they should be deeply involved and in substantial agreement in any proposed modifications.[16]

What should be one's view of the industrial relations and collective bargaining the nation will need in the 1990s, and will the present legal framework get us there? I urge the application of a test: the potential for agreement between labor and management to proposals advanced in this volume.

Dr. David A. Hamburg, a psychiatrist by profession and now president of the Carnegie Corporation of New York, has well asked "whether human groups (labor organizations or management hierarchies) can ever achieve internal cohesion without harsh depreciation of other groups."[17] He happily reminds us that "the existence of multiple loyalties, rather than single-minded loyalty to one group only, makes it possible to line people of very different groups together."

The legal framework of the 1990s must be built on the intent and dedication of labor and management concerned with the

---

[16] Dunlop, *Trends and Issues in Labor Relations in the Transportation Sector,* TRN NEWS (TRB) 1–8 (1985).

[17] *Prejudice, Ethnocentrism, and Violence in Age of High Technology,* CARNEGIE CORPORATION OF NEW YORK ANNUAL REPORT 8, 11 (1984).

economic performance of this country. The Statement of Purpose of our Labor-Management Group is a good starting place:

> The uniqueness of America lies in the vitality of its free institutions. Among these a free labor movement and a free enterprise economy are essential to the achievement of social and political stability and economic prosperity for all. It is destructive to society and to business and organized labor, if in our legitimate adversarial roles, we question the right of our institutions to exist and perform their legitimate functions. In performing these legitimate functions, we recognize that both parties must respect deeply held views even when they disagree.[18]

I am reminded of a poem by Robert Frost, "The Road Not Taken":

> Two roads diverged in a yellow wood,
> And sorry I could not travel both
> And be one traveler, long I stood
> And looked down one as far as I could
> To where it bent in the undergrowth;
>
> *   *   *
>
> I shall be telling this with a sigh
> Somewhere ages and ages hence:
> Two roads diverged in a wood, and I—
> I took the one less traveled by,
> And that has made all the difference.[19]

In 1935 we took the road dictated by the opportunity of the moment, perhaps inevitably so, but the road was the wrong one for the long term; let's make a better choice for the 1990s, the road less traveled.

---

[18] *Statement of Purpose,* March 4, 1981, *reprinted in* J. Dunlop, *supra* note 7, at 264–66.
[19] THE POETRY OF ROBERT FROST 105 (E. Lathem ed., 1979).

CHAPTER 1

THE ACT'S IMPACT ON EMPLOYMENT, SOCIETY, AND THE NATIONAL ECONOMY

F. RAY MARSHALL*

This symposium comes during a period of ferment and controversy for the NLRB, the American industrial relations system, and the American economy. The controversy over the Board's change of direction since 1981 is symptomatic (and related to) disagreements over economic and industrial relations policy. Nor is this surprising; the industrial relations system is a subset of the larger society, so the industrial relations policies developed during the 1940s, 1950s, and 1960s naturally reflected the basic economic policies of that day. Moreover, industrial relations policy, as reflected in the Wagner Act, became an integral component of overall New Deal depression and war policies. Labor relations policy was modified by the Taft-Hartley and Landrum-Griffin acts, and, many would argue, the present conflict surrounding the Board is at least in part a reflection of the need to adapt industrial relations policies to new economic realities.

My main purpose, however, is to discuss the broader economic forces interacting with the industrial relations system, not to enter into the current debates about the Board, although I will make some comments after outlining the interactions between the economy and the U.S. industrial relations system.

I. Industrial Relations and Economic Policy

There are close relationships between an industrial relations system and the economic performance of an enterprise or economy. The enterprise's productivity, competitiveness, and ability to adapt to change depend heavily on the relationships between

* Bernard Rapoport, Centennial Professor of Economics and Public Affairs, LBJ School of Public Affairs, University of Texas, former Secretary of Labor.

workers and managers. Moreover, what happens in enterprises determines overall economic performance on such matters as productivity, economic growth, employment and unemployment, international competitiveness, and levels of living. By the same token, there are close relationships between public policies and the competitiveness of enterprises. Public policies set the external rules for the industrial relations system; affect the cost of capital, labor, and raw materials; help determine exchange rates, the quality of the work force, and the prices of goods and services in domestic and international markets; and influence the ability of labor and other resources to adjust to changing demand as well as the flexibility or rigidity of wages and prices. International and historical experiences make it very clear that economic policy that ignores labor and industrial relations will be incomplete and ineffective, if not counterproductive. Moreover, the mediating, negotiating, consensus-building, and human-resource-oriented tools of industrial relations could do much to improve economic policymaking, especially in the United States.

This section outlines some of the basic relationships between the industrial relations systems and the economy. My main theme is that the industrial relations system and supporting domestic and international economic policies put in place during the 1930s, 1940s, and 1950s facilitated, and were strengthened by, the growth in productivity, output, and real incomes. However, these positives concealed certain weaknesses in the traditional industrial relations system for dealing with the problems created by internationalization, changing technology (especially the information revolution), changing demographics (especially the increased labor force participation of women and the emergence of a younger, better-educated work force), and changing the occupational composition of the work force—especially the growth of services relative to the goods-producing sectors, where the traditional industrial relations system had its roots.

These developments call for a reconsideration of the basic assumptions upon which the traditional industrial system was based, producing new viability conditions and procedures. The new system must combine the positive and still viable principles and features of the old system and the viability and growth requirements of the internationalized information world. The basic purpose of labor relations policy should be to facilitate the achievement of these adjustments in a manner compatible with national policies and institutions.

A. *The Traditional Industrial Relations System*

The traditional American industrial relations system had three principal characteristics in common with those of other industrial nations: (1) a demand management approach to macroeconomic policy; (2) a commitment to a "free" labor movement;[1] and (3) the same basic structure where representatives of labor, management, and specialized government agencies were the main actors in the system. There were close interrelationships between the industrial relations systems in the industrial market economies (IMECs) and demand management economic policies, which conceived the primary national economic problem to be to achieve adequate aggregate demand to maintain high levels of growth and relatively low levels of unemployment. Growth helped both companies and unions, and unions were justified partly because by sustaining wages they helped maintain aggregate demand. Collective bargaining, unemployment compensation, social security, and other income support systems, were justified as ways to prevent recessions or moderate their impact by sustaining purchasing power.

The traditional industrial relations system established the work rules and assured some flexibility in response to changes in the basic forces affecting the system. As John Dunlop demonstrated in his classic and pathbreaking *Industrial Relations Systems* (1958), these contextual forces were technology, budget or market constraints, and the power status among those involved in the system. The traditional system's ideology (body of common ideas holding the system together) involved management's recognition of the right of workers to organize and bargain collectively and the dominant union leaders' acceptance of the prevailing economic and political system.

In addition to these features it had in common with other industrial nations, the American industrial relations system was distinguished by the following main characteristics:

1. *Exclusive representation,* whereby the union recognized as the bargaining agent has bargaining rights for all employ-

---

[1] A free labor movement is free from control by outside political or religious organizations and emphasizes democratic control by its members and the right to strike.

ees, whether or not they are members of the union. The legal right of workers to vote for or against unions in government-supervised elections has had a strong influence on the American industrial relations system, creating competition between the union and nonunion sectors and between unions and employers for the workers' allegiance. There is little doubt that the behavior of both unions and employers is influenced by this legal right; nonunion employers treat their workers better and unions have modified such practices as race and sex discrimination and adjusted other policies to appeal to minorities and women in representation elections.

2. *Decentralized bargaining,* with heavy emphasis on wages, hours, and working conditions in particular firms, industries, and labor markets. But pattern bargaining has been very important—wage comparisons between companies and occupations have been major elements in wage determination—with only a loose relation to economic conditions in particular firms or industries in the short run. Pattern bargaining, cost-of-living adjustments, and wage structures within enterprises were strongly influenced by equity, as well as product and labor market considerations.

3. *American employers are more hostile to unions than their counterparts in other major industrial nations.* This surprises some people in other countries because the American labor movement has been relatively unique in embracing the capitalist system and has demonstrated relative flexibility in accommodation to employers' interests. The reasons for this greater employer hostility here are not clear, but undoubtedly relate to the greater political power of unions in other countries, which causes them to be more of a threat to hostile employers, and the greater individualism and fluidity in the American economy.

4. In manufacturing enterprises, the traditional American industrial relations system also was characterized by an *authoritarian management system* and adversarial, confrontational relationships between labor and management. This system was rooted in American industrial history. The "scientific management" system, developed in the beginning of America's industrial revolution for relatively uneducated and inexperienced (often immigrant) workers in goods-producing activities, subdivided work into discrete tasks

and sought to maintain strict management control over work processes; this management system assumed, in addition, that workers had little other than brawn to contribute to the work process, that there was one best way to do a task, and that management's responsibility was to determine what that one best way was and to impose it on employees. This model provided limited security for or participation by workers, and workers had limited commitment to or identification with the enterprise. Workers often assumed that a major function of unions was to protect workers from exploitation by elitist managements more interested in profit maximization than workers' welfare. This adversarial, confrontational industrial relations system therefore tended to reduce management's (and labor's) flexibility through a detailed system of rules that carefully specified such matters as job content, promotion and layoff procedures, and management's rights and prerogatives.

5. *A nonsocialist political orientation.* American unions are unique in not having formed a labor party; a lower degree of class consciousness has caused the American labor movement to be organized mainly around the *job* for economic purposes rather than around the *working class* for political purposes.

In the United States, unions have been strongest in large oligopolistic firms, urban areas, regulated industries, and among male blue-collar workers and workers who occupy strategic locations in the economy—such as transportation. Craft union bargaining power was based mainly on skills and the control of labor supplies and training processes. In the construction, garment, and printing industries, the craft industrial relations system was more flexible and less authoritarian than in the large-scale manufacturing firms that were unionized mainly during the 1930s and 1940s. A number of features aided the unionization of oligopolies (control of a commodity or service in a given market by a small number of companies): public opinion (which turned against the oligopolies in the 1930s), oligopolistic profits (oligopolies resisted wage increases less than competitive firms because they had greater control over their prices and therefore could pass wage increases through to consumers in the form of higher prices), size, and location in key labor markets. By the 1960s, except for industries like clothing and garments, which were relatively concentrated geographically, and those retaining craft principles (like printing and some specialty machine shops), very few highly competitive industries or small employers were unionized.[2]

Other industries which were unionized but had limited competition because of regulations (*i.e.*, trucking and other transportation) existed where unions and companies accommodated each other within the framework of adversarial relations. By taking wages out of competition, the unions helped companies to regulate markets, and employer participants in the industrial relations system recognized the right of workers to organize and bargain collectively; and free collective bargaining helped legitimize the free enterprise system. Moreover, management's right to freely lay off workers during economic recessions was justified, in part, by unemployment compensation and the assumption that Keynesian policies would cause the layoffs to be temporary. This was an informal "social compact," which had broad public support, not only as a part of the demand management macroeconomic rationale, but also because of a prevailing assumption that labor market competition was not good for workers or the economy.

The government consolidated the "traditional" industrial relations system during World War II through the War Labor Board. Recalcitrant companies and unions were brought in line by the military. The economy's performance during the war also justified the assumption that Keynesian policies could achieve full employment.

There were a number of economic consequences of the traditional American industrial relations system:

1. That system, together with the Keynesian economic policies to which it was closely related, and the expanding international economy facilitated by the Bretton Woods institutions, contributed to a long period of relatively high growth in productivity and total output. American firms also have had higher short-run profit requirements than their Japanese competitors, partly because of their sources of finance but also because the more adversarial and less

---

[2] However, R. Freeman & J. Medoff in their book WHAT DO UNIONS DO? (1984) present evidence that in recent times unions have won a greater proportion of their representation elections in relatively small enterprises.

coordinated economic policy processes in the United States cause greater uncertainty and risk. As noted, the main characteristic of the system was to promote growth within the framework of relatively stable prices, wages, and exchange rates. Within this system, collective bargaining made it possible for most union members to achieve middle-class incomes.

2. The American system was not as flexible in adjusting to change as the Japanese system, but was more flexible than most European industrial relations systems. The main indicators of flexibility in the American system relative to the European, were the greater decline in real wages and increase in employment in the United States during the 1970s and the greater increase in long-term unemployment in Europe during the 1970s and 1980s. The factors providing for greater flexibility in the United States than in Europe included: the principle of exclusive bargaining rights; a more decentralized bargaining system; lower levels of income support for those not working; lower degrees of unionization and the resulting competition between union and nonunion companies; the American economy's greater openness to immigration and imports; the greater internal displacement of labor from American agriculture, which created pools of underemployed workers; and the greater ease with which American employers could close plants and lay off workers.

3. The evidence of flexibility in the Japanese system is suggested by higher growth in productivity, total output, and real wages than in either the United States or Europe; the maintenance of relatively low levels of unemployment; and the greater ease in bringing inflation down after the oil price shocks of the 1970s without generating high levels of unemployment. Large Japanese enterprises have adjusted to declining demand by maintaining output and reducing labor compensation and prices. The factors making for greater flexibility in the Japanese system than in either the American or European systems include: highly interrelated consensus-based economic policies that have emphasized the upgrading (in terms of productivity and value added) of the Japanese industry mix; an enterprise management system stressing labor-management cooperation, participation, and consensus; mechanisms to absorb shocks in

demand, including a bonus compensation system based on the enterprise's performance, production sharing (whereby low-wage work is done in third world countries), sub-contracting, and the use of temporary workers; one of the world's most effective positive adjustment programs to shift resources from noncompetitive to more competitive industries; an industrial relations system that stresses "lifetime" employment, continuing education of an already well-educated work force (education and training make *individuals* more flexible), concentration of collective bargaining at the enterprise instead of the industry or sectoral levels, and the annual adjustment of wages through a "spring wage offensive" that minimizes whipsawing and leapfrogging; the heavy reliance on consensus mechanisms at every level (in national, as well as enterprise policymaking) rather than the detailed regulations that characterize the American and European systems; the bonus wage payment system, which prevented wage increases based on temporary factors from becoming imbedded in the wage base; and the flexibility in job assignments and training made possible by the "lifetime employment" system, which caused workers to have *employment* security rather than *job* security, caused workers to be less concerned about protecting particular jobs, and made companies more willing to finance long-term education and training for their employees. The growing importance of human resources for economic competitiveness in an internationalized information world made this last point particularly significant.

4. The traditional industrial relations systems in the United States and Europe contained inflationary biases: these systems gave inadequate attention to productivity and efficiency; the decentralized American system was conducive to whipsawing (raising wages by playing one employer off against another) and leapfrogging (union leaders escalating wages in competition with each other); long-term contracts with cost-of-living adjustments and annual improvement factors tended to cause temporary factors to increase the wage base and therefore ratchet the compensation base upward; the "safety nets" of unemployment compensation and income maintenance programs for those who were unemployed or not expected to work reduced the impact of labor supplies on wages, as did the

growth of families with multiple wage earners; and the "full employment" policies pursued by governments created less incentive for employers to resist wage increases or for unions to hold wages down, since wage and price increases were likely to be offset by government monetary-fiscal policies.

5. The American and European industrial relations systems had some participatory features that improved productivity, which is one of the reasons many studies tended to show higher productivity (but not necessarily *competitiveness*, *i.e.*, changes in wages could exceed changes in productivity) in union than in nonunion firms in the same industry.

II. Consequences of Internationalization and Other Trends

A number of trends have disrupted the traditional American and IMEC industrial relations systems. The most important of these have been related to the emergence of a more integrated world economy, but other simultaneous trends tending to alter the relationships between the actors in the industrial relations system include: the decline in productivity growth after the middle of the 1960s, and especially after the oil price shocks of the 1970s, which made it much more difficult to sustain the increase in output and real wages; stagflation, which upset the economic policy framework that had sustained the industrial relations system; technological changes (especially the information revolution) which made scale less important (and adaptability to change both more possible and more important) to an enterprises' viability and competitiveness and shifted employment out of heavily unionized industries, companies, and places into smaller firms, rural areas, white-collar work, services, and the sunbelt, where unions are weaker; and the increased labor force participation rates of women, who generally are less well-organized than men and whose presence as permanent, integral parts of the work force put pressure on traditional work rules and compensation systems oriented to male heads of households and based on the assumption that women were temporary, peripheral labor market participants. In 1950, 70 percent of American households were headed by men whose income was the sole source of income; by 1984, less than 15 percent of households fell into this category. Moreover, between 1950 and 1984, the proportion of the work force in the information occupations had increased from less than 20 percent to about 60 percent.

All of these trends tended to interact with internationalization to weaken unions, strengthen the relative power of multinationals, and change the traditional industrial relations system. In 1950 only about 9 percent of America's GNP entered international trade; by 1980, 25 percent of the GNP entered international trade.

The American system—as it was established in the 1930s, 1940s, and 1950s, was partly justified as a stabilizing system that took wages out of competition, thus reducing product-market competition, but internationalization made it more difficult for collective bargaining to insulate labor from competition. Stagflation, declining real wages, and the slow growth of real incomes caused people to be more price conscious, leading to deregulation of economic activity, especially in airlines and trucking, where unions were strong; because of greater mobility of capital relative to labor, multinational corporations can play workers of different countries against each other, making it much more difficult for unions to sustain wages above those of competing workers in other countries. Nationalism and worldwide joblessness (which is 40–50 percent in third world countries and at post-depression highs in Western Europe) weaken organized responses to multinational corporations by unions or governments. Unions have turned to such international agencies as the International Labor Organization, but these organizations, while very important, have limited power relative to the multinationals.

The demand-management macroeconomic policies which reinforce the traditional industrial relations systems have important limitations in an internationalized information world. These policies assume a closed economy—or at least work best under those conditions. Moreover, the system assumes downwardly inflexible wages. The basic policy objective of Keynesian economics—low levels of unemployment—means that wages and prices can escalate, but cannot fall very much.

Of course, most of the inflation of the 1970s originated outside American product and labor markets mainly from external shocks, but the industrial relations system did not have the wage and price flexibility to achieve the real wage and income reductions required to achieve external equilibrium in the face of low or declining productivity growth and the external energy and commodity price shocks. Real wage cuts were therefore achieved through inflation, followed inevitably by rising unemployment.

Monetarism and supply-side economics, by contrast, emphasize competitive labor and product markets and therefore are more hostile to the traditional labor relations system. I believe the Keynesian assumptions and policies still are more valid than supply-side–monetarist prescriptions, but macroeconomic policy must be modified to fit the realities of an internationalized information world. While demand is still the driving force in market economies, greater attention must be given to inflation; productivity; resources; flexibility; technology; selective labor market, anti-inflation, and industrial policies; and industrial relations, all of which receive inadequate attention from the Keynesians.

Nevertheless, internationalization makes it more difficult for the United States to carry out monetary-fiscal policies of whatever variety. Efforts to stimulate the economy are much less effective if other economies are not also growing; in that case, increases in immigration and imports will limit expansion in our economy. Similarly, with floating exchange rates, checking inflation through restrictions on the growth of the money supply increases interest rates and the value of the dollar, leading to worldwide economic problems, which, in an increasingly interdependent global economy, boomerang back to the United States. An overvalued dollar makes it more difficult to export, and therefore costs millions of Americans jobs, though it reduces the price of imports and therefore helps with inflation.

The main impact of internationalization has been to transform a system that was geared primarily to American product and labor markets into one that must address the requirements of international competition.

International competition has not only influenced macroeconomic policies and wage and prices, but also has called into question the effectiveness of the traditional American management and industrial relations systems. Other countries, especially Japan, have developed management and industrial relations systems that appear to be much more competitive than the systems used in the United States.

While the Japanese system has received a lot of attention, it is not superior across the board; after all, productivity and living standards are still higher in the United States than in Japan. Moreover, most American companies (outside the basic industries dominated by oligopolies) have been fairly competitive, and some Japanese sectors like agriculture and consumer distribution are not very efficient, and only about 15–20 percent of the work force has "lifetime" employment to age 55; older workers and women have less security than prime-working-age males. Nevertheless, the Japanese have developed a very competitive system in the industries they have targeted—*e.g.*, automobiles, steel, consumer electronics, and computer chips. The Japanese system likewise provides rising real incomes and security to all, even though some people have more security than others. Moreover, the Japanese system is much more egalitarian than the American system, in the sense that the income differentials between managers and workers are much smaller. The Japanese also have developed a system where workers perceive their benefits to be much more closely related to productivity improvements than is the case with American workers. For example, a 1983 Chamber of Commerce survey found that only 9 percent of American workers thought that increasing productivity would benefit them; 93 percent of comparable Japanese workers thought they benefited from increased productivity.

Finally, the Japanese provide an economic environment for their enterprises that is conducive to flexibility and productivity growth. Coordinated economic policy based on public-private cooperation and consensus creates greater stability and predictability, as well as flexibility. Japanese public policy socializes much economic risk, making it possible for enterprises to be satisfied with lower rates of return. The Japanese financial system is particularly beneficial: the consumer credit, social security, compensation, consumer price and tax systems all encourage a high level of savings; the government has kept interest rates relatively low to producers; and Japanese corporations rely much more heavily on debt financing than their American counterparts, who rely more heavily on stocks; bank financing relieves the Japanese of the need to be concerned about short-run stock market quotations, enabling them to develop longer-term strategies based on the latest technologies. Moreover, Japanese banks and related companies are likely to be the enterprises' main stockholders. These related companies are less likely than individual or institutional investors to be concerned about short-run returns on their stock; they are more interested in their long-term business relations with the enterprise than in their stock dividends. Finally, Japanese corporations are likely to give higher priority to the concerns of their workers than to their stockholders. This makes the Japanese firm more interested in market share than profit maximization, the main driving force of the stockholder-oriented American enterprise. The Japanese firm, in order to enlarge market share, gives much greater attention to quality and productivity than has been the case with large oligopolistic American firms in basic goods-producing industries.

Finally, the absence of energy and other physical resources has caused the Japanese to emphasize human resource development. Indeed, some observers even believe education to be the Japanese's *main* economic advantage—even more important than its management and industrial relations systems. However, the components of the Japanese system are so closely interrelated that it would be very difficult to single out any one of them as *mainly* responsible for the overall outcome. I am persuaded, though, that Japan's principal advantage relative to the United States is its comprehensive consensus-based economic policy, though its industrial relations system provides important advantages in the basic industries.

A. *Implications for Industrial Relations System*

What are the implications of these trends for America's traditional industrial relations system?

1. In a relatively open trading system and increased international competition, labor cannot be as insulated from competition as it was during the 1950s, and oligopolistic pricing is much more difficult.

2. Because technology can be standardized and capital and material prices are determined mainly by international markets, unit labor costs become a more important and strategic element in the viability of economic enterprises. The oligopolistic-pattern bargaining wage premium becomes less tenable, as do long-term contracts, pattern bargaining, and fragmented work assignments.

3. Weaknesses in flexibility, productivity, and quality output, which previously had been concealed by economic growth, become more obvious in a slow-growth global economy. Competition with the more flexible and productive Japanese industrial relations system reveals weaknesses in the American system. The lessons learned from the Jap-

anese (as well as more competitive American enterprises) include the following:

a. The importance of quality to productivity. Quality affects management and worker morale, market share, the ability to maintain steady production, and therefore optimal resource mixes and utilization levels.

b. The importance of the source and terms of credit on long-run economic viability; the need to free management from the "tyranny of Wall Street" (preoccupation with short-run earnings statements designed to satisfy equity investors) while permitting greater attention to technology development and long-run economic viability.

c. Maximizing market share rather than profits gives the Japanese firm a competitive edge. It is very difficult for oligopolies to compete with the Japanese model which adjusts to declining demand by reducing relative prices and increasing market share while the oligopolist attempts to keep prices high and reduce output. It could be, however, that employee-owned enterprises would be more competitive because of higher productivity resulting from greater employee involvement and lower profit requirements because workers are likely to be more concerned with employment preservation than profit maximization.

d. The relationship of human resource development, cooperation, and consensus building (labor-management, public-private) to productivity, quality, flexibility, and stability.

e. The correlation between *employment security*, worker commitment, and good management. Employment security provides greater flexibility. With labor as a relatively fixed cost, education, training, and job rotation allow more flexibility. As some American companies have discovered, providing employment security makes it more difficult to shift the costs of change to workers in the form of unemployment and forces management to better plan production and labor utilization.

f. The adversarial/confrontational mode of labor relations places American enterprises at a disadvantage when competing with more cooperative models like those in large Japanese firms. Adversarial/confrontational relations make it difficult for labor and management to establish the kind of cooperation and mutual trust required for quality output, productivity, and flexibility in adjusting to change. In the internationalized information world where workers have higher levels of education, authoritarian, adversarial management systems deprive enterprises of the productivity and creativity of workers who know their jobs better than anyone else in the organization. Strong visible links have been established between the viability of enterprises, labor-management cooperation, employment security, and worker participation. In this new environment, unions must give greater attention to the enterprises' economic viability and management must give greater attention to workers' security and involvement in decision making. This is, however, a matter of balance and emphasis: adversarial relations are inevitable and can be constructive forces, but they also can become functionless in the sense that they do more damage to the parties' common interests than they benefit either of them.

It is important to stabilize the core of the labor-management system through instruments of flexibility or "shock absorbers" such as the sharing of information and flexible compensation systems, but this should be done in a way that maintains upward economic mobility and does not rigidly polarize or segment the work force. Coordination of economic policy and industrial relations policy is an important part of the system. An economic policy with low interest rates, high savings, research and development, and information sharing protects domestic producers.

Public policy with respect to industrial relations systems must be concerned about creating the environment within which enterprises can compete. There is a need for flexibility in the external or "tradeables" sector of most economies. The Japanese keep prices and interest rates low and encourage flexible systems in order to absorb shocks, while maintaining output and employment. Small, open European systems (like the Austrians) have developed wage and price policies that keep prices competitive in the sectors that depend on exports, as well as those that are most affected by import competition. The lack of coordinated trade and economic policy in the United States makes it difficult to sustain low levels of unemployment at stable prices. Our macro and micro systems are too prone to let output and employment absorb demand shocks, at considerable cost to real output.

Public policy must therefore be concerned with maintaining an economic environment that permits and encourages productivity and flexibility. This requires some consensus-building processes, balanced macroeconomic policies, and selective measures to deal with inflation, labor-market problems, and industrial upgrading through more explicit industrial policies.

III. Implications for National Labor Relations Policy

While we need to make our legal framework more compatible with the requirements of the emerging industrial relations system, I am persuaded that the NLRA's basic assumptions are still largely valid. Encouraging collective bargaining and protecting the workers' rights to decide for themselves whether or not they want to be represented by unions are as important, or perhaps even more important, today as they were in 1935. Individual workers still have inadequate bargaining power relative to most of their employers. Moreover, collective bargaining and other forms of worker participation are perhaps even more important in an internationalized information world than they were in the mainly domestic goods-producing world of 1935. Similarly, despite the supply-side rhetoric accompanying the 1981 tax cuts, the clear failure of those measures to achieve their promised results reaffirms the importance of adequate aggregate demand for economic growth and prosperity. Increased consumer and military spending were mainly responsible for the recovery from the 1981–82 recession, not increased savings and investment, which declined in 1981–84 relative to 1977–81. Nor is there any evidence of a weakening of the relationships between free and democratic societies and free and democratic labor movements.

The main problem, however, is the *implementation* of national labor policy, not its underlying philosophy. Even before the Reagan Board tilted Board decisions more against unions, employers' interests were much better protected in the American system than those of workers or unions. The Board and the courts have been much more effective in restricting such union self-help activities as secondary boycotts than they have been in restricting such employer practices as boycotting union contractors, helping each other during strikes, discharging workers for union activity, or stonewalling during contract negotiations. Moreover, time delays, expensive legal maneuvers, and weak penalties for violations all bias the Board's procedures against unions and workers. Especially devastating is the finding by Paul Weiler of the Harvard Law School that the odds were 1 in 20 that union supporters would be fired illegally in 1980 and 1981.[3] In addition to these weaknesses, legalisms have damaged industrial relations by forcing the parties to consider "legalities" rather than the spirit of their proposals and relationships.

The Board's effectiveness also is diminished by politicization. Some politicization is inevitable, of course, but it has become even more of an issue since the Reagan Board appointments. These appointments not only represent probably the sharpest philosophical change in the Board's history, but also represent the sharpest departure in terms of membership continuity.

Much of the decline in union strength since the 1960s is attributable to increased employer opposition which, in turn, undoubtedly is attributable to the Board's enforcement limitations. This has been documented by Richard Freeman, who has studied the reasons for declining union success in representative elections very thoroughly. Freeman concludes that "perhaps 40 percent is due to increased management opposition; perhaps 20 percent is due to reduced union organizing effort per nonunion worker; the remaining 40 percent is due to structural changes in the economy and in part to unknown forces."[4]

The Reagan Board has relaxed rules making it an unfair labor practice for employers to make threats or promises during organizing campaigns; made it more difficult to sign up union members on company premises during the workday; discontinued protections for employees for turning in employers who violate safety and health laws; and has made it more difficult for labor organizations to discipline their members for violating union rules during strikes. Supporters of the present Board claim that it is merely reversing decisions of the "free wheeling" Carter Board. Since I was President Carter's chief labor adviser, I naturally disagree with this characterization. The Carter Administration's policy was to maintain *continuity* by appointing board members with long experience who believed in the purposes of the Act.

Additionally, an examination of the present Board's decision shows that the Reagan Board has done much more than merely

---

[3] Bus. Wk., July 16, 1984, at 29.
[4] *Why Are Unions Faring Poorly in NLRB Representative Elections?*, CHALLENGES AND CHOICES FACING AMERICAN LABOR 63 (T. Kochan ed., 1985).

reverse Carter Board decisions. Most of the Board's reversals were of precedents that predated the Carter Board.[5] Such analyses are admittedly hard to make because each case is unique and all cases are not equally important. However, it would really be difficult for even its most ardent supporters to argue that the Reagan Board has leaned over backward to strengthen the workers' rights to express timely preferences for or against collective bargaining.

As the House Subcommittee on Labor-Management Relations concluded in a highly critical 1984 report, the Reagan Board's bias is suggested as much or more by its day-to-day decisions, as in its reversals of established precedent. After all, the main thrust of labor policy is sufficiently well established that even the most biased Board would risk reversal by the courts if it departed too far from precedent. Despite judicial review, however, biases influence Board decisions, because the courts defer to the Board's presumed expertise in labor matters. Some indication of the present Board's departure from precedent in day-to-day cases is suggested by the fact that the Nixon-Ford Board decided for employers in unfair labor practice and representation cases 29 percent of the time, which was about the same as the Carter Board (27 percent). The Reagan Board, by contrast, has decided for employers in 60 percent of the cases and against unions 86 percent of the time.[6] It is hard to believe that differences of this magnitude could be by chance.

There was, however, considerable disillusionment with the NLRA even before the Reagan Board appointments. This disillusionment was exacerbated by the failure of even the relatively mild procedural and penalty-strengthening reforms to the NLRA proposed in 1978–79. Despite passage by an almost 100-vote majority in the House and a clear majority in the Senate, business and antiunion forces mounted such an intensive campaign against the reform bill that its supporters were unable to muster the 60 (out of 100) votes needed to break a filibuster in the Senate. Pro-reform forces were particularly concerned that no important business organization was willing to support the measure publicly, though some were willing to do so privately.

---

[5] See S. Kaynard, *Recent Developments and Current Trends Under the NLRA or the Golden Anniversary of the NLRA: Will the Marriage Survive?*, paper presented at the 50th Anniversary NLRA Conference, Rutgers University, April 24, 1985.

[6] D. Silberman, *Labor Law Turned Upside Down*, speech to the Labor-Management Conference, Northern Kentucky University, May 22, 1985; AFL-CIO News, June 1, 1985.

The Reagan Board's actions, added to this frustration, have caused growing union support for either repeal of the NLRA or nonuse of the Board. Some observers think union leaders are only posturing on these matters, but I believe they are very serious.

Experts disagree, however, over whether unions would be better off without the NLRA. Some, including almost all lawyers who represent unions, argue that they would be. In this view, the Board's procedures sap financial and leadership resources with the delusion that workers' and unions' interests are being protected. These critics also contend that the unions' ultimate success rests on their ability to exert economic and political power, and to strike successfully, not their ability to win representation elections. Repeal of the NLRA probably would strengthen the unions' economic power, especially the strong unions' ability to help weak ones through secondary boycotts and other means. Critics of this position contend that the NLRA has in fact done much to protect workers' rights and that unions are too weak and divided to attempt to organize without the Board's help.

It is, of course, impossible to resolve this dispute. My own view is that *unions* probably would be better off without the NLRA, which, as noted, does more to protect employers' interests than to help unions or workers. Indeed, the NLRA had only marginal impact on union growth, even before the Taft-Hartley (1947) and the Landrum-Griffin (1959) amendments tilted the Act against unions.[7]

Moreover, even a stronger, highly motivated, more efficient Board would not necessarily solve the unions' problems. As noted, most basic economic, technological, and political trends have tended to weaken the unions' relative strength. Labor organizations will therefore have to change their traditional policies and procedures and gain greater economic and political power in order to reverse their decline. They must develop special ways to respond to the needs of workers in occupations, firms, industries, and demographic groups that are becoming larger porportions of the work force: services, women and minorities, small firms, and nonmetropolitan areas. Unions, in addition, must find ways to deal with multi-national corporations and gain greater public approval. Many unions already are beginning to do these things through increased political action,

---

[7] *See* R. Marshall, LABOR IN THE SOUTH (1967).

corporate campaigns, more effective use of their substantial economic resources (especially pension funds and stock ownership) and their ability to determine the viability of enterprises through concessions or greater cooperation. For example, the Machinists (IAM) and Pilots (ALPA) played a major role in avoiding the takeover of TWA by Texas Air chief Frank Lorenzo, whom the unions considered to be a "ruthless union buster."[8] Against all odds, the unions helped financier Carl Icahn gain control of TWA by skillful negotiations and by granting wage concessions in exchange for stock and a profit-sharing program.

The TWA and other company and industrial restructurings show how important unions can be in protecting the workers' interest in the current economic environment. Protecting workers' interests in an internationalized information economy also will require greater attention to flexibility, sound management practices, quality output, and productivity. Flexibility can be achieved through flexible compensation systems (combining bonuses and ownership earnings as well as wages). Unions must give management more flexibility in work assignments and compensation in exchange for job security and a larger role in management decisions. Above all, the critical importance of human resource development in the emerging workplace will require improved education and training systems. Instead of the traditional union organizing principle of the common rule, greater attention must be given to individual differences to fit a more heterogeneous, better education work force primarily employed in information and services occupations rather than the production of goods. Detailed economic analyses show human resource improvements to be responsible for almost all of the advances in productivity since 1929. All of these matters require greater cooperation and consensus, but in most cases effective consensus probably requires some means for workers to protect their interests through organizations which they control.

Thus, the preservation of the NLRA is desirable not because it would strengthen unions, but because it is in the public interest. It would not be in the public interest to encourage a return to the law of the jungle with its risk of debilitating "functionless con-

---

[8] Salpukas, *The Long Fight for TWA: Unions Decided the Winner*, N.Y. Times, Aug. 31, 1985, at 1.

flict." National labor relations policy should be neither pro-union nor pro-employer, but *pro-worker*. Strengthening the workers' right to timely decisions about whether or not to bargain collectively would cause unions *and* employers to be more responsive to the workers' interests. The workers' right to bargain collectively has been compromised by the Board's inability or unwillingness to hold timely elections and prevent unfair labor practices, especially the discharge of workers for union activity.

Effective national labor relations policy also requires less politicization of the Board. As noted, some politicization is inevitable, but wide swings in Board decisions with successive national administrations are not in the public interest. Indeed, it is doubtful that the Board could survive many such swings. We should therefore attempt to build a new consensus about the desirability of collective bargaining and workers' rights to organize and bargain collectively and either insulate the Board more from the political process or establish new machinery to resolve representation issues and prevent prohibited conduct by unions and employers. Industrial relations professionals who understand the value of the industrial relations system to a free society as well as the nature and importance of human resource management, dispute settlement, and consensus building, should take the lead to build bipartisan consensus for a more effective national labor relations policy compatible with the requirements of an internationalized information world.

Responses

FIVE MODEST PROPOSALS

HOWARD JENKINS, JR.*

Though the point tends to be obscured by overriding concern with detail, there can be no doubt that one of the most potent bulwarks against governmental wage and price controls has been the development of the system of establishing wage levels privately through bargaining between private industry and free labor unions. Those whose concern is most deeply committed to preservation of management's right to be free from governmen-

---

* Former member, National Labor Relations Board; arbitrator and mediator.

tal price-fixing would do well to reflect on the role of the trade union movement in preserving a free economy. Industrial relations, like politics, make strange bedfellows.

In a very real sense, the problems of the industrial community are a reflection in miniature of the problems of our nation. The socio-economic problems that beset us in the human relations field, which are the concern of all Americans, are not unlike the socio-economic problems that constitute grist for the industrial relations mill. Underlying both sets of problems are the major political and legal tasks of testing and readjusting doctrine so as to harmonize two fundamental democratic principles, namely: preservation of the rights of the individual and preservation of free democratic institutions. Upon reflection, it should not be surprising to find that neither set of problems can be solved in isolation. Whatever judgments form the base from which doctrine emerges in the one area will also by logic and necessity dictate doctrine in the other. Those whose primary concern is with the strengthening and expanding of our economy, as well as those whose efforts are directed toward elimination of social and economic inequities in the broader sense, need clearly to recognize the fact that neither group can achieve its goals if one group disregards the other.

During my 20 years of service as a member of the Labor Board I held firmly to the view that it was not the proper function for Board members to be about the business of telling Congress how to write legislation. I made no recommendations for amendments or changes in the law and indeed refused invitations from both the House and Senate to comment on legislative proposals then pending before the Congress. I felt it to be inappropriate for a person with decisional responsibilities under a federal statute to undertake to describe how the statutes ought to be written; just as I would have thought it inappropriate had members of the Congress undertaken to advise me on how to decide cases. Incidentally, at no time during my service on the Board did any member of the Congress or any President undertake to influence any Board case or the manner in which that case would be decided.

Now that I am free from those constraints, I am willing to share my views on ways in which I think the work of the Board could be improved by some changes in the statutes.

With that comment I move with some trepidation into the political arena—an area where I have been more of an observer than a participant.

Experience teaches that achieving changes in the labor statutes is extremely difficult. No change comes easily. For example,
the last substantive change in the law occurred in 1974, and a
major effort to overhaul the statute in large part in 1978 completely failed. In my view there are several basic reasons for this
difficulty. The first is that the National Labor Relations Board
has no constituency. It is unlike some regulatory agencies whose
impact is felt through its direct power to regulate a given industry or, as with other agencies, the power to award franchises, to
grant licenses, and to take action that will benefit people subject
to the regulation of that agency. In the course of events, most
people who come before the Board lose, and those who do not
feel they should not have been there in the first place. Of course,
I should quickly add that the Labor Board should not have a
constituency, and it is appropriate that it not have one primarily
because of the nature of the Board's responsibilities. Nevertheless, the plain political fact is the Board lacks clout in the
legislative process and has no one to speak for it either in the
appropriations process or in the legislative process itself. One
could hardly expect disappointed litigants to go on to the Hill
and urge the Congress to help this agency and provide it with
more resources and funds or to take action that would be beneficial to the agency.

A second basic reason for the difficulty lies in the fact that both
labor and management have their own partisan positions for
which they lobby and their own separate legislative goals. Thus
consensus among those most directly affected does not come
easily; moreover, there is wide diversity within both groups.
Contrary to what some political cartoonists would have us
believe, organized labor is not a monolith. Neither is management monolithic in its views. Leadership positions in both
groups are held by persons of differing political philosophies,
party affiliations, organizational goals, and personal ambitions,
to say nothing of the size and character of the constituent organizations.

A further complicating factor is the legislative system itself. It
has been suggested that the genius of our system lies in the fact
that the legislative process is a process of accommodation to
competing points of view and that seldom does any one point of
view prevail to the exclusion of all others. It has been described
in terms of a horse race, with the suggestion that in the socio-
economic area there is never a clear victory but rather always a

photo finish with the debate going on for years as to who won. Nothing said here is intended either in word or spirit to be critical of the legislative process, because I think Congress is doing exactly what it should do in reacting to the kinds of problems facing it. Rather, the thrust of my observation is that the likelihood of significant substantive changes in our labor laws is slight.

Despite that rather negative and dismal forecast concerning substantive changes, there are some procedural changes that I think could be made if they obtain the support and backing of the organized bar. I recognize at the outset that the line between what is procedural and what is substantive is not always clear. To me, however, the differences are real. I will briefly outline the proposals and my reasons for suggesting the changes.

The first has to do with a little known provision which makes it impossible for the Board to employ economists. For many years there has been a rider on the NLRB Appropriation Bill which forbids the Board to expend any of its funds to employ economists.[1] Without going into detail, this dates back to a time when some felt that there were employed by the Board economists who also were either communists or fellow travelers. The consequence of this rider is that the Board's knowledge of economic matters comes through happenstance, briefs filed by parties, or whatever incidental reading Board members happen to do. But obviously, for much of what the Board does in the area of determining appropriate units and in handling the problems of collective bargaining generally, knowledge of the industrial economy is key. For example, when the health care amendments were passed and for the first time the Board started looking at hospitals, nursing homes, and other health care institutions on a broad basis, we needed to know what the industry was like and we needed information about employment in the industry. The kind of information which, if we had had economists capable of doing some research and gathering data for us, would have made our task a great deal easier, and perhaps the results in the cases might well have been more useful and more acceptable to the parties. In any event, it is almost ludicrous for the National

---

[1] The Taft-Hartley Act amended §4 of the statute to provide: "Nothing in this Act shall be construed to authorize the Board to appoint individuals for the purpose of . . . economic analysis."

Labor Relations Board to be flying blind in dealing with the industrial economy of our nation.

A second area in which change would be beneficial, in my view, deals with the existence of Board vacancies. As we know, when a Board member's term expires, at midnight of that day his authority ends. Until a new member is appointed and confirmed or brought into office through a recess appointment, that seat remains vacant and the staff which reported to the member whose term expired is taken over by the Chairman or a senior member. The Chairman or the senior member, or as it now exists, both, must operate and direct two staffs. I have experienced that situation and know that it is an unnecessary burden on the senior member, in my case, or the Chairman in another case, to have the burden of giving direction to two staffs while trying to carry on one's normal duty.

There obviously is no way in which a president of the United States can be compelled to act quickly in filling vacancies, and I certainly do not suggest any criticism of any president for delay in the appointment process; that is his prerogative and I make no suggestion with regard to it. I do, however, feel that if the Board is to function effectively there should be five members, and one way to encourage the prompt filling of vacancies is to provide in the law that a member whose term has expired shall remain in office until a successor is appointed. Most other agencies have such a provision. The Labor Board is almost alone in this regard.

I might add that the holdover provision should also be changed with regard to the General Counsel. As we know, on the day a General Counsel's term expires, if no new General Counsel has been appointed, the work of the field offices grinds to a halt. No complaints can issue, no briefs can be filed, no enforcement actions can be taken because they must be taken by the authority of the General Counsel; and it is necessary, therefore, for the President to appoint an Acting General Counsel, which is usually done very quickly. A Regional Director or a senior staff member on the General Counsel staff is named as Acting General Counsel. But that is a caretaker function, and the occupant understands that as the Acting General Counsel he or she is in a caretaker role. So it would be useful, I think, to change the law at the same time as the Board law is changed to apply it also to the General Counsel.

The law currently requires that all lawyers employed by the Board work for a specific Board member. They are not employed to work generally for the Board, and this too needs modification so as to permit general employment by attorneys of the Board and not require that each Board member hire a staff independently.

This change would enable the Board members to restructure their staffs so as to retain the right to employ senior members of the staff for themselves independently and to have a pool of attorneys who could do the research, read records, prepare memoranda, and analyze the cases for the use of the entire Board. As matters stand, there is a great deal of duplicative effort expended by Board member staffs, and each Board member currently has about 20 or so attorneys on his staff. I would think that this could be restructured so as to permit each Board member to have four or five senior attorneys who would report to him individually, and the remainder would be working for the Board as a whole. This could be done quite easily.

The final two proposals for change are somewhat more controversial, I would think, than the others. These have to do with the appeals to the Board from decisions by administrative law judges and appeals or enforcement of Board decisions in the courts.

The problems to be addressed in the first proposal are time delays in case processing and Board case load. The fact that these problems exist needs no documentation. Neither is there any doubt that these problems continue to frustrate those who seek to use the Board's processes. Under current law governing unfair labor practice cases, any party has an automatic right of appeal to the Board and the Board has no discretion with respect to these appeals. It must accept all of them no matter how frivolous. I would urge legislative action designed to provide greater finality to administrative law judge decisions and discretionary review by the Board. I am well aware that proposals of this type have been considered in the past and rejected for a variety of reasons. I bring them up again because I think that the need is clear, and the possibility that minds have changed may warrant a reconsideration of these proposals. I shall not, at this time, attempt to outline in detail how the proposal should be drafted. I shall only state what I believe to be the desired goal of balancing full Board consideration of cases and expeditious processing of the case load.

We should not devote as much time as we have to minor problems and frivolous problems—problems which the litigants are almost 90 percent certain at the time they file the appeal that there will be no reversal of the administrative law judge decision. Based on experience, it is my firm belief that Board time can be better spent on important issues and problem areas in which clarification is needed and on careful crafting of decisions that will ultimately go before the courts.

Moving on to the last of these proposals, dealing with court enforcement of Board decisions, it is my view that there is need for clarification of the role of the General Counsel and the role of the Board in the enforcement area.

When Congress separated the prosecutorial and the decisional responsibilities, giving to an independent General Counsel the prosecutorial function and reposing in the Board the decisional function, it properly made it impossible for the Board to usurp or interfere in any manner with the role and function of the General Counsel. At that time, insufficient thought was given to the question of where the enforcement function should be carried out. As a consequence, internal accommodation had to be sought, and early on the function was exercised by the General Counsel. So long as the relationship between the Board and the General Counsel is aimiable and cooperative, the problems can be resolved without controversy. However, the General Counsel is in an awkward position. He is a prosecutor before the Board, urging positions which the Board may reject in its decision; the General Counsel then puts on his enforcement hat and goes to court seeking to enforce the very decision he opposed in litigation.

It is a tribute to the many persons who have served as General Counsel and Board members, that seldom has controversy arisen. But the fact that it has arisen from time to time is reason enough for Congress to clarify the role of each, the General Counsel and the Board, so that it is not left to good men and women to do good. Let the law specify how the function should be carried out. Having served as a Board member during peaceful times and also when controversy arose, I am firmly of the view that this is a problem which is best solved by the Congress rather than by accommodation between the Board and the General Counsel.

The decisions rendered by the Board are the Board's decisions, and what happens to them in court is a matter of concern to the Board. The General Counsel—all whom I have known—have undertaken to keep separate their role as prosecutor and their role as enforcer of Board decisions, so that it is not to impugn the integrity of the occupant of the office, neither is it to assert that the Board knows better how its decision should be handled. It is simply a question of the propriety and right of the Board to supervise the enforcement of its decisions, if that is what Congress wants. On the other hand, if Congress is more comfortable with the function being exercised under the supervision and control of the General Counsel and desires to have the Board excluded from that role, then it behooves Congress to clarify its intention. Here again I outline no specific detailed proposal. I state merely the obvious—that lack of clarity has lead to controversy from time to time, and since the lack of clarity originates with the legislation, the corrective step is to clarify the legislation in some manner so that the work of the agency will not be disruptive or dependent only upon good will.

I conclude these comments by repeating a point made earlier, that the preservation of the rights of the individual and the preservation of free democratic institutions are linked in their goals and that those whose primary concern is with the strengthening and expanding of our economy, as well as those whose efforts are directed toward elimination of social and economic inequities in a broader sense, need clearly to recognize the fact that neither group can achieve its goals if one group disregards the other. The discussions in this volume will be helpful in further analyzing those points.

WHAT THE NLRB IS ALL ABOUT

PETER G. NASH*

It is a pleasure and an honor to respond to Secretary Marshall's paper. I think the last time he and I met was during an extended debate (which he referred to as a filibuster) in the Senate on a piece of legislation called Labor Reform. We were appearing together on the "Today" show. As I recall it, we had

* Former General Counsel, National Labor Relations Board; senior partner, Ogletree, Deakins, Nash, Smoak and Stewart, Washington, D.C.

seven minutes, and he took six! I was hardly in a position then to object to his filibuster, but I am delighted to have an opportunity to respond more fully on this occasion. The problem is that I agree with most of what he has said.

I am prepared to make three basic points, jumping from one to the other during this brief commentary. However, I remember the advice given by Lloyd George, who once counseled that it is relatively dangerous to attempt to leap a deep chasm in two bounds. Nevertheless, I shall attempt to leap three in much the same fashion.

I agree with the Secretary's assertions, at least as I understand them, that international competition in both goods and labor has changed collective bargaining in the United States. I listened to an economist not too long ago trying to teach those of us who do not know much about economics how international competition has changed collective bargaining. He took as his example the automobile industry. For decades the participants within the automobile industry would lock themselves in a room every two or three years. The management participants each wanted to make at least $100,000; the shareholder participants each wanted at least a 50 percent return on investment per year; and the employee participants (through their union representative) each wanted to make at least $30.00 an hour. Every time they met they would sit for days. Ultimately, they would come together with a package which they would take out and dump on a little fellow standing outside the door—the consumer. One year when those three participants got together in that room, worked out their package, and then walked out to dump it on that little consumer—there was no consumer. They looked up and saw him driving down the road in his little Japanese car. So as a consequence, they had to go back into their room and rearrange their package.

To a noneconomist, I think that story defines the kind of changes that international competition requires in collective bargaining today. I do not, however, subscribe to the notion that has been expounded by some (but not by Secretary Marshall) that collective bargaining is not equal to the task before it. Indeed, cooperative problem solving through collective bargaining, as anticipated by the National Labor Relations Act, is, in my judgment, equal to the task of meeting foreign as well as domestic competition. Which leads me to my second point.

The Secretary commented about recent Labor Board decisions which he seems to read as evidencing a lack of enthusiasm for collective bargaining: a Labor Board tilt to the management side of the bargaining table. He even mentioned a few case examples. His examples are consistent with present union rhetoric but do not, in my view, accurately describe the particular Labor Board decisions to which he refers. I shall discuss two sample decisions.

In one case decision the Secretary contends that the Labor Board has now made it more difficult for employees to sign up union adherents on the employer's work premises. I assume by that he is referring to the recent decision of the Labor Board dealing with no-solicitation and no-distribution rules. However, what the Labor Board said in that case is that the law is, and shall remain, what it has been for some 40 years. Thus, employees shall have the opportunity to solicit support for a labor union during nonworking time on the employer's premises. The only thing the Labor Board said that could possibly excite friends of labor is that the solicitation notice an employer puts on its bulletin board does not have to detail what is "nonworking time." However, the solicitation law remains exactly the same as it has been for 40 years.

The second example is the topical contention that today's Labor Board acted inappropriately by making it easier for employers to transfer work from union plants to nonunion plants. That, I assume, refers to the *Milwaukee Spring II*[1] decision of this Board, which reversed the *Milwaukee Spring I*[2] decision of its immediate predecessor Board. In the *Milwaukee Spring I* decision, the Labor Board held that during the term of a collective bargaining agreement an employer may not transfer work from the unit covered by that collective bargaining agreement to another unit in order to take advantage of lower wages in the second unit. Apparently, the Board read into every collective bargaining agreement some sort of implicit management promise not to have work done at a cheaper wage than that agreed upon in the collective bargaining agreement. That decision, I submit, changed the law that had existed since the National Labor Relations Act was passed. That Act basically established

---

[1] Milwaukee Spring, Div. of Ill. Coil Spring Co., 268 NLRB 601, 115 LRRM 1065 (1984).
[2] Milwaukee Spring, Div. of Ill. Coil Spring Co., 265 NLRB 206, 111 LRRM 1486 (1984).

that if employees, through their union, wished to restrict management's right to transfer work, they could bargain such restrictions into a collective bargaining agreement. However, absent bargaining of such restrictions, an employer maintained its management right to make work transfers. Indeed, if it were true that management, by agreeing to a particular wage rate in a collective bargaining agreement, made an implied promise not to transfer work in order to take advantage of lower wages, it would seem to me that employees would likewise have committed themselves not to quit that employer to go elsewhere to earn a higher wage. Whatever the merits of the Board's decision, in the oral argument before the Board, the AFL-CIO declined to make the argument that the collective bargaining agreement somehow implicitly restrains the employer from making work transfers. And in the D.C. Circuit, the Automobile Workers (the charging party) dropped that argument from its case. As a consequence, with the reversal of the *Milwaukee Spring I* decision, the law now is in accord with the way the law has been read for the last 50 years, and would also seem to be in accord with what both the Automobile Workers and the AFL-CIO thought the law was when they were litigating *Milwaukee Spring*.

On to my third topic which concerns the furor that has developed over the years about the ineffectiveness of Board remedies. It is argued that the NLRA is not an effective labor-management statute because the remedies under that statute are ineffective and not sufficiently tough or punitive to require employers to obey the dictates of that law. The problem with that contention, however, is that it loses sight of what the National Labor Relations Act is all about. It is not the primary purpose and function of the Act to beat unions and employers over the head when they commit unfair labor practices. The primary purpose of that Act is eventually to guide those parties into a room where they may freely bargain to an agreement which will set wages, hours, and terms and conditions of employment. And Congress structured the Act in a way best designed to make that bargaining work effectively.

For example, suppose I sit down with a union representative to bargain a collective bargaining agreement, and he or she says: "It's a buck an hour—take it or leave it." I could file a Section 8(b)(3) charge with the Labor Board, and, assuming additional punitive remedies were available under the Act to correct that blatant violation, I could seek an order fining the union and throwing its official in jail for three months. My guess is that when that official came back to the bargaining table, there would be at least a 50 percent chance that I would not get very far in a cooperative collective bargaining discussion. Congress knew that when it decided to impose only make-whole remedies under the National Labor Relations Act, and, accordingly, chose not to impose punitive penalties which would be disruptive of the basic purpose of the Act—which was the encouragement of cooperative collective bargaining.

There is an old adage that effectively explains Congress' approach to bargaining under the National Labor Relations Act: "You can lead a horse to water but you can't make him drink." Presumably, the purpose of leading a horse to water is to make him drink. There are two ways to do that. One is to cajole, work with that horse over a period of time, and ultimately convince that horse not only that he should be led to the water, but that he ought to drink. Although it may take hours to get him there, when he finally gets to the water he is likely to take a drink. The second way is to hit the horse on the head, knock him out, drag him to the water by his halter, then let go (which, of course, is what the law says you do with an employer and a union when they get to the bargaining table), stand over him with a club, and when he wakes up, watch to see if he drinks. Under this second scenario, however, there is a strong chance that the horse will jump up and run away rather than drink. Thus, the consequence of using the punitive but easy way to get that horse to the water is not likely to produce the ultimate result desired. And when Congress passed the Labor Act, it understood that adage. One simply does not get effective, cooperative, problem-solving bargaining from employers and unions when they are knocked out and dragged to the bargaining table.

In summary, the overriding purpose of the Act—cooperative collective bargaining—is better served by a law that does not punish but, instead, merely remedies unfair labor practices. I concur wholeheartedly with Secretary Marshall's view that that kind of cooperative collective bargaining is more essential today in an internationally competitive world than it has ever been before.

THE NLRA: WHAT NEEDS TO BE DONE?

ELLIOT BREDHOFF*

Looking back fleetingly over the 50 years of the National Labor Relations Act, what is there to celebrate or commemorate?

* General Counsel, Industrial Union Department, AFL-CIO; partner, Bredhoff & Myers, Los Angeles, California. The author is grateful to his colleague Barbara Bergman for her invaluable assistance in the preparation of this paper.

I believe that the Act, at least in its earlier years, played a major role in the establishment or expansion of workplace rights for millions of workers. The fundamental protections still embedded in the Act—the right of employees to organize into unions, to bargain collectively, to engage in concerted activities, and to be free from employer unfair labor practices—facilitated a massive growth of unionism and industrial democracy. Workers thereby obtained a voice and a sense of participation in determining the terms and conditions of their employment, as well as procedures for resolving contract grievances. The quality of their lives thus was substantially enhanced. The gradual increases in purchasing power achieved by workers through collective bargaining helped to fuel the vast expansion of the economy in the past 50 years.

At the same time, unionism has enhanced the lives of non-union employees as well. They have benefited from the economic expansion and the protections and improved conditions obtained through union efforts. For example, unions have been in the forefront in supporting both federal and state legislation to protect the American worker. The minimum wage laws, Social Security, the Occupational Safety and Health Act, pension reform through ERISA, and Equal Employment Opportunity legislation are only a few examples. The unions have also played a vital role in enforcing the rights guaranteed by these laws. Some say that this legislation has diminished the scope of collective bargaining and that unions by supporting such laws have sounded their own death knell. That simply is not true. I am firmly convinced that such legislative protections complement rather than supplant collective bargaining.

But getting back to the impact of the NLRA—those employers who accepted the mandate of the Act and engaged in good-faith collective bargaining, achieved stable labor relations, which helped substantially to increase their production and profits.

Indeed, the institution of collective bargaining in organized industries blossomed to a greater degree in the United States than in almost any other country. The genius of our system of collective bargaining is the ability it affords employers and unions to devise and fashion responses and solutions tailored to the infinite variety of problems and disputes which arise daily in the multitude of bargaining units throughout our land. For this salutary development, we accord substantial credit to the National Labor Relations Act.

Unfortunately, however, the practice of good-faith collective bargaining has applied in more recent years to a declining proportion of the nation's work force. Despite the urgent need for greater labor-management cooperative efforts to meet the ever-escalating challenges of world trade and competition, we have witnessed increased employer resistance to unionization and collective bargaining. This is, indeed, unfortunate and constitutes a major roadblock in what should be joint efforts to improve the competitive posture of American industry.

With that in mind, I have been asked to comment on Professor Marshall's presentation on "The Act's Impact on Employment, Society, and the National Economy." Because I am an attorney and not an economist, I will limit my remarks to that portion of Professor Marshall's paper which discusses the NLRA's effectiveness in providing a viable legal framework for achieving our national labor policy goals.

Let me begin by agreeing with two of Professor Marshall's basic premises. First, unions *must* be responsive to modern-day economic realities. As George Meany said in 1979, "the labor movement cannot be content with defending the status quo, or reliving past glories. We must constantly look to the future, develop new leadership, adapt policies to changing conditions and new technologies . . . ."[1] That advice is especially pertinent today. As a 1985 BNA Special Report noted, "Unions are facing the most serious challenges to their power and influence in the United States since passage of the Wagner Act some 50 years ago."[2]

Those challenges are the result of changes in the demographics of the work force, new technology, decline of highly organized industries, and a growing resistance to unionization on the part of management. Specifically, the growth of the work force has occurred in those sectors of the economy and geographic areas that have not traditionally been highly organized. These developments have, in part, been the result of technological

---

[1] Speech by George Meany at the 1979 AFL-CIO Convention, reprinted in *A Report by the AFL-CIO Committee on the Evolution of Work: The Changing Situation of Workers and Their Unions* 32 (1985).

[2] UNIONS TODAY: NEW TACTICS TO TACKLE TOUGH TIMES, 1985, 1.

advances that have eliminated scores of jobs, created entirely new jobs, and altered the requirements of others.

In response to these changes, unions have begun to develop new strategies and techniques. The AFL-CIO Executive Council in August 1982 established the Committee on the Evolution of Work "to review and evaluate changes that are taking place in America in the labor force, occupations, industries and technology."[3] This Committee has proposed specific recommendations for structural changes within the labor movement: improved communications, increased members' participation in their unions, development of new techniques for improving organizing activities, and other new methods for advancing the interests of workers.

Unions have adopted some of those suggestions. For example, the Industrial Union Department of the AFL-CIO, which I have the pleasure of serving as General Counsel, has taken the offensive in developing coordinated corporate campaign strategies. These corporate campaigns identify and apply various techniques to points of vulnerability in a target company. These techniques, in turn, are intended to convince the company, which presumably is opposing organizing efforts or meaningful collective bargaining, to deal fairly and equitably with the union. Despite these new tactics, much remains to be done. Unions today—to survive—must respond quickly and innovatively to the new "economic realities."

The second premise with which I agree is that the central goal of the NLRA—collective bargaining with employees represented by an exclusive bargaining representative—reflects the optimal "American" system for conducting labor relations. (Whether economic warfare represents the best way to resolve labor-management disputes is an issue which warrants serious reexmination at another time. It may well be that some form of interest arbitration may be more effective and stable, given the current "economic realities.")

In recent years, however, the NLRA has not been able adequately to achieve its primary goal—collective bargaining by the broad spectrum of American employers with exclusive bargaining representatives selected by the employees. Problems have arisen because (1) the techniques by which the Act can be frus-

---

[3] A Report by the AFL-CIO Committee on the Evolution of Work: The Changing Situation of Workers and Their Unions, at 2.

trated are now well-known, and (2) more and more employers are willing to use those techniques to circumvent the Act.

As we all are aware, a declining percentage of the American work force is unionized. And that decline is traceable to fundamental defects in the NLRA—as professor Paul Weiler convincingly demonstrated in his 1983 article.[4] While the pro-management tilt of the Reagan NLRB has exacerbated these problems, the principal defects are ingrained in the NLRA and were apparent even before any of the recent Reagan appointments.

Before I turn to a more specific discussion of the NLRA's defects, I would note that the NLRA does perform two constructive functions. First, it enables many illegally discharged employees ultimately to secure reinstatement and back pay. Even though such relief is provided far too late to repair meaningfully the damage to the union's organizing efforts, eventual reinstatement and back pay do have remedial effects. Second, in any certification election, someone has to set the rules and count the votes, and the Board performs that job reasonably well.

These beneficial aspects of the NLRA are overshadowed by the NLRA's defects—defects that exist at both the organizing and the bargaining stages of the process. Initially, under the NLRA, unions are frustrated in their organizing attempts when they are denied access to employees. Some employers require employees to attend meetings on company time at which anti-union speeches or films are presented. Many who have attended such "captive audience" sessions have found them to be inherently coercive and destructive of free choice. Nevertheless, the NLRA has not been construed as prohibiting the captive audience tactic. By contrast, unions often are not entitled under the NLRA to meet with employees even in the employer's parking lot during the employee's own time—and thus are restricted in many instances to trying to communicate with employees at their homes or other nonplant sites. This doctrine was established by the Supreme Court in the *Babcock & Wilcox*[5] case decided in 1956. The Court held in that case that employers may prohibit access to nonemployee union organizers if "reasonable efforts . . . through other available channels of communication

---

[4] *Promises to Keep: Securing Workers' Rights to Self-Organization Under the NLRA*, 96 HARV. L. REV. 1769 (1983).

[5] NLRB v. Babcock & Wilcox, 351 US 105, 38 LRRM 2001 (1956).

will enable [the union organizers] to reach the employees"[6] and the employer does not allow access by other nonemployees.

At the same time, not only are unions denied equal *access* at the organizing stage, but under the existing system, the NLRA provides employers with ample opportunity—which more and more employers are using—to coerce employees before they make their decision about unionization. And, most importantly, the remedies provided by the NLRA are wholly inadequate and untimely to deter these increasing abuses.

According to Board statistics, union victory rates in Board elections have been steadily declining. Before 1974 on the average, unions never lost more than half of the elections in which they participated. Since 1974, they have *never won* more than half. According to Professor Weiler, unions won 74 percent of the certification elections in 1950. By 1980 that victory rate had fallen to 48 percent.[7]

Professor Weiler persuasively argues that this decline can in large part be attributed to deficiencies in the NLRA. He concludes that "evidence suggests that the current certification procedure does not effectively insulate employees from the kind of coercive antiunion employer tactics that the NLRA was supposed to eliminate.[8] The time lag of roughly two months between the filing of a representation petition and the vote (which is much shorter than the time lag in contested cases), gives an employer far too much opportunity to try to frighten its employees—more and more successfully—out of selecting a union.

The most ruthless tactic used by employers to bust the organizing efforts of their employees is the discriminatory discharge of the most active union adherents at the height of the campaign, frequently on the eve of the election. This tactic is often so successful in intimidating the rest of the employees that the election is lost by the union, even though it is clear that most employees in fact desire organization. A Board order for reinstatement and back pay two or three years later does little to lessen such intimidation. To antiunion employers, a back-pay award is merely a good investment.

---

[6] *Id.* at 112.
[7] *Supra* note 4, at 1775.
[8] *Id.* at 1777.

And a *Gissel*[9] bargaining order—even if such an order can be obtained, which is not an easy task—is most often not a viable solution. Employees who are so terrified by the employer's coercive acts that they will not vote for a union in the secrecy of a voting booth are hardly likely candidates for the degree of open solidarity necessary to convince an employer that it must make concessions in collective bargaining. Not surprisingly, the vast majority of *Gissel* bargaining orders do not result in the achievement of a collective bargaining agreement.

In this regard we can learn a valuable lesson from our Canadian neighbors. They have avoided this problem of employer intimidation at the organizing stage in two ways. The provinces either (1) certify a union when it presents signed authorization cards from a majority of the employees in a unit or (2) hold an election immediately once a union presents enough cards to indicate substantial employee interest. Under this statutory framework, employers have little or no opportunity to campaign against a union. Thus, because coercive tactics are useless, there is no temptation to use them. At the same time, such a system is not unfair to employers because they have had plenty of time to demonstrate any advantages of individual bargaining long before a union ever comes on the scene. Thus, the Canadian approach at the organizing stage avoids the inherent defects of the NLRA and merits our consideration.

The NLRA is not only defective at the organizing stage, but it suffers from serious flaws during the bargaining stage as well. For example, under the NLRA, although employees have a right to bargain over the *effects* of certain entrepreneurial decisions, they do not have a right to bargain about the actual decisions themselves—even though it is those decisions that often have a direct and substantial impact upon the preservation of their jobs. The Supreme Court made this clear in 1981 in its decision in *First National Maintenance Corp.* v. *NLRB*.[10] The Supreme Court stated in that case:

> Management must be free from the constraints of the bargaining process to the extent essential for the running of a profitable business. . . . [I]n view of an employer's need for unencumbered decisionmaking, bargaining over management decisions that have a

---

[9] NLRB v. Gissel Packing Co., 395 US 575, 71 LRRM 2481 (1969).
[10] 452 US 666, 107 LRRM 2705 (1981).

substantial impact on the continued availability of employment should be required only if the benefit, for labor-management relations and the collective-bargaining process, outweighs the burden placed on the conduct of the business.[11]

Under the model posited by Professor Marshall, given today's economic realities, the most important issues affecting workers are likely to involve just such management decisions. Yet, under the NLRA, American workers have no right to bargain over those issues. And the right to bargain about the effects of such decisions is insufficient because it provides too little, too late.

In addition, the NLRA provides no *effective* remedy if an employer simply refuses to bargain in its efforts to resist unionization. The Labor Board's only remedy when an employer refuses to bargain is to issue an order directing the employer to bargain forthwith—the legal system's equivalent of a slap on the wrist. Thus, an employer who refuses to bargain incurs no financial penalty whatsoever, but reaps the gains of avoiding the obligations that a union contract would impose.

Indeed, in the famous *Ex-Cell-O*[12] case a three-member majority of the Board stated:

> We have given most serious consideration to the Trial Examiner's recommended financial reparations Order, and are in complete agreement with his finding that current remedies of the Board designed to cure violations of Section 8(a)(5) are inadequate. A mere affirmative order that an employer bargain upon request does not eradicate the effects of an unlawful delay of two or more years in the fulfillment of a statutory bargaining obligation. It does not put the employees in the position of bargaining strength they would have enjoyed if their employer had immediately recognized and bargained with their chosen representative. It does not dissolve the inevitable employee frustration or protect the Union from the loss of employee support attributable to such delay.[13]

The Board concluded, however, that it lacked statutory authority to order an employer to make employees whole for losses caused by a refusal to bargain. The D.C. Circuit disagreed, as did many scholars of the law, but the Board has adhered to its views. As a result, under the Board's interpretation of the NLRA, there remains no effective remedy to an employer's refusal to bargain.

---

[11] *Id.* at 678–79 (footnotes omitted).
[12] Ex-Cell-O Corp., 185 NLRB 107, 74 LRRM 1740 (1970).
[13] *Id.*, 74 LRRM at 1741.

Finally, the NLRA's promise of equalizing bargaining power has proven illusory as well, given the economic realities of today's labor market. The employer's right, under the NLRA, permanently to replace economic strikers means that, with diminishing exceptions, a strike often is destined to lose. In an economy with large numbers of people looking for work, employers frequently have no trouble finding permanent replacements. And if pilots and air traffic controllers can be replaced wholesale, as Continental Airlines and President Reagan have proved, even highly skilled employees no longer can strike with the confidence that their jobs will not be lost. Some employers, in fact, have even trained "shadow" work forces in anticipation of a strike, ensuring that substantial risks attach when a union even plans to use its primary economic weapon.

As these examples show, fundamental defects in the NLRA have in more recent years become major problems which we must address. This 50th anniversary of the Wagner Act is an especially appropriate time for us seriously to consider possible modifications or alternatives. My practical preference would be for federal labor law reform along the modest lines which failed by a hair during the Carter Administration. However, I recognize that such reform may not be attainable in the near future. As an alternative, I offer the following tentative suggestions for your consideration. I stress that I am not quite yet at the point of directly advocating these suggestions, which require further study and reflection. Moreover, I am not oblivious to the formidable legislative challenges posed by the suggestions.

First, the existence of the NLRA preempts the states from legislating in this area. If the NLRA were at least partially repealed, it is likely that state law would fill the vacuum. In fact, many states have already shown their willingness to enact legislation to protect workers. Twenty-five states have enacted "right-to-know" laws requiring companies to divulge information about hazardous substances in the workplace. Nineteen states have laws prohibiting any mandatory retirement age, and three states by law require notice of plant shutdowns and severance pay for affected workers.[14] Allowing the states to take a more active role in this field would be similar to the approach followed

---

[14] *Beyond Unions: A Revolution in Employee Rights Is in the Making*, BUS. WEEK, July 8, 1985, at 72, 73.

in Canada, where each province has developed its own set of labor laws.

While *some* state laws would probably be better than the current NLRA for unions and employees, others might well be worse. To achieve a better balance, I would suggest the possibility of maintaining federal law to guarantee certain basic rights. Federal law could preserve three central features of current labor policy, leaving the rest of the labor law to be developed by the states. Congress might well need only to guarantee the following:

1. exclusive representation by a union selected by a majority of the members of a bargaining unit;

2. prohibition of any discrimination for union activities; and

3. the employer's duty to bargain (with the content of this bargaining to be prescribed by state law).

These three rights could be enforced by the Board or in the federal courts. Such federal legislation might well preserve the basic goals of the American labor relations system while diminishing the problems inherent in the NLRA.

At the same time, there would be no reason to tamper with federal law governing the *enforcement* of collective bargaining agreements once they have been achieved. The law in that area (Section 301), which is not administered by the NLRB, already works well and should be maintained.

Let me conclude with the caveat that I do not suggest these proposals would necessarily solve all the problems facing American workers. But in 1935 Congress charted the course of this nation's labor policy by passing the Wagner Act. Recent experience has demonstrated that the NLRA contains serious flaws which have prevented the policies of the Act from adequately being realized. The Act has become a snare and a delusion. For thousands of workers, the freedom and security promised by the legal framework of our labor system have been replaced by fear, insecurity, and deprivation. It is time to make substantial changes to our entire approach to regulating labor relations so that we can deal more flexibly and effectively with today's "economic realities."

Commentary

DAVID LEWIN*

In his paper "The Act's Impact on Employment, Society, and the National Economy," Professor Marshall offers a useful macroeconomic—or, more accurately, macrolevel—perspective in U.S. industrial relations. The perspective is useful because it reminds us that while a regulatory statute may affect the behavior of parties toward whom it is directed, such behavior is also and perhaps more fundamentally shaped by economic forces. In recent years, and with respect to labor-management relations in particular, these forces include rapid technological change and increased domestic and international competition, which have been supported, respectively, by public policies favoring deregulation and "free" trade. Indeed, the main purpose of Professor Marshall's paper "is to discuss the broader economic forces interacting with the industrial relations system, [and] not to enter the current debates about the Board . . . ."

But, of course, the odds of an industrial relations scholar and former Secretary of Labor *not* commenting on the NLRB, especially at a symposium on "The Labor Board at Mid-Century," are probably about the same as those of an employer not commenting about unions when faced with a representation election—that is, p = < .01! And, to be sure, Professor Marshall does comment on the NLRB. What are these comments and what questions do they raise for the study of and policy-making about U.S. industrial relations?

First, Professor Marshall says that the National Labor Relations Act's (NLRA's) "basic assumptions"—that is, encouraging collective bargaining and protecting workers' rights to decide whether or not they wish to be represented by unions—"are still largely valid." But the validity of other, less explicit assumptions underlying the Act may be questioned.

One of these assumptions is that union-induced wage increases will exceed price increases and thereby raise purchasing power in the economy. While the prevalence of this assumption during the depression-ridden 1930s is certainly understandable, the "proactive" use of the several instruments of macroeconomic policy (*i.e.,* fiscal and monetary policy) since

* Professor, Graduate School of Business, Columbia University.

then strongly suggests that a "union-driven wage-thrust" economy is a relic of the past, if it ever existed at all.

Moreover, it seems undeniable that the larger the union-
imposed wage gain and the greater the union-nonunion pay
differential for comparable or identical work, the greater the
incentive for employers to substitute capital *and* nonunion labor
for union labor. Recent evidence from the construction, mining,
trucking, and auto industries, to name but a few, support this
point.[1] True, some scholars argue that unionism serves to
reduce turnover, enhance human capital, and, most important,
improve productivity.[2] If these things are "true," they appear to
work in the firm's favor and, therefore, employers should
encourage or at least be neutral about employee unionization.
But, of course, virtually all U.S. employers, including unionized
employers, have undertaken to ward off or contain employee
unionization. Thus in a most fundamental sense, the productiv-
ity-improvement argument in favor of unionism is less compelling than the employee rights-workplace democracy argument
in favor of unionism. The latter argument is well developed in
Eliot Bredhoff's response to Professor Marshall.

This last point is especially relevant to another, largely
implicit, assumption underlying the NLRA, namely, that U.S.
unionism is a narrow wage-oriented movement that eschews or
at least should not be encouraged to pursue an enlarged role in
enterprise management. As with the wage push-purchasing
power enhancement theory, the concept of a limited union role
in the enterprise is understandable in light of the concern about
company-dominated unions expressed in the 1930s by legislative framers of the NLRA. But is such a limited union role
appropriate for the 1980s and beyond? The answer seems to be
no, based on Professor Marshall's extolling of the "cooperative"
labor-relations systems prevailing in Japan and elsewhere, the
actions of some U.S. employers who (admittedly in the context of
labor cost concessions) have invited certain unions to play
enlarged roles in management of the enterprise, and the comments of both Peter Nash and Eliot Bredhoff. Putting the point
in sharp relief, certain (implicit) assumptions underlying the
NLRA may be so inappropriate for the 1980s as to suggest that

---

[1] *See, e.g.,* COLLECTIVE BARGAINING: CONTEMPORARY AMERICAN EXPERIENCE
G. Somers ed., (1980).

[2] R. Freeman & J. Medoff, WHAT DO UNIONS DO? (1984).

U.S. unions and industrial relations may be better off if the NLRA were eliminated rather than, and as Professor Marshall advocates, retained. In this regard, and as Professor Marshall properly notes, the "elimination" or "deregulation" argument offered by some U.S. labor leaders should not be casually dismissed.[3]

A second observation offered by Professor Marshall is that "[t]he NLRB's effectiveness . . . is diminished by politicization," and he cites the "Reagan Board's" extensive reversals of the decisions reached by the "Carter Board" and it predecessors to support this point. But it is hardly surprising that the Board is political; after all and as with judicial appointments Board members are appointed by U.S. Presidents and, therefore, should be expected to be political, whatever this term may mean. Indeed, a close historical reading of Board and court decisions concerning picketing shows how the "allowable" circle of acceptable union actions to exercise free speech via picketing was increasingly circumscribed following the Supreme Court's celebrated *Thornhill*[4] decision of 1940. Were these decisions "political"? Yes, to some extent, but what else could they be? The way to avoid political decisions is to eliminate regulatory institutions and "let the market decide," but Professor Marshall argues eloquently for the retention of the NLRA and the Board. This proregulation position can be supported on several grounds, but whatever particular supporting rationale is advocated it then becomes inconsistent to decry the political decisions of the regulators. A more pressing question, perhaps, one recently raised by Delaney, Lewin, and Sockell in their appraisal of 50 years of research on the Wagner (and Taft-Hartley) Act,[5] is "how does the changing political composition of the Board affect the behavior and decisions of NLRB regional offices and the Board's professional personnel?" Note that former Board Member Howard Jenkins' response to Professor Marshall suggests that Board employees are highly professional and thus may be more or less inured to the changing political composition of the Board.

Third, Professor Marshall decries the courts' deferral to the Board because of its "presumed expertise in labor matters." But

---

[3] *See, e.g.,* Apcar, *Kirkland's Call to Void Labor Laws Ignites a Growing Debate,* Wall Street J., Sept. 6, 1984, at 33.

[4] Thornhill v. Alabama, 310 US 88, 6 LRRM 697 (1940).

[5] *The NLRA at 50: A Research Appraisal and Agenda,* 39 INDUS. & LAB. REL. REV. 46.

what is the alternative? The history of court decisions in labor relations matters in the United States is largely a history of favoring employer "real" property rights over workers' "incorporeal"[6] (*i.e.*, intangible) property rights. Lest one think that this was true only of the 19th and early 20th centuries, consider various recent court decisions favoring employer bankruptcy petitions to overturn labor agreements.[7] These decisions hardly support the view that if only the Board (or, for that matter, the courts) were "properly" constituted, a more evenhanded approach to regulating industrial relations would result.

Finally, suppose that the NLRA and the Board were dissolved; what then? The consequence, I submit, would be a patchwork of state regulations, some strongly supporting, some mildly supporting, some neutral about, some mildly opposing, and some strongly opposing, private sector unionism and collective bargaining. In this sense, the private sector experience might closely mirror the recent public sector experience in terms of the regulation of labor relations.[8] In other words, the public policy choice in U.S. industrial relations is not between regulation and no regulation. Rather, it is between regulation at the federal level and regulation at the state level. Indeed, this is true of human resource regulation more broadly, not just labor relations regulation. In an era of deregulation, we would do well to anticipate that debate will ensue about the appropriateness of not just the NLRA, but the ERISA, OSHA, Civil Rights Act, Age Discrimination in Employment Act, and many other federal human resource statutes.[9] To the extent that Professor Marshall's comments, as well as those of Messrs. Jenkins, Nash, and Bredhoff, about the NLRA alert us to the potential of a major debate about human resource regulation more broadly, we are unquestionably and usefully in their debt.

---

[6] The term "incorporeal" is taken from J. Commons, LEGAL FOUNDATIONS OF CAPITALISM 388 (1924).

[7] *See* NLRB v. Bildisco & Bildisco, 465 US 513, 115 LRRM 2805 (1984).

[8] Public sector labor relations are presently regulated by individual states, 38 of which have enacted one or another type of public sector bargaining law. Other industrial relations/human resource management issues presently being debated and subjected to legislation at the state level include comparable worth, unjust discharge, and plant closings.

[9] *See* Lewin & Lipsky, *Research on IR Regulation, Bargaining Power and Theory, and Progressive Discipline*, in ADVANCES IN INDUSTRIAL AND LABOR RELATIONS, Vol. 3 (D. Lipsky & D. Lewin eds., forthcoming).

CHAPTER 2

ESTABLISHMENT AND DISESTABLISHMENT OF UNION REPRESENTATION

WILLIAM P. MURPHY*

I have interpreted my topic to comprehend the total representation process. What I will endeavor to do is highlight and comment briefly on some aspects of that process over the 50-year span of the Act's existence.

I. The Right to Representation

Section 1 of the Act states that it is the policy of the United States to protect interstate commerce "by encouraging the practice and procedure of collective bargaining and by protecting the exercise by workers of full freedom of association, self-organization and designation of representatives of their own choosing." These two purposes are congruent only to the extent that workers exercise their freedom of choice in favor of union representation. In 1935 the assumption was that they would do so, and for 15–20 years this was the reality. Today it can be maintained persuasively that neither purpose is being effectuated.

Discussion of the representation process may properly take note of restrictions on access to it. From the beginning the purposes of the statute have been limited by denying large numbers of employees any right under the Act to union representation. Congress defined the terms "employer" and "employee" to exclude many categories of employees. Notable among these are agricultural laborers. In 1935 farm employers could distinguish the family farm from factories and plausibly argue that interstate commerce was not affected by farm work. Both legal doctrine and economic change have long since dissipated the validity of these arguments. The development of "agribusiness" has created a large class of farm workers, an

---

* Paul B. Eaton Professor of Law, University of North Carolina.

estimated half to a full million, whose economic status is that of corporate employees. Countless studies have documented the oppressive conditions under which many of them work. This is especially true of migratory workers. This past summer in my state a farm employer spokesman asserted publicly that these people did not need toilet facilities; they could relieve themselves in the trees and bushes. The bills to delete the exclusion of farm workers from the Act have been introduced and the hearings have been held, but the exclusion remains. A handful of states have enacted farm labor laws, but obviously only extension of the NLRA would provide all farm workers a uniform right to choose union representation. Small family farms could still be exempt by a number of employees standard. I find it impossible to reconcile in principle Congress' continued unwillingness to extend coverage to farm workers with its 1974 extension of union representation rights to more than a million workers in nonprofit hospitals.

It is one thing for Congress by statute to deny employees of a particular group the right to union representation. It is quite another thing for the Board and the courts, on the basis of their own policy considerations, to deny protection to other groups of employees. But, despite Congress' careful examination of the conflict-of-interest problem and its studied exclusion and definition of supervisors, we know that by NLRB and Supreme Court decisions, some confidential employees (but not all, only those engaged in labor relations) are excluded from the Act, although it is not altogether settled whether they are excluded from Section 8 or Section 9 or both.[1] After some characteristic waffling by the Board, so-called "managerial" employees have been gratuitiously excluded by the Supreme Court.[2] The concept of "managerial" employees, once created, has proved capable of supporting an expansive Supreme Court extension to university faculty, who were at first excluded, then later included, by Board decision. The statutory exclusion of state subdivisions clearly applied to faculty in state universities. In *Yeshiva*[3] the Supreme Court judicially excluded faculty in private universities. As a professor with real doubts about faculty unions, I think both the

---

[1] NLRB v. Hendricks County Rural Elec. Membership Corp., 454 US 170, 108 LRRM 3105 (1981).

[2] NLRB v. Bell Aerospace Co., 416 US 267, 85 LRRM 2945 (1974).

[3] NLRB v. Yeshiva Univ., 444 US 672, 103 LRRM 2526 (1980).

result and, more importantly, the process of judicial exclusion are altogether wrong.

As we know, by Board decision, medical interns, although employees in an economic sense, are not so in a legal sense since they are still students.[4] This is an approach which fortunately has not been applied generally to on-the-job trainees and apprentices. Among the least persuasive of these gratuitous additions to the statute are the Board's early exclusion of the employees of unions, reversed by the Court,[5] and the Supreme Court's decision in the *Catholic Bishop* case[6] holding that secular employees of religious schools are excluded for the novel and bizarre reason that Congress did not expressly intend to include them.

I suggest that both the Board and the Court have been entirely too free-wheeling in this area. Respect for congressional judgment and separation of powers doctrine both support a general approach that employees in an economic sense are covered unless Congress has excluded them. A basic and oft reiterated maxim is that a statute should be interpreted and applied so as to further its policy and purpose. Freedom to choose union representation is maximized by expanded coverage. Exclusion denies employee choice altogether.

The Board's jurisdiction and the demand for its services have increasingly exceeded its resources. The jurisdictional standards were thus born of necessity. They nevertheless deny some employees representational rights under the NLRA. Section 14(c) froze the standards in effect in 1959, but the impact on employees excluded by the standards has been minimized by inflation, a happy illustration of the ill wind that blew some good.

Some years ago, a leading labor law authority estimated that only about half of the work force in America was legally entitled to the protections of the NLRA. The law's promise of freedom to choose union representation is thus less than wholehearted. If the percentage of employees who choose union representation is measured against half the work force instead of all of it, we can fairly conclude that expansion of coverage would encourage collective bargaining, if that indeed is any longer a component of our national policy.

---

[4] Cedars-Sinai Medical Center, 223 NLRB 251, 91 LRRM 1398 (1976).
[5] Office Employees Local 11 v. NLRB, 353 US 313, 40 LRRM 2020 (1957).
[6] NLRB v. Catholic Bishop of Chicago, 440 US 490, 100 LRRM 2913 (1979).

II. Some Special Section 9 Problems

The representation process is the fundamental basis of the entire statutory scheme. Before the NLRA was enacted in 1935, there was no formal, legally sanctioned method for a union to establish a bargaining relationship, and this was a principal source of labor disputes. One of the great innovations of American labor law is the representation election whereby workers decide whether they wish to be represented by a union which, if it wins the election, is certified as the legal bargaining representative.

A Board press release this past July informed us that since 1935 over 32 million employees have voted in some 345,000 elections. This statistic on its face manifests what formerly could be sincerely and proudly referred to as "industrial democracy." For the past 20 or more years, however, the process has come under increasing criticism. Obviously, the representation process is affected by many of the unfair labor practice provisions, so I apologize in advance to succeeding speakers if I sometimes poach on their preserves.

A. Appropriate bargaining units

From the beginning the concept of the appropriate bargaining unit has been central to the representation process. The unit initially determines the constituency which votes in the Board election and, in most cases, the employees the union will represent if it wins the election. Section 9 empowers the Board to decide what the appropriate unit shall be, but it gives the Board very little guidance on how to go about deciding. Over the years the Board has identified many factors which may be considered, all of which are subsumed under the general standard that the employees in the unit must have "community of interest" with each other. In passing, I will say that I have never understood why one of these factors—the employer's administrative structure—should have any bearing upon the matter. It is possible to have more than one appropriate unit and it is not necessary that the Board determine the most appropriate unit. It is apparent that the Board has great flexibility and discretion in its unit determinations. Judicial review is generally deferential.

In the earlier years of the statute there was fierce dispute over craft versus companywide units, engendered by the advent of the CIO in the late 1930s and its threat to the craft unit basis of AFL unions. Mercifully, I will spare you any discussion of the tortuous meandering in the Board's dealing with this problem— *Globe* elections,[7] *American Can,*[8] Section 9(b)(2), *National Tube,*[9] *and American Potash.*[10] It seems fair to conclude that, except during the years of the Eisenhower Board, the tendency was to favor the larger unit which maximized collective bargaining and incidentally favored the more aggressive CIO unions. The AFL-CIO merger in 1955 and the Board's 1967 *Mallinckrodt*[11] decision have largely domesticated this once unruly area. What were once strictly craft unions now commonly represent plant-wide units.

A unit determination problem of continuing controversy arises when a union seeks a single-location unit in the context of a multi-plant store or office employer. Typically the union seeks a single-location unit and the employer some larger grouping of locations, each party's position being determined by its desire to win the Board election. Again, I will spare you the details of the Board's zig-zag course in rationalizing the application of the "community of interests" concept to this problem. Viewing the matter over time, it seems apparent to me, and I think to most observers, that the Board's approach to this problem has always depended upon the composition of the Board, whether it is generally union or management oriented. The analysis of all of the many factors in the Board's opinions come across as rationalizations of policy preferences to facilitate either union or employer election victories. The adoption of the presumption that a single-location unit is appropriate[12] merely shifts the focus to the sufficiency of the evidence to rebut the presumption. Today's Board will find no more difficulty in rationalizing larger units to minimize unionization than earlier Boards have had in maximizing it. In short, the process is basically manipulative, and at all times the policy has been about as covert as U.S. operations in Nicaragua.

Currently the most controversial area of unit determination is in health care facilities, a problem generated by the 1974 amend-

---

[7] Globe Mach. & Stamping Co., 3 NLRB 294, 1-A LRRM, 122 (1937).
[8] American Can Co., 13 NLRB 1252, 4 LRRM 392 (1939).
[9] National Tube Co., 76 NLRB 1199, 21 LRRM 1292 (1948).
[10] American Potash & Chem. Corp., 107 NLRB 1418, 33 LRRM 1380 (1954).
[11] Mallinckrodt Chem. Works, 162 NLRB 387, 64 LRRM 1011 (1966).
[12] *E.g.*, Frisch's Big Boy, 147 NLRB 551, 56 LRRM 1246 (1964).

ment extending coverage to nonprofit hospitals. While Congress admonished the Board to prevent proliferation of units, at the same time it rejected a proposal to limit health care units to four specified employee groups—professional, technical, clerical, and service and maintenance. The Board struggled with the problem for 10 years under the "community of interest" rhetoric, identifying as many as seven different units. In *St. Francis II*[13] in 1984, the Board, reversing its 1982 *St. Francis I*[14] decision, abandoned the community of interests approach and adopted a disparity of interests standard which must be met in order to justify a unit smaller than an overall professional or nonprofessional unit. The legislative history certainly does not require this result, and arguably is contrary to it. What I think is clear is that it is an approach which will make union organization more difficult and minimize union election victories, the policy result one would expect from the current Board.

The Board has not done everything it could to improve the unit determination problem. In 1976–77 a Task Force on the NLRB created by then Chairman Betty Murphy considered ways in which the Board might improve its R and C case procedures. It was my privilege to chair the committee on R cases, which had an equal number of prominent union and management lawyers. These adversary attorneys were able to agree on many recommendations which were endorsed by the entire Task Force. One recommendation agreed upon was that the area of unit determination was a prime area in which the Board should use its rule-making authority to reduce the frequency of hearings. As you know, for many years, numerous authorities, on the basis of considerations which to me are compelling, have been urging the Board to engage in more rule making in suitable areas. With minor exceptions, the Board stubbornly refuses to acquiesce, and relies almost entirely on adjudication. Rule making in unit determination could well reduce the delay in the election process, as well as the frequency of post-election 8(a)(5)'s by employers to obtain judicial review of the Board's unit determination.

It should be noted that one effect of basing collective bargaining on the concept of an appropriate unit is to decentralize collective bargaining and to fragment and disperse union

---

[13] St. Francis Hosp., 271 NLRB 948, 116 LRRM 1465 (1984).
[14] St. Francis Hosp., 265 NLRB 1025, 112 LRRM 1153 (1982).

strength. Thus, American labor law does not provide for industrywide bargaining, a fact which distinguishes it from systems in many other countries. Unit bargaining does not, however, preclude "pattern" bargaining which has emerged in some areas, nor has it prevented the development of a more widespread and important phenomenon, the multi-employer bargaining unit. Although not specifically mentioned in the statute, the validity of such units has been finally recognized at least since the Supreme Court's *Buffalo Linen*[15] decision in 1957. The importance of this development is underscored by reliable estimates that multi-employer units include about 40 percent of all employees covered by collective agreements.

Opinions differ as to whose bargaining power is increased by such bargaining, but practical considerations must persuade both the employers and the union that they will benefit, for the creation of multi-employer units quite properly rests on mutual consent. In my judgment, the standards for withdrawal by one employer from the unit are too strict. In its *Charles Bonanno*[16] decision, the Supreme Court upheld the Board's rules that a bargaining impasse does not justify withdrawal, which seems fair enough. But the Court gratuitously (since it was not an issue in the case) upheld the Board's position that not even an interim agreement between the union and an employer who had suffered a whipsaw strike is ground for withdrawal. Such interim agreements seem to me to be thoroughly inconsistent with multi-employer bargaining. Fortunately, the Court's majority opinion, piously grounded on deference to Board judgment, does not preclude the Board from reconsidering the issue. In closing on this matter, I think the boat was missed in *Buffalo Linen* by not declaring the whipsaw strike to be an unprotected concerted activity, thus obviating the need to determine whether the employer's response was an unfair labor practice.

B. *Campaign Propaganda*

One of the most controversial aspects of the representation process for the past 25 years has been the extent to which the Board should police the use of speech and propaganda of the parties. In 1947, Congress, following the Supreme Court's lead

---

[15] NLRB v. Truck Drivers Local 449, 353 US 87, 39 LRRM 2603 (1957).
[16] Charles D. Bonanno Linen Serv., Inc. v. NLRB, 454 US 404, 109 LRRM 2257 (1982).

in its 1941 *VEPCO*[17] decision, concluded that the Board had been too restrictive of employer speech. Accordingly, Section 8(c) of the Taft-Hartley amendments provided that the expression of views, arguments, and opinion should not constitute or be evidence of an unfair labor practice, unless they contained a threat of force or reprisal or a promise of benefit. Such speech it called coercive, and there has never been any doubt that its use may be the basis for setting aside an election.

In its *General Shoe*[18] decision in 1948, the Board held three to two that its elections should be conducted under what is called "laboratory conditions" and set aside an election in which the company president had delivered a strong antiunion speech to groups of employees in his own office. Although the speech was not coercive and therefore not an unfair labor practice, the Board held that the president's conduct went far beyond the accepted manner of conducting campaigns and thus interfered with the "laboratory conditions." Section 8(c), the Board said, applied only to unfair labor practice cases under Section 8 of the statute and did not limit the Board's power over representation cases under Section 9. Note that it was not the content of the speech, but the manner in which it was delivered, that the Board found objectionable.

In later cases, however, the Board expanded the *General Shoe* doctrine and held that speech which was not coercive could interfere with "laboratory conditions" and be the basis for setting aside an election because of the content of speech. The two leading cases came in 1962—*Hollywood Ceramics*,[19] involving misrepresentation of comparative wage rates by a union, and *Sewell Mfg. Co.*,[20] in which an employer used racial propaganda. Happily, racial propaganda of an inflammatory nature is less used these days than it was in the 1960s. Misrepresentation as is well known, engendered a record series of Board flip-flops. *Shopping Kart*[21] in 1977 overruled *Hollywood Ceramics*. *General Knit*[22] in 1978 overruled *Shopping Kart*, and was itself overruled in 1982 in *Midland National Life Insurance Co.*,[23] a decision likely to stand so

---

[17] NLRB v. Virginia Elec. & Power Co., 314 US 469, 9 LRRM 405 (1941).
[18] General Shoe Corp., 77 NLRB 124, 21 LRRM 1337 (1948).
[19] Hollywood Ceramics Co., 140 NLRB 221, 51 LRRM 1600 (1962).
[20] 138 NLRB 66, 50 LRRM 1532 (1962).
[21] Shopping Kart Food Kts., Inc., 228 NLRB 1311, 94 LRRM 1705 (1977).
[22] General Knit of Cal., Inc., 239 NLRB 619, 99 LRRM 1687 (1978).
[23] 263 NLRB 127, 110 LRRM 1489 (1982).

long as Reagan nominees have a majority on the Board. In case the reader got lost, misrepresentation today is not grounds for setting aside an election.

The current Board does not accept the assumption that misleading campaign propaganda interferes with employee freedom of choice. The view is that employees should be viewed as mature individuals who are capable of recognizing campaign progaganda for what it is and discounting it. The two major studies of campaign tactics have been then Professor Bok's 1964 analysis[24] and the Getman-Goldberg study published in 1976.[25] It is worth noting that both these studies, albeit for somewhat different reasons, support the Board's present position.

For a long time now I have disagreed with the practice of setting aside elections under Section 9 because of noncoercive speech which is not an unfair labor practice because it is protected by Section 8(c). In many speech cases under the First Amendment, the Supreme Court has distinguished between time, place, and manner in regulation of the exercise of speech rights, and regulation of the substantive content of the speech. Time, place, and manner regulations are permissible if they are carefully tailored to protect important public interests. Regulations of content, however, are generally prohibited as constituting censorship. There is no doubt that under Section 9 the Board can properly regulate the time, place, and manner of campaigning. Examples are *General Shoe*[26] (a place and manner regulation), and the *Peerless Plywood*[27] 24-hour rule (a time regulation).

But I have never been convinced of the need and desirability of the Board's regulation of the content of propaganda beyond the line drawn by Congress between coercive and noncoercive speech. To me that practice is inconsistent with the language and purpose of the statute, and with free speech principles generally. The Board finesses Section 8(c) because on its face it speaks only of unfair labor practices. The reason is that in the pre-1947 years employers objected to the Board's propensity to find speech coercive and therefore an 8(a)(1). But clearly Section 8(c) was

---

[24] Bok, *The Regulation of Campaign Tactics in Representation Elections Under the National Labor Relations Act*, 78 HARV. L. REV. 38 (1964).

[25] J. Getman, S. Goldberg, & J. Herman, UNION REPRESENTATION ELECTIONS: LAW AND REALITY (1976).

[26] *Supra* note 18.

[27] Peerless Plywood Co., 107 NLRB 427, 33 LRRM 1151 (1953).

intended to protect noncoercive speech, and it is only in the preelection period that an employer is apt to engage in anti-union propaganda. If an employer confines itself to noncoercive speech and defeats the union in the election, it can reasonably feel sandbagged when it is deprived of its victory with the explanation that this is an R case and Section 8(c) does not apply. This is about as fair and sensible as telling a striker he hasn't been discharged, he's only been replaced. As to coercive speech, employers, because of their economic power, clearly have an advantage over unions. But in the area of noncoercive speech, especially misrepresentation, unions are fully capable of competing on equal terms.

More broadly, the whole concept of "laboratory conditions" is artificial, fictional, and inconsistent with the robust and free-wheeling rhetoric we have long expected and tolerated in labor disputes in this country. I do not agree that it is unrealistic to compare Board elections with political elections, where voters have long been aware that the only time one can be sure a politician is telling the truth is when he says another politician is lying. In my judgment, there is no compelling public interest which justified the Board to police its elections as though they were sheltered workshops.

C. Access Rules

Having criticized the Board for having exercised its Section 9 power improperly in one area, I will now criticize it for not having exercised it broadly enough in another area. It has long been assumed that employee freedom of choice presupposes access to employees by employer and union to communicate their respective messages. The most convenient time and place for the union and the employees to campaign is at the place of business while the employees are there. Presently the law permits the employer, because he owns the property and runs the enterprise, to impose on his employees campaign limits by which he himself is not bound. Employers may validly prohibit employees from engaging in union solicitation during working time and from the distribution of union literature in working areas, thus confining them to their free time and to nonworking areas. The leading cases are *Republic Aviation*[28] in 1945 and *Stoddard-Quirk*[29]

---

[28] Republic Aviation Corp. v. NLRB, 324 US 793, 16 LRRM 620 (1945).
[29] Stoddard-Quirk Mfg. Co., 138 NLRB 615, 51 LRRM 1110 (1962).

in 1962. In addition, under the Supreme Court's 1956 decision in *Babcock & Wilcox*[30] employers do not, absent unusual circumstances, commit an unfair labor practice when they deny nonemployee union organizers access to company property, even to nonwork areas when access would not interfere with the operation of the enterprise.

One practice of employers which is particularly vexatious to unions is the so-called "captive audience" antiunion speech made by the employer to his employees on company time. In 1946 the Board in *Clark Brothers*[31] held such speeches to be unfair labor practices. In 1951 the Board changed the law and held in *Bonwit Teller*[32] that noncoercive captive audience speeches were permissible, but it was an unfair labor practice for the employer to deny the union equal time. In 1953 the Board changed its mind again, this time holding in *Livingston Shirt*[33] that neither the speech nor the denial of equal time was an unfair labor practice. The Supreme Court approved this approach in its 1958 *Nutone*[34] decision, and it is still the rule.

It seems to me perfectly obvious that the result of the foregoing is to give management a lopsided advantage over unions in getting its message to employees. It seems naive to suppose that this advantage can ever be offset by any or all of the off-premises techniques such as union meetings, home visits, and mailings. It is easily possible to provide controlled access to company property in ways which do not interfere with operations. The only management right then at stake is the mere property right accruing from ownership of the premises.

It seems to me the problem of unequal access is one which could be dealt with under the Board's Section 9 power to make time, place, and manner regulations. It is certainly easier to justify than the laboratory conditions fiction, since there is no property right provision in the statute similar to Section 8(c). Both practically and legally, a stronger case can be made for access regulations under Section 9 than the speech regulations which have been upheld by the courts. The time was propitious for dealing with the access problem in the 1960s, shortly after

---

[30] NLRB v. Babcock & Wilcox Co., 351 US 105, 38 LRRM 2001 (1956).
[31] Clark Bros. Co., 70 NLRB 802, 18 LRRM 1360 (1946), *enforced*, 163 F2d 373, 20 LRRM 2436 (CA 2, 1947).
[32] Bonwit Teller, Inc., 96 NLRB 608, 28 LRRM 1547 (1951).
[33] Livingston Shirt Co., 107 NLRB 400, 33 LRRM 1156 (1953).
[34] NLRB v. Steelworkers, 357 US 357, 42 LRRM 2324 (1958).

Babcock and *Nutone* and a time when the membership of the Board was generally sympathetic with responding to legitimate union complaints. The Board's failure to move more boldly under Section 9 was a major disappointment. The Board skirted the area in its *Excelsior*[35] decision but an *Excelsior* list is not really needed in the small unit elections which have been the norm for many years.

It will be recalled that the Labor Reform Bill of 1978, which passed the House but was filibustered to death in the Senate, would have made a modest approach to the problem by requiring the Board to adopt a rule dealing with the captive audience situation. Although the Board in my view already had the authority to act, clearly a statutory mandate would have been a powerful argument in support of the legality of the rule when challenged in court. The bill did not provide that an employer's failure to comply with any such rule would be an unfair labor practice. Thus presumably, violation of any Section 9 rule would be the basis for setting an election aside if the union lost. Aside from the possibility of the judicial enforcement of Section 9 rules, the mere existence of such rules would be a salutary step forward in rectifying the unfairness of the present imbalance in the access area. Obviously, neither the Board nor Congress is going to do anything about unequal access in the foreseeable future. But, if history is any guide, one day the political pendulum will swing and perhaps the access problem will eventually be addressed, assuming the labor movement is still around by then.

III. Majority Rule and Exclusive Representation

The concepts of majority rule and exclusive representation embodied in the language of Section 7 are basic to American labor law, again distinguishing it from systems in other countries. Together with the concept of the appropriate bargaining unit, they have precluded the establishment in the United States of any collective bargaining on a members-only basis, even in the context of voluntary recognition. You may recall that Justice Douglas in his dissenting opinion in the *Bernhard-Altmann*[36] case

---

[35] Excelsior Underwear, Inc., 156 NLRB 1236, 61 LRRM 1217 (1966).
[36] Garment Workers v. NLRB (Bernhard-Altmann Tex. Corp.), 366 US 731, 47 LRRM 1616 (1961).

would have recognized the propriety of members-only bargaining. But this minor loss to the union movement is more than overcome by the status and prerogatives accruing from exclusive representation following majority choice. Indeed, union power has been viewed by the law as so great that there has been much concern, and properly so, over protecting the rights of individual employees within the system of exclusive representation. The principal check is the duty of fair representation, which is covered in detail in Professor Aaron's paper.

In one respect, unnecessary solicitude for individuals has prohibited what to my mind is a natural corollary of exclusive representation. I refer to the problem of the free rider. Section 7 recognizes the right of employees not to join unions, subject to union or agency shop agreements negotiated pursuant to the Section 8(a)(3) proviso. Absent such agreements, nonunion members of the bargaining unit obtain cost-free the benefits of bargaining and protection against unfair representation.

Efforts by unions to obtain security agreements historically have caused serious bargaining disputes and work stoppages. I think the whole issue would better be removed from the bargaining table. The power and duty flowing from exclusive representation point logically toward requiring membership or dues payment. It is not a question of individual rights or voluntary unionism, since present law authorizes compulsion, but only with the employer's agreement. Since the issue is one between the union and the employees, no good reason appears why the employer should have control over its resolution. To me it would seem more consistent with the principle of exclusive representation for the statute itself to require membership or dues payment and automatic checkoff. Employers would still have control over the hiring process. Union shop authorization elections, which were required for a few years after Taft-Hartley was enacted, demonstrated that employees who wanted a union also wanted a union shop, and today a substantial majority of collective agreements do contain union-security clauses. Think how much bargaining travail and litigation we would have been spared if the statute had dealt with the matter forthrightly as I have suggested.

IV. Pollution of the Representation Process

Today the entire statutory scheme is under serious indictment. The principal charge is that in too many cases the normal intended operation of the representation process is defeated by employers who commit unfair labor practices for which the law provides no prompt or adequate remedies. This problem has been under periodic investigation by Congress for about 25 years, and has been the subject of commentary in countless forums. Perhaps the best documentation of the magnitude of the problem is Professor Paul Weiler's 1983 analysis in the *Harvard Law Review*.[37]

When it is not infected by unfair labor practices and operates as intended, the representation process stands up well after 50 years. Historically, about 80 percent of Board elections have been held on a consent basis within about 45 days of the filing of the petition. Even when a hearing is held or there is a request for review by the Board, the election is not often delayed more than about three months. Frequently, as in the case of challenged ballots, the election is held promptly and the ballots impounded pending resolution of the legal issue. This procedure was the result of a recommendation by the Task Force I mentioned earlier. A union which cannot hold its support until election day, in the absence of unfair labor practices, has no real cause for complaint. The declining percentage of union victories in prompt and clean elections must find its explanation in reasons other than the inadequacy of the representation process.

The question is whether the pollution of the process by employer unfair labor practices is of sufficient incidence and effect to call for remedial legislation. The case was persuasive in the 1960s; today I think the arguments are overwhelming. Whether unfair labor practices charges are filed before or after the election, several years may elapse before final resolution. The inadequacy of remedies is notorious. These matters are treated in subsequent papers.

Is it possible to deal with the problem through change in the representation process itself? The Board could improve the situation only modestly by tightening its own post-election procedures, since the principal period of delay and union attrition is during judicial review. Professor Weiler has suggested that the way to deal with the problem is to eliminate the preelection campaign period. Theoretically, the election itself could be eliminated and unions certified on the basis of membership or autho-

---

[37] Weiler, *Promises to Keep: Securing Workers' Rights to Self-Organization Under the NLRA*, 96 HARV. L. REV. 1769 (1983).

rization cards, as indeed was the practice in the early years under the Wagner Act. About 1942 the Board began to opt for elections, and the 1947 amendments to Section 9 clinched the matter. Professor Weiler's proposed change, drawn from Canadian experience, is the "instant" election held within five to seven days after the filing of the petition. The premise is that this period is too brief for employer unfair labor practices to destroy union support. Instant elections reject the assumption that employee freedom of choice requires exposure to employer antiunion appeals. This assumption finds support in the Getman-Goldberg study which concluded that preelection propaganda has little effect on the outcome of the election. If this is so, then nothing is lost under the instant election, and employee choice will be determined by whether or not they are generally satisfied or dissatisfied with their employment conditions. Section 8(b)(7) affords a statutory precedent for an expedited election, in that case in order to protect the interests of employers against union picketing. Why not instant elections to protect the interests of employees?

V. Nonunion Representation

Unionization and collective bargaining are not ends in themselves. They are means through which employees achieve some voice in their economic destiny and the assurance of fair compensation and humane working conditions. Because of the history of company unionism, the Wagner Act broadly proscribed, through Section 8(a)(2) and the definition of labor organization in Section 2(5), virtually all forms of employee representation except full-fledged independent unions. The Supreme Court's 1959 decision in *Cabot Carbon Co.*,[38] with its expansive reading of Section 2(5), has been a powerful impediment to the legal establishment of nonunion employee representation plans.

Since that decision, a small body of case law has developed on the question. There are a handful of decisions[39] in which particular plans have been upheld despite the language of the statute and *Cabot Carbon*. This result has been achieved through strained distinctions. Thus, while Section 8(a)(2) prohibits

---

[38] 360 US 203, 44 LRRM 2204 (1959).
[39] *E.g.*, NLRB v. Steamway Div., Scott & Fetzer Co., 691 F2d 288, 111 LRRM 2673 (CA 6, 1982).

employer support, it does not prohibit "cooperation," and while Section 2(5) prohibits "dealing" (which the Supreme Court said was broader than bargaining), it does not prohibit communicating. These relatively few appellate decisions clearly manifest an unwillingness to confine employees to a choice between a union or nothing.

Recent years have witnessed a substantial amount of scrutiny of the adversarial nature of labor relations which characterizes collective bargaining. Some proposals seek to alleviate the confrontation within the union/bargaining contexts. Examples are union membership on the company board of directors; FMCS underwriting of labor-management committees as authorized in Section 205(a) of the Act, added by the Labor Management Cooperation Act of 1978; and the involvement of unions in joint intra-plant programs. At the other end of the spectrum, separable from the bargaining context, protection of employee interests is urged through such techniques as profit-sharing, stock ownership, or outright employee ownership of the enterprise.

Intermediate are a variety of employee representation plans and committees whose legal status is under the constant jeopardy of a Section 8(a)(2) charge. Surely not all of these schemes have been foisted by unscrupulous employers on gullible employees in order to frustrate unionism. Surely there should be room in our industrial relations system for bona fide methods of employer-employee problem solving other than the union/collective bargaining model. In 1935 the single-minded focus on unions and collective bargaining was understandable. Today it seems an anachronism to confine employee freedom of choice to union representation or no representation at all. In order to broaden employee choice the procrustean state of the law should be changed. It is not beyond our legal capacity to develop criteria and standards which will distinguish between legitimate nonunion employee representation plans and spurious schemes whose ancestry is the company union. What is needed is a green light—either a Supreme Court decision modifying *Cabot Carbon* or a statutory amendment.

VI. Conclusion

Now I will return to where I started. In 1935 the labor policy of the United States was set forth in the stated purposes of the statute: to protect employee freedom of choice and to encourage collective bargaining. The assumption was that employees would choose unions. While the Taft-Hartley law did not delete these stated purposes, it seems fair to conclude that its overall labor policy was to contain unionism and check the growth of collective bargaining. It is clear that Taft-Hartley has achieved this purpose, while at the same time creating an excessively and obsessively legalistic labor relations system.

It seems to me that for many years there has been no labor policy of the United States. Rather, there have been a lot of labor policies dealing with discrete problem areas, emanating from different sources—legislative, executive, judicial, and private as well as governmental. These policies are administered by a number of different departments, boards, commissions, and services. They are frequently inconsistent and in conflict with each other. The LMRA is just one statute and the NLRB just one decisionmaker among many in the field of labor law, performing limited functions in limited areas. It is an important but independent factor exerting some unmeasurable influence on activities which are also affected by numerous other legal and nonlegal forces. Sometimes I think that we Board watchers inflate the role of the Board and exaggerate its influence on labor relations and the economy. Perhaps what we need is a Labor Code of the United States, which would synthesize and regularize all of the present disparate statutes and policies. This might give us more clarity of purpose and consistency of achievement than we now have. But only Congress can bring this to pass. Until it happens, the Board still has a function to perform.

The year 1985 marked the 50th year since the enactment of the National Labor Relations Act. What should have been a joyful golden anniversary instead has been a year characterized by a number of sad ironies.

It is a sad irony that the statute which in its early years encouraged the growth of unionism has increasingly become a promise to the ear broken to the hope and is today viewed in many respects as a hollow mockery.

It is a sad irony that the statute passed to promote unionism and collective bargaining is today consciously turned against itself to defeat the statutory objectives by the most blatantly antiunion Board in history.

It is a sad irony that in the nation which has the world's most conservative labor movement, one which has consistently rejected political and economic radicalism, there should exist the world's most intense, widespread, and frequently illegal employer opposition to unions.

It is a sad irony that American unions are victims of their own success, that the general enhancement of labor standards, attributable in large part to unionism, has minimized a felt need and desire for unions in nonunion sectors.

It is a sad irony that the public at large perceives unions as having "too much power" when in fact union power is negligible compared with corporate economic power. Union power relates only to terms and conditions of employment, whereas corporate economic decisions exploit and allocate resources, create and satisfy consumer desires, and affect the nation, its economy, and the lives of people as fully as do decisions by government.

It is an irony, although not a sad one, that the union movement, which is an apparent state of decline in the United States, continues to be a symbol and beacon of hope and inspiration to employees in nations with emerging and developing economies.

But perhaps we are being unduly pessimistic. After all, Cassandra was a false prophet and the reports of Mark Twain's death were greatly exaggerated. Human events move in unpredictable and sometimes cyclical patterns. Our forecasts of the future are frequently wrong. So it is altogether possible that forces as yet not peceived or even existent may bring about a renaissance of unionism in America. It may be that the darkest hour for unions in 50 years is just before the dawn of a new day.

Responses

A RESPONSE TO MURPHY'S LAW

CHARLES G. BAKALY, JR.*

Professor Murphy in his paper presented a view of the Board and its work which, without more, would leave one with the impression that the current Board is "the most blatantly anti-union Board in history" and is failing to carry out its obligations under the Act. It is my belief that the current Board, within the

* Partner, O'Melveny & Myers, Los Angeles, California. The author acknowledges the assistance of David J. Hamilton in the preparation of this paper.

bounds prescribed by Congress, has done as much or more than any of its predecessors to fulfill its statutory mandate.

The scope of the mandate bears further examination.

Under the Wagner Act, passed in 1935, the policy of the Act was twofold—to encourage collective bargaining and to protect the workers' right to organize and designate representatives of their own choosing.[1]

Twelve years later, in 1947, Congress recognized the one-sidedness of the Wagner Act and realized that in order to insure the employees' freedom of choice it was essential to guarantee not only the right of employees to self-organize and join labor organizations but that it was equally necessary to insure that employees have the right to refrain from such activity.[2] Thus, while Section 1 still remains in the Act, Section 7 is clearly the centerpiece of the Act; and the Board, the courts, and Congress have all focused on the balance to be struck under Section 7. Therefore, for almost 40 of the 50 years of the Board's existence, the policy of the Act in reality has been to encourage collective bargaining as a method of resolving labor disputes *only* when the workers involved have clearly exercised their franchise in favor of the establishment of such a regime—a mandate which past and current Boards have in large measure fulfilled within their jurisdictional limits.

In fulfilling its Congressional mandate, the current Board has been subjected to a great deal of criticism by the labor establishment, charging that the Board is attempting to dismantle many of labor's gains of past years. However, if one takes a more objective view of this Board's work, one finds that there is nothing new or sinister in the current Board's rulings regarding representation.

With the coming and going of each administration, the Board has tended to shift its stance depending upon the political affiliation of the incumbent president. With each such change, the cry has gone up from the partisans that the Board is being unduly politicized by the party in power. The grumbling first came from management in the early years of the Board. For example, in 1938, *Fortune* magazine launched an attack on the Board in an article entitled "The Goddamned Labor Board." In the late

---

[1] 29 USC §151.
[2] 29 USC §157.

1940s a great howl of discontent was heard from the union side regarding the Taft-Hartley amendments.[3]

In the late 1950s, a committee from the House of Representatives attacked the record of the "Eisenhower" Board because of its allegedly pro-management decisions. A decade later the pendulum had swung the other way and the so-called Kennedy-Johnson Board was subjected to attacks that it had "disregarded fraud and gross misrepresentations on the part of unions and rewarded strikers for flagrant misconduct . . . ."[4]

Through the early 1970s the Board again came under attack by unions. But, by the turn of the decade, the decisions of the Board were again being criticized by management groups as containing "result oriented reasoning" and an excess of "zeal and unreasonableness."[5]

History repeats itself and, now, predictably, the attacks go the other way. One labor leader was recently quoted as stating that the Board had been "packed with radical conservatives who frustrate (union) organizing and discourage collective bargaining and delay and deny justice to workers" and that unions may now "take to the streets" to enforce their rights because of their inability to receive satisfaction from the Board.[6]

An examination of the history of a few of the rules applicable to union organizing quickly dispels the validity of such charges. In the 1940s the Board adopted the so-called "contract-bar" rule which barred the filing of a representation petition during the period of time in which a collective bargaining agreement was in effect, so long as the period of this contract was not unduly long.[7] If the contract period was overly long, the bar would be effective only for a reasonable period, which would vary with the custom of the industry in which the contract was signed. The test applicable then was an "all the circumstances" test.[8]

By the late 1950s the contract-bar rule had become increasingly unworkable and burdensome because of the difficulty encountered by the parties to the contract in determining at

---

[3] A. McAdams, POWER AND POLITICS IN LABOR LEGISLATION 29 (1964).

[4] LABOR RELATIONS YEARBOOK—1969 273 (BNA Books, 1970).

[5] Irving, *New Directions: Recent Trends and Developments in NLRB Cases*, LABOR LAW DEVELOPMENTS 1981 (Twenty-Sixth Annual Institute on Labor Law, Southwestern Legal Foundation) 25 (1981).

[6] Los Angeles Times, Sept. 3, 1985, at I-1.

[7] General Box Co., 82 NLRB 678, 23 LRRM 1589 (1949).

[8] Reed Roller Bit Co., 72 NLRB 927, 19 LRRM 1227 (1947).

what point the contract-bar rule would cease to apply. As a result, the Board implemented a *per se* rule in which a written contract for a period of two years or longer would receive the protection of the contract-bar rule through the first two years of the contract only; thereafter, representation petitions could be filed by any party and the contract would not serve as a bar to an election.[9]

By the early 1960s, the composition of the Board had changed from an "Eisenhower" Board to a "Kennedy" Board with the additions of Chairman McCulloch and Member Brown. The Kennedy Board extended the contract bar from two years to three years in which the filing of a petition would be barred.[10] This rule is one which, after several years of refinement, has remained relatively stable through the last two decades. Despite having the opportunity to do so, the Nixon, Carter, and Reagan Boards have left the rule intact.

There are, of course, a number of rules which have been far less stable during the last two decades. The most glaring area of instability involves misrepresentations. Under the Wagner Act, the Board, with rare exceptions, did not inquire into the content of speech of either party. Virtually any preelection campaign speech by management was unlawful.[11] On the other hand, virtually all union campaign propaganda was permissible, regardless of accuracy.[12]

With the addition of Section 8(c) to the Act in 1947,[13] employer speech that had previously been considered unlawful no longer constituted an unfair labor practice. Nevertheless, the Board still exhibited a concern for the impact of employer speech upon employee choice in representation elections. Thus, the Board developed the *General Shoe*[14] doctrine and held that speech, even though it may not violate Section 8(c), could be sufficiently coercive, misleading, or untruthful to upset election results. The upshot of Section 8(c) and *General Shoe* was a basic change in Board policy which resulted in the application of a stricter standard against preelection communications by all par-

---

[9] Pacific Coast Ass'n of Pulp & Paper Mfrs., 121 NLRB 990, 42 LRRM 1477 (1958).
[10] General Cable Corp., 139 NLRB 1123, 51 LRRM 1444 (1962).
[11] Rockford Mitten & Hosiery Co., 16 NLRB 501, 5 LRRM 244 (1939).
[12] Maywood Hosiery Mills, Inc., 64 NLRB 146, 17 LRRM 90 (1945).
[13] 29 USC §158(c).
[14] General Shoe Corp., 77 NLRB 124, 21 LRRM 1337 (1948), *enforced*, 192 F2d 504, 29 LRRM 2112 (CA 6, 1951), *cert. denied*, 343 US 904 (1952).

ties, and by the early 1950s the Board began to hold that it would overturn election results based upon union campaign statements involving gross misrepresentations related to speech.[15] Nevertheless, the Board continued to refrain from policing campaign statements unless the ability of the employees to evaluate such statements had been so impaired by the use of forged campaign material or other campaign trickery that the uninhibited desires of the employees could not be determined.[16]

The Eisenhower Board was somewhat ambivalent about the *General Shoe* doctrine and retracted from it. It tended to use Section 8(c) as the outer limit of permissible conduct in election cases.[17] Interestingly, the courts were generally more zealous in applying the "laboratory conditions" standard, and many of the circuit courts undertook to insure that the standard would be applied as strictly against campaign abuses by unions as against those by management.[18]

In 1962, the reconstituted "Kennedy" Board returned to a more restrictive view of the laboratory condition standard, holding in *Dal-Tex Optical Co., Inc.*[19] that conduct which was not an unfair labor practice could upset the laboratory conditions of the election.

After several adverse judicial decisions, the Board in late 1962 attempted to restate, and to some extent codify, its rules regarding misrepresentations in election campaigns and at the same time create some flexibility in its laboratory condition standards. The result was *Hollywood Ceramics*[20] in which the Board held that an election could be set aside for misrepresentation if there was a substantial departure from truth at a time when the opposing party could not effectively reply and the misrepresentation would reasonably be expected to have a significant impact on the election. However, if the voters had an independent source of knowledge or the misrepresentation was so extreme as to put voters on notice, the Board would not interfere.

---

15 West-Gate Sun Harbor Co., 93 NLRB 830, 27 LRRM 1474 (1951).
16 Merck & Co., Inc., 104 NLRB 891, 32 LRRM 1160 (1953); Gummed Prods. Co., 112 NLRB 1092, 36 LRRM 1156 (1955).
17 National Furniture Co., 119 NLRB 1, 40 LRRM 1442 (1957).
18 Celanese Corp. v. NLRB, 279 F2d 204, 46 LRRM 2445 (CA 7, 1960); NLRB v. Houston Chronicle Publishing Co., 300 F2d 273, 49 LRRM 2782 (CA 5, 1962).
19 137 NLRB 1782, 50 LRRM 1489 (1962).
20 Hollywood Ceramics Co., Inc., 140 NLRB 221, 51 LRRM 1600 (1962).

The *Hollywood Ceramics* rule was adopted by the full Board. The rule held through the remainder of the Kennedy Administration and through the Johnson and Nixon administrations. However, the rule was subjected to sharp criticism by the courts,[21] commentators,[22] and by some Board members.[23] Derek Bok, now the president of Harvard University, stated in 1964 that "such restrictions [regarding misrepresentation] resist every effort at clear formulation and tend inexorably to give rise to vague and inconsistent rulings which baffle the parties and provoke litigation."[24]

By 1977, the composition of the Board had changed significantly with the appointment of Chairman Murphy and Member Walther by President Ford. In *Shopping Kart*,[25] the Board reversed *Hollywood Ceramics* and held that it would no longer set aside representation elections solely because of misleading campaign statements or misrepresentations of fact. The Board stated that it would continue to intervene only where a party improperly involved the Board or its processes or forged documents were used to render the voters unable to recognize the propaganda for what it was.

The *Shopping Kart* case was not a unanimous decision, with Members Fanning and Jenkins dissenting. By late 1977, the Board composition had again changed slightly with the appointment of Member Truesdale by President Carter to replace Member Walther. The misrepresentation issue again came before the Board; the Board, in *General Knit*,[26] again reversed itself and returned to the *Hollywood Ceramics* rule. As might be expected, Members Murphy and Penello (who had voted with the majority in *Shopping Kart*) dissented, indicating that they would have retained the *Shopping Kart* rule; thus, the appointment of Member Truesdale proved to be the key to the vote.

By 1982, President Reagan had the opportunity to appoint two members of the Board, Chairman Van de Water and Mem-

---

[21] NLRB v. Cactus Drilling Corp., 455 F2d 871, 79 LRRM 2551 (CA 5, 1972).

[22] Bok, *Regulating NLRA Election Tactics*, 7 HARV. L. REV. 38 (1964); J. Getman, S. Goldberg, & J. Herman, UNION REPRESENTATION ELECTIONS: LAW AND REALITY (1976).

[23] Modine Mfg. Co., 203 NLRB 527, 83 LRRM 1133 (1973), *enforced*, 500 F2d 914, 86 LRRM 3197 (CA 8, 1974).

[24] Bok, *supra* note 22, at 92.

[25] Shopping Kart Food Mkt., Inc., 228 NLRB 1311, 94 LRRM 1705 (1977).

[26] General Knit of Cal., 239 NLRB 619, 99 LRRM 1687 (1978).

ber Hunter. Those two, together with Member Zimmerman, a Carter appointee, returned to the *Shopping Kart* rule in *Midland National Life Insurance Co.*[27] As would be expected, Members Fanning and Jenkins dissented.

There are many who claim that the *Midland National* decision is one of the current Board's "union-busting" decisions. However, there is little factual or legal underpinning to that claim. I believe that the vast majority of workers are sufficiently sophisticated to understand and react to misrepresentations. If anything, the *Midland National* rule favor unions. In an unscientific review of the cases, it appears to me that a significant majority of the misrepresentation cases involve claims by employers that the union made misrepresentations during the course of the campaign. If, in fact, most of the cases involve misrepresentations by unions, it is unions, not employers, that are most likely to benefit from the current rule. Unions can now make misrepresentations without committing an unfair labor practice or having the election set aside. Even if my review of the cases is not correct, unions should still favor the current rule. Union leaders have long charged that employers file baseless objections to elections simply to prolong the period of time prior to commencing bargaining. If those accusations have any basis in fact, it is evident that the current rule will remove at least one basis for objecting to the outcome of an election.

If the *Midland National* rule regarding misrepresentations favors unions, what of the current Board's other decisions that its critics claim are "contrary to the purposes of the Act" and reverse "longstanding precedents?" Such claims have little factual basis. In reality, the previous administration's view of labor relations was much more interventionist, and it was the Carter Board that was responsible for reversing a number of long-established principles.[28] The truth of the matter is that the current Board has effected a return to a centerist position *vis-à-vis* union and management.

In *TRW Bearings*,[29] decided by Chairman Fanning and Members Jenkins and Zimmerman in 1981, the Carter Board over-

---

[27] 263 NLRB 127, 110 LRRM 1489 (1982). The *Midland National* holding was further expanded in *Riveredge Hospital*, 264 NLRB 1094, 111 LRRM 1425 (1982) in which the Board held that it would treat a party's misrepresentations of Board actions the same as any other misrepresentations.

[28] Irving, *supra* note 5, at 28.

[29] 257 NLRB 442, 107 LRRM 1481 (1981).

ruled *Essex International*.[30] *Essex International* established 10 years ago that in-plant rules prohibiting union solicitation during "working time" were presumptively valid, while rules prohibiting such solicitation during " working hours" were presumptively invalid. The *Essex International* case had essentially codified principles regarding employee solicitation in the workplace that were well known to both management and labor alike since the *Peyton Packing*[31] decision in 1943 and approved by the Supreme Court in *Republic Aviation* v. *NLRB*[32] in 1945. The Carter Board's *TRW* decision, which abandoned the "working time" and "working hours" distinction and the attendant presumptions as ambiguous, unraveled years of stability and certainty in the area. The current Board reversed *TRW* and returned to the certainty of the previous distinctions in *Our Way, Inc.*[33] Contrary to the statements of one commentator, that the *Our Way* decision amounted to a "dismantling of the pro-union provisions the previous *Boards* had written into labor management law,"[34] the *Our Way* case overruled the decision of only *one* Board, the Carter Board, which had departed from a long, familiar precedent.

Another area where there has been a recent change in the law involves the interrogation of open union adherents. Thirty years ago in *Blue Flash Express, Inc.*,[35] the Board adopted a test to evaluate cases involving interrogation. The test was whether under all the circumstances the interrogation reasonably tended to restrain, coerce, or interfere with the rights guaranteed by the Act. The Carter Board threw that test out the window in favor of a *per se* rule and held that any questioning, even though addressed to an open and active union supporter and without threats or promises, was inherently coercive. The Carter Board's decision in *PPG Industries*[36] reversed 30 years of Board precedent and ignored circuit court rulings. For instance, the Seventh Circuit said in *Midwest Stock Exchange*[37] that "It is well established

---

[30] 211 NLRB 749, 86 LRRM 1411 (1974).
[31] 49 NLRB 828, 12 LRRM 183 (1943), *enforced*, 142 F2d 1009, 14 LRRM 792 (CA 5), *cert. denied*, 323 US 730 (1944).
[32] 324 US 793, 16 LRRM 620 (1945).
[33] 268 NLRB 394, 115 LRRM 1009 (1983).
[34] Sawyer, *New NLRB Undoing Past Pro-Union Decisions*, St. Louis, Mo. Post-Dispatch, Apr. 10, 1984.
[35] 109 NLRB 591, 34 LRRM 1384 (1954).
[36] 251 NLRB 1146, 105 LRRM 1434 (1980).
[37] 635 F2d 1255, 1267, 105 LRRM 3172, 3182 (CA 7, 1980).

that interrogation of employees is not illegal *per se* . . . . [E]ither
the words themselves or the context in which they are used must
suggest an element of coercion or interference." The Third
Circuit, in *Graham Architectual Products* v. *NLRB*,[38] spoke in a
similar vein and raised the possibility that a *per se* approach
forbidding noncoercive questioning raised First Amendment
issues: "If Section 8(a)(1) of the Act deprived the employers of
any right to ask non-coercive questions of their employees during such a campaign, the Act would directly collide with the
Constitution." Thus, the current Board's decision in *Rossmore
House*[39] does not establish a new principle but rather effects a
return to years of Board and court precedent.

Another area of recent concern involving the organizational
process is nonmajority bargaining orders.

Since the *Gissel*[40] decision, it has been clear that a bargaining
order could be issued without an election in limited circumstances. However, both before and after *Gissel*, the Board had
declined to issue nonmajority bargaining orders.[41] In fact, the
Board's Associate General Counsel in *Gissel*, Dominick Mannoli,
indicated in oral argument before the Supreme Court that
majority status was still an essential predicate to a bargaining
order.[42]

In 1979, when the Carter Board was first presented with the
issue of nonmajority bargaining orders, it split three ways.[43]
Member Penello held that the Board did not have such authority. Chairman Fanning and Member Jenkins held that the Board
did have such authority, and Members Murphy and Truesdale
found that the Board may have such authority. Finally in early
1982, Members Fanning, Jenkins, and Zimmerman held in *Conair Corp.*[44] (over the dissents of Chairman Van de Water and
Member Hunter) that the Board did have the authority to issue

---

[38] 697 F2d 534, 541, 112 LRRM 2470, 2475 (CA 3, 1983).

[39] 269 NLRB 1176, 116 LRRM 1025 (1984), *aff'd*, 760 F2d 1006, 119 LRRM 2624 (CA 9, 1985).

[40] *NLRB v. Gissel Packing Co.*, 395 US 575, 71 LRRM 2481 (1969).

[41] H.W. Elson Bottling Co., 155 NRLB 714, 60 LRRM 1381 (1965), *enforced as modified*, 379 F2d 223 (CA 6, 1967); Fugua Homes Mo., Inc., 201 NLRB 130, 82 LRRM 1142 (1973); GTE Automatic Elec., 196 NLRB 902, 80 LRRM 1155 (1972); Loray Corp., 184 NLRB 557, 74 LRRM 1513 (1970).

[42] *Proceedings of the Supreme Court*, Gissel Packing, oral argument, at 21–22.

[43] United Dairy Farmers Coop. Ass'n, 242 NLRB 1026, 101 LRRM 1278 (1979), *aff'd and remanded*, 633 F2d 1054, 105 LRRM 3034 (CA 3, 1980).

[44] 261 NLRB 1189, 110 LRRM 1161 (1982), *enforcement granted in part and denied in part*, 721 F2d 1355, 114 LRRM 3169 (CA DC, 1983), *cert. denied*, 467 US 1241 (1984).

nonmajority bargaining orders. In *Conair*, the Board's choice was denominated as the employee's real choice, that is, that the employees would have selected union representation but for the employer's misconduct. However, one can only speculate that that was the true employee choice, particularly in light of the fact that the union had never demonstrated majority support.

In 1984, with the appointment of new members by President Reagan, the Board overruled the *Conair* decision. In *Gourmet Foods, Inc.*[45] the Reagan Board abandonded the Carter Board's attempt to remedy employer unfair labor practices by imposing a collective bargaining regime by administrative fiat and held that a bargaining order would not be appropriate unless the union had demonstrated majority support at some relevant time. I think that Professor Murphy would have to agree that the current Board's ruling avoids the situation where the Board would replace employee freedom of choice with a government agency's educated guess that the employees would fare better with the union than without one.

This Board, as all of the Boards preceding it, has little control over its jurisdiction. As noted by Professor Murphy, the Act does not cover agricultural laborers.[46] However, that is not to say that agricultural workers are totally without rights. California provides protection to agricultural laborers which in many respects is more expansive than that covered by the Act.[47] A number of other states have provided similar, though less extensive protection. However, as an attorney who has had to work with the California Agricultural Labor Relations Board, I would certainly favor the coverage of the Act being extended to agricultural workers, although I am sure that employers in other states would disagree with that proposition.

The coverage of the Act does not extend to most governmental workers.[48] Nevertheless, the government employees receive some protection in regard to collective bargaining rights. Federal workers have the protection of the Federal Labor Relations Authority.[49] Most of the states have similar protection for government workers and in many jurisdictions the right to strike has been extended to public employees. Thus, even though the

---

[45] 270 NLRB 578, 116 LRRM 1105 (1984).
[46] 29 USC §152(3).
[47] *See* CAL. LAB. CODE §1140 *et seq.*
[48] 29 USC §152(2).
[49] 5 USC ch. 71 (Civil Service Reform Act of 1978).

coverage of the Act extends to only about 50 percent cf all workers, well over 80 percent of the workers in the United States have protection with respect to collective bargaining rights.[50]

The Board has been afforded some discretion with respect to jurisdiction. Under Section 14(c)(1) Congress ratified the Board's decision to decline jurisdiction over certain industries and over very small enterprises.[51] Unfortunately, Section 14 also locked in the jurisdictional dollar amounts existing under the Board's rules in 1959. With an increase in the cost of living of over 300 percent[52] since the enactment of Section 14, I think the Board would be well-advised to return to Congress and advocate an increase in the jurisdictional thresholds to permit the Board to get out of an area which does not impact on interstate commerce and lift some of the bureaucratic burden off of small businessmens' backs.

The Board has also excluded certain classes of employees from the Act's coverage (or at least from Section 9), most notably managerial[53] and confidential employees.[54] Both of these excluded classes involve small numbers and, conceptually, I think that the determination of the Board to exclude these classes is absolutely correct. Managerial and confidential employees, because of their close relationship to the decision-making process, should not be placed in the compromising position of dividing their loyalty between the employer's legitimate expectations and the union's demands for solidarity. The policies underlying the Board's decisions regarding medical interns and secular employees of religious schools are also compelling, and the Board was justified in its actions.[55]

There are other areas in which coverage has been denied which Professor Murphy has not questioned, such as race tracks and dog tracks.[56] The Board did not hesitate to take jurisdiction over other gambling enterprises such as casinos.[57] I fail to see a

---

[50] C. Gifford, DIRECTORY OF U.S. LABOR ORGANIZATIONS: 1984–85 EDITION 3 (BNA Books, 1984).

[51] 29 USC §164(c)(1).

[52] See, e.g., Bureau of Labor Statistics, Consumer Price Index for 1985.

[53] NRLB v. Bell Aerospace Co., 416 US 267, 85 LRRM 2945 (1974).

[54] Westinghouse Elec. Corp. v NLRB, 398 F2d 669, 68 LRRM 2849 (CA 6, 1968).

[55] See, e.g., Cedars-Sinai Medical Center, 223 NLRB 251, 91 LRRM 1398 (1976).

[56] NLRB Rules and Regs. §103.3; Centennial Turf Club, Inc., 192 NLRB 698, 77 LRRM 1894 (1971).

[57] El Dorado Club, 151 NLRB 579, 58 LRRM 1455 (1965), overruled on other grounds, El Conquistador Hotel, Inc., 186 NLRB 123, 75 LRRM 1289 (1970); NLRB v. Anthony Co., 557 F2d 692, 95 LRRM 3239 (CA 9, 1977).

factual or policy distinction which would justify the Board's reluctance to exercise jurisdiction over racing. Here is one area where I can agree with former Chairman Fanning that the NLRB would better serve the public if it exercised jurisdiction.

The subject of appropriate bargaining units has also been a subject frequently before the Board. The issue which has generated the most controversy recently involves the establishment of health care units. After several years of adverse decisions from the Courts of Appeal, in *St. Francis II*[58] the current Board has adopted a "disparity of interest" approach in establishing health area units as opposed to the traditional "community of interest" approach. Certainly the change in direction was justified in light of the clear congressional intent to avoid the proliferation of units in the health care area and the frequent judicial rejection of the Board's health care unit determinations.[59]

One area in which I would disagree with both Chairman Dotson and Professor Murphy is that unit determination is an area that would be appropriate for rule making. This may be the only other area in which former Chairman Fanning and I can agree. For 50 years the Board, regardless of who the members were, has consistently rejected the idea of substantive rule making. I would concur in that decision. The area of bargaining units is of particular concern. Variations in operating procedure and management structure within American business are almost limitless. Not only do the needs of different industries compel different organizational structures but the management styles adopted by various institutions also mandate different types of organization.

If the Board were to engage in rule making in this area, it could well result in a standardization of organization which would amount to putting the area of labor relations into much the same quagmire that the tax laws are in. In the tax area, the regulations promulgated by the IRS have frequently resulted in the establishment of enterprises and projects with the sole goal of benefiting from the tax laws rather than with the more proper goal of establishing a profitable entity which provides needed goods and services. The use of rule making by the Board in the

---

[58] St. Francis Hosp., 271 NLRB 948, 116 LRRM 1465 (1984).

[59] *See, e.g.*, NLRB v. St. Francis Hosp., 601 F2d 404, 101 LRRM 2943 (CA 9, 1979); St. Luke's Medical Center v. NLRB, 653 F2d 450, 107 LRRM 2953 (CA 10, 1981), *modified on other grounds*, 688 F2d 697, 111 LRRM 2384 (1982); NLRB v. Frederick Memorial Hosp., 691 F2d 191, 111 LRRM 2680 (CA 4, 1982).

unit determination area could easily have much the same effect. That is, that actions could be taken by employers simply to comply with (or circumvent) rules rather than for the purpose of providing goods and services to the public in an efficient manner and advancing employee rights. I would leave the area of unit determinations to the *ad hoc* approach currently used by the Board, tempered by the use of certain guiding principles.

Overall, the Board's rules regarding the representation election process are working well. In fiscal year 1984, a record 84 percent of all elections were held by agreement of the parties. Elections are typically held within 47 days of the filing of the petition.[60] Professor Murphy's suggestion for an expedited election process is not well-founded. Employee support for unions is ostensibly at its peak at the time petitions are filed. However, much of that support has been generated in a vacuum, in the absence of any input of opposing views. If employees are to make a rational choice regarding representation, it is imperative that they have adequate time to hear and consider both sides of the story. The expedited election would preclude such deliberation.

I think Professor Murphy's assertion that the Getman-Goldberg study found that preelection propaganda had little effect on the outcome of elections is not entirely accurate. That study found that roughly 80 percent of the vote of employees could be predicted prior to the commencement of campaigning and that those employees were not swayed by subsequent propaganda. However, 20 percent of the electorate were undecided and presumably voted on the basis of the campaign presentations of unions and employers.[61] Given the closeness of most elections, that undecided 20 percent is clearly decisive and should be given an adequate opportunity to listen and reflect before making a decision.

Professor Murphy's argument that unions should be given more access to employers' property during the election campaign ignores the real-world problems facing employers. Unions admittedly have less access to employees in the workplace but clearly have a counterbalancing exclusive right to visit employees in their homes. Moreover, the employers' right to

---

[60] *NLRB General Counsel's Summary of Operations for FY 1984*, LABOR RELATIONS YEARBOOK—1984, 323 (BNA Books, 1985).

[61] J. Getman, S. Goldberg, & J. Herman, *supra* note 22, at 72.

maintain production and discipline must be of paramount concern when analyzing nonemployee access rules. While bald statements that the presence of union organizers on employers' property would not be unduly intrusive may have some surface appeal in the ivory towers of academe, no proposal yet drafted, when applied to the real-world workplace, would insure noninterference with production.

Moreover, many such proposals present free speech implications. Employers have a constitutional right to refrain from speaking and, with certain limitations, a right to refrain from providing a forum for another's message which they find repugnant.[62] A Board rule compelling employers to provide a forum and a paid audience for the presentation of the unions' message may well exceed the Board's constitutional authority.

In sum, in the area of establishment of collective bargaining relationships, the Reagan appointees are merely returning to precedents that had been abandoned by the Carter Board; and the Board is working in much the same way as it has for the last 20 years or so. More importantly, most of the recent decisions have very little impact on whether employees vote for the union. As for the charges that the current Board is the most destructive of unions since the inception of the Act, again, one must separate reality from rhetoric.

Unionism was on the decline for 30 years before President Reagan appointed a single member to the Board. Unions hit their peak in the mid-1950s (during the tenure of another allegedly antiunion Board) when roughly 34 percent[63] of the nonagricultural work force was represented by unions. Since that time, unions have been in a long decline and although their memberships and actual numbers continued to increase until the mid-1970s,[64] the percentage of union members in the work force has declined steadily until union members now comprise less than 18 percent[65] of the civilian work force. Concomitantly, union victories in representation elections have declined from a high of over 80 percent[66] in the 1940s to only about 40 percent

---

[62] Wooley v. Maynard, 430 US 705 (1977); Miami Herald Publishing Co. v. Tornillo, 418 US 241 (1974).

[63] LABOR RELATIONS YEARBOOK—1967 353 (BNA Books, 1968).

[64] C. Gifford, *supra* note 50, at 2.

[65] *Id.* at 3.

[66] *See, e.g.,* 1941 NLRB ANN. REP. 37 (1942).

today.[67] Moreover, roughly 30 million employees voted in NLRB elections in the first 42 years of the Board,[68] while only about 3 million have voted in the last 8 years. There are a number of factors, all unrelated to the current Board's rulings, which are responsible for the decline in union strength.

As society has become more complex, the workers have become more sophisticated and the nature of the work force has changed dramatically. Unlike the 1930s, there is no labor "movement" or demand for collective action existing among most of today's employees. Very few of today's workers can remember the Great Depression. The closest thing for most is the recession of 1981–82. The majority of today's workers have never been through a cataclysmic war such as World War II. In fact, almost all of the workers under 35 have had no military service whatsoever. This is clearly the best educated work force in history. According to one recent study as much as 25 percent of the work force has a college degree[69] and a much higher percentage than that has had at least some college education. The workers today are the most affluent and most independent workers of all time. I believe that the prevailing attitude among workers is that they do not need or want others to help them when they can help themselves.

Co-extensive with the changes in the work force, there has been a change in employers. Most employers have now realized that the combative union-busting attitudes of the 1930s were counterproductive. As Professor Murphy acknowledged, the vast majority of employers know that the best way to avoid unionization and at the same time increase productivity is simply to treat employees right. Employees who are treated fairly and paid well will rarely have an interest in organizing.[70] In that same light, we have seen a rapid increase in employee benefit plans granting many of the same rights and benefits formerly found only in a union contract.

Many of the employees in the United States have also realized that unions are a largely impotent force in the 1980s. Deregula-

---

[67] See, e.g., supra note 60.

[68] LABOR RELATIONS YEARBOOK—1977 339 (BNA Books, 1978).

[69] Young, One-fourth of the Adult Labor Force Are College Graduates, MONTHLY LAB. REP., 43, February 1985.

[70] See, e.g., Los Angeles Times, Sept. 30, 1985, at I-3. (Restaurant workers in Berkeley, California, show little interest in organizing because wage and benefit levels equal or exceed most union contract terms.)

tion has had a dramatic impact upon unions in both the airline and trucking industries. Unions were impotent to stop such deregulation and the fierce competition it has engendered.

Virtual total unionization in the auto and steel industries has been unable to halt the decline in membership in those areas. Both unions have lost hundreds of thousands of active members since the mid-1970s. Currently, there are only about 625,000 steelworkers working in the United States.[71] Of that number, only about 200,000 are employed in the steel industry.[72] This is not to say that unions are entirely responsible for the decline. Clearly, foreign imports are in large measure responsible for the decline in the number of auto and steelworkers working in the United States. However, at least some of the decline in the domestic work force can be attributed to the shortsightedness of both management and labor and their joint failure to develop and implement new processes and to update the antiquated work rules which would have kept the price and quality of U.S. products at a competitive level.

The big economic weapon of the union movement—the strike—has become increasingly ineffective. Employers have learned that they can continue to operate during a strike. One need only examine the copper industry in that regard. A continued high unemployment rate coupled with massive foreign imports enabled Phelps Dodge to continue operations during a strike in Arizona and to replace strikers with no impact on its production. The employers' success in strike situations is attributable, in part, to the ability of the employer to replace striking employees from an overcrowded labor pool, but more importantly it also stems from the realization by many employers and employees that if they wish to remain part of a viable enterprise they must be willing to take the necessary steps to keep labor costs at competitive levels.[73]

Finally, I think the efficacy of other solutions to many of the workers grievances should be noted. Fifty years ago many employees may have been working for virtual slave wages with no expectation of increases or improved working conditions. With the advent of minimum wage and overtime laws, some of those concerns were alleviated. Discrimination against women

---

[71] LABOR RELATIONS YEARBOOK—1984, 285 (BNA Books, 1985).

[72] 1985 DAILY LAB. REP. (BNA), 158:A-15.

[73] *See, e.g.,* Jones, *Company Gives Edge in Press Strike,* N.Y. Times, Oct. 25, 1985, at 16.

and minorities has been in large measure rectified by Title VII and other antidiscrimination laws, an area of concern which was largely untouched by unions. Many of the health and safety problems have been rectified by OSHA. The recent increase in litigation regarding wrongful discharge has also reduced the viability of the unions' claims that they alone could achieve fair grievance and discharge procedures. In sum, there are a number of viable solutions to employee problems that do not require $20 to $25 per month in dues to resolve.

Where does the current Board fit in all of this? It is self-evident that the Board is not responsible for foreign imports or deregulation. Nor is it directly responsible for the recent ability of employers to operate during strikes. For the most part, the issues confronting the Board involve typical Sections 8(a)(1), 8(a)(3), and occasional 8(b) cases. These cases are being processed in much the same way as they have in the last 20 years. Admittedly, unions are not winning 84 percent of the cases against employers as they were during the Carter years. Nevertheless, even the AFL-CIO's attorneys concede that unions still win over 50 percent of all the cases against employers before the current Board.[74] To argue that this Board is not fullfiling its statutory obligations is simply without foundation. Under Section 7 the Board's job is to protect the individual employees' right to engage in or refrain from engaging in collective action. Within the jurisdictional and procedural framework set out by Congress, the Board has done an admirable job of returning the law to normalcy and away from the undisguised prounion position of the late 1970s. This Board is not "blatantly anti-union" rather, it is pro-employee choice and noninterventionist.

Where does the Board fit in the future? So long as it continues in a moderate stance, the Board will continue to function as an effective force in protecting employee rights and maintaining labor peace in the private sector. Nevertheless, as the proportion of union representation in the private sector continues to decline the Board will become less of a force in American society.

Professor Murphy is correct in his statement that both the Board and unions must reassess the old adversarial aspect of collective bargaining and look less to confrontation and put more emphasis on cooperative endeavors as a method of resolv-

---

[74] *See, e.g.*, Gold & Silberman, *Reagan NRLB Reveals "Double Standard" at Work*, The Legal Times, Aug. 26, 1985, at 8.

ing labor problems. It is time for unions to stop attempting to make the Board the scapegoat for their own inadequacies and to concentrate on new methods of cooperation with industry for the good of all. The great challenge of future Boards will be to accommodate new concepts of industrial relations. We can only hope that Congress and the Board will encourage employers and unions to move beyond the mindset of the 1930s, that collective bargaining is the only solution to employee relations, and allow American business to develop new and less adversarial relationships that will result in a more productive and prosperous economy.

A Voice From the Trenches

Edwin H. Benn*

The recent changes in the membership and doctrines of the National Labor Relations Board have sparked a debate in labor-management circles[1] that approaches the fervor of the debates currently raging over such issues as abortion and the Israeli-Palestinian dilemma. If one takes the time to analyze the arguments on both sides of the abortion and the Israeli-Palestinian debates with as much objectivity as possible (if one can be objective over such issues) the conclusion easily reached is that the arguments may be irreconcilable. The premises for the arguments are too far apart. There may be no common ground upon which to agree.

With respect to the abortion issue, in very basic terms, the prolife advocates urge that no one has the right to end a life. The prochoice advocates argue that women have the inherent right to choose what happens to their bodies. With respect to the Israeli-Palestinian argument, the pro-Israeli urges with great passion that the land of Israel was given to the Jews and makes all appropriate references to the Bible. The pro-Palestinian argues with equal passion that the Palestinians have existed in that troubled land for centuries and no one has the right to evict them from their homeland.

Although we all dream of a reconciliation between the arguments espoused on all sides of the debates, it is not hard to

---

* Arbitrator.
[1] *See, e.g., NLRB at 50: Labor Board at the Crossroads* (BNA Special Report, 1985).

conclude that such a goal may never be achieved. When these difficult topics are raised, too many social gatherings have ended with red faces, clenched fists, and more.

So too, perhaps to a lesser degree, is the debate that has stirred as a result of past Board memberships and the decisions of the current appointees of President Reagan. If unions suffer as a result of a Board decision, then, according to those espousing the attributes of the labor movement, the Board has cannibalized the Act, resulting in decisions that are antilabor, anti-employee, or intellectually dishonest. If management prevails as a result of a change in doctrine, then the law has been restored to what was originally intended.[2] Some academicians take the mid-course and tell us that the decisions of the present Board and past Boards are all equally defensible no matter which way they come out. Those decisions, according to the objective observers of the war, are but fine shadings on either side of a gray line.[3] Academicians can make those kinds of observations since they generally do not have to give advice.

From my perspective, it would serve no good for the purpose of this volume either to laud or criticize the current Board's decisions. That function has been amply served by other papers contained herein. In any event, the views of the clients I have represented over the years are well known. Therefore, although labor lawyers are perceived as bringing with them certain biases and perceptions stemming from those with whom they associate, I will attempt objectivity. I will discuss facts and the perceptions of a lawyer who represents unions in Chicago, Illinois—certainly a view from the trenches.

I. Statistics

Since my first association with the Board, I have been fascinated with the Board's penchant, indeed its obsession, with statistics. It seemed a bit ironic to me that amorphous goals of seeking industrial peace and stability and protecting the right to engage or refrain from engaging in protected concerted activity could somehow directly translate into numbers. One person's concept of "justice" is apparently another's "median case han-

---

[2] *See, e.g.*, the papers of my esteemed co-panelists John Irving and Charles Bakaly.

[3] Remarks of Prof. Theodore J. St. Antoine, *Labor Law—The Next Fifty Years*, Chicago Kent College of Law (April 9, 1985). *See also* St. Antoine, *Federal Regulation of the Work Place in the Next Half Century*, 61 Chi.[-]Kent L. Rev. 631 (1985).

dling time." The Board's Annual Reports are filled with pie graphs, bar graphs, tables, and charts. The invention of the personal computer must have those who generate those statistical tables in a state of sheer ecstasy.[4]

I recently took a journey through the Board's past annual reports. For those who think that the Board's delight in statistics is a recent phenomenon, that thought is erroneous. The Annual Reports from the 1930s bear striking resemblance to the more recent Reports.[5] I was curious to find out who has been utilizing the Board's representation processes and to what degree. Specifically, I wanted to know how many employees have voted in NLRB elections and how that figure compared with the general growth of the private sector work force. To make the comparison between the numbers of employees voting in NLRB elections and the growth of the private sector work force, it was necessary also to consult the Bureau of Labor Statistics' figures on the growth of the private sector work force.[6]

The underlying question I had was, if we put aside the philosophical arguments concerning the Board's current or past compositions, the apparent decline of the strength of the labor movement and the asserted reasons why employees or labor organizations use or do not use the Board: Does the comparison between the numbers of employees using the representation process, as contrasted with the growth in the private sector work force, give us some indication of whether the Board is still a viable force after 50 years of regulating the representation process in the private sector? In other words, is the Board responding, in fact, to the changes in the private sector work force?

An analysis of the data in Table 1[7] shows that for whatever

---

[4] When I was with the Board I was once ushered into the infamous Chart Room in the General Counsel's office. The Chart Room at the time consisted of walls of magnetic charts showing statistics for various aspects of the Board's regional case handling functions. I inadvertently bumped into one of the charts, causing the jostling and movement of several magnetic pieces. I imagine that a regional director somewhere either got an unexpected bonus or a severe tongue-lashing.

[5] As of this writing, the last official Board Annual Report was published in 1982.

[6] Those figures are found in Bureau of Labor Statistics, EMPLOYMENT AND EARNINGS, June 1985, at 61.

[7] The number of employees in the private sector work force are based on BLS figures, which include the following categories of employers: mining, construction, manufacturing, transportation and public utilities, wholesale, retail, finance, insurance, and real estate sevices. Excluded from the totals are those employees who are employed by federal, state, and local employers and agricultural employees. Further, it should be noted (for the

Table 1

Number of Employees Voting in NLRB Elections Compared With Number of Employees in Private Sector Work Force

Year	Number of Employees		Percentage
	Voting in NLRB Elections	In Private Sector Work Force	
1938	350,960[a]	25,311,000	1.3
1944	1,072,594[b]	35,822,000	2.9
1950	789,867[c]	39,170,000	2.0
1954	458,762[d]	42,238,000	1.1
1958	324,510[e]	43,483,000	0.7
1962	482,558[f]	46,660,000	1.0
1966	540,000[g]	53,116,000	1.0
1970	531,402[h]	58,325,000	0.9
1974	482,414[i]	64,095,000	0.8
1977	511,336[j]	67,344,000	0.8
1980	458,114[k]	74,166,000	0.6
1981	392,157[l]	75,126,000	0.5
1982	257,599[m]	73,727,000	0.3
1983	181,307[n]	74,330,000	0.2
1984	218,191[o]	78,477,000	0.3
1985	261,262[p]	81,275,000[q]	0.3

[a] 1938 NLRB ANN. REP. 49 (1939).
[b] 1944 NLRB ANN. REP. 20 (1944).
[c] 1950 NLRB ANN. REP. 13 (1951).
[d] 1954 NLRB ANN. REP. 7 (1955).
[e] 1958 NLRB ANN. REP. 6 (1959).
[f] 1962 NLRB ANN. REP. 18 (1963).
[g] 1966 NLRB ANN. REP. 20 (1967).
[h] 1970 NLRB ANN. REP. 15 (1971).
[i] 1974 NLRB ANN. REP. 16 (1974).
[j] 1977 NLRB ANN. REP. 17 (1977).
[k] 1980 NLRB ANN. REP. 16 (1980).

[l] 1981 NLRB ANN. REP. 18 (1981).
[m] 1982 NLRB ANN. REP. 12 (1982).
[n] Preliminary figures obtained from the General Counsel's office.
[o] Preliminary figures obtained from the General Counsel's office.
[p] Preliminary figures for first 6 months of the fiscal year projected on a 12-month basis.
[q] Preliminary figures. Bureau of Labor Statistics, EMPLOYMENT AND EARNINGS, June 1985, at 61.

---

sake of the purists) that the private sector figures of BLS in all likelihood do not correspond precisely with the exact number of employees who fall within the definition of employee under the Act. For example, the policy kinds of exclusions (*e.g.*, relatives of management, managerial employees, and confidential employees), which are typically excluded from collective bargaining units under Board law, may well exist in the figures of the BLS. In light of the total numbers of employees in the private sector work force, those kinds of exclusions were deemed to be negligible and any adjustments would be proportionate to the actual numbers of employees falling under Board jurisdiction.

reasons, good or bad depending upon one's point of view, while there is a straight line increase in the growth of the private sector work force since the passage of the Act, there is no corresponding increase in the numbers of employees using the Board's representation processes. Indeed, if anything, there is a dramatic decrease in usage of the Board's representation procedures. To debate the reasons for such a decline will only get us into the irreconcilable arguments mentioned earlier. The fact remains rather glaring that after 50 years of the Board's existence, each year a very miniscule percentage of the private sector work force actually utilizes Board representation procedures. Therefore, the question must be asked again: Looking at the entire scheme of the trends in the private sector work force, is an agency still viable when it is not being used? Have the changes that have occurred, be they good or bad, simply invalidated the function of this Agency no matter how much historical importance it has? Is there an alternative? The Board's penchant for statistics may have been a subliminal effort to justify its own existence, but ironically the resulting statistics may well be an indicator of the Board's own demise.

Professor Murphy speculates in his paper: "Sometimes I think that we Board watchers inflate the role of the Board and exaggerate its influence on labor relations and the economy."[8] The above figures certainly substantiate that well-placed suspicion.

II. Perceptions From the Trenches

The dramatic decrease in use of the Board and the questions raised concerning continued viability in light of that decrease leads one to ask more questions concerning viability.

A. Is An Agency Viable When Throughout Its History It Has Continually Changed Its Doctrines?

In the representation area alone, throughout the Board's history those subject to the Board's jurisdiction, those practicing before it, and the Board's objective observers have suffered through continually changing doctrines.[9] As examples, we have

---

[8] *See* Murphy, *supra*, in Chapter 2.
[9] *See generally*, C. Morris, THE DEVELOPING LABOR LAW 2d ed., at 309–412 (BNA Books, 1983).

run full circle in the areas of "laboratory conditions,"[10] captive audience speeches,[11] the period for objectionable conduct,[12] initiation fee waivers,[13] discrimination on the basis of race or sex,[14] effect of elections by private or state agencies,[15] the period for a contract bar,[16] what is the window period for filing petitions,[17] misrepresentations,[18] defining independent contractors,[19] or defining relatives of management.[20] Professor Murphy calls these types of changes a "zig-zag" course, "flip-flops," or "tortuous meanderings."[21] If one dares to consider the law that has developed in the health care field concerning appropri-

---

[10] General Shoe Corp., 77 NLRB 124, 21 LRRM 1337 (1948); National Furniture Co., 119 NLRB 1, 40 LRRM 1442 (1957); Dal-Tex Optical Co., Inc., 137 NLRB 1782, 50 LRRM 1489 (1962).

[11] Clark Bros. Co., 70 NLRB 802, 18 LRRM 1360 (1946), enforced, 163 F2d 373, 20 LRRM 2436 (CA 2, 1947); Babcock & Wilcox Co., 77 NLRB 577, 22 LRRM 1057 (1948); Bonwit-Teller, Inc., 96 NLRB 608, 28 LRRM 1547 (1951), modified, 104 NLRB 497, 32 LRRM 1102 (1953); Livingston Shirt Co., 107 NLRB 400, 33 LRRM 1156 (1953); Peerless Plywood Co., 107 NLRB 427, 33 LRRM 1151 (1953).

[12] Great Atl. & Pac. Tea Co., 101 NLRB 1118, 31 LRRM 1189 (1952); F.W. Woolworth Co., 109 NLRB 1446, 34 LRRM 1584 (1954); Ideal Elec. & Mfg. Co., 134 NLRB 1275, 49 LRRM 1316 (1961); Goodyear Tire & Rubber Co., 138 NLRB 453, 51 LRRM 1070 (1962).

[13] The DeVilbiss Co., 102 NLRB 1317 (1953); Labue Bros., 109 NLRB 1182 (1954); DIT-MCO, 163 NLRB 1019, 64 LRRM 1476 (1967); enforced, 428 F2d 775, 74 LRRM 2664 (CA 8, 1970); NLRB v. Savair Mfg. Co., 414 US 270, 84 LRRM 2929 (1971).

[14] NLRB v. Mansion House Corp., 473 F2d 471, 82 LRRM 2608 (CA 8, 1973); Bekins Moving & Storage Co., Inc., 211 NLRB 138, 86 LRRM 1323 (1974); Bell & Howell Co., 213 NLRB 405, 87 LRRM 1172 (1974); Handy Andy, Inc., 228 NLRB 447, 94 LRRM 1354 (1977); Bell & Howell Co., 230 NLRB 420, 95 LRRM 1333 (1977).

[15] National Container Corp., 87 NLRB 1065, 25 LRRM 1234 (1949); Punch Press Repair Corp., 89 NLRB 614, 26 LRRM 1012 (1950); West Indian Co., 129 NLRB 1203, 47 LRRM 1146 (1961).

[16] Cushman's Sons, Inc., 88 NLRB 121, 25 LRRM 1296 (1950); Pacific Coast Ass'n of Pulp & Paper Mfrs., 121 NLRB 990, 42 LRRM 1477 (1958); General Cable Corp., 139 NLRB 1123, 51 LRRM 1444 (1962).

[17] General Elec. X-Ray Corp., 67 NLRB 997, 18 LRRM 1047 (1946); Deluxe Metal Furniture Co., 121 NLRB 995, 42 LRRM 1470 (1958); Leonard Wholesale Meats Co., 136 NLRB 1000, 49 LRRM 1901 (1962).

[18] Hollywood Ceramics Co., 140 NLRB 221, 51 LRRM 1600 (1962); Shopping Kart Food Mkts., Inc., 228 NLRB 1311, 94 LRRM 1705 (1977); General Knit of Cal., 239 NLRB 619, 99 LRRM 1687 (1978); Midland Nat'l Life Ins. Co., 263 NLRB 127, 110 LRRM 1489 (1982).

[19] Seafarers Local 777 v. NLRB, 603 F2d 862, 99 LRRM 2903 (CA DC, 1978), opinion accompanying denial of reh'g, 603 F2d 891, 101 LRRM 2628 (CA DC, 1979) and cases cited therein.

[20] Foam Rubber City No. 2 of Fla., Inc., 167 NLRB 623, 66 LRRM 1096 (1967); Cerni Motor Sales, Inc., 201 NLRB 918, 82 LRRM 1404 (1973); Marvin Witherow Trucking, 229 NLRB 412, 95 LRRM 1089 (1977); NLRB v. Caravelle Wood Prods., Inc., 466 F2d 675, 80 LRRM 3411 (CA 7, 1972), remanded, 200 NLRB 855, 82 LRRM 1004 (1972), enforced, 504 F2d 1181, 87 LRRM 2579 (CA 7, 1974).

[21] See Murphy, supra.

ate units,[22] the fact remains that as of this writing, 11 years have passed since the enactment of the 1974 Health Care Amendments and we still cannot say with any certainty what constitutes an appropriate health care bargaining unit.

With such constant changes, how can managers effectively manage to avoid potentially volatile labor situations? Similarly, how can unions effectively plan organizing campaigns and strategies? Last, how can labor lawyers, be they management or union, effectively give advice? With the recent changes in the current Board, upon inquiry by a client if a proposed course of conduct is acceptable, a standard response from counsel may well be: "It sounds fine to me, but I haven't seen today's *Daily Labor Report*."

In light of all of the flip-flops, zig-zags, and meanderings I spoke of, there is a good case for the exercise of rule making. Stability in industrial relations requires that the parties know what the rules are. As a practitioner, I was tired of being thunderstruck by the *Daily Labor Report* as new changes in the law were so often reported.

B. Is an Agency Viable When Its Procedures Provide for Immense Delay?

In *DelCostello* v. *Teamsters*,[23] the Supreme Court reemphasized that the national labor policy involves the "relatively rapid final resolution of labor disputes."[24] The Board's procedures provide the antithesis of this policy. From the Board's own preliminary figures[25] in the representation area, the following statistics are reported:

Petition to Board Decision

Year	No. of Days
1980	295
1981	215
1982	193

If one considers the statistics in the unfair labor practice area, the delay is even greater:

---

[22] *See* St. Francis Hosp., 265 NLRB 1025, 112 LRRM 1153 (1982); St. Francis Hosp., 271 NLRB 948, 116 LRRM 1465 (1984).

[23] 462 US 151, 113 LRRM 2737 (1983).

[24] *Id.*, 113 LRRM at 2743.

[25] Obtained from the General Counsel's office.

Charge to Board Decision

Year	No. of Days
1980	484
1981	490
1982	633

We all know too well the strategy of defeating a union organizing campaign through the litigation of nonmeritorious unit questions, raising objections that lead to hearings with appeals to the Board and eventually to the Courts of Appeal. Even though the union may weather the storm of delay, by the time the appeals are exhausted years have gone by and the union's once strong support base has dwindled, or ceased to exist. The employees are left in a state of limbo. Employers suffer due to unstable employee morale and uncertainty that changes made during the period of litigation may result in further unfair labor practices. However, on balance, the reward to the employer is obvious. Through the filing of appeals and delays it has only had to expend costs for attorneys, which although perhaps high, pale in comparison to the increased costs that an early union contract may bring. In short, it makes good business sense to delay and stall. What happens to the policy of the rapid disposition of labor disputes when a simple cost-benefit analysis dictates abuse of the Board's procedures?

The delay which can exist is shown by the documentation of the time elements in the following example. In 1977 the Cement, Lime and Gypsum Workers Union commenced an organizing drive at the San Antonio Portland Cement Company in San Antonio, Texas. A petition was filed and a stipulation for an election was reached. The election was held on March 17, 1978. The results of the election were that 98 employees voted in favor of the union, 72 voted against the union, and 39 votes were challenged. To cover itself in case the challenges were adversely decided, the company filed objections. The main objection was that a low-level supervisor participated in the organizing campaign.[26] On May 24 and 25, 1978, a hearing was held before a Board hearing officer on the challenges and objections. On July 13, 1978, the hearing officer issued his report recommending that the objections be overruled and that, as a result of the

---

[26] The Company thus sought to benefit from the alleged misconduct of its own agent.

decision on challenged ballots, the union should be certified as the employees' collective bargaining representative. On September 8, 1978, the Board adopted the hearing officer's report and certified the union. Because the company refused to bargain, on October 13, 1978, the union filed a Section 8(a)(5) charge. On March 5, 1979, the Board found a technical Section 8(a)(5) violation.[27] After briefs and arguments in the Fifth Circuit, on February 15, 1980, the Board's order was enforced.[28] On April 8, 1980, the Fifth Circuit denied the company's petition for rehearing. On October 6, 1980, the Supreme Court denied the company's petition for certiorari.[29] During the period of the Board's proceedings and the certification test, the company made a series of unilateral changes without notification to or bargaining with the union. These changes included wage increases, medical benefit changes, elimination of jobs causing layoffs, reclassification of employees, elimination of shifts, changes in discipline practice, and forced retirement of an employee. The company readily admitted to the changes but defended them by asserting that the union was improperly certified. Additionally, there were several discharges in alleged violation of the *Weingarten*[30] rule along with a constructive discharge. In September 1979, an administrative law judge heard the unfair labor practice allegations. On May 21, 1980, the administrative law judge issued his decision. Exceptions and cross-exceptions followed.

Notwithstanding all of the above, the company agreed to commence bargaining with the union, and the first bargaining session was held on August 22, 1980. On July 10, 1981, the last bargaining session was held. No agreement was reached. On August 5, 1981, a decertification petition was filed. Upon learning of the decertification petition, the company canceled the previously scheduled bargaining sessions set for August 6 and 7, 1981, and filed an RM petition. More unfair labor practice charges followed. On July 15, 1983, another administrative law judge found the company had violated Section 8(a)(5) by withdrawing recognition from the union, noting especially that the previous unresolved unfair labor practices precluded it from

27 San Antonio Portland Cement Co., 240 NLRB 1168, 100 LRRM 1445 (1979).
28 NLRB v. San Antonio Portland Cement Co., 611 F2d 1148, 103 LRRM 2631 (CA 5, 1980).
29 449 US 844 (1980).
30 NLRB v. J. Weingarten, Inc., 420 US 251, 88 LRRM 2689 (1975).

challenging the union's majority status. As of the date of this writing the Board had not decided these cases.[31] In short, almost *eight years* had gone by as of the date of this symposium (or 16 percent of the Board's existence), and the Board could not ultimately resolve a case that essentially concerns a representation matter. Certain court review will follow. Rapid disposition of labor disputes? No valid excuses exist for these kinds of delays or a system that fosters and indeed encourages such delay.

C. Is the Board Viable After 50 Years When Its Decisions Have Led Unions to Take Action That Will Only Lead to Industrial Strife?

Because of adverse decisions in the eyes of the labor movement and the inherent delays in the Board's procedures, coupled with the uncertainty that exists about well-accepted doctrines being subject to reversal, the course of action now being considered by unions and the advice given by union attorneys are more aggressive than before.

1. The Initial Organizing Campaign. Because of the potential delay and uncertainty as to what will happen should a union proceed to the Board with a petition, the option of the recognitional strike is being given more consideration. To a greater extent, organizing campaigns are now planned with the recognitional strike as a more certain option. The recognitional strike is devised with an eye toward quick recognition or implementation of the expedited election procedure in Section 8(b)(7)(C) of the Act. That kind of planning can only lead to increased industrial strife.

2. The Plant and Bargaining Unit Movement Cases. Although perhaps more appropriate for noting under the topic of unfair labor practices rather than the current subject of representation, the Board's recent decisions in *Milwaukee Spring*[32] and *Otis Elevator Co.*[33] have an indirect bearing on the representation process since those decisions obviously will have

---

[31] In an act which I am sure was coincidental, the Board issued its decision in these cases on November 12, 1985—approximately one month after I spoke at this symposium concerning the delay in these cases. *See* San Antonio Portland Cement Co., 277 NLRB No. 36, 121 LRRM 1234 (1985). *See also,* Alamo Cement Co., 277 NLRB No. 33, 121 LRRM 1268 (1985); 277 NLRB No. 34, 121 LRRM 1266 (1985); 277 NLRB No. 35, 120 LRRM 1288 (1985); and 277 NLRB 108, 121 LRRM 1131 (1985).

[32] Milwaukee Spring, Div. of Illinois Coil Spring Co., 268 NLRB 601, 115 LRRM 1065 (1984).

[33] 269 NLRB 891, 115 LRRM 1281 (1984).

an effect on the representative capacity of a union. The backlash effect from these types of decisions will be a conscious effort by those unions which do not have work preservation language in their collective bargaining agreements to seek such language. Because of the devastating effect that these decisions have on existing units, more strikes may result from unions seeking to obtain sufficient work preservation language in their contracts to avoid the application of those cases. Actions in other areas by the current Board may lead to the same result. We have seen recent changes in Board law concerning the protection traditionally accorded to sympathy strikers (*Indianapolis Power & Light Co.*[34]); diminishing the definition of "concerted" activity (*Meyers Industries*[35]); lessening the standards for discharge for picket line misconduct (*Clear Pine Mouldings*[36]); and the increased use of deferral of many issues to arbitration (*United Technologies Corp.*[37] and *Olin Corp.*[38]). The reaction of organized labor should be obvious. Unions will seek in the collective bargaining process to insert clauses that regain what the current Board has taken away and may find it necessary to strike to obtain that protection. The result will be *increased* agitation and industrial strife, *not* a lessening of it. The Board may have been myopic in its view if the agenda was to afford employers more protection and leeway. In the long run employers may be hurt, especially the small businessman. The antithesis of labor peace could be achieved from those decisions, be those decisions right or wrong.

D. Labor's Overall Perception

It is the perception of organized labor that the current administration has purposely sought to dismantle the effectiveness of the Board. There is no excuse for the President to take as long as he did to fill appointments for vacant positions on the Board. Indeed, some of the delays referred to earlier are a direct result of the Board not being at full staff. Why would this administration wait when cases were backed up and justice from the Board

---

[34] 273 NLRB No. 211, 118 LRRM 1201 (1985).
[35] 268 NLRB 493, 115 LRRM 1025 (1984), *enforcement denied and remanded sub nom.* Prill v. NLRB, 755 F2d 941, 118 LRRM 2649 (CA DC, 1985).
[36] 268 NLRB 1044, 115 LRRM 1113 (1984).
[37] 268 NLRB 557, 115 LRRM 1049 (1984).
[38] 268 NLRB 573, 115 LRRM 1056 (1984).

became, in many instances, a joke as a result of unconscionable delay? Apparently, the phenomenon of working at less than full capacity is not something of recent vintage. Former Board Member Howard Jenkins in his paper alluded to the fact that for one-third of the time in the Board's history, the Board has operated at less than full capacity. No excuse exists for shackling the Board in this fashion.

It is my understanding that recently the current Board Chairman indicated that he would like to see the Board's jurisdictional standards changed to reflect an inflation factor.[39] Aside from the statutory hurdles that such a change would face,[40] a definite backlash would result. The smaller employers who now fall under the Board's jurisdictional umbrella and who, under the Chairman's inflation plan, would benefit from not having the restrictions of Board jurisdiction for elections and unfair labor practice proceedings, may in reality suffer. The advice to unions that will be given and the actions that will follow will cause more labor strife. Although the smaller companies may be theoretically freed from Sections 8(a) and 9 of the Act, these new found freedoms may prove to be negligible. Along with freedom from Board jurisdiction comes the realization that there may be a lessened ability to invoke the recognitional picketing provisions of Section 8(b)(7) or, in some cases, the secondary boycott provisions of Sections 8(b)(4). Those sections invoke the notions of effect on a statutory "employer." Thus, such a change may permit more economically powerful unions to picket without limitation. Hence, the Chairman's desire to limit the Board's jurisdiction by increasing the dollar amounts for jurisdictional purposes may well lead only to increased strikes and picketing. At a time when there is a decided decrease in the use of the Board's procedures, especially in the representation area, the issue of continued viability of the Board must be raised when steps are considered to further limit access to the Board.

Because a number of unions have determined that the current Board is antiunion and antiemployee, they have made a conscious decision to avoid using the Board and to seek relief in different fashions. Indeed, it has become a common tactical

---

[39] See also Charles Bakaly's paper, supra. The Board's jursidictional standards were generally set in 1958. See Siemons Mailing Serv., 122 NLRB 81, 43 LRRM 1056 (1958).

[40] See §14(c)(1) of the Act, 29 USC §164(c)(1) ("the Board shall not decline to assert jursidiction over any labor dispute over which it would assert jurisdiction under the standards prevailing upon August 1, 1959.").

decision to avoid using the Board if the issue to be presented is not clear, will result in further delay, or has any degree of uncertainty that will present a small degree of downside risk to a current organizing campaign or to a disciplinary matter that can be handled through other means including arbitration. The all too common response to an inquiry about obtaining a fast and certain outcome from the Board is: "Forget about using the Board on this one—it is no friend." That there is a plan to limit access to the Board and to increase the use of alternative procedures, and the fact that labor organizations are making a conscious effort to avoid the Board and are publicizing that decision, only serves to undermine the perception of continuing viability of that Agency.

To argue that the labor movement is dead is really a social and not a legal issue. I do not believe that to be the case, however. Human beings have gathered together for mutual aid and protection throughout their entire existence. To argue that today more sophisticated managers exist who are more attuned to the needs of employees, thereby making the need for unions obsolete, is, in my view, to ignore history. The paternalistic employer, no matter how well intentioned in providing for all of the basic needs of its employees, will always have hard choices to make when the economy, based on competition, requires that the most fluid factor of its costs—the cost of labor—be cut to permit competition. George Pullman tried the concept and it did not work.[41] I believe that the increased nonunion environment created by more sophisticated management techniques would not have thrived as it now does if the economic time were not so favorable.

In closing, I would like to refer to another comment made by former Board Member Jenkins. He stated that unbeknownst to many, there is a provision in the Board's appropriations prohibiting the Board from hiring economists and the Board is thereby deprived of consulting in an obvious area of useful expertise. While I believe that such restrictions should not exist, I can think of one other profession that perhaps should also be given some negative consideration, though facetiously: maybe lawyers should be barred from the collective bargaining process. They tend to complicate the process unnecessarily. The whole process has become too litigious—something that brings with it the

---

[41] *See* Lindsey, THE PULLMAN STRIKE (1942).

delays which cause workers, management, and unions all to suffer. Indeed, the legalistic nature of the system invites legal abuse of its process.

THE BOARD'S REPRESENTATION PROCESS: ANOTHER VIEW

JOHN S. IRVING*

I shall make some observations about Professor Murphy's remarks and conclusions. I noticed a number of inconsistencies, contradictions, and nonsequiturs that are worth mentioning.

I. Informed Employee Choice vs. Instant Elections

On the one hand, Professor Murphy recognizes the importance of informed employee choice concerning union representation. He would allow union access to employer property to make captive audience speeches in response to those of management. He acknowledges that employers have a legitimate interest in responding to union propaganda and recognizes that employees may benefit from exchanges between labor and management. He would not regulate the content of campaign propaganda unless it contained unlawful threats or promises.

On the other hand, Professor Murphy is a proponent, along with Professor Weiler of Harvard, of "instant elections." These are elections which force employees to a choice concerning union representation within five to seven days after a union election petition is filed.

I do not understand how one can be in favor of free speech and informed employee choice and, at the same time, an advocate of quickie elections which deny to employees the benefit of the employer's point of view. That is exactly what instant elections would accomplish.

II. Employee Rights vs. Compulsory Unionism

On the one hand, Professor Murphy professes concern for employee rights and free choice. However, it is interesting to see

* Former General Counsel, National Labor Relations Board; partner, Kirkland & Ellis, Washington, D.C.

what happens to these concerns when forced to choose between employee free choice and union institutional interests.

Thus, Professor Murphy advocates legislative extensions of the Act's coverage to, among others, farm workers and managers. He would do this to promote employee "freedom to choose union representation."

On the other hand, Professor Murphy would favor other legislative amendments which would force employees to become and remain union members and which would require the deduction, or checkoff, of union dues from employee paychecks.

So much for employee freedom of choice.

III. The Alleged Antiunion Board

The biggest nonsequitur of all is Professor Murphy's out-of-context claim that the present Board is the "most blatantly antiunion Board in history." No foundation can be found for this serious charge in the text of Professor Murphy's remarks.

Thus, Professor Murphy decries the NLRA's limited coverage, but admits that these are limitations which reflect the will of Congress and the Supreme Court, not the Board. He acknowledges that appropriate unit determinations have been manipulated historically. He would legislatively bar whipsaw strikes designed to undermine multi-employer units, but makes no suggestion that the current Board has interfered with the multiemployer bargaining which he views as beneficial. He agrees with the current Board's reluctance to regulate campaign propaganda and that the promotion of "laboratory conditions" is unrealistic. He regrets the current rules on captive audience speeches, but acknowledges that they have been in force since 1957. He acknowledges that his suggestions on compulsory unionism, dues checkoff, and instant elections, would require legislative change. Finally, he suggests that ambiguities in the law concerning employee committees which have existed since 1959 should be clarified by the Supreme Court or by Congress.

Nowhere in his text, then, does Professor Murphy provide a basis for his accusation that the present Board is the "most blatantly antiunion Board in history." In fact, his lightning bolt comes to us out of a clear blue sky. It is almost as if it was injected for press consumption or for the benefit of certain congressional leaders who are always on the lookout for quotations from professors to support their politically motivated criticisms of the Board.

IV. The Frustrated Leap to Erroneous Conclusions

What has happened, I think, to Professor Murphy, has happened to other advocates of institutionalized unionism. Without critical analysis, they have fallen for the misleading and inaccurate "analysis" of Harvard Professor Weiler, who, with little more than a magic wand, declared that employer resistance to unionization is so massive that "the current odds are about one in twenty that a union supporter will be fired for exercising rights supposedly guaranteed by federal law a half century ago."[1] Weiler's outrageous conclusions have been echoed across the land as gospel to support the claims of union advocates in Congress and elsewhere that employer unfair labor practices are to blame for the difficulties unions face in organizing employees. Professor Murphy calls Weiler's study "the best documentation of the magnitude of the problem."

Professor Weiler's "analysis" is seriously flawed. In the November 1984 edition of the *Northwestern Law Journal*, Professors Stephen Goldberg and Jeanne Brett of Northwestern Law School, and Julius Getman of Yale Law School, debunk Professor Weiler's result-oriented conclusions.[2] After pointing out the errors in Weiler's analysis and the statistical data on which he relies, these professors reaffirm their conclusion "that election outcomes are unlikely to be affected by unlawful campaigning."

As the article points out, the only other recent empirical study confirms their findings.[3] In that study, Northwestern Professor Laura Cooper studied the files of all elections conducted by one of the Board's regional offices between 1978 and 1980. Professor Cooper found (1) no evidence that unions lost a significantly higher proportion of elections when employers committed unfair labor practices than when they did not, regardless

---

[1] *Promises to Keep: Securing Workers' Rights to Self-Organization Under the NLRA*, 96 HARV. L. REV. 1769, 1781 (1983).

[2] *The Relationship Between Free Choice and Labor Board Doctrine: Differing Empirical Approaches*, 79 Nw. U.L. REV. 721 (1984).

[3] Cooper, *Authorization Cards and Union Representation Election Outcome: An Empirical Assessment of the Assumption Underlying the Supreme Court's Gissell Decision*, 79 Nw. U.L. REV. 87 (1984).

of the size of the unit; and (2) no evidence that union support declined more between the signing of authorization cards and the election when employers committed unfair labor practices than when they did not, regardless of whether the election outcome was close.

Equally flawed is Professor Weiler's conclusion that "the current odds are about one in twenty that a union supporter will be fired." This shocking and erroneous conclusion was music to the ears of those who would blame employers for union misfortunes. Weiler reached it by attempting to equate the number of workers voting in Board elections in 1980 to the number of unlawful discharges which he says were "found" by the Board during that year. In fact, comparing voters and discriminatory discharges is like comparing apples and oranges. Even the Board does not attempt to equate the two. Moreover, the vast majority of the 10,000 employees for whom reinstatement was "secured" by "the Board," according to Weiler, were reinstated through voluntary settlement agreements without any final determination by the Board or anyone else that the law had, in fact, been violated. Most frequently, those settlements are agreed to by employers as matters of economy and convenience, and they contain specific provisions acknowledging that no violation is admitted or "found."

In short, it is astounding to me that Professor Murphy and many others are so willing to accept Professor Weiler's alarmist and misleading conclusions. It must be that their instincts make them unwitting disciples of those who would distort reality to prove a point or gain advantage.

Since a basis for Professor Murphy's charge that the current Board is "blatantly antiunion" cannot be found in the balance of his remarks or in the Weiler study, perhaps it can be found in the way this Board handles elections.

What has changed since Professor Murphy chaired the representation case subcommittee of the NLRB Task Force in 1976? In 1976, 8,643 Board elections were conducted. Voluntary election agreements entered into by employers were obtained in 76 percent of those election proceedings.[4]

Improvements recommended by Professor Murphy's Task Force subcommittee and adopted by the entire bipartisan Task

---

[4] *NLRB General Counsel's FY 1977 Operations Report*, LABOR RELATIONS YEARBOOK—1977, 313 (BNA Book, 1978).

Force were few and minor in nature. Nowhere in the Task Force report are there allegations of Board mismanagement or dire predictions about the future of the Agency or the administration of the Act. In fact, Professor Murphy, and the other two Task Force subcommittee chairmen observed in a letter to the Board:

> Although we have identified various areas in which we believe the Board's procedures could be improved, we have come away from our endeavors with a healthier respect than ever for the efficiency and fairness of one of the federal government's most effective agencies.[5]

Last year, fiscal year 1985, 5,181 NLRB elections were conducted and a record 84 percent were held pursuant to election agreements voluntarily entered into by employers.[6] Elections were conducted in a median of 47.6 days from the date on which the election petition was filed, which is close to an agency record.

The only real difference between 1976 and 1985 is a 40 percent decline in the number of union election petitions filed, and the loss by unions of a larger percentage of Board elections. Certainly nothing in the current Board's handling of elections suggests that Professor Murphy should reach a different conclusion today. Certainly the Board is not responsible if unions file fewer election petitions, and neither can the Board be blamed for union election losses.

More than likely, the charges leveled at the Board by advocates of institutional unionism are generated by their frustrations over the lack of success unions are having in marketing their services. The Board, particularly one appointed by a political opponent, makes a convenient whipping boy for the misfortunes of unions.

In fact, the causes for the decline in union membership and the inability of unions to market their product, are much more complex and deep-seated than mere changes in Board composition. Some of these causes are external to unions, like foreign competition, technological developments, fluctuations in the economy, the strength of the dollar, the swing toward political conservatism, and the new independence of workers. Other

---

[5] *1976 Interim Report and Recommendations of the Chairman's Task Force on the NLRB*, LABOR RELATIONS YEARBOOK—1976, 327 (BNA Books, 1977).

[6] *NLRB General Counsel's Summary of Operations for FY 1984*, LABOR RELATIONS YEARBOOK—1984, 323 (BNA Books, 1985).

causes of union misfortunes are internal, just as many unions themselves recently have conceded.

In any event, however, it simply cannot be said that the Board is responsible for union misfortunes, and thus, it startles me when Professor Murphy hurls such serious charges without citing any basis for his accusations.

V. Changing the Rules

In conclusion, it seems to me that the NLRA remains a viable and valuable legislative landmark. I disagree with those who suggest irresponsibly that the Act should be scrapped and that workers would be better off protesting in the streets. I also disagree with those who seek to reverse union misfortunes by repealing those portions of the law which inhibit coercive organizing tactics, such as the prohibitions against secondary boycotts, the restrictions on picketing to compel recognition without an election, and the right of employees to refrain from union activity.

The Redskins fans who have seen their team go from Super Bowl champions to the league cellar in three years might like to see the rules of that game changed too. They might like to see a rule requiring all Redskins games to be played at home. Perhaps there should be a rule giving ex-Super Bowl champions five downs instead of four. Perhaps there should be a rule prohibiting any interference with John Riggins as he seeks free access to an opponent's end zone.

Obviously, no one is foolish enough to suggest that the rules of football be changed merely because his team has fallen from glory. And yet, it seems that is exactly what union advocates suggest to reverse the misfortunes of unions: "Quickie" or "instant" elections, repeal of Section 8(c) free speech provisions, union access to employer property even if employees are accessible through alternative means, automatic injunctions in discharge cases even where evidence of unlawful conduct is, at best, unclear, and compulsory union membership and dues checkoff.

The danger, as with football, is that with a few changes of this sort, no one will recognize the game. Advocates of fundamental change should think twice before upsetting a law which has worked well for 50 years.

The balance inherent in our system of labor laws is the envy of the world. As NLRB General Counsel, I regularly met with representatives of other countries, even developed countries, who were here to study our labor-management system so that all or portions of it could be transplanted to their countries. They came not because our system is a failure, but because it works. Before we cast it aside or modify it in ways that make it unrecognizable, we should be certain that proposals for change have balance and substance, and are not merely designed to bestow tactial advantages to the proposing parties.

To date, I have seen no proposals for change that reflect this requisite balance and substance. Not even those suggested by Professor Murphy would qualify. Accordingly, my view is that more attention should be devoted to making the present system work and less attention devoted to tearing at the law's foundations and attacking the integrity of those who are but temporary custodians of the NLRA.

Commentary

REGINALD H. ALLEYNE, JR.*

Professor Murphy's paper and the responses of panelists Benn, Irving, and Bakaly, highlight for us the incipient nature of the NLRA's representation process. It is the beginning point in the statutory scheme. Union failure at that stage leaves the involved employer free to remain nonunion for the then time being. How has this important aspect of the NLRA served union and employer interests?

All panelists would agree that the preamble to the National Labor Relations Act[1] encourages collective bargaining as a means of safeguarding commerce from "industrial strife and unrest." The panelists are sharply divided on a question implicitly raised by their discussion: At what point in the NLRA statutory procedure does it become the obligation of the Board to render decisions that "encourag[e] the practice and procedure of collective bargaining . . ."?[2] Is it the point following which a union wins a representation election or the point at which a union files a representation petition? If the sweeping language of the NLRA's preamble may be read as supporting the encouragement of collective bargaining at the point of filing

---

* Professor of Law, University of California at Los Angeles.
[1] NLRA §1, 29 USC §151.
[2] *Id.*

a representation petition, it would seem to follow that the Board's unit decisions, among others, should be those that facilitate union representation-election victories; the Board's decisions on organizing campaign conduct, among others, should establish rules with presumptions favoring unionization. If, on the other hand, the statutory encouragement of collective bargaining is to begin after the union has won a representation election, the Board's unit and organizing campaign decisions ought to establish a more neutral analytical framework, free of presumptions in favor of union representation.

We have no doubt where Professor Murphy stands on the issue. His analysis of the representation process has as its beginning point the NLRA's basic coverage. He uses statutory coverage—"access" to the system—as a partial means of measuring the effectiveness of the representation process. "From the beginning," he argues, "the purposes of the statute have been limited by denying large numbers of employees any right under the [NLRA] to union representation." He then makes a strong case that Congress excluded too many classes of employees from NLRA coverage.

One might agree that too many classes of employees were excluded from the Wagner Act's coverage, but only by disagreeing with the legislative policy. On the interpretation of the NLRA, it seems nearly impossible to conclude that the Act was intended to include those it expressly excluded. It is equally difficult to conclude that the Act's intended objective of encouraging collective bargaining is weakened by its express exclusions of certain classes of employees. We can only read the Act as providing that its objective of encouraging collective bargaining is limited to those classes of employees who are within the Act's defined coverage, though we might debate the wisdom of the exclusionary policy.[3]

---

[3] NLRA §2(3), 29 USC §152(3). There are of course disputes over what constitutes an "agricultural employee." See, e.g., Di Giorgio Fruit Corp., 80 NLRB 853, 23 LRRM 1188 (1948), adopting the Fair Labor Standards Act definition, 29 USC §203(f), of "Agriculture." Four states—California, Arizona, Idaho, and Kansas—have enacted statutes authorizing collective bargaining for farm workers. See, e.g., CAL. LAB. CODE §1140 et seq. Mr. Bakaly's paper states that "as an attorney who has had to work with the California Agricultural Labor Relations Board, I would certainly favor the coverage of the [NLRA] being extended to agricultural workers, although I am sure that employers in other states would disagree with that proposition." In California, the Agricultural Labor Relations Act, though patterned closely after the NLRA, has been viewed over the years as being

Other Board exclusions from NLRA coverage are not expressly required by the statute. Professor Murphy decries the exclusion by the Board of confidential employees, managerial employees, certain university faculty members, and those employed by religious institutions. His objection has the support of the arguably applicable maxim that exclusions from statutory coverage should not extend beyond expressed exclusions. To Professor Murphy, as I understand him, there may be sound policy reasons for excluding classes of employees not expressly excluded by Congress (a point I suspect he would make on an arguendo assumption), but the Board has no authority to indulge them in the absence of clear congressional direction. Not surprisingly at this stage of the debate, Mr. Bakaly takes the policy reasons for excluding the not-expressly-excluded class of employees, and uses them in support of their exclusion by Board decisional law. For him the exclusion of managerial and confidential employees is based on "their close relationship to the decision-making process."[4] Mr. Bakaly does not directly meet Professor Murphy's argument that the expressly excluded classes are the only classes of employees Congress intended to exclude from NLRA coverage.

The panelist's debate illustrates the wide range of respectable views the NLRA is able to absorb. Even when the Act is as specific as it is in setting out excluded classes of employees, fair argument can be made for restricted or liberal interpretation of the exclusionary language. On matters such as unit determination, and of course other portions of the Act, the statutory standard is so deliberately vague as to be a complete congressional abdication to the case-by-case authority of the Board. The statute is highly elastic. The view that it was always intended to be interpreted in a manner most favorable to unions, in order to encour-

---

tougher on employers than the NLRB—and certainly the current Board—would be. With a recent majority of Agricultural Labor Relations Board appointments by a Republican governor, that view may no longer be the general view. Indeed, the current Agricultural Labor Relations Board is being boycotted by the United Farm Workers of America, AFL-CIO, a union that accounts for about 50% of the cases filed with the California ALRB. Los Angeles Times, May 22, 1986, at A-3. Currently, the UFW views the California ALRB as too "pro-employer" to serve UFW interests. Id.

[4] More pointedly, the managerial employee exclusion policy is based on the same "divided loyalties" rationale that supports the NLRA's express exclusion of supervisors from its coverage. See NLRB v. Bell Aerospace Co., 416 US 267, 85 LRRM 2945 (1974). The Board's exclusion of "confidential employees" is based on their participation in labor-management relations activity for the employer. That is a narrower ground than the divided loyalties rationale in support of the exclusion of supervisors.

age collective bargaining, is one that is difficult to maintain. More statutory specificity on the side of fostering collective bargaining would be required to support that view.

With its enactment in 1935, the NLRA certainly accommodated union interests during a time of the union movement's most dire needs. Unions moved from a position of having no legal standing to compel relations with employers to one in which employers became obligated to bargain for a contract they would not have bargained for or entered into without the kind of extraordinary compulsion provided by the NLRA.[5] At that time, the imbalance of employer and worker power in favor of employers was undeniable and graphic.[6] For years following the NLRA's enactment, the statute looked good to union and employee interests. The bargaining imbalance was addressed. Inevitably, though, the Act's susceptibility to wide-ranging case-by-case interpretations began to work against union interests. Board members appointed by presidents not of the Roosevelt tradition began to interpret the Act in a manner not to the unions' liking. Mr. Bakaly traces these swings in the outlook of different groups of Board members. Among other lines of cases, he traces the history of the *Hollywood Ceramics*[7] rule on campaign misrepresentations. He concludes that the latest rule on misrepresentations—that the Board will not consider them a ground for setting aside a representation election[8]—is one favoring union interests. "Unions," he says, "can now make misrepresentations without committing an unfair labor practice or having the election set aside." In addition, and perhaps more accurately, he notes that employers can no longer file baseless objections to election conduct on grounds of union misrepresentations. The overruling of Board case "A" with case "B" and a subsequent return to the law of case "A" with the overruling of case "B," runs throughout the Labor Board's history.

The large question addressed by the panel is: What is the effect that decisions going against union organizing efforts might have on the current decline in union fortunes? To what extent have Board decisions favoring employers contributed to

---

[5] *See* NLRA §§9, 29 USC §159, and 8(a)(5), 29 USC §158(a)(5), and Magruder, *A Half Century of Legal Influence Upon the Development of Collective Bargaining*, 50 HARV. L. REV. 1071 (1937).

[6] *See* Magruder, *supra* note 5.

[7] Hollywood Ceramics Co., Inc., 140 NLRB 221, 51 LRRM 1600 (1962).

[8] Midland Nat'l Life Ins. Co., 263 NLRB 127, 110 LRRM 1489 (1982).

the record low 17.8 percent of private sector employees who are now represented by unions? Mr. Bakaly, supported by Mr. Irving, points out that "[u]nionism was on the decline for 30 years before President Reagan appointed a single member to the Board." Professor Murphy suggests that certain Board decisions have considerably hastened unionism's decline.[9] Panel Member Benn concludes that the current line of cases going against union interests will produce increased agitation and industrial strife. His argument, though, is not entirely convincing, given the increasingly effective use of employers' power to replace permanently employees who strike, and the increasing growth of the nonunion sector over the unionized sector.[10]

Mr. Benn adds a fresh perspective to the discussion by identifying the percentages of the private sector work force that have taken part in NLRB representation elections from 1938 to 1985. The high was 2.9 percent in 1944; the low was 0.2 percent in 1983. He concludes that "there is a dramatic decrease in usage of the Board's representation procedures." Dismissing the arguments on cause as "irreconcilable," he questions whether the Board is viable if it is not being used. Seemingly, he then answers his own question by noting the long delays associated with Board processes and the sometimes used employer strategy of defeating a union by litigating "nonmeritorious unit questions" and objections. His example of the time consumed by the Board and the courts in the *San Antonio Portland Cement Co.*[11] litigation is sobering and compelling. It suggests that the Board's ability to aid unionism may suffer from institutional problems that will not go away when a future President appoints Board members who are inclined to read into the Act a statutory mandate to promote the interests of unionism and collective bargaining.

---

[9] Others are of the same view. *See* Weiler, *Promises to Keep: Securing Workers' Rights to Self-Organization Under the NLRA*, 96 HARV L. REV. 1769 (1983).

[10] *See* Craver, *The Vitality of the American Labor Movement in the Twenty-First Century*, 1983 U. ILL. L. REV. 633.

[11] 240 NLRB 1168, 100 LRRM 1445 (1979), *enforced*, 611 F2d 1148, 103 LRRM 2631 (CA 5, 1980) *and* 277 NLRB No. 36, 121 LRRM 1234 (1985).

Chapter 3

RIGHTS OF INDIVIDUAL EMPLOYEES UNDER THE ACT

Benjamin Aaron*

On March 1, 1934, Senator Robert Wagner of New York introduced into the U.S. Senate his proposed Labor Disputes Act.[1] In his brief introductory remarks he stressed that equality of bargaining power between employers and workers "is the central need of the economic world today,"[2] and that only through collective bargaining could such equality be attained. Among the evils that his bill was designed to eliminate, he said, were employer domination of unions and the interpretation of Section 7(a) of the National Industrial Recovery Act (NIRA)[3] "to mean that any employee at any time may . . . elect to deal individually with his employer," a construction that "strikes a death blow at the practice and theory of collective bargaining."[4] "No real advocate of collective bargaining," he continued, "would argue that a worker should be free to bargain individually even after an overwhelming [sic] majority of his co-workers desire an agrccment covering all."[5]

As it finally emerged from the Congress and was signed by President Roosevelt, the National Labor Relations (Wagner) Act (NLRA), Section 1, declared it to be the policy of the United States in part to protect "the exercise by workers of full freedom of association, self-organization, and designation of represen-

---

*Professor of Law, University of California at Los Angeles.

[1] S. Rep. No. 2926, 72d Cong., 2d Sess. (1934).

[2] 78 Cong. Rec. 3443 (1934), *reprinted in* 1 Legislative History of the National Labor Relations Act, 1935 [hereinafter Leg. Hist. NLRA], at 15 (1949).

[3] 48 Stat 195 (1933). Sec. 7(a) provided in part: "Every code of fair competition, agreement, and license . . . shall contain the following conditions: (1) That employees shall have the right to organize and bargain collectively through representatives of their own choosing, and shall be free from the interference, restraint, or coercion of employers . . . or their agents, in the designation of such representatives or in self-organization or in other concerted activities for the purpose of collective bargaining or other mutual aid or protection. . . ."

[4] Leg. Hist. NLRA 16.

[5] *Id.*

tatives of their own choosing, for the purpose of negotiating the terms and conditions of their employment or other mutual aid or protection."[6] Section 8(1) made it an unfair labor practice for an employer "to interfere with, restrain, or coerce employees in the exercise of the rights guaranteed by Section 7," and Section 8(3) forbade employer "discrimination in regard to hire or tenure of employment to encourage or discourage membership in a labor organization," except for that authorized by valid union-security clauses.

Thus, from the outset the emphasis was on the rights of the collectivity of employees, rather than on the rights of individuals. As the Supreme Court pointed out many years later, the rights protected by Section 7 "are, for the most part, collective rights, rights to act in concert with one's fellow employees; they are protected not for their own sake but as an instrument of the national labor policy of minimizing industrial strife 'by encouraging the practice and procedure of collective bargaining.' "[7] In the administration of the Wagner Act, whenever the claims of the individual ran counter to the interests of the group or those of its union representative, the latter almost always prevailed.

The changes in the NLRA brought about by the Labor Management Relations (Taft-Hartley) Act, 1947 (LMRA)[8] profoundly affected the relative emphases on individual and group rights. During the 12-year interim between the Wagner and Taft-Hartley Acts, unions had grown much more powerful, politically and economically, and it was the sense of the Congress that their use of this power against both employers and individual employees should be curbed. Much of the focus in the congressional debates was on the closed and union shop. In place of Section 8(3) of the Wagner Act, which permitted but did not require employers and unions to enter into closed or union shop agreements, Congress substituted Section 8(a)(3), which prohibits discrimination by an employer against an employee for nonmembership in a labor organization:

> if he has reasonable grounds for believing that such membership was not available to the employee on the same terms and conditions generally applicable to other members, or . . . that membership was

---

[6] 49 Stat 449 (1935).

[7] Emporium Capwell Co. v. Western Addition Community Org., 420 US 50, 62, 88 LRRM 2660 (1975).

[8] 61 Stat 449 (1945), 29 USC §§151–168 (1982).

denied or terminated for reasons other than the failure of the employee to tender the periodic dues and the initiation fees uniformly required as a condition of acquiring or retaining membership.

The LMRA also added Section 8(b)(2), making it an unfair labor practice for a union to cause or attempt to cause an employer to discriminate against an employee in violation of Section 8(a)(3), or itself to discriminate against an employee denied admission to, or retention of, membership on some grounds other than those specified in Section 8(a)(3). Section 8(b)(3) was added to impose upon unions the same duty to bargain as that previously applicable only to employers.

An even more important change in the Wagner Act wrought by Taft-Hartley was the amendment to Section 7 guaranteeing the right of employees "to self-organization, to form, join, or assist labor organizations, to bargain collectively through representatives of their own choosing, and to engage in concerted activities for the purpose of collective bargaining or other mutual aid or protection." The amended Section 7 added the following significant clause: "and shall also have the right to refrain from any or all such activities except to the extent that such right may be affected by a [union security] . . . agreement . . . as authorized in section 8(a)(3)."

Thus, the LMRA not only announced a new policy of congressional indifference as to whether or not workers joined unions, but also laid the basis for a new emphasis on the rights of individual workers. As I shall show, however, the individual employee rights enunciated in the Taft-Hartley amendments to the NLRA and subsequently expanded by decisions of the National Labor Relations Board (NLRB or Board) and the courts, were not so much a defense against discrimination, intimidation, restraint, or coercion by employers, designed to prevent the exercise of their employees' right to organize and to bargain collectively, as they were the means of enabling employees to refrain from or to oppose union activity.

It is undoubtedly true that in administering the amended NLRA, which for the first time prohibited a number of union unfair labor practices, including, in Section 8(b)(1), the restraint or coercion of employees in the exercise of their Section 7 rights, the Board provided needed protection against certain abusive union practices against members and nonmembers. My thesis,

however, is that in recent years employee statutory rights originally conceived of as protections against abuses of employer
power have been increasingly enforced in ways that weaken
unions, reduce the effectiveness of collective bargaining, and
leave individual employees vulnerable to the hostile acts of
employers.

Moreover, I believe that the expanding concept of the union's
duty of fair representation and the enactment of the Labor-
Management Reporting and Disclosure (Landrum-Griffin) Act
of 1959 (LMRDA),[9] has had an uneven effect on the relationship
between unions, on the one hand, and their members and union
members of the bargaining unit, on the other, sometimes
providing the latter with insufficient protection against the former, and sometimes unwisely elevating individual rights over
the interests of the group represented by the union. Limitations
of space preclude a lengthy list of examples supporting this
contention. I shall, therefore, confine my discussion to the following areas: exclusive representation, majority rule, and the
adjustment of grievances; the union's duty of fair representation; individual rights at the workplace; and individual rights
and union discipline.

I. The Principle of Exclusive Representation

A. Majority Rule

Section 9(a) of the Wagner Act provided in part:

> Representatives designated or selected for the purposes of collec-
> tive bargaining by the majority [not the "overwhelming majority"[10]]
> of the employees in a unit appropriate for such purposes, shall be
> the exclusive representatives of all the employees in such unit for the
> purposes of collective bargaining in respect to rates of pay, wages,
> hours of employment, or other conditions of employment.

A corollary of this provision was Section 8(5), which made it
an unfair labor practice for an employer "to refuse to bargain
collectively with the representatives of his employees, subject to
the provisions of Section 9(a)."

The principle of exclusive representation had a history dating
back to World War I and had been reaffirmed under the NIRA

---

[9] 73 Stat 519 (1959), 29 USC §§401–531 (1982).
[10] *See* comments of Senator Wagner, *supra* note 5.

by the National Labor Board (NLB),[11] which despite its lack of enforcement powers, began to develop a "common law" in its application of Section 7(a) of the NIRA, the precursor of Section 7 of the Wagner Act. One principle thus enunciated was that representatives elected by a majority of valid votes cast bargained for all workers in the unit, even when the union asked to represent only its own members or a minority.

On June 19, 1934, Public Resolution No. 44 was enacted by Congress.[12] A few days later, the President issued an executive order[13] abolishing the NLB and creating a National Labor Relations Board of three public members. Decisions of this new Board continued the development of the "common law" of Section 7(a) of the NIRA, and reaffirmed the principle of exclusive representation, which eventually became part of the national labor policy embodied in the Wagner Act.[14] The Board based its stand on majority rule. It did so "the more willingly because the rule is in accord with American traditions of political democracy, which empower representatives elected by the majority to speak for all the people,"[15] and because "[s]imilar interpretations of similar provisions [to Section 7(a)] have been made whenever the question has presented itself."[16]

The right of any employee or group of employees to "present grievances [and] to confer with their employer" was subsequently incorporated in the proviso to Section 9(a) of the Wagner Act: "*Provided,* that any individual employee or a group of employees shall have the right at any time to present grievances to their employer."

---

[11] *See* generally for a description of the machinery established under the NIRA, L. Lorwin & A. Wubnig, LABOR RELATIONS BOARDS Chs. I–XI (1935).

[12] 48 Stat 1183 (1934).

[13] EXEC. ORDER NO. 6763, June 29, 1934.

[14] *See, e.g.,* Houde Eng'r Corp., 1 NLRB (old series) 35 (1935).

[15] *Id.* at 43.

[16] *Id.* at 40. The Board traced the majority rule principle back as far as decisions of the National War Labor Board created by President Wilson in the spring of 1918. *See also,* the testimony of Professor Edwin E. Witte before the Senate Committee of Education and Labor on S. 2926: "In industrial government, just as in political government, there has to be a majority rule, when it comes to actual government. . . . [I]n industrial government, the right of petition, the right to lay grievances before the employer seems to me . . . a right that every group should be accorded, and every individual . . . but if it comes to determining conditions of employment . . . there obviously has to be a determination on the basis of majority rule, or you have pure anarchy, just as you would have in government." LEG. HIST. NLRA 273.

The principle of majority rule embodied in the Wagner Act got off to a shaky start in *NLRB* v. *Jones & Laughlin Steel Corp.*,[17] in which the Supreme Court upheld the constitutionality of the Act. Quoting from its decision in *Virginia Railway* v. *System Federation No. 40, Railway Employees Department*[18] construing Section 2, Ninth of the Railway Labor Act (RLA),[19] the analogue of Section 9(a) of the NLRA, the Court said of the exclusive representation provision:

> It was taken "to prohibit the negotiation of labor contracts generally applicable to employees" in the described unit with any other representative than the one so chosen, "but not as precluding such individual contracts" as the Company might "elect to make directly with individual employees." We think this construction also applies to Section 9(a). . . .[20]

Any uncertainty about the status of the majority-rule principle created by those two cases was dispelled, however, by subsequent decisions of the Supreme Court in *J.I. Case Co.* v. *NLRB*[21] and *Medo Photo Supply Corp.* v. *NLRB.*[22] In the former, the issue was whether lawful individual contracts of employment were a bar to collective bargaining demands by a duly certified exclusive bargaining representative of all employees in the bargaining unit. With only one dissent, the Court, in an opinion by Justice Jackson, answered that question in the negative. The employer's reliance on *Virginia Railway* and *Jones & Laughlin* was almost summarily rejected.[23] Likening a collective bargaining contract to a trade agreement, rather than to a contract of employment, Justice Jackson explained that the individual hiring contract "is subsidiary to the terms of the trade agreement and may not waive any of its benefits, any more than a shipper can contract away the benefit of filed tariffs. . . .[24] The very purpose of providing by statute for the collective agreement, he continued, "is to supersede the terms of separate agreements of employees

---

[17] 301 US 1, 1 LRRM 703 (1937).

[18] 300 US 515, 548, 549, 1 LRRM 743 (1937).

[19] 44 Stat 577 (1926), *as amended,* 48 Stat 926 (1934) (current version at 45 USC §§151–168 (1982)).

[20] 301 US at 45.

[21] 321 US 332, 14 LRRM 501 (1944).

[22] 321 US 678, 14 LRRM 581 (1944).

[23] *Supra* note 21, at 336.

[24] *Id.* at 335.

with terms that reflect the strength and bargaining power and serve the welfare of the group."[25]

Justice Jackson also dealt specifically and at length with the argument that individuals might be able to secure greater employment benefits for themselves than a union could obtain for the bargaining-unit employees as a group. Prefacing his remarks with the observation that "[t]he practice and philosophy of collective bargaining looks with suspicion on such individual advantages,"[26] Justice Jackson continued:

> [A]dvantages to individuals may prove as disruptive to industrial peace as disadvantages. They are a fruitful way of interfering with organization and choice of representatives. . . . The workman is free, if he values his own bargaining position more than that of the group, to vote against representation; but the majority rules, and if it collectivizes the employment bargain, individual advantages or favors will generally in practice go in as a contribution to the collective result. . . .[27]

In *Medo Photo Supply* an employer recognized a union as the exclusive representative of its employees. Shortly thereafter, without repudiating the union, a group of employees told the employer they were dissatisfied with the union and would abandon it if their wages were increased. The employer negotiated with them, without the intervention of the union, granted a wage increase, and thereafter refused to recognize or bargain with the union. In upholding the Board's findings that the employer had interfered with the exercise of its employees' bargaining rights in violation of Sections 7 and 8(1) of the Act, and had also violated Section 8(5) by refusing to bargain with the union, the Court declared: "Bargaining carried on by the employer directly with the employees, *whether a minority or a majority*, who have not revoked their designation of a bargaining agent, would be subversive of the mode of collective bargaining which the statute has ordained."[28]

Taft-Hartley amended the Section 9(a) proviso in the Wagner Act by adding the following words:

> and to have such grievances adjusted, without the intervention of the bargaining representative, as long as the adjustment is not

---

[25] *Id.* at 338.
[26] *Id.*
[27] *Id.* at 338–39.
[28] *Supra* note 22, at 684 (emphasis added).

inconsistent with the terms of a collective-bargaining contract or agreement then in effect: *Provided further,* That the bargaining representative has been given opportunity to be present at such adjustment.

The report of the Senate Committee on Labor and Public Welfare explained the change as follows:

[T]he revised proviso for Section 9(a) clarifies the right of individual employees or groups of employees to present grievances. The Board has not given full effect to this right as defined in the present statute since it has adopted a doctrine that if there is a bargaining representative he must be consulted at every stage of the grievance procedure even though the individual employee might prefer to exercise his right to confer with his employer alone. . . . The revised language would make it clear that the employee's right to present grievances exists independently of the rights of the bargaining representative, if [it] . . . has been given an opportunity to be present at the adjustment, unless the adjustment is contrary to the terms of the collective-bargaining agreement then in effect.[29]

Hopes that the amended Section 9(a) proviso would eliminate existing ambiguities in the right of individual employees or groups of employees to "present grievances" were temporarily dashed by the Second Circuit in *Douds* v. *Retail, Wholesale & Department Store Union Local 1250.*[30] That court, in an opinion by Judge Learned Hand, held that a union other than the exclusive bargaining representative had the right to represent discharged bargaining-unit employees in their efforts to obtain reinstatement. Conceding that in granting to electoral minorities in the bargaining unit the measure of individual representation that it did, Congress may have "clogged, and perhaps even frustrated, the venture as a whole,"[31] Hand asserted that the language of the revised proviso was too plain to allow consideration of that argument. He also raised another point that was to be emphasized by others in the years to come, namely:

The present Act provides for the intervention of the certified agent, and he will seldom, if ever, intervene if he is in sympathy with the minority's "grievance"; for if he is, they are likely to ask him to do the

---

[29] S. Rep. No. 105 on S. 1126, 80th Cong., 1st Sess. 24 (1947), *reprinted in* 1 Legislative History of the Labor Management Relations Act, 1947, [hereinafter Leg. Hist. LMRA] at 430 (1948).
[30] 173 F2d 764, 23 LRRM 2424 (CA 2, 1949).
[31] *Id.* at 771.

"adjusting." Hence they will ordinarily be called upon to face two opponents, each better qualified in such negotiations than they. It appears to us extremely unreasonable to impute that purpose to Congress.[32]

The Board, however, refused to follow the Second Circuit's *Local 1250* decision. In *Federal Telephone & Radio Co.*,[33] which also involved the question of whether or not, under Section 9(a), when the employee is in a bargaining unit represented by a certified bargaining agent, he may designate a rival union of his own choice to present an individual grievance to his employer. It declared that the Second Circuit had read more than was warranted into the Section 9(a) provisos, and continued:

> Concededly, the effect of the new provisos is necessarily an added encroachment on the majority rule principle . . . in that the bargaining representative's participation in grievances is further circumscribed. However . . . these provisos could not have been intended to confer rights upon the minority union: Indeed, to read such a broad meaning into the proviso would effectively disrupt the peaceful application of the majority rule inherent in the Board's certification and would lead to instability in industrial relations not consonant with the spirit and objectives of the 1947 amendments.[34]

B. Adjustment of Individual Grievances

After a careful review of the legislative history of the Section 9(a) proviso in the Wagner Act, Ruth Weyand concluded:

> The fact that Congress inserted a proviso respecting grievances in . . . [Section 9(a)] and chose the word "present" to define the extent of the right it denied to preserve to the individual employee or group of employees shows it intended all aspects of grievance adjustment other than presentation to be vested exclusively in the majority representative. . . .[35]

The Board's initial approach to the question of adjusting individual grievances was consistent with that view. In *Hughes Tool Co.*[36] the employer accorded a minority union the right to present and negotiate the adjustment of grievances for its members, and did so without affording the duly certified Steel-

---

[32] *Id.* at 772.
[33] 107 NLRB 649 (1953).
[34] *Id.* at 653.
[35] *Majority Rule in Collective Bargaining*, 45 COLUM. L. REV. 556, 584 (1945).
[36] 56 NLRB 981 (1944).

workers the opportunity to negotiate in respect of their
disposition. The Board held that the employer had violated
Section 8(1) and (5) of the Act. Specifically, the Board stated:

> We interpret the proviso of Section 9(a) . . . to mean that individual
> employees and groups of employees are permitted "to present griev-
> ances to their employer" by appearing in behalf of themselves—
> although not through any labor organization other than the
> exclusive representative—at every stage of the grievance procedure,
> but that the exclusive representative is entitled to be present and
> negotiate at each such stage concerning the disposition to be made of
> the grievance.[37]

The Board explained:

> The Act makes it clear that the right to bargain collectively concern-
> ing the establishment of a grievance and to conduct all bargaining
> for each and every employee in the unit is vested solely in the
> statutory representative. After the execution of a contract, any
> adjustment of a grievance constitutes, if the subject matter involved
> is dealt with in the contract, an interpretation and application of the
> contract, or, if the subject matter is not dealt with in the contract,
> bargaining respecting a condition of employment. Again it is clear
> that these rights are vested exclusively in the statutory
> representative.[38]

Hughes Tool was decided before the Supreme Court decided
Steele v. *Louisville & Nashville Railroad*,[39] which may partially
explain why the Board considered evidence proffered by the
employer and a minority independent union "immaterial," but
rejected by the trial examiner, that the exclusive bargaining
representative had refused to present grievances for employees
who were not members. According to the Board, "the rights of
the individual employees or groups of employees . . . to present
grievances on their own behalf affords adequate protection for
their interests."[40] With no further clarification, the Board
ordered the following sentence deleted from the trial examiner's

[37] *Id.* at 982.

[38] *Id.* The Board's decision thus ran counter to that of the Ninth Circuit in NLRB v.
North Am. Aviation, Inc., 136 F2d 898, 12 LRRM 806 (CA 9, 1943), in which that court
construed the §9(a) proviso to allow the employer to process all grievances without the
presence of the union at the request of individual employees. The court approved dual
grievance procedures: one provided by the collective agreement and the other provided
by the employer's notice that it would process grievances independently of the agreement.

[39] 323 US 192, 15 LRRM 708 (1944).

[40] 56 NLRB at 985.

intermediate report: "The right to see that a grievance is presented by the recognized representative for the employer's consideration is not an empty right."[41]

Upon review, the Fifth Circuit enforced the Board's order as modified.[42] The court first emphasized the distinction between collective bargaining over wages, hours, and other conditions of employment and grievances, which it characterized as "usually the claims of individuals or small groups that their rights under the collective bargain have not been respected."[43] It agreed with the Board that "individuals and groups may . . . fully prosecute their grievances through all stages and appeals," observing that "[n]o one would think a case in court was 'presented' by merely filing it."[44] It also agreed that the right did not include a presentation of a grievance by a union other than the exclusive bargaining representative, but added:

> We think an inexperienced or ignorant griever can ask a more experienced friend to assist him, but he cannot present his grievance through any union except the [exclusive] representative. On the other hand, the representative, when not asked to present the grievance, but is attending to safeguard the collective bargaining, cannot exclude the griever, and withdraw his grievance or destroy it by not permitting its consideration.[45]

By the time the Fifth Circuit decided *Hughes Tool*, the Supreme Court had handed down its seminal decision in *Steele*, holding, among other things, that an exclusive bargaining agent under the RLA has a duty "to represent non-union or minority union members of the craft without hostile discrimination, fairly, impartially, and in good faith,"[46] Although a decade was to elapse before the duty of fair representation enunciated in *Steele* was applied by the Supreme Court to unions under the NLRA,[47] the Fifth Circuit applied it in *Hughes Tool,* and expressly repudiated the Board's statement that evidence that

---

[41] *Id.* at 993.

[42] Hughes Tool Co. v. NLRB, 147 F2d 69, 15 LRRM 852 (CA 5, 1945).

[43] *Id.* at 72. In this regard the court thus anticipated a Supreme Court decision later that year, which emphasized the same distinction. Elgin, Joliet & Eastern Ry. v. Burley, 325 US 711, 16 LRRM 749 (1945).

[44] *Supra* note 43, at 73.

[45] *Id.*

[46] 323 US at 204.

[47] *See* Syres v. Oil Workers Local 23, 350 US 892, 37 LRRM 2068 (1955) (*mem. per curiam*).

the bargaining representative had refused to present the grievances of nonmembers was "immaterial." "We think," said the court, "a meritorious grievance is entitled, if desired, to the aid and countenance of the bargaining representative. If the griever is a member of another union, and cannot be represented by his own union, it is more necessary that he have the aid of the representative."[48] It decided, however, that because that issue had not been presented in the case before it, it would not order the evidence to be taken, and contended itself with the statement: "We will assume that conduct so plainly at war with the bargaining agent's duty will not be repeated, if it has occurred in the past.[49]

Also relevant to the question of the adjustment of grievances by arbitration was a new provision introduced by Taft-Hartley, Section 301, which provided in part:

> (a) Suits for violation of contracts between an employer and a labor organization representing employees in an industry affecting commerce . . . may be brought in any [federal] district court . . . having jurisdiction of the parties, without respect to the amount of controversy or without regard to the citizenship of the parties.

Questions involving both presentation to the employer and arbitration of a grievance arose in *Black-Clawson Co.* v. *Machinists*,[50] a suit for a declaratory judgment that a demand by a discharged employee that the employer arbitrate his grievance was not arbitrable.[51] The collective agreement between the employer and the certified bargaining representative provided for a four-step grievance and arbitration procedure: step one specified the oral presentation of the grievance to the department foreman by the grievant, with or without the assistance of the shop committee; the next two steps permitted the shop committee to carry the grievance to higher levels of management. Step four provided in part:

> In the event the grievance or dispute is not settled in a manner satisfactory to the grieving party then the grieving party may submit

---

48 147 F2d at 74.

49 *Id.*

50 313 F2d 179, 52 LRRM 2038 (CA 2, 1962).

51 The court decided, as a preliminary matter, that an action for declaratory judgment may be brought under §301(a) of the LMRA, as implemented by the Federal Declaratory Judgment Act, 28 USC §2201 (1982). For further discussion of this question, *see* Aaron, *Arbitration in the Federal Courts: Aftermath of the Trilogy,* COLLECTIVE BARGAINING AND THE ARBITRATOR'S ROLE 60, 76–81 (M. Kahn ed., 1962).

such grievance or dispute to arbitration. Whomever requests arbitration shall serve notice to the other party. . . .

The court concluded that the rights of the grievant under the collective agreement were limited to step one, and that "party" in step four was limited to the employer or the certified bargaining agent. The court also held, anticipating the Supreme Court's decision five years later in *Vaca* v. *Sipes*,[52] that Section 9(a) does not confer upon an individual grievant the power to compel the employer to arbitrate the grievance. In the court's view,

rather than conferring an indefeasible right upon the individual employee to compel compliance with the grievance procedure up to and including any arbitration provision, Section 9(a) merely sets up a buffer between the employee and his union, "permitting" the employee to take his grievances to the employer to hear and adjust them without running afoul of the "exclusive bargaining representative" language of the operative portion of Section 9(a).[53]

The latest word to date on the subject of the right of individuals to present their own grievances, rather than through the certified bargaining agent, was pronounced by the Supreme Court in *Emporium Capwell Co.* v. *Western Addition Community Organization*[54] in which several black employees were discharged for pursuing their grievances against the employer's alleged racial discrimination by conducting a press conference, distributing leaflets attacking the employer, and picketing the store entrances, instead of waiting for the exclusive bargaining agent to process their grievances through the contract grievance and arbitration procedures.

Although one of the claims advanced by the discharged employees was that they had merely attempted to present a grievance to their employer within the meaning of the first proviso to Section 9(a), the Board found that their course of conduct "was no mere presentation of a grievance but nothing short of a demand that the [employer] bargain with the picketing employees for the entire group of minority employees."[55] It concluded that protection of such an attempt would undermine the statutory system of collective bargaining.

---

52 386 US 171, 191–92, 64 LRRM 2369 (1967).
53 313 F2d at 185.
54 420 US 50, 88 LRRM 2660 (1975).
55 The Emporium, 192 NLRB 173, 185, 77 LRRM 1669 (1971).

The D.C. Circuit reversed and remanded the Board's decision.[56] It directed the Board to inquire, on remand, "whether the union was actually remedying the discrimination to the *fullest extent possible, by the most expedient and efficacious means*," and observed that when a union's efforts "fall short of this high standard, the minority group's concerted activity cannot lose its Section 7 protection."[57]

The Supreme Court reversed. Rejecting the claim of the discharged employees that they were protected by the Section 9(a) proviso, Justice Marshall, for the Court, stated:

> The intendment of the proviso is to permit employees to present grievances and to authorize the employer to entertain them without opening itself to liability for dealing directly with employees in derogation of the duty to bargain only with the exclusive bargaining representative, a violation of §8(a)(5). . . . The Act nowhere protects this "right" by making it an unfair labor practice for an employer to refuse to entertain such a presentation; nor can it be read to authorize resort to economic coercion. . . .[58]

The discharged employees had also relied on the antidiscrimination policies enunciated in Title VII of the 1964 Civil Rights Act.[59] The Court rejected this argument as well, saying that it confused the employee's substantive right to be free of racial discrimination with procedures available under the NLRA for securing those rights. Whether those rights depend upon Title VII or have an independent source in the NLRA, said the Court, "they cannot be pursued at the expense of the orderly collective-bargaining process contemplated by the NLRA."[60]

As of this writing, the situation regarding the presentation of grievances by an individual employee or by a union other than the exclusive bargaining representative under the amended NLRA appears to be generally as follows:

An individual employee may present a grievance to his employer and have it adjusted in a manner consistent with the collective agreement, without the intervention of the exclusive bargaining agent, so long as the latter has an opportunity to be

---

[56] Western Addition Community Org. v. NLRB, 485 F2d 917, 83 LRRM 2738 (CA DC, 1973).

[57] *Id.* at 931 (emphasis in original).

[58] *Supra* note 54, at 61, n.12.

[59] 78 Stat 241, as amended, 42 USC §§2000e to 2000e-17 (1982).

[60] *Supra* note 54, at 69.

present at such adjustment. An individual employee has no right, however, to demand that the employer meet with him to adjust a grievance; the employer commits no unfair labor practice by refusing to do so.[61] Similarly, subject to its duty of fair representation, discussed below, a union cannot be compelled by an employee to present and adjust his grievance,[62] or to arbitrate it.[63] If an employee wishes to have a minority union process his grievance, he may do so if, but only if, both the employer and the exclusive bargaining representative consent.[64] A resort by the minority union to economic pressure to force the employer to deal with it concerning an employee's grievance, if unaccompanied by any further demands, such as for continuing negotiations on other matters encompassed by Section 9(a), will probably not be an unfair labor practice, but will not affect the employer's right to resort to self-help.[65]

C. The Union's Duty of Fair Representation (DFR)

Long before the *Steele* case was decided in 1944, it had been apparent that, by virtue of their right of exclusive representation under the NLRA and the RLA, majority unions could and sometimes did abuse that authority by discriminating against members as well as nonmembers for a variety of invidious or irrelevant reasons. After *Steele*, most of the cases involving a breach of a union's DFR continued to arise under the RLA, and most of them grew out of charges of racial discrimination.[66] The Board, under the Wagner Act, however, took no action in any case on the basis of a union's alleged breach of its DFR, although it frequently threatened to revoke the certification of any union

---

[61] *Supra* note 54, at 50, 61 n.12 (1975); Black-Clawson Co. v. Machinists, *supra* note 50, at 185 (CA 2, 1962).

[62] Pekar v. Brewery Workers Local 181, 311 F2d 628, 52 LRRM 2123 (CA 6, 1962), *cert. denied,* 373 US 912 (1963).

[63] Vaca v. Sipes, 386 US 171, 191, 64 LRRM 2369 (1967).

[64] Douds v. Local 1250, Retail, Wholesale & Dep't Store Union, 173 F2d 764, 23 LRRM 2424 (CA 2, 1949), although never overruled, must thus be regarded as a sport. Even the worthy Hand sometimes nodded.

[65] Laborers Local 840 (C.A. Blinne Constr. Co.), 135 NLRB 1153, 1167–68, 49 LRRM 1638 (1962) (*dictum*) (if uncertified union had conformed its picketing to protest discriminatory transfer of an employee and against payment of wages at a rate lower than that prescribed by law, it would not have violated NLRA, §8(b)(7)(c), prohibiting organizational picketing without filing a representation petition for a reasonable period of time not to exceed 30 days).

[66] *See* Aaron, *The Union's Duty of Fair Representation Under the Railway Labor and National Labor Relations Acts,* 34 J. Air L. & Com. 167, 175–85 (1968).

which, as a matter of internal policy, refused to grant equal status to all employees in the bargaining unit for which it was the exclusive representative.[67] Indeed, there was considerable doubt if the Board had such power under the Act.[68]

Seven years after the Supreme Court inferred a union DFR under the NLRA in *Syres*,[69] the Board decided for the first time, in a series of cases, that unfair, irrelevant, or invidious treatment of employees by their exclusive bargaining representative violates rights guaranteed by Section 7 of the NLRA and constitutes an unfair labor practice within the meaning of Sections 8(b)(1)(A), 8(b)(2), and 8(b)(3) of the Act.[70]

In *Vaca* v. *Sipes*[71] the Supreme Court assumed, without actually deciding, that a union's breach of its DFR is an unfair labor practice, although not one within the exclusive jurisdiction of the Board. It declared that a breach of the DFR occurs "only when a union's conduct toward a member of the collective bargaining unit is arbitrary, discriminatory, or in bad faith . . . [or] arbitrarily ignore[s] a meritorious grievance or process[es] it in perfunctory fashion."[72] The Court also reiterated prior holdings that an employee who alleges a violation of a collective agreement by the employer and a breach by the union of its DFR, may sue for a remedy under Section 301(a) of the LMRA;[73] that he must first exhaust his contractual remedies,[74] and that a "wide range of reasonableness must be allowed a statutory representative in serving the unit it represents, subject

---

[67] *See* Aaron & Komaroff, *Statutory Regulation of Internal Union Affairs—I*, 44 Nw. U.L. Rev. 425, 440–42 (1949), and cases cited therein.

[68] *See, e.g.*, Cushman, *The Duration of Certifications by the National Labor Relations Board and the Doctrine of Administrative Stability*, 45 Mich. L. Rev. 1, 33–37 (1946); and Justice Jackson, dissenting in Wallace Corp. v. NLRB, 323 US 248, 268, 15 LRRM 697 (1944), stated: "Neither the . . . [NLRA] nor any other Act of Congress explicitly or by implication gives to the Board any power to supervise union membership or to deal with union practices, however unfair they may be to members . . . [or] to minorities. . . . This may or may not have been a mistake, but it was no oversight."

[69] Syres v. Oilworkers Local 23, *supra* note 47.

[70] Miranda Fuel Co., 140 NLRB 181, 51 LRRM 1584 (1962), *enf. denied*, 326 F2d 172, 54 LRRM 2715 (CA 2, 1963); Metal Workers Local 1 (Hughes Tool Co.), 147 NLRB 1573, 56 LRRM 1289 (1964); Longshoremen Local 1367 (Galveston Maritime Ass'n), 148 NLRB 897, 57 LRRM 1083 (1964), *enforced*, 368 F2d 1010, 63 LRRM 2559 (CA 5, 1966), *cert. denied*, 389 US 837 (1967); Rubber Workers Local 12 (Business League of Gadsden), 150 NLRB 312, 57 LRRM 1535 (1964), *enforced*, 368 F2d 12, 63 LRRM 2395 (CA 5, 1966), *cert. denied*, 389 US 837 (1967).

[71] *Supra* note 63, at 186–87.

[72] *Id.* 190–91.

[73] Humphrey v. Moore, 375 US 335, 55 LRRM 2031 (1964).

[74] Republic Steel Corp. v. Maddox, 379 US 650, 58 LRRM 2193 (1965).

always to complete good faith and honesty of purpose in the exercise of its discretion."[75] Finally, the Court declared that if the union had breached its DFR, it would have been liable only for increases, if any, in the employer's damages caused by the union's wrongful conduct.

Space does not permit a discussion of the Niagara of DFR cases that have flooded the courts since *Vaca* was decided.[76] It appears, however, that despite the broad discretion accorded unions in the exercise of their DFR, courts are increasingly finding ways to hold them liable for breaches, for example, by disjunctively applying the *Vaca* test, so that a breach will be found if a union has acted in bad faith, *or* in an arbitrary, *or* discriminatory, *or* perfunctory manner. In addition, some courts have found breaches of the DFR if a union acted negligently or irrationally; while others have extended the scope of judicial review to include basic union policies, such as the handling of competing seniority claims by union members.[77]

Perhaps the most damaging blow to unions was the decision by the Supreme Court in *Bowen* v. *United States Postal Service*,[78] in which the Court held that a union found guilty of a breach of its DFR by virtue of its refusal to arbitrate the discharge of a bargaining-unit employee was liable for all back pay awarded to the employee from the date on which it was presumed an arbitrator would have issued an award in the grievant's favor.

It seems fair to conclude that, on the whole, the courts have contributed as much confusion as clarity to the process of defining the nature of a union's DFR.

In this necessarily abbreviated and selective account of the adoption of the principle of majority rule, exclusive bargaining rights, and the presentation and adjustment of grievances, I have followed "conventional labor historiography," which, according to Professor Klare,

> has tended to equate the aspirations and goals of working people with those of the leadership of organized labor and . . . has assumed widespread consensus among working people as to what was desired: legal protection of the right to organize; equalization of

---

[75] Ford Motor Co. v. Huffman, 345 US 330, 338, 31 LRRM 2548 (1953).

[76] *See* Aaron, *An Overview*, THE CHANGING LAW OF FAIR REPRESENTATION 15 (J. McKelvey ed., 1985).

[77] *Id.*, sample cases are listed at 16–26.

[78] 459 US 212, 112 LRRM 2281 (1983).

bargaining power by—and to the extent of—promoting unions as units of countervailing economic power; use of this power to achieve higher standards of living through wage-bargaining; and an industrial democracy limited to the notion that the bargaining unit is a political constituency to which should be extended the traditional democratic right to vote for or against representation, but that democratic participation is largely exhausted by that choice.[79]

With the exception of the final clause of this quotation, to which I take exception, I think it is an accurate characterization of conventional historiography, and one with which I agree. Klare also asserts that

the Act by its terms apparently accorded a governmental blessing to powerful workers' organizations that were to acquire equal bargaining power with corporations, accomplish a redistribution of income, and subject the workplace to a regime of participatory democracy. The Act's plain language was susceptible to an overtly anticapitalist interpretation.[80]

Of course, whether a statute is "susceptible to" a given interpretation depends upon the premises of the interpreter. The quoted passage does not accord with my interpretation of what the Congress intended, but I do concede that probably, as Klare asserts, "the Act meant many different things to different people and groups on the labor side and that for a substantial number . . . it . . . symbolized a significant opening in the direction of radical change."[81]

A critique of Klare's thesis that the Act was "deradicalized" by the judiciary is not within the scope of this paper.[82] My own view is that the principle of majority rule embodied in Section 9(a) of the Act was adopted primarily to prevent the continued efforts by employers or electoral minorities to fractionize workers within a plant or enterprise, thereby preventing them from creating, in a single, exclusive bargaining representative, an , effective countervailing bargaining power to that of their employer. To have permitted bargaining-unit employees to bargain individually or in groups over wages, hours, and working

---

[79] *Judicial Deradicalization of the Wagner Act and the Origins of Modern Legal Consciousness, 1937–1941*, 62 MINN. L. REV. 265, 289 (1978).

[80] *Id.* at 285.

[81] *Id.* at 290.

[82] Others have undertaken this task; *see, e.g.*, Finkin, *Revisionism in Labor Law*, 43 MD. L. REV. 23, 48–54 (1984).

conditions, to adjust grievances involving the interpretation or application of a collective agreement without the knowledge and consent of the exclusive bargaining representative, almost certainly would have "clogged . . . and frustrated the venture as a whole."[83] The same is true if minority unions had been allowed to bargain or adjust grievances for bargaining-unit employees. This view, once generally accepted, has been challenged in recent years, notably by Professor Schatzki;[84] but I continue to adhere to it.

What the Congress overlooked, however, was that ignorance, prejudice, and the corrupting influence of power could erode the protections that the two Section 9(a) provisos were designed to provide and subject individuals and minority groups to the tyranny of the majority. The judicial invention of a union DFR therefore became necessary. The DFR was intended to protect those individuals and groups against unfair treatment by unions, or by unions and employers acting collusively, in the employment context. Although breaches of the DFR are unfair labor practices, the development of the DFR doctrine has very largely been by the courts. In my view this development has been seriously flawed in at least two respects.

First, the requirement laid down in *Vaca* that an employee wishing to sue an employer under Section 301 for violation of a collective agreement must first prove that his union representative violated its DFR in the processing of the employee's grievance, or by refusing to process it, weights the scales heavily against the employee's chances of recovery. There is some merit in Justice Black's statement in his dissent in *Vaca* that the Court's decision "while giving the worker an ephemeral right to sue his union for breach of its . . . [DFR], creates unsurmountable obstacles to . . . his [exercise of the] far more valuable right to sue his employer for breach of the collective bargaining agreement."[85] Thus, although the rights of individual employees against their exclusive bargaining representatives have received added protection by virtue of the imposition on the latter of the DFR, that protection has in many instances proved to be illusory.

---

[83] *Supra* note 30, at 771.

[84] *Majority Rule, Exclusive Representation, and the Interests of Individual Workers: Should Exclusivity Be Abolished?*, 23 U. PA. L. REV. 897 (1975).

[85] *Supra* note 63, at 171, 197.

Second, in overcoming the obstacles to employee recovery in DFR cases, some courts have broadened the unions' duty beyond reasonable or practicable limits; moreover, unions have been made increasingly vulnerable to substantial damages, while employers in some instances have been shielded from the normal consequences of their own wrongdoing.[86] In *Bowen*, for example, the Supreme Court apportioned the liability of the union and the employer in a grotesque fashion.

II. Individual Rights at the Workplace

A. Employer Interrogation

Sections 8(1) and (3) of the Wagner Act outlawed employee interference with, restraint, or coercion of employees in the exercise of their Section 7 rights, or discrimination for the purpose of discouraging or encouraging union membership. This, in time, brought about a sharp reduction in the more egregious unlawful practices of employers, such as physical violence, use of labor spies, blacklisting, and the like. So zealous was the Board to eliminate perceived interference with workers' Section 7 rights that it attempted to outlaw any statements by an employer on the question of unionism.[87] That policy, under pressure from the courts, yielded to one more tolerant of employers' rights of free speech. However, the borderline between threats and intimidation, on the one hand, and neutral expressions of opinion, explanation of legal positions, predictions, and the like, on the other, has remained a vague and shifting one, the characterization of an employer's speech depending largely upon the makeup of the Board.[88]

---

[86] Exactly how the judiciary, under the leadership of the Supreme Court, arrived at the present unsatisfactory state of the law is brilliantly illuminated in Feller, *A General Theory of the Collective Bargaining Agreement*, 66 CALIF. L. REV. 663 (1973). *See*, particularly, his six propositions for defining the legal status of collective agreements and the rights created by them, *id.* 773–74, the adoption of which would result in a much more equitable and understandable system than that which presently exists.

[87] *See, e.g.*, Union Pac. Stage, Inc., 2 NLRB 471, 1 LRRM 61 (1937), *enf. denied*, 99 F2d 153, 3 LRRM 699 (CA 9, 1938); 1936 NLRB ANN. REP. 73 (1936); Aaron, *Employer Free Speech: The Search for a Policy*, PUBLIC POLICY AND COLLECTIVE BARGAINING 28, 29–30 (J. Shister, B. Aaron, & C. Summers eds., 1962).

[88] The cases are too numerous to list. *See generally*, R. Gorman, BASIC TEXT ON LABOR LAW 148–68 (1967); Aaron, *supra* note 87; Bok, *The Regulation of Campaign Tactics in Representation Elections Under the National Labor Relations Act*, 78 HARV. L. REV. 38, 66–92 (1964).

The policies regarding employer interrogation of employees concerning union sympathies or activities have also altered over time. Under the Wagner Act, the Board early characterized direct interrogation as "a particularly flagrant form of intimidation of individual employees,"[89] and said that its effect "is to create immediate, personal fear of loss of employment in present and prospective members of the Union, and . . . obviously constitutes, therefore, flagrant and unlawful interference, restraint, and coercion of employees."[90]

The Taft-Hartley amendments, besides prohibiting unions, as well as employers, from restraining or coercing employees in the exercise of their Section 7 rights, also added in a new provision, Section 8(c), which stated:

> The expressing of any views, argument, or opinion, or the dissemination thereof, whether in written, printed, graphic, or visual form, shall not constitute or be evidence of an unfair labor practice under any of the provisions of this Act, if such expression contains no threat of reprisal or force or promise of benefit.

This provision had the immediate effect of allowing employers much greater freedom in what they told their employees, the Board taking the position that Section 8(c) granted an "immunity beyond that contemplated by the free speech guarantees of the Constitution."[91] The new provision, however, did not immediately affect the Board's policies on employer interrogation. The Board at first held that because interrogation is not the expression of an opinion, but rather a process of gathering information, it is not protected by Section 8(c).[92] As late as 1949, in *Standard-Coosa-Thatcher Co.*,[93] the Board brushed aside an employer's claim that employees who openly professed their union sympathies and affiliation by wearing union buttons could properly be interrogated on union matters, saying that this argument lost sight of the "essential character of the restraint involved." "The subtle pressure created by interrogation," the Board continued, "results from the realization by the interro-

---

[89] 1936 NLRB ANN. REP. 76 (1936).

[90] Botany Worsted Mills, 4 NLRB 292, 297–98, I-A LRRM 299 (1937), *enforced as modified*, 106 F2d 263, 267, 4 LRRM 595 (CA 3, 1939).

[91] 1948 NLRB ANN. REP. 49 (1948).

[92] *See, e.g.*, Ames Spot Welder Co., Inc., 75 NLRB 352, 355, 21 LRRM 1040 (1947); Wollett & Rowen, *Employer Speech and Related Issues*, 16 OHIO ST. L.J. 380, 395 (1955).

[93] 85 NLRB 1358, 24 LRRM 1575 (1949) (emphasis in original).

gated employee that his employer is *concerned* with his union affiliation or activities and will, therefore, act to the employee's detriment."[94]

Modifications in the policy, however, soon began to appear. For example, in a case in which the employer interrogated employees in violation of that *Standard-Coosa-Thatcher* standard, the Board found that because of the "isolated nature" of the interrogation, no useful purpose would be served by issuing a cease-and-desist order based upon it.[95] Less than a year later, in *Blue Flash Express, Inc.*,[96] the Board overruled *Standard-Coosa-Thatcher*, noting that "the courts of at least six circuits have explicitly or by necessary implication condemned the rationale" of that case.[97] It announced a new test:[98] "whether particular interrogation interferes with, restrains, and [sic] coerces employees must be found in the record as a whole. And . . . 'The time, the place, the personnel involved, the information sought and the employer's conceded preference . . . must be considered.' "[99]

Although the *Blue Flash* test was never rejected by the courts, some questioned the Board's application of it in specific cases. In *Strucksnes Construction Co.*,[100] the D.C. Circuit reversed and remanded the Board's decision that an employer's poll of his employees' attitude toward a union accorded with the *Blue Flash* test. Upon remand, the Board abandoned the *Blue Flash* test and substituted the following:

> Absent unusual circumstances, the polling of employees by an employer will be violative of Section 8(a)(1) . . . unless the following safeguards are observed: (1) the purpose of the poll is to determine the truth of the union's claim of majority, (2) this purpose is communicated to the employees, (3) assurances against reprisal are given, (4) the employees are polled by secret ballot, and (5) the employer has not engaged in unfair labor practices or otherwise created a coercive atmosphere.[101]

---

[94] *Id.* at 1363.

[95] Walmac Co., 106 NLRB 1355, 1357, 33 LRRM 1019 (1953).

[96] 109 NLRB 591, 34 LRRM 1384 (1954).

[97] *Id.* at 593.

[98] This test was based on one laid down in NLRB v. Syracuse Color Press, 209 F2d 596, 599, 33 LRRM 2334 (CA 2, 1954).

[99] 109 NLRB at 594.

[100] 148 NLRB 1368, 57 LRRM 1158 (1964), *rev'd and remanded sub nom.* Operating Eng'rs v. NLRB, 353 F2d 852, 60 LRRM 2353 (CA DC, 1965).

[101] Strucksnes Constr. Co., 165 NLRB 1062, 65 LRRM 1385 (1967).

Assuming a fairly rigorous and consistent application of this test, it appeared to provide adequate protection to employee rights and employer interests in those cases in which an employer genuinely desired to confirm whether or not a majority of its employees desired a union. The need for such confirmation was virtually eliminated, however, when the Board modified its *Joy Silk* doctrine[102] and held that an employer will no longer be required to give reasons for rejecting a union bargaining demand and insisting upon an election.[103] In any case, *Blue Flash* is not dead; the Board continues to determine the legitimacy of casual or isolated interrogations on the basis of "all the surrounding circumstances."[104] Furthermore, despite the apparent approval of the Board's *Strucksnes* standards by the Supreme Court,[105] at least some lower courts have shown hostility to any attempt by the Board to find a *per se* violation when any of the five *Strucksnes* requirements is not met.[106]

As recently as 1980, in *PPG Industries*,[107] the Board held that employer questioning constituted coercive behavior even when addressed to known union sympathizers and even in the absence of threats of retaliation or promises to improve working conditions. Four years later, however, in *Rossmore House*,[108] the Board overruled *PPG*, saying:

> We conclude that *PPG* improperly established a per se rule that completely disregarded the circumstances surrounding an alleged interrogation and ignored the reality of the workplace. Such a per se approach had been rejected by the Board [in *Blue Flash*] 30 years ago. . . . Accordingly, we overrule *PPG* and similar cases to the extent they find that an employer's questioning open and active union supporters about their union sentiments, in the absence of

---

102 Joy Silk Mills, Inc. v. NLRB, 85 NLRB 1263, 24 LRRM 1548 (1949), *enforced*, 185 F2d 732, 27 LRRM 2012 (CA DC, 1950) (employer must have "good-faith doubt" as to union's majority status before insisting on election).

103 Aaron Bros., 158 NLRB 1077, 1078, 62 LRRM 1160 (1966).

104 *See, e.g.*, B.F. Goodrich Footwear Co., 201 NLRB 353, 82 LRRM 1262 (1973).

105 NLRB v. Gissel Packing Co., 395 US 575, 609, 71 LRRM 2481 (1969).

106 *See, e.g.*, General Mercantile & Hardware Co. v. NLRB, 461 F2d 952, 80 LRRM 2622 (CA 8, 1972).

107 251 NLRB 1146, 105 LRRM 1434 (1980). The Board also overruled prior decisions in which it had declined to find violations in such circumstances: Stumpf Motor Co., 208 NLRB 431, 85 LRRM 1113 (1974); B.F. Goodrich Footwear Co., *supra* note 104.

108 269 NLRB 1176, 116 LRRM 1025 (1984), *enforced sub nom.* Hotel & Restaurant Employees Local 11 v. NLRB, 760 F2d 1006, 119 LRRM 2624 (CA 9, 1985).

threats or promises, necessarily interferes with, restrains, or coerces employees in violation of Section 8(a)(1) of the Act.[109]

On the other hand, neither the Board nor the courts have shown much sympathy for an employer's alleged solicitude for the right of employees to be free from interrogation by unions regarding their views on union representation. In *Louis-Allis Co.* v. *NLRB*,[110] the Seventh Circuit found

> no merit in the Company's argument that, because . . . [a union] poll might have been coercive if conducted by the Company, it is likewise coercive when conducted by the Union. The employer occupies a far different position with regard to the coercive impact of its actions upon employees than does a Union.[111]

I am inclined to agree that employees who openly avow their union support are not likely to be intimidated by questions from management that are unaccompanied by threats of reprisal. The trouble with *Rossmore House,* however, is that the Board has failed to demonstrate why any interrogation is necessary. As previously noted, employers may demand secret ballot elections conducted by the Board to determine whether their employees support a union; their insistence in interrogating employees about their sentiments is therefore gratuitous and is likely to arouse concerns about the possibility of unlawful retaliation in the minds of their more fearful employees.

B. *"Concerted" Activity*

As noted earlier, the Board's protection of various forms of union activity by workers is quite broad; if construed literally, Sections 7 and 8(a)(1) would cover some conduct in support of collective bargaining, such as destruction of property, which they were never intended to protect. The courts have therefore deemed it necessary to add their own gloss to the statutory language. In *Boeing Airplane Co.* v. *NLRB*,[112] for example, the employer discharged an engineer who had acted as an employment agent to procure offers from other employers for his fellow engineers at Boeing. This activity was undertaken as a means to put pressure on Boeing during contract negotiations.

---

[109] *Id.*, 116 LRRM at 1026.
[110] 463 F2d 512, 80 LRRM 2864 (CA 7, 1972).
[111] *Id.* at 517.
[112] 238 F2d 188, 38 LRRM 2276 (CA 9, 1956).

The Ninth Circuit refused to enforce a Board order that the discharged engineer be reinstated. It held that the dischargee's refusal to cease his activity, when requested to do so by Boeing, constituted disloyalty, and fell "in the classification of a slow-down, sit-down strike, damage to business or to plant and equipment, trespass, violence, refusal to accept work assignment, physical sabotage, refusal to obey rules and other such activities,"[113] all of which were, presumably, unprotected. Although the court felt that the dischargee's conduct should be treated as individual, it said that even if the conduct were regarded as part of a concerted activity, "still the whole combination to destroy or damage the business of the employer would seem collectively disloyal and illegal."[114]

In *Shelly & Anderson Furniture Manufacturing Co.* v. *NLRB*,[115] however, the same court agreed with the Board that a demonstration away from the plant at the start of the workday to protest the employer's alleged dilatory negotiation tactics was protected concerted activity. In so doing it set forth the following four-point test to determine when such activity is protected:

> (1) there must be a work-related complaint or grievance; (2) the concerted activity must further some group interest; (3) a specific remedy or result must be sought through such activity; and (4) the activity should not be unlawful or otherwise improper.[116]

As can be seen from the dictum in *Boeing,* the category of "otherwise improper" activities is a broad one.

It now seems well established that some concerted activities by employees are protected even if they are not aimed at union organization or collective bargaining. For example, a spontaneous walkout by unorganized employees to protest against working conditions was held by the Supreme Court to be protected.[117] Similarly, a work stoppage in the plant to protest

---

[113] *Id.* at 193.

[114] *Id.*

[115] 497 F2d 1200, 86 LRRM 2619 (CA 9, 1974).

[116] *Id.* at 1202–1203.

[117] Washington Aluminum Co. v. NLRB, 370 US 9, 50 LRRM 2235 (1962). Significantly, the Court rejected the argument that the workers lost the protection of §7 merely because they had not presented a specific demand upon their employer to remedy the condition to which they objected. *Id.,* 50 LRRM at 2237.

against the discharge of a fellow employee, even if unrelated to union organization, is protected.[118]

In recent years, however, the focus has been on the protection, if any, for employees who act alone: can such persons ever be considered to have engaged in "concerted" activity? To this question the Board and the courts have given changing answers over time.

In *Interboro Contractors, Inc.*[119] the Board held that complaints made by an individual employee against the alleged violation of terms of a collective agreement "are grievances within the framework of the contract that affect the rights of all employees in the unit, and thus constitute concerted activity which is protected by Section 7 of the Act."[120] The Board adhered to that policy in *City Disposal Systems,*[121] a case involving the discharge of a truck driver for refusing to drive a truck with defective brakes. The Sixth Circuit refused to enforce the Board's order of reinstatement, as it had also done in a previous case of the same type.[122] That court concluded that the refusal was an action taken solely on the dischargee's own behalf and was not concerted activity within the meaning of Section 7. The Supreme Court, by a vote of five to four, reversed.[123]

In upholding the *Interboro* doctrine, the majority reiterated its professed deference to the Board's "expertise," whereas the dissenters refused to do so because of their belief that the Board had attempted to exercise undelegated legislative authority.[124] In the view of the minority, Congress, by refusing to amend the

---

[118] NLRB v. Pepsi-Cola Bottling Co. of Miami, 449 F2d 824, 78 LRRM 2481 (CA 5, 1971), *cert. denied*, 407 US 910 (1972). The court stressed that the workers left the plant as soon as they were ordered to do so by the police, and that there was no procedure for the handling of grievances.

[119] 157 NLRB 1295, 61 LRRM 1537 (1966).

[120] *Id.* at 1298.

[121] 256 NLRB 451, 107 LRRM 1267 (1981).

[122] Aro, Inc. v. NLRB, 596 F2d 713, 101 LRRM 2153 (CA 6, 1979). The other circuit courts of appeal were divided on this issue, three favoring the Board's position and four supporting that taken by the Sixth Circuit. *See* NLRB v. City Disposal Systems, Inc., 465 US 822, 115 LRRM 3193, 3195, n.4 (1984).

[123] *Supra* note 122.

[124] This deference is not imposed by the statute, §10(e) of which requires only that the findings of the Board "with respect to questions of fact if supported by substantial evidence on the record considered as a whole shall be conclusive." The Supreme Court had declared, however, in *Universal Camera Corp.* v. *NLRB*, 340 US 474, 27 LRRM 2373 (1951), that a reviewing court should give special deference to Board findings that relate to a matter in which the Board's industrial experience and expertise gives it a special competence, and should also defer in other matters if the Board's finding is reasonable.

NLRA to provide that every violation of a collective bargaining agreement is an unfair labor practice, had inferentially deprived the Board of authority to treat as an unfair labor practice a violation of purely individual contract rights on the theory that the individual claim is, constructively, "concerted" activity protected by Section 7. The fundamental difference between the majority and the dissenters was made clear by Justice O'Connor, in her opinion for the latter:

> [W]hen an employee acts alone in expressing a personal concern, contractual or otherwise, his action is not "concerted;" in such cases, the statute instructs him to seek vindication through his union, and where necessary, through the courts. . . . Under either scenario, the integrity of the rights won in the collective bargaining process and the rights of all other employees are preserved. The question is whether these rights will be vindicated by administrative or by private and judicial practices.[125]

Justice O'Connor came down strongly on the side of the latter.

But what of the individual worker in an unorganized plant who complains about unsafe working conditions: is he protected by Section 7? Ten years ago, in *Alleluia Cushion Co.*,[126] the Board's answer was affirmative. It held that

> when an employee speaks up and seeks to enforce statutory provisions relating to occupational safety designed for the benefit of all employees, in the absence of any evidence that fellow employees disavow such representation, we will find an implied consent thereto and deem such activity to be concerted.[127]

In 1984, however, a newly constituted Board viewed the issue differently. In *Meyers Industries*[128] an employee was discharged for making safety complaints, refusing to drive an unsafe truck, and reporting a safety violation to a state public service commission. Relying on *Alleluia*, the administrative law judge concluded that the employer had violated Section 8(a)(1) of the Act. A majority of the Board reversed and also overruled *Alleluia*. The Board first distinguished *Interboro* from *Alleluia*: the focal point of the former was an attempted implementation of a collective agreement, whereas in the latter there was no collective agree-

---

125 *Supra* note 122 at 845–46, 115 LRRM at 3203–3204.
126 221 NLRB 999, 91 LRRM 1131 (1975).
127 *Id.* at 1000.
128 268 NLRB 493, 115 LRRM 1025 (1984).

ment or any attempt to enforce one. Next, the Board repudiated the reasoning in *Alleluia* and its progeny, saying:

> Instead of looking at the observable evidence of group action to see what men and women in the workplace in fact choose as an issue about which to take some action, it was the Board that determined the existence of an issue about which employees *ought* to have a group concern.[129]

Finally, the Board stated that it was returning to the standard approved by the courts prior to *Alleluia* and announced the following new definition of "concerted" activity:

> In general, to find an employee's activity to be "concerted," we shall require that it be engaged in with or on the authority of other employees, and not solely by and on behalf of the employee himself. Once the activity is found to be concerted, an 8(a)(1) violation will be found if, in addition, the employer knew of the concerted nature of the employee's activity, the concerted activity was protected by the Act, and the adverse employment action at issue (e.g., discharge) was motivated by the employee's protected concerted activity.[130]

The Board also emphasized that the new standard places on the General Counsel the burden of proving the elements of a violation, saying: "It will no longer be sufficient . . . to set out the subject matter that is of alleged concern to a theoretical group and expect to establish concert of action thereby."[131]

With one judge dissenting, a panel of the D.C. Circuit concluded that the Board had acted on the basis of an erroneous view of law and, consequently, had failed to exercise the discretion delegated to it by Congress. Accordingly, the court remanded the case to the Board for further consideration of the scope of concerted activities under Section 7.[132] The court of appeals faulted the Board's decision in *Meyers* on two principal grounds: first, it held that the Board had "erred in assuming that the NLRA *mandates* its present interpretation of 'concerted activities' . . . except as indicated in the *Meyers* test"; second, the court, contrary to the Board, held that "the *Meyers* test does not represent a return to the standard relied on by the courts and by

---

[129] *Id.* at 496 (emphasis in original).

[130] *Id.* at 497.

[131] *Id.*

[132] Prill v. NLRB, 755 F2d 941, 118 LRRM 2649 (CA DC, 1985).

the Board before *Alleluia,* but instead constitutes a new and more restrictive standard."[133]

The most novel and interesting feature of the court's opinion in *Meyers* is its insistence that the Board exercise "its own policy judgment and expertise" in determining the proper definition of concerted activities. The court cited the Supreme Court's observations in *City Disposal Systems,* that although the phrase, "to engage in concerted activities," could be interpreted "to refer to a situation in which two or more employees are working together at the same time and the same place toward a common goal, the language of §7 does not confine itself to such a narrow meaning,"[134] and that "[t]here is no indication that Congress intended to limit this protection [of §7] to situations in which an employee's activity and that of his fellow employees combine with one another in any particular way."[135] The Board had failed, said the court of appeals, to exercise its "substantial responsibility to determine the scope of protection in order to promote the purposes of the NLRA," for example, by neglecting "even to consider whether the discharge of an employee because of his safety complaints would discourage other employees from engaging in collective activity to improve working conditions."[136]

My conclusion is that although the present Board may have lost a battle, it will probably win the war on this issue. It's interpretation of "concerted" activities need not depend upon the law as it was prior to *Alleluia,* and it is clear that reasonable persons can and do reach different conclusions as to both the original intent of Congress and the lessons to be learned from the experience under the Act. If the courts continue to rely upon the Board's assumed expertise in these matters, a revised opinion, based not so much on statutory interpretation as on the Board's weighing of the factors mentioned in the Supreme Court's majority opinion in *City Disposal Systems* and in the D.C. Circuit's majority opinion in *Meyers,* but adhering to its initial conclusion, might pass muster the second time around. Furthermore, if the present Board is faced with another case similar to *City Disposal Systems,* I think there is a strong likelihood that it will

---

[133] *Id.* at 948 (emphasis in original).
[134] *Supra* note 122, 115 LRRM at 3197.
[135] *Id.* at 3199.
[136] *Supra* note 132, at 953.

reconsider the views it set forth in that case in the light of those expressed by the Supreme Court dissenters.

III. Individual Rights and Union Discipline

The NLRA's prohibition in Section 8(b)(1)(A) of union restraint or coercion of employees in the exercise of their Section 7 rights is subject to the following proviso: "*Provided,* That this paragraph shall not impair the right of a labor organization to prescribe its own rules with respect to the acquisition or retention of membership therein." There are, of course, other limitations on a union's power to discipline its members set forth in the LMRDA, but those are beyond the scope of this paper.

Under the NLRA, the Board and the courts have built up a body of case law that goes much further than the literal meaning which the Section 8(b)(1)(A) proviso seems to suggest. The major cases have involved union efforts to suspend or expel members or to sue them in court to collect fines for engaging in conduct arguably protected by Section 7. The logic of their various decisions, when they are compared, is sometimes difficult to follow.

The Supreme Court has interpreted Section 8(b)(1)(A) as outlawing only two forms of union discipline: coercive threats of reprisal and attempts to affect adversely the relationship between an employee and his employer through job discipline. Accordingly, it held in *NLRB* v. *Allis-Chalmers Manufacturing Co.*[137] that a union may fine members who, in violation of the union's constitution and bylaws, cross a picket line during a legal strike, and may sue to collect those fines in a state court, despite the fact that the proviso to that section speaks only of rules relating to "the acquisition or retention of membership." Obviously, in this kind of case it is self-defeating for a union to expel an erring member, but a substantial fine and a lawsuit to recover it might well be regarded as a reprisal not permitted by the proviso, as the dissenters in *Allis-Chalmers* insisted. The Court majority concluded, however, that the fined members were fully bound by an obligation voluntarily undertaken (*i.e.,* each had executed the pledge of allegiance to the union constitution and had taken the oath of full membership), and thus stood

---

[137] 388 US 175, 65 LRRM 2449 (1967).

in essentially the same position as that of a citizen who is sued for nonpayment of taxes. Suppose, however, that an employee's membership is limited to paying the standard initiation fee and monthly dues:[138] can he, too, be disciplined for crossing the picket line? In *Alllis-Chalmers* the Court refused to express an opinion on that issue, but in accordance with its reasoning in subsequent cases, the answer must surely be in the negative.

Many unions provide in their constitutions and bylaws that any member aggrieved by an action of the union or its officers must exhaust all remedies and appeals provided for in the constitution before resorting to any other court or tribunal outside of the union. In *Operating Engineers Local 138 (Charles S. Skura)*[139] the Board found the union had violated the Act by fining a member who had filed an unfair labor practice charge against the union without first exhausting his internal union remedies. In *NLRB* v. *Marine & Shipbuilding Workers,*[140] the Supreme Court upheld a similar determination by the Board that a union which expelled a member for filing an unfair labor practice charge against it without first exhausting his internal union remedies had violated Section 8(b)(1)(A) of the Act. The Court concluded that the case involved considerations of public policy as well as purely internal union affairs, and that the proviso to Section 8(b)(1)(A) "is not so broad as to penalize a member who invokes the protection of the Act for a matter that is in the public domain and beyond the internal affairs of the union."[141] I find it difficult to distinguish logically between the obligation freely undertaken by union members in *Allis-Chalmers* not to cross the union picket line and that undertaken by union members in *Marine & Shipbuilding Workers* to abide by the terms of the union's constitution. As the Court pointed out in the latter case, however, the six-month limitation on the filing of unfair labor practice charges in Section 10(b) of the NLRA and the incapacity of the Board to initiate such charges underscore the

---

[138] In *NLRB* v. *General Motors Corp.*, 373 US 734, 53 LRRM 2313 (1963), the Supreme Court held that under the form of union security permitted by §8(a)(3) of the Act, an employee's obligation is "expressly limited to the payment of initiation fees and monthly dues. . . . 'Membership' as a condition of employment is whittled down to its financial core." *Id.* at 742.

[139] 148 NLRB 679 (1964).

[140] 391 US 418, 68 LRRM 2257 (1968).

[141] *Id.* at 425.

importance of removing union barriers to access to the Board by its members.

Given a public policy against enforcing union barriers to access to the Board by individual members, there are problems in explaining the Board's decision in *Tawas Tube Products, Inc.*[142] that a union's expulsion of two members for filing a decertification petition was protected by the proviso to Section 8(b)(1)(A). The Board justified its decision on these grounds: (1) no employment interests were involved, that is, the expulsions did not result in the loss of jobs; (2) the reason for the expulsions was clearly related to a matter of legitimate concern ("even a narrow reading of the proviso would necessarily allow a union to expel members who attack the very existence of a union as an institution"[143]); and (3) it would be difficult for the union to carry on an election campaign if two such hostile members were allowed to exercise all of the rights now guaranteed by Section 101(a)(1) of the LMRDA.[144]

The first and third grounds relied upon by the Board are unpersuasive. In neither *Marine & Shipbuilding Workers* (expulsion) nor in *Skura* (fine) did the union member lose his job. And in *Skura* the disciplined member would, if he paid his fine, be entitled to all the privileges of membership protected by Section 101(a)(1) of the LMRDA. The Board was on sounder ground, however, in pointing out that in *Tawas* union members "resorted to the Board for the purpose of attacking the very existence of their union rather than as an effort to compel it to abide by the Act."[145] Nevertheless, the result of *Tawas* seems to be that only a nonunion member of a bargaining unit is free to file a decertification petition under Section 9(c)(A)(ii) of the Act[146] without incurring the risk of lawful union discipline ranging from a fine to expulsion.

---

[142] 151 NLRB 46, 58 LRRM 1330 (1965).

[143] *Id.* at 47–48.

[144] Sec. 101(a)(1), 29 USC §411(a)(1), provides: "every member of a labor organization shall have equal rights and privileges within such organization to nominate candidates, to vote in elections or referendums . . ., to attend membership meetings, and to participate in the deliberations and voting upon the business of such meetings, subject to reasonable rules and regulations in such organization's constitution and bylaws."

[145] *Supra* note 142, at 48.

[146] Sec. 9(c)(1)(A)(ii), 29 USC §159(c)(1), provides in part: "Whenever a petition shall have been filed . . . (A) by *an employee or group of employees* or any individual or labor organization acting in their behalf alleging that a substantial number of employees . . . (ii) assert that the individual labor organization, which has been certified or is being currently recognized by their employer as the bargaining representative, is no longer a representative as defined in section 9(a) . . . the Board shall investigate. . . . If the Board finds . . . that . . . a question of representation exists, it shall direct an election by secret ballot and shall certify the results thereof." (Emphasis added)

Perhaps the least controversial of the Supreme Court's decisions in this area was that in *Scofield* v. *NLRB*,[147] holding that a union could lawfully fine and suspend members for violating a rule limiting the amount of production for which they could be paid on a given day. The purpose of the rule was to protect piecework rates from undercutting by "rate-busters," who, by exceeding the daily limit, created pressures on the employer to lower the piecework rates. Noting that the employer had signed contracts recognizing the union-imposed ceiling and had cooperated in the administration of the plan by banking each employee's earnings in excess of the daily limit and paying them out on days when they fell below the allowable daily maximum, the Court declared that Section 8(b)(1) "leaves a union free to enforce a properly adopted rule which reflects a legitimate union interest, impairs no policy Congress has imbedded in the labor laws, and is reasonably enforced against union members *who are free to leave the union and escape the rule.*"[148] The central importance of the underscored phrase in the preceding quotation became more apparent in *NLRB* v. *Granite State Joint Board, Textile Workers Union*,[149] which involved union attempts to fine ex-members who had resigned during a lawful strike and then had crossed a union picket line to return to work. Significantly, there was no restriction on the right to resign in the union's constitution or bylaws. The Supreme Court was careful not to decide to what extent "the contractual relationship" between union and member may curtail the freedom to resign; it limited its holdings to the proposition that when there are no restraints on the resignation of members, "the vitality of §7 requires that the member be free to refrain in November from the actions he endorsed in May and that his §7 rights are not lost by a union's plea for solidarity or by its pressures for conformity and submission to its regime."[150]

Justice Blackmun, in dissent, questioned the refusal of the majority to find any limitation on a member's right to resign. In his view it seemed likely that the three factors of a member's strike vote, his ratification of strikebreaking penalties, and his

---

[147] 394 US 423, 70 LRRM 3105 (1969).

[148] *Id.* at 493 (emphasis supplied).

[149] 409 US 213, 81 LRRM 2853 (1972).

[150] *Id.* at 217–18.

actual participation in the strike, would be far more reliable indicia of his obligation to the union and its members than the presence of boilerplate provisions in a union's constitution.[151]

The Supreme Court, in a *per curiam* opinion, decided in *Machinists Booster Lodge 405* v. *NLRB*[152] that the union's fining of members who had gone back to work during a strike and who had resigned either before or after returning to work, constituted a violation of Section 8(b)(1)(A) of the Act. The union's constitution and bylaws contained no provisions either permitting or prohibiting resignations during a strike, but the constitution did impose on members an obligation to refrain from strikebreaking, a fact that the union argued should distinguish this case from *Granite State*. The Court rejected this argument, however, pointing out that nothing in the record indicated "that Union members were informed prior to the bringing of the charges that were the basis of the actions, that the provision [against strikebreaking] was interpreted as imposing any obligation on a resignee."[153]

Justice Blackmun, the sole dissenter in *Granite State*, explained his vote with the majority in *Booster Lodge* on the ground that in the latter case none of the employees who resigned from the union had been given notices of a strikebreaking penalty before the strike vote or before their participation in the strike, nor was the imposition of a penalty ever formally ratified by the union membership. "Without effective notice of obligations that are supposed to be assumed," he concluded, "there can be no waiver of a member's §7 right to refrain from participation in a legal strike."[154]

After *Booster Lodge,* the only question remaining in respect of a union member's right to resign was the effect, if any, of a union rule or constitutional provision preventing members from resigning in specific circumstances or at specified times. The debate over this issue has been hot and prolonged, and has centered on conflicting interpretations of the Supreme Court's decisions in *Allis-Chalmers, Scofield, Granite State,* and *Booster Lodge.*

---

[151] *Id.* at 220.
[152] 412 US 84, 83 LRRM 2189 (1973).
[153] *Id.* at 89.
[154] *Id.* at 91.

Following the Supreme Court's decision in *Booster Lodge*, the union had adopted, in 1974, a constitutional provision declaring that resignation would not relieve a member of his obligation to refrain from accepting employment at a struck establishment for the duration of a strike or lockout or within 14 days preceding its commencement, or of his obligation to observe a primary picket line for its duration if the resignation occurred during the period the picket line was maintained or within 14 days preceding its establishment. In *Machinists Local 1327 (Dalmo Victor)*[155] (*Dalmo Victor I*) the Board, by a vote of three to two, held it to be a violation of Section 8(b)(1)(A) of the Act for the union to fine former members who had resigned and then gone back to work for an employer being struck by the union. In the view of the majority, the language of the constitutional provision "places no clear restriction, no subtle restriction, no restriction by implication, and in sum, no restriction whatsoever upon an employee's right to resign";[156] its application was therefore an unfair labor practice under the policy laid down by the Supreme Court in *Scofield* and *Granite State*. Conceding that unions have legitimate interests in restricting resignation or post-resignation activity, the majority insisted, nevertheless, that those interests are not absolute, and that the real issue is whether union attempts to protect those interests impermissibly intrude on other matters of concern under the national labor policy.

The Ninth Circuit refused to enforce the Board's order and remanded the case. By a divided vote, the court rejected the Board's reading of the union's constitution as "hyper-technical." In the court's view the provision plainly imposed a restriction on the members' right to resign, and thus squarely placed in issue the question specifically reserved by the Supreme Court in *Booster Lodge*. The court accepted the union's argument that when a strike is in progress or in immediate prospect, a member who resigns should not thereby be relieved of his obligation not to act as a strikebreaker. Accordingly, the court concluded that the union's constitutional amendment in this case was valid.

Upon reconsideration on remand, the Board revised its decision (*Dalmo Victor II*), which was split three ways.[157] Members

---

[155] 231 NLRB 719, 96 LRRM 1160 (1977), *enf. denied and remanded*, 609 F2d 1219, 102 LRRM 2583 (CA 9, 1979).

[156] *Id.* at 720.

[157] Machinists Local 1327 (Dalmo Victor), 263 NLRB 984, 111 LRRM 1115 (1982), *enf. denied*, 725 F2d 1212, 115 LRRM 2972 (CA 9, 1984), *cert. granted, vacated and remanded* for further consideration in light of Pattern Makers League v. NLRB (Rockford-Beloit Pattern Jobbers), 473 US___, 119 LRRM 2992 (1985).

Fanning and Zimmerman concluded that a union rule limiting the members' right to resign only to nonstrike periods constitutes unreasonable restriction on members' Section 7 rights in violation of Section 8(b)(1)(A) of the Act, but they also held that the right of union members to resign is not absolute, and that a union may place "some reasonable limitation on the right to resign so long as such rules are applicable during both strike and nonstrike periods."[158] They therefore proposed as "a reasonable accommodation between the right of union members to resign . . . and return to work, and the union's responsibility to protect the interests of employees who maintain their membership, as well as its need to dispose of administrative matters arising from such resignations,"[159] a rule that restricts a union member's right to resign for a period not to exceed 30 days after the tender of resignation. Member Jenkins dissented, insisting that the union's rule was a reasonable restriction on the right to resign.

Chairman Van de Water and Member Hunter, while concurring in the conclusion reached by Fanning and Zimmerman, rejected any restriction on an employee's right to resign from a union. They condemned the proposed 30-day restriction as a sham, representing "nothing more than arbitrary compromise over how far a union can unilaterally abrogate individual statutory rights and the congressional scheme of labor relations."[160]

Once again the Ninth Circuit refused to enforce the Board's order. In the court's opinion, the union's rule disapproved by the Board met the three tests laid down by the Supreme Court in *Scofield*.[161] It declared:

> Because *both* the employee's right and the union's interest are policies that have been "embedded" in the labor laws for over 35 years, neither can "impair" or "override" the other within the meaning of *Scofield*. They must—and do—coexist.[162]

The court also rejected the Board's so-called "30-day rule," saying that it "frustrates federal labor policy in important respects,"[163] and concluded not only that the union rule was

---

158 *Id.*, 263 NRLB at 986–87.
159 *Id.* at 987.
160 *Id.* at 992.
161 *See* text at note 148 *supra*.
162 725 F2d at 1217 (emphasis in original).
163 *Id.* at 1215.

valid but also that collecting fines from those members who broke it was a reasonable, and indeed the only practicable, way to enforce it.

Meanwhile, in reliance on *Dalmo Victor I,* the Board, in *Pattern Makers (Rockford-Beloit Pattern Jobbers Association),*[164] again by a divided vote, had held that the union's League Law 13, which provided that "no resignation or withdrawal from an Association [local] or from the League, shall be accepted during a strike or lockout, or at a time when a strike or lockout appears imminent," violated Section 8(b)(1)(A) of the Act. The issue in that case arose when the union fined ex-members who had tendered resignations and returned to work during the course of a strike. And despite the second rebuff from the Ninth Circuit, the Board, in *Machinists Lodge 1414 (Neufeld Porsche-Audi, Inc.),*[165] adopted an even more uncompromising interpretation of Section 8(b)(1)(A) than it had in *Dalmo Victor II.* Indeed, by a vote of three to one, it expressly overruled *Dalmo Victor II* and adopted the position taken by Van de Water and Hunter in that case that *any* restriction on the right to resign violates the Act.

To resolve the conflict between the Ninth and Seventh circuits, the Supreme Court granted *certiorari* in *Pattern Makers* and affirmed the decision of the Seventh Circuit enforcing the Board's order.[166] The decision produced four opinions. Justice Powell, writing for the four-member plurality, basically relied on the Board's expertise, and agreed that League Law 13 was not covered by the proviso to Section 8(b)(1)(A) of the Act, which was intended to protect only union rules involving admission and expulsion. He also accepted the Board's conclusion that the union rule, by restricting the right of "employees" to resign,[167] impaired the congressional policy of voluntary unionism implicit in Section 8(a)(3) of the Act.

Justice White, concurring in the result, was of the opinion that the Board's reading of Section 7 and 8(b)(1)(A) was a permissible construction of the Act, but not the only possible one. He deferred to the Board's expertise, stating, however, that if that agency

---

[164] 265 NLRB 1332, 112 LRRM 1030 (1982), *enforced,* 724 F2d 57, 115 LRRM 2264 (CA 7, 1983).

[165] 270 NLRB 1330, 116 LRRM 1257 (1984).

[166] Pattern Makers League v. NLRB (Rockford-Beloit Pattern Jobbers), *supra* note 157.

[167] This was obviously an error; the union's rule purported to be binding only on voluntary members.

had reached the opposite conclusion, he would similarly have supported its construction of the Act.

In an unusually sharp dissent Justice Blackmun, speaking for Justices Brennan and Marshall as well, accused the Court of "supinely" deferring to the Board.[168] In brief, he drew a distinction between two kinds of union rules: those representing "obligations voluntarily incurred by members [which] were intended to be free from federal regulation under §8," and those seeking "to coerce an employee by utilizing the employer's power over his employment status, or . . . relationship between the union and his employer."[169] He argued that because League Law 13 fell in the former category, it did not violate the Act. Blackmun stressed that no employee was obliged to join the union; that those who did so voluntarily promised their co-workers, as a *quid pro quo* for the benefits they received as union members, not to resign during a strike; and that those who broke that promise suffered no loss of employment as a result. He also relied in part on the legislative history of the Taft-Hartley Act, pointing out that a provision in the House bill that would have made it a union unfair labor practice "to deny any member the right to resign from the organization at any time" was rejected by the Senate.[170]

Justice Stevens, in a brief dissent, relied principally on the legislative history of the LMRA related by Blackmun, "coupled with the plain language in the proviso to §8(b)(1)(A) . . . ."[171]

It is ironic that the Supreme Court's decision in *Pattern Makers* did not purport to overrule *Allis-Chalmers;* so long as employees do not resign their union membership, they may be fined for returning to work during a strike. But the Board's crabbed construction of the Section 8(b)(1)(A) proviso approved by the Court undermines that decision, as well as the right to strike effectively, thus substantially diminishing the right to engage in concerted activity heretofore protected by Sections 7 and 13[172] of the Act. I have noted on previous occasions[173] that the Court

---

[168] 119 LRRM at 2938.

[169] *Id.* at 2939.

[170] §8(c)(4), H.R. REP. NO. 3020, 80th Cong., 1st Sess. (1947); S. REP. NO. 105, 80th Cong., 1st Sess. 2 (1947).

[171] *Supra* note 157, 119 LRRM at 2944.

[172] §13, 29 USC §163, provides: "Nothing in this Act, except as specifically provided for herein, shall be construed so as either to interfere with or impede or diminish in any way the right to strike, or to affect the limitations or qualifications of that right."

[173] *See, e.g.,* Aaron, *The Supreme Court 1982–1983 Term,* LABOR LAW DEVELOPMENTS 1984 (30th Annual Institute on Labor Law, Southwestern Legal Foundation) 73–74, n.208 (1984).

is insufficiently conversant with how collective bargaining actually works, and Justice Powell's opinion in *Pattern Makers* is yet
another example of that unfortunate fact. Thus, in a footnote he
states: "The Board does not believe, and neither do we, that it's
interpretation of §8(b)(1)(A) impedes the right to strike."[174] The
Board surely knows better, and the Court should know better.
So long as individual union members, who voluntarily accepted
membership with the knowledge that they thereby assumed an
obligation to their fellow members and to their union not to
return to work for the duration of a valid strike, are free to
violate that commitment, the right of unions to strike effectively
is seriously undermined. The obviousness of that conclusion
may not be apparent to the Court, but it will not be overlooked by
selfish or timid workers, and especially not by employers.

IV. Concluding Observations

Scholars of widely differing persuasions[175] are in general
agreement that the Wagner Act was designed to replace the
increasing disruption of interstate commerce caused by labor
disputes with a regime of industrial peace. Congress concluded
that this could be established only by instituting a system of
collective bargaining, whereby the concerted power of workers,
represented exclusively by one freely chosen union in each
appropriate bargaining unit, could approximately balance the
power of the employer. It was also anticipated that the combined
strength of the collectivity of workers would result in improved
wages, hours, and working conditions, and increased purchasing power, which would speed the return to a prosperous economy. The keystone of the entire system was the right of workers,
guaranteed by Section 7 of the Act, to organize and to bargain
collectively through representatives of their own choosing, and
to engage in concerted activities.

At least one of these objectives was never attained: collective
bargaining did not pull the country out of the depression; it took
World War II to do that. Industrial peace was also slow in
coming, largely because of the all-out resistance by employers

---

[174] *Supra* note 157, 119 LRRM at 2934, n.18.

[175] *See, e.g.,* Klare, *supra* note 79, at 281–84; A. Cox, LAW AND THE NATIONAL LABOR
POLICY 8–12 (1960); G. Taylor, GOVERNMENT REGULATION OF INDUSTRIAL RELATIONS
3–7 (1948).

against the basic principles of the Act. Nevertheless, a system of collective bargaining was established, and the general lot of organized workers was greatly improved as a consequence.

Establishing the right of workers freely to choose their own representatives was a historic change of immense significance. As Cox has pointed out, this principle was "antithetical to the Holmesian philosophy of competition"[176] and to the old AFL practice of "top-down" organizing, based upon the theory of union jurisdiction as property.[177] Once the right of free choice had been exercised, however, the emphasis switched to the rights of the collectivity, as compared with those of the individual. This did not necessarily mean, as Klare has contended, that "since union activity was denominated as something separate from members' self-activity in the workplace, unions could not function as participatory institutions in which workers continuously articulated and redefined their aspirations for the governance and transformation of the work-process."[178] The unions' need to establish and maintain an institutional life of their own, apart from the individual objectives of their members, did not prevent them from functioning as "participatory institutions"; but the system of exclusive representation and majority rule did permit them to present a united front against the resistance of the employers.

It is true that despite the proviso to Section 9(a) of the Wagner Act and the second proviso added by Taft-Hartley, unions remained in control of the grievance procedure, and in many instances they ignored or deliberately frustrated legitimate claims of right of individual bargaining-unit members. Such misuses of power have been substantially, but probably not sufficiently, restrained by the expanding doctrine of the unions' DFR. I believe, however, that far greater damage to the entire system of collective bargaining would have resulted if individual bargaining-unit members had been allowed to present and adjust their grievances up to and including arbitration without

---

[176] Cox, *supra* note 175, at 10–11.

[177] This theory was succinctly stated in Barnett, *The Causes of Jurisdictional Disputes in American Trade Unions*, 9 HARV. BUS. REV. 400, 401 (1935), as follows: "Complete sovereignty resides in the national union. Every local union in the particular trade or group of trades represented by the national union must belong to the national union or it is an outlaw (dual) organization. Only one national union in the territory covered . . . can be a legitimate union. Any rival local, sectional or national union is an outlaw (dual) union. . . ."

[178] *Supra* note 79, at 321.

regard to an exclusive bargaining representative's construction of the collective agreement, or had been permitted to authorize a rival, minority union to represent them in such proceedings.

As I have previously stated, the Taft-Hartley amendments to the NLRA placed additional emphasis on the rights of individual employees. The primary congressional purpose, however, was to protect them from perceived abuses by unions rather than from those by employers; for the only important new right given directly to individual employees was to refrain from collective bargaining activities. I think Schatzki exaggerates when he declares that "employees are the primary victims in an effort to keep employers strong vis à vis unions, and . . . are similarly victimized to keep unions strong vis à vis employers,"[179] although there is some truth in the statement. Perhaps the strongest support for the first part of the quoted passage, as Klare has so well demonstrated,[180] is the Supreme Court's determination in *NLRB* v. *Mackay Radio & Telegraph Co.*[181] that a struck employer has the right to offer permanent positions to strikebreakers so long as the strike was not provoked or prolonged by the employer's unfair labor practice. I disagree, however, with Schatzki's characterization of *Emporium Capwell* as an example of the "very narrow scope [given by the Supreme Court] to section 7's promise of protection to employees in their concerted activities for better working conditions,"[182] presumably "to keep unions strong vis à vis employers." That case, which I believe to have been rightly decided, did reconfirm the union's exclusive authority to process grievances beyond their initial presentation; but it did not, in my view, "victimize" the grievants. Indeed, if a union is not permitted to insist that bargaining-unit members follow orderly grievance procedures in a collective agreement, at least so long as the union observes its DFR, its status as the exclusive bargaining representative will be undermined.

I disagree even more strongly with Schatzki's assertions that, even in the absence of a union security agreement, "employees are coerced (induced?) into joining their exclusive representative because, once having the union imposed upon them, they

---

[179] *Supra* note 84, at 901.
[180] *Supra* note 79, at 301–303.
[181] 304 US 333, 2 LRRM 610 (1938).
[182] Schatzki, *supra* note 84, at 900.

might as well join and have some voice in selecting their spokesmen and in determining what policies the union should follow,"[183] and that the Supreme Court's decision allowing a union to fine its members for crossing a picket line during a strike, contrary to union rules, is "another example of vindicating the institution of exclusive representation at the expense of individual employee interests."[184] The notion that employees are joining unions against their wishes is belied by the steadily declining union membership in the private sector. Moreover, I think that the principle of majority rule necessarily and properly leads to the vindication of exclusive representation at the expense of some individual interests.

Although I strongly advocate a liberal interpretation of rights granted to union members by the LMRDA, when it comes to pursuing bargaining objectives and administering collective agreements, I think that, subject to principles of due process and fair representation, the claims of individuals must be subordinate to those of the group. Although we all know of some instances in which a tyranny of a union has proved to be as bad or worse than that of an employer, I still believe that the more enduring danger to individual employee rights lies in Board and court decisions in cases like *Pattern Makers* that seriously undermine a union's ability to maintain a united front against an employer during an industrial dispute.

Responses

ON MISREADING THE ACT

KATHY L. KRIEGER*

I agree with Professor Aaron's conclusion that the NLRB and the federal courts have applied the NLRA inconsistently with respect to individual workers. On the one hand, the Board vigorously defends the rights of individual employees against perceived infringement by labor organizations. On the other hand, the Board displays little concern for shielding individual employees from coercion and retaliation by their employers.

---

[183] *Id.* at 914.
[184] *Id.* at 915.

*Associate General Counsel, United Brotherhood of Carpenter's, AFL-CIO.

This superficial inconsistency masks a simple and consistent purpose that becomes apparent when one focuses on collective action rather than on individual rights. That is, in each case the government seeks the result that will hinder if not preclude altogether the collective empowerment of workers that the NLRA encourages as a matter of national labor policy. Today the NLRB construes the Act to ensure that workplace activism does not spread among unorganized employees by denying protection to individuals who protest working conditions and assert employment rights. Where employees have succeeded in organizing, the Board, with court approval, undermines their chosen unions by giving paramount status to individual interests. Thus the current statutory regime deters workers from acting individually to better their condition, and makes the alternative—collective action—as ineffectual as possible. The intended result of these policies is to strengthen employers' control over a more docile and powerless work force.

Granting all of the above, one might ask what is gained by highlighting the problem in this volume. If deficiencies in our labor relations statute itself dictate such outcomes, then detailing the Board's pro-business agenda and the hypocritical means by which the agency pursues it would not suffice to prove unprincipled adjudication. If we confirm that the fault lies not in the statute but in its administration by political appointees, what relief can we expect from a judiciary evolving in the same political direction? Though a number of well-reasoned critiques from the labor bar have shown the current NLRB to be the most antilabor and result-oriented to date, it is not apparent that anyone outside our community of advocates—with the exception of conscientious scholars—cares whether or not the NLRB reaches its results in a principled fashion. I suspect that our assessments may make a difference only to union members and other concerned workers who, like the employees of whom Senator Wagner spoke 50 years ago, placed their trust in the federal government and now recognize their betrayal.

With those reservations, I will comment on selected decisions, four in particular, that deliberately misread the NLRA so as to prevent employees from attaining power over their working conditions. Although the NLRA, as amended, provides the weakest imaginable system for advancement of employee interests, it does not in my view require the extreme results embodied in recent decisions addressing individual rights. Considering the

Board's and the Supreme Court's elevation of individual over collective interests in *Machinists Local 1414 (Neufeld Porsche-Audi, Inc.)*[1] and *Pattern Makers League* v. *NLRB (Rockford-Beloit Pattern Jobbers)*,[2] I conclude that neither the statutory language, the legislative history, nor the relevant Court precedent justifies the condemnation of union restrictions on resignations of members. Turning to the NLRB policy set forth in *Meyers Industries*[3] and *Sears, Roebuck & Co.*,[4] I conclude that the Board strains both the statute and legislative history in ruling that the Act denies protection to individuals against employer retaliation in connection with work-related grievances. By way of background, this paper first summarizes some of the relevant legislative history and viewpoints concerning protection of individual employees. In the discussion of key cases I attempt to identify some of their consequences for, and unarticulated attitudes toward, the collective power of workers.

I. The Wagner Act

Section 7 of the Wagner Act afforded employees the right "to self-organization, to form, join or assist labor organizations, to bargain collectively through representatives of their own choosing, and to engage in concerted activities for the purpose of collective bargaining or other mutual aid or protection." Those were, of course, individual rights in the sense that the statute guaranteed them to each individual employee. The conduct apparently contemplated by Section 7, however, was collective in nature. The express terms of the statute made "concert" of action, in some form, an essential element. The legislative history demonstrates the vision of worker dignity and empowerment through collective action that formed the original National Labor Relations Act.

The legislative proposals that led to the Wagner Act were based on the premise that "cooperation between employer and employee, on the basis of equal bargaining power," was essential for the economic well-being of the country.[5] Congress had

---

[1] 270 NLRB 1330, 116 LRRM 1257 (1984).

[2] 473 US ___, 119 LRRM 2928 (1985).

[3] 268 NLRB 493, 115 LRRM 1025 (1984), *remanded sub. nom.* Prill v. NLRB, 755 F2d 941, 118 LRRM 2649 (CA DC, 1985).

[4] 274 NLRB No. 55, 118 LRRM 1329 (1985).

[5] 78 Cong. Rec. 3525–26 (1934).

already concluded that employees could achieve such equality of power only by uniting for collective bargaining purposes. Thus the Norris-LaGuardia Act declared, as a matter of national policy, that since "the individual unorganized worker is commonly helpless to exercise actual liberty of contract and to protect his freedom of labor . . . it is necessary that he have full freedom of association, self-organization, and designation of representatives of his own choosing."[6] Consistent with this principle, the futility of individual action was repeatedly cited in the hearings, statements, and reports underlying the Wagner Act.[7] As Senator Wagner stated, in a public address explaining his proposed labor bill

> it was perfectly obvious to every observer of modern large-scale enterprise that it would be impossible for employees individually to deal directly with their employers. One cannot imagine an isolated worker cooperating with the United States Steel Co. . . . Cooperation depends upon the free and untrammeled right of workers to organize for that purpose.[8]

In the decision upholding the constitutionality of the Act, *NLRB v. Jones & Laughlin Steel Corp.*,[9] the Supreme Court reiterated that "a single employee was helpless in dealing with an employer; . . . [a] union was essential to give laborers opportunity to deal on an equality with their employer."[10]

The legislative history reflects not only the assumption that workers as individuals lacked the power to deal effectively with their employers, but also the view that excessive individualism posed a significant detriment to society. Senator Wagner, for example, attributed the nation's continued economic crisis in part to employers pursuing "a blind and unchecked form of individualism, with each enterprise working at cross purposes, and with many of them cutting prices, slashing wages, and indulging in other unfair methods of competition."[11] He fur-

---

6 29 USC §102.

7 S. REP. No. 573, 74th Cong., 1st Sess. 3 (1935) ("The relative weakness of the isolated wage earner caught in the complex of modern industrialism has become such a commonplace of our economic literature and political vocabulary that it needs no exposition.") See also 70 CONG. REC. 2332 (1926) ("His helplessness as an individual in bargaining with his employer is recognized."); 78 CONG. REC. 3443 (1934) ("Genuine collective bargaining is the only way to attain equality of bargaining power.").

8 79 CONG. REC. 6184 (1935).

9 301 US 1, 1 LRRM 703 (1937).

10 *Id.* at 33.

11 79 CONG. REC. 6183 (1935).

ther asserted that individual employees, subjugated by employers and "without any unifying influences to direct their efforts, were demoralizing standards by assenting to sweatshop conditions, thus knocking the props of purchasing power from beneath the structure of business."[12] The predecessor National Industrial Recovery Act was enacted, Wagner explained, because the nation "came to the sound conclusion that everyone would profit by subordinating narrow and selfishly conceived interests to a nation-wide plan for general revival."[13]

Moreover, Wagner cited undue deference to individualism as one of the defects in the NIRA. In particular, he noted that the guarantee that "employees shall be free to choose their own representatives" had been interpreted to mean that "any employee at any time may choose his own representative or may elect to deal individually" with his employer:

> Such an interpretation, which illegalizes the closed shop, strikes a death blow at the practice and theory of collective bargaining. . . . It allows the unscrupulous employer to divide the workers against themselves. No real advocate of collective bargaining would argue that a worker should be free to bargain individually even after the overwhelming majority of his co-workers desire an agreement covering all.[14]

An additional problem, the proliferation of employer-dominated "employee representation committees" and "company unions" under the NIRA, was deplored not primarily because of its repressive effect on individual workers, but rather because such "masquerade" organizations precluded the rank and file's free choice of stronger, more comprehensive forms of collective representation. As Wagner explained, company unions made employee power a "sham" by narrowly "restricting employee cooperation to a single employer unit at a time when business men are allowed to band together in large groups, and by cutting off employees' access to outside "experts" in collective bargaining and representation.[15]

Against this background, the conferral of rights on employees as individuals did not become an important objective of the proposed labor legislation. Although questions of individual or

---

[12] *Id.*
[13] *Id.*
[14] 78 CONG. REC. 3443 (1934).
[15] *Id.*

minority rights arose in connection with matters such as the closed shop and the majority rule principle of representation, the legislators found substantial accommodation to individual interests unnecessary. Responding to such concerns, the Senate Report on the Wagner bill stated that "since the bill specifically prevents discrimination against anyone either for belonging or for not belonging to a union, the representatives selected by the majority will be quite powerless to make agreements more favorable to the majority than to the minority" in the absence of a closed-shop clause.[16] The closed shop was characterized as a benign, historically common industry practice resulting from voluntary agreement between labor and management. Congress thus adopted a neutral approach that essentially maintained the status quo, leaving the states free to continue regulating in that area.[17] As for exclusivity of bargaining rights, Wagner Act proponents emphasized the essentially democratic character of majority rule, together with the "grievance proviso" to Section 9 that preserved "the right of minorities or individuals to confer and discuss grievances with their employer" even after the majority has "acted in accordance with democratic procedure."[18]

Some commentators did urge Congress to provide greater affirmative protection to individual workers. For example, Professor Harold Shapiro, of New York Law School, declared his sympathy for "the individual member of a Local Union, whose silence has been due to an economic helplessness arising from fear that he may offend the officers of his union." Shapiro proposed that the Wagner bill include provisions requiring bonding of union officers, maintenance of proper financial accounts and records, periodic audits and annual elections of officers by secret ballot, as well as prohibitions on excessive union dues and inequitable admission restrictions whenever a closed shop is permitted.[19] The proposed regulation of internal union affairs, however, gained few adherents. A second approach to individual rights, in the form of proposed prohibitions on interference with and coercion of employees by fellow employees and unions, received greater attention. But Congress

---

[16] S. Rep. No. 573, 79th Cong., 1st Sess. 13 (1935).

[17] Id. at 11–12.

[18] 79 Cong. Rec. 6184 (1935); supra note 16, at 13–14.

[19] 2 Legislative History of the National Labor Relations Act, 1935 [hereinafter Leg. Hist. NLRA], at 2085–86 (1949).

rejected such measures, concluding that protecting individual employees from "interference" by fellow workers in organizing campaigns would defeat the purpose of the bill, usurp state and local police powers, and overwhelm the NLRB with "counter-charges and recriminations" that would frustrate the representation process.[20]

Even the rhetoric of individual rights took on a collective emphasis, as proponents of the Wagner Act repeatedly invoked the principles of democracy and civil liberties to support the right to organize collectively. In arguing for the Act, for example, Representative Mead asserted that it "creates a democracy within industry which gives our industrial workers the same general idea of freedom which the founding fathers conferred upon citizens of the United States."[21] Testifying in favor of the bill, Robert Hale, Professor of Law at Columbia University, employed a pragmatic notion of liberty to dismiss the argument that the closed shop "destroys the freedom of the worker to be 'independent'" from a union if he so desires:

> Well, to a certain extent, of course it does, but in a complicated modern society like ours, nobody is going to be entirely free. If a man wants to work in a steel plant, he does not just go out and work according to his own ideas about how it should be worked. . . . Normally, in the case of a steel plant, he becomes an employee of a Steel Company, and then he has no freedom as to the details of his work whatsoever; he is a non-voting member of a society. If he joins a closed-shop union, he has a little more freedom through the brotherhood of his union against the restraint imposed upon him by the employer. . . .[22]

Wagner similarly translated the language of abstract freedom and liberty into arguments for organizing and collective bargaining:

> [T]he national labor relations bill does not break with our traditions. It is the next step in the logical unfolding of man's eternal quest for freedom. . . . Today, with economic problems occupying the center of the stage, we strive to liberate the common man from destitution, from insecurity, and from human exploitation.
>
> . . . [T]he isolated worker is a plaything of fate. Caught in the labyrinth of modern industrialism and dwarfed by the size of corpo-

---

20 *Supra* note 16, at 16–17; H.R. Rep. No. 1147, 74th Cong., 2nd Sess. 16–18 (1935).
21 Leg. Hist. NLRA at 3180–81 (1949).
22 Leg. Hist. NLRA at 81.

rate enterprise, he can attain freedom and dignity only by cooperation with others of his group.[23]

Reviewing the Wagner Act a decade later, a former aide to
Senator Wagner identified collective action as a means of achieving true individual liberty:

> In a free society it is not enough that there is a large freedom of
> group action. In a free society, each individual must also feel free. So
> many have given eloquent expression to the connection between the
> individual worker's sense of freedom and his opportunity to affiliate
> with others. . . .[24]

Wagner himself, in a 1937 article, portrayed the collective right
of workers to organize as the linchpin of political democracy:

> Let men become the pawns of their masters in the factories of the
> land and there will be destroyed the bone and sinew of resistance to
> political dictatorship. . . . But let men know the dignity of freedom
> and self-expression in their daily lives, and they will never bow to
> tyranny in any quarter of their national life.[25]

II. The Taft-Hartley Amendments

Twelve years after the Wagner Act's passage, the rhetoric of
individual liberty provided the rallying cry for the legislative
attacks on trade unionism that culminated in the Taft-Hartley
amendments. In speech after speech, the oppression of the
individual employee by his peers supplanted the coercive power
of monopoly capital over the lone worker as the principal threat
to the public welfare. In reporting Congressman Hartley's bill to
the House, the Committee on Education and Labor presented a
stinging indictment of collective action, using the very terms that
once described the workers' need to organize:

> For the last 14 years, as a result of labor laws ill-conceived and
> disastrously executed, the American workingman has been
> deprived of his dignity as an individual. . . . His whole economic life
> has been subject to the complete domination and control of unregu-
> lated monopolists. . . . He has been denied any voice in arranging
> the terms of his own employment. . . . In short, his mind, his soul,

---

[23] 79 CONG. REC. 7565 (1935).
[24] Keyserling, THE WAGNER ACT: AFTER TEN YEARS 13 (L. Silverberg ed., 1945).
[25] *Id.* at 23.

and his very life have been subject to a tyranny more despotic than one could think possible in a free country.[26]

Hartley intended through his legislation to provide a comprehensive "bill of rights" for individual employees, prescribing their entitlements as members of a union and proscribing numerous forms of "interference" and coercion by fellow workers as well as unions.[27] Among the provisions of his bill were severe restrictions on the grounds of as well as the manner of union discipline and membership decisions; detailed regulation of union operations and finances; and an unqualified ban on "[denying] to any member the right to resign from the organization at any time," set forth as Section 8(c)(4). The bill further added to Section 7 of the Wagner Act the right "to refrain from any or all" of the activities affirmatively protected therein.[28]

Taft's bill, in contrast, contained no new provisions expressly prescribing members' rights within their union, no prohibition on restraint or coercion of employees by a union or other employees, and no guarantee in Section 7 of the right to refrain from concerted activity.[29] The Senate Committee bill, instead, sought to accommodate individual rights by modifying and strengthening existing limitations on collective action. "In the interests of assuring complete freedom of choice to employees who do not wish to be represented collectively," the bill "reformed" the NLRA's representation provisions to permit challenges to a union's status as bargaining agent and give differences among employees greater significance in unit determinations.[30] Additionally, the bill outlawed the closed shop and gave employees the collective power to authorize or preclude negotiation of union-shop provisions.[31] And the bill indirectly affected unions' dealings with members and individual employees by forestalling enforcement of union-shop clauses against individuals disciplined or denied membership for reasons other than financial delinquency or activity challenging the unions'

---

[26] H.R. REP. NO. 245, 80th Cong., 1st Sess. 4 (1947).

[27] H.R. 3020, §§7(b), 8(b), 8(c), reprinted in 1 LEGISLATIVE HISTORY OF THE LABOR-MANAGEMENT RELATIONS ACT, 1947 [hereinafter LEG. HIST. LMRA], at 31, 49–56 (1974); *supra* note 26, at 319–24; 93 CONG. REC. 2521 (1947).

[28] H.R. 3020, §7(a), LEG. HIST. LMRA at 49.

[29] S. 1126, LEG. HIST. LMRA at 99–157.

[30] S. REP. NO. 105, 80th Cong., 1st Sess. 3, 10–12 (1947).

[31] S. 1126, §8(a)(3), LEG. HIST. LMRA at 110–11; *supra* note 30, at 5–7.

status as majority representative.[32] Finally, Taft sought to assure individual workers an "independent" right to present grievances to their employer.[33] Compared with "such completely repressive measures as the Hartley bill," the Senate bill,[34] as reported, appeared in some respects a preemptive effort at moderation.[35]

Dissenting legislators denounced the proposed NLRA amendments as an ill-disguised attempt by the economic elite, "masquerading as protesters against monopoly," to repress workers and cripple trade unions, "the remaining barrier to concentration of industrial power."[36] The revisions to Section 7, together with the individual rights aspects of Sections 8(b) and 8(c), were characterized as a deliberate effort to destabilize labor relations, "to invite disruption of unions and render them powerless against the tactics of 'boring from within.' "[32] The hypocrisy underlying various "employee rights" measures provoked justifiable criticism in floor debate:

[I]t strikes me as a little inconsistent for many of our friends to be such champions of free enterprise in certain spheres, and to believe so strongly that the Government must protect people against one another in other spheres. When we talk about regulating business, those persons take the position that the Government must not interfere. . . . But those same staunch defenders of private enterprise, when it pertains to business in America and the way it works . . . become the champion of public intervention in the internal affairs of labor organizations.[38]

As it moved through the Senate, Taft's bill retained its relatively moderate character regarding individual rights. An attempt was made to proscribe in general terms the coercion of employees by unions, a provision that had earlier been rejected in committee. Senator Ball offered the provision as an amendment to Section 8(b)(1), adding "employees in the exercise of the rights guaranteed in Section 7," to the bill's existing prohibition on interference, restraint, or coercion of employers.[39]

---

[32] S. 1126, §§8(a)(3), 8(b)(2), LEG. HIST. LMRA at 110–12; *supra* note 30, at 5–7.

[33] S. 1126, §9(a), Leg. Hist. LMRA at 116–17; *supra* note 30, at 24.

[34] S. 1126.

[35] LEG. HIST. LMRA at 466.

[36] Senate Minority Rep. No. 105, PART 2, 80th Cong., 1st Sess. 4 (1947).

[37] House Minority Rep. No. 245 at 75–77, 80–81.

[38] Remarks of Sen. Pepper, LEG. HIST. LMRA at 1097.

[39] LEG. HIST. LMRA at 1018.

Responding to objections that the new provision would restrict legitimate organizing activity, however, the Senate deleted the term, "interfere" from Section 8(b)(1) before disposing of the amendment.[40] Additionally, the Senate adopted Senator Holland's amendment to the Ball amendment, adding the proviso to Section 8(b)(1)(A) stating that "this subsection shall not impair the right of a labor organization to prescribe its own rules with respect to the acquisition or retention of membership therein."[41] That proviso confirmed the Senators' understanding that Section 8(b)(1)(A) "would have no application to or effect upon the right of a labor organization to prescribe its own rules of membership either with respect to beginning or terminating membership."[42] As Senator Holland stated:

> I have had some discussion with the Senator from Minnesota [Mr. Ball] and the Senator from Ohio [Mr. Taft] and with other Senators in reference to the meaning of the pending amendment and as to how seriously, if at all, it would affect the internal administration of a labor union.
>
> Apparently it is not intended by the sponsors of the amendment to affect at least that part of the internal administration which has to do with the admission or expulsion of members, that is with the question of membership.[43]

Senator Ball confirmed with respect to the body of Section 8(b)(1) that "[i]t was never the intention of the sponsor of the pending amendment to interfere with the internal affairs or organization of unions."[44]

Congress ultimately rejected the regulation of internal union affairs and the individual rights measures originally sought by the House in Sections 7(b), 8(b), and 8(c). The House conferees agreed to eliminate all of the House bill's Section 8(c) except for the prohibition on excessive initiation fees, noting:

> The other parts of this subsection are omitted from the conference agreement as unfair labor practices, but Section 9(f)(6) of the con-

---

[40] LEG. HIST. LMRA at 1022–32, 1138–40.

[41] LEG. HIST. LMRA at 1139–43.

[42] LEG. HIST. LMRA at 1141.

[43] LEG. HIST. LMRA at 1139.

[44] LEG. HIST. LMRA at 1141. Sen. Ball subsequently reiterated that through his amendment as "modified" by Sen. Holland, "we are not trying to interfere with the internal affairs of a union which is already organized. All we are trying to cover is the coercive and restraining acts of the union in its efforts to organize unorganized employees. . . . The modification covers the requirements and standards of membership in the union itself." LEG. HIST. LMRA at 1200.

ference agreement requires labor organizations to make periodic reports with respect to many of these matters as a condition of certification and other benefits under the Act.[45]

Concurrently, Hartley's Section 7(b)—guaranteeing union members freedom from discriminatory financial demands, freedom from discipline for expression of any views, and the right to have union affairs conducted fairly and in accord with the majority's free will—was deleted in conference without comment in the Report.[46] Hartley's Section 7(a) "right to refrain" was retained in Section 7 of the conference bill.[47] But despite the final bill's inclusion of a purpose in Section 1(b) "to protect the rights of individual employees in their relations with labor organizations," Congress retained without qualification the Wagner Act's preeminent national policy of "encouraging the practice and procedure of collective bargaining" by protecting the exercise of workers' organizational rights.[48]

III. Advancement of Individual Interests to Diminish Employees' Organizational Strength

Despite the drastic revisions made to the NLRA in 1947, the Act as amended was not designed to regulate the internal affairs and operations of unions or to grant members statutory rights within their organizations. In *NLRB* v. *Allis-Chalmers*,[49] the Supreme Court reviewed the legislative history summarized above and confirmed that "the body of Section 8(b)(1)—that is, the prohibition on restraint or coercion—does not reach a union's discipline of its members for noncompliance with the union's legitimate internal rules."[50] The Court identified the proviso to Section 8(b)(1)(A) as an additional shield against intervention in the internal affairs of unions.[51]

---

[45] CONF. REP. No. 510, 80th Cong., 1st Sess. 46 (1947).

[46] H.R. REP. No. 510 at 38–40.

[47] *Id.* at 39–40.

[48] *Id.* at 1, 2–3.

[49] 388 US 175, 65 LRRM 2449 (1967).

[50] *Id.* at 184–90, 191–92. The Court relied not only on the statements directly explaining the Ball amendment, but also on assurances from the Senate Report and statements by Sen. Taft discussing §8(b)(2): "The pending measure does not propose any limitations with respect to the internal affairs of unions." LEG. HIST. LMRA at 1097. *See* S. REP. No. 105 at 20.

[51] *Supra* note 49, at 191–92.

Central to the *Allis-Chalmers* decision was the Court's recognition that the terms of Section 8(b)(1)(A) are not to be read in a literal manner that would undermine the "national labor policy" encouraging collective bargaining through organization and concerted action.[52] The Court repeatedly emphasized that subordination of individual employees to the lawful collective rule of their peers, acting as a labor organization and exclusive bargaining agent, inheres in the NLRA. As the Court explained in particular:

> Integral to this federal labor policy has been the power in the chosen union to protect against erosion of its status under the policy through reasonable discipline of members who violate rules and regulations governing membership. That power is particularly vital when the members engage in strikes. The economic strike against the employer is the ultimate weapon in labor's arsenal for achieving agreement upon its terms, and the power to fine or expel strikebreakers is essential if the union is to be an effective bargaining agent. . . .[53]

In *Machinists Local 1414*,[54] and *Pattern Makers League*,[55] the Board and Court have adopted the approach to Section 8(b)(1)(A) condemned in *Allis-Chalmers*. To divide workers and increase management's economic clout in labor disputes, these tribunals have ignored or misread legislative intent and have produced results that undermine fundamental policy embodied in the NLRA. These failings can be demonstrated most clearly by examining the Supreme Court decision in *Pattern Makers*.

The Court betrays its stance at the very outset of its substantive discussion of controlling principles in Part II-A of the decision. There the majority takes pains to emphasize that Section 8(b)(1)(A) presumptively condemns virtually all forms of control by a union over its membership: "Indeed, if the terms 'restrain or coerce' are interpreted literally, fining employees to enforce compliance with any union rule or policy would violate the Act."[56] Absent from this discussion is any hint that the Court in *Allis-Chalmers* had authoritatively rejected such literalism and

---

52 *Id.* at 179–81.
53 *Id.* at 181.
54 *Supra* note 1.
55 *Supra* note 2.
56 *Id.*, 119 LRRM at 2931.

had concluded that the legislative intent underlying Section 8(b)(1) required just the *opposite* presumption. And in reluctantly acknowledging that discipline of current members is lawful "[d]espite this language from the Act,"[57] the Court disregards the source of that conclusion in the Act's policy concerning collective activity. Instead, this preface to the Court's reasoning suggests that the Section 7 "right to refrain" is wholly isolated from an equally important policy encouraging concerted activity, and indeed enjoys a superior status under the Act.

At Part II-B, the Court acknowledges the *Allis-Chalmers* decision's interpretation of the terms "restrain or coerce," yet avoids the implications of that interpretation. In *Allis-Chalmers* the Court concluded that a union's use of the legal process to enforce a "contractual obligation voluntarily undertaken"—that is, the UAW members' agreement to participate in concerted activity—does not "restrain or coerce" within the meaning of Section 8(b)(1). The obligation not to withdraw from the union during a strike, accepted by individuals joining the Pattern Makers, is as much a voluntary contractual undertaking as the UAW member's agreement not to abandon a strike. The *Pattern Makers* Court, however, fails to explain why enforcement of the former obligation "coerces" and "restrains" employees in the exercise of Section 7 rights, while enforcement of the latter agreement does not.

The Court next derives an affirmative "freedom to resign" from the "language and reasoning" of two other decisions, *Scofield* v. *NLRB*[58] and *NLRB* v. *Textile Workers Local 1029, Granite State Joint Board*.[59] Here the Court is engaged in pure bootstrapping. In *Scofield*, the Court did not have before it any issue as to the conditions or procedures for terminating union membership. The *Scofield* language cited by Justice Powell was merely part of a general characterization of case precedent to the effect that Section 8(b)(1)(A) proscribes all "external" enforcement of union rules to affect employment status, but only such purely "internal" enforcement as frustrates an overriding labor law policy:

---

[57] *Id.*
[58] 394 US 423, 70 LRRM 3105 (1969).
[59] 409 US 213, 81 LRRM 2853 (1972).

Under this dual approach, §8(b)(1) leaves a union free to enforce a properly adopted rule which reflects a legitimate union interest, impairs no policy Congress has imbedded in the labor laws, and is reasonably enforced against union members who are free to leave the union and escape the rule.[60]

On the facts before it, the *Scofield* Court found only that the record contained "no showing" that "the membership of petitioners in the union was involuntary."[61]

Justice Powell similarly mischaracterizes the citations taken out of context from *Textile Workers*. In that decision, the Court observed that the union's constitution and laws did not define or limit the circumstances under which a member may resign from the union, and thus that the individuals who had lawfully resigned from the union were *nonmembers* at the time they engaged in the conduct for which the union sought to discipline them.[62] Accordingly, the *Textile Workers* Court concluded that the union's adverse actions against nonmembers were not internal union affairs excluded from the reach of Section 8(b)(1). The *Textile Workers* majority further rejected the argument (endorsed by Justice Blackmun in his dissent) that the ex-members had made an enforceable contract of "mutual commitment" with their fellow members by participating in the strike vote. It was in that context that the Court stated:

> We do not now decide to what extent the contractual relationship between union and member may curtail the freedom to resign. But where, as here, there are no restraints on the resignation of members, we conclude that the vitality of §7 requires that the member be free to refrain in November from the actions he endorsed in May and that his §7 rights are not lost by a union's plea for solidarity or by its pressures for conformity and submission to its regime.[63]

Thus, the *Textile Workers* decision simply refused to find an implied contractual restriction in the absence of any express obligation to which the members had knowingly consented.[64] No plausible reading of that case could make it stand for a negative answer on the question it expressly left open.

---

[60] 394 US at 430.
[61] *Id.*
[62] 409 US at 216–17.
[63] *Id.* at 217–18.
[64] *Id.* at 217 & n.5.

From that ephemeral basis, however, Justice Powell proceeds in Part III to the further conclusion that restrictions on resignation contravene "the policy of voluntary unionism implicit in §8(a)(3)," thus failing the requirement that a validly enforced union rule must "impair no policy Congress has imbedded in the labor laws."[65] The Court's reasoning here simply begs the question. Section 8(a)(3)'s relevant policy is only that union membership cannot be compelled by affecting an individual's *employment* status, and the union's actions in this case involved no employment-related enforcement implicating that policy. To bridge that gap the Court equates discipline involving monetary exactions with impairment of employment rights, presumably because the member's wages provide money he will use to pay his union financial obligations. Such absurd reasoning would convert every union fine of current members into an "external" employment-related enforcement of union policy, a result obviously inconsistent with *Allis-Chalmers* and *Scofield*.

Most significantly, the majority completely ignores the "national labor policy" supporting collective action that *Allis-Chalmers* identified as the essential context in which the courts must construe Section 8(b)(1)(A).[66] As previously indicated, *Allis-Chalmers* expressly stated that a union's power to prohibit strikebreaking and to "protect against erosion of its status" was "essential" to the union's effectiveness as bargaining agent and "[i]ntegral to . . . federal labor policy."[67] That recognized Congressional policy, which gave rise to the NLRA in 1935, is as much "imbedded in the labor laws" as the implied "voluntary unionism" policy advanced by Justice Powell. See *Machinists Local 1327, District 115* v. *NLRB*.[68] To apply *Scofield's* "impairment" test without reference to the federal policy lying at the heart of the Act can only be deemed unprincipled.

The least defensible aspect of the *Pattern Makers* decision, however, is the majority's treatment of the plain language and legislative history of the proviso to Section 8(b)(1)(A). In Part IV-A, the Court erroneously finds that the Pattern Makers League Law 13 is not a rule "with respect to the acquisition or retention of membership" within the terms of the proviso. Here

---

[65] 394 US at 430.

[66] *See* discussion *supra* at notes 49–53 and Justice Blackmun's dissent in *Pattern Makers*, 119 LRRM at 2938.

[67] 388 US at 181 (emphasis added).

[68] 725 F2d 1212, 1217, 115 LRRM 2972 (CA 9, 1984).

the majority eschews a literal reading of the Act that would vindicate national labor policy. As discussed above, the Union's rule barring withdrawal during a strike is one of the specific obligations voluntarily undertaken in acquiring membership, and it concerns retention of membership in that it prescribes circumstances in which continuation of membership is required. In short, League Law 13 is nothing if not a rule "with respect to the acquisition or retention of membership." To escape the clear import of that express statutory language, the majority must distort the relevant legislative history. This the Court accomplishes by isolating two legislative references to "expulsion" from membership, while ignoring equally pertinent statements explaining that Section 8(b)(1)(A) protects Union rules "with respect to beginning or *terminating membership*" (Sen. Holland),[69] and that the proviso "covers *the requirements* and standards of membership in the union" (Sen. Ball).[70]

This misreading of the Taft-Hartley legislative history continues in Part IV-B, where the Court dismisses the union's persuasive showing that Congress deliberately rejected the enactment of a protected right to resign from union membership. In the original Hartley bill, as noted above, the House proposed two parallel statutory schemes for protecting individuals. Initially, Section 7(a) of H.R. 3020 set forth in general terms the rights of employees, including the right to "refrain" from concerted activities. To implement those rights, the Hartley bill provided a Section 8(b), which made it an unfair labor practice for any "employee" or employee representative:

> (1) by intimidating practices, to interfere with the exercise of employees of rights guaranteed in Section 7(a) or to compel or seek to compel any individual to become or remain a member of any labor organization. . . .[71]

---

[69] LEG. HIST. LMRA at 1141 (emphasis added).

[70] LEG. HIST. LMRA at 1200 (emphasis added). *See also* text accompanying notes 41–44 *supra*.

[71] LEG. HIST. LMRA at 49–52. The House Committee Report made it clear that §8(b)(1) provided a narrowly qualified ban on "interference *by intimidation*," so that union adherents could not "*harass* or *abuse* employees into joining labor organizations." H.R. REP. No. 245, 80th Cong., 1st Sess. 30 (1947) (emphasis added). With respect to the §7(a) right to "refrain," moreover, the committee explained: "[W]hen the law states that employees are to have the rights guaranteed in Section 7, *the Board* will be prevented from compelling employees to exercise such rights as it has consistently done in the past. In other words, when Congress grants to employees the right to engage in specified activities, it also means to grant them the right to refrain from engaging therein if they do not wish to do so." *Id.* at 27 (emphasis added).

In a separate and differently focused Section 7(b), Hartley set forth the rights of *union members* with respect to their labor organizations; to implement those rights, a corresponding Section 8(c) enumerated 10 forbidden practices by unions, including a Section 8(c)(4) making it unlawful for a union "to deny to any member the right to resign from the organization at any time."[72] Clearly the Section 7(a) "right to refrain" from concerted activity, together with the implementing Section 8(b), did not apply to a union's institutional relations with its members, such as a union rule limiting resignation. Sections 7(b) and 8(c), on the other hand, expressly addressed that subject. Thus in deleting Sections 7(b) and 8(c), while adopting a Section 8(b)(1) that on its face disclaims regulation of internal union membership matters, Congress confirmed that the NLRA does not bar enforcement of a union rule embodying a member's obligation not to resign during a strike. The majority plainly errs in reducing such manifestations of legislative intent to "a summary statement in the House Conference Report."[73]

Moreover, the legislative history does not support the majority's suggestion that Congress eliminated H.R. 3020's proposed Section 8(c)(4) only because the same "right to resign" was adequately protected in other sections of the bill.[74] As Justice Blackmun points out in his dissent, Senator Taft made it clear that the conferees had expressly refused to agree to the proposed "bill of rights" measure because

> they felt that it was unwise to authorize an agency of the Government to undertake such elaborate policing of the internal affairs of unions as this section contemplated without further study of the structure of unions.[75]

And while the Conference Report affirmatively indicated that one of the Section 8(c) provisions had been included in the conference bill, it specifically stated that "the other parts of this

---

[72] Leg. Hist. LMRA at 52–53. As the House Committee explained:
[W]hen, under the Labor Act, we confer upon unions the power they have as exclusive bargaining agents, . . . it is incumbent upon us, by the same law, to assure to the employees whom we subject to union control some voice in the union's affairs. This we do by the general provisions of Section 7(b), which are implemented by the provisions of Section 8(c).
H.R. Rep. No. 245, 80th Cong., 1st Sess. 28 (1947).

[73] 119 LRRM at 2935.

[74] *Id.*

[75] 93 Cong. Rec. 6443, quoted in 119 LRRM at 2940.

subsection are omitted from the conference agreement as unfair labor practices. . . ."[76] Justice Blackmun correctly condemns the majority's disingenuous attempt to equate prohibition of the closed shop, to which the Senate agreed, with prohibition of rules restricting resignation, which the Senate specifically rejected:

> [T]he Senate was not willing to impose conditions on the contractual relationship between the union and its members, including a rule giving members a right to resign at will, insofar as such regulation did not affect the employment relationship. . . . Perhaps the House believed that the proscription against the closed shop and the proscription on limitations on a member's right to resign were aimed at the same evil. But the Senate obviously did not, and it prevailed.[77]

In short, the majority pays lip service to, but ultimately repudiates, "the crux of Allis-Chalmers' holding" concerning the scope of Section 8(b)(1)(A)—that is, "the distinction between 'internal and external enforcement of union rules. . . .' "[78]

Finally, the majority errs in rejecting the argument that the union's restriction on resignation is a valid, common law contract between a voluntary association and its members. Here the Court cites *NLRB* v. *Marine & Shipbuilding Workers*,[79] for the propositions that "union discipline cannot be analyzed primarily in terms of the common law of contracts," and the "many union rules, although valid under the common law of associations, run afoul of §8(b)(1)(A) of the Act."[80] In fact, the *Marine & Shipbuilding Workers* decision merely held that a union rule requiring exhaustion of internal appeals before resort to outside tribunals may not be enforced so as to impair access to NLRB processes for vindication of public statutory rights. As the Court observed in that case, the NLRB cannot initiate its own proceedings but depends completely upon the actions of private parties to set in motion the machinery for protection of nonprivate rights.[81] The Court further found that coercion employed to defeat such access is "beyond the legitimate interest of a labor organization."[82] At the same time, however, the Court reaffirmed that

---

[76] *Supra* note 45.
[77] 119 LRRM at 2940–41.
[78] *Id.* at 2932, quoting from Scofield v. NLRB, 394 US at 428.
[79] 391 US 418, 68 LRRM 2257 (1968).
[80] 119 LRRM at 2936 & n.26.
[81] 391 US at 424.
[82] *Id.*

union rules designed to preserve a union's institutional strength during a strike, and thus its effectiveness in collective bargaining, involve "legitimate internal affairs" as to which Section 8(b)(1)(A) "assures a union freedom of self-regulation."[83] Thus *Marine & Shipbuilding Workers* supports the validity of the union rule in *Pattern Makers.*

In summary, *Pattern Makers League* v. *NLRB*[84] vindicates an overriding purpose, unrestrained by the terms and policy of the NLRA, of undermining the ultimate collective power of workers, the strike weapon. The illusory short-term freedom accorded to individual employees under this NLRB doctrine is instrumental, but secondary, to the objective of subordinating all employees, individually or collectively, to the enhanced power of management.

Although the recent resignation-at-will cases strike the most publicized blow to workers' organizational solidarity, the Reagan Board has been exploring other equally fruitful avenues for diminishing the effectiveness of unions. One such approach is to give management a significant role in individual employees' exercise of the resignation option, as in *Greyhound Lines, Inc.*[85] There the Board allowed an employer to offer to pay union reinitiation fees for employees who had resigned from union membership in order to work during a strike. In the agency's view the payments were justified because the employees believed management had misled them into resigning, and the company merely sought to undo the economic harm for which it assumed responsibility. Notwithstanding the display of compassion for employee victims, this Board serves only employers' interests by inviting management to propagate error or confusion that turns union members into strikebreakers, and then protects the strikebreakers from the consequences of abandoning their union.

This Board also finds ways of cutting off or restricting unions' financial support. For example, though a dues checkoff authorization has traditionally been considered an individual contract separate and distinct from union membership and therefore revocable only pursuant to its own terms, the Agency will construe the wording of an authorization form so as to find that it is canceled automatically by resignation from full union mem-

---

[83] *Id.* at 423–24.
[84] *Supra* note 79.
[85] 275 NLRB No. 166, 119 LRRM 1257 (1985).

bership.[86] Moreover, the Board has begun to chip away at the dues obligations of even full union members. In *Carpenters Local 455*,[87] it ruled that a member subject to a union security clause could not be compelled to pay that portion of monthly dues that had been allocated by the union for use in strike and picketing activities. Although the union had increased its regular monthly dues from $16.00 to $18.00, and the increase had already been in effect for one year when the issue as to the member's union-security obligation arose, the Board nonetheless found an insufficient basis for concluding that the amount of the increase constituted "periodic dues" within the meaning of the Act. While the Board has not yet adopted the doctrine of *Ellis* v. *Railway Clerks*,[88] the agency may be signaling its intent to police the uses of union dues money under Sections 8(a)(3) and 8(b)(2).

It seems likely that the agency will not long remain content merely to grant all employees the privilege of "at whim" union membership, in violation of specific and voluntary commitments undertaken as a condition of membership. Under the Board's current approach to Section 8(b)(1)(A), protection of individual rights may further require that employees who repudiate their union membership or decline to join be afforded, nonetheless, the same internal union privileges granted to union members.

In *Teamsters Local 670*,[89] for example, the NLRB recently held that a union violated Sections 8(b)(3) and 8(b)(1)(A) of the Act by denying employees who had resigned from membership during a strike the internal benefits of access to union-sponsored medical services and assistance in meeting the job-search requirements of state unemployment compensation regulations. Chairman Dotson and Member Dennis, in agreement with the administrative law judge, predicated the Section 8(b)(1)(A) violation on a finding that the union violated its statutory bargaining duty by breaching a strike settlement contract which provided that no employee or supervisor would be penalized or discriminated against for lawful activity in connection with a strike.[90] In so ruling, the majority necessarily concluded that the union's provision or withholding of its own benefits concerned a

---

[86] Machinists Local 2045, Dist. 102, 268 NLRB 635, 115 LRRM 1092 (1984).

[87] 271 NLRB 1099, 117 LRRM 1082 (1984).

[88] 466 US 435, 116 LRRM 2001 (1984).

[89] Teamsters Local 670 (Stayton Canning Co. Coop.), 275 NLRB No. 127, 119 LRRM 1236 (1985).

[90] Slip Op. at p. 2, n.2.

mandatory subject of bargaining by virtue of a general "amnesty clause" in the collective bargaining agreement.[91] That conclusion, however, is contrary to NLRB and federal court precedent.[92] The ALJ, whose analysis was adopted by the Board, apparently reasoned that breach of an amnesty clause directly contravenes the Act's fundamental policy of "encouraging the practice and procedure of collective bargaining" as a peaceful means of resolving labor disputes.[93] Given the Board's licensing of employers to vitiate their collective bargaining agreements in cases such as *Milwaukee Spring II,*[94] and *Otis Elevator Co.*[95] the professed concern for the integrity of voluntary agreements in *Teamsters Local 670* rings false.

In a separate concurring and dissenting opinion, Member Hunter found that the benefits in question were "union-provided and were completely outside the collective bargaining contract."[96] He therefore correctly concluded that such benefits "did not in any fashion concern a term and condition of employ-

---

[91] *Id.*

[92] A permissive subject of bargaining does not become mandatory merely by inclusion in a collective bargaining agreement; breach of unilateral modification of a permissive contract term, therefore, does not violate §8(d) of the Act. *See* Chemical Workers v. Pittsburgh Plate Glass Co., 404 US 157, 78 LRRM 2974 (1971). It has long been settled that internal union matters such as the granting of union privileges to members or nonmembers are permissive bargaining subjects. *See* NLRB v. Corsicana Cotton Mills, 178 F2d 344, 24 LRRM 2494 (CA 5, 1949) (participation and voting in union meetings by nonmembers); NLRB v. Superior Fireproof Door & Sash Co., 289 F2d 713, 47 LRRM 2816 (CA 2, 1961); Houchens Mkt. v. NLRB, 375 F2d 208, 64 LRRM 2647 (CA 6, 1967) (voting on contract). The Board, with court approval, has ruled that an "amnesty clause" barring a union from penalizing employees for refraining from concerted activity is not a mandatory subject to bargaining. Universal Oil Prods. Co., 179 NLRB 657, 72 LRRM 1475 (1969), *enforced,* 445 F2d 155, 77 LRRM 2005 (CA 7, 1971) (withdrawal of fines for crossing picket line); Allen-Bradley Co., 127 NLRB 44, 45 LRRM 1505 (1960), *enforcement denied,* 286 F2d 442, 47 LRRM 2562 (CA 7, 1961). The Seventh Circuit in *Universal Oil* overruled its earlier decision denying enforcement in *Allen-Bradley.*

Without discussion of the above principles, the Board subsequently ruled that a union violated §8(b)(1)(A) by breaching such an amnesty clause included in a collective bargaining agreement. *See* Operating Eng'rs Local 39 (San Jose Hosp. & Health Center, Inc.), 240 NLRB 1122, 100 LRRM 1388 (1979); Hospital & Institutional Workers Local 250, 254 NLRB 834, 106 LRRM 1284 (1981). Although violation of §8(b)(3) was not at issue in those cases, the ALJ in *Teamsters Local 670* relied on them in finding that the union had breached its statutory bargaining obligation under §§8(d) and 8(b)(3) of the Act. ALJ decision at 13–16.

[93] ALJ decision at 11–12.

[94] Milwaukee Spring, Div. of Illinois Coil Spring Co., 268 NLRB 601, 115 LRRM 1065 (1984).

[95] 269 NLRB 891, 115 LRRM 1281 (1984).

[96] *Supra* note 90, at p. 4.

ment and thus are not mandatory subjects of bargaining."[97] Hunter, however, proceeded to find that the union nonetheless violated Section 8(b)(1)(A) by withholding those "wholly internal," nonemployment-related benefits from ex-members, because the union acted in "reprisal" for the members' resignation. I find the implications of that reasoning even more disturbing than the majority's ruling. Virtually any denial of purely internal economic benefits to employees who decline to join or who resign from a union would constitute "a form of economic reprisal" that could restrain employees in the exercise of their Section 7 right to refrain from concerted activity. Such a construction of Section 8(b)(1)(A) completely disregards the congressional intent underlying the Taft-Hartley amendments and makes the proviso to Section 8(b)(1)(A) a nullity.

Although the Board majority in *Teamsters Local 670* carefully refrained from deciding whether Section 8(b)(1)(A) would confer on nonmembers the privileges of union membership absent an amnesty or strike settlement agreement, such fine distinctions may be academic. Independently of Section 8(b)(1), the Board has already taken a major step toward rendering union membership a mere formality in *Amoco Production Co.* ("Amoco IV").[98] Under the guise of fully protecting individual employees' rights to select their collective bargaining representative, the Board there ruled that a union forfeits its collective bargaining rights under the Act if it fails to allow nonmembers the privilege of voting on the internal union question of affiliation with an international union. (See also *Seattle-First National Bank*.[99]) While the affiliation in *Amoco IV* did not alter the identity of the bargaining agent and did not in itself raise a question concerning representation justifying an NLRB election under Section 9 of the Act, the Board nonetheless established a "due process" right of nonmembers to participate in a purely internal union decision that could affect the "interests" of all represented employees.[100] The Board has applied the same rationale to terminate the

---

[97] *Id.*

[98] 262 NLRB 1240, 110 LRRM 1419 (1982).

[99] 265 NLRB 426, 111 LRRM 1637 (1982). [**Editor's Note:** On February 25, 1986, in a unanimous decision, the Supreme Court, affirming the Ninth Circuit, reversed the NLRB in this case. NLRB v. Financial Institution Employees of Am. Local 1182, 475 US ___, 121 LRRM 2741 (1986). The Court came to the same conclusion as Ms. Kreiger regarding the right of a union to affiliate with another union without requiring a vote of the nonunion employees.]

[100] 262 NLRB at 1241.

bargaining agent status of a union because nonmembers were denied a vote on the merger of two local unions within the same international.[101]

The irrationality of the *Amoco IV* doctrine is obvious in that union decisions concerning organizational affiliation have no inherently greater bearing on employee interests than do other internal matters, such as election of officers and contract ratification, with which the Board does not yet interfere. And the Board's solicitude for individual employees' representation choices is unnecessary, as the statutory election process remains available to nonmembers who are dissatisfied with the results of union affiliations or mergers. Regardless of the future implications of *Amoco IV* for any remaining matters of union discretion, the Board's *Amoco* policy alone inflicts the intended damage to collective bargaining and employees' collective interests. At a time when consolidation of resources and achievement of greater unity are essential to trade unions' effectiveness as collective bargaining agents, the very act of securing the necessary institutional strength will permit employers to repudiate their contracts and collective bargaining relationships. Unless a union gives up the fundamental justification for voluntary membership—that is, the right of members alone to govern their organization—the union must remain a weak and ineffectual entity. Indeed, the union's institutional strength and significance suffers in either event. Thus the purported vindication of individual rights merely provides the vehicle for protection of employer interests.

IV. Subjection of the Individual Employee to Unjustifiable Employer Retaliation

The current case law governing protection of an individual employee who asserts her rights in the workplace presents an unusual dichotomy. Under the NLRB doctrine of *Interboro Contractors, Inc.*[102] reaffirmed by the Supreme Court in *NLRB* v. *City Disposal Systems, Inc.*,[103] a worker employed in an organized workplace engages in presumptively concerted action under Section 7 when she individually claims a right secured by a

---

[101] F.W. Woolworth Co., 268 NLRB 805, 115 LRRM 1120 (1984).
[102] 157 NLRB 1295, 61 LRRM 1537 (1966).
[103] 465 US 822, 115 LRRM 3193 (1984).

collective bargaining agreement. So expansive is the construction of the "concerted" activity requirement in such circumstances that the lone worker enjoys protection despite her failure to act through the exclusive bargaining agent, and regardless of whether she invokes the contract or even knows of the contractual basis for her claim. In contrast, under the doctrine of *Meyers Industries*,[104] the worker in a nonunion setting is excluded as a matter of law from the ambit of Section 7 when he individually invokes a statutory right, even if his claim addresses the conditions affecting his fellow workers. With *Meyers Industries,* the Board has abruptly reversed the decisional authority that had developed as *Interboro's* equivalent for the unorganized worker.

A similar dichotomy appears in the treatment of individual workers who initiate the literal concert of action recognized in *NLRB* v. *J. Weingarten, Inc.*[105] The employee in an organized workplace enjoys Section 7 protection when requesting the presence of a co-worker union witness in a potential disciplinary interview with management. Under the rationale of *Sears, Roebuck & Co.,*[106] an employer in an unorganized shop may lawfully interfere with or obstruct an employee who requests the presence of a co-worker witness in such an interview. Again, the Board has reversed an evolving interpretation of Section 7—approved in at least one circuit—that had given nonunion and union workers comparable protection under the Act. See *Materials Research Corp.*[107] and *E.I. du Pont de Nemours & Co.* v. *NLRB.*[108]

On initial examination, the above decisions might seem to encourage unionization by teaching individual workers that their only protection lies in overtly making common cause with their fellow employees and obtaining a collective bargaining agreement. I summarily dismiss any such objectively "prounion" implications of the Board's current policy, however, for they are as illusory as they are unintended. As Professor Aaron and other commentators have recognized, the Board's decisions increasingly permit management to chill the very action employ-

---

[104] *Supra* note 3.

[105] 420 US 251, 88 LRRM 2689 (1975).

[106] *Supra* note 4.

[107] 262 NLRB 1010, 110 LRRM 1401 (1982).

[108] 724 F2d 1061, 115 LRRM 2153 (CA 3, 1983), *vacated and remanded,* 733 F2d 296, 116 LRRM 2343 (CA 3, 1984). [**Editor's Note:** *See* Slaughter v. NLRB (E.I. du Pont de Nemours & Co.), 104 Lab. Cas. §11858 (CA 3, 1986).]

ees must take under *Meyers* in order to gain Section 7 protection. And the steps taken by the Board to weaken unions and undermine collective bargaining relationships effectively nullify any decisional references to the privileged status of concerted activity. I think that the intended object of *Meyers Industries* and similar individual rights cases can only be to assure management's control of a more docile work force. Simultaneously, the Agency's policies effect a kind of administrative reform. By turning away unorganized workers, while adopting a deferral policy that makes Section 8(a) effectively off limits to employees covered by collective bargaining agreements, the Board significantly reduces its case load and frees up agency resources for more effective enforcement of Section 8(b).

As I have previously stated, the Board's decision in *Meyers Industries* embodies an unduly restrictive reading of the Act. The D.C. Circuit has persuasively detailed the Board's errors in *Prill* v. *NLRB*.[109] That decision, among other things, essentially confirms the analysis set forth by former Member Zimmerman in his *Meyers* dissent. While concurring with Member Zimmerman's reasoning, I tend to agree with Professor Aaron that *Prill* may represent only a temporary setback to the Board if the agency chooses to preserve the *Meyers* result while exercising its "discretion" and "expertise" in interpreting Section 7.

One of the puzzling aspects of *Meyers* is that the Board chose to present its rationale as a decision *mandated* by the Act, rather than as the agency's preferred statutory interpretation. It may be that the Board hoped thereby to lock in the *Meyers* result permanently. I think, however, that the Board majority must have recognized that such an approach invited at least a remand, and that even an enforcing court need go no further than to accept the Board's rationale as permissible. Perhaps a partial failure of nerve explains the Board's approach in *Meyers*. That is, the Board may not worry about being labeled antiunion, but it may be reluctant to admit publicly that although the law authorizes protection of individual, nonunion workers under Section 7, it nevertheless chooses to withhold such protection. And it is certainly easier to justify a sudden about-face as an outcome dictated by the statute rather than as a result of a change in the composition and politics of the tribunal.

---

[109] 755 F2d 941, 118 LRRM 2649 (CA DC, 1985).

To bolster its construction of Section 7, the Board in *Meyers* also pretends that pre-*Alleluia Cushion Co.*[110] decisions consistently required a showing of actual or literal concert of action by two or more employees. Here, again, the Board is unnecessarily categorical. More than 30 years ago, a commentator reviewed the Board's "policy-minded approach" to construing the term "concerted," and concluded that "the Board and the courts have largely read it out of the Act" by assuming the concerted nature of an individual's action taken in furtherance of employees' common interests.[111] Subsequent reviews of this issue have confirmed the Board's flexible application of Section 7 to further the Act's policy of encouraging self-determination by workers.[112] The D.C. Circuit was correct in concluding that *Meyers Industries* does not simply return to the state of the law that obtained before *Alleluia Cushion.*

In addition to relevant Board precedent and the Supreme Court's approval of the *Interboro* doctrine, congressional intent appears to favor an interpretation of Section 7 encompassing the employee conduct at issue in *Meyers.* Though the Wagner Act legislative history does not specifically explain the choice of the term "concerted" in Section 7, its lineage can be traced through the major preceding labor laws. In the Clayton Act, Congress sought to forestall use of the criminal conspiracy and restraint of trade doctrines against employees who combined for legitimate ends, by barring injunctions to prohibit "any person or persons, individually or in concert," from striking and other enumerated activities.[113] The Norris-LaGuardia Act utilized related language in declaring, as the public policy of the United States, that the "individual unorganized worker . . . shall be free from the interference, restraint or coercion of employers . . . in self organization or in other concerted activities for the purpose of collective bargaining or other mutual aid or protection. . . ."[114] That policy was carried over into Section 7 of the

---

[110] 221 NLRB 999, 91 LRRM 1131 (1975).

[111] Note, *The Requirement of "Concerted" Action Under the NLRA,* 53 Colum. L. Rev. 514, 522, 530 (1953).

[112] *See* Gorman & Finkin, *The Individual and the Requirement of "Concert" Under the National Labor Relations Act,* 130 U. Pa. L. Rev. 286 (1981); Note, *Individual Rights for Organized and Unorganized Employees Under the National Labor Relations Act,* 58 Tex. L. Rev. 991 (1980); and the Supreme Court's decision in NLRB v. City Disposal Sys., Inc., *supra* note 103.

[113] 29 USC §52.

[114] 29 USC §102.

National Industrial Recovery Act in substantially the same terms. It subsequently became enforceable positive protection in Sections 7 and 8(1) of the Wagner Act.

Clearly, Congress initially protected concerted activity in order to assure that "lawful individual action should not become unlawful when engaged in collectively."[115] It does not follow, however, that in strengthening federal labor law Congress ultimately intended to authorize employer retaliation against an employee for individually taking action that would be lawful if taken by a group. As I have acknowledged, the Wagner Act's proponents did believe that individual workers in general could not effectively deal with their employers on an equal basis. But such reasoning in no way demonstrates a deliberate decision to abandon any lone worker brave enough to stand up to his employer for collective interests.

Moreover, the Taft-Hartley amendments, which purported to give balance to the Act by protecting workers whether or not they chose to organize into unions, support a broad reading of Section 7. By its terms, the right to "refrain from any or all" of the activities specified in Section 7 would include not only the right to eschew "concerted" action entirely, but also the right to attempt unspecified forms of "self organization" while refraining from traditional unionizing activity. Finally, the context as well as the generality of the language employed by Congress counsels a flexible interpretation of Section 7 that accommodates a changing industrial reality. That evolving reality includes more protective regulation affecting employment than existed in 1935, more reliance on worker initiative as part of a comprehensive enforcement scheme, and an increasingly significant role for individual action in the empowerment of workers on the job. In short, unless the Board is willing to say that the NLRA protects only those particular forms of employee action known to Congress at the time it legislated, it makes no sense to halt the development of Section 7 doctrine at the point selected in *Meyers Industries*.

The consequences of the *Meyers* decision for organizing are readily apparent. The activist employee who successfully enforces legal rights in the workplace demonstrates how to stand up to management, raises fellow employees' consciousness of their own power, and enhances the climate for organizing; fur-

---

[115] Gorman & Finkin, *supra* note 112, at 336, 331–46. *See also, supra* note 111, at 514–16.

thermore, she obviously makes a good prospect for leadership. *Meyers* permits the employer to weed out the employee "troublemaker" and stifle potential organizing activity at its inception. To sanction this result the Board must disregard precedent by denying legal significance to the chilling effect that retaliation against the employee activist has on *other* employees' exercise of their rights. Section 8(a)(1)'s ban on interference and restraint unquestionably includes adverse action by an employer calculated to have such a deterrent impact. Indeed, the Board has reaffirmed essentially the same rationale in penalizing strikers for conduct that "may reasonably tend to coerce or intimidate employees in the exercise of rights protected by the Act."[116] Under the *Clear Pine* doctrine, a picket's verbal threats even to supervisors, management personnel, or other nonemployees could be deemed improper because of their probable effect on employees. Unconcerned by its obvious double standard, however, the Board has simply chosen to ignore the "effects" rationale whenever an employer's, rather than an employee's or union's, conduct is at issue.[117]

Even more offensive is how *Meyers Industries* and its progeny treat as irrelevant the fact that the employer has fired, or taken other reprisals against, an employee in clear contravention of public policy expressed in statutes. Here again, the Agency manifests a blatant double standard. The Board's Section 8(b)(1)(A) decisions consistently emphasize that "the Board is charged with considering the full panoply of congressional labor policies in determining the legality" of a union's conduct toward its members.[118] At the same time, in its Section 8(a)(1) individual rights cases the Board relinquishes all responsibility for "the full panoply of congressional labor policies" governing employers, such as OSHA, Title VII, or other statutes invoked by individuals. Moreover, regardless of public policy, the fact remains that an employer has no legitimate justification whatsoever for the conduct at issue in *Meyers*. The Board manages to sidestep this issue by displacing and avoiding the "balancing" test properly employed under Section 8(a)(1) to measure the legality of an employer's infringement of Section 7 rights. In *Meyers* the

---

[116] Clear Pine Mouldings, 268 NLRB 1044, 115 LRRM 1113 (1984).

[117] *See* Rossmore House, 269 NLRB 1176, 116 LRRM 1025 (1984); Parker-Robb Chevrolet, Inc., 262 NLRB 402, 110 LRRM 1289 (1982).

[118] *E.g.*, Carpenters Local 22 (Graziano Constr. Co.), 195 NLRB 1, 2, 79 LRRM 1194 (1972) (LMRDA rights).

Board prematurely weighs and resolves a range of competing interests, acknowledged and unarticulated, in order to decide whether the employee's action falls within Section 7. Under the correct approach, the Board would first recognize that Section 7 protects the employee's action, and then determine whether the employer committed *unlawful* interference or restraint. At that point the Board's task would be to weigh the employee's statutory rights against the legitimate business needs or justifications, if any, advanced by the employer. Thus the Board would be forced either to publicly condemn the employer's retaliation because it serves no cognizable interest, or else openly place its stamp of approval on the employer's egregious conduct. I find the *Meyers Industries* approach dishonest because it seeks to conceal the Board's actual reasoning.

V. Conclusion

In addition to the foregoing points, I find in the cases discussed above an attitude of profound hostility and distrust toward collective self-governance by workers. That bias is easily discerned in the union discipline cases. It is less obvious, but equally strong, in the Section 8(a)(1) decisions considered as a group. Those cases, in effect, tell us that employees need statutory protection and individual avenues for enforcing their interests only where they are already represented by a union.

In 1947, proponents of Hartley's repressive antilabor bill complained that the Wagner Act, and the worker organization it fostered, forced employers to deal with their employees as a separate "caste" or "class."[119] The House champions sought to expunge such class consciousness from federal law as an invidious concept foreign to American labor relations. In fact, the most deeply rooted "caste" or "class" bias fueled the legislative efforts to revise the Wagner Act, and is reflected in the current regressive interpretations of the NLRA. For despite the majority rule and union self-governance principles integral to the Act, democratic control of employees by and among their peers in the form of a labor organization is treated as unnatural and presumptively evil. No legislative commands can significantly alter the perceived natural order dictating the continued domi-

---

[119] H.R. REP. No. 245, 80th Cong., 1st Sess. 5 (1947).

nation of employees by their natural superiors, the employing class. While these lessons are not new, they are administered with uncommon force to workers today.

A FRAMEWORK FOR PROTECTION OF LIBERTY

WILLIAM F. JOY*

In his paper, Professor Aaron has set forth a short history of the conditions existing prior to the enactment of the National Labor Relations Act in 1935[1] and the evolution of that statute through the Taft-Hartley Act,[2] with some passing reference to the Labor-Management Reporting and Disclosure Act,[3] with particular emphasis on how Congress, by statutory enactment, envisaged the rights of individuals within the framework of the national labor policy. His central thesis is "that in recent years employees' statutory rights originally conceived of as protection against abuses of employer power have been increasingly enforced in ways that weaken unions, reduce the effectiveness of collective bargaining, and leave individual employees vulnerable to the hostile acts of employers." As part of his thesis, he postulates that "the expanding concept of the union's duty of fair representation and the enactment of the Labor-Management Reporting and Disclosure (Landrum-Griffin) Act of 1959 (LMRDA)[4] has had an uneven effect on the relationship between unions, on the one hand, and their members and non-union members of the bargaining unit, on the other, sometimes providing the latter with insufficient protection against the former, and sometimes unwisely elevating individual rights over the interests of the group represented by the union."

In support of his thesis, Professor Aaron deals with the following areas:
1. The principle of exclusive representation;
   a. Majority rule;
   b. The adjustment of grievances;
   c. The union's duty of fair representation
2. Individual rights at the workplace; and
3. Individual rights and union discipline.

---

* Senior Partner, Morgan, Brown & Joy, Boston, Massachusetts.
[1] Ch. 372, 49 Stat 449 (1935), 29 USC §§151–166 (1982).
[2] Ch. 120, Title I, Sec. 101, 61 Stat 136 (1947), 29 USC §§151–167 (1982).
[3] 73 Stat 519 (1959), 29 USC §§153, 158, 159, 160, 164, 186, 187, 401, 402, 411–415, 431–440, 461–466, 481–483, 501–504, 521–531 (1982).
[4] *Id.*

As a Respondent, I conceive it to be my function to indicate those areas where I agree, disagree, or suggest a different point of view. Professor Aaron's paper is an incisive, in-depth review supported by agency and judicial decisions illustrating his position on the three areas which he has delineated for consideration in support of his thesis. In the interest of expedition and order, I shall follow the same format, with brief responses on each of his three areas and his basic thesis.

A brief word, however, is in order at the outset to indicate that in my view the rights of individuals received more than passing attention when Congress enacted the Wagner Act and received special emphasis and attention in the Taft-Hartley and the Landrum-Griffin acts. Perhaps at this point also, a brief reference would be in order to the basic philosophical preconceptions which influenced the founders of this country and are embodied in the Declaration of Independence and the Constitution of the United States. I refer specifically to the theories of John Locke, the English philosopher, with his emphasis on individual liberty in the political and social sphere, and similarly those of Adam Smith in the economic sphere.[5] I think it goes without saying that their views of the rights of individuals have to a large degree permeated the social, political, and economic history of the United States. It is true that any system of social justice must look not only to the rights of the individual in relation to the state, but to the rights of the individual in relation to the common good or to the society or the group as a whole. It may be argued that this relationship between the individual and the state, known as distributive justice, and the relationship of the individual to the common good, known as general justice, finds expression in the National Labor Relations Act and its progeny in the sense that the rights of individuals are given consideration as well as those of the collectivity. Further, it may be pertinent to observe that some scholars believed that the Taft-Hartley Act did not represent a policy of congressional indifference as to whether or not workers joined unions. Professor Sumner Slichter said: "the act has greatly invigorated the trade union movement." Also, he stated, "the act specifically recognizes the right not to organize

---

[5] Weber, *Labor Unions and Two Concepts of Social Justice*, ISSUES IN THE LABOR-MANAGEMENT DIALOGUE—CHURCH PERSPECTIVE, Ch. 9 (A. Maida ed., 1982).

and the right not to strike, as well as the right to organize and to strike and undertakes to protect all these rights from interference by either employers, unions or agents of unions."[6]

As to the first point—*the principle of exclusive representation,* Professor Aaron considers *majority rule, adjustment of individual grievances,* and the *duty of fair representation.* Majority rule has been well established from the beginning, despite later litigation about the rights of minority unions. As to adjustment of individual grievances, he deals primarily with Section 9(a) of the Act, with emphasis on the exclusivity reference and the two provisos relating to the rights of individuals to present grievances to their employers without the intervention of the bargaining agent. I concur with his analysis of the rights of individuals in this regard. I would have preferred some additional comment on the case of *Emporium Capwell Co.* v. *Western Addition Community Organization,*[7] a case in which the Supreme Court upheld the discharge of several black employees for pursuing their grievances against the employer's alleged racial discrimination. The employees conducted a press conference, distributed leaflets attacking the employer, and picketed the store entrances instead of waiting for the exclusive bargaining agent to process their grievances through the contract grievance and arbitration procedures. The conduct of the union in that situation as well as in similar situations should not be shielded by a strong commitment to the grievance and arbitration process. Inquiries should be made as to whether or not the union is engaging in delay, frustrating the legitimate rights of minorities, or whether, to use the words of the D.C. Circuit in the same case, it is trying to "the fullest extent possible, by the most expedient and efficacious means" to remedy the discrimination. If the union is not performing its duties properly, the Board should consider such sanctions as revocation of certification or unfair practice findings against the union if charges are filed under the duty of fair representation doctrine.

We now turn to Professor Aaron's treatment of the union's duty of fair representation (DFR). It is my opinion that this development in the law is an anomaly and one which should be remedied by legislation. The American Bar Association Section of Labor and Employment Law appointed a distinguished com-

---

[6] Schlicter, *The Taft-Hartley Act,* 63 Q.J. Econ. 1, 8, 16 (1949).
[7] 420 US 50, 88 LRRM 2660 (1975).

mittee to report its recommendations on this subject.[8] After exhaustive study, the report of the committee was made, but not favorably acted upon because of disagreement on both sides of the table. Nevertheless, there was a good deal of sentiment for the general proposition that legislation was preferable to the existing situation of litigating both the employer's action against an employee and the union's duty of fair representation in federal court before a jury. Until the six month's statute of limitations under Secton 10(b) of the NLRA was determined by the Supreme Court in *DelCostello*[9] to be the appropriate limitations period, there was confusion in several jurisdictions as to which statute applied. The First Circuit applied the state contract statute of limitation to the employer, which was six years, and the tort statute, which was three years, to unions. Thus, in one case, *Figueroa de Arroyo* v. *Sindicato de Trabajadores Packinghouse*,[10] a union was dismissed from the case because of untimeliness and the employer was left in the case, giving the employer the burden of proving the union's actions were in compliance with its duty, and then, if the case went to the jury, defending its own action in a forum not contemplated by either the employer, the union, or the employee.

I disagree with Professor Aaron that the decision of the Supreme Court in *Bowen* v. *United States Postal Service*[11] was "perhaps the most damaging blow to unions." That case made it clear that unions, as defendants in DFR cases, were subject to damages which were caused by the union's failure to perform its DFR. In analyzing the basis for its decision, the court reviewed its decision in *Vaca* v. *Sipes*[12] as well as the state of the law in the circuits. What apparently rankled union adherents was that prior to this decision they had assumed, incorrectly, that they had no liability for damages in a DFR case. It is interesting to note also that among the judges in the majority was Justice Brennan, not unfriendly to unions, and in the minority, Justice Rehnquist, not considered by the unions as their champion.

---

[8] Cheit, *Competing Models of Fair Representation—The Perfunctory Processing Cases*, 24 B.C.L. Rev. 1, 7, n.34 (1982).

[9] DelCostello v. Teamsters, 462 US 151, 113 LRRM 2737 (1983).

[10] 425 F2d 281, 74 LRRM 2028 (CA 1, 1970), *cert. denied sub nom.* De Arroyo v. Puerto Rico Tel. Co., 400 US 877 (1970).

[11] 459 US 212, 112 LRRM 2281 (1983).

[12] 386 US 171, 64 LRRM 2364 (1967).

It seems that Professor Aaron is overly expansive in his treatment of two points arising out of *Vaca*. He states that the burden on the employee in a DFR case, to prove that the union violated its DFR, weighs the scale heavily against the employee's chances of recovery. In a meritorious case it certainly does not. In a tenuous case it certainly does. The burden indeed is a heavy one, but it should be if the labor policy of encouraging collective bargaining and arbitration is to remain viable. Consider the large number of cases disposed of by unions in the grievance procedure by settlement or abandonment, which is part and parcel of grievance and arbitration processing. The courts have protected unions against suits for doing their job well or even mistakenly. It is only where the conduct is arbitrary, discriminatory, or in bad faith that the union has failed in its duty. And what about the employer in this situation? Why should the employer who has negotiated a contract containing a grievance and arbitration procedure and has resolved a grievance with the majority representative find itself in court in a trial before a jury subject to damages because of the suggested failure of the union representative to perform its duty of fair representation? If the theory has any right to existence in our system of labor law, it is right and proper that these restrictions on employee recovery exist.

With respect to the second point in that case, Professor Aaron takes a look at the other side of the coin and states that in overcoming obstacles to employee recovery in DFR cases some courts have broadened the union's duty beyond practical or reasonable limits and have made them increasingly vulnerable to substantial damages, while employers in some instances have been shielded by the normal consequences of their own wrongdoing. This position seems at odds with his position on the first point (the principle of exclusive representation), and his comments on *Bowen* would indicate that he believes that unions who violate the DFR should be insulated from liability. With this I disagree.

With respect to *individual rights at the workplace*, Professor Aaron deals with employer interrogation and concerted activity. Although the law on employer interrogation has had a checkered career, it is my view that the present state of the law is appropriate and protects employee rights. *Blue Flash Express,*

Inc.[13] and *Rossmore House*[14] regarding interrogation generally, and *Strucksnes Construction Co.*[15] regarding polling of employees to confirm whether or not a majority desires a union, illustrate the present state of the law.

As to concerted activity, I believe that the language of Section 7 is clear and that Justice O'Connor in the dissent in *City Disposal Systems*[16] was correct when she stated, "when an employee acts alone in expressing a personal concern, contractual or otherwise, his action is not concerted. . . ." I agree with Professor Aaron's observation that the present Board's initial conclusion in *Meyers Industries*[17] may pass muster the second time around by the Board weighing the factors in the decision in *City Disposal Systems* and the D.C. Circuit's opinion in *Meyers Industries.*

As to *individual rights and union discipline*, Professor Aaron traces the case law development of a union's discipline of a member or former member who abandons a strike and returns to work. *Allis-Chalmers*[18] is still the law in the case of an employee who does not resign his membership before returning to work. In *Pattern Makers*,[19] the Supreme Court held that a union constitutional provision providing "no resignation or withdrawal from an association or from the League, shall be accepted during a strike or lockout, or at a time when a strike or lockout appears imminent," which made resignations ineffective when tendered by employees during a strike and under which the employees were fined by the union, violated Section 8(b)(1)(A). Thus, the right to resign from a union by an employee is clearly established in the law.

Professor Aaron reads into this decision dire consequences for the right to strike and an example of the Supreme Court's lack of familiarity with collective bargaining. He reaches further to "selfish or timid workers" and "especially. . . employers" who will see this decision as seriously undermining the right to strike.

---

[13] 109 NLRB 591, 34 LRRM 1384 (1954).

[14] 269 NLRB 1176, 116 LRRM 1025 (1984), *aff'd sub nom.* Hotel Employees Local 11 v. NLRB, 760 F2d 1006, 119 LRRM 2624 (CA 9, 1985).

[15] 165 NLRB 1062, 65 LRRM 1385 (1967).

[16] NLRB v. City Disposal Sys., 465 US 822, 115 LRRM 3193 (1984).

[17] 268 NLRB 493, 115 LRRM 1025 (1984), *rev'd sub nom.* Prill v. NLRB, 755 F2d 941, 118 LRRM 2649 (CA DC, 1985).

[18] NLRB v. Allis-Chalmers Mfg. Co., 388 US 175, 65 LRRM 2449 (1967).

[19] Pattern Makers v. NLRB (Rockford-Beloit Pattern Jobbers), 469 US ___, 119 LRRM 2928 (1985).

Despite such rhetoric and the assumptions of the minority, Justices Blackman, Brennan, and Marshall, let us take a look at the resigning employees. The first one was on strike for four months. The remaining 10 were out an additional period over the next three months. Apparently, they questioned the prudence of remaining on strike, which they had a right to do. In *NLRB* v. *Textile Workers Local 1029*,[20] Justice Douglas, writing for the Court stated:

> The Court of Appeals gave weight to the fact that the resigning employees had participated in the vote to strike. We give that factor little weight. The first two members resigned from the Union from one to two months after the strike had begun. The others did so from seven to 12 months after its commencement. And the strike was still in progress 18 months after its inception. Events occurring after the calling of a strike may have unsettling effects leading a member who voted to strike to change his mind. The likely duration of the strike may increase the specter of hardship to his family; the ease with which the employer replaces the strikers may make the strike seem less provident. We do not now decide to what extent the contractual relationship between union and member may curtail the freedom to resign. But where, as here, there are no restraints on the resignation of members, we conclude that the vitality of § 7 requires that the member be free to refrain in November from the actions he endorsed in May and that his § 7 rights are not lost by a union's plea for solidarity or by its pressures for conformity and submission to its regime.

Conclusion

Congress and the National Labor Relations Board have worked out a good framework for protecting individual rights and the rights of the collective in the national labor policy as embodied in the NLRA as amended. The time has come for an in-depth review of the entire statutory framework of labor and employment law in the federal sphere. As a beginning point, it is appropriate to consider a unitary system in which all such laws would be placed under the umbrella of a specialized system of courts or under the umbrella of one agency with limited resort to courts. Professor Charles Morris wrote a scholarly article some

---

[20] 409 US 213, 81 LRRM 2853, 2855 (1972).

years ago on this very subject,[21] and I think that this would be an excellent starting point for this consideration. If one looks at the plethora of statutes in the federal sphere in developing theories that have come along—just to list a few: the NLRA, OSHA, ERISA at least in part, EEOC, Wage and Hour, Federal Employee Labor Laws, and the Age Discrimination in Employment Act—it seems that the time has come that they should be treated in a uniform unitary system.

Collective Rights Versus Individual Rights

Don A. Zimmerman[*]

Professor Aaron's analysis of the rights of individual employees under the Act serves as a useful reminder that despite five decades of labor law litigation filling close to 300 volumes of Board decisions, many of which have been reviewed by the courts of appeal and the Supreme Court,[1] some fundamental issues have only recently been squarely addressed and others still remain unresolved. When Congress wrote the Act it left many major questions to be determined by judicial interpretation, and the Board and the reviewing courts over the years have not been eager to supply the required answers. This is partly a reflection of the deep political conflict engendered by the long-standing antagonism between labor and management that has prevailed throughout the history of the Act, a law that is itself modeled on conflict rather than cooperation. As Justice Frankfurter once observed, the Taft-Hartley Act represents a "compromise between strong contending forces" in our national life, which strive before the Board, the courts, and the Congress to have the statutory balance struck anew in their respective interests.[2]

---

[21] Morris, *The Case for Unitary Enforcement of Federal Labor Law—Concerning a Specialized Article III Court and the Reorganization of Existing Agencies*, 26 Sw. L.J. 471 (1972).

[*] Former Member, National Labor Relations Board; associate, Covington and Burling, Washington, D.C.

[1] For many years, Board decisions have been responsible for more federal appellate litigation than any other federal agency, including the Department of Justice.

[2] Carpenters Local 1976 v. NLRB (Sand Door & Plywood Co.), 357 US 93, 99–100, 42 LRRM 2243 (1957).

Only twice in its history has the Act been subject to major amendment—the Taft-Hartley Amendments of 1947,[3] and the Landrum-Griffin Amendments of 1959.[4] Thus, the failure to resolve basic statutory issues can hardly be blamed on frequent congressional meddling. Indeed, quite the opposite is true. This brief but complex law is subject to widely varying interpretation, and the Board, which in the first instance is responsible for the interpretation, is comprised of members whose terms are limited to five years. Thus, even when the Board does interpret the statute, neither unions nor employers can be certain that any given decision will survive the changing composition of the Board. Fifty years of case-by-case adjudication have left us without a clear, comprehensive, and reliable code for the conduct of labor relations.

The problem faced by the Board and the courts is more than filling in statutory gaps. As Professor Aaron explains, Congress did not enact this law with a single-minded purpose. Consequently, the Board is often forced to balance the competing interests of labor and management to which Justice Frankfurter referred. As a member of the Board, I was struck by how frequently that "balancing" was viewed by unions, employers, and the lawyers who represent them, as reflecting no more than an inherent bias toward one side or the other.

Whatever the merits of that view, surely it ignores deeper problems faced by those charged with interpreting the law. In the individual rights context, it fails to take into account the tensions within the Act between the individual rights of employees and the rights of those employees who choose to act collectively through labor organizations to enhance their economic power vis-à-vis their employers. In the present statutory scheme, Congress has framed legislation that expresses *both* interests, and in important respects has failed to reconcile them.

The collective thrust of the Act is found in the very first section. The last sentence of Section 1 declares that "encouraging the practice and procedure of collective bargaining" is the policy of the United States, as is "protecting the exercise by workers of full freedom of association, self-organization, and designation of representatives of their own choosing. . . ." Sections 8 and 9 back this policy up by mandating collective bargain-

---

[3] 61 Stat 449 (1945), 29 U.S.C. §§151–168 (1982).
[4] 73 Stat 519 (1959), 29 U.S.C. §§401–531 (1982).

ing when a majority of employees have selected a bargaining representative, and by setting forth procedures for that selection. In Section 7, the heart of the Act, Congress set forth these rights, but then went further in its 1947 amendments by protecting the rights of employees "to *refrain* from any or all such activities . . . ."[5] As Professor Aaron has noted, the 1947 language provides the underlying basis for those who believe that the Act thereafter was meant to emphasize the rights of *individual* employees as against the collective rights of unions.

Since 1947, and perhaps earlier, it has been clear that the statutory rights of individual employees to refrain from engaging in collective activities are in conflict with the Act's provisions encouraging and protecting collective bargaining.

In some situations the conflict has been resolved sharply in favor of collective interests. For example, Section 9 confers upon unions not just the right but the obligation to function as the exclusive representative of all employees in an appropriate bargaining unit. An individual employee, no matter how strongly he or she may be opposed to having a collective bargaining representative, has no right to bargain, separately from the union, over terms and conditions of employment. If a contract is negotiated by the union establishing a wage scale based entirely upon seniority, and a junior employee has the highest skills and pay level, he or she will be subordinated to the contract terms. Even prior to the Taft-Hartley Amendments, the Supreme Court stated, "the majority rules, and if it collectivizes the employment bargain, individual advantages or favors will generally in practice go in as a contribution to the collective result."[6] In this context, the Board and the courts have clearly elevated the statutory purpose of furthering collective bargaining over any individual employee rights.

It took another 41 years, however, for the Supreme Court to address squarely an equally acute conflict between individual and collective rights. The problem was resolved in the *Pattern Makers* case,[7] which involved the rights of employees who are union members to resign their membership and return to work during a strike. Just three years earlier, the Board in *Dalmo Victor*

---

[5] Emphasis supplied.

[6] J.I. Case Co. v. NLRB, 321 US 332, 14 LRRM 501 (1944).

[7] Pattern Makers League v. NLRB (Rockford-Beloit Pattern Jobbers), 473 US __, 119 LRRM 2928 (1985).

II[8] had addressed this question for the first time in its history. Not surprisingly, the Board was unable to muster a majority for any single position on this issue, and the sharply divided Board issued three separate opinions.

The Board in *Dalmo Victor* struggled with prior Supreme Court decisions holding that a union acts lawfully when it imposes fines on union members who violate the union's internal rules against crossing picket lines during a strike,[9] and that a union member may nonetheless resign from the union at any time and be free of any union discipline.[10] Perhaps more than any prior decision, the Board's decision in *Dalmo Victor* highlighted the competing interests expressed in the Act. Two of us found that the union's absolute ban on resignations during strike periods was unlawful; that some accommodation between the conflicting interests was necessary. We thought that the Section 7 right to refrain from collective activity did not reach so far as to rule out all restriction by resignations and, rather arbitrarily, we stated that a union should be permitted, through a clearly announced rule, to require a member to give 30 days' notice before his or her resignation becomes final. Three of my colleagues, however, rejected any need to balance individual and collective interests. Two members found that Section 7 conferred an absolute right to resign on union employees, and the fifth member took exactly the opposite tack, finding that the union's rule restricting resignations for the duration of the strike was reasonable—thus, he would have required the individual's right to yield entirely to the collective interests.

We now know, of course, that the Supreme Court resolved this matter by a decision that almost mirrored the Board's 1982 divisions in *Dalmo Victor*. In the *Pattern Makers* decision[11] the Supreme Court found itself almost equally divided, with Justice White concurring with the majority's rejection of any union restriction on resignation only on the basis of complete deferral

---

[8] Machinists Local 1327 (Dalmo-Victor), 263 NLRB 984, 111 LRRM 1115 (1982), *enforcement denied*, 725 F2d 1212, 115 LRRM 2972 (CA 9, 1984), *cert. granted, vacated, and remanded*, ___ US ___, 119 LRRM 2992 (1985), *enforcement granted*, 773 F2d 1070, 120 LRRM 2864 (CA 9, 1985) (Board's original order enforced after Supreme Court's decision in *Pattern Makers*).

[9] NLRB v. Allis-Chalmers Mfg. Co., 388 US 175, 65 LRRM 2449 (1967).

[10] NLRB v. Textile Workers Local 1029, Granite State Joint Bd. (International Paper Box Mach. Co.), 409 US 213, 81 LRRM 2853 (1972); Scofield v. NLRB, 394 US 423, 70 LRRM 3105 (1969).

[11] *Supra* note 6.

to the "expertise" of the Board. By that time the Board's composition had changed because of appointments made by the current Administration, and the new majority had no inclination to find that any competing interests needed to be balanced.

The holding in *Pattern Makers* stands in contrast to an earlier Supreme Court decision in which the Court found that the presence of a collective bargaining representative extinguishes an individual's rights in favor of the collective majority. In *Emporium Capwell,*[12] the Court addressed attempts by a group of employees to circumvent their bargaining representative and deal directly with the employer. This involved efforts by a group of black employees to protest employer hiring and promotion policies that they believed were racially discriminatory. The employer refused to deal directly with these employees, insisting that they address the matter through their collective bargaining representative. The employees proceeded to distribute leaflets attacking the employer's policies, and they also picketed the employer. The employer discharged the employees for engaging in those activities. There can be no doubt that in the absence of a collective bargaining representative, the employees would have been found to be engaged in concerted activity protected by Section 7 of the Act. But, because they had selected a bargaining representative, the Court found that these employees were attempting to bargain with their employer in derogation of the exclusive representation status of the union. It therefore found that their activity was unprotected by the Act and that the employer's discharge of those employees was lawful. That decision can only be logically explained on the basis that the employees had surrendered certain Section 7 rights to the union.

Professor Aaron also discusses the union's duty of fair representation, which the Board and the court have imposed despite the absence of any specific language in the Act. The effect of this duty is to restrain majority rights by imposing upon the collective bargaining representative the obligation to represent fairly all employees in the bargaining unit. The years of debate over the extent of this duty clearly illustrate differing views as to the proper balance between collective and individual interests.

Another situation in which individual rights are weighed against collective rights, although it is not normally thought of in

---

[12] Emporium Capwell Co. v. Western Addition Community Org., 420 US 50, 88 LRRM 2660 (1975).

that context, involves the Board's policy of deferring to the arbitration awards rendered under contractual grievance procedures. Over the years, the Board's deferral to arbitration policies has been the subject of considerable controversy among practitioners and within the Board itself. Interestingly, however, that controversy has focused on the development and application of a deferral standard rather than on the question of whether the Board ought to have a deferral policy at all.

Perhaps no individual's right is more fundamental to the scheme of the NLRA than the right to file charges before the Board, and if those charges are found meritorious, to have them addressed in a Board unfair labor practice proceeding. Yet the Board's deferral policy, at least as to cases found appropriate for deferral, denies individuals the statutory forum for adjudication of unfair labor practice issues, and instead substitutes the almost unreviewable discretion of an arbitrator under private resolution procedures established pursuant to contract. I do not mean to suggest that deferral is not a sound policy, but only to point out that it is another example of a situation in which the Board has focused on the statutory purpose of furthering collective bargaining in a way that derogates individual rights that would otherwise be protected and safeguarded by the Act.

Finally, Professor Aaron quite thoroughly discusses the still unresolved fundamental question of whether the Act offers protection for employees who act alone with respect to terms and conditions of employment. Is such activity "concerted" within the meaning of the Act? Once again, a sharply divided Supreme Court has answered that question in the affirmative in *NLRB* v. *City Disposal Systems*. [13] We do not yet know, however, if in the absence of protective language in a collective bargaining agreement, an employee acting alone will similarly be deemed to be engaged in concerted activity when his or her "collective" support may be found only in another protected statute. This, of course, was the situation of employee Prill in *Meyers Industries*. [14]

Upon review by the D.C. Circuit, the court left to the Board the task of rationalizing its decision in light of its "error" in holding that its statutory interpretation was mandated by the statutory language. Like Professor Aaron, I have no doubt that

---

[13] 465 US 822, 115 LRRM 3193 (1984).
[14] 268 NLRB 493, 115 LLRM 1025 (1984), *remanded sub nom.* Prill v. NLRB, 755 F2d 941, 118 LRRM 2649 (CA DC, 1985).

the current Board, on remand, will reach the same result that it did originally. What is perhaps of even greater significance than the substantive question of the proper interpretation of "concerted" activity, is the obvious, if unstated, intention of the court to prevent the Board from obtaining approval of its holding as a "mandatory" interpretation. In its decision remanding *Meyers,* the court is insisting that the Board rule through exercise of its discretionary authority instead of finding a statutory mandate. This judicial reaction to the current Board seems designed to assure that at some time in the future a Board comprised of different members will have the opportunity to change the law once again.

The framers of the NLRA left it to the Board to interpret the statute, to fill in the many gaps, and to reconcile the competing rights and obligations that were established in conflict with each other. After 50 years, I believe most observers would have to concede that the task was more than the Board has been able to handle effectively. One might think that Congress would intervene to save the Board from any continuing misery. The political outlook for that prospect, however, remains as bleak as ever. The reaction to virtually any legislative proposals will no doubt continue to reflect the adage of the gored ox; and for the near future, at least, we can expect contentious parties to continue to press their views on the Board and courts in furtherance of their respective interests.

Commentary

Eleanor Holmes Norton*

The right to organize and bargain collectively required not only a struggle against industry but also against deep traditions in American law. The individualist ideal, perhaps the most pervasive in American life and law, is reflected in common law notions. Thus, it was natural for the common law to resist collectivist impulses, which seemed to impede developmental commerce. When craft and industrial workers tried to organize unions, the courts easily adapted protective common law commercial notions to the burgeoning industrial economy.[1]

---

* Professor of Law, Georgetown University.
[1] *See* Vegelahn v. Guntner, 44 NE 1077 (1896).

Thus, the legal embrace of the collectivist ideal now embodied in the Labor Management Relations Act (LMRA) was difficult. In 1921 Justice Brandeis claimed for the courts a "reversal of . . . common law," declaring that "the change in the law by which strikes once illegal and even criminal are now recognized as lawful was effected in America largely without the intervention of legislation."[2] This pre-Wagner Act claim is not without some validity. Yet the very claim, made in a dissenting opinion as the Supreme Court applied the Sherman Act to union activity, only serves to illuminate the law's deep instincts against the collectivist premises of labor organization.[3]

Despite the triumphant passage of the Wagner Act in 1935, the tension between individualist and collectivist notions has never been fully resolved. If the Taft-Hartley additions to the Act strengthening the rights of individuals did not make that clear, subsequent debate and interpretation have. Today, judicial and administrative balancing of the individual rights of workers and the collective prerogatives for unions—both conferred by the Act—yields such confusion that one despairs of extracting a principled interpretation without either legislative guidance or a different mode of legal analysis. I argue for the latter in this Commentary because it is the more likely and more practical route for achieving clarification.

Professor Aaron and respondents Joy, Kreiger, and Zimmerman document the confusion over individual rights in the labor context. Even after 50 years of statutory experience, notions of individual rights in the unionized setting are in disarray.

In light of the maturity of the Act, it is fair to ask why this question remains so unsettled. Locating the reasons for such a dilemma may be difficult and even perilous, but it must be pursued if a satisfactory approach to the problems raised is to be found. In this Commentary, I first will examine whether the current Board's sharp departures adequately explain the tensions generated by individual rights cases today. Second, I will look at an attempt at a more principled analysis of individual rights and similar issues by Board Member Patricia Diaz Dennis. Third, I will discuss some of the economic and social issues that

---

[2] Duplex Printing Press Co. v. Deering, 254 US 443 (1921).

[3] See Epstein, Common Law for Labor Relations: A Critique of New Deal Labor Legislation, 92 YALE L.J. 1357 (1983), suggesting that a return to common law contract notions would protect the interests of employees, employers, and society better than the present statutory scheme.

have fed the legal issues raised. Finally, I will suggest that resolving the balance between individual rights and union prerogatives requires a more complex and balanced analysis, drawing more systematically upon the underlying purposes of the labor statute. Otherwise, individual rights, a notion with particular power in our law, achieves an easy dominance, eclipsing the policies of a collectivist statute. For purposes of illustration, I will use perhaps the most basic of the statutory policies, the promotion of labor peace as an alternative to economic warfare,[4] and one of the most troublesome areas of individual rights, the duty of fair representation (DFR).

Given the perception many have of the present Board, it is reasonable to ask the extent to which individual rights issues today are a case of management bias. I do not dispute the contention made especially by Aaron and Kreiger that the present Board has shown such consistent regard for management concerns as to cast doubt upon its apparent solicitude for the rights of workers, especially in DFR cases. Seen in this way, decisions upholding individual rights appear to be a tool to strengthen management and weaken labor, with incidental benefits to some individual workers but long-term disadvantages to unions, which alone are charged with systematic and coherent worker protection. This view is not without force. However, over the life of the statute, the courts have also played an important role in the tension that has developed between individual and group rights. This suggests that several forces have been at work.

Even at the Board, Member Dennis, has applied her philosophy that "the Board should administer the Act to promote nongovernmental solutions to problems in labor-management relations,"[5] to reach both pro-management and pro-labor results in individual rights and similar cases. Thus, she has voted with the majority to require deferral to arbitrators' decisions in a broad range of circumstances, including Section 8a(3) discrimination cases involving discharge and discipline, which had been

---

[4] "The statute can best be understood as an effort by Congress to create the conditions of individual peace in interstate commerce by removing obstacles to—indeed, encouraging—the formation of labor unions as an effective voice for the individual worker." Robert A. Gorman, BASIC TEXT ON LABOR LAW: UNIONIZATION AND COLLECTIVE BARGAINING, (1976).

[5] Dennis, *Principles That Guide My Decision-Making*, 15 STETSON LAW REV. 1 (1985).

excepted from deferral by the prior Board.[6] Member Dennis has lamented that her view of deferral, which often implicates individual rights, "has been criticized as 'pro-management.'"[7]

However, employing the same principle of noninterference by the Board, she has dissented in a series of recent decisions in which management had put in issue the rights of individual workers against the rights of unions. In each of these cases, recognition of workers' rights strengthened management against the unions, and in each case Member Dennis voted with the unions. In *Owens-Illinois,*[8] she voted against the majority and would have upheld a union election victory in spite of the union's distribution to employees of union jackets valued at $16. Significantly, she relied on a case in which the majority had rejected the union's objection to a similarly valued company distribution.[9] In *Kraft, Inc.,*[10] Member Dennis opposed the Board's refusal to certify a union victory, ruling that the ballot, which was translated into three foreign languages, was too confusing to English speakers because of mistakes in translation that affected three of the 238 employees. In *S & C Security,*[11] she dissented when the Board overturned a union victory on the ground that the union observer believed he would be paid in the election at issue because he had been paid in an earlier election, even though there was no evidence of misconduct.

These cases do not necessarily mean that Member Dennis has found a principled approach to labor law decision making or the appropriate balance between individual and union prerogatives. Such a judgment would require a more systematic examination of her decisions. Nor is her government deregulation philosophy neutral or broadly appealing. What is noteworthy, however, is her conscious use of a readily ascertainable philosophy or

---

[6] *See* Olin Corp., 268 NLRB 573, 115 LRRM 1056 (1984) *and* United Technologies Corp., 268 NLRB 557, 115 LRRM 1049 (1984). *Olin* relaxes the *Spielberg-Raytheon* requirements for deferral in two important ways. First, it interprets the "clearly repugnant" *Spielberg* standard to mean that the arbitrator's award need not be "totally consistent with Board precedent" but is acceptable so long as it is not "palpably wrong." Second, it accepts the arbitrator's disposal of the unfair labor practice if "(1) the contractual issue is factually parallel to the unfair labor practice issue, and (2) the arbitrator was presented generally with the facts relevant to resolving the unfair labor practice." 268 NLRB at 574.

[7] *Supra* note 5, at 7.

[8] Owens-Illinois, Inc., 271 NLRB No. 194, 117 LRRM 1104 (1984).

[9] R.L. White Co., 262 NLRB 575, 111 LRRM 1078 (1982).

[10] Kraft, Inc., Retail Food Group, 273 NLRB No. 184, 118 LRRM 1242 (1985).

[11] S & C Sec., Inc., 271 NLRB No. 211, 117 LRRM 1154 (1984).

standard that appears to have produced more principled results than those of some others on the Board.

Whatever the standard, individual rights issues, like other issues in labor law, have always been affected by economic and social trends. Rapidly changing economic conditions today have undermined some of the salient premises of the Wagner Act. Respondent Kreiger makes a convincing case that the Wagner Act was a consciously collectivist statute that deliberately subordinated individual rights as the only way to protect the rights of workers against the inherent power of management. The result was functionally a bargain between management and labor amounting to a *de facto* pact of coexistence. As a result, by 1950 one-third of the work force was organized, compared with under 20 percent today.[12]

The fact is, during the 1940s and 1950s, when union strength was at its peak, business did not systematically avail itself of tactics routinely used today, such as corporate campaigns to prevent unionization[13] and the employment of permanent strike replacements.[14] At first this seems quite remarkable, given the turbulent history of labor relations before the enactment of the Wagner Act. It is understandable only in light of the economic forces in operation at the time.

The Wagner Act was not only a charter guaranteeing the right to organize and bargain collectively. It was also a weapon in the New Deal arsenal for stimulating a depressed economy and reinvigorating American capitalism itself. The Act was meant to promote labor peace and stability in order to encourage labor-management cooperation to help end the Depression.[15]

Similarly, the Taft-Hartley Act was passed in part in reaction to perceived economic excesses by unions, including prolonged

---

[12] The Economist, October 29, 1983, at 71.

[13] *See* NLRB v. J.P. Stevens & Co., 563 F2d 8, 96 LRRM 2150 (CA 2, 1977), *and* J.P. Stevens & Co., 244 NLRB 407, 102 LRRM 1039 (1979).

[14] For example, after successfully filing for bankruptcy, Continental Airlines resumed business with a nonunionized labor force. N.Y. Times, September 24, 1984.

[15] However, the Wagner Act was embraced belatedly by President Roosevelt who "delayed until after the bill had been passed by the Senate and passage by the House was a certainty." *See* C. Morris, ed., THE DEVELOPING LABOR LAW 2d ed. 27 (1983). The Act's economic purposes were made explicit. In the Findings and Policies, Congress found "[t]hat inequality of bargaining power between employees . . . and employers . . . tends to aggravate recurrent business depressions, by depressing wage rates and the purchasing power of wage earners in industry and by preventing the stabilization of competitive wage rates . . . ." 49 Stat 449, §1 (1935), 29 USC §151.

strikes and the use of the secondary boycott.[16] Labor had become far more muscular, and some of the Wagner Act protections seemed to many to be unnecessary paternalism.

Still, the Taft-Hartley amendments did not by themselves produce changes in management behavior. The robust management challenges seen so frequently today emerged in the 1970s, not in the immediate post-Taft-Hartley period. Economic forces set loose by the Depression and the post-war conditions of a growing economy kept in place much of the basic compact between management and labor. Economic forces of a different kind, but equally powerful, have led to a breach of that compact.

These forces are so familiar they do not require extensive elaboration here. They include the rise of the international economy and the multinational corporation. Escalating international economic competition has created both problems and opportunities for management, but only problems for labor. "Capital is mobile and labor is not," Lane Kirkland, President of the AFL-CIO, has said. "Capital has no flag, and no country. Labor is locked not just into its country, but its community."[17] The rapidly growing service economy has not offset losses in union membership in manufacturing, because organizing in the service and white-collar sectors has always been more difficult. Structural economic and demographic changes, recession, inflation, and technological transition have all served to encourage business disengagement from the old Wagner Act detente.

It was virtually inevitable that labor law would be deeply affected by these economic changes. This is especially the case with Board interpretation because, historically, the Board has been far more sensitive to political and economic changes than the courts, sometimes making a mockery of traditional notions of *stare decisis*.[18] In any case, the changing economy has encour-

---

[16] A. Cox, D. Bok, & R. Gorman, CASES & MATERIALS ON LABOR LAW, 91 (1986).

[17] Bob Kuttner, *Can Labor Lead*, THE NEW REPUBLIC, March 12, 1984, at 25.

[18] The Board's history on the question of whether campaign misrepresentations should be grounds for overturning an election is perhaps the most notorious example. Hollywood Ceramics Co., 140 NLRB 221, 51 LRRM 1600 (1962), delineated the circumstances when an election could be overturned because of misrepresentations. The Board overruled *Hollywood Ceramics* fifteen years later in *Shopping Kart Food Mkt., Inc.*, 228 NLRB 131, 94 LRRM 1705 (1977), but a new Board overruled *Shopping Kart* less than two years later in *General Knit of Cal., Inc.*, 239 NLRB 619, 99 LRRM 1687 (1978), returning to the *Hollywood Ceramics* standard, which in turn was rejected again four years later by a new Board in *Midland Nat'l Life Ins. Co.*, 263 NLRB 127, 110 LRRM 1489 (1982). Consequently, today the Board will not overturn an election because false statements were made during an election campaign.

aged business to make use of whatever weaknesses could be found in the Act. Unlike other sections of the LMRA,[19] however, most of the provisions affording individual rights can only be indirectly exploited by management, because usually they must be raised by the employees affected.

Clearly then, external forces encouraged individual rights to be claimed in the labor context, quite apart from management concerns. One of the most determined of these was the quest for individual rights in the society-at-large. The black civil rights movement set off a stream of similar demands by other excluded groups.[20] It is no wonder that workers analogized slogans and grievances that tapped universal themes of individual rights.

Faced with an assortment of unprecedented claims seeking to vindicate individual rights, the Board and the courts have often proceeded without consistent labor law reference points or guiding principles. Without such principles, individual claims will often seem compelling and overriding in our system of law. This is especially the case with courts, because both their bedrock function and their most cherished ideal is the resolution of individual claims.[21] Professor Aaron looks at several quite diverse areas of labor law from which individual rights issues have emerged. One of the most vexatious is the duty of fair representation jurisdiction.

The courts inferred[22] and then developed DFR as an obligation flowing from the status of exclusive bargaining agent, conferred by statute on certified unions, and the Board followed suit. As a consequence, without regard to the effect on the union or on other workers, employees can allege unfair labor practices under Sections 8(b)(1)(A), 8(b)(2), and 8(b)(3) for perfunctory or arbitrary handling of a meritorious grievance or for conduct

---

[19] *See, e.g.*, §8(c) affording free speech rights to employers; §8(a)(3) barring the closed shop; §8(b)(3) imposing a duty on unions to bargain like that imposed by the Wagner Act on employers; and §8(b)(4) barring secondary boycotts.

[20] There are perhaps some analytic reasons for, but nevertheless some irony in, the fact that the LMRA never became a major vehicle for challenging the most pervasive denial of rights in the workplace, race and sex discrimination by companies and unions. Many actions brought under Title VII of the 1964 Civil Rights Act have successfully challenged such discrimination.

[21] It is noteworthy that the Board initially refrained from developing the DFR jurisdiction when it might have done so. The Board appears to have been concerned by the implications of the development of an important individual rights jurisdiction in a labor statute. The courts moved into the vacuum.

[22] *See* Syres v. Oil Workers Local 23, 390 US 892, 37 LRRM 2068 (1959); Steele v. Louisville & Nashville R.R. 323 US 192, 15 LRRM 708 (1944).

that is "arbitrary, discriminatory, or in bad faith."[23] If anything, the courts in DFR cases sometimes have ventured beyond the Board.[24]

Nevertheless, the standards, as articulated and applied, seek to erect a barrier in recognition of a union's need for discretion to choose and process grievances in light of its responsibilities to individuals and the group alike. But in practice, the results have often been confusing, unpredictable, or worse. Because the LMRA is not primarily an individual rights statute, standards such as "arbitrariness" and "discrimination" cannot operate in the way they do in more traditional areas without doing damage to the statutory purpose of the Act to promote group interests and cooperation. The applicable concepts of individual rights need to be anchored more specifically to the underlying purposes of a labor statute.

I have suggested that the promotion of labor peace is one statutory purpose that might be used in appropriate cases involving individual rights. This statutory policy is useful to illustrate the kind of analysis that might be helpful, both because of the fundamental place labor peace has in the statutory framework and because of its potential usefulness as a tool for bringing about the necessary balance between individual and union concerns.

Labor peace is perhaps the most basic and abiding purpose of the LMRA. It was of fundamental importance to the framers of both the Wagner Act and the Taft-Hartley Act. The Wagner Act did much to end labor-management turmoil during the Depression and to promote critical labor stability during the years of the Second World War. It conferred the right to organize and bargain collectively, authorized the closed shop, provided for exclusive representation, and barred unfair labor practices by employers. After the war, concern that the Wagner Act was then inadequate to encourage labor peace led to the enactment of the Taft-Hartley Act. At the time, Congress viewed labor, not business, as rambunctious and powerful. In the Declaration of Policy to the Taft-Hartley Act, the dominant theme was again labor

---

[23] Vaca v. Sipes, 386 US 171, 191, 64 LRRM 2369 (1967).

[24] Unintentional acts have been found by courts to violate the duty of fair representation. For example, in *Dutrisac* v. *Caterpillar Tractor Co.*, 749 F2d 1270, 113 LRRM 3532 (CA 9, 1983), a union was found to have breached the duty of fair representation by negligently failing to perform a ministerial act.

peace.[25] Congress sought to achieve this purpose by authorizing injunctions against a number of activities it believed encouraged unnecessary economic warfare: secondary boycotts, violence and intimidation, strikes to compel unfair labor practices, and jurisdictional strikes over work assignments. The amended Act, moreover, sought to encourage labor peace by specifically restricting labor's power in several ways, including barring the closed shop and balancing management's unfair labor practice obligations with corollary union obligations.

Thus, in suitable cases, the labor peace principle provides a legitimate statutory anchor against which to test individualist principles that otherwise can assume a life of their own and defeat the purposes of a collectivist statute. To be sure, the labor peace principle would require rigorous analysis and application in the very different areas of labor law in which individual rights arise—from concerted activity to union discipline. Moreover, as an analytic tool, such a principle is likely to prove of differential value, depending on the particular rights at issue and the context. Nevertheless, the peace principle has the virtue of being consistently dominant in both the original Act and the Taft-Hartley Amendments, which on questions of individual rights often appear to move in contrary directions.

The DFR jurisdiction is a paradigm that captures several aspects of the individual rights dilemma and thus is helpful to demonstrate how the peace principle might be used analytically. DFR provides a strong test for principled analysis because of its loose and disjointed character. It is an inferred rather than an explicitly conferred right. Jurisdiction on the merits may be exercised by the courts, the Board, an arbitrator, or the union through its internal procedures. The jurisdiction is developmental and unusually volatile, and the results are sometimes bizarre.

Bowen v. *United States Postal Service*[26] invites an effort to test a more principled analysis. Whether or not one agrees with Professor Aaron that the result in *Bowen* was "grotesque," the case can hardly be considered analytically satisfying. The union was held primarily liable in damages for failing to arbitrate an employee's grievance concerning a wrongful discharge implicat-

---

[25] Pub. L. 101, 80th Cong., 1st Sess. (1947) 61 Stat 136, 141, as amended by Pub. L. 257.
[26] 459 US 212, 112 LRRM 2281 (1983).

ing only the employer. The Court's analysis often seems mechanical in its use of standards, including an admittedly hypothetical date when arbitration of the underlying grievance might have occurred had the union arbitrated the grievance. The increase in damages was charged to the union, with the result that, of the $52,954 in liability, the district court charged $30,000 to the union.

The decision of the Court is notable for the consistent deference it gives individual rights concepts over standards that relate to the underlying labor policies reflected in the Act. The Court relies on such notions as the "paramount . . . right of the employee . . . to be made whole"[27] without addressing resulting anomolies that seem inconsistent with the purposes of a labor statute. Similarly, the Court cites the obligation of the union for the "natural consequences"[28] of its breach without persuading us that it is "natural" to allow a hypothetical arbitration date to leave a union with the damages accruing during the lengthy court process. These concepts are, of course, entirely relevant to the issue. But the Court ignores contract principles that appear equally relevant in this context.[29]

The Court discusses labor policy defensively. The damages apportioned to the union are justified as consistent with the allocation of responsibilities under the grievance mechanism. The Court is concerned that by imposing total liability on the employer, "incentives to comply with the grievance procedure will be diminished"[30] and, worse, "the willingness of employers to agree to arbitration clauses" could be affected.[31] Nowhere is the corollary disincentive to unions mentioned except to note, remarkably, that "requiring the union to pay damages . . . will provide an additional incentive for the union to process its members' claims where warranted."[32]Had labor policy been more deeply analyzed, the perverse incentive to unions to avoid rather than adopt a grievance mechanism that could bankrupt their treasuries would more likely have been discussed. One effect of a more balanced discussion of labor policy might have

---

[27] *Id.* at 222.
[28] *Id.*
[29] *Id.* at 238 (opinion of White, J., concurring in the judgment) (citing 5 A. Corbin, Contracts §999 [1964]).
[30] *Supra* note 26 at 227.
[31] *Id.*
[32] *Id.*

been some attempt to distinguish among factual settings that might qualify for a *Bowen*-type remedy and those that might not. This analysis would have been aided by a discussion of the merits of the prevailing view before *Bowen*—that unions are liable for the costs of collecting damages, but not for damages. Even if the result in *Bowen* had not been different, the analysis would have been more credible had such issues of labor policy been faced forthrightly.

The danger of *Bowen* is precisely the potential harm to the grievance mechanism, it seeks to avoid. *Bowen* puts at risk the grievance machinery, which is the alternative to strikes and thus the primary keeper of labor peace. The decision unintentionally trivializes the system by encouraging the processing of marginal grievances and, worse, by risking the flooding and thus the breakdown of the grievance and arbitration process altogether. Julius Getman, a leading labor scholar who also counsels unions, notes that "[e]xpanding the duty of fair representation convinces unions to be cautious," and he reports that "[m]any [unions] are currently taking all discipline cases to arbitration."[33] Getman notes not only the costs involved but also the impression given arbitrators that "unions are just going through the motions."[34] How long can this impression escape workers? These and similar results could rob the grievance process of the vital credibility it needs if workers are to regard it as the preferred way to resolve disputes. The primary purpose of the dispute resolution system is to provide an outlet for resolving disagreements short of strikes or other economic warfare. Thus, the peace principle, which undergirds the Act, is profoundly affected over time by how the courts and the Board balance the equities in DFR cases.

It is not certain that a more conscious and systematic use of labor policy concepts would produce results different from the *Bowen* holding. What *Bowen* reveals is how much the relative place of individual and group rights remain enigmatic and unsettled in the Labor Management Relations Act. The courts as well as the Board have developed some salutary principles, but

---

[33] Getman, *Is the Labor Act Doing Its Job?* 15 STETSON LAW REV. 93, 96 (1985).

[34] *Id.* The cost of processing frivolous grievances may well be less than a large damage claim. Prohibitive compensatory damages could amount to punitive damages, although the Supreme Court held that unions are not liable for punitive damages in *Electrical Workers* v. *Foust,* 442 U.S. 42 (1979).

the underlying purposes of the statute have been insufficiently exploited.

Diverse trends outside of the law—including structural economic changes that have encouraged management hostility to labor and a national climate that is particularly sensitive to individual rights—have raised questions about the accommodation between individual and group concerns in the Act. The answers must be found by the Board, the courts, or Congress. The most likely actors are the courts and the Board. The most realistic approach appears to be a studied attempt by the interpreters of the Act to find the proper balance between individual and group rights. To do this, the strong and explicit statutory purposes, among them labor peace, should be plumbed. While underlying statutory policies do not guarantee that a more satisfactory balance will be found, they hold more promise than the uncharted present course of the courts and the Board.

The need for reconciliation of individual and group rights is as old as the Taft-Hartley Act, which explicitly imposed the individual rights vision. On the 50th anniversary of the Wagner Act, after many years of actions that have appropriately vindicated individual rights, there is no reason to regret the introduction of individual rights as a concern of the statute. Rather, there is a need for a systematic search for a more principled analysis.

CHAPTER 4

THE COLLECTIVE BARGAINING PROCESS

THEODORE J. ST. ANTOINE*

A half century after the passage of the Wagner Act[1] the right
to bargain collectively remains a glowing but imperfectly realized promise for American workers. In recent years even the
theoretical dimensions of the right have been markedly com-
pressed. Yet collective bargaining was conceived in the widespread belief that both the cause of industrial peace and the
welfare of the individual employee would be promoted if workers were given a genuine voice in determining their employment
conditions.[2] Why has the process apparently lost so much
appeal? Does it still hold hope for the future?

In this paper I shall review briefly the major policy choices
confronting the early formulators of collective bargaining law,
trace some of the more important doctrinal and practical developments over the intervening decades, and ruminate a bit about
where we should go from here.

I. Bargaining in Good Faith

Right at the outset Congress faced the question of whether a
formal duty to bargain should be imposed on employers. There
were influential voices on both sides of the issue. Although
Senator Wagner's original "labor disputes bill" of 1934 did not
speak explicitly of an obligation to "bargain collectively," one
provision would have made it an unfair labor practice "to fail to

---

* James E. and Sarah A. Degan Professor of Law, University of Michigan.
[1] 49 Stat 449 (1935) (codified as amended at 29 USC §151 (1982)).
[2] *See, e.g.,* 78 CONG. REC. 3443 (1934) *rerpinted in* 1 LEGISLATIVE HISTORY OF THE
NATIONAL LABOR RELATIONS ACT, 1935 at 15 (1949) (remarks of Sen. Wagner); [here-
inafter cited as LEG. HIST. NLRA], *id.* at 10351, 10559, *reprinted in* 1 LEG. HIST. NLRA, at
1117, 1122 (remarks of Sen. Walsh).

exert every reasonable effort to make and maintain agreements with [employees'] representatives."[3]

At the committee hearings Sumner Slichter of Harvard opposed this requirement as a "pious wish," declaring contemptuously: "You might almost enact that the lions and lambs shall not fail to exert every reasonable effort to lie down together."[4] But persons with more practical experience, both inside and outside of academia, insisted that failure to mandate collective bargaining would "omit . . . the very guts"[5] of the organizational process, and that it was "exceedingly important" to provide that employers must "make an earnest effort"[6] to reach an agreement with unions representing their employees. This group included Lloyd K. Garrison, Dean of the Wisconsin Law School and former Chairman of the old National Labor Relations Board; William M. Leiserson, then Chairman of the Petroleum Labor Policy Board; and Francis Biddle, Chairman of the old NLRB.[7] Their views prevailed. Section 8(5) was added to the Wagner-Connery bill in 1935, making it an unfair labor practice for an employer to "refuse to bargain collectively with the representatives of his employees."[8] The same language appeared in the National Labor Relations Act as finally adopted and has remained unchanged ever since.[9]

---

[3] S. REP. NO. 2926, 73d Cong., 2d Sess. (1934), *reprinted in* LEG. HIST. NLRA, *supra* note 2, at 3.

[4] *To Create a National Labor Board: Hearings on S. 2926 Before the Senate Comm. on Education and Labor,* 73d Cong., 2d Sess. 59 (1934), *reprinted in* LEG. HIST. NLRA, *supra* note 2, at 89. Dr. Slichter's opinion carried enough weight that the bill as reported from committee omitted the language he criticized. S. REP. NO. 2926, 73d Cong., 2d Sess. (1934), as reported, *reprinted in* LEG. HIST. NLRA, *supra* note 2, at 1070.

[5] *National Labor Relations Board: Hearings on S. 1958 Before Senate Comm. on Education and Labor,* 74th Cong., 1st Sess. 137 (1935), *reprinted in* LEG. HIST. NLRA, *supra* note 2, at 1517 (statement of Lloyd K. Garrison).

[6] *To Create a National Labor Board: Hearings on S. 1958 Before the Senate Comm. on Education and Labor,* 73d Cong., 2d Sess. 234 (1934), *reprinted in* LEG. HIST. NLRA, *supra* note 2, at 264 (statement of William M. Leiserson).

[7] *See supra* notes 5–6; *Labor Disputes Act: Hearings on H.R. supra 6288 Before the House Comm. on Labor,* 74th Cong., 1st sess. 175 (1935), *reprinted in* LEG. HIST. NLRA, *supra* note 2, at 2649 (statement of Francis Biddle); *National Labor Relations Board: Hearings on S. 1958 Before Senate Comm. on Education and Labor,* 74th Cong., 1st Sess. 79–80 (1935), *reprinted in* LEG. HIST. NLRA *supra* note 2, at 1455–56 (statement of Francis Biddle).

[8] S. REP. NO. 1958, 74th Cong., 1st Sess. (1935), as reported, *reprinted in* LEG. HIST. NLRA, *supra* note 2, at 2290; H.R. REP. NO. 7978, 74th Cong., 1st Sess. (1935), *reprinted in* LEG. HIST. NLRA, *supra* note 2, at 2862. *See also* S. REP. NO. 573, 74th Cong., 1st Sess. 12 (1935), *reprinted in* LEG. HIST. NLRA, *supra* note 2, at 2312; H. R. REP. NO. 1147, 74th Cong., 1st Sess. 20 (1935), *reprinted in* LEG. HIST. NLRA, *supra* note 2, at 3069.

[9] 49 Stat 449, 453 (1935) (codified as amended at 29 USC §158(a)(5) (1982)). *See generally* Cox, *The Duty to Bargain in Good Faith,* 71 HARV. L. REV. 1401 (1958); Duvin, *The*

The debate has never ended on the wisdom of what Congress did, or indeed on exactly what it was that had been done. The two principal congressional architects of the legislation differed considerably over its meaning. The Act's sponsor, Senator Wagner, thought it would obligate an employer to "negotiate in good faith" and "make every reasonable effort to reach an agreement."[10] Senator Walsh, the Chairman of the Senate Labor Committee, felt instead that the parties would merely be required to get together, to meet and confer. "The bill," said he, "does not go beyond the office door."[11] In 1950 the powerful voices of Archibald Cox and John Dunlop spoke out to insist that the Wagner Act was concerned only with "*organization for bargaining*—not with the scope of the ensuing negotiations."[12] They lamented that the NLRB, with judicial endorsement, had undertaken the task of "defining the scope of collective bargaining."[13] As late as 1961 a distinguished labor study group headed by Clark Kerr labeled the bargaining requirement "unrealistic," commenting that the "provisions designed to bring 'good faith' have become a tactical weapon used in many situations as a means of harassment."[14]

Meanwhile, in 1947, the Taft-Hartley amendments finally defined collective bargaining. In addition to subjecting unions as well as employers to the duty to bargain, Congress added a new section, Section 8(d)[15] to the NLRA, declaring that to "bargain

---

Duty to Bargain: Law in Search of Policy, 64 COLUM. L. REV. 248, 252–53 (1964); Fleming, *The Obligation to Bargain in Good Faith*, 47 VA. L. REV. 988 (1961); Gross, Cullen, & Hanslowe, *Good Faith in Labor Negotiations: Test and Remedies*, 53 CORNELL L. REV. 1009 (1968); Latham, *Legislative Purpose and Administrative Policy Under the National Labor Relations Act*, 4 GEO. WASH. L. REV. 433 (1936); Murphy, *Impasse and the Duty to Bargain in Good Faith*, 39 U. PITT. L. REV. 1 (1977); Smith, *The Evolution of the "Duty to Bargain" Concept in American Law*, 39 MICH. L. REV. 1065, 1084–86 (1941).

[10] 79 CONG. REC. 7571 (1935), *reprinted in* LEG. HIST. NLRA, *supra* note 2, at 2336 (remarks of Sen. Wagner, citing Houde Eng'g Corp., 1 NLRB (old) 35 (1934)).

[11] 79 CONG. REC. 7659 (1935), *reprinted in* LEG. HIST. NLRB, *supra* note 2, at 2373 (remarks of Sen. Walsh).

[12] Cox & Dunlop, *Regulation of Collective Bargaining by the National Labor Relations Board*, 63 HARV. L. REV. 389, 394 (1950) (emphasis in the original).

[13] *Id.* at 397.

[14] LABOR STUDY GROUP, COMM. FOR ECONOMIC DEVELOPMENT, THE PUBLIC INTEREST IN NATIONAL LABOR POLICY 82 (1961). The members of the Study Group, besides Chairman Clark Kerr, were Douglas V. Brown, David L. Cole, John T. Dunlop, William Y. Elliot, Albert Rees, Robert M. Solow, Philip Taft, and George W. Taylor.

[15] 61 Stat 136, 142–43 (1947) (codified as amended at 29 USC §158(d)(1976)), *reprinted in* 1 LEGISLATIVE HISTORY OF THE LABOR MANAGEMENT RELATIONS ACT, 1947 [hereinafter cited as LEG. HIST. LMRA], at 8 (1948). At the same time §8(b)(3) made it a reciprocal duty of unions to bargain collectively with employers, and §8(5) was renumbered as §8(a)(5). 29 USC §158 (a)(5), (b)(3)(1982).

collectively" meant the "mutual obligation" of employer and union to confer "in good faith" with respect to "wages, hours, and other terms and conditions of employment." Section 8(d) also took pains to state that no party would be under a compulsion to "agree to a proposal" or make any "concession." There is probably no principle of national labor policy about which the Supreme Court has been so emphatic and so consistent over the years as this "free opportunity for negotiation";[16] the Labor Board may not "sit in judgment upon the substantive terms of collective bargaining agreements."[17]

Inevitably there will be tension when a government agency that is totally precluded from intruding upon or assessing the parties' ultimate bargain must nonetheless determine in many cases whether the negotiations were carried on in "good faith," that is, with a "*bona fide* intent" to adjust differences and "to reach an agreement if agreement is possible."[18] Apart from examining such obvious procedural factors as the parties' willingness to have duly authorized representatives meet and confer at reasonable times and places, how can the NLRB inquire into "good faith" without looking at what proposals and counterproposals are made during the course of bargaining? And how can taking such a look avoid tipping the scales in favor of some types of contract provisions and against others? The problem becomes especially acute, as we shall discuss shortly,[19] when the NLRB proceeds to tell the parties that they must bargain about certain subjects, and need not bargain about others.

Section 8(d)'s definitional provision contains essentially two elements, the "how" of bargaining—"in good faith"—and the "what" of bargaining—"wages, hours, and other terms and conditions of employment." In practice these elements sometimes merge. Occasionally, an employer's substantive proposals have been treated as evidence of bad faith, especially when combined with other conduct such as delaying tactics. So classified were an

---

[16] NLRB v. Jones & Laughlin Steel Corp., 301 US 1, 45, 1 LRRM 703 (1937).

[17] NLRB v. American Nat'l Ins. Co., 343 US 395, 404, 30 LRRM 2147 (1952). *See also* NLRB v. Insurance Agents, 361 US 477, 487, 45 LRRM 2705 (1960); H.K. Porter Co. v. NLRB, 397 US 99, 108, 73 LRRM 2561 (1970) ("freedom of contract" as fundamental policy of NLRA).

[18] Atlas Mills, 3 NLRB 10, 21, 1 LRRM 60 (1937); NLRB v. Highland Park Mfg. Co., 110 F2d 632, 637, 6 LRRM 786 (CA 4, 1940). *See also* National Licorice Co. v. NLRB, 309 US 350, 358, 6 LRRM 674 (1940) (accepting good-faith requirements under original Wagner Act).

[19] *See infra* Part II.

insistence on an "open shop" and absolute employer control over wage rates,[20] and an offer of little or no wage increase during a period of double-digit inflation.[21] Besides the classic case of a bad-faith refusal to bargain, which involves a subjective state of mind (the lack of *bona fide* intent), the Board and the courts have also held that there may be certain *per se* refusals to bargain, regardless of a party's good faith or bad faith. The theory in such instances is that in effect there has been no bargaining at all, or at least insufficient bargaining to satisfy the obligation to persist to the point of "impasse" or deadlock in the negotiations. The party's frame of mind is thus immaterial. Examples of *per se* violations include a party's taking unilateral action without prior negotiations concerning a matter, like wages or hours, on which bargaining is required,[22] or, conversely, a party's insisting on negotiations concerning a matter on which bargaining is *not* required.[23]

More typically, a finding of a refusal to bargain in good faith is based on the "totality of conduct" exhibited by a party.[24] Perhaps the most celebrated and controversial decision on the subject is *General Electric Co.*,[25] often referred to as the "Boulwarism" case. Lemuel R. Boulware was a vice president of GE who in the late 1940s devised a new three-step bargaining strategy.[26] It consisted of a systematic research program to determine what benefits employees wanted and what the company could afford; the preparation of a "fair and firm" offer for presentation to the union with no room for change unless the company had overlooked critical facts; and a massive communications campaign to convince the employees and the public

---

[20] NLRB v. Wright Motors, Inc., 603 F2d 604, 102 LRRM 2021 (CA 7, 1979).

[21] K-Mart Corp. v.'NLRB, 626 F2d 704, 105 LRRM 2431 (CA 9, 1980).

[22] NLRB v. Katz, 369 US 736, 50 LRRM 2177 (1962); *cf.* NLRB v. Crompton-Highland Mills, Inc., 337 US 217, 24 LRRM 2088 (1949) (unilateral action as manifestation of bad faith).

[23] NLRB v. Wooster Div. of Borg-Warner Corp., 356 US 342, 42 LRRM 2034 (1958); *see infra* Part II.

[24] *See* General Elec. Co., 150 NLRB 192, 193, 196, 57 LRRM 1491 (1964), *enforced*, 418 F2d 736, 72 LRRM 2530 (CA 2, 1969), *cert. denied*, 397 US 965 (1970). The general approach of looking at the "whole complex" of a party's activities to determine their legitimacy under the NLRA may be derived from NLRB v. Virginia Elec. & Power Co., 314 US 469, 477–78, 9 LRRM 405 (1941).

[25] *Supra* note 24.

[26] *See generally* H. Northrup, BOULWAREISM (1964); Cooper, *Boulwareism and the Duty to Bargain in Good Faith*, 20 RUTGERS L. REV. 653 (1966); Note, *Boulwareism and Good Faith Collective Bargaining*, 63 MICH. L. REV. 1473 (1965).

that GE would "do right voluntarily," without the need for union intervention. The Board, supported by a divided Second Circuit, found this procedure as employed in these particular circumstances at odds with the "shared process" of collective bargaining mandated by the NLRA. More specifically, the Board held that GE had failed to bargain in good faith through (1) its failure to furnish information requested by the union, (2) its attempts to deal separately with locals while engaged in national negotiations, (3) its presentation of an accident insurance proposal on a take-it-or-leave-it basis, and (4) its overall approach to and conduct of bargaining.[27]

Although the trial examiner treated GE's proposal of its insurance plan on a take-it-or-leave-it basis as a separate violation, the Board majority declared it was simply indicative of the company's overall bad faith.[28] Nevertheless, the scrupulously balanced treatise produced by the American Bar Association's Section of Labor and Employment Law is surely correct in summing up the majority's attitude toward the bargaining obligation: "The duty refers to a *bilateral* procedure whereby the employer and the bargaining representative *jointly* attempt to set wages and working conditions for the employees."[29] If *General Electric* did not outlaw take-it-or-leave-it bargaining as such (and I conclude it did not), it clearly did not place its imprimatur on the technique either.

However hard it may be to identify "good faith" and to classify such particular tactics as "take-it-or-leave-it" bargaining, there has been considerable evidence over the years that the statutory duty to bargain has had a positive practical effect. One survey in the 1960s, for example, revealed that successful bargaining relationships were eventually established in 75 percent of the cases sampled that went through to a final Board order, and in 90 percent of the cases that were voluntarily adjusted after the issuance of a complaint.[30] Although a recalcitrant offender can drag its heels with relative impunity, because a Board order to

---

[27] General Elec. Co., *supra* note 24, at 193.

[28] *Id.* at 196.

[29] American Bar Association, Section of Labor and Employment Law, THE DEVELOPING LABOR LAW 2d ed. 574 (C. Morris, ed., 1983) (emphasis in the original) [hereinafter cited as DEVELOPING LABOR LAW].

[30] P. Ross, THE GOVERNMENT AS A SOURCE OF UNION POWER 180–230 (1965); *see also* McCulloch, *The Development of Administrative Remedies*, 14 LAB. L.J. 339, 348 (1963) (then NLRB Chairman discussing effectiveness of Board remedies).

bargain operates only prospectively and ordinarily does not furnish any monetary relief,[31] the happy reality during most of the past half century is that the vast majority of American employers and unions bowed to the law's demands, cheerfully or otherwise. Unfortunately, the last decade has seen an ominous new pattern of unlawful employer behavior. Professor Paul Weiler estimates that about 10,000 employees were discharged in 1980 for their activities in representation campaigns; since 200,000 employees voted for unions that year, this meant that one out of every 20 union supporters paid for her allegiance with her job.[32] By my own calculations from Professor Weiler's figures, that represents about a sixfold increase in the rate of employer illegality during organizing drives since the mid-1950s.

Not surprisingly, a recent study by Professor William Cooke concerning union success in a sample of first-contract negotiations indicates that while agreements were reached in about 77 percent of all the cases in which the union had won an election, employer discrimination reduced the probability of a contract by nearly 44 percent, and a refusal to bargain reduced that probability by as much as 25 percent.[33] Despite these gloomy tidings, I retain my belief that a properly constructed and properly enforced law can reclaim the salutary role it played in the balmier labor relations climate of the 1950s and the 1960s. For the remainder of this paper I shall concentrate on the substantive area of collective bargaining law that I consider the most deficient: the regulation of the subject matter of negotiations.

II. The Subject Matter of Bargaining

If the House of Representatives had had its way, Section 8(d) of the NLRA, as added by the Taft-Hartley amendments, would have been much more specific, even definitive, in enumerating

---

[31] See NLRB v. Food Store Employees Local 347 (Heck's Inc.), 417 US 1, 86 LRRM 2209 (1974); Ex-Cell-O Corp., 185 NLRB 107, 74 LRRM 1740 (1970); Tiidee Prods., Inc., 194 NLRB 1234, 79 LRRM 1175 (1972), enforced, 502 F2d 349, 86 LRRM 2093 (CA DC, 1974), cert. denied, 421 US 991 (1975).

[32] See Weiler, Promises to Keep: Securing Workers' Rights to Self-Organization Under the NLRA, 96 HARV. L. REV. 1769, 1780–81 (1983).

[33] Cooke, The Failure to Negotiate First Contracts: Determinants and Policy Implications, 38 IND. US. & LAB. REL. REV. 163, 164, 170, 174–75 (1985) (analyzing data from 118 elections in Indiana in 1979 and 1980).

the subjects of bargaining. In so doing the Act would have made clear, as the House Labor Committee put it, that a union had "no right to bargain with the employer about . . . how he shall manage his business. . . ."[34] The more general language that was finally adopted was seen as confirmation of the course that the Labor Board had been following.[35] That course was for the Board itself to define for employers and unions the "mandatory" subjects of bargaining, about which either party could be required to bargain at the behest of the other.[36]

If a topic is mandatory, moreover, a party may demand agreement on it as the price of any contract. Stated differently, negotiations could be carried to the point of impasse or stalemate on such an issue, and economic pressure could be brought to bear to back up the demands. Matters outside this charmed circle of mandatory subjects are merely "permissive." The parties may negotiate concerning such topics if both sides are willing, but neither party may insist on bargaining over them if the other party objects. These permissive subjects could not be the grounds for an impasse or breakdown in the negotiations.[37]

The Supreme Court was eventually called upon to appraise this scheme in *NLRB* v. *Wooster Division of Borg-Warner Corp.*[38] The facts of *Borg-Warner* were curiously atypical. An employer demanded that its collective bargaining agreement contain, *inter alia,* a clause requiring a vote of the employees by secret ballot before the union could go on strike. A majority of the Supreme Court held first that the "ballot" clause related to a matter of purely internal union concern, and was thus not a mandatory subject of bargaining. Then, in a step not logically necessitated by Section 8(d) and highly dubious as a matter of healthy industrial relations, the Court agreed with the Board that the

---

[34] H. REP. NO. 245, 80th Cong., 1st Sess. 22–23 (1947), *reprinted in* LEG. HIST. LMRA, *supra* note 15, at 313–14.

[35] *See* Cox & Dunlop, *supra* note 12, at 400–401. *See also* post-1947 cases cited *infra* note 36.

[36] Inland Steel Co., 77 NLRB 1, 21 LRRM 1310 *enforced,* 170 F2d 247, 22 LRRM 2506 (CA 7, 1948), *cert. denied,* 336 US 960, (1949) (pensions); J.H. Allison & Co., 70 NLRB 377, 18 LRRM 1369 (1946), *enforced,* 165 F2d 766, 21 LRRM 2238 (CA 6), *cert. denied,* 335 US 814 (1948) (merit increases). For varying assessments of the Board's performance in defining what is mandatory, *compare* Modjeska, *Guess Who's Coming to the Bargaining Table,* 39 OHIO ST. L.J. 415 (1978), *with* Walther, *The Board's Place at the Bargaining Table,* 28 LAB. L.J. 131 (1977).

[37] *See generally* DEVELOPING LABOR LAW, *supra* note 29, at 761–64; R. Gorman, BASIC TEXT ON LABOR LAW: UNIONIZATION AND COLLECTIVE BARGAINING 496–98 (1976).

[38] 356 US 342, 42 LRRM 2034 (1958).

employer's insistence on a "permissive" clause as a condition of agreement amounted in effect to an unlawful refusal to bargain on mandatory subjects.

At least two other approaches might have made more sense. The lead attorney for the company in *Borg-Warner* told me that he seriously considered arguing for the most straightforward solution, which would have been the obliteration of the whole mandatory-permissive distinction.[39] Under this approach, any topic put on the table by either party would have triggered the duty of good-faith negotiating. The other party, it should be emphasized, would never be obligated to agree, only to bargain. Why, after all, should a federal agency, rather than the parties themselves, determine whether a particular item is so important that it is worth a strike or a lockout? The subject matter of collective bargaining ought to be flexible rather than frozen into rigid molds by governmental fiat.[40] Indeed, does not *Borg-Warner* in a real sense cut against the parties' "freedom of contract," which lies at the core of national labor policy? Furthermore, the Board's doctrine encourages hypocrisy in negotiations. If a party deeply desires a concession on a permissive subject that may not legally be carried to impasse, it will be tempted to hang the bargaining up on a false issue that happens to enjoy official approbation as a mandatory topic. Candor would have been enhanced by a different rule, and unresolved disputes would have been recognized for what they ordinarily become in any case—matters to be decided by economic muscle.

Making all topics subject to the duty (and therefore the right) of good-faith bargaining would of course have won the case for the company in *Borg-Warner*. But it is readily understandable why the employer there shrank from such strong medicine. Ordinarily it would be the union, not the employer, that would profit the most from an expanded range of negotiations. The right to force good-faith bargaining on any topic would enable the union to demand bargaining over those most sensitive of

---

[39] Conversation with James C. Davis, Esq., of Cleveland, Ohio (*circa* 1960).

[40] Contemporaneous criticisms of *Borg-Warner* along these lines were expressed by Cox, *Labor Decisions of the Supreme Court at the October Term, 1957*, 44 VA. L. REV. 1057, 1083–86 (1958); Wollett, *The Borg-Warner Case and the Role of the NLRB in the Bargaining Process*, NYU TWELFTH ANNUAL CONFERENCE ON LABOR 39, 46–51 (1959); Note, *The Impact of the Borg-Warner Case on Collective Bargaining*, 43 MINN. L. REV. 1225, 1233–36 (1959); Note, *Bargaining on Nonmandatory Topics Constitutes Refusal to Bargain*, 11 STAN. L. REV. 188, 193 (1958).

issues, basic business decisions now classified as managerial pre-rogatives. Borg-Warner's counsel was much too sophisticated not to be aware of all this. His position was that having to bargain to an impasse over a business decision would not be the worst thing that could happen to an employer. Much worse is to be told, after the fact, that a business decision unilaterally imple-mented without prior negotiation with the union involved a mandatory subject of bargaining, and that the unilateral change therefore constituted an unfair labor practice which must now be undone at some substantial expense to the company.[41] Such indeed was the ill fortune of numerous employers during the 1960s, when the Board significantly enlarged the scope of required bargaining.[42] The wiser course might well have been to end the confusion and uncertainty by treating all lawful subjects as mandatory. But that was the road not taken.

A second, more modest approach would also have allowed the employer in *Borg-Warner* to prevail. That was the position adopted by Justice Harlan and three other Justices,[43] who would have retained the mandatory-permissive distinction, but with a difference. Either party would still be required to bargain to an impasse about mandatory subjects but not about permissive subjects, as is the case under existing law. At the same time, however, either party under the Harlan formulation could per-sist in pursuing any lawful demand, regardless of how the Board might categorize it, and could refuse to contract absent agree-ment on that item. In short, Justice Harlan read Section 8(d) of the NLRA to mean exactly what it says, and only that: A party is obligated to bargain about wages, hours, and other employment terms, but an insistence on bargaining about more is not the equivalent of a refusal to bargain about a mandatory subject. A union, for example, could dismiss out of hand an employer's demand for a secret-ballot strike vote procedure, but the

---

[41] *See, e.g.*, Fibreboard Paper Prods. Corp. v. NLRB, 379 US 203, 57 LRRM 2609 (1964); American Needle & Novelty Co., 206 NLRB 534, 84 LRRM 1526 (1973) (rejecting management's unilateral decisions and requiring that the issues be resolved by collective bargaining). In the exercise of its discretion, however, the Board might not order a financially troubled employer to restore the status quo ante. *E.g.*, Renton News Record, 136 NLRB 1294, 49 LRRM 1972 (1962).

[42] One of the reasons Borg-Warner counsel Davis leaned toward the elimination of the mandatory-permissive distinction was his anticipation of this trend.

[43] NLRB v. Wooster Div. of Borg-Warner Corp. *supra* note 38, at 350–51 (Frankfurter, J., concurring in part and dissenting in part; Harlan, J., joined by Clark, J., and Whit-taker, J., concurring in part and dissenting in part).

employer would not commit an unfair labor practice if it remained adamant.

Either of those two approaches would probably have comported better with the realities of collective bargaining than does the law as now propounded. If it is too late in the day to press for fundamental changes, except through unlikely legislation, at least a recognition of past missteps may help us chart a sounder future course.

III. Management's Rights vs. Employees' Jobs

Under Section 8(d) of the amended NLRA the mandatory subjects of bargaining are wages, hours, and other conditions of employment.[44] It is now well established that wages include compensation in almost every conceivable form, from straight hourly earnings[45] through the most complex pension plan.[46] Hours cover not only the total number of hours in a day or a week, but also the times of particular shifts,[47] the scheduling of overtime,[48] and the like. Working conditions plainly encompass such physical aspects of the job as heat and cold, dirt and noise, lighting, safety hazards, and other assorted stresses and strains.[49] But over the last two decades, the most controversial

---

[44] See text accompanying note 15 supra. A further distinction depends on the persons for whose immediate benefit the contract terms are being negotiated. Only current members of the bargaining unit are "employees" entitled under the NLRA to be represented by the union in collective bargaining. Allied Chem. & Alkali Workers Local 1 v. Pittsburgh Plate Glass Co., 404 US 157, 78 LRRM 2974 (1972) (retirees or pensioners not employees). But the benefits to be accorded persons outside the unit may still be mandatory subjects of bargaining if they "vitally affect" the employment conditions of unit employees. Compare Teamsters Local 24 v. Oliver, 358 US 283, 43 LRRM 2374 (1959) (rental rates of owner-drivers in trucking industry were a mandatory subject because of integral relationship to wage structure of covered employee-drivers), with Pittsburgh Plate Glass Co., supra (health insurance of retired workers was not a mandatory subject of bargaining). The fairly stringent "vitally affects" test only applies to nonunit persons or their benefits, and not to matters directly involving bargaining-unit employees. Ford Motor Co., v. NLRB, 441 US 488, 101 LRRM 2222 (1979) (prices charged by third-party concessionaire in plant cafeteria and vending machines were mandatory subject; "triviality" argument rejected).

[45] Gray Line, Inc., 209 NLRB 88, 85 LRRM 1328 (1974), enforced in part, 512 F2d 992, 89 LRRM 2192 (CA DC, 1975).

[46] Inland Steel Co., supra note 36, noted in 43 ILL. L. REV. 713 (1948) and 58 YALE L.J. 803 (1949).

[47] Timken Roller Bearing Co, 70 NLRB 500, 18 LRRM 1370 (1946), enforcement denied on other grounds, 161 F2d 949, 20 LRRM 2204 (CA 6, 1947); see also Meat Cutters Local 189 v. Jewel Tea Co., 381 US 676, 691, 59 LRRM 2376 (1965).

[48] Colonial Press, Inc., 204 NLRB 852, 860–61, 83 LRRM 1648 (1973).

[49] E.g., NLRB v. Gulf Power Co, 384 F2d 822, 66 LRRM 2501 (CA 5, 1967) (safety rules).

issue concerning the duty to bargain has been the extent to which employers must negotiate about managerial decisions that result in a shrinkage of job opportunities for employees. Under the *Borg-Warner* rubric, the crucial question is whether a subject is classified as a condition of employment or as a management right.[50]

For a long time the Board held that in the absence of antiunion animus, employers were not required to bargain over decisions to subcontract, relocate operations, or introduce technological improvements. The only obligation was to negotiate regarding the *effects* of such decisions on the employees displaced. Layoff schedules, severance pay, and transfer rights were thus bargainable, but the basic decision to discontinue or change an operation was not.[51] Under the so-called Kennedy-Johnson Board, however, a whole range of managerial decisions were reclassified as mandatory subjects of bargaining. These included decisions to terminate a department and subcontract its work,[52] decisions to consolidate operations through automation,[53] and decisions to close one plant of a multi-plant enterprise.[54] The key seems to have been whether the employer's action would result in a "significant impairment of job tenure, employment security, or reasonably anticipated work opportunities for those in the bargaining unit."[55]

In *Fibreboard Paper Products Corp.* v. *NLRB*,[56] the Supreme Court gave limited approval to this shift of direction. The Court sustained a bargaining order issued when a manufacturer wished to subcontract out its maintenance work within a plant. The Court emphasized that the subcontracting did not alter the company's "basic operation" or require any "capital investment."[57] It simply involved a replacement of one group of employees with another group to do the same work in the same place under the same general supervision. Bargaining would not

---

[50] *See* NLRB v. Wooster Div. of Borg-Warner Corp., *supra* note 38 at 349–50 (1958).

[51] *E.g.*, Brown-Dunkin Co., 125 NLRB 1379, 45 LRRM 1256 (1959), *enforced*, 287 F2d 17, 47 LRRM 2551 (CA 10, 1961); Brown-McLaren Mfg. Co., 34 NLRB 984, 9 LRRM 50 (1941).

[52] Town & Country Mfg. Co., 136 NLRB 1022, 49 LRRM 1918 (1962), *enforced*, 316 F2d 846, 53 LRRM 2054 (CA 5, 1963).

[53] Renton News Record, *supra* note 41.

[54] Ozark Trailers, Inc., 161 NLRB 561, 564, 63 LRRM 1264 (1966).

[55] Westinghouse Elec. Corp., 150 NLRB 1574, 1576, 58 LRRM 1257 (1965).

[56] 379 US 203, 57 LRRM 2609 (1964).

[57] *Id.* at 213.

"significantly abridge" the employer's "freedom to manage the business."[58]

One court of appeals, elaborating on this rationale, held that there was no duty to bargain about subcontracting involving a "change in the capital structure."[59] Other courts of appeal, in cases of partial shutdowns and relocations, attempted to balance such factors as the severity of any adverse impact on unit jobs, the extent and urgency of the employer's economic need, and the likelihood that bargaining would be productive.[60] This approach had the attraction of maximizing fairness in individual situations, but it could often lead to uncertainty and unpredictability.

The Supreme Court revisited the issue in *First National Maintenance Corp.* v. *NLRB*,[61] with rather puzzling results. The Court held that a maintenance firm did not have to bargain when it decided to terminate an unprofitable contract to provide janitorial services to a nursing home. The Court first stated broadly that an employer has no duty to bargain about a decision "to shut down part of its business purely for economic reasons."[62] It then pointed out that in this particular case the operation was not being moved elsewhere and the laid-off employees were not going to be replaced. The employer's dispute with the nursing

---

[58] *Id.* An unusually influential separate concurrence by Justice Stewart, joined by Justices Douglas and Harlan, limited *Fibreboard* to its facts and emphasized that the Court was not deciding that "subcontracting decisions are as a general matter subject to [the] duty [to bargain]." 379 US at 218. Specifically, *Fibreboard* did not involve one of the "managerial decisions . . . which lie at the core of entrepreneurial control." *Id.* at 223.

[59] NLRB v. Adams Dairy Co., Inc., 350 F2d 108, 111, 60 LRRM 2084 (CA 8, 1965), *cert. denied,* 382 US 1011 (1966). *See also* Automobile Workers Local 864 v. NLRB (General Motors Corp.), 470 F2d 422, 81 LRRM 2439 (CA DC, 1972) (manufacturer's "sale" of dealership); NLRB v. Transmarine Navigation Corp., 380 F2d 933, 65 LRRM 2861 (CA 9, 1967) (relocation); NLRB v. Royal Plating & Polishing Co., 350 F2d 191, 60 LRRM 2033 (CA 3, 1965) (plant shutdown).

[60] NLRB v. Production Molded Plastics, Inc., 604 F2d 451, 102 LRRM 2040 (CA 6, 1979) and Brockway Motor Trucks v. NLRB, 582 F2d 720, 99 LRRM 2013 (CA 3, 1978) (closing one of several plants); Garment Workers v. NLRB (McLoughlin Mfg. Corp.), 463 F2d 907, 80 LRRM 2716 (CA DC, 1972) (relocation). *See generally* Goetz, *The Duty to Bargain About Changes in Operations,* 1964 Duke L.J. 1; Harper, *Leveling the Road from Borg-Warner to* First National Maintenance: *The Scope of Mandatory Bargaining,* 68 Va. L. Rev. 1447 (1982); Heinsz, *The Partial-Closing Conundrum: The Duty of Employers and Unions to Bargain in Good Faith,* 1981 Duke L.J. 71; Schwartz, *Plant Relocation or Partial Termination—The Duty to Decision-Bargain,* 39 Fordham L. Rev. 81 (1979); Comment, *Duty to Bargain About Termination of Operations,* 92 Harv. L. Rev. 768 (1979); Note, *Partial Closings: The Scope of an Employer's Duty to Bargain,* 61 B.U.L. Rev. 735 (1981).

[61] 452 US 666, 107 LRRM 2705 (1981).

[62] *Id.* at 686. The Court stated, however, that there was "no doubt" the employer had an obligation to bargain about the "results or effects" of its decision to halt the operation. *Id.*

home concerned the size of a management fee over which the union had no control, and because the union had only recently been certified there was no disruption of an ongoing relationship.[63] The decision thus left unanswered important questions regarding the more typical instance of a partial closing or the removal of a plant to a new location.[64]

The majority in *First National Maintenance* purported to apply a balancing test in reaching its conclusion. Stressing that employers must be free from the "constraints" of collective bargaining when that is necessary for running a profitable business, the Court declared that in conflicts between employees' job security and management's interest in "the scope and direction of the enterprise," negotiations should be required "only if the benefit, for labor management relations and the collective bargaining process, outweighs the burden placed on the conduct of the business."[65] The proposed subject of negotiation must be "amenable to resolution through the bargaining process."[66] In dissent, Justices Brennan and Marshall argued forcibly that the majority's test failed to take into account "the legitimate employment interests of the workers and their union."[67] Furthermore, even if the union had no control over the management fee involved in the case, sufficient wage concessions might have enabled the employer to receive a satisfactory percentage return on its investment.

In *Otis Elevator Co.*[68] the NLRB gave *First National Maintenance* a broad reading, placing no weight on the possible limiting effect of the latter's peculiar facts. An employer's decision to terminate its research and development functions at a facility in New Jersey and to relocate and consolidate those functions at another facility in Connecticut was held not to be a mandatory subject of bargaining. Although there were three separate opinions, the Board plurality emphasized that the employer's decision "did not turn upon labor costs" but rather "turned upon a fundamental change in the nature and direction of the business."[69] The

---

[63] *Id.* at 687–88.
[64] The Court expressly reserved the questions of bargaining over plant relocations and sales. *Id.* at 686 n. 22.
[65] *Id.* at 677–79.
[66] *Id.* at 678.
[67] *Id.* at 689.
[68] 269 NLRB 891, 115 LRRM 1281 (1984).
[69] *Id.* at 892, 115 LRRM at 1282–83.

decision was thus not "amenable to bargaining," regardless of its "effect on employees [or] a union's ability to offer alternatives."[70]

Otis Elevator was not mandated by *First National Maintenance*, but it was an entirely defensible extension of the Supreme Court majority's rationale. At the same time the Reagan Board's approach represents almost the polar opposite of the Kennedy-Johnson Board's emphasis on "employment security" in the bargaining unit.[71] In my opinion either position is supportable under the language and history of the statute, which fairly leaves the issue for resolution as a matter of sound industrial policy. We should remember that at the time of the Taft-Hartley debates, a determined effort was made to spell out explicitly the subjects of bargaining, and that effort was defeated.[72] NLRB Chairman Paul Herzog advised the Senate Labor Committee that the scope of bargaining might "vary with changes in industrial structure and practice," and recommended that the task of defining the range of bargaining should remain with the Board, subject to judicial review.[73] In enacting Section 8(d) Congress adopted that approach.[74]

We are so used to speaking of the mandatory subjects of bargaining as embracing wages, hours, and "working conditions" that we tend to forget that Section 8(d) does not say that. It speaks of "other terms and conditions of employment." Moreover, the theoretically almost infinitely expansible "terms" was an addition to the phrase, "wages, hours of employment, or other conditions of employment," which has always appeared in Section 9(a)[75] of the NLRA, dealing with a majority union's power of exclusive representation for purposes of collective bargaining. When Congress has desired to treat "working condi-

---

[70] *Id. See also* Gar Wood-Detroit Truck Equip., Inc., 274 NLRB No. 23, 118 LRRM 1417 (1985); Hawthorn Mellody, Inc., 275 NLRB No. 55, 119 LRRM 1079 (1985).

[71] *See* text accompanying note 55 *supra.*

[72] *See* text accompanying notes 15–16 *supra.*

[73] *Hearings on S. 55 and S.J. Res. 22 Before Senate Comm. on Labor and Public Welfare*, 80th Cong., 1st Sess. 1914 (1947). *Cf.* Ford Motor Co. v. NLRB, 441 US 488, 101 LRRM 2222 (1979) (current industrial practices as general guideline for mandatory subjects of bargaining).

[74] *See* H.R. REP. NO. 245, 80th Cong., 1st Sess. 71 (1947) (minority report), *reprinted in* LEG. HIST. LRMA, *supra* note 15, at 362; H.R. CONF. REP. NO. 510, 80th Cong., 1st Sess. 34–35 (1947), *reprinted in* LEG. HIST. LMRA, *supra* note 15, at 538–39; First National Maintenance Corp. v. NLRB, *supra* note 61 at 675 & n.14; Fibreboard Paper Prods. Corp. v. NLRB, *supra* note 56 at 219 n.2 (Stewart, J., concurring).

[75] 49 Stat 453 (1935) (codified as amended at 29 USC §159(a)(1982)).

tions" as such it has known how to do so.[76] I do not wish to press this point too far. The Supreme Court, speaking through Justice Brennan, has accepted the notion that Section 8(d) "does establish a limitation," and that it "includes only issues which settle an aspect of the relationship between the employer and employees."[77] And it is especially doubtful that the Taft-Hartley Congress harbored any intention of making a union "an equal partner in the running of the business enterprise."[78]

Nevertheless, I am satisfied that at least there is ample legislative justification for the standard which the Kennedy-Johnson Board was apparently evolving, namely, that negotiations are mandatory when managerial decisions affecting unit work may jeopardize employees' job security.[79]

The policy question in these situations is how to reconcile management's interest in running its own business as it sees fit with the workers' claim to a voice in shaping their industrial lives. Before I set forth my own views on how such a reconciliation may be effectuated, one further important technical distinction must be understood. Whether a particular item is a mandatory subject of bargaining may arise in two quite different contexts. First, the union may be seeking a certain provision, either as part of a new labor contract that is open for negotiation or as an addition to an existing agreement in midterm. Second, an employer may wish to make a unilateral change in its operations, either in the absence of or in the face of a current collective agreement, without first having to bargain with the union about the matter.

In both of these contexts the Supreme Court has seemed to assume, with little or no analysis, that the scope or ambit of mandatory subjects is the same.[80] That is to say, if the item in question is one about which the union could demand bargaining, then generically it is the sort of matter that an employer may not unilaterally change at any time without prior notice to the union and good-faith efforts to negotiate an agreement con-

---

[76] See, e.g., §6(d) of the Fair Labor Standards Act, 77 Stat 56 (codified at 29 USC §206(d) (1982) (Equal Pay Act).

[77] Allied Chem. & Alkali Workers Local 1 v. Pittsburgh Plate Glass Co., supra note 44.

[78] First Nat'l Maintenance Corp. v. NLRB, supra note 61 at 676.

[79] An employer seems to have no duty to bargain about a decision to go out of business completely, even if it is for antiunion reasons. See Textile Workers v. Darlington Mfg. Co., 380 US 263, 267 n.5, 58 LRRM 2657 (1965).

[80] Allied Chem. & Alkali Workers Local 1 v. Pittsburgh Plate Glass Co., supra note 44 at 185–88.

cerning it. This doctrine is susceptible to several refinements depending on the terms of the existing agreement, the extent of precontract discussions, and the scope of any union waivers or management rights clauses.[81] For our purposes, however, the important point is that in determining the range of mandatory subjects of bargaining, we are not merely deciding what the parties are obligated to deal with at the time a contract is initially negotiated or subsequently amended. To a significant degree we are also deciding what limits shall be imposed on the employer's freedom and business flexibility during the two or three years of the contract's life. What principles and practical considerations should govern this determination?

IV. Collective Bargaining in Operation

Imposing a duty to bargain about managerial decisions such as plant removals, technological innovation, and subcontracting or "outsourcing" would obviously delay transactions, reduce business adaptability, and perhaps interfere with the confidentiality of negotiations with third parties. In some instances bargaining would be doomed in advance as a futile exercise. Nonetheless,

---

[81] *See, e.g.,* LeRoy Mach. Co., 147 NLRB 1431, 56 LRRM 1369 (1964) (waiver through management-rights clause); Proctor Mfg. Corp., 131 NLRB 1166, 1169, 48 LRRM 1222 (1961); Jacobs Mfg. Co., 94 NLRB 1214 (1951), *enforced,* 196 F2d 680 (CA 2, 1952). *See also* R. Gorman, *supra* note 37, at 466–80 (on waiver). *Cf.* NLRB v. C & C Plywood Corp., 385 US 421, 64 LRRM 2065 (1967).

The most fascinating recent decision on an employer's power to make unilateral changes during the term of a contract is Automobile Workers v. NLRB (Milwaukee Spring), 756 F2d 175 (CA DC, 1985). The court of appeals, per Edwards J., held that where a labor contract contained a broad management-rights clause and no work-preservation clause, an employer did not violate §8(a)(5) by its decision to relocate operations at a nonunion plant in order to increase return on investment. The move was sanctioned either by the management-rights clause or by implied management-reserved rights. (The relocation decision was bargained to impasse with the union, but that seems immaterial under the court's theory.) Much more significant than the particular holding in *Milwaukee Spring,* however, was the court's novel treatment of the "zipper" clause, whereby each party waived all further bargaining rights. In effect, the court equated this with a "maintenance of standards" clause, precluding the employer from instituting any unilateral changes during the term of the contract (except under a management-rights theory), regardless of whether it had bargained to impasse. While perhaps startling at first blush, this conclusion seems eminently sound. If not otherwise authorized (by a union's express or implied waiver) to make midterm unilateral changes in a bargainable item, an employer would first have to bargain to impasse over the matter. But, if by a zipper clause the employer has relinquished the capacity to fulfill the condition precedent to the change, it could never make the change without the union's consent. Hereafter, presumably, employers will seek zipper clauses in which only the union, and not management, waives the right to demand bargaining.

the closer we move toward recognizing that employees may have something akin to a property interest in their jobs,[82] the more evident it may become that not even the employer's legitimate regard for profit-making or the public's justified concern for a productive eonomy should totally override the workers' claim to a voice in the decisions of ongoing enterprises that will directly affect their future employment opportunities. A moral value is arguably at stake in determining whether employees may be treated as pawns in management decisions.[83]

On a crasser, tactical level, a leading management attorney of my acquaintance once said that long before the Supreme Court's decision on in-plant subcontracting, he *"Fibreboarded"* the unions he dealt with simply as a matter of sound personnel relations. Indeed, ignoring technical distinctions between mandatory and permissive topics seems characteristic of mature bargaining relationships. Retirement benefit levels of retired workers may be nonmandatory,[84] but they are of intense concern to the United Automobile Workers. So the union and the major auto manufacturers negotiate about them routinely.

From the workers' perspective, the opportunity to bargain before a decision is made could be crucial. Unions will lose considerable leverage in bargaining about even the effects of a business change if the employer can present them with a *fait accompli* in the change itself. Oftentimes negotiations may benefit both parties by producing a less drastic solution than a shutdown or a relocation. For example, one of the most dramatic moments during the 1982 Ford-UAW negotiations occurred when a union representative from the plant level and his opposite number from the management side agreed that not once had the two of them failed to find a way to adjust operations so as to keep work within the shop and not have it contracted out.

---

[82] *See e.g.*, Association of the Bar of the City of New York, Committee on Labor and Employment Law, *At-Will Employment and the Problem of Unjust Dismissal*, 36 RECORD ASS'N BAR CITY N.Y. 170 (1981); *Symposium, Individual Rights in the Workplace: the Employment-at-Will Issue*, 16 U. MICH. J.L. REF. 199 (1983); C. Bakaly & J. Grossman, MODERN LAW OF EMPLOYMENT CONTRACTS (1983); H. Perritt, THE LAW OF WRONGFUL DISMISSAL (1984); St. Antoine, *The Twilight of Employment at Will? An Update*, in FIRST ANNUAL LABOR AND EMPLOYMENT LAW INSTITUTE 1 (W. Dolson ed., 1985); W. Holloway & M. Leech, EMPLOYMENT TERMINATION: RIGHTS AND REMEDIES (1985). *Cf.* F. Meyers, THE OWNERSHIP OF JOBS (1964).

[83] *See.* N. Chamberlain, THE UNION CHALLENGE TO MANAGEMENT CONTROL 8–9 (1948).

[84] *See supra* note 44.

At the very least, bargaining may serve a therapeutic purpose. As the Supreme Court stated in *Fibreboard*, in words that might sound platitudinous but for the grim historical reality behind them, the NLRA "was framed with an awareness that refusals to confer and negotiate had been one of the most prolific causes of industrial strife."[85]

Despite these advantages of collective bargaining, neither organized labor nor collective bargaining has ever enjoyed full acceptance in this country. Unions are feared by many employers and distrusted by much of the public.[86] Their support today even among workers is lower than at any time during the past half century. For several years they have lost over 50 percent of all the representation elections conducted by the Board, and their membership has shrunk to less than one-fifth of private nonagricultural employment, not even half the proportionate strength of unions in most of Western Europe.[87]

There is keen irony here. Ours is the most conservative, least ideological of all labor movements, traditionally committed to the capitalistic system and to the principle that management should have the primary responsibility for managing.[88] Yet employers will pay millions of dollars to experts in "union avoidance" in order to maintain their nonunion status.[89] In part this resistance is attributable to the highly decentralized character of American industrial relations. Because of this decentralization, an employer typically must confront a union on a one-to-one basis, without the protective shield of an association to negotiate on behalf of all or substantially all the firms in a particular industry, as is true in Western Europe. In part the resistance to union organization here may result, among both employers and workers, from ingrained American attitudes of rugged individualism and the ideal of the classless society.[90]

---

85 Fibreboard Paper Prods. Corp. v. NLRB, *supra* note 56 at 211.

86 Opinion polls in the 1970s showed that there was no other major institution in our society whose leadership so consistently lacked the confidence of the general public. Ladd, *The Polls: The Question of Confidence*, 40 Pub. Opinion Q. 544, 545 (1977).

87 1980 NLRB Ann. Rep. 270–72 (1980). In 1954 over 38% of private nonagricultural employees were unionized. The figure fell to 30% by the mid-1960s and to 24% by 1980. R. Freeman & J. Medoff, What Do Unions Do? 211–22 (1984). The union segment has apparently now dipped below 20%. 177 Lab. Rel. Rep. (BNA) 81 (Oct. 1, 1984).

88 *See* Labor and American Politics Rev. ed. 4–5 *passim* (C. Rehmus, D. McLaughlin, & F. Nesbitt eds., 1978).

89 *See* Weiler, *supra* note 32, at 1776–86.

90 *See* Bok, *Reflections on the Distinctive Character of American Labor Laws*, 84 Harv. L. Rev. 1394, 1458–62 (1971).

In any event, it seems plain that aversion to unionism can hardly be supported by a dispassionate analysis of the actual impact of collective bargaining in this country. Indeed, for many years labor economists wrangled over whether *any* significant economic effect could be demonstrated. Today, however, there is an emerging consensus. Unionism cannot be proven to have brought about any substantial redistribution of wealth as between labor and capital. It has achieved a wage level that is roughly 10 to 20 percent higher for union workers,[91] but that differential is largely offset by increased efficiency and greater productivity in unionized firms. Furthermore, unions have not been an initiating cause of inflation in the post-World War II period, although they may have hampered efforts to combat it.[92]

For many observers of the labor scene, the major achievement of collective bargaining has not been economic at all. It has been the creation of the grievance and arbitration system, the formalized procedure whereby labor and management may resolve disputes arising during the term of a collective agreement, either by voluntary settlements between the parties themselves or by reference to an impartial outsider, without resort to economic force or court litigation.[93] The mere existence of a grievance and arbitration system helps to eradicate such former abuses as favoritism, arbitrary or ill-informed decisionmaking, and outright discrimination in the workplace.

My conclusion from all this is that collective bargaining has promoted both industrial peace and broader worker participation in the governance of the shop, while simultaneously stimulating higher productivity and causing only modest dislocations in the economy generally. At the same time I believe that the full potential of collective bargaining has not been tapped. Because law serves such an important legitimating function in our society, collective bargaining may have been seriously undermined when the courts began to cut back the scope of

---

[91] Freeman & Medoff, *The Impact of Collective Bargaining: Illusion or Reality?* U.S. INDUSTRIAL RELATIONS, 1950–1980: A CRITICAL ASSESSMENT 50–56 (J. Stieber, R. McKersie, & D. Mills eds., 1981) [hereinafter cited as U.S. INDUS. REL.]. *See also* A. Rees, The Economics of Trade Unions 2d ed. 74, 89–90 (1977).

[92] Mitchell, *Collective Bargaining and the Economy,* U.S. INDUS. REL., *supra* note 91, at 25–26, 33–35.

[93] *See, e.g.,* D. Bok & J. Dunlop, LABOR AND THE AMERICAN COMMUNITY 463–65 (1970); A. Rees, *supra* note 91, at 187; Freeman & Medoff, *The Two Faces of Unionism*, PUB. INTEREST, Fall 1979, at 69, 70.

mandatory bargaining to exclude managerial decisions even though they might have a substantial effect on employees' job security.

Far better, it seems to me, would have been an open-ended mandate that lets the parties themselves decide what their vital interests are. The only exclusions from compulsory bargaining that I would readily admit are matters going to the very existence or identity of the negotiating parties, such as the membership of a corporation's board of directors, and perhaps the integrity of their internal structure and procedures. Those limitations would preserve the holding in *Borg-Warner*,[94] which adopted the mandatory-permissive dichotomy in the first place. Ironically, the legal duty to bargain is now more hindrance than help to a well-entrenched union. Without it, the union could demand bargaining on anything it wished; with it, bargaining is by leave of the employer on everything outside the prescribed list of "wages, hours, and other terms and conditions of employment."

A thoughtful, more conventional solution has been proposed by Professor Michael Harper. He would exclude from the scope of mandatory bargaining only "product market decisions," which he defines as "all decisions to determine what products are created and sold, in what quantities, for which markets, and at what prices."[95] He bases this principle on a "social policy allowing consumers, and only consumers, to influence management's product market decisions."[96] There is much merit in Professor Harper's thesis, and he demonstrates its feasibility and conformity to precedent in a variety of contexts. Nonetheless, as he seems to recognize, it may unduly circumscribe bargaining for a class of employees that will become increasingly significant in the post-industrial world—artists and artisans, educators, entertainers, and customer service personnel generally—in short, all those employees "whose identity and behavior . . . define the product."[97] Thus, Professor Harper would not make safety rules a mandatory topic for professional football players, or the scantiness of costume for cocktail waitresses.[98] The logic here

---

[94] *See* text accompanying note 38 *supra*. Under my test, however, First Nat'l Maintenance Corp. v. NLRB, *supra* note 61 (termination of maintenance at nursing home), would have to be overruled or treated as a sport.

[95] Harper, *supra* note 60, at 1463.

[96] *Id.*

[97] *Id.* at 1467–68.

[98] *Id.* at 1466.

may be impeccable, but it leads one to question the soundness of the premise which so exalts consumer interests over employee interests.[99]

My own argument for a more sweeping and wide-open duty to bargain is grounded in two considerations, one a matter of economics and industrial relations policy, and the other a matter of social policy, if not of ethics. I shall deal with them in turn.

V. Participative Management: Economics, Ethics, and Social Policy

During the late 1960s American management became alarmed by signs of growing alienation, even militancy, on the part of workers. Although this unrest was much exaggerated, it fueled an effort by many companies to enhance the quality of work life (QWL) by increasing employee participation in job-centered decisionmaking. The interest in such programs was intensified during the 1970s by glowing accounts of the capacity of Japanese industry to improve both the quantity and quality of production by fostering an almost filial relationship between employee and employer. Altogether, it is estimated that one-third of the companies in the *Fortune 500* have established programs in participative management.[100] Furthermore, in certain countries, such as Sweden and West Germany, worker participation is guaranteed by statute.[101] More and more studies attest that it is

---

[99] Professor Harper's proposal for a product market principle might also have the theoretical advantage of providing a rational basis for distinguishing between union-employer activity that is and is not subject to the antitrust laws. But the Supreme Court has apparently rejected the notion of such a sharp labor market-product market dichotomy; even an agreement concerning wages may violate the Sherman Act if "predatory intent" is present; Mine Workers v. Pennington, 381 US 657, 59 LRRM 2369 (1965), *on remand sub nom.* Lewis v. Pennington, 257 F Supp 815, 62 LRRM 2604 (ED Tenn 1966), *aff'd in part, rev'd in part*, 400 F2d 806, 69 LRRM 2280 (CA 6), *cert. denied*, 393 US 983 (1968); Smitty Baker Coal Co. v. Mine Workers 620 F2d 416 (CA 4, 1980), *cert. denied*, 449 US 870 (1981). *See generally* Handler & Zifchak, *Collective Bargaining and the Antitrust Laws: The Emasculation of the Labor Exemption*, 81 COLUM. L. REV. 459 (1981); Leslie, *Principles of Labor Antitrust*, 66 VA. L. REV. 1183 (1980); St. Antoine, *Connell: Antitrust Law at the Expense of Labor Law*, 62 VA. L. REV. 603, 610 (1976). If predatory intent is indeed the key to a union-employer antitrust violation, then of course the particular subject matter of the agreement is not a crucial factor.

[100] Wallace & Driscoll, *Social Issues in Collective Bargaining*, in U.S. INDUS. REL., *supra* note 91, at 199, 241.

[101] Berqvist, *Worker Participation in Decisions Within Undertakings in Sweden*, 5 COMP. LAB. L. 65 (1982); Richardi, *Worker Participation in Decisions Within Undertakings in the Federal Republic of Germany*, 5 COMP. LAB. L. 23, 29–31 (1982).

simply smart business to heed the voice of the individual employee and to give him or her a stake in the successful operation of the enterprise.[102] The worker on the production line will spot flaws that have escaped the eye of the keenest industrial engineer.

Participative management or QWL programs have undoubtedly been used by some companies to counter the appeal of labor unions.[103] Nevertheless, several major international unions have become involved in such projects. As of 1980 General Motors and the UAW had programs under way in 50 separate plants;[104] I am told there are now programs in approximately 90 of 150 bargaining units. Some locations have registered remarkable gains in employee morale and performance. In addition, the contract signed in 1982 by Ford Motor Company and the UAW provided for "Mutual Growth Forums," at both national and local levels, consisting of joint union-management committees for the "advance discussion of certain business developments of material interest and significance to the union, the employees, and the company."[105] This past year GM's new Saturn project and the UAW extended the concept of shared decisionmaking far beyond the conventional limits of collective bargaining, with the company securing increased operational flexibility in return for guaranteed job security.[106]

The anomaly is that many of these developments, evidently so beneficial to management, might well be classified as "permissive" subjects of bargaining by the Board or the courts. A union could not bring them to the bargaining table without the acquiescence of the employer. Of course, as long as the parties are cooperative, that is a moot point. But the law should be structured to deal with the case where regulation is necessary, not where it is superfluous. Even on so-called managerial decisions, such as revising the layout of a trim department in an auto

---

[102] Wallace & Driscoll, *supra* note 100, at 238, 241. For varying appraisals *see* Goodman, *Quality of Work Life Projects in the 1980s*, 31 LAB. L.J. 487 (1980); Locke & Schweiger, *Participating in Decision-Making: One More Look*, in 1 RESEARCH IN ORGANIZATION BEHAVIOR 271 (B. Staw ed., 1979); Merrifield, *Worker Participation in Decisions Within Undertakings*, 5 COMP. LAB. L. 1 (1982); Summers, *Worker Participation in the U.S. and West Germany: A Comparative Study from an American Perspective*, 28 AM. J. COMP. L. 367 (1980); *Workers' Participation in Management: An International Comparision*, 18 INDUS. REL. 247 (1979).

[103] Wallace & Driscoll, *supra* note 100, at 242–51,

[104] *Id.* at 245.

[105] SOLIDARITY, Mar. 1982, at 8.

[106] 119 LAB. REL. REP. (BNA) 275–76 (Aug. 5, 1985).

assembly plant, the workers' input has often proved valuable.[107] The law ought not insulate an employer from bargaining merely because it rejects that lesson.

One worrisome objection to my prescription is that it may unduly restrict a company's autonomy after a contract has been agreed upon. If an item is a mandatory subject of bargaining, the employer is not only obligated to negotiate when a contract is executed but may also be precluded from instituting a unilateral change during the life of the agreement.[108] This result would be opposed by those who believe that once an employer has fulfilled its duty to bargain and has signed a contract, it should be entitled to treat all contract terms as settled.[109] Unless restricted by some particular provision, a company should be entirely free, under this view, to act unilaterally without further bargaining. Two answers can be given to this objection. First, an employer can preserve its autonomy by securing a suitably broad "management rights" clause as part of the initial settlement. Second, even if the employer must bargain, there is no obligation to agree. After a good-faith effort has been put forth, and the negotiations carried to impasse, the employer may proceed to make the changes it desires. The union and the employees would have had their say, and the law requires no more.

The period of bargaining may be short if the circumstances warrant. I have examined nine contested Board cases during the 1970s in which an employer instituted unilateral changes after bargaining "to impasse." Elapsed times from the employer's initial notification of an impending change or first meeting with the union to the implementation of the change ranged from three weeks to six months. Three cases took three weeks; five took between four and eight weeks; and one took six months. The median was six and one-half weeks, which in the usual situation would hardly seem very onerous. More empirical data on the practical effect of such delays would plainly be desirable.

A quarter century ago a classic study on industrial relations concluded: "An important result of the American system of collective bargaining is the sense of participation that it imparts

---

[107] Wallace & Driscoll, *supra* note 100, at 246.

[108] *See* text accompanying notes 80–81 *supra*.

[109] *Cf.* Cox & Dunlop, *The Duty to Bargain Collectively During the Term of an Existing Agreement*, 63 HARV. L. REV. 1097, 1116–20 (1950) (labor contract should be construed as requiring continuance of major terms of employment existing at time agreement was executed; differing management and union views are discussed).

to workers."[110] For me, in the end, the issue may come down to this sort of social or humane value. It is good to know that giving the individual a voice in the shaping and operation of his or her job may be enlightened industrial relations and may enhance efficiency and productivity. But I think there is considerably more at stake than simply economic concerns. My emphasis on noneconomic factors is neither novel nor quixotic. A generation ago a hard-headed labor expert, Neil Chamberlain, declared that "the workers' struggle for increasing participation in business decisions . . . is highly charged with an ethical content . . . . [L]egal and economic arguments, technological and political considerations must give way before widely held moral convictions."[111]

It is primarily work that defines a man or woman. Thus, studies have found that "most, if not all, working people tend to describe themselves in terms of the work groups or organizations to which they belong. The question 'Who are you?' often elicits an organizationally related response. . . . Occupational role is usually a part of this response for all classes: 'I'm a steelworker,' or 'I'm a lawyer.' "[112] Leisure-time activities, however pleasurable in themselves, can seldom rise to such a level of significance. If it is also true, as the underlying premise of the Wagner Act proclaims, that collective action on the part of employees best ensures "equality of bargaining power"[113] with employers, then in setting the metes and bounds of mandatory negotiations we are engaged in far more than a pragmatic exercise in industrial relations policy. We are performing a task of profound moral consequence. We may be, in substantial effect, determining the capacity of American workers for fullest self-realization—for finding out, in this one life they have to live, who they really are.

---

[110] S. Slichter, J. Healy, & E.R. Livernash, THE IMPACT OF COLLECTIVE BARGAINING ON MANAGEMENT 960 (1960).

[111] N. Chamberlain, *supra* note 83, at 8–9.

[112] SPECIAL TASK FORCE TO THE SECRETARY OF HEALTH, EDUCATION, AND WELFARE, WORK IN AMERICA 6 (1973). *Cf.* S. Terkel, WORKING 177 (1974) (quoting an auto worker on his love-hate relationship with the car: "I think of a certain area of proudness. . . . I put my labor in it.").

[113] NLRA §1, 49 Stat 449 (1935) (codified as amended at 29 USC §151 (1982)). *See also* 78 CONG. REC. 3443 (1934) ("Genuine collective bargaining is the only way to attain equality of bargaining power.") (remarks of Sen. Wagner), *reprinted in* LEG. HIST. NLRA, *supra* note 2, at 15.

Responses

NEW DIRECTIONS IN COLLECTIVE BARGAINING

EUGENE L. HARTWIG*

Professor St. Antoine has discussed the Board and court decisions in *Otis Elevator*[1] and *Milwaukee Springs II*.[2] From a management standpoint, these are favorable and welcomed holdings. They represent a dramatic shift in the tenor of Board decisions from as little as three years ago when the Board decided *Milwaukee Springs I*,[3] holding that the Act was violated because the employer decided without the union's consent to transfer its assembly operations.

While the recent pronouncements of the Board and courts have generally been applauded by the management community, a much more fundamental shift in emphasis in collective bargaining relationships has been occurring which requires attention. In examining this change, I will be referring principally to the industry with which I am most familiar—the automobile industry—although much of what I have to say is equally applicable to what have been termed the "smokestack industries" (e.g., steel and rubber).

The problems these "low tech" industries are encountering have been well documented by scholarly reviews and in the media. Rising materials and parts costs, stagnant or falling demand, outdated factories, high wage and benefit costs, and inflexible work rules hamper efficiency and diminish the ability of these companies to compete in the international marketplace. These problems have been masked, to a certain extent, by the recent economic surge that has followed the most severe recession since the 1930s. But hard times and another retrenchment for American industry are looming on the horizon. Imports continue to account for a large portion of the U.S. market. Recently (September 1985) it was reported that for the first time

---

* Vice President and Associate General Counsel, General Motors Corporation.
[1] Otis Elevator Co., 269 NLRB 891, 115 LRRM 1281, *corrected*, 269 NLRB 891, 116 LRRM 1075 (1984).
[2] Milwaukee Spring, Div. of Ill. Coil Spring Co., 268 NLRB 601, 115 LRRM 1065 (1984), *aff'd sub nom.* Automobile Workers v. NLRB, 765 F2d 175, 119 LRRM 2801 (CA DC, 1985).
[3] Milwaukee Spring, Div. of Ill. Coil Spring Co., 265 NLRB 206, 111 LRRM 1486 (1982), *remanded mem.*, 718 F2d 1102, 114 LRRM 2376 (CA 7, 1983).

since World War II, the United States had become a debtor nation with a $37 billion dollar foreign trade imbalance for the month of August. Clearly, something must be done to enable U.S. companies to compete more effectively in the world marketplace. Suggestions range from imposing wide-ranging import quotas to weakening the strength of the U.S. dollar in order to reduce the cost of exported goods. These policies have proven to be either ineffective or costly in the past. There is another approach that can and should be utilized to the mutual benefit of employers, unions, and employees.

I. The Historical Setting

Historically, labor-management relations in the United States have been conducted on an adversarial basis. The basic relationship had its genesis in the volatile history surrounding the introduction of unionism in this country. With passage of the National Labor Relations Act, collective bargaining was legitimatized as the means to secure industrial peace. Workers were given the right freely to choose unions as their bargaining representatives under that Act. While both parties have had a statutory obligation to bargain in good faith, the final detriment in the collective bargaining process has been and continues to be economic power. So long as both parties abided by the statutory requirements, the manner and atmosphere in which they bargained—be it adversarial or cooperative—was their own concern.

The legalistic, rule-driven structure governing labor-management relations and collective bargaining erected over the years in decisions by the Board and the courts has only served to reinforce the view that management and labor are adversaries in the process of cutting up the economic pie—adversaries rather than joint venture partners each with a vital stake in the success of the business undertaking. Certain subjects called for mandatory bargaining, others were permissive or illegal. Unions could waive some employee rights but only if a precise formulation was written into the contract. Management was required to provide financial data substantiating a claim of a noncompetitive wage structure, but unions were free to cause economic disaster with a strike regardless of what the data showed.

Concessions made by either side were by and large dictated by sheer economic power rather than by any rational attempt to seek mutual accommodation geared to the long-term health of the enterprise. Where the parties miscalculated regarding the degree of economic power at their disposal, strikes resulted, in many cases to the ultimate detriment of the best interests of both management and employees. Management was, of course, a contributor to this destructive system preferring, often with an eye on the quarterly report, to settle at any cost rather than to resist exorbitant demands with a longer view in sight.

As a result of the severe economic downturn in 1981–83, and the reality of worldwide competition, recent labor negotiations have offered some encouragement that a more cooperative approach at the bargaining table can become a reality. Unions, albeit reluctantly, have accepted management proposals on wage and benefit concessions and work rule changes. In return, employers have agreed to profit-sharing arrangements, to improvements in job security, and to more participatory forms of management decision making. In the automobile industry, these changes were formally adopted in the 1982 National Agreements between the Automobile Workers and General Motors and Ford.

In 1984 negotiations between General Motors and the UAW, the parties built on and expanded the changes first introduced in 1982. An innovative job security program was established to insure that eligible employees would not be laid off during the course of the agreement because of the introduction of new technology and outsourcing. In addition, a $350 million dollar training fund was created to aid in the personal growth and development of employees. Of perhaps even greater significance, General Motors agreed to recommend to the GM Board of Directors that it authorize the funds and take action necessary to proceed with implementation of the Saturn project *in the United States*.

II. The Saturn Project

Sometime prior to 1984, General Motors and the Automobile Workers conducted a joint study to evaluate the feasibility of manufacturing a small car in the United States, one which could compete on an equal footing with foreign imports. The parties realized that the automobile industry's inability to compete in the small car market meant that foreign competition would ultimately dominate the midsize and large car markets. It was this study which led to the joint GM-UAW Project Saturn.

The success of Project Saturn depended upon the integration and coordination of all of the disciplines involved in the business toward the goals of improved quality at low cost. That success could not be realized without the cooperation of an experienced work force to build the new products. What was needed was a new commitment by management and labor, both of whom would participate as partners, each contributing its energies and talents in a new approach to building fuel-efficient, high quality small cars.

To ensure that GM's human resources—its employees—were totally integrated into the new system, GM and the UAW embarked on an unprecedented union-management part-nership. For the first time in their nearly 50-year relationship, GM and the UAW worked together as a team on a new vehicle program at the conceptual stage. A GM-UAW Study Center was formed to review the socio-technical system design process and those business-related factors which impacted on the ability of General Motors to produce world class automobiles. The Study Center mission statement reflects the direction of this joint effort:

> To identify and recommend the best approaches to integrate the people and the technology to competitively manufacture small cars in the United States.[4]

A total of 99 participants, from 55 GM plants and 41 UAW locals, were actively involved on a full-time basis at the Study Center. The 35 plant management personnel included, among others, plant managers, production managers, and general superintendents. Local union presidents, shop chairmen, com-mitteemen, die makers, assemblers, among others, were included in the 42 UAW-represented plant personnel. The remaining 22 members were from GM and UAW central office staffs and negotiating teams.

The GM-UAW Study Center was organized into seven func-tional committees. The joint union-management committees matched the prospective Saturn business units which would be responsible for areas from product design to component man-ufacturing, as well as subassembly and assembly of the com-pleted vehicle. The basic objective was to investigate new ways to "leapfrog" the competition in quality, cost, and scheduling in the

---

[4] GM-UAW Study Center, Dec. 19, 1983.

production in the United States of small cars of high customer value before the end of this decade. The analysis included 82 joint management-UAW trips to 49 different GM plants and 75 visits to 60 companies outside GM, such as Hewlett-Packard, Volvo in Sweden, VW in West Germany, and Kawasaki in Japan. Committee members traveled an estimated two million miles and made over 170 company, academic, and GM plant contacts.

Following this study and analysis, the participants again met in committee to set down their recommendations regarding the ways in which the "people systems" should be established in order to achieve the Saturn mission.

Interestingly, no one called this process collective bargaining, and yet what was happening, was collective bargaining in a very genuine, indeed in a most sophisticated sense.

This study group, made up of people with varying points of view representing the traditional environments from which they came, used a consensus decisionmaking process where any one of the participants could block a decision. The result was a set of recommendations unanimously adopted by the Study Center. In January 1985, the Board of Directors approved the formation of Saturn Corporation as a wholly-owned subsidiary to assume the responsibilities, obligations, and goals of Project Saturn.

III. The Saturn Agreement

What emerged from this joint undertaking with the Automobile Workers was a Memorandum of Agreement establishing the framework of the collective bargaining relationship between Saturn Corporation and the union. The agreement was in some respects traditional; mainly, however, it was nontraditional in the sense that it was not a compromise resulting from confrontation, but was, instead, the product of a joint effort by the parties, each with a stake in the enterprise, who recognized that the problem which confronted them could not be solved by individual divided efforts. The agreement reflected a completely new approach—a "clean sheet" approach—to industrial relations and to manufacturing. It was a response as novel as the challenge itself.

Consistent with its persisting concern for job security and its desire to preserve work for the employees it represents, the UAW urged that the Saturn workforce be drawn from among

GM bargaining unit employees. (The UAW made no secret of the circumstance that it considered the Saturn plant in particular and the Saturn concept in general to be replacing presently existing GM automobile production.) The agreement reflected the consensus of GM and the UAW that the chances of Saturn's success would be enhanced by the employment of GM's experienced and skilled autoworkers.

The parties recognized that the initial agreement defining their relationship would not and could not be all-inclusive and complete. It would not be written in the pattern of traditional collective bargaining agreements, which historically carefully prescribe the responsibilities and rights of the parties. This agreement would provide direction and serve as a guide, but remain flexible enough for the parties to refine and develop their relationship within its framework.

There are no rigid rules or dates for the opening or closing of negotiations to modify the agreement, since it is contemplated that the parties will modify the agreement as needed, on an ongoing basis.

The agreement not only addresses the environment and culture of the workplace, but also sets the tone for the relationship between employee and employer. Gone are references to management and labor, as such. Saturn was conceived as a team project and its constituents are to be treated as team members. Instead of references to "management rights," there are references to Saturn people philosophy, Saturn corporation philosophy, Saturn symbols, and Saturn mission.

The organizational structure contemplates nonadversarial methods of decisionmaking and problem solving. Provision is made for full participation of team members in consensus decisionmaking. Most of the authority and decisionmaking is expected to be exercised at the work unit level, which is an integrated group of approximately 6–15 members.

The team concept inherent in Saturn is reinforced by the organizational structure which insures full participation in all decisions by its members, work units, work unit modules, business units, manufacturing and strategic advisory committees, with full participation of union representatives in the role of counselors and as advisors at all levels of the enterprise.

The UAW's role in the development of Saturn is literally without precedent. Never before has a union been involved to this extent in designing work stations, business and people systems, and in selection of the site where its members will be asked to work and relocate their families. Saturn would not and could not exist without the participation of the UAW.

How does all of this fit into traditional labor law concepts of proper subjects for bargaining and the rights of employees and labor organizations under the Act? I wonder. As I indicated earlier, the process that resulted in Saturn reflects, in my judgment, collective bargaining at the most sophisticated level. It was collective bargaining based not on an obsolete ideological, adversarial mind-set, but rather on finding practical ways to solve real problems in order to maximize employment opportunities in this country and preserve an important U.S. manufacturing base. It is a type of collective bargaining which results in employees, through the instrumentality of their union, becoming participants in the enterprise rather than simply contributing their labor to the production process.

A Saturn-type collective bargaining agreement may not be the right answer in many labor-management settings, but in those industries which find themselves threatened by worldwide competition, the Saturn approach to collective bargaining may be the only way to preserve jobs for American workers without resort by the government to an unacceptable regime of protectionism.

COLLECTIVE BARGAINING: A PROCESS UNDER SIEGE

ROBERT J. CONNERTON*

Professor St. Antoine has given us an excellent discussion and analysis of the changing contours of collective bargaining over the past half century. Starting from the legislative genesis of the good-faith bargaining requirement, he reminds us that our present assumption that the bargaining duty depends preliminarily on our characterization of a particular subject as mandatory or permissive does not follow necessarily from the statutory language, but rather from difficult and debatable crossroad choices that the Supreme Court made in *Borg-Warner*.[1] Clearly Professor St. Antoine is correct in observing that collective bargaining would appear far different if the *Borg-*

* General Counsel, Laborers' International Union, AFL-CIO; partner, Connerton, Bernstein & Katz, Washington, D.C.
[1] NLRB v. Wooster Div. of Borg-Warner Corp., 356 US 342, 42 LRRM 2034 (1958).

Warner Court had chosen other equally defensible readings of the statute.

For Professor St. Antoine, the historical review leads to an expansive view of the bargaining duty and "participative management." Professor St. Antoine finds that considerations of economics, ethics, and social policy fully support his view. He correctly notes that in our society men and women are defined by and derive their sense of self-esteem from their work. Thus, he concludes "that negotiations [should be held] mandatory when managerial decisions affecting unit work may jeopardize employees' job security." Otherwise, employees are treated as little more than unthinking pawns whose employment rights are unjustifiably sacrificed to the property rights of employers. With this conclusion I concur wholeheartedly. In addition, I acknowledge with appreciation Professor St. Antoine's thoughtful assessment of the possibilities for opening up and extending the concept of bargaining to involve workers more deeply in the decisions that affect their working lives.

In a better world, enlightened self-interest would lead employers, for the reasons suggested by Professor St. Antoine, to accept bargaining over a wide array of what are possibly only permissive subjects. His examples demonstrate the mutual advantages which are available to both labor and management when bargaining is fully accepted rather than begrudgingly extended only as required by law. Unfortunately, enlightenment is always in notoriously short supply.

I. The Future of Collective Bargaining

Recent Board cases, however, bode ill for the very foundations of collective bargaining. Professor St. Antoine sees the glass half full; I see it three-quarters empty. I confess at the outset that I am deeply concerned about the impact of the current Board's assault on collective bargaining. Recent cases substantially narrow the arena of mandatory "terms and conditions of employment" other than wages and hours. The subjects covered in this category, such as plant relocation, sale or partial sale of a business or assets, and consolidation or transfer of operations,[2] often include critical issues going directly to job security. To be frank, I

---

[2] Otis Elevator Co., 269 NLRB 891, 115 LRRM 1281, 1283 n.5 (1984), *rev'g* 255 NLRB 235, 106 LRRM 1343 (1981).

must tell you that the Board's shortcomings in this as well as other areas lead me to question whether it continues to serve the purposes for which it was originally chartered.

After *Fibreboard Paper Products* v. *NLRB*,[3] the framework of mandatory/permissive analysis favored a finding that "terms and conditions of employment" covered a wide area of matters crucial to employees. In determining subcontracting to be a mandatory subject, the *Fibreboard* Court observed that subcontracting was a "vital concern to labor and management;"[4] that as a matter of empirical fact it was frequently the subject of bargaining;[5] and that it was amenable to the bargaining process.[6] These factors tend to favor, if not to compel, the conclusion that issues such as plant relocation and transfer of operations are mandatory subjects. Indeed, in terms which come within striking distance of Professor St. Antoine's thesis that the bargaining duty should extend to all decisions affecting job security, the *Fibreboard* Court held:

> The words ["condition of employment"] even more plainly cover termination of employment which, as the facts of this case indicate, necessarily results from the contracting out of work performed by members of the bargaining unit.[7]

If I am correct that *Fibreboard* created a presumption as a matter both of law and of subsequent practice that the topics we are discussing are mandatory subjects of bargaining, that presumption nonetheless came to an end in *First National Maintenance*.[8] There, the Court discovered an additional factor in *Fibreboard* of which we had previously been unaware:

> [B]argaining over management decisions that have a substantial impact on the continued availability of employment should be required only if the benefit, for labor management relations and the collective bargaining process, outweighs the burden placed on the conduct of the business.[9]

In the hands of the current Board this balancing principle quickly led to a series of *per se* rules so that, in an astonishingly

---

[3] 379 US 203, 57 LRRM 2609 (1964).
[4] *Id.* at 211.
[5] *Id.* at 211–12.
[6] *Id.* at 213–14.
[7] *Id.* at 210.
[8] First Nat'l Maintenance Corp. v. NLRB, 452 US 666, 107 LRRM 2705 (1981).
[9] *Id.* at 679.

wide range of contexts, the burden on business would always outweigh the impact on collective bargaining and therefore bargaining should never be required.

In *Milwaukee Spring II*,[10] reversing a contrary decision found in *Milwaukee Spring I*,[11] the Board held that an employer does not violate its bargaining duty by transferring its operations to a nonunion facility in retaliation for a union's failure to grant midterm wage concessions. On appeal the D.C. Circuit affirmed, holding that where the transfer of operations was permitted by the existing management rights clause, the unilateral transfer of operations and resulting abolition of union jobs did not violate Section 8(d).[12] However, said Judge Edwards, if the contract does not grant the company broad discretion in transferring its operations, it would violate Section 8(d) for the employer to transfer work unilaterally for the purpose of gaining wage concessions.[13]

After *Milwaukee Spring* the rout was on. In *Otis Elevator II*,[14] again reversing its own decision in *Otis Elevator I*, the current Board declared that an employer had no duty to bargain over a midterm decision to close one facility and transfer and consolidate remaining operations in another. The Board plurality read *First National Maintenance* to justify this *per se* rule so long as the decision to transfer operations did not "turn on" labor costs. In its list of the types of decisions covered by the *Otis Elevator* rule, the Board included such decisions as the sale of the business, the consolidation or restructuring of operations, the introduction of

---

[10] Milwaukee Spring, Div. of Ill. Coil Spring Co., 268 NLRB 601, 115 LRRM 1065 (1984), *enforced sub nom.* Automobile Workers v. NLRB, 765 F2d 175, 119 LRRM 2801 (CA DC, 1985).

[11] Milwaukee Spring, Div. of Ill. Coil Spring Co., 265 NLRB 206, 111 LRRM 1486 (1982).

[12] 765 F2d 175, 119 LRRM 2801 (CA DC, (1985).

[13] Judge Edwards' analysis turns upon the effect to be given the standard zipper clause. The zipper clause, says Judge Edwards, not only waives the parties' rights to bargain over otherwise mandatory subjects but also their rights to make midterm unilateral changes without bargaining. If the employer fails to obtain contractual language permitting relocation or subcontracting, the standard zipper clause may on the one hand excuse the employer from having to bargain over that decision. But, on the other hand, that clause will prohibit the company from changing the terms and conditions of employment by unilaterally acting without bargaining. Accordingly, where a standard zipper clause appears in the contract, the D.C. Circuit's *Milwaukee Spring* decision puts the bargaining onus on the employer—not the union—to obtain affirmatively the right to engage in such midcontract changes.

[14] *See supra* note 4.

labor-saving technology, and advertising.[15] The Board plurality implicitly suggested that, notwithstanding *Fibreboard,* even the duty to bargain over subcontracting was imperiled.

The attack on meaningful bargaining over "other terms and conditions of employment" continues.[16] The consolation prize in *Milwaukee Spring* and *Otis Elevator* appeared to be the requirement that before undertaking a unilateral, midterm change intended to reduce labor costs, an employer must at a minimum bargain to impasse. Later cases have proven that assumption far too optimistic. In *Hawthorn Melody*[17] the Board held that there is no bargaining duty even if labor costs are a factor so long as they are not determinative. Showing its versatility in *Gar Wood-Detroit Truck Equipment,*[18] the Board nullified the duty in yet another fashion. By the facile device of labeling as a decision to reduce overhead costs, one obviously motivated by the employer's intent to reduce labor costs, the bargaining duty disappeared.

Similarly indicative of the present posture of the bargaining duty are two other recent decisions. The first held that a unilateral decision to discontinue giving employees a Christmas dinner or ham is lawful because it does not involve compensation or a term or condition of employment.[19] The second held that a three-day notice to the union that the employer intended to close a division of the business satisfied the employer's duty to engage in *effects* bargaining, given the employer's reasonable need to maintain secrecy to preserve its competitive position.[20]

In sum, the picture at mid-century is that the NLRA is no longer a source of employee protection for many critical mid-contract changes which go to the very existence of employment and job security. One might expect unions to respond by negotiating the protections which have been read out of the statute. For example, if the Board no longer reads the NLRA to prevent a midterm unilateral decision to transfer work without bargain-

---

[15] *Id.*

[16] Indeed, the scope of recent cases goes beyond "other terms and conditions of employment." The *Milwaukee Spring* employer was after all seeking wage reductions. Thus the effect, if not the explicit holding, of the Board's decisions in this area is to arm employers with the license to demand midterm renegotiation of wages and hours as well as other terms and conditions.

[17] 275 NLRB No. 55, 119 LRRM 1079 (1985).

[18] 274 NLRB No. 23, 118 LRRM 1417 (1985).

[19] Benchmark Indus., Inc., 270 NLRB 22, 116 LRRM 1131 (1984).

[20] Creasey Co., 268 NLRB 1425, 115 LRRM 1131 (1984).

ing, unions would be expected to negotiate such provisions in their collective bargaining agreements.

Unfortunately, *Milwaukee Spring, Otis Elevator,* and their progeny do not simply permit midterm changes. They declare plant relocations, work transfers, and the like to be nonmandatory subjects of bargaining. If they are nonmandatory midterm, they are nonmandatory in contract negotiations. Unions generally will therefore find it difficult to replace the nullified statutory rights with collectively bargained rights because the Board has clearly announced its intention to remove these issues from the bargaining duty. In sum, the Board has removed the statutory prohibition against employer unilateral changes of core job security and job preservation issues while at the same time prohibiting unions from negotiating compensating contract protections.

II. The Construction Industry: An Example

Certainly, the current retreat from *Borg-Warner* should concern all labor practitioners committed to the continued viability of collective bargaining. Unfortunately the threat is not confined to the issues discussed above. St. Antoine has addressed collective bargaining as it is presented primarily in the mature industrial setting. In other collective bargaining settings, the debate over mandatory versus permissive subjects of bargaining seems almost an academic luxury. In many cases the attack on collective bargaining comes at a more fundamental level. For example, in the construction industry, with which I have been heavily involved for more than 30 years, collective bargaining has been completely "deregulated" in favor of employer free choice. Even where a long-standing and stable collective bargaining relationship has existed, as a practical matter the National Labor Relations Board has decreed that a contractor is at liberty to walk away from that relationship or contract at any time.

The NLRA was originally drafted to address the industrial or other fixed-plant setting. The construction industry, on the other hand, as a rule consists of many short-term projects, built by a multiplicity of contractors and staffed in large part through referrals by various craft unions. From the beginning, Congress recognized that the Act as a regulator of labor relations in the industrial sector was ill-suited for direct application to the construction industry.[21] Instead, Congress found that the primary purposes of the Act, promoting concerted activity and collective bargaining, could be secured only through rules specially tailored to the industry's situation.

For example, the lengthy election procedures of the NLRA, regardless of their utility or lack thereof in the typical long-term industrial setting, have never been satisfactory in the construction industry with its many short-term projects. Labor relations in the construction arena initially grew out of the realities of the industry, with little reference to the industrial model underlying the NLRA. Indeed, before 1947 there was already a long history of collective bargaining in the construction industry. Prehire agreements were routinely negotiated and enforced. Accordingly, before Taft-Hartley the Board concluded that it would not effectuate the purposes of the Act to exercise jurisdiction over construction projects.[22] Unfortunately, the Board's post-1947 application of the Taft-Hartley amendments to the construction industry created serious problems for the existing stability of labor relations in that field.

It was to remedy these difficulties and restore the pre-Taft-Hartley status quo that Congress passed Section 8(f) in 1959. Over the strenuous objections of construction employers and contractors, Congress adopted Section 8(f) expressly (1) to remove any shadow on the enforceability of prehire agreements which were standard industry practice and (2) to place such agreements on an equal footing with agreements in the indus-

---

[21] "[T]he occasional nature of the employment relationship makes this industry markedly different from manufacturing and other types of enterprise. An individual employee typically works for many employers and for none of them continuously. Jobs are frequently of short duration depending upon various stages of construction." S. REP. NO. 187, 86th Cong., 1st Sess. 27 (1959), *reprinted in* I LEGISLATIVE HISTORY TO THE LMRDA OF 1959 [hereinafter LEG. HIST. LMRDA], at 423; LEG. HIST. LMRDA, at 777 (H.R. REP. NO. 741).

The National Labor Relations Act was written with a view to places of more or less fixed employment, factories, mines, mills, and so forth.

The theory is that you have a payroll, a working force, that you then conduct an election among the working force, and then you choose a bargaining representative and the bargaining representative then negotiates the terms and conditions of employment.

Now in the construction industry, in 95% of the cases none of that works.

Hearings before the Senate Committee on Labor and Public Welfare, 83d Cong., 2d Sess. 386 (1956) (statement of Archibald Cox, as relied upon in LEG. HIST. LMRDA, at 424 (S. REP. No. 187)).

[22] LEG. HIST. LMRDA, at 423, 777 (H.R. REP. NO. 741).

trial sector.[23] Congress also was careful to accommodate employees' free-choice rights by including a proviso to Section 8(f) that exempts construction workers from conventional contract-bar principles and permits such employees to file representation and decertification petitions during the term of a prehire agreement.

Until 1971, when the Board decided *R.J. Smith Construction Co.*,[24] Congress' intent had been given effect and there was no challenge to the enforceability of prehire agreements. In that case, however, the Board turned Section 8(f) upon its head. Contrary to congressional intent, the Board decreed that Section 8(f) requires employers to abide by collective bargaining agreements only with a *majority* representative. No longer did that section evoke the outrage of contractors and the gratitude of workers. Overnight, construction employers applauded Section 8(f) as an employer emancipation proclamation; contractors now were free to repudiate prehire agreements despite the apparent Section 8(a)(5) violation, or even more apparent enforceability via a Section 301 action. The only limitation on this newly created right was and remains a practical consideration: whether the contractor can locate sufficient numbers of skilled nonunion craft workers. The Board thus transformed Section 8(f) into a boon for employers and a bust for employees. The Board's attempt to rationalize this result by paying lip service to employees' Section 7 rights cannot disguise the effect of its holdings, namely, virtually to destroy construction workers' rights to engage in concerted activity.[25]

---

[23] In further recognition of the industry's unique situation, Congress also enacted the construction industry proviso to §8(e) to permit wide latitude in the industry's subcontracting practices and amended §302 to permit the pooling of certain fringe benefit funds common in the industry.

[24] R.J. Smith Constr. Co., 191 NLRB 693, 77 LRRM 1493 (1971). In NLRB v. Ironworkers Local 103 (Higdon Contracting Co.), 434 US 335, 97 LRRM 2333 (1978), the Supreme Court deferred to the Board's expertise and accepted this reading of the statute. *Higdon* was subsequently both expanded and limited in Jim McNeff, Inc. v. Todd, 461 US 260, 113 LRRM 2113 (1983), in which the Supreme Court held that a prehire agreement was enforceable under §301 even by a minority union but only until such time as it was repudiated by the employer.

[25] A simple analogy demonstrates the audacity of the Board's logical leap in *R.J. Smith.* Areawide collective bargaining agreements are commonplace in the construction industry. Such agreements promote industrial stability and prevent "whipsawing" by providing uniform terms for all union construction workers and their employers in a particular region. If a signatory union were to adopt the approach the Board applied to employers in *R.J. Smith,* then it might repudiate that area agreement with impunity for projects at which contractors were especially vulnerable. In essence, then, *R.J. Smith* and its progeny permit employers to do precisely that which §8(f) was designed to prevent: destabilize labor relations and wreak havoc upon an entire industry.

As if the repudiation of prehire agreements did not provide a wide enough loophole, the NLRB has also seen fit to allow contractors through "double-breasting" to avoid their collective bargaining agreements and obligations by freely establishing a separate nonunion enterprise to which the agreement does not apply. Whether a second enterprise is a continuation of the operation covered by the union contract theoretically depends upon an analysis of four factors: interrelation of operations, common management, centralized control of labor relations, and common ownership.[26] But in a line of cases commencing with *Gerace Construction, Inc.,*[27] the Board has repeatedly found that construction operations or divisions are not a single employer so long as the same person does not exercise the day-to-day control of labor relations. It has not troubled the Board that the two divisions are commonly controlled and owned, use the same offices, equipment, storage yards, estimators, and technical people, and compete for the same type of construction projects. Thus, the union contract is frequently found not to apply to the new enterprise because of the legal fiction that it is a different employer.[28] The result is that any contractor can choose with impunity and without cost whether to operate on a union or nonunion basis at any particular job site.

Accordingly, at midcentury the NLRB has made a joke of collective bargaining in the construction industry. Contractors are freely allowed either to repudiate their prehire agreements or to go double-breasted. By manipulating their work force selection or corporate structure, contractors can work either union or nonunion as they choose. The Act's underlying objective of promoting employee free choice, and Section 8(f)'s enact-

---

[26] Electrical Workers (IBEW) Local 1264 v. Broadcast Serv. of Mobile, Inc., 380 US 255, 256, 58 LRRM 2545 (1965).

[27] 193 NLRB 645, 78 LRRM 1367 (1971).

[28] The D.C. Circuit rejected this constricted view of the bargaining duty in Operating Eng'rs Local 627 v. NLRB (Perter Kiewit Sons Co.), 518 F2d 1040, 90 LRRM 2321 (CA DC, 1975), *vacating and remanding* 206 NLRB 562, 84 LRRM 1356 (1973), *aff'd in part and remanded in part sub nom.* South Prairie Constr. Co. v. Operating Eng'rs Local 627, 425 US 800, 92 LRRM 2507 (1976), *on remand*, 231 NLRB 76, 95 LRRM 1510 (1977), *aff'd*, 595 F2d 844, 100 LRRM 2792 (CA DC, 1979). On remand, however, the Board held firm to its result if not its theory, deciding that even if the union and nonunion employers were deemed a single employer, the collective bargaining agreement of the union company did not bind the nonunion company. The Board relied on essentially the same analysis of the single employer issue that the court of appeals had rejected, to hold that the work forces of the union and nonunion entities lacked a community of interest and, therefore, did not constitute a single bargaining unit.

ment to fulfill that objective in the unique circumstances of the construction industry, have been perversely transformed into a statutory provision which denies employee free choice in order to exalt employer free choice. Thus, whether a particular topic is a mandatory or permissive subject of bargaining appears a remote intellectual enterprise for construction trade unions. These parties confront the ever-present threat that the employer will, with apparent Board approval, walk away from a collective bargaining obligation tomorrow, if not today.

III. Noncollective Bargaining Methods

As Professor St. Antoine trenchantly points out, the labor movement in the United States has historically been among the most conservative trade union movements in the world. American unions have passively and silently accepted many types of managerial decisions. They did so on the basis of an implicit pact with management: A deal was a deal and so-called managerial decisions would not be employed to destroy the labor agreement. In substantial measure, management has now repudiated that basic premise and declared war on the trade union movement.

Today's unions are discovering that the NLRA and the NLRB are all too frequently irrelevant to the problems they face. The current antiunion climate and the push toward deregulation of industry on all fronts have helped, finally, to radicalize the American labor movement. Unions in this country are no longer willing to sit by idly while management—largely unconstrained by any effective legal process—blithely eliminates workers' hard-won jobs and protections. Instead, the labor movement is acknowledging and insisting upon its right to participate in managerial decisions of critical importance to employees. Faced with the limits of collective bargaining, unions are reaching for tools outside the realm of collective bargaining. The result is a far more progressive trade union movement than that which Senator Wagner envisioned 50 years ago.

Expanding categories of union membership is one example. In recent years some unions have permitted workers at unorganized facilities to become "associate" union members in order to obtain health and educational benefits and legal services otherwise not available. The AFL-CIO has taken the lead in recommending that unions give serious consideration to "providing direct services and benefits to workers outside of a collective bargaining structure."[29] Creating new types of membership encourages workers to take advantage of the vast array of services that modern unions provide, and may prove an aid to more conventional organizing strategies as well. The practice also draws on the roots of the labor movement; trade unions historically served primarily as benefit societies, providing death benefits and the like to their members.

Unions today are also reaching out to the general public in an effort to accomplish their goals. Innovative strategies such as corporate campaigns have had tremendous success in helping workers obtain union recognition, reach agreement on contracts, and fight plant closings and relocations. These campaigns succeed by applying external pressure to recalcitrant employers. Thus the J.P. Stevens campaign, for example, involved a massive consumer boycott as well as actions to cut the ties between the company, two insurance companies, and a bank. Other campaigns have targeted employers' dependency on—and consequent vulnerability to—government licensing schemes. In still other instances, unions have protested corporate anti-unionism at shareholder meetings and withdrawn union funds from banks connected with intransigent employers. Union officials now sit on boards of directors in the automobile and airline industries. Unions in other industries are likely soon to follow suit. All these tactics entail cooperation and coordination both among unions and between unions and other organizations, that is, community, minority, feminist, religious, and political groups.[30]

As the Board labors to reduce collective bargaining to an anachronism, the battle moves on to other fronts. The *Bildisco*[31] and Continental Airlines bankruptcies have suggested to management a new divice to extract themselves from unwanted labor agreements while retaining corporate control. But as the chairman of Wheeling-Pittsburgh found out, trade unions have also learned the bankruptcy game. In April 1985 Wheeling-Pittsburgh went into voluntary bankruptcy and in July it abrogated the collective bargaining agreement. The Steelworkers struck,

---

[29] AFL-CIO Committee on the Evolution of Work, THE CHANGING SITUATION OF WORKERS AND THEIR UNIONS 20 (1985).

[30] *See generally,* Mishel, *Strengths & Limits of Non-Workplace Strategies,* 7 LAB. RESEARCH REV. 69, 72–74 (1985).

[31] NLRB v. Bildisco & Bildisco, 465 US 513, 115 LRRM 2805 (1984).

and on September 30 it was Wheeling-Pittsburgh's chairman who was without a job.[32]

The extraordinary steps taken by airline unions in the TWA takeover situation illustrate the imaginative tactics trade unions are using in the financial arena. In July 1985 the Air Line Pilots Association announced the creation of a $100 million contingency fund. The fund's purpose went beyond merely supporting a traditional strike. Instead, the fund was meant to provide the "financial clout" with which to pursue "innovative strategies."[33] In addition, ALPA, the Machinists, and the Flight Attendants subsequently announced an agreement with Carl Icahn, with whom they had previously been locked in combat, to exchange wage concessions for stock. This measure was designed to improve Icahn's position as a suitor for TWA over that of Frank Lorenzo, whom the union viewed as an antiunion corporate raider.[34] Although the TWA Board of Directors had previously supported Lorenzo, in part because of his hostility to unions, the Board then accepted Icahn's offer precisely because of the prospects for labor stability.

The striking effectiveness of labor parties' involvement in the TWA takeover campaign will not be an isolated situation if Jesse Unruh's newly formed Council of Institutional Investors achieves its purposes. Formed in January 1985, the Council intends to encourage pension fund trustees to take a more active role in corporate mergers and takeover campaigns.[35] At its formation, Council members, representing primarily public funds, controlled over $100 billion. The Council's recognition of the funds' duty to assess the impact of merger or takeover offers rather than simply selling their voting rights to the highest bidder was endorsed by Robert Monks, former Administrator of the Labor Department's Office of Pension and Welfare Benefit Programs.[36]

---

[32] Wash. Post, Oct. 3, 1985, at E1, col. 1. [**Editor's Note:** On May 28, 1986, the Third Circuit struck down a Bankruptcy Judge's approval of the company's rejection of its collective bargaining contract. Wheeling-Pittsburgh Steel Corp. v. Steelworkers, 122 LRRM 24-25.]

[33] 1985 DAILY LAB. REP. (BNA) 128: A-11.

[34] 1985 DAILY LAB. REP. (BNA) 153: A-9.

[35] 12 PENSION REP. (BNA) No. 4 at 146, Jan. 28, 1985.

[36] 12 PENSION REP. (BNA) No. 3 at 121, Jan. 21, 1985.

Pension funds are also beginning to engage in socially conscious investment practices. For example, some funds are actively seeking to invest in all-union construction projects that otherwise meet ERISA's fiduciary standards. On another front, other fund trustees are reversing their historic neutrality with respect to voting the hundreds of billions of dollars in stock portfolios. That neutrality had the effect of supporting incumbent corporate management. The recent upsurge of anti-unionism in the boardrooms has led many trustees to realize that their fiduciary duty requires them to exercise these voting rights aggressively in order to fulfill their duty to act in the best interest of their beneficiaries—the workers.

Thus, trade unions are reaching out to new allies and fashioning new tools in order better to serve the interests of their constituency. The shrinking legal protection for collective bargaining has not crippled the American labor movement. On the contrary—labor unions have shifted focus from the legal/regulatory arena into other areas. By innovating within the structure of existing trade unions, and by reaching out to involve other types of organizations in the common struggle, the labor movement is returning to its motivating principle: to promote the common good through solidarity.

The System Works Well

Peter D. Walther*

In appraising the National Labor Relations Board at midcentury, I undoubtedly am in the minority in saying I am very optimistic and very positive. As I said a year ago at Cornell, the Labor Board has had a magnificent 50 years and will have another. For a Philadelphian from the Keystone State, it is appropriate to be assigned to appraise "collective bargaining" in regard to the Board's 50 years, since collective bargaining is the keystone of the Act. The Act revolves around, and is supported by, collective bargaining; and frankly, for our present purposes, the Labor Board and the Act are synonymous. The labor law, whether one calls it the Wagner Act, the Taft-Hartley Act, or both, is basically a remedial process. Congress, in order to

* Former Member, National Labor Relations Board; partner, Drinker Biddle & Reath, Philadelphia, Pennsylvania.

accomplish certain objectives, established several primary premises and assigned the carrying out of those premises and the fulfilling of those objectives to the National Labor Relations Board with power of remedial action.

The primary underlying premises of the Act, I think, are clear, and I should hope, beyond question: the encouraging of collective bargaining and the guarantee and protection of employee free choice. While most will agree with these two premises, the resultant opinions of where this leads are often divergent. Many seem to feel the Act is not a success because collective bargaining has not become more acceptable to employees in the exercising of their free choice, because collective bargaining is still a minority, not a majority factor in industrial relations in this country. This is based on a mistaken belief, or a failure to understand, the original intent of Senator Wagner and the supporters of the Wagner Act back in 1935. I ask you not to accept just my word on this, but also that of General Counsel Larry Gold of the AFL-CIO, who, before the Labor section in Washington in July 1985 made it very clear that the basic premise in 1935 was not that everyone should be organized, but that employees should have the right of free association. If employees do have the right of free association, do have the right of free choice, there is no requirement or even intent that they necessarily have to go one way or the other—that is left to the wishes and desires of the individual employees, as declared through majority vote.

If one studies the history of the Act, there is no evidence that Senator Wagner or Congress, either in 1935, 1947, or at any other time, provided that all employees, or a majority, or any, should be organized in labor unions, though in 1935 Congress did intend to encourage workers to join unions. Again, I ask you not necessarily to accept just my opinion, but the objectives of the Act as set forth by Leon Keyserling before the Capitol Labor Historical Society in his November 1984 speech commemorating the 50th anniversary of the Wagner Act. To those who do not recognize the name of Leon Keyserling, as administrative assistant to Senator Wagner in the mid-1930s he was in fact the author of the Act. It was Senator Wagner who almost single-handedly devised the policies and the objectives of the Act, but it was Leon Keyserling who put them into words and provisions on paper. He presented the four objectives of Senator Wagner behind the Act.

The first objective was to remove labor disputes—strikes—arising out of an employer's refusal to recognize or accept collective bargaining from the industrial complex in this country. As Mr. Keyserling commented in this regard, there can be no question that the Act has been extremely successful and has met its objective beyond any question. While there is some contrary talk today, let us be honest: with very few and rare exceptions, it is still successful; but this is one area where there may be some problems in the future.

The second objective was to free the American worker and to create a free workplace, freeing him primarily from harrassment and control of the employer. This is where, in my opinion, the Taft-Hartley Act did amend the objectives by also establishing provisions which would free the American worker from harrassment or improper control by labor unions.

The third objective was to bring about the redistribution of wealth and the raising of wages for employees, thereby increasing buying power. By increasing buying power, there would be a greater need for production, and therefore a creation of more jobs. The underlying objectives of the Wagner Act were not directed just at employment relations, but were a major part of the economic program to solve the Depression and to reduce the possibilities of recession in the future.

The last objective set forth by Professor Keyserling in his speech was to correct these actions without governmental interference and involvement directly in the industrial community. By accomplishing these objectives through the collective bargaining premise, it was believed that they would be able to forestall or prevent government interference—socialism—as Senator Wagner clearly defined it, from becoming more involved in the employment situation and industry.

As Senator Wagner stated:

Modern nations have selected one of two methods to bring order into industry. The first is to create a super government. Under such plans, labor unions are abolished or become the creatures of the state. Trade associations became the cartels of the state . . . . The second method of coordinating industry is the democratic method. It is entirely different from the first. Instead of control from the top, it insists on control from within. It places the primary responsibility where it belongs and asks industry and labor to solve their mutual problems through self-government. That is industrial democracy, and upon its success depends the preservation of the American way of life.[1]

There is no question that Senator Wagner's objective was to follow the second route, to leave the solution of industrial problems in a democratic industrial society to management and labor, keeping government as far removed as possible. It is also quite evident that the United States is in fact the only nation in the world that has really tried to follow that route. While Japan is to some extent closer to the democratic process than Senator Wagner's "super government" process, and Canada is as close to us as it is to the European system, there can be no question that he was following a different course than that which has been followed throughout Europe.

This fourth objective is the only one that has not been completely, and beyond anyone's fondest dreams, successful. There has been a great deal of both federal and state legislation over the last 15 or 20 years—ERISA, OSHA, and many others—that has moved into and brought government closer to and more involved in industrial relations situations.

While I will not make a major point of it, if you give it just a little bit of thought, I am sure you can agree with me that in both the areas of safety and pensions, OSHA and ERISA came about because collective bargaining was not able to successfully deal with those areas and bring about the proper and necessary protection of the rights of the employees.

There should be no question, and it is my strong conviction, that the Act, and therefore the Labor Board, has been unbelievably successful in meeting and fulfilling the objectives of the Act; and that we can establish its tremendous success by viewing it in comparison with any and every other democratic or undemocratic industrial nation in the world.

Does anyone really believe that any other worker anywhere in the world is freer, has more rights, and is more greatly respected in his workplace and in his job, overall, than the American worker? How can he be freer, when in most other nations, he is either under the direct Communist-type approach, where he does not even have the right to strike, has no real rights or freedom in his workplace; or as has been clearly demonstrated in

---

[1] Keyserling, THE WAGNER ACT: AFTER TEN YEARS 13 (L. Silverberg ed., 1945).

recent years, he is under a system which is based on super government. His wages are not bargained by his chosen representatives and his employer, but are bargained somewhere off on a national scale, on a minimum basis, by a national union and a big employer's association, and with a third-party government right in the middle. The super government approach does not permit a free employee in the workplace.

Stop for a minute and look at Sweden, where union officials are elected for life and do not stand for reelection. Is this a situation, where those national union officials have a great deal of control over the wages, benefits, and working conditions of the employee, that is conducive to employee freedom? In Sweden, as in Japan, it is very difficult for an employee who is dissatisfied with his employment relationship to change jobs. We all hear about the lifetime guarantee for employment in Japan, but do not forget, you only get that once; and if you do not like your job and decide to leave and try something else, you will never again obtain any form of lifetime guarantee of employment. The very structure of Japanese society puts a great many restrictions and prohibitions on the rights of the individual employee in the workplace.

In many of the countries in the European Economic Community and throughout the world, with the exception of the United States, the closed shop is legal and enforceable. Does the closed shop really provide a free workplace? England and Japan have court systems which enforce wrongful discharge procedures; but in both countries, reinstatement is extremely rare. The quasi-judicial system for handling wrongful discharge cases in those countries does not believe in reinstatement and does not use that as a remedy except in very rare situations. Can worker freedom in the workplace be provided absent reinstatement? Even further, one finds that the monetary rewards are extremely small. In England, the average back pay is in the area of 300 pounds, not $300,000, which is what I understand is becoming the average judgment for wrongful discharge cases in California.

What other country in the world has established such extensive personnel communication programs, has in fact turned from personnel relations to human resource relations, and with justification for the use of that title? In the United States, most companies no longer have just personnel relations, we do have human resources. No other country has followed those programs, although it is true that in Great Britain communications are starting to become a more interesting and active pursuit from the point of view of the employers. No worker anywhere else in the world has been given such a free and unrestrained workplace—whether it is viewed from the standpoint of his individual rights and his ability to make his own decisions, or from the standpoint of his working conditions—as has the American.

How about the third objective—the redistribution of wealth? Have we been successful in that regard? Tremendously. And in the last four years under the Reagan administration, unbelievably successful in comparison to the other industrial nations of the world. The closest possible comparisons we can make are to the nations of the European Community—countries such as West Germany, Sweden, The Netherlands, England, and France. As regards wages, there is no question that the average American worker is paid much higher than any other worker in the world. The Bureau of Labor Statistics in July 1985 informed us that the closest in comparable manufacturing wages to the American is the West German, who earned approximately 75 percent of what the American earned in manufacturing as of 1984. It is interesting to note that just three years before, in 1981, the West German was earning 97 percent of what the American earned. In fact, in 1981, the Swedish manufacturing worker was earning 108 percent of what the American earned in comparable buying power, but by 1984 this figure had fallen to 72 percent. We have, in fact and in truth, the highest paid workers in buying power and standard of living of anywhere in the world in this country today. This has represented a tremendous jump and progress in just the last four years.

I mention that because, in my opinion, one of the major reasons for the success of the Reagan administration in solving the economic problems has been its encouragement of the same approach to industry that was behind the Wagner Act—let the parties work it out themselves and keep government interference out of the industrial community. As we all know, one of the major pledges—and he has been quite successful in keeping it—of President Reagan was to get government off the businessman's back. It may be strange for you to realize that the Reagan philosophy was the underlying objective or philosophy of the original Wagner Act in 1935, and it has been the most successful approach in accomplishing the objectives of redistribution of wealth, jobs, and worker freedom in the entire world since that time.

Okay. Wages are good, but what about unemployment? The European communities have unemployment; there, where much of our work is going in the manufacturing area, they have 11 percent unemployment, compared with our 7 percent. In fact, it is in the area of the creation of jobs that the success of our system, and especially its tremendous success in comparison to the socialistic systems that have been put in place in the European communities, stands out.

In the last year, there have been several studies of the increase in jobs in the United States in comparison with the European Community covering a span of 15 years. One must first recognize that during that 15-year period, the United States underwent a tremendous influx into its job force from two sources—a baby boom and the housewife. In those 15 years we underwent an influx of baby boomers that no other country could match in percentage or numbers. While there was a baby boom to some extent in other countries, it never was as great as in the United States. Also, we underwent a tremendous influx of housewives, American women moving from the home into the work force, an increase estimated from approximately the high 30s into the low 50s percentage wise. No other country went through this to any extent at all, and it is just now in the mid-1980s starting to become a factor in Great Britain. But even with those tremendous influx effects, we still held our unemployment level down to the lowest in the industrial world today, 7 percent. During this 15-year period, econometric studies show we created at least 18 million or, more probably 28 million, jobs. During that same period, how many jobs did the European Community—nine leading industrial nations of the world (the only exception, Japan)—create? you may be shocked to know that in 15 years, their socialistic systems of handling industrial relations were successful in affecting 1½ to 2 million jobs, but there is a minus sign before it. In 1985, there were 1½ to 2 million fewer jobs in the European Community than in 1970.

So let us get one understanding straight: Appraising the Act and the Board at midcentury, on the basis of the objectives of the Act and congressional intent, their success has been magnificent beyond anyone's expectations.

The only objective that has not been reached and maintained is keeping governmental interference out of labor relations, and that cannot be blamed on either the Act or the Board.

Collective bargaining, the keystone of the Act, is and has been successful; perhaps not as common or accepted as expected, but it has done the job of fulfilling the objectives of the Act and providing a free workplace, higher wages, and more jobs. It has worked so well, employers have struggled mightily to reach those objectives through human resource programs without unionization and in the absence of collective bargaining.

Not only is collective bargaining working very successfully in bringing about the objectives of the Act, where it exists, but also it works well. There are problems and always will be. During the late 1960s and early 1970s, unions ruled the bargaining table and got most, perhaps too many of their demands. Naturally, the situation changed; and by the early 1980s, we find employers sitting at the head of the concession bargaining tables. That does not mean collective bargaining does not work; in truth, it is a clear demonstration of how well it does work and meets the pressures and needs of the times.

How can anyone argue collective bargaining is not working when we see the Saturn and General Motors-Toyota agreements, and the General Electric contract with a 12-union coalition headed by, and GE praised by, Lane Kirkland? One remembers the number one company in the union's "hate book" under the "Boulwarism" heading of not too many years ago.

I submit the Act works extremely effectively, collective bargaining works effectively, and the Board is doing its job effectively. Unless we wish to change the objectives of the Act, their successes cannot be denied. How would we change those objectives? Stop encouraging collective bargaining and substitute government fiat or control—let the Board write our labor agreements? Do away with free choice and democratic principles in the workplace? In 1984 at Cornell, I heard a former Board Chairman propose, and two other recent former Chairmen agree, that the way to further "free choice" was to do away with the freedom-of-speech guarantees in the Act.

Do we continue down the road to super government that so concerned Senator Wagner, with more and more legislative solutions, such as in the European systems? If we really set our minds to it, we too can lose 2 million jobs by the year 2000; instead, our present system of semifree enterprise is expected to produce 3½ million new jobs in 1985. A very appropriate commendation for the 50th anniversary of the Act and the Board— 3½ million more jobs for the working people of America. For it is the working people of America whom the Act and the Board are meant to serve, not employers and not just unions.

With all of this, I have much agreement with what Professor St. Antoine has said. I must agree that the system fashioned by Congress is in jeopardy because, for collective bargaining to continue working, labor unions are essential. I frankly must admit that the majority of employers, as fair and wise as they may be, cannot be expected or trusted to maintain free workplaces, high wages, and fair distribution of wealth, absent the threat of viable union organizing. If you agree with me that the Act has worked well for working people, that further socialization of the employment relationship and government interference is counterproductive, you must realize that steps are needed to strengthen and maintain collective bargaining and viable labor unions as a meaningful part of our industrial complex. While I do not agree fully with the solution, I agree that collective bargaining has problems and that one of the major problems is the result of too much governmental interference by the Board and the courts. *Otis Elevator II*[2] is a fair reading of *First National Maintenance*,[3] but I personally do not accept it as the proper way to go; much less, I cannot, in any way, agree with the *Gar Wood-Detroit Trucking*[4] decision.

I see several problems and even a few contradictions in the unlimited duty-to-bargain theory. Perhaps we are continuing the problem the Supreme Court got into in *First National Maintenance*. Instead of continuing to look at where and when we will apply the duty to bargain, I believe it would be more fruitful to follow the course hinted at by the Supreme Court in *Fibreboard*,[5] and suggested by Professor Charles J. Morris back in my days on the Board. Do not worry about when the duty applies, but look to what duty or what degree of duty will apply. Whether it should be a less demanding "consultive bargaining," as Professor Morris suggested,[6] or some variation thereof is not important here. By varying the requirements of full discussion to impasse, or the need to supply any and all possibly related information, we can in fact have at least discussion, if not full bargaining, whenever

---

[2] Otis Elevator Co., 269 NLRB 891, 115 LRRM 1281 (1984).
[3] First Nat'l Maintenance Corp. v. NLRB, 452 US 666, 107 LRRM 2705 (1981).
[4] Gar Wood-Detroit Truck Equipment, 274 NLRB No. 23, 118 LRRM 1417 (1985).
[5] Fibreboard Paper Prods. Corp. v. NLRB, 379 US 203, 57 LRRM 2609 (1964).
[6] *A Fresh Look at Conventional Wisdom and Unconventional Remedies*, 30 VAND. L. REV. 661, 667–76 (1977).

any union could reasonably request; and we would still protect the employer's needs as recognized in *First National Maintenance* and *Otis.*

I happen to agree with Professor Morris' comments[7] that the Board presently has the power and capacity, with the exercise of some imagination and careful analysis and evaluation, to bring about changes and improvements in remedies and remedial procedures that are essential if we are to keep collective bargaining viable. And more importantly, such an approach is essential if we are to maintain viable labor unions as the bulwark against more socialism.

I submit that Senator Wagner was right in 1935 when he decided that the way to keep super government out of business and bring about a cessation of strikes and labor disputes, a freer workplace, and a redistribution of wealth—through higher wages, more buying power, and more jobs for the American worker—was to encourage collective bargaining and free choice. Collective bargaining and the fear thereof, or the desire to avoid it and unions, has fulfilled those objectives beyond anyone's right to expect or predict. But if either collective bargaining or organizing by viable labor unions ever fails and ceases to exist as a threat to employers, the European socialistic systems of governmental regulations already being preached by many as the wave of the future, will rapidly fill the vacuum.

Collective bargaining works and works well.

Labor unions are our only bulwark against socialism in industrial relations.

As regards the multitude of suggestions for amendments to the Act or changes in our labor policy that seem to appear almost weekly, often in the *Harvard Law Review,* let me discount them all with another *Harvard Law Review* quotation from then-Dean Bok:[8]

> And finally, most of the professors and other critics who evaluate the laws are likely to continue in their unwillingness and inability to study the actual impact of the laws upon workers, unions, and employers in ways that will identify rules that fail to achieve their

---

[7] Morris, *The NLRB at 50: Labor Board at the Crossroads,* 26 (BNA Special Report, 1985). *See also* Professor Morris' paper in this volume.

[8] Bok, *Reflecting on the Distinctive Character of American Labor Laws,* 84 HARV. L. REV. 1394, (1971).

intended result or rest upon fallible suppositions of human behavior.[9]

Commentary

CARIN A. CLAUSS*

Professor St. Antoine starts and ends with a premise that is shared by all three of the response panelists: that collective bargaining has served us well. Professor St. Antoine points out that the United States has achieved substantial industrial peace and that broad worker participation, that is, workers having a voice in the industrial workplace, has not resulted in any adverse economic cost to the economy. We have attained this success in collective bargaining despite the absence of effective Board remedies applicable to employers who have engaged in unfair labor practices by either refusing to bargain or by illegally discharging union organizers. He notes that although collective bargaining has been successful and has served us well, it is still very much an imperfectly realized promise. He is especially critical of the restrictions which the Supreme Court and the Board have placed upon the scope of bargaining and argues for an open-ended mandate which would permit the parties to bargain about whatever they deem appropriate.

Eugene Hartwig's description of the bold Saturn experiment, with its emphasis on nonadversarial relations, is an exciting look into the wishful future. While he cautions that what General Motors and the United Automobile Workers were able to do with the Saturn project might not work elsewhere, I prefer to believe like Charles Wilson that what is good for GM is good for the country. There is no reason why shared decisionmaking cannot be as beneficial in other industrial settings as it is at GM.

Of all the respondents, Robert Connerton comes off as the least optimistic regarding the ability of the NLRB system to emerge from the morass of *Otis Elevator*[1] and *Milwaukee Spring*[2]

---

[9] *Id.* at 1462.

* Assistant Professor of Law, University of Wisconsin.

[1] 269 NLRB 891, 115 LRRM 1281 (1984), *rev'g* 255 NLRB 235, 106 LRRM 1343 (1981).
[2] Milwaukee Spring, Div. of Ill. Coil Spring Co., 268 NLRB 601, 115 LRRM 1065 (1984), *enforced sub nom.* Automobile Workers v. NLRB, 765 F2d 175, 119 LRRM 2801 (CA DC, 1985).

onto the high ground of meaningful worker participation. It would seem that the problems he describes in the construction industry would indeed require legislative adjustment. But because he views the Labor Board as increasingly irrelevant, he presents a description of a labor movement that is reaching out to new allies and using new kinds of tools to achieve its social and economic objectives.

Peter Walther is of course the most optimistic of all the panelists about the past, present, and future of the NLRA. He sees success in the system not only where collective bargaining is established, but also where it is not; for he concludes that "[c]ollective bargaining and the fear thereof, or the desire to avoid it and unions, has fulfilled [the Act's] objectives beyond anyone's right to expect or predict."

Professor St. Antoine and his respondents, notwithstanding their different perspectives, all foresee the possibility of a healthy and vigorous industrial relations system. It remains to be seen whether the Board will be important or irrelevant in shaping the future contours of that system.

CHAPTER 5

THE REGULATION OF UNION ECONOMIC POWER

WALTER E. OBERER*

When I was asked to present this paper on the occasion of the 50th year of the National Labor Relations Act, I thought, "They have given me the show." Union economic power and the regulation thereof is what our system of labor relations is all about. The rest is peripheral, indeed parasitic.

Those initial provocative remarks are premised, I assure myself, on some rock-bottom of speculative analysis. I shall now probe for that rock-bottom. Aha, it has three elements. The first is that the American system of collective bargaining is predicated on economic warfare. The second is that the role of government in such combat is umpire: (a) to protect the right of employees to form a "team" (to organize); (b) to establish and enforce rules for the playing of the "game." The third, a concomitant, is that we want to protect innocent bystanders from unnecessary involvement. What these three elements boil down to is this: *free* collective bargaining under a rule of law designed largely to establish the contest and to domesticate the strife.

That which distinguishes "labor relations" from other relations is, I would argue, the potential of lawful economic warfare. Indeed, if you strip the union's arsenal of the strike and supportive picketing and boycotts—that is, of the legal right to bring

* Professor of Law, University of Utah.

In the preparation of this paper, particularly the historical part, I have borrowed freely, without attribution, from the casebook on labor law written jointly with my then Cornell colleague Kurt Hanslowe, updated in a second edition in which my then Utah colleague Jerry Andersen joined. I wish these dear, now-departed friends thus to share in any credit the reader may conclude the paper deserves, but none of the blame; any misjudgments are mine. The books are: W. Oberer and K. Hanslowe, CASES AND MATERIALS ON LABOR LAW: COLLECTIVE BARGAINING IN A FREE SOCIETY (1972); W. Oberer, K. Hanslow & J. Andersen, *id.* 2d ed. (1979). I also wish to acknowledge the contributions of Timothy Heinsz, who read much of the paper in draft form (while working with me on the third edition of the casebook, in process) and played the angels' advocate, sometimes on morning jogs.

collectivized pressure to bear on targeted employers—you reduce labor relations to the level of all other strongly contested disputation. "I am right and you are wrong" becomes the postulation, with no mutually acceptable means for resolving the dispute, except the courtroom. "Collective begging" some unionists in supposedly strike-free areas of public employment have called it.

In the beginning of this country, the "I am right and you are wrong" postulation stated the issue, and the law resolved that issue in favor of the employer. The *Philadelphia Cordwainers' Case* of 1806,[1] America's first labor case, declared the union's framing of that issue a criminal conspiracy, even though framed in core terms—a strike for higher wages. Most of what has happened in the United States since that time with regard to the formulation of a model labor code has been a retreat from the criminal conspiracy doctrine. The quest has been, inexorably, for a balance in the economic warfare between capital and labor—a quest, when viewed historically, of the parties themselves, seeking to move the machinery of government into a neutral position.

A *balance* in *warfare*? That the parties should seek to achieve such a balance is a kind of contradiction in terms. But here the alternative to a mutually acceptable balance in governmental intervention is a willy-nilly swinging back and forth of governmental power that is unacceptable from either side because of its uncertainty.

In a free society, in short, the freely contesting parties in the labor relations arena prefer ultimately, whatever their interstitial niggling, order over disorder, predictability over chaos, governmental neutrality over political defeat. They therefore accept neutral conditions of warfare as a preference to warfare with a governmental thumb on the grenade.[2]

Having thus premised a "free society," let me define it in relevant terms. A free society is one the rules of which allow the

---

[1] Commonwealth v. Pullis (Mayor's Court of Philadelphia, 1806), *reprinted in* 3 J. Commons, DOCUMENTARY HISTORY OF AMERICAN INDUSTRIAL SOCIETY 59 (1958). The case is fascinatingly discussed in Nelles, *The First American Labor Case*, 41 YALE L.J. 165 (1931).

[2] The Railway Labor Act of 1926, the seminal statute in the existing scheme of labor relations in the United States, was the product of a broad consensus among railroads and railroad brotherhoods, so much so as to be fairly characterized as an industrywide collective bargaining agreement which was ratified into law by congressional enactment. *See* Texas & New Orleans R.R. v. Railway Clerks, 281 US 548, 563 n.2 (1930).

collectivizing of individual weakness into organized strength for the sake of countering a power center of otherwise incontestable proportions.[3] The power center may be public or private. No matter; the need for the countervailing power of collectivization remains constant.

But, and this is an important *but* in the current and increasingly *international* economic scene, the premise for effective exercise of union economic power is the possession by the union of a monopoly or a near monopoly on the supply of labor in the relevant market. Deregulation of our domestic airline and trucking industries has demonstrated the cataclysmic impact of sudden loss of that monopolistic power by the relevant unions (and also by the relevant employers). And the lack of monopolistic position of American unions, as well as American employers, in the *world* market has undercut our union power in such now internationalized industries as steel and motor vehicles. In a nutshell, where our unions lack monopolistic power in the relevant market, economic warfare by those unions is a losing fight. The regulation of union economic power in such circumstances is not by law, but by life.

But let us reserve the present and future for a moment in consideration of the past. The criminal conspiracy doctrine held sway for much of the 19th century, seeking to muzzle union power at the point of gestation. The very *combination* of workers for the purpose of improving their most basic employment conditions—higher wages, shorter hours—was itself a crime against the state. The situation in the United States during that period was not greatly unlike the situation in Poland today where the Solidarity movement presents unacceptable challenge to the primacy of an autocratic state. But the United States and its constituent bodies were not autocratic. Indeed, their premise was freedom, and much of the labor history of this country entails an exploring for the meaning and bounds of "freedom" in the labor context. In so testing those bounds, the American labor movement has provided an invaluable contribution to a free society in search of itself.

The death knell of the criminal conspiracy doctrine was tolled in *Commonwealth* v. *Hunt*,[4] an 1842 decision of the Massachusetts

---

[3] *See, e.g.*, J. Galbraith, AMERICAN CAPITALISM: THE CONCEPT OF COUNTERVAILING POWER (1952).

[4] 45 Mass. (4 Metc.) 111, 38 AM. DEC. 346 (1842).

Supreme Judicial Court. Chief Justice Shaw defined the doctrine in a way which presaged the analytic structure of all subsequent regulation by law of union economic power in this
country. He said that such a conspiracy was: "a combination of
two or more persons . . . to accomplish some . . . unlawful purpose, or to accomplish some purpose, not in itself . . . unlawful,
by . . . unlawful means."

The lawfulness of the *purpose* and/or of the *means* was thus
focused upon. The controlling questions are: (1) *What* did the
actors do? (2) *Why* did they do it? The what and the why are then
measured against a yardstick of current social acceptability (as
perceived by the particular court, legislature, agency). There is
nothing unique, of course, in this process; the lawfulness of all
human conduct is so measured.

Commonwealth v. *Hunt*, incidentally, is an artifact of our labor
law history worthy of archaelogic attention by all of us now-
professed "legal realists." Legal realism proceeds on the premise
that environment is more important than legal doctrine in deciding cases, particularly landmark cases. As defined by one of the
pioneers of legal realism, Leon Green (one of my mentors when
I was a youthful member of the law faculty at the University of
Texas), there are three ingredients in the decisional mix:
(1) environmental facts, (2) litigated facts (those introduced into
evidence), and (3) legal doctrine.[5] Their importance to decisionmaking is in the order stated. The order is, however, inverted in
judicial opinions. Doctrine dominates, litigated facts appear in
highly abstracted form only, environmental facts are seldon seen
at all. The farther removed one is, therefore, from the time and
place of a particular decision, the more difficult it becomes to
understand the real rationale. Indeed, the more one studies the
opinion of the court, the more misled one may be. A study of the
trial record would flesh out the litigated facts but not necessarily
communicate much of the environment.

The opinion and statement of facts in the official report of
Commonwealth v. *Hunt* run 25 pages, dedicated to a highly legalistic examination of the criminal indictment in the case and it is
found wanting because neither an unlawful purpose nor an
unlawful means had been adequately alleged. The following
paragraph from Charles Gregory's monumental book, LABOR

---

[5] Green, *Tort Law: Public Law in Disguise*, 38 TEX. L. REV. 1 (Part I), 257 (Part II)
(1959–60).

AND THE LAW, does more to explain the difference in result between the *Philadelphia Cordwainers' Case* and *Commonwealth* v. *Hunt* than all 25 of those pages:

> [N]umerous . . . criminal convictions of workers [between 1806 and 1842] for taking advantage of what they regarded as their ordinary civil privilege to exercise their right to work or not to work, under such terms as they saw fit, bred ill-feeling throughout the East. Mobs of laborers held mock trials of judges and hung them in effigy to show their resentment at being treated as common criminals for having done what they believed they had a perfect right to do. Juries were refusing to convict in some of these prosecutions, in spite of clearly proved cases of criminal conspiracy under the prevailing law.[6]

Once the criminal law lost sanctity as a control on the exercise of union economic power, employers resorted to the law of torts. *Walker* v. *Cronin*,[7] a Massachusetts case of 1871, is an interesting artifact here. The prima facia tort doctrine was wheeled into place. The declaration of the plaintiff alleged that the defendant union had, through its picketing, "wilfully persuaded and induced a large number of persons who were in the employment of the plaintiffs," and others "who were about to enter into" their employment, "to leave and abandon the employment of the plaintiffs, without their consent and against their will."

By a wonderful elucidation of the common-law approach to such a problem, the *Walker* v. *Cronin* court found controlling guidance in the ancient English case of *Keeble* v. *Hickeringill*,[8] where a tort had been held to exist by reason of the defendant's frightening of wild ducks out of the plaintiff's decoy and preventing those and *other* wild ducks from returning to the decoy. The amusing force of the *Keeble* v. *Hickeringill* precedent can be seen in the following analogy between the two cases. In both cases, two sets of objects of the tortious conduct of the defendants could be seen to be present, through which the defendants harmed the plaintiffs: (1) objects already present, in the one case in the plaintiff's employ, in the other case in the plaintiff's decoy; (2) objects not yet, but desirous of being, in the employ or decoy, as the case might be.

---

[6] C. Gregory, LABOR AND THE LAW 27 (2d rev. ed., 1961).
[7] 107 Mass. 555 (1871).
[8] *See id.* at 562–63 for the several ancient reports of the case cited.

The defendant union had thus, the court held, caused intentional loss to the plaintiff employer without justifiable cause.

The problem with this tort remedy was that the union, an unincorporated association, could not be reached except through the suing of its members, who were largely impecunious. Moreover, the torts were typically continuing, and invited a multiplicity of suits.

Then, through a kind of accident of labor regulatory history, the seed for the labor injunction was sown. The year was 1877, and the union involved had forcibly stopped the trains of a railroad company in the possession of a receiver appointed by an Illinois federal court. In *Secor* v. *Toledo, Pacific & Western Ry.*,[9] that court held that summary punishment for contempt of its authority was in order. It was a short step from *Secor* to a judicial recognition that a court order restraining strike activity, even absent a prior receivership, was enforcible by summary contempt procedures.[10] The "government by injunction" phase of our regulation of union economic power had thus been conceived.[11]

The subsequent application of the Sherman Act of 1890[12] to regulate labor activities, as evidenced in *Loewe* v. *Lawlor*,[13] and again in *Duplex Printing Press Co.* v. *Deering*[14] despite the abortive efforts of the Clayton Act of 1914[15] in Sections 6 and 20 to free labor from the antitrust laws, augmented the control of the labor movement by federal injunctions.

The colorfully stated "yellow-dog contract" doctrine, first endorsed by the Supreme Court in *Adair* v. *United States*,[16] further constrained the unionizing of American workers. That doctrine, pursuant to which employers were free to extract promises from employees not to join unions at risk of loss of employment, provided the basis for courts to find that efforts by a union to organize employees who had signed such contracts constituted the tort of inducing breach of contract. In *Hitchman*

[9] 21 Fed. Cas. 968, 971 (Cir Ct, ND Ill, 1877).

[10] *See* Nelles, *A Strike and Its Legal Consequences—An Examination of the Receivership Precedent for the Labor Injunction*, 40 YALE L.J. 507, 533 (1931).

[11] The first labor injunction in the United States was granted in Sherry v. Perkins, 147 Mass. 212, 17 NE 307 (1888). *See* Nelles, *supra* note 10, at 508 n.2.

[12] 26 Stat 209, as amended, 15 USC §§1–7 (1982).

[13] 208 US 274 (1908).

[14] 254 US 443 (1921).

[15] 38 Stat 730 (1914), as amended, 15 USC §§12 *et seq.* (1982).

[16] 208 US 161 (1908).

Coal & Coke Co. v. *Mitchell,*[17] the Supreme Court held that this tort provided rationale for enjoining the efforts of the Mine Workers to organize employees who had entered such contracts, even though their employment was "at will."

I. Paternal Protection

The Norris-LaGuardia Act of 1932,[18] taking the federal courts out of the labor-injunction business, even in secondary-boycott cases, and also proscribing the yellow-dog contract, provided the pivot for a dramatic reversal in the role of government in the regulation of union economic power. The triumverate of that Act, the Railway Labor Act of 1926,[19] and the Wagner Act of 1935[20] produced a brand new era in labor regulation—the era of paternalist protection. As interpreted in *United States* v. *Hutcheson,*[21] the Norris-LaGuardia Act exempted unions from the antitrust laws "so long as a union acts in its self-interest and does not combine with non-labor groups."

This exemption of labor from the application of the antitrust laws was no mere act of grace by the Supreme Court. Simultaneously, it exempted that Court from the excruciatingly difficult task of differentiating (1) so-called "local" strikes which cut off goods destined for interstate markets *at the source* from (2) labor disputes which somehow interdicted interstate commercial competition in a way more befitting the vague language of the Sherman Act.[22] In short, the continued application of Sections 1 and 2 of the Sherman Act to such "local" strikes threatened the throwback of organized labor a hundred years, to the environment of the *Philadelphia Cordwainers' Case.* This, of course, was untenable in a free society in search of the very meaning of freedom.

The period of paternal protection of the labor movement reached its zenith in the years from 1935 to 1947, dramatized in

---

17 245 US 229 (1917).

18 47 Stat 70 (1932), 29 USC §§101–15 (1982).

19 44 Stat, Part II 577 (1926), as amended, 46 USC §§151–88 (1982).

20 National Labor Relations Act, 49 Stat 449 (1935), as amended, 29 USC §§151–68 (1982).

21 312 US 219, 7 LRRM 267 (1941).

22 For an understanding of the Court's problem, *see* Coronado Coal Co. v. Mine Workers, 268 US 295 (1925), and Apex Hosiery Co. v. Leader, 310 US 469, 6 LRRM 647 (1940).

inception by the use of the sit-down strike in retaliation for the civil disobedience of employers in contesting the constitutionality of the Wagner Act.[23] In the *Jones & Laughlin*[24] decision of 1937, the Supreme Court responded to the environment of the Great Depression and the New Deal efforts to cope with it— but just barely, five to four. This landmark decision put in place a new labor policy which, fostered by the fortuitous intervention of World War II, was to culminate in the most profound changes in labor relations of any era in the history of the United States. Union membership increased fivefold, from 3 million to almost 15 million.

It oversimplifies to attribute this change solely to the protective policies enhanced by the Wagner Act, but those policies were certainly the catalyst of the new mix. As a result of those policies, union organizers could and did say to prospective recruits: "FDR wants you to join a union!" The further circumstance, that the Wagner Act placed no constraints on unions and that the Norris-LaGuardia Act relaxed existing controls in the federal antitrust laws, contributed substantially to the environment for change.

Major change of the sort generated by the Wagner Act is invariably accompanied by strong protest on the part of those whose interests are adversely affected. Complaints fell into three major categories. First, the Act was criticized for its one-sidedness. It protected only employees, and through them their unions; it placed restraints only upon employers. The interests claimed to have been neglected were principally those of employers and of the public, although complaint was also made that big, strong, unregulated unions on occasion dealt perversely with individual and minority employee interests. Second, it was charged that this one-sided statute was administered in an overzealous and one-sided fashion. The NLRB and its staff were inveighed against as missionaries of a faith not entirely the creation of Congress—collective bargaining the message and evangelism the mood. A third category of complaint was the hard-core resistance on the part of many employers and their sympathizers to the central theme of the Wagner Act—the pro-

---

23 *See* NLRB v. Fansteel Metallurgical Corp., 306 US 240, 4 LRRM 515 (1939); Hart & Pritchard, *The Fansteel Case: Employee Misconduct and the Remedial Powers of the National Labor Relations Board,* 52 HARV. L. REV. 1275 (1939).

24 NLRB v. Jones & Laughlin Steel Corp., 301 US 1, 1 LRRM 703 (1937).

priety and propagation of collective bargaining. Complaints against the Act at this basic level were frequently camouflaged in the garb of the first two categories of complaint.

No requiem for the Wagner Act would be complete without an additional commentary upon its impact. It enabled a largely peaceful revolution in the industrial relations of a capitalist society. The system of collective bargaining which it fostered constitutes a major oversight of socialist philosophers, such as Karl Marx, who failed to foresee the accommodating potential of a private-enterprise economy.[25] But organized labor, the new power center produced by the Act, like every other locus of power in a free society, invited and shortly received the disciplinary attention it now deserved.

II. Government as Umpire

The Taft-Hartley Act of 1947[26] constituted a major overhaul of the national labor policy. Whereas in the Wagner Act days union organizers could and did tell American workers that the President wanted them to join a union, under the Taft-Hartley Act the accurate paraphrase was: "The President doesn't care whether or not you join a union." This change in policy was most basically demonstrated in the amendment of Section 7, the heart of the National Labor Relations Act. To the three Wagner Act rights there declared—the right to engage in self-organization, the right to engage in collective bargaining, and the right to engage in concerted activities in support thereof—Congress added a *fourth* right: the right to *refrain* from any or all of such activities.

The new role of government, that of umpire rather than paternal protector, was further manifested in related provisions of the Act. A set of *union* unfair labor practices was created. The neutrality of the government in the new scheme was also evidenced in the so-called "free speech" provision, Section 8(c), which, in its most obvious application, encourages employers to compete more vigorously with unions for the loyalty of their

---

[25] For an exposition of "the significance of collective bargaining to freedom of enterprise," *see* Frey, *The Logic of Collective Bargaining and Arbitration*, 12 LAW & CONTEMP. PROBS. 264 (1947).

[26] Labor Management Relations Act, 61 Stat 136 (1947), as amended, 29 USC §§141–97 (1982).

employees than they had previously felt free to do. Other important changes in policy were effectuated by the Taft-Hartley Act, most of them related in one way or another to the shift in the role of government from "drive" to "neutral."

The chief agency for the carrying out of the new policy continued to be the National Labor Relations Board, but with significant changes in its structure and mode of operation. The changes were designed to better fit the Board for its new role as umpire. First, the membership of the Board was increased from three to five members, with staggered five-year terms.[27] Each of these members was provided with a large and independent staff of attorneys. The purpose of this was to afford each Board member the wherewithal for independence of judgment in deciding cases, thereby permitting abolition of the much-maligned "Review Section" which had been established during the administration of the Wagner Act.[28] The Review Section was a group of approximately 90 lawyers employed by the Board, as an entity, to review transcripts of hearings and prepare drafts of opinions. This faceless group was charged with exerting undue influence on Board policies and decisions without any accountability.

A second fundamental change in the Board's structure and functioning was the creation of the office of General Counsel, to be filled, as with the Board itself, by the President with the advice and consent of the Senate. The General Counsel, appointed for a four-year term, is charged with performing the prosecutorial function, that is, investigating charges, issuing complaints, prosecuting cases. Accordingly, the General Counsel has "general supervision over all attorneys employed by the Board (other than trial examiners and legal assistants to Board members) and over the officers and employees in the regional offices."[29] The purpose of this change was to separate the prosecutorial function from the judicial one. Consistent with this purpose and demonstrating the degree of independence of the General Counsel from the Board, the statute vests in that office final authority in the determination of whether or not a complaint should issue in unfair labor practice cases.[30]

---

[27] NLRA §3(a), 29 USC §153(a) (1982).
[28] The Review Section was abolished by §4(a) of the Act, 29 USC §154(a) (1982).
[29] NLRA §3(d), 29 USC §153(d) (1982).
[30] *Id.*

From the standpoint of specific change in the regulation of union economic power, the major contribution of the Taft-Hartley Act lay in two areas: the outlawing of the closed shop and of secondary boycotts. The first was accomplished through the amendment of the proviso to Section 8(a)(3) and the addition of Section 8(b)(2). Whereas under the "closed shop" union-security agreement permitted under the Wagner Act, the union determined who the employer's employees would be, under the newly created concept of the "union shop" agreement, the employer determines who the union's members will be. The unions were thus deprived of the power to control access to employment. Moreover, in Section 14(b), the so-called (and *mis*called) "right-to-work" provision, the states were given authority to outlaw even *union*-shop agreements.

Secondary boycotts were prohibited in some wonderfully convoluted language of Section 8(b)(4) which put the Board and the reviewing courts in the business of drawing that often mystical line between "primary" pressure, which is lawful, and "secondary" pressure, which is unlawful. In concept, the line between primary and secondary pressure makes considerable sense as a limit on the scope of the arena and the weaponry to be permitted in the economic warfare of free collective bargaining. The strife is thus domesticated to an extent rendering it socially palatable. But creative lawyering by union counsel soon discovered and exploited loopholes in the Taft-Hartley provisions—including the so-called "hot-cargo" agreements, a tribute to Teamster lawyers.

As a tribute to this tribute, Congress sought in the Landrum-Griffin Act of 1959[31] (in the first quarter-century of the National Labor Relations Act we were on a 12-year cycle—1935, 1947, 1959) to plug the loopholes in the secondary-boycott provisions. My own assessment of these efforts, which included the banning of hot-cargo agreements in Section 8(e), is that Congress did a commendable job of reforming and balancing our labor code. But, as ever, life overtakes law; technological innovations have blurred the primary-secondary line-drawing.

Perhaps the most fundamental question distillable out of the post-Landrum-Griffin-Act Supreme Court decisions in second-

---

[31] Labor-Management Reporting and Disclosure Act, 73 Stat 519 (1959), as amended, 29 USC §§401–531 (1982).

ary-boycott cases—*National Woodwork*,[32] *Pipefitters*,[33] the container cases[34]—is: Has the primary-secondary test for lawfulness of union economic pressure been stretched beyond its reach? I will come back to this question later. Before doing so, I want to introduce the second major qualification of union economic power introduced by Landrum-Griffin.

Union pressure is invoked for two essential purposes in our system of collective bargaining. The first purpose, chronologically, is to unionize a target group of employees. The second purpose is to obtain or renew a collective bargaining contract. The primary-secondary test is relevant to both of these stages. With regard to the first stage, however, that of unionization, the Landrum-Griffin Act imposed, in Section 8(b)(7), substantial limitations on the use of *primary* pressure. This provision, aimed at the core evil of "blackmail picketing," restricts both the occasions when a union may lawfully picket a primary employer for recognitional or organizational purposes and, where the occasion is appropriate, the length of time the picketing may continue without the filing of a Section 9 petition.[35] Section 8(b)(7) thus protects the target employer and those of its employees who do not favor the picketing union from unnecessarily prolonged union pressure. It also protects the rest of society from the burdens of gratuitous labor-management warfare. The publicity proviso[36] and area-standards[37] exceptions provide the Board and reviewing courts with rather neatly contrived doctrinal devices for fine-tuning of the restrictions.

In its main thrust, the Landrum-Griffin Act, of course, further regulates union power by imposing on the internal government of unions citizenship rights of members akin to those possessed by members of society at large[38]—thus creating a kind

---

[32] National Woodwork Mfrs. Ass'n v. NLRB, 386 US 612, 64 LRRM 2801 (1967).

[33] NLRB v. Plumbers Local 638 (Enterprise Ass'n), 429 US 507, 94 LRRM 2628 (1977).

[34] NLRB v. Longshoremen, 447 US 490, 104 LRRM 2552 (1980); NLRB v. Longshoremen (American Trucking Ass'n), 473 US ___, 119 LRRM 2915 (1985).

[35] The general working of §8(b)(7) is explained in Laborers Local 840, (C.A. Blinne Constr. Co), 135 NLRB 1153, 49 LRRM 1638 (1962).

[36] *See, e.g.*, Hotel & Restaurant Employees Local 681 (Crown Cafeteria), 130 NLRB 570 (1961), *supplemental decision and order*, 135 NLRB 1183, 49 LRRM 1648 (1962), *aff'd sub nom.* Smitley v. NLRB, 327 F2d 351, 55 LRRM 2302 (CA 9, 1964).

[37] *See, e.g.*, Houston Bldg. & Constr. Trades Council (Claude Everette Constr. Co.), 136 NLRB 321, 49 LRRM 1757 (1962).

[38] *See, generally*, Cox, *Internal Affairs of Labor Unions Under the Labor Reform Act of 1959*, 58 MICH. L. REV. 819 (1960).

of free society within a free society. These rights were greatly augmented by Title VII of the Civil Rights Act of 1964[39] providing nondiscriminatory *entry* rights into unions and further assuring nondiscrimination within the union.[40] Since enforcement of these rights to admission to unions and to internal rights therein is left largely to the federal courts and to the Equal Employment Opportunity Commission, and only peripherally to the Board, I will not dwell upon them.

But a closely related right, belatedly recognized by the Board as emanating from the National Labor Relations Act, and intimately implicating, both philosophically and practically, the exercise and regulation of union power demands attention here. I have reference to the duty of fair representation. The duty of fair representation first saw the light of day in 1944 in the Supreme Court's decision in *Steele* v. *Louisville & Nashville R.R.*,[41] a RailwayLabor Act case. It was soon expanded to encompass the National Labor Relations Act.[42] The Court was presented with the constitutional question of whether the arbitrarily discriminatory exercise by a union of the power of exclusive representation, possessed by it under the auspices of congressional enactment, constituted a denial of due process or equal protection to those adversely affected. To avoid this constitutional question, the Court interpreted the statutes so as to impose the duty of fair representation. The most uniquely American concept of collective bargaining, that of exclusivity, was thus held to have a flip side.

Some 20 years after the *Steele* decision, the Board found the violation of the duty of fair representation to be an unfair labor practice under Section 8(b)(1).[43] It restrains employees in the exercise of their Section 7 right to "bargain collectively through representatives of their own choosing," such representation being exclusive pursuant to Section 9(a), and exclusivity carrying with it the duty of fair representation as declared in *Steele*.

---

[39] 78 Stat 253 (1964), as amended, 42 USC §§2000e *et seq.* (1982).

[40] The type of discrimination targeted by Title VII is "race, color, religion, sex, or national origin." *See id.* §703, 42 USC §2000e-2.

[41] 323 US 192, 15 LRRM 708 (1944).

[42] Syres v. Oil Workers Local 23, 223 F2d 739, 36 LRRM 2290 (CA 5, 1955), *rev'd and remanded per curiam*, 350 US 892, 37 LRRM 2068 (1956); *cf.* Wallace Corp. v. NLRB, 323 US 248, 15 LRRM 697 (1944).

[43] NLRB v. Miranda Fuel Co., 326 F2d 172, 54 LRRM 2715 (CA 2, 1963); Rubber Workers Local 12 v. NLRB, 368 F2d 12, 63 LRRM 2395 (CA 5, 1966), *cert. denied*, 389 US 837 (1967).

Because of the Johnny-come-lately connection of the Board with the duty of fair representation and of the original judicial recognition of the duty, the enforcement of the duty was held by the Supreme Court in *Vaca* v. *Sipes*[44] not to be subject to the preemption declared in *San Diego Building Trades Council* v. *Garmon*.[45]

The federal preemption doctrine, brought to peak fruition in *Garmon*, is itself an important aspect of the regulation of union economic power under the American scheme. That doctrine, at its *Garmon* peak, grants to the Board the exclusive primary jurisdiction for the adjudication of the issue of whether the subject union activity is either protected or prohibited under the Act, and, if prohibited, the remedy to be provided. The more recent erosion of the doctrine merits attention in the present context.

While the declared function of the labor preemption doctrine was to achieve a uniform national labor policy, presided over at least preliminarily by the Board, the underlying purpose, I submit, was to protect a nascent labor movement from inexpert and unfriendly local tribunals. The early exceptions to the doctrine were narrowly and sharply defined. A "compelling state interest" was required to be present, such as in the violence cases of *Laburnum*[46] and *Russell*,[47] or a "merely peripheral federal concern" as in *Gonzalez*.[48] These narrowly drawn exceptions were then expanded so as to include state libel actions as in *Linn*,[49] state actions for "outrageous conduct causing severe emotional distress" as in *Farmer*,[50] and state trespass actions as in *Sears*[51] where the aggrieved party has no access to the Board. The expansion of the exceptions has been accompanied by a loosening of the rationale. The "compelling state interest" and the "merely peripheral federal concern" tests have been merged and subsumed under the following analytic inquiries: (1) Is there a substantial state interest in regulating the subject activity?

---

[44] 386 US 171, 64 LRRM 2369 (1967).

[45] 359 US 236, 43 LRRM 2838 (1959).

[46] Construction Workers v. Laburnum Constr. Corp., 347 US 656, 34 LRRM 2229 (1954).

[47] Automobile Workers v. Russell, 356 US 634, 42 LRRM 2142 (1958).

[48] Machinists v. Gonzales, 356 US 617, 42 LRRM 2135 (1958).

[49] Linn v. Plant Guard Workers, 383 US 53, 61 LRRM 2345 (1966).

[50] Farmer v. Carpenters Local 25, 420 US 290, 94 LRRM 2759 (1977).

[51] Sears, Roebuck & Co. v. San Diego County Dist. Council of Carpenters, 436 US 180, 98 LRRM 2282 (1978).

(2) Does such state regulation constitute unacceptable interference with the federal regulatory scheme?[52] What has
evolved, in short, is a new kind of balancing test, less preemptive
of state regulation and, conversely, more invasive of Board
jurisdiction. Since, as I said earlier, the *Garmon* preemption
doctrine is, for me, best understood as a device for the protection
of the labor movement from relatively uninformed and hostile
local tribunals, it follows, at least in my jurisprudence, that the
later Supreme Court decisions reflect judgments about the
maturity and self-protective capacity of unions which may at this
point in time seem ironic.

III. The Primary-Secondary Morass

While the Board has, through the curtailment of the preemption doctrine, suffered a curtailment of its control over union
economic pressure, it is still up to its ears, indeed over its head, in
some of the most critical regulatory waters. The advent of technological change in the way some of our most basic industries do
business has set the stage for this Board Gethsemane. The primary-secondary litmus for Board resolution of the problems
thus produced is the second element in this conundrum. The
therapy of collective bargaining as the solvent for resolving these
problems is the third element in this decisional mix. The Board
has labored, in my view heroically, in seeking to manage these
problems of accommodation, instructed, largely inadequately,
by the reviewing courts, ultimately by the Supreme Court, all
levels of regulation inadequately guided by the existing law.

Let us take as an example the construction industry where the
problems of applying the primary-secondary test in the context
of technological change are at white heat, and let us also review
the founding wisdom of the primary-secondary test. The
rationale is that union pressure should be confined to parties
immediately involved in the pertinent controversy so as to protect "neutral parties," that is, "innocent bystanders." The current problem is that the primary-secondary dichotomy no
longer provides an apt criterion for distinguishing proper combatants from proper noncombatants. Taking *NLRB* v. *Plumbers
Local 638 (Enterprise Association)*,[53] the so-called *Pipefitters* case,

---

[52] *See, generally,* the *Farmer* and *Sears* cases, *supra* notes 50 and 51.
[53] *Supra* note 33.

decided by the Supreme Court in 1977, as a point of departure, let us review the facts there involved.

Austin Company, the general contractor, had entered a contract with Norwegian Home for the Aged, the owner, for the construction of a project. The contract between Austin and Norwegian Home called for the purchase by Austin of certain climate control units manufactured by Slant/Fin Corporation. The contract further provided that the internal piping in the climate control units was to be cut, threaded, and installed at the Slant/Fin factory. Austin subsequently awarded, on the basis of competitive bidding, a subcontract to the Hudik-Ross Company to perform the heating, ventilation, and air-conditioning work for the Norwegian Home project. The employees of Hudik were represented by the Enterprise Association, a plumbing and pipefitting union. The collective bargaining agreement between Hudik and Enterprise contained a Rule IX to the effect that pipe threading and cutting were to be performed on the jobsite. Accordingly, when the prethreaded and cut climate control units from Slant/Fin arrived on the job, the union steamfitters refused to install them, pursuant to Rule IX. Austin, the general contractor, then filed a Section 8(b)(4)(B) charge with the Board, claiming that the union, Enterprise, had engaged in a strike to force Hudik, the subcontractor, to cease doing business with Austin and to force Hudik and Austin to cease dealing with the products of Slant/Fin. The union's position was that it was merely seeking to enforce its contract with Hudik and to preserve the jobsite cutting and threading work covered by Rule IX.

The Board held that, while the Pipefitters Union had not violated Section 8(e) in the eliciting of Rule IX in the agreement with Hudik because that was a valid work-preservation clause a la *National Woodwork*, the union had, nonetheless, violated Section 8(b)(4)(B) in refusing to install the climate control units.[54] The rationale for the secondary-boycott finding was that Hudik, as subcontractor, did not have the "right of control" over the use of prethreaded and precut climate control units. Therefore, the union was exerting prohibited secondary pressure on Hudik with an object of either forcing a change in Austin's, the general contractor's, manner of doing business or forcing Hudik to cease doing business with Austin. This pressure on Hudik was under-

---

[54] 204 NLRB 760, 83 LRRM 1396 (1973).

taken for its effect on other employers and was therefore secondary.

A divided Court of Appeals for the District of Columbia, sitting en banc, set aside the Board's order. The Supreme Court, six to three, reversed, agreeing with the Board.[55]

Now for our analysis. While Hudik can, on the basis of the primary-secondary test, be fairly assessed as a secondary target, Hudik is most difficultly categorized as an innocent victim. The problem here is the product of technological advance, complexity of business relationships, and ingenuity of organizational strategy and tactics of the various categories of interest groups involved in the pertinent labor disputes. This problem is aggravated in the construction industry by the fact that conflicting contractual obligations are negotiated, in varying time sequence, between (1) owners and general contractors; (2) general and subcontractors; (3) general and subcontractors and unions. (The contractor-union contracting is frequently the product of multi-employer bargaining between associations of employers, general and/or sub, and building trades unions or regional councils of such unions.) The dominant interests at each of these levels of contracting differ; the contractual provisions accordingly clash; the resolution of the clashes is left to the decisional processes of the Board, reviewing courts, contractual grievance and arbitration procedures, and self-help.

Against this backdrop, both the majority and dissenting positions in the *Pipefitters* case are tenable under primary-secondary analysis.[56] Indeed, that analysis may be said to be irrelevant. Which is to say that the present state of federal labor relations law is inadequate to cope with these sophisticated problems, produced as they are by the underlying sophisticated institutional arrangements described above. Two solutions suggest themselves: (1) amendment of the federal labor code so as to define in more refined fashion the licit and the illicit; (2) consignment, by default, of the anticompetitive problems involved to the federal antitrust law—a sufficiently shorthanded body of proscriptions to allow enough judicial elbow room for federal

---

[55] 521 F2d 885, 89 LRRM 2769 (CA DC, 1975), *rev'd*, 429 US 507, 94 LRRM 2628 (1977).

[56] The dissent contended that Hudik was not a neutral in the sense contemplated by Congress as warranting protection, nor by reason of being powerless to deal with the union demands since it might have negotiated some substitute for full compliance with Rule IX, such as premium pay.

judges to "enact" their own version of social justice as these questions of labor policy are litigated.[57]

The former is, of course, preferable to the latter—more specific and therefore providing better guidance to all of the interest groups involved.[58] But I have no better talisman, nor have I seen any suggested by others, which would provide an improved statutory surrogate for the primary-secondary test. Indeed, the most useful tool in drawing that line seems, by the repetitive reliance upon it by the Supreme Court, to have been fabricated by our law-professing colleague Howard Lesnick in an article[59] which has thus far stood the test of time. In a phrase often quoted by the Court, he posed, with regard to the ubiquitous problem of defining secondary pressure, this criterion: Whether the "cessation of business [by the union] was being used tactically, with an eye to its effect on conditions elsewhere"[60]—a test sufficiently inscrutable to withstand confounding when applied to the ambiguous circumstances typically found in these cases. As my former mentor Leon Green used to say: "We need dead ends in the law—limits to the spinning out of reason." The Lesnick postulation has admirably served this purpose. It speaks to the inscrutable with sufficiently authoritative inscrutability to cut off further argument whichever way the decision goes.

IV. The "Reagan Board" in Institutional Perspective

Since a central focus of this volume is upon the National Labor Relations Board "at mid-century," I want to pay my respects to the Board in its front-line role of regulating union economic power, including, but certainly not limited to, the defining of unlawful secondary pressure. Much of the current maligning of the Board by labor groups is misdirected at the so-called "Reagan Board." The criticism, to the extent valid, is more properly to be directed at the institutional architecture involved in the original blueprint, as amended in Taft-Hartley. The Board is *not* a "labor court"; if it were, it would be presided over by judges

---

[57] On the application of federal antitrust law to such problems, *see, e.g.,* Connell Constr. Co. v. Plumbers Local 100, 421 US 616, 89 LRRM 2401 (1973).

[58] For relevant comment, *see* St. Antoine, *Connell: Antitrust Law at the Expense of Labor Law,* 62 VA. L. REV. 603 (1976).

[59] Lesnick, *Job Security and Secondary Boycotts: The Reach of NLRA §§8(b)(4) and 8(e),* 113 U. PA. L. REV. 1000 (1965).

[60] *Id.* at 1017–18.

with life-tenure or long-term appointments. It is, for better or for worse, a political body. The "Eisenhower Board," as those of us old enough will recall, was similarly inveighed against by labor. Management representatives were, in turn, strongly agitated by the "Kennedy Board." It is simply a fact of governmental life that each new administration places its own political stamp on the Board. Critics who argue for a "labor court" have the obvious purpose of making the Board more impartial, less subject to political influence, more constant in its policies. While these arguments can be, indeed have been, strongly made,[61] there is another side which has thus far carried the day. The kind of body Congress created in the Board is not intended to be as insulated as a court from the political environment. The five members of the Board each serve, in staggered terms, for five years. This means that the President (with the advice and consent of the Senate) has at least one vacancy each year to fill. As a consequence, a new President can by the third year of his term at the latest (sooner if the Board was previously split or if there are fortuitous vacancies) establish a new majority for the resolution or reresolution of the perennial close questions of statutory interpretation. This gives a new administration a degree of control over labor policy (a major component of domestic policy) which would not be available were Board members appointed for longer terms or for life. Thus, the national will, as expressed quadrennially, is more quickly reflected in those aspects of national labor policy over which the Board has control. The Board, in short, the rationale runs, is not supposed to feel as politically invulnerable as a federal judge with life tenure or as a member of the Federal Reserve Board with a 14-year appointment. In the latter cases different considerations are thought to obtain.

The foregoing institutional observations are not meant to condemn the condemning of the "Reagan Board." The fact is that such criticism by the adversely affected interest group, be it labor or management, is itself part of the institutional plan. Board members are thus called to account publicly and politically for their alleged "leaning" to the right or the left, as the case may be. The General Counsel of the Board is also on occasion hailed into this informal public "dock." We have all witnessed at

---

[61] The arguments are reviewed in Booker & Coe, *The NLRB and Its Critics*, 17 LAB. L.J. 522 (1966), and *The Labor Board and Its Reformers*, 18 LAB. L.J. 67 (1967).

conferences or read of these defenses of current policies, impugned by the gorees and justified by the gorers. This kind of political challenging and defense against the challenging is reflective of the implicitly acknowledged character of the Board as a quasi-political body; by contrast, judges, a fortiori Supreme Court justices, traditionally, and properly, shun such political hustings. While I have no personal knowledge of the impact of such outings on the Board's decisional process, I am sure, as a sometimes arbitrator and as an all-times student of human nature, that *some* impact there must be. And I am further sure that this impact is therapeutic, because it *should be* therapeutic; the Board has a clientele, a sharply defined and divided clientele, and should accordingly feel an institutional responsibility to keep that clientele sufficiently *acceptive* of its process, however unhappy or discontent with some aspects of it, to want to continue to engage in the economic war game in accordance with the umpire's calls. A playful analogue is baseball. An analogue closer to the experience of many in the reading audience of this volume is that of a permanent arbitrator under a collective bargaining agreement.

V. Deregulation

Further speaking to the present and future with regard to the regulation of union economic power, I believe the pillorying of the Board for current labor restrictions, while understandable, to be essentially misguided. A free society is premised, in its economic aspects, upon free markets. Much of the recent trauma to the labor movement is the product of the deregulation of the airline and trucking industries—the removal of a regulatory wall which permitted employers and unions to inflate prices and wages artificially, in defiance of free-market concepts. The consequence was that pilots, truck drivers, and supportive employees were sustained at a level inconsistent with their market worth. While I fully sympathize with the trauma suffered by these employees as a result of the sudden "cold shower" of deregulation, as a student of the labor movement and of a free society, I see no philosophical or moral basis for continuing their sinecure. It is true, of course, that a primary function of our national labor and antitrust laws is to protect American workers from free-market competition based upon *sub*-labor standards. But pursuit of this goal is a far cry from the creation and defense of artificial market barriers which protect *super*-labor standards; the employers have been as badly hurt by deregulation as the employees and their unions. Someone once said that the capitalist system is a hell of a system, and you better not try to take all of the hell out of it. The same is true, I believe, of our system of collective bargaining.

VI. Industrial Internationalization

The deregulation of some of our industries is but one aspect of our current labor malaise. Another, as I have earlier observed, is the internationalizing of many manufacturing industries. For a decade or two following World War II, American manufacturers enjoyed a kind of world monopoly occasioned by the war-destruction of the productive capacity of almost all other industrialized countries. American unions could, as a consequence, demand and get "more" in each new contract go-round. As early as the late 1950s, a new writing began to appear on the world industrial wall. It began, at least in the eyes of Walter Reuther, with the industrial resurgence of West Germany. When asked how the Automobile Workers and other American unions should respond to this challenge, his answer was by creating truly international unions—for example, a *world* union of automobile workers. Such was the overpowering optimism of that admirable man. But a quarter of a century later there is little evidence, in my perhaps myopic view, of such a development. National unions, their members and adherents, like most of the rest of us, still are governed by the short-range view of their sharply conflicting interests. Short of national tariff walls, anathema to free-market thinking, I see no answer to the dilemma of those American unions which represent workers in internationalized industries other than the facing-up to the real-life constraints which such internationalizing places upon both them and their American employers.

In this context, complaining about the Board for policies thought to be too restrictive of the exercise of union economic power is simply irrelevant. American labor law, however permissive it might be in this regard, simply lacks the jurisdictional reach to alter *world* economic life. American employers are as much caught in this web of life as their American employees.

I am as incurably optimistic as was Walter Reuther, but with a different twist. Where he fantasized, grandly, of making the rest of the world conform to the designs of the American labor movement, I fantasize, modestly, of making the American labor movement conform to the rest of the world. As I have suggested at several points in this paper, the ultimate regulation of American union economic power is not the National Labor Relations Board or the reviewing courts administering a labor code which I perceive to be, in core if not in every detail, a *model* labor code, but rather *life*.

A remarkable example of this effort to conform to world life is revealed in a fundamental change in policy on the part of the Steelworkers several years ago in dealing with the steel industry. Like most American unions, the Steelworkers have long cherished their right to strike in support of contract renewal demands. Accordingly, again like most American unions, while acceptive of the notion of the submission of disputes as to "rights" under an existing contract to final and binding arbitration, they have been most chary about submitting "interest" disputes, that is, disputes as to what the provisions of a new contract should be, to arbitration. Resolution of these renegotiation-of-contract disputes the union zealously reserved to strike pressures. The long-lasting strike of 1959 educated both the union and the steel companies that they were cutting off their noses to spite their faces. Customers of the struck steel producers turned to foreign suppliers of steel to meet their needs. In so doing, these customers were in some instances sufficiently impressed by the quality of product, price, and service of the foreign suppliers to continue doing business with them even after the strike had ended. The product of this long lesson from life was acceptance of interest arbitration as a substitute for the strike, and incorporation of compulsory arbitration of these disputes into steel industry collective bargaining agreements.[62]

VII. The Remaining Employment Arena

What I have said about deregulated industries and industries drawn into internationalized competition does not, of course,

---

[62] This provision, which has been referred to as the "Experimental Negotiation Agreement," effective in 1974, is discussed in Fischer, *The Significance of the Steel No-Strike Arbitration Agreement*, NYU TWENTY-SIXTH ANNUAL CONFERENCE ON LABOR 93 (1974). *See also* LAB. REL. YEARBOOK 81—1974, 81 (BNA Books, 1975); LABOR RELATIONS YEARBOOK—1980, at 103 and 254 (BNA Books, 1981). The ENA plan included, as part of the consideration for the union's acceptance of it, a one-time bonus payment of $150, a guaranteed 3% increase each year of the three-year contract, and a cost-of-living escalation clause. *Id.* These "sweeteners," viewed by the employers as too costly in the 1980s economic environment, caused the recent abandonment of ENA in the steel industry.

dispose of *all* American industry nor of the desirable controls to be placed on the exercise of union power in these other industries. The evolution of much of American industry from "smokestack" to the "services" area is in the process of documentation.[63] The service industries are not as vulnerable to internationalization as the production industries and, at the same time, are not typically so regulated as to have the sword of deregulation dangling over them. Labor relations in these industries might, therefore, be reasonably expected to respond to the American industrial norms in a labor relations sense—that is, unionization and collectively bargained terms and conditions of employment. That they have not done so, at least to an extent deemed desirable by aficionados of unionism, has been an additional current frustration of the American labor movement. I do not intend to dwell on the classical explanations advanced for this phenomenon—for example, that white-collar workers have been traditionally harder to organize, that there is an increased number of women in this employment area and that they, too, have been traditionaly harder to organize. I simply accept, arguendo, the foregoing contentions of empiricists in this field.[64]

What I do intend to dwell upon is the philosophic, indeed romantic, notion that these, indeed *all* American employees *should* be unionized. When I was young, very young, I had a halo view of unions and of the process of collective bargaining as a generic panacea. Experience, age also perhaps, has disabused me.

Workers are moved to organize, a very difficult and sometimes traumatic effort, by deeply felt grievances. Where these deeply felt grievances exist, the workers involved, and the unions which aspire to represent them, should have the cover of law in seeking to collectivize individual weakness into organized strength. The protective shield of the law around this effort to collectivize, to establish this countervailing power, is the quintessence of a free society in the sense here relevant. What I perceive to be the dilemma of the American labor movement today is that the workers they seek to organize do not deeply enough feel the

---

[63] This and other of the emerging dilemmas for unionization are ambitiously, and optimistically, explored in Craver, *The Vitality of the American Labor Movement in the Twenty-First Century*, 1983 U. ILL. L. REV. 633.

[64] *Id.*

sense of grievance or truly enough trust unions to optimize union efforts to collectivize them. This is, of course, frustrating to unions; the blame for this state of affairs may be attributed by them to the Board and the law which it administers.[65] But I, for one, would not consider it freedom-enhancing for our labor code to be amended, to take the arguments of the aficionados to their ultimate end, so as to *mandate* unionization in all employment contexts. There is an underside to unionization as well as an overside, and free employees ought to be free to view the costs and the abrasions as more burdensome than the benefits, even if they mistakenly so balance the accounts. That underside would be even darker, I fear, if unionization were to be made compulsory. Indeed, there is reason for American society to feel gratified by an assessment of lot by American workers which is largely acceptive of the status quo, however bemusing such acceptance may seem to some of us more farsighted observers, some with vested interests in "improving" this status quo.

Now for a cautioning word as to what I am *not* saying. I am not saying that the American labor movement should be cast upon the ash-heap. Free labor unions are an utterly essential component of a free society, a truth evidenced by their absence behind the "Iron Curtain." Nor am I saying that American workers who eschew unionism are better off for the eschewing. What I am saying is that I do not think the law of a free society would allow them to be bullied into the heaven of unionism and of more militant collective bargaining through, for example, judicially enforced fines for crossing picket lines even after they have unsuccessfully attempted to resign from the union in the face of restrictive provisions in the union constitution. I am pleased to see my position in this regard very recently endorsed by the Supreme Court.[66] If union activists have not been able in the current relatively free state of things to convert employees into true believers, they should be free to disbelieve. There will be other days and other times when other Walter Reuthers may

[65] For a tandem of articles meticulously arguing for changes in the National Labor Relations Act which will aid American unions in their efforts to organize and to obtain effective first-contracts with antiunion employers, borrowing largely from the Canadian experience, *see* Weiler, *Promises to Keep: Securing Workers' Rights to Self-Organization Under the NLRA*, 96 HARV. L. REV. 1769 (1983), and *Striking a New Balance: Freedom of Contract and the Prospects for Union Representation*, 98 HARV. L. REV. 351 (1984). *See also* Modjeska, *The Reagan NLRB, Phase I*, 460 OHIO ST. L.J. 95 (1985).

[66] Pattern Makers League v. NLRB (Rockford-Beloit Pattern Jobbers), 469 US ___, 119 LRRM 2928 (1985).

find it more propitious to take us to the top of the mountain where the sun is bright. If so, the ascent will be, in my jurisprudential view, under a body of law and process not greatly different from that presently in place.

The other days and other times will, however, require a change in the *felt need* for unions and in the public perception of unions—a return to a view of them as underdogs heroically representing underdogs who have begun to growl, a view of the leadership in a Reuther mold rather than a Hoffa mold, a view of the union rank-and-file as something other than major-league baseball players earning an average salary of $300,000 plus a year and still not satisfied, presenting, unfortunately, the most visible union "crisis" on the scene at this writing. What a comedown for American unionism, once the idealist's symphonic dissonance!

But maybe not a comedown for American society? At least not a comedown fairly attributable to a weakening American labor movement. Our basic freedoms are still strongly intact. We still live, most of us, the good life. Our economic problems derive from a dollar which is too strong, interest rates which are too high, an incredible imbalance in trade, an incredible budget deficit, a world free-trade policy more honored by us than by the world, a high unemployment rate conjoined paradoxically with noncompetitive labor standards in certain key industries. All of these constitute dilemmas which the National Labor Relations Board "at mid-century" can do preciously little to alleviate, even were it to swing sharply left in the small compass of discretion it has to exercise in establishing labor policy. Indeed, this complex of problems has thus far proved intransigent even to the much vaster sway of congressional power.

VIII. The "Saturn Project"

There is a recent ray of hope, however, the product of creative collective bargaining within the existing legal mold. The freshly conceived "Saturn project"[67] of the General Motors Corporation has resulted in a collective bargaining agreement with the Automobile Workers designed to enable the production of smaller cars of a quality and price which will be effectively

---

[67] *See* N.Y. Times, July 27, 1985, at 1; Time, Aug. 5, 1985, at 42; Newsweek, Aug. 5, 1985, at 42.

competitive with, most importantly, Japanese imports in the American market. The agreement is premised upon a reduction in the wage rates currently extant in the American car-producing industry, but with the substitution of salaries and an income-enhancing program conditioned upon product quality and profit at the plant. The arrangement entails the surrender by the union not only of the prevailing wage standards, but also of the traditional straightjacketing job-classification restrictions, in return for job-security assurances, a greater union voice in production policies, and the profit-sharing scheme. Overall, the experiment entails a "different" relationship between the workers and management—a difference perhaps most accurately described as "Japanized." While I am, as a practicing skeptic, wary about the potential of "Japanizing" American workers, I applaud this avant garde endeavor of one of our most forward-looking unions, responding, open-mindedly, to a profound change in its environment. And I cannot help remembering in this context the Automobile Workers bargaining-strategy convention I attended in Detroit in the late 1950s when I was Executive Director of its newly created Public Review Board, a supreme court for the union as to internal disputes.

The convention was attended by delegates from all of the 3,000 and more local unions of the Automobile Workers; its purpose was to develop the bargaining strategy of the union in its then-impending new bargaining go-round with the auto industry. It was a time of early concern with inflation, then at a level of two or three percent a year, but nonetheless the subject of considerable media attention. Walter Reuther, that consummate master of the convention console, was at the keys, and he had an important message to impart to his audience. That message was that the hierarchy of the union wanted to take the inflationary heat off the union, produced by the media's wage-push analysis of the inflationary development. He proposed, therefore, that the Automobile Workers present the following demand to the auto industry: a profit-sharing arrangement pursuant to which any increase in the workers' pay would be determined not at the time of contracting, but rather at the end of each year of the contract, at which time it could be ascertained what the profit of each employer had been. That profit, he suggested, could then be allocated in accordance with the following formula: one-third to the employees, one-third to the stockholders, and one-third in the form of rebates to the purchasers of the cars. In that way, he argued, the Automobile Workers could not legitimately be charged with contributing to the currently much-feared inflation.

His proposal met with a fascinating response from the floor. Delegate after delegate arose to challenge Reuther's proposal. What they said was that that would be playing the boss's game, that the boss would have one arm around the worker's shoulders and the other hand in his pocket. Other concerns as to equity were expressed—GM might be expected to have more profits than American Motors. In short, Reuther's plan not only did not fly, it never got airborne, despite his protestation in defense that a profit-sharing scheme extracted from the boss through the exercise of union power in collective bargaining was a much different animal from one unilaterally imposed through employer beneficence.

What a contrast a quarter of century later to review the GM-Automobile Workers agreement covering the plant to be constructed for the Saturn operation in Spring Hill, Tennessee! Whatever reservations one may have about the viability of a seeming effort to convert American workers to a foreign work ethic, the very courting of it in the current context is applaudable. That courting, however, raises a question which goes to the essence of the meaning of a free-labor movement—a question I confront in closing.

For me, the central responsibility our labor movement holds in trust is alertness to injustice in the employment sphere, arguably the single most sensitive sphere for the arising of justice-injustice issues in any society, but particularly a free society, and maintenance of the will and organizational apparatus to respond to alarms in that sphere. That responsibility, when triggered, is to step into the vacuum of individual employee weakness and to organize it into collectivized strength. In so doing, the labor movement also provides a model for parallel movements to confront injustice in other spheres of a free society in perennial search of itself. The civil rights movement and the women's movement are two such parallel movements in American, indeed world, society.

A crucial question for the Saturn-type experiment is thus this: How compatible is the independent labor union model, so essential to a free society, particularly to a heterogeneous society such as ours, with the Japanese model of familial cooperation? What our unions cannot give up, consistent with their independence, is their economic power. Will the fact, as argued by Walter Reuther a quarter of a century earlier, that familial cooperation is the product of hard collective bargaining, carry the day? A related question of fundamental proportion: Does free collective bargaining, with its institutionalizing of conflict as well as the resolution of conflict, have enough flex to weather the need for "embracing the boss"?

I dare say, only time will tell—perhaps gently, with a bow.

IX. A Postscript: "Pension Fund Leverage"

While I would like to stop here, completion of my mission, even in the inherently curtailing context of a volume such as this, requires a postscript. In a fascinating book published in 1978, entitled, intriguingly, *The North Will Rise Again,* and subtitled, more informatively, *Pensions, Politics and Power in the 1980s,* authors Jeremy Rifkin and Randy Barber advance a thesis not unsupportive of Saturn-type experiments, but more pointed at union-resistant renegades such as J.P. Stevens & Co. The stunning seed from which their thesis springs is that American employee pension funds have become the largest pool of private capital in all the world[68]—totaling at present perhaps a trillion dollars and constituting, by far and away, the major source of financing for American industry.[69] A substantial portion of this vast sum is the fruit of collective bargaining, the beneficiaries of which are still-active and retired union members.

These pension funds wind up, almost universally, in the control of investment managers, typically the nation's largest banks and insurance companies, under trust and group-annuity contract arrangements. They are invested, accordingly, by these fiduciaries pursuant to the "prudent man," highest return for the least risk, principles which have traditionally governed such fiduciaries. The irony is that, pursuant to these trust-investment standards, literally millions of dollars of these funds are invested in the stock and other corporate paper of companies such as J.P. Stevens. To mince no words, vast funds "owned" by union beneficiaries, as a form of delayed wages, are invested without

---

[68] J. Rifkin and R. Barber, THE NORTH WILL RISE AGAIN: PENSIONS, POLITICS AND POWER IN THE 1980s 10 (1978).

[69] *Id.;* Kaiser, *Labor's New Weapon: Pension Fund Leverage—Can Labor Legally Beat Its Plowshares Into Swords?,* 34 RUTGERS L. REV. 409 (1982).

their consent by the financial institutions which "control" the funds in some of the bitterest corporate enemies of unions! As a character in the old comic strip, "Pogo," once said: "We have met the enemy, and he is *us*!"[70]

The frustration felt by American unionists over this un-planned, indeed unanticipated, side effect of a humanely con-ceived program to protect employees in their post-retirement years is utterly understandable. That this irony should galvanize union leaders, labor sympathizers, scholars, political activists, justice-seekers to a microscopic examination of the pertinent law in search of "pension fund leverage," to supplement or supplant more traditional labor economic power, is not only understand-able but laudable. The pertinent law includes ERISA (Employ-ees Retirement Income Security Act of 1974),[71] Section 302(c)(5) of the Taft-Hartley Act,[72] certain provisions of the Internal Revenue Code,[73] the common law of fiduciary duty,[74] the secondary boycott provisions of the National Labor Rela-tions Act,[75] and the federal antitrust laws.

The several potential uses to which pension fund leverage might be put, *assuming* in each instance the existence of union power to prompt the particular leveraging, include: (1) refusing to lend such funds to offending employers; (2) withholding or withdrawing funds from pension fund managers (banks, insur-ance companies) who do lend to offending employers; (3) refus-ing to invest such funds in offending employers; (4) withholding or withdrawing funds from pension fund managers who do invest in offending employers; (5) buying the stock of offending employers for the purpose of establishing leverage through the voting of the stock; (6) withholding or withdrawing funds from pension fund managers who refuse to buy such stock for such purpose.[76]

---

[70] Referred to in Rifkin & Barber, *supra* note 68, at 106.

[71] 29 USC §§1001–1381 (1982).

[72] 29 USC §186(c)(5)(1982), requiring, among other things, *joint* employer-union administration of any pension funds over which unions or their representatives have any control.

[73] Title II of ERISA amended the Internal Revenue Code. *See* 29 USC §§1201 *et seq.* (1982). Most importantly, qualified pension funds are exempted from federal taxation. *See* I.R.C. §501. The criteria for exemption are set forth in §401(a).

[74] For some notion of the "prudent man" rule as applied to trust investment, *see* Restatement (Second) of Trusts §§227–231 (1957).

[75] NLRA §8(b)(4)(ii)(B), 29 USC §158(b)(4)(ii)(B) (1982); NLRA §8(e), 29 USC §158(e) (1982); LMRA §303, 29 USC §187 (1982).

[76] *See, e.g.,* Kaiser, *supra* note 69.

Quite frankly, no one has yet offered to retain me at the fee it would require to prepare a legal analysis of any one of the manifold questions of law which repose on the manifold facets of the foregoing pension-leverage ploys. My survey of the legal literature already extant on the subject[77] leaves me in a not uncustomary mist. I can report to you with semiconfidence only that the subject is a whole can of worms, that almost none of the strategic questions have yet been authoritatively answered, and that there will be considerable collective bargaining palaver, learned conference ensembling, and lengthy litigative backup before the matter is entirely put to rest.

I hazard, however, this prediction, worth every penny you will pay me for it: "The North Will *Not* Rise Again," nor will American labor, on the basis of a revisionist view of the "prudent man" test, adjusted for the "social" criterion of "invest union." At least not without congressional imprimatur.

Responses

THE DECLINE OF UNION APPEAL AND POWER

Timothy P. O'Reilly*

It seems appropriate to have a Philadelphia attorney comment on Professor Oberer's paper, for he notes that the first labor case

---

[77] Much of the relevant literature is rallied in Rifkind & Barber, *supra* note 68, and Kaiser, *supra* note 69. *See also, e.g.*, Note (Cunningham), *The Employee Retirement Income Security Act of 1974 and Union Influence in Pension Fund Investment Decisions*, 12 FORDHAM URB. L.J. 151 (1984).

Unions will attempt in the future to preserve jobs through bargaining over the right to recommend investment policies to money managers. The fiduciary status of money managers conservatively influences their investment posture and thus discourages their support for such a program by organized labor. It is submitted that any recommendations made must be narrowly formulated. One proposal, for example, could be to recommend that pension funds be used to "invest in unionized companies where such investments are economically competitive." If the persons making such recommendations do not make their interest in job preservation the *paramount* interest, they will not have violated their fiduciary duties under ERISA. The test of whether fiduciary duties have been violated can never be whether the investments were equal, because such absolute equality is rarely found. Courts should apply a materiality standard when interpreting the fiduciary duty provision of ERISA. The issue should be whether the investment decision was materially affected by the "pro union" factors. Some flexibility in the decision-making process should be allowed as long as the paramount interest of all fiduciaries remains the retirement income security of employees, past and present. *Id.* at 174.

* Partner Morgan, Lewis & Bockius, Philadelphia, Pennsylvania.

ever reported was the *Philadelphia Cordwainers'*[1] case. But be assured, in Philadelphia the courts no longer regard unions as criminal conspiracies.

We are here to discuss union economic power in the private sector. Professor Oberer has accurately and thoroughly traced the history of the American labor laws in his excellent paper. I certainly concur with his analysis of such subjects as voluntary unionism. Mandatory unionism is not the solution to the dilemma caused by the fact that unions, as principally national organizations, may have less economic power than an employer operating on an international basis.

Unions are to be commended for recent innovative approaches to collective bargaining, such as the Steelworkers' approach to interest bargaining to avoid strikes and such as the Saturn project cited in the Professor's paper. Solutions developed by the parties are far preferable to legislatively imposed restraints.

Before turning to the pension fund issue, I would like to comment briefly on the status of labor policy today.[2] The U.S. labor policy today is consistent with the wishes of the majority of the electorate which so overwhelmingly voiced its opinion in November 1984. Today, there is considerable support for individual rights. Thus, the erosion of the employment-at-will concept. However, there is less support for greater union power. The recent Supreme Court decision in *Pattern Makers*[3] is evidence of this fact.

The factors that have influenced today's labor policy include, first, the public attitude toward unions. This attitude has been on a decline for some time, possibly from the time of the criminal convictions of leaders of the Paper Workers and Teamsters unions. *Second*, the economy. Unions were perceived to be the saviour during the depression in the late 1930s and the early 1940s when union membership grew so substantially. However, during the more recent recessions, employees perceived unions as toothless tigers, unable to help them or to protect them in job security issues. Unemployment remains high, and this is an

---

[1] Commonwealth v. Pullis (Mayer's Court of Philadelphia, 1806), *reprinted in* 3 J. Commons, DOCUMENTARY HISTORY OF AMERICAN INDUSTRIAL SOCIETY 59 (1910).

[2] *See* J. Siegal address to American Bar Association Labor and Employment Law Section, Washington, D.C., reported in the Wall Street J., Sept. 4, 1985, at 24.

[3] Pattern Makers League v. NLRB (Rockford-Beloit Pattern Jobbers), 473 US ___ , 119 LRRM 2928 (1985).

economic factor for which many blame the unions. The *third* and least important factor, I believe, is the political climate. That is, the appointees to the Board and to the judiciary who shape the interpretation of the Act. But because I am confident that this process has been amply covered elsewhere, I shall not add my comments on this factor.

The *fourth*, and I believe the most important factor in shaping U.S. labor policy, is the attitude of employees themselves. Today, the most significant aspect of that is the attitude of young workers. Over one-half of the workers in this country today are under age 35, but only 14 percent of them are unionized. Why? A number of reasons have been cited by various commentators.

First, I believe that the independence of the young workers, especially those in the service and white-collar areas, is a key factor. Generally, these workers are better educated and have more difficulty identifying with union leaders, most of whom are twice their age.

Second, management has become more sophisticated in its dealings with its employees, and it has taken away the need in many companies for a union.

Third, the mobility of the young work force. Those workers who are under age 35, according to a recent survey, stay in their jobs an average of 2.5 years. Those over age 45, on the other hand, stay in their jobs an average of 12 years.

Fourth, the two-tier wage systems that are becoming more and more popular. I find they are correctly perceived by the older workers as an alternative to taking a cut in pay, but at the same time they may be turning off the young workers to unions.

What can the unions do to regain some of their former economic power? As a management representative, I encourage the union leaders to adopt some of the suggestions offered by many commentators, otherwise we management-labor lawyers may find ourselves writing wills in a few years!

In order to appeal to young workers, unions need to appoint and elect younger organizers and leaders, and include more women in the ranks. Several must clean their own houses of corrupt officials. Where they represent the employees, they need to continue to work with companies to develop innovative projects, such as Saturn and the refinancing solutions that assisted Chrysler, Eastern, and Pan Am.

Unions must also focus on the needs of the young workers. These include day care centers, job training, quality of work and life programs, and cafeteria approaches toward benefits. Blind allegiance to the union health and welfare and pension plans will no longer suffice.

Finally, I would like to turn to Professor Oberer's treatment of pension investments. This topic has not yet received the attention that it merits and will receive in the next couple of years.

The Department of Labor estimates that there will be three trillion dollars in pension fund assets by 1995. The unions, as joint trustees in many multi-employer funds, have considerable control over investment decisions that are made daily by investment advisors to these funds. Recently, unions have tried to affect investment decisions for a variety of social reasons. Some examples include union construction projects, withdrawing funds from companies that are perceived to be antiunion, such as J.P. Stevens, withdrawing money from companies that have activities in South Africa, or supporting various women's movement issues.

Generally there are three categories of investment policies. There is a "socially neutral policy," where the only concern of the investment advisor is the safety of the principal and the rate of the return. Second, there is the "socially sensitive" or "desirable policy." That is, selecting from a number of potential investments that are substantially equal the ones that are most socially desirable. And third, there is a "socially dictated" investment approach. Under this approach, rate of return, safety, and diversification are sacrificed for the social benefits.

As discussed in the Professor Oberer's paper, there are a number of statutory limitations that may impact on the selection of investment policy. While the antitrust laws may come into play, the focus is on the Employee Retirement Income Security Act (ERISA). ERISA Section 404 sets forth limits and fiduciary requirements for plan fiduciaries. Basically, fiduciaries must act solely in the interest of the participants and beneficiaries. The regulations require that the fiduciaries comport to the "prudent man rule," that they diversify the plan assets, and that they demonstrate loyalty to the plan document, participants, and beneficiaries.

Furthermore, ERISA Section 406 lists prohibited transactions. Basically, with some few exceptions, these prohibit transactions between parties in interest, including unions and contributing employers.

Although the case law is still in an embryonic stage, some general principles can be gleaned. *First*, investment actions must be taken primarily for the purpose of benefiting the participants and beneficiaries. *Second*, "dual loyalty" is permissible. Initially the Department of Labor (DOL) had a *per se* rule against dual loyalty. The issue came to light in the *Grumman Corporation*[4] pension plan case, where stock was purchased to thwart a takeover. The district court held that the DOL *per se* rule was inappropriate. However, it found the purchase of the stock to be imprudent.

Injunctions have recently been issued against stock purchases to resist corporate takeovers, and injunctions have been issued against unions for receiving loans from pension plans to finance construction of union office complexes. On the other hand, summary judgment was recently granted trustees who made 11 percent mortgages available when the prevailing interest rates were from 12½ to 17 percent.

In conclusion, it is my opinion that the socially sensitive investment policy will be permitted by the DOL and the courts, and this will have a substantial impact on the unions' economic power in the coming decades, as long as a few guidelines are met: (1) the rate of return is reasonable, (2) the risk of principal is not appreciably greater than any alternative investments available, (3) the diversification is maintained, and (4) the social benefit is the indirect result of the investment. A suggestion to accomplish this is to make the investment policy passive, not active. That is, do not direct the investment advisor to make an investment in a particular project, but direct him instead to avoid undesirable investments, however those are perceived, unless there is no comparable investment opportunity available.

LABOR AT A CROSSROADS

BRUCE H. SIMON*

I would like to extract from Professor Oberer's broadly based and seemingly objective paper the hard-core assumptions that in

---

[4] Grumman Corp.

* General Counsel, National Association of Letter Carriers, AFL-CIO; partner, Cohen, Weiss and Simon, New York, New York.

my view characterize much of the "iron fist and velvet glove" approach that has virtually emasculated the trade union movement. First, he states that in the absence of monopoly or near monopoly control of the supply of labor in the relevant labor market, economic warfare by unions is a losing battle. Unions are regulated, Professor Oberer avers, not by law, but by life. And after an excursion starting with *Philadelphia Cordwainers*,[1] through the 19th century, criminal syndicalism, and such, he briefly mentions "yellow-dog" contracts. One would have thought that a reference to *Belknap*[2] as the 1980s reincarnation of the creative use of individual employee contracts to thwart union rights might have been appropriate as an honorable mention.

Professor Oberer then pays ritualistic obeisance to the Norris-La Guardia and Wagner Acts' paternalism. He notes in an aptly phrased requiem that our capitalist society successfully circumvented Karl Marx's prognostications by co-opting America's workers. But then, the law's benevolent paternalism turned to the inevitable, but still fatherly, discipline.

The real world, according to Professor Oberer, is one where strife is tempered by Taft-Hartley, rendering it socially acceptable. A brief flurry of life from our Taft-Hartley tamed labor force in the guise of creatively lawyered "hot-cargo" clauses led to yet another dose of discipline: Landrum-Griffin. And to make sure that labor remains powerless, we have a series of pronouncements from the Board and the Supreme Court circumscribing the boundaries of the labor movement's political, social, and economic power.[3]

After all of the secondary boycott and antitrust decisional obfuscation, the net result is that the original concept of shielding only the "wholly unconcerned" has been lost. The corporate

---

[1] Commonwealth v. Pullis (Mayor's Court of Philadelphia, 1806), *reprinted in* 3 J. Commons, DOCUMENTARY HISTORY OF AMERICAN INDUSTRIAL SOCIETY 59 (1958).

[2] Belknap, Inc. v. Hale, 463 US 491, 113 LRRM 3057 (1983). Employer offered strike replacements permanent jobs to replace economic strikers. Employer breached his contract with replacements when he displaced the replacements with the former strikers. The Court held that the NLRA did not preempt the replacement employees' state breach of contract action.

[3] The 1947 Taft-Hartley Amendments to the Wagner Act included the prohibition against secondary boycotts culled from the language of §8(b)(4)(A). Defining the parameters of proscribed secondary activity has inspired litigation, line drawing, and dubious distinctions. Electrical Workers (IUE) v. NLRB (General Elec. Co.), 366 US 667, 48 LRRM 2210 (1961). *See also* NLRB v. Denver Bldg. & Constr. Trades Council, 341 US 675, 28 LRRM 2108 (1951); Sailors Union of the Pac. (Moore Dry Dock Co.), 92 NLRB 547, 27 LRRM 1108 (1950).

veil, however gossamer the fabric, is an impenetrable wall. As the Supreme Court stated in *NLRB* v. *Longshoreman (ILA) (American Trucking Ass'n)*[4] "[t]he various linguistic formulae and evidentiary mechanisms we have employed to describe the primary/secondary distinction are not talismanic nor can they substitute for analysis. . . . The inquiry is often an inferential and fact-based one, at times requiring the drawing of lines 'more nice than obvious.'"[5] Those who can interpret that and advise clients accordingly must be acolytes of Justice Frankfurter rather than mere lawyers.

An excursus of the Court's examination of work preservation clauses illustrates the confusion. *National Woodwork Mfrs. Ass'n* v. NLRB[6] is one of the first in a series of cases in which the Supreme Court examined work preservation provisions in collective bargaining agreements. The Court formulated a test to determine whether the work preservation clause was lawful primary activity or proscribed secondary activity: "The touchstone is whether the agreement or its maintenance is addressed to the labor relations of the contracting employer *vis-a-vis* his own employees."[7] Only if the conduct was directed toward another employer would those actions be considered having a "secondary" effect.

In *NLRB* v. *Plumbers Local 638 (Austin Co.)*,[8] the Court continued to refine the distinction between primary protected activity and the statutorily prohibited secondary boycott. The Court reformulated the *National Woodwork* test by emphasizing another part of the decision: "The issue is whether 'an object' of the inducement and the coercion was to cause the cease-doing-business consequences prohibited by Section 8(b)(4), the resolution of which in turn depends on whether the product boycott was 'addressed to the labor relations of [the secondary employer] . . . *vis-a-vis* his own employees' or whether the union's conduct was tactically calculated to satisfy [its] objectives elsewhere.' "[9]

In *NLRB* v. *Longshoremen (ILA)*,[10] the controversy at issue concerns the most recent technological innovation in the

---

[4] 473 US ___, 119 LRRM 2915 (1985) (hereinafter *Longshoreman II*).
[5] *Id.*, 119 LRRM at 2923.
[6] 386 US 612, 64 LRRM 2801 (1967).
[7] *Id.* at 645.
[8] 429 US 507, 94 LRRM 2628 (1977) (hereinafter *Pipefitters*).
[9] *Id.* at 528.
[10] 447 US 490, 104 LRRM 2552 (1980) (hereinafter Longshoremen I).

shipping industry, "containerization." Containers are metal boxes which can carry up to 30,000 pounds of freight. They can be lifted in one piece from the container ship and transferred directly to a truck, thereby consolidating the time-consuming process of unloading and loading many separate pieces of cargo. The increased use of containers precipitated the concomitant decline in the amount of work available for longshoremen who previously loaded and unloaded the cargo, piece by piece, from conventional vessels to trucks and from the trucks to the ships.[11]

To determine whether a work preservation agreement is violative of either the secondary boycott or "hot-cargo" provisions of the NLRA (Sections 8(b)(4)(B) and 8(e)) the Court prescribes the following test: "the inquiry must be carefully focused: to determine whether an agreement seeks no more than to preserve the work of bargaining unit members, the Board must focus on the work of the bargaining unit employees, not on the work of other employees who may be doing the same or similar work, and examine the relationship between the work as it existed before the innovation and as the agreement proposes to preserve it."[12] "The legality of the agreement turns, as an initial matter, on whether the historical and functional relationship between this retained work and traditional longshore work can support the conclusion that the objective of the agreement was work preservation rather than the satisfaction of union goals elsewhere."[13]

Longshoremen II,[14] focuses on the issue of whether the work preservation agreement was one simply designed "to forestall" the possibility of adverse effects on workers by technological innovations. The Court in *Longshoremen II*, refocuses the inquiry of *National Woodwork* by adopting as its approach Justice Harlan's concurrence in *National Woodwork:* "'The only question thus to be decided . . . is whether Congress meant, in enacting §§8(b)(4)(B) and 8(e) of the National Labor Relations Act, to prevent this kind of labor-management agreement designed to forestall possible

---

[11] *See generally*, 447 US at 495 ff.
[12] *Id.* at 508.
[13] *Id.* at 511.
[14] *Supra* note 4.

adverse effects upon workers arising from changing technology. . . . [W]e must be especially careful to eschew a resolution of the issue according to our own economic ideas and to find one in what Congress has done.'"[15] Having found that Congress, since the *National Woodwork* decision, altered neither Section 8(b)(4)(B) nor Section 8(e), the Court held that work preservation clauses must therefore be considered within the lawful parameters of activity proscribed in the secondary boycott and hot-cargo section of the Act.[16]

To return to my review of Oberer: To insure that the labor movement's naturally combative instincts have an outlet, the Supreme Court implied the duty of fair representation.[17] Then, with Court-imposed limitations on the Board's preemption of state laws, one is led, Professor Oberer argues, to question the final utility of the Act.[18]

Although Oberer presents an arguable recital of the course of the history of organized labor, it is necessary to reexamine fundamental principles. First, while union strength requires monopoly control of labor, the law has been directed, and very successfully so, to the prevention of unions having almost any influence on the relative labor market, let alone monopoly control.

Having made reference to the disutility of the Section 8(b)(4) analysis to the problem of technological advance and the complexity of business relationships, Professor Oberer then proposes two options to confront the proposition that present labor relations law "is inadequate to deal with these sophisticated problems": (1) to amend the labor laws to be more specific, or (2) to use the federal antitrust laws. In what is surely a gesture of "noblesse oblige," Professor Oberer eschews use of the antitrust laws, but then confesses he has no better talisman for a statutory primary/secondary test.

Professor Oberer leaves us with the conclusion that "authorative inscrutability" is the best the labor movement can expect. I look forward to using the "authoritative inscrutability" technique in advising one of my local union clients faced with a labor dispute with a multinational conglomerate consisting of

---

[15] *Id.*, 119 LRRM at 2924.

[16] For the antitrust aspect of this idea, *see* Connell Constr. Co. v. Plumbers Local 100, 421 US 616, 89 LRRM 2401 (1975), *reh'g denied*, 423 US 884 (1975).

[17] Vaca v. Sipes, 386 US 171, 64 LRRM 2369 (1967).

[18] Belknap, Inc. v. Hale, *supra* note 2.

mysterious divisions utilizing sophisticated upstreaming of profits from a facially independent profit center, or confronted with an employer utilizing "independent contractors" carefully crafted from guidelines culled from the right Board panels, or faced with a double-breasted employer, or having to deal with some variant of containerization.

To illustrate the inanity of such an analysis, consider the following: When the assembly line robot breaks down will it be the production line employees' union, or the machine repair union, or the American Medical Association that will have a legitimate work preservation objective under *Longshoremen I*[19] and *Longshoremen II*?[20] Or if the robots are leased to the factory by the robot maker with no right of control given to the factory, will *Enterprise*[21] and *Pipefitters*[22] step in? Or will the union's attempt to bargain over the question of robots be met with *Otis Elevator's*[23] position of nonmandatory subjects of collective bargaining.

I shall advise my client, no doubt, that the best I can do is to share with him a few moments of transcendental meditation upon the "authoritatively inscrutable." "I'll inscrutable you" is likely to be his response. And he will be right.

The next basic principle is that the tribunal established to interpret and apply the "inscrutable" is, by design, a political body to be used by each national administration to implement its own political agenda. Those of us who would have as our purpose "making the Board more impartial, less subject to political influence, more constant in its policies," to use Professor Oberer's phrase, are presumably "naive simpletons." I

---

[19] *Supra* note 6.

[20] *Supra* note 4.

[21] NLRB v. Plumbers Local 638 (Enterprise Ass'n), 429 US 507, 94 LRRM 2628 (1977).

[22] *Supra* note 6.

[23] Otis Elevator, 269 NLRB 891, 893 n.5, 115 LRRM 1281 (1984). The Board in *Otis* held that a decision to move a plant from New Jersey to Connecticut was not a mandatory subject of bargaining, "even though . . . [labor costs] . . . may have been one of the circumstances which stimulated the evaluation process which generated the decision." *Id.*, 115 LRRM at 1282. The Board concluded that decisions which affect the nature of the business, including *inter alia* those "decisions to sell a business or a part thereof, to dispose of its assets, to restructure or to consolidate operations, to subcontract, to invest in labor-saving machinery, to change the methods of finance or of sales, advertising, product design, and all other decisions akin to the foregoing" lie outside of the scope of mandatory subjects of bargaining included in §8(d). The Board's *Otis Elevator* decision was drawn from the Supreme Court's opinion in *First Nat'l Maintenance Corp. v. NLRB*, 452 US 666, 107 LRRM 2705 (1981).

respectfully submit that a system which uses a frankly political tribunal not expected to render principled decisions, to administer a law described as "authoritatively inscrutable," is the very antithesis of what our system was designed to be. It is, quite simply, antidemocratic. "Not to worry," Professor Oberer would tell us.

My exercise, in this paper, is part of the "institutional plan" (a chilling phrase, I submit). Criticism of the Board by the "adversely affected interest group," is and should be therapeutic. Allowing us to ventilate at forums like this, Oberer would argue, is part of the hegemonic process, its institutions, and doctrines.

Returning to basic principles, now that we have been taught that we are covered by an indecipherable rule of law that will be applied to us by a political body expected to use a political stamp, we are reminded once again of the real world of supply and demand, the free market. Professor Oberer sympathizes with those who would suffer from deregulation and foreign competition, but sees no "philosophical or moral basis for continuing workers' sinecures" earned under those systems.

Would not at least a mention of the willingness of the system to bend its laudable "free market" concepts to save distressed employers be appropriate here? Or perhaps the abuse of the bankruptcy law to permit employers to dispose of union contracts?[24] Is it the free market and the glory of deregulation that has permitted Continental Airlines to come roaring back from the edge of insolvency with cheap fares based upon a 50 percent slash in wage rates permitted by the repudiation of its collective bargaining agreement by a bankruptcy court?[25] Or is it the perversion of Chapter XI's interference with the free market? Is it simply deregulation and the free market that has caused chaos in the trucking industry, or was it the perversion of the doctrine of "independent contractor" that permitted union-busting employers to erode the business of union truckers through the use of owner-operators? How does the free market deal with

---

[24] In re Wheeling-Pittsburgh Steel Corp., 50 Bankr. 969 (Bankr. WD Pa., 1985). But note the Third Circuit's recent rejection of the district court's approval of Wheeling-Pittsburgh's rejection of its collective bargaining agreement with the union: Wheeling-Pittsburgh Steel Corp. v. Steelworkers, 122 LRRM 2425 (CA 3, 1986).

[25] In re Continental Airlines, 119 LRRM 2752 (SD Tex., 1985); In re Continental Airlines, 40 Bankr. 299, 115 LRRM 2364 (SD Tex., 1984).

tobacco farmers? Oil companies? Lockheed? Continental Illinois Bank?

What is Professor Oberer's prescription for American unions representing workers in internationalized industries? He avers that they must "face up to real life constraints." American labor law simply cannot alter macroeconomics. The Professor's fantasy is making the American labor movement "conform to the rest of the world." Conform to what? Child labor at 25 cents an hour? Employers seek the lowest common denominator available in the world market.

Professor Oberer claims that this is merely a "modest fantasy." However, one cannot help but recall Jonathan Swift's "A Modest Proposal."[26] Swift's ironic answer to perceived overpopulation of the world was the consumption of the newborn. I speculate that in a free market with true libertarianism and a minimum of government intrusion into our personal lives, Swift's is a theoretically acceptable approach.

Professor Oberer offers the 1970s Steelworkers' "experimental negotiation" model as an example of union response to the real world. With hindsight, one may question how well in today's world that agreement served the Steelworkers.

Big steel diversified and committed its major capital to non-steel areas. The industry has splintered. Wheeling-Pittsburgh tried to use bankruptcy to void its labor contract, only to be met with an enormously successful strike. That may be viewed as less than successful in terms of meeting the problems of the free marketplace.

Let me now turn to my view of an appropriate labor movement response to a philosophy that has rendered the Board virtually irrelevant, and certainly no longer a forum for the protection of worker or union rights. Lane Kirkland has suggested a repeal of all labor laws and a return to the law of the jungle.[27] If one really wants a free market, let us be free to operate in the free market. Lest anyone forget, we are not incapable of responding to predators with fangs of our own.

On a more civilized note, I would point to a few recent developments that may guide us to a revitalized labor movement, using strategies and techniques which even the current brand of

---

[26] A MODEST PROPOSAL (1969).

[27] See generally, Estreicher, Worker's Still Need Labor Law's Shield, N.Y. Times, July 21, 1985, §3, at 2.

"authoritative inscrutability" may not breach. In the steel industry, perhaps one of the most successful companies operating today is Wierton, 100 percent owned by its employees. The use of ESOPs to rescue and then control distressed companies may be very much a last resort and, as *Rath*[28] meatpacking unfortunately shows, may be a snare and a delusion for workers. Yet, Wierton is evidence that employee stock ownership plans can work.[29]

In fairness, Professor Oberer asks in a slightly different context whether collective bargaining has enough flex to weather the need for "embracing the boss." I suppose here the question is whether it will have enough flex to weather labor *becoming* the boss.

A second and related example is the union's role in the recent takeover battle for TWA. Here, too, playing on the free market field so beloved of our entrepreneurial gurus, the unions were able to carve out a significant piece of the equity action by aligning themselves with one of a number of corporate raiders. The resulting agreement is a wonderful amalgam of securities law, corporate merger minutia, and collective bargaining items, negotiated by as unlikely a cast of characters as was ever assembled: investment bankers, corporate, SEC, ESOP, and labor lawyers, green mailers, shop stewards, and billionaires.

Since "takeover" mania appears to be with us for a while, and leveraged buy outs seem to be the order of the day, labor should understand that it can leverage the labor costs and productivity components of its contracts into an equity bargaining kit and it can trade its affection to the corporate rival offering the best proposal. To be sure, many of the legal questions and legal issues raised with reference to the investment of pension funds will be applicable here as well. The answers are, if anything, even less clear than they are in the pension field.

Another "success," is the United Airlines pilots' strike. By spending an awful lot of time and an awful lot of money and the most sophisticated techniques available to communicate with a widely spread work force (closed circuit television, family meetings, all manner of prestrike communications), the union was

---

[28] Rath Packing Co., 275 NLRB No. 42, 119 LRRM 1063 (1985).

[29] *See generally*, EMPLOYEE OWNERSHIP: A HANDBOOK FOR UNIONS (1982); *Steelworkers Ratify Concessionary Pact at LTV Steel, Settle with National Steel*, 13 PENSION REP. (BNA) No. 15, at 721 (Apr. 14, 1986); *Unions May Want to Get Heavily Involved in Establishment of Plans for Concessions*, 13 PENSION REP. (BNA) No. 11 at 466 (Mar. 17, 1986).

able to thwart the efforts of the employer to coerce a group of over 500 pretrained, newly hired pilots to cross the picket line.[30]

Labor's use of "corporate campaigns" deserves close attention. That technique neither began and nor ended with J.P. Stevens, and it appears to be a strategy toward which unions will turn with increasing frequency.[31] Additionally, labor unions will increasingly negotiate with investment bankers, public relations experts, and others in an effort to offer solutions and bargains which attempt to meet the problems national and international companies confront.

The regulation of union power in the past 50 years has seen a steady decline from the high point of the Wagner Act, where unions were recognized as having something significant to contribute to the American way of life, where a social compact was struck between a government concerned about the potential for revolution which grew out of the greatest depression ever experienced by this country and an emerging "labor movement," where recognition and fostering unionism was traded for peace.

In the last 50 years we have seen that social compact destroyed, chip by chip, leaving labor unions today with a sense of despair. That despair will manifest itself either in destructive activity by labor unions or will be met with constructive measures by a society that will recognize the value of labor and collective action.

I think that we are at a crossroads. And I must say that the next few years, at least, do not give me a great sense of optimism as to which path this country will take.

ACCOMMODATING SURVIVAL

JOHN H. FANNING*

I want to compliment Professor Oberer for his very fine paper on the provocative subject, "The Regulation of Union Economic Power." I would have added some comment on the Health Care

---

[30] *See* Airline Pilots Ass'n Int'l v. United Airlines, 614 F. Supp 1020, 119 LRRM 3483 (ND Ill., 1985).

[31] The most recent example of the "corporate campaign" technique is the strike by the Hormel workers (Food & Commercial Workers Local P-9) in Austin, Minn. The P-9 campaign indicates that here, too, there are limits to the usefulness of any technique.

*Former Chairman and Member, National Labor Relations Board; of counsel, Hinckley, Allen, Tobin & Silverstein, Providence, Rhode Island.

Amendments of 1970. They did extend the Act into the very large health care field, generating many problems, producing considerable economic impact, and also some further regulation of union economic power. But that would be a minor addition.

I am more concerned about his statement that "union economic power and the regulation thereof is what our system of labor relations is all about." It seems to me that misses the management phase of the problem, but, of course, that was not included in his topic, so I do not fault him. I am also concerned by his observation that the American system of collective bargaining is predicated on economic warfare. That may have been the norm over the past 50 years, but there are indications the antagonisms of the past may be giving way to the acquired wisdom of the past for the collective security of the future.

I am not going to go into a section-by-section analysis of the Act in respect of its regulation of union economic power, a term which incidentally does not appear in the statute. I would be repeating much of what Professor Oberer has pointed out. But as one who served on the Board for a quarter of a century, I will pursue a few, I think relevant, though not directly subject-connected, observations.

Initially, I would observe and emphasize that the National Labor Relations Act was not enacted to regulate union economic power—whatever that phrase might encompass. The Act is very clear in Section 1 wherein it declares it

> to be the policy of the United States to eliminate the causes of certain substantial obstructions to the free flow of commerce and to mitigate and eliminate those obstructions when they have occurred by encouraging the practice and procedure of collective bargaining and by protecting the exercise by workers of full freedom of association, self-organization, and designation of representatives of their own choosing, for the purpose of negotiating the terms and conditions of their employment or other mutual aid or protection.

Sometimes I think we forget this section because all the other esoteric sections of the Act grab our attention. In the year before enactment of the Wagner Act there were almost 3,000 work stoppages on the issue of representation alone. Too many employers were unwilling to recognize or bargain with their employees through their employees' representatives about their terms and conditions of employment. The situation was perceived as a threat to the economic, and possibly political, health of the nation and so, for the first time the federal government brought employees under the protection of the Constitution in the incidents of their employment. The congressional purpose since then has been to protect as effectively as possible the legal rights and protections given employees, their representatives, and employers under the statute. The statute did not say workers and their employers have to have equal economic power, and they rarely do, or that they have to agree; but the incidence of peaceful settlement of disputes will be higher when employees can freely select bargaining representatives, and parties are required to bargain in good faith toward the resolution of the dispute, with the threat of legitimate economic sanctions by one being a factor in the bargaining. No one questions the ultimate use of sanctions to resolve a dispute, and that involves use of economic power, whether strike or boycott. But what is a legitimate sanction and a nonlegitimate sanction has been a problem since the beginning. These are difficult concepts to grasp, even more difficult to administer, and very much influenced by subjective analysis. This the Congress, the Board, and the courts have been trying to do with varying degrees of success—depending largely on one's own subjective philosophy of labor-management relations—for the past 50 years. Varying degrees of success, I say, because the need for protective policies and the administration thereof is perceived and implemented by people, and people are a variable lot. And so the regulation of union activity to gain economic power by statute, Board, or court decisions becomes a debatable issue.

But the basic policy has not been modified by the Congress of the United States in the 50 years that the Act has existed, although its application has been refined from time to time. By the Congress in its two major amendments—Taft-Hartley in 1947 and Landrum-Griffin in 1959, when the Congress felt one or both of the parties had departed from the original purpose of the Wagner Act, and hence a refining series of limitations on what labor and management can do with respect to each other and with respect to the public were added to the regulatory scheme.

But, notwithstanding the statute, the basic "economic power" on either side of the labor-management equation varies pretty much with prevailing economic conditions. Unions, which have the priceless commodity of their members' labor to sell but whose members need jobs to support themselves and their families, as much as any other component in the industrial production relationship, are subject to the shifting tides of the economic fortunes of the nation. This was clearly established during the industrial production period encompassing World War II and the post-World-War-II period when civilian supplies needed replenishing and the country needed workers to do the production work incident to the process. These years saw the greatest growth in union membership, that is, in "union economic power," in our history. The reverse has been true in periods of recession. Unions are as strong or as weak as the economy, and the policing resrictions of Taft-Hartley and Landrum-Griffin are a restriction on union activity, in large part their organizational activity, rather than a regulation of their economic power.

Some unions are economically strong today, but their industries are strikeproof because of technical developments in the industry. I believe that is true of telephone communications in the United States today. Because of technical developments in that industry, I believe it is virtually impossible for employees and unions in that industry to effectively strike employers in that industry. Economic power? Hardly. There are other measures available in other national industries to combat the nationwide impact of work stoppages. Threatened work stoppages in railroads, as we all know, can be stopped by the President's designation of fact-finding boards to help produce a settlement. The impact of national airline work stoppages can be markedly diminished by other airlines which are not involved in labor problems and which can expand to serve the customers of the strike-bound airlines. Government seizure is even a reluctant possibility. Shortly after the end of World War II, I was involved in the seizure by the government of 300 railroads after the exhaustion of peaceful statutory methods, and those railroads were operated by the government for two years—with conditions of employment set by the government—because of an unresolved labor dispute that was affecting the national economy and defense needs. During World War II, I was involved in the government seizure and operation of several individual facilities which were engaged in labor disputes where production was vital to national defense. This practice goes back to President Lincoln. Economic power did not help those unions. Nor did it help much in the organization of the J.P. Stevens Co.

I once worked for Charles Wilson, formerly president of General Motors, when he was Secretary of Defense. We were quite friendly and I said to him one day, "Mr. Wilson, what do you think your biggest accomplishment was in the field of labor relations while you were at General Motors?" He replied, "The cost of living clause in our labor contracts, without question." And I said to him, "But it does not seem to me necessarily good labor relations from a management viewpoint to commit yourself to long-term wage increases, and it also is built-in inflation. If you have a cost of living clause, you start a potentially built-in inflationary cycle, and once the clause is in your contract I imagine it would be very difficult to get rid of it." And I probably had some other equally theoretical arguments. And he said to me, "All you say is true, but at the time I adopted the cost of living policy, it was after the War, and I could sell every car I could make and for almost any price I wanted to place on it. The one thing I couldn't stand was a work stoppage or a strike." And that probably is the essence of labor-management relations. The "economic power" of labor and management is largely determined by the needs of the marketplace.

This is what collective bargaining is all about; and even though there may be some accidental impact on neutrals—such as higher prices on cars—which competition will control, I believe it is the best industrial relations system in the world. Many foreign visitors have told me that.

I think one of the reasons may be that we have a different system of industrial relations in this country than anywhere else in the democratic world. Except where it is otherwise agreed to by the parties, unit bargaining is the norm. A union can only require the employer whose employees it represents to bargain with it about the terms and conditions applicable to the plant or plants of that employer. And one union has exclusive right of representation of all employees in the unit, unlike the practice in many other countries. True, in some industries there are multi-employer units and contracts by agreement, and there have been attempts to produce so-called nationwide master contracts. Whether if there were a nationwide strike in the transportation industry, for example, there would be a situation that would require some national action, I do not know. But there never has been. The fact is, if some unions do have this economic power we are talking about, it too is combated by general economic conditions in the country and the world, and by the attitude of many citizens. We are all familiar with the situation in the automobile industry a couple of years ago and the course of "concession" collective bargaining which ensued because of the Japanese automobile import threat and "concession bargaining" elsewhere for comparable reasons. It is a question of both labor and management recognizing their co-dependency, and I think there is a trend in that direction.

We may be in for a new kind of industrial relations era. The era of "economic warfare" may come to be replaced by an era of "accommodating survival"—not necessarily tomorrow, but certainly sooner than appeared likely 50 years ago.

The "Saturn Project" discussed by Professor Oberer is but one example of what I consider a new reflection of union economic power. I happen to be on the board of directors of two national business companies. Both companies were experiencing financial difficulties. In both cases, free and open discussion with the unions representing the employees resulted in what is known today as "employee stock ownership plans." In one case, the union reduced its wages by 12½ percent in exchange for 12½ percent in stock, so that at the end of five years, the employees would own 49 percent of the stock of the company, but with no rights of management. In the second case, the union—that is, the employees—gave up 15 percent of their wages in exchange for 15 percent of the stock of the company, plus 15 percent of the profits before taxes, in a three-year plan, and also agreed to an increased productivity factor. Neither of these companies is a small company. Both were able to acquire in this manner immediate and continuing new capital, which has helped them presently; but more significant to me is the fact that the attitude of both employee groups has changed. Both now regard the companies as "their" companies, and their interest in and loyalty to their companies is much higher. The employees desire to help their companies and to add more security to their jobs. They are a more loyal, productive, and committed work force. I think this may be the best long-range benefit of such an accord and a way to harness union economic power.

The Act, of course, provides for the regulation of management economic power and its use as well as union economic power. I regret that our current topic considered only one phase of the regulatory aspect of the Act. A comparison would have been interesting and possibly even more provocative.

I would also like to indicate that I agree with Professor Oberer's observations on "pension fund leverage." If unions can ever devise a system to use these funds, or at least their share, to accomplish traditional trade union objectives and values, consistent with their fiduciary responsibilities, then they will have achieved true economic power.

Commentary

Thomas C. Kohler*

Writing in 1776, Adam Smith, in his treatise, *The Wealth of Nations*, observed that

> [w]e rarely hear . . . of the combinations of masters, though frequently of those of workmen. But whoever imagines, upon this account, that masters rarely combine, is as ignorant of the world as of the subject. Masters are always and every where in a sort of tacit, but constant and uniform combination, not to raise the wages of labour above their actual rate. To violate this combination is every where a most unpopular action, and a sort of reproach to a master among his neighbors and equals.[1]

Smith further observed that, when workers do organize themselves

> [t]he masters upon these occasions . . . never cease to call aloud for the assistance of the civil magistrate, and the vigorous execution of those laws which have been enacted with so much severity against the combinations of servants, labourers, and journeymen.[2]

The economic power of workers has been an enduring object of legal regulation. Indeed, since at least the time of the 1349 Ordinance of Laborers,[3] Anglo-American law has in varying ways and to varying degrees attempted to control this power and its expression. Though he at once seemingly characterizes it as hyperbole, Professor Oberer's opening comment that giving him this topic was tantamount to "giving him the show," comes much closer to the truth that he modestly suggests.

Professor Oberer's useful paper presents a thoughtful overview of his theories and opinions on the manner in which both the law and market forces have regulated the economic power of

---

* Assistant Professor of Law, Boston College.
[1] A. Smith, An Inquiry into the Nature and Causes of the Wealth of Nations 75 (1976).
[2] *Id.* at 75–76.
[3] Ordinance of Laborers, 1349, 25 Edw. III, I Statutes of the Realm, 307.

unions. Such an effort defies comprehensive summary. Consequently, the first part of this paper will present a cursory interpretive summary of what constitute—at least to this commentator—Professor Oberer's major themes and premises. A critique of and commentary upon these themes will be offered in the second part of the paper. It will conclude with a brief consideration of some possible implications of legal and social trends for collective bargaining as an institution, and what these may portend for democracy in general.

I. Review

Professor Oberer's paper consists of two parts. In its first portion, he states his theory of the development of collective bargaining in the United States, and of the law that regulates it. The underlying theme of this history as he views it is the mutual, if not necessarily simultaneous, efforts of labor and capital to put the force of governmental power into equipoise between them. To use Professor Oberer's words, this history can be characterized as "the search for balance." As he conceives it, this search has gone forward in a nearly dialectical progression. Implicit in this view is the suggestion that the development of the institution of collective bargaining, and the enactment and content of the statutes concerning it, are entirely predictable, if not absolutely historically preordained occurrences.

The era of a common law regulation, Oberer states, is the first phase of this search. This period, he observed, is characterized by the use of governmental power on capitals' behalf through the judiciary to restrict the expression of workers' economic power. The enactment of a triad of statutes—the Railway Labor, Norris-LaGuardia, and the Wagner Acts—Oberer posits, caused governmental authority to be swung into a position antipodal to that which obtained during the previous era. This second phase of development Oberer characterizes as the era of paternalistic protection of unions. Although he stops short of suggesting that this period of "paternalism" was alone responsible for the growth in union membership and bargaining strength, he states that the shift of governmental power which he perceives to have occurred during this period was its primary cause.

The paternalistic policies of the 12-year period after 1935, Oberer suggests, necessarily led to demands for a curbing of the power legislatively awarded labor. As a result, governmental favor was once again shifted and came to rest in a position of synthesis, or equipoise. This third, or synthetic phase he characterizes as "government as umpire." Under this regimen, government's role is to assist neither party. Instead, its power is to be used to demark (in a neutral fashion) the bounds within which the parties' economic struggle may occur and to confine as closely as possible the impact of economic pressure tactics to the parties themselves. Legislative amendments to the Wagner Act, Professor Oberer suggests, are not alone responsible for the transformation of government's role; two sets of Supreme Court decisions also made important contributions. The Court's development of the union's duty of fair representation, which began with the Court's 1944 opinion in *Steele* v. *Louisville & Nashville Railroad*,[4] Oberer points out, has had an important influence on the ways in which union power is exercised. (Although he does not mention it, the extensions and applications of this doctrine have also permitted substantial judicial intervention into both arbitration and the internal decisionmaking process of unions, as the Eighth Circuit's *Smith* v. *Hussmann Refrigerator Co.*[5] decision exemplifies.) The preemption doctrine, Oberer states, has also played a significant role in the regulation of union economic power. That doctrine, he posits, was intended to protect unions in their nascent stage from unfriendly local tribunals, and its erosion has been correlative with the maturation of the labor movement.

In the second part of his paper, Professor Oberer discusses a series of topics related to the administration of the Act and the future of unions and collective bargaining. Innovations in enterprise organization and in ways of performing work, he contends, have outstripped the Act's secondary boycott provision, leaving the Labor Board with no useful criteria for distinguishing between primary parties to disputes and neutrals. Citing *NLRB* v. *Plumbers Local 638 (Austin Co.)*,[6] as exemplary of the problems in this area, he calls for legislative amendment of the outmoded provisions of Section 8(b)(4).

Criticisms both of recent appointees to and decisions by the Board, Oberer suggests, are misdirected. The Board, he reminds us, is by design a political body, not a court, and its

---

[4] 323 US 192, 15 LRRM 708 (1944).
[5] 619 F2d 1229, 103 LRRM 2321 (CA 8, 1980).
[6] 429 US 507, 94 LRRM 2628 (1977).

decisions have perenially (and properly) been a reflection of the policies of the party in power. Deregulation of the market, and the growing internationalization of manufacturing industries, he asserts, not the Board's administration of the Act, is responsible for much of the "malaise" that currently affects unions. Oberer sees no reason to re-erect regulatory controls of internal markets to assist labor. Such restrictions, he asserts, are inconsistent with the nature of a free society and are wasteful of societal resources.

The dwindling size and strength of American unions today, Professor Oberer concludes, are a function not of legal policy, but of the lack of a perceived need among the unorganized, particularly those employed in the growing service sector of the economy, for unions and the collective bargaining process. It is Oberer's (admittedly impressionistic) sense that today's workers lack what he terms the "sense of grievance" that characterized employees of an earlier era.

While unions are an essential part of a free society, he asserts that our society has retained its basic freedoms despite the decline in their strength and membership. Indeed, he claims, American society has reason "to feel gratified" by its workers' assessment of their position, which accepts "the status quo." Professor Oberer concludes his paper by questioning whether unions and collective bargaining will be sufficiently flexible to endure the necessity for cooperation with management that international economic competition has imposed.

II. Three Queries

Professor Oberer's paper provoked a number of questions and concerns for me. I have framed three broadly thematic queries as a means to organize and sketch the outlines of some of the more pressing of these.

Initially, I question whether it is accurate to characterize the New Deal triad of labor legislation, the Railway Labor, Norris–LaGuardia, and Wagner Acts, as paternalistic. The principal thrust of these statutes was the removal of impediments to worker self-association that common law courts had erected or recognized and justified through formalistic notions of contractual freedom. This is the foundational aim of the Norris-LaGuardia Act, which outlawed the use of the yellow-dog device that employers had used, with judicial approbation, as a means to squelch employee self-organization. It is also the heart of the Wagner Act's provisions.[7] Similarly, the Railway Labor Act's objective, as the Supreme Court recognized in its landmark *Texas & New Orleans Railroad*[8] opinion, was to prevent interference with worker self-organizational activities. None of these statutes either directs or provides workers' incentives to organize. Rather, they merely extend to workers the same associational freedoms that had been constitutionally guaranteed to citizens who wished to form other types of groups such as churches, political parties, fraternal clubs, and corporations. The existence of the last of these, it should be recalled, had been made possible during the 19th century though the law's recognition and acceptance of flexible contract and organizational devices like the trust.

In considering the question of the paternalistic character of these acts, it is also important to reflect upon the nature of collective bargaining itself—my second query. As the Supreme Court has observed,[9] and as Professor Dunlop notes in the Introduction to this volume, the Wagner Act was innovative neither of the institution nor of the practices of collective bargaining. To expand on some ideas suggested by Willard Wirtz,[10] at the time of the Wagner Act's passage, Congress was forced, after years of vacillating,[11] to make a difficult choice. The existing model for the ordering of the employment relationship, which the common law had developed during the latter part of the 19th century, was premised upon a (mostly fictional) ideal of individual bargaining and justified by formalized notions of

---

[7] Nor is this exemplified by or confined to the operation of the Act's §7 alone. Thus, for instance, like the prohibition against the use of the yellow-dog device, §8(a)(2)'s provisions are designed to bar employers from the use of schemes of collective relations other than through employee organized and controlled groups since these other means serve to obstruct or blunt efforts at work self-association. *See*, Kohler, *Models of Worker Participation: The Uncertain Significance of Section 8(a)(2)*, 27 B.C.L. Rev. ___ (1986) (forthcoming).

[8] Texas & New Orleans R.R. v. Railway Clerks, 281 US 548 (1930).

[9] NLRB v. American Nat'l Ins. Co., 343 US 395, 30 LRRM 2147 (1952).

[10] *Government by Private Groups*, 13 La. L. Rev. 440 (1953).

[11] As early as 1898, the U.S. Industrial Commission that Congress had established in 1894 recommended that the law be changed to permit labor to organize freely and endorsed the idea of collective bargaining. U.S. Industrial Commission, 5 Report of the Industrial Commission on Labor Legislation, H.R. Doc. No. 95, 56th Cong., 1st Sess. (1900). Fifteen years later, another congressionally appointed committee again strongly endorsed collective bargaining in the course of recommending extensive changes in the law governing the employment relationship. *See* U.S. Commission on Industrial Relations, Final Report of the Commission on Industrial Relations (1915).

contractual freedom. Because of the unilateral control this regimen permitted employers over the ordering of the employment
relationship—in effect transferring lawmaking authority into
their hands alone[12]—it was widely regarded as unacceptable and
demand for change was high. The choices lay between a system
of public ordering of the type that exists in Western Europe,
characterized by comprehensive regulation of and strong and
pervasive state intervention in the employment relationship,
and a private ordering system in which workers and their
employers jointly establish and adjust the terms governing their
relationshp through collective agreement. Congress, of course,
chose the latter. In so doing, it merely adopted a model for
ordering that workers themselves had initiated, the characteristics of which had been shaped jointly in an evolutionary
fashion by labor and management.[13] In essence then, collective
bargaining is an institution in which state decisional authority is
delegated to those directly affected to determine, within the
range set by market forces, the law that will govern the employment relationship. In a setting in which the primary form of
wealth and determinant of status is usually one's job, bargaining
affords workers the means to participate directly in the framing
and administration of the law that has the greatest impact on
their daily lives. Self-association for the purposes of bargaining
thus provides employees a means for group self-determination.
In short, taken together, the statutes in question remove some
impediments to, but do not require or encourage employee self-
association. They (secondarily) protect the ordering process,
which developed and proceeds from the "bottom up," but they
do not determine its substantive outcomes.[14] To characterize
this legislation as paternalistic, I find most problematic.

I am also troubled by Professor Oberer's characterization of
the Taft-Hartley amendments as establishing a regimen of "government as umpire." Certainly, this is the way these provisions
are often portrayed in the legal and industrial relations literature. An important question that arises is whether, either by

---

[12] *See generally,* M. Weber, ECONOMY AND SOCIETY 666–70, 705–31 (1978); Rheinstein,
Introduction to MAX WEBER ON LAW AND ECONOMY IN SOCIETY lx–lxi (1954).

[13] For a useful discussion of this development, see M. Derber, THE AMERICAN IDEA OF
INDUSTRIAL DEMOCRACY, 1865–1965 (1970).

[14] For a thoughtful description of collective bargaining as a system of "reflexive" law,
see, Tuebner, *Substantive and Reflexive Elements in Modern Law,* 17 LAW & SOC. REV. 239
(1983).

intent or effect, the Taft-Hartley provisions have been impartial. It is not my purpose to undertake a comprehensive examination of these amendments. As background, however, it is useful to remember that the enactment of the Taft-Hartley amendments culminated a decade's worth of efforts directed at repealing, modifying, confining, or undercutting the Wagner Act's provisions.[15] The bill eventually enacted was the direct heir of these earlier efforts, and consequently many provisions of Taft-Hartley bear their stamp. As Professor Emily Brown has written in evaluating the whole of Taft-Hartley, while some of its provisions have acted to eliminate abuse and to fill in gaps in the existing legislation, "too much of the Act shows that it was the product of men who did not know how things work in industry or in the administration of the NLRA, and of some who wished to weaken the position of all labor organizations in the economic and political scene."[16]

Indeed, one of the more curious things about Taft-Hartley has been the increasingly restrictive effect that its prohibitions against secondary economic activity have had on union rights to speech and freedom of expression. This is best typified by the Supreme Court's recent opinion in *Longshoreman (ILA)* v. *Allied International, Inc.*[17] There, at the members' insistence, the president of the ILA ordered longshoremen to cease handling goods arriving from or destined for the Soviet Union to protest the Russian invasion of Afghanistan. No picket lines were established and no other employees prevented from working. In its review, the Supreme Court found that the ILA's protest was purely political in nature and had no labor relations objectives. Nevertheless, stated the Court, where, as in the case at bar, such union activity "can reasonably be expected to threaten" a neutral with substantial economic loss, it necessarily has the unlawful object of coercing them.[18] Thus, it concluded that the ILA's activity was proscribed by Section 8(b)(4) and, as a consequence, unprotected by the First Amendment. The Court's rationale for permitting the restriction of the union's speech activities con-

---

[15] *See* J. Gross, The Reshaping of the National Labor Relations Board: National Labor Policy Transition, 1937–1947 187–99, 251–59 (1981); H. Millis & E. Brown, From the Wagner Act to Taft-Hartley: A Study of National Labor Policy 241–362 (1965).

[16] Millis & Brown, *supra* note 15, at 665.

[17] 456 US 212, 110 LRRM 2001 (1982).

[18] *Id.* at 224.

sisted in an *ipse dixit:* It simply stated that the application of
Section 8(b)(4) would "not infringe upon the First Amendment
rights of the ILA and its members."[19]

In the wake of this case, it appears that whether the speech
activities of a union or its members gain constitutional protection
depends solely upon their expected economic impact on third
parties. This works a substantial departure from established
First Amendment doctrine, and the trend in the cases is most
troubling. When compared with cases involving other organizations, it becomes clear that unions as associations, and their
members when acting through them, enjoy far fewer speech
rights than do other types of associations and their members.
This point is perhaps most clearly made by contrasting *Allied*
with a decision handed down in the same term, *NAACP* v.
Clairborne Hardware Co.[20] There the Court held that all non-
violent aspects of a boycott of white-owned businesses by blacks
that had both primary (the hiring of blacks by the merchants) but
predominantly secondary (influencing through pressure on the
merchants changes in governmental policies) goals constituted
protected expression under the First Amendment. The Court
acknowledged that "the petitioners certainly foresaw—and
directly intended—that the merchants would sustain economic
injury as a result of their campaign."[21] Nevertheless, the Court
ruled that the boycott was not subject to state regulation because
of its political nature. This is not the occasion for a thoroughgo-
ing analysis of all the pertinent cases in this area. In passing,
however, it might be noted that the Court has also shown a
greater solicitude for the speech rights of corporations and for
commercial speech in general than it has when a union is
involved, as the Court's opinions in *First National Bank of Boston* v.
Bellotti[22] and *Central Hudson Gas & Electric Corp.* v. *Public Service
Commission*[23] exemplify.

Upon brief reflection, the isolation of unions from the extent
of First Amendment protections afforded other types of associations is not surprising. As Justice Frankfurter observed in his
dissent in *Machinists* v. *Street,*[24] the notion that there is no connec-

---

[19] *Id.* at 226.
[20] 458 US 886 (1982).
[21] *Id.* at 914.
[22] 435 US 765 (1978).
[23] 447 US 557 (1980).
[24] 367 US 740, 48 LRRM 2345 (1961).

tion between economic power and political voice is "pre-Victorian."[25] The Taft-Hartley amendments have provided government with substantial power to control the manner in which unions can employ their economic strength; the possibility for the use of that power has also been extended to employers through the damage action provided for in the Act's Section 303. Significantly, these provisions only apply to unions, not to other groups or associations like corporations. That the exercise of this power has resulted in the narrowing of the scope of union speech rights is perhaps not wholly to be unexpected. The likelihood that a statute so constructed can be impartial in its effects seem slight indeed.

III. Law as Narrative

In a recent, insightful essay, James Boyd White reminds us of the constitutive nature of law.[26] By it, relational patterns are shaped, duties announced and defined, expectations created; in all, it is a means through which a society makes itself to be what it is. Law is also didactic; thus, as it shapes what we are, so it helps to determine what we as a society will become. Law then is not a static thing, but a reflexive process, one means by which society continually remakes itself. As such, law is also a carrier of meanings. To borrow White's phrasing, it is at heart a "narrative," a way society has of "telling a story" about itself.[27]

So conceiving law, I was pleased by Professor Oberer's reference to Dean Leon Green who emphasized the importance of being attentive to the "environmental facts," by which he meant the patterns of community mores, beliefs, and values that are reflected in and form the core of law and legal doctrine.[28] Consistent with Dean Green's admonition, I turn here to consider briefly what kind of a story the law may be telling us about the future of collective bargaining as a social institution, and what that may portend for democratic ordering more generally. My inquiry consists of three strands, which through their intertwining make up the object of my concern.

---

[25] *Id.* at 814 (Frankfurter, J., dissenting).
[26] *Law as Rhetoric, Rhetoric as Law: The Arts of Cultural and Communal Life*, 52 U. Chi. L. Rev. 684 (1985).
[27] *Id.* at 691–92.
[28] *Tort Law Public Law in Disguise*, 38 Tex. L. Rev. 22, 24 (1959).

I begin by looking at the *first strand, the impact the law regulating union activity has had on the institution of collective bargaining.* As a society, we have never been very comfortable with the idea of truly free collective bargaining, that is, permitting the parties, free of governmental intervention, to frame and administer privately the order of their relationship. As is attested by its development and continued existence in a setting often hostile to it, and as the recent Saturn plant agreement between General Motors and the Automobile Workers illustrates, collective bargaining can be a flexible and resilient system for ordering. It permits and requires the parties themselves to determine the pattern and form of their relationships, and to adapt its order to changing conditions. It thus can truly be a means for "grass-roots" self-constitution.

Though in theory its role is limited to protecting the mechanisms for ordering, government has long intruded itself into the substance of the process and thereby affected both its shape and its outcomes. It has done this, often unwittingly, in a variety of ways. One means has been through judicial intervention into bargaining. The Court's *Borg-Warner*[29] opinion, of course, provided the judiciary with a large portal into a process from which it had been excluded. The significance of *Borg-Warner,* while hard to overstate, is difficult to portray accurately. Its import, I believe, does not lie primarily in any effects its holding might be thought to have on the allocation of power in bargaining between the parties themselves. As Professor Feller notes,[30] the line between mandatory and permissive topics is an illusory one; in actual practice, parties constantly bargain and apply economic pressure over the latter. In one respect then, *Borg-Warner* merely places a premium upon skilled bargaining. To me, the insidious aspect of *Borg-Warner* is that, through it and its progeny, the Court has been enabled to shape for itself—and for other readers of legal opinions—a view about the nature of the process and the types and character of issues appropriate to and capable of being arranged through it. In turn, it also shapes views about the types of concerns about which unions and their members acting through them may appropriately and legitimately speak. To a large extent, *Borg-Warner* and its progeny have created a vicious ratiocinative circle in which the source of

---

[29] NLRB v. Borg-Warner Corp., 356 US 342, 42 LRRM 2034 (1958).
[30] Feller, *Response,* 11 N.Y.U. Rev. L. & Soc. Change 136, 137–38 (1982).

the Court's understanding of the purposes and roles of the institution of bargaining and of labor unions is largely based upon its own characterization of them. Unfortunately, the sterile medium of appellate opinions has been the school for much of what the judiciary (and the bar) know about these subjects and through which they inform society about them. An important contributing factor to this problem has been the loss of institutional memory within the Court about the nature and goals of bargaining.[31] The habits of practice and mind that the *Borg-Warner* progeny inculcate and encourage are many and often subtly expressed. While my thesis can only be briefly sketched here, some examples may suggest the contours of the effects on bargaining that I believe these holdings have had.

The narrowness with which its self-instruction has taught the Supreme Court to conceive of the nature of bargaining and the role of unions goes far in helping to explain the restrictive approach it has taken toward union speech rights. For example, in the *Allied International* case, the Court approvingly quoted the First Circuit's statement that the "random political objective" of the Longshoremen's boycott was objectionable because it was "far removed from what has traditionally been thought to be the realm of legitimate union activity."[32] Since *Borg-Warner,* these activities have been defined with increasing restrictivity, as a comparison of the holding and policies of the Court's *Fibreboard*[33] opinion with its recent decision in *First National Maintenance*[34] reveals. Indeed, the trend in these cases shows an ever-narrowing vision of the types of matters that are susceptible to arrangement by the parties through their own lawmaking. It also perforce demonstrates an increasing skepticism and lack of confidence on the Court's part about the ability of the parties to arrange their own affairs and the capacity of private ordering as the means to do it. Increasingly, the trend has been that the state, through the judiciary, has attempted to determine the agenda for ordering rather than permitting the parties to shape and decide it themselves, based on their own views of what its subject matter should be free from the obstruction and distortion that

---

[31] For two cases that reflect this loss, *compare* NLRB v. Insurance Agents Int'l Union, 361 US 477, 45 LRRM 2705 (1960) with First Nat'l Maintenance Corp. v. NLRB, 452 US 666, 107 LRRM 2705 (1981).

[32] *Supra* note 17, 456 US at 225–26.

[33] Fibreboard Paper Prods. Co. v. NLRB, 379 US 203, 57 LRRM 2609 (1964).

[34] *Supra* note 31.

may result through state efforts to control the substance of the process. That the Court's self-generated views about that subject matter has distorted the manner in which the private ordering process works seems clear. For example, as noted, the *Borg-Warner* dichotomy promotes confusion and subterfuge in bargaining by requiring a party to appear to go to impasse over a Court-approved mandatory topic to gain discussion of, or change in, an issue adjudged to be permissive in nature. The Court's choice of strategy over candor advances a view of collective bargaining that tends to undercut faith in it as a rational means for ordering; it also acts to shape behavior in ways that tend to confirm the portrayal.

Legislation, of course, has also been responsible for enlarging the government's role in and influence over bargaining. Statutory regulation of the expression of union economic power again provides a prominent example. As Professor Clyde Summers has pointed out,[35] the objective of protecting neutrals that was sought through Sections 8(b)(4) and 303 are wholly inconsistent with the inherent character of collective bargaining. The use of economic pressure tactics, he observes, is a part of the private-ordering system, and resort to them should not be viewed as pathologic.[36] In an integrated economy, however, uninterested parties are inevitably affected by their use; the impact of the application of these tactics spreads like the concentric rings that ripple around a stone cast into still water. This, Professor Summers states is the price society pays for free collective bargaining. Some of the costs of its avoidance through increased governmental intervention have already been mentioned; another will be discussed shortly. Legislation has also had the effect of removing issues from the parties by making them the subject of direct regulation, or by indirectly shaping the outcome of ordering through the influence of adjacent statutory schemes.

As the trend toward public ordering of the employment relationship continues, the American labor law scheme is tending to converge with those that obtain in Western European countries, which, as noted, are characterized by pervasive state control of and intervention in the relationship. This trend toward convergence, and the growth in state influence over the relationship

---

[35] *A Summary Evaluation of the Taft-Hartley Act*, 11 INDUS. & LAB. REL. REV. 405 (1957).
[36] NLRB v. Insurance Agents' Int'l Union, *supra* note 31.

generally, was forecast by the comparative economic studies conducted by Professors Kerr, Dunlop, Harbison, and Myers.[37] Ironically, however, at a time when confidence in and the practice of collective bargaining are on the decline in the United States, interest in collective bargaining is growing among some major Western European nations. For example, an effort is being made in France through law reform to introduce and encourage its practice along lines familiar to Americans.[38]

The *second strand* of the narrative the law tells concerns a closely allied phenomenon: The *reentry of common law courts into the regulation of the employment relationship* through their modifications of the employment-at-will doctrine. The courts have relied on various theories by which to effect these changes, including public policy exceptions to the rule's operation and approaches rooted in contract and tort.[39] Though their discussion is out of place here, such theories raise fascinating legal process and source of law problems, and the area in general provides a unique perspective upon the manner in which common law courts operate.

Significantly, these developments at common law are occurring at a time when union membership and the practice of bargaining have been steadily declining and when the private ordering process has become increasingly rigidified and constricted in scope through legislative and judicial intervention. As was demonstrated 50 years ago, in a society in which job, wealth, and status are so closely bound it is not a societally acceptable notion to permit unilateral control over the relationship to rest in the hands of the employing entity. When private governance through self-associated groups declines, direct state intervention is inevitable. Indeed, as common law courts have begun to step into the vacuum, many commentators and groups have called for statutory schemes to restrict dismissals save in circumstances where just cause exists.[40] That such protections have

---

[37] C. Kerr, J. Dunlop, F. Harbison, & C. Myers, INDUSTRIALISM AND INDUSTRIAL MAN RECONSIDERED: SOME PERSPECTIVES ON A STUDY OVER TWO DECADES OF THE PROBLEMS OF LABOR AND MANAGEMENT IN ECONOMIC GROWTH (1975).

[38] *See* Glendon, *French Labor Law Reform 1982–83: The Struggle for Collective Bargaining,* 32 AM. J. COMP. L. 449 (1984).

[39] For a brief overview of these theories, *see* Wagenseller v. Scottsdale Memorial Hosp., 119 LRRM 3166 (Ariz., 1985).

[40] *See, e.g.,* State Bar of California, Labor and Employment Law Section, TO STRIKE A NEW BALANCE: A REPORT OF THE AD HOC COMMITTEE ON TERMINATION AT WILL AND WRONGFUL DISCHARGE APPOINTED BY THE LABOR AND EMPLOYMENT LAW SECTION OF THE STATE BAR OF CALIFORNIA (1985).

only been available to the increasingly small portion of the work force covered by collective bargaining agreements, it is force-fully argued, is unfair and inconsistent with societal needs.[41]

Due to costs associated with litigation, the primary benefici-aries of the developing common law protections, thus far, seem to have been mid- and upper-level managerial employees. Growing opinion, however, suggests that the existence of these protections and the extension of their availability throughout the work force by statute, coupled with the growth of other protective legislation, will do away with the need for employee self-association and collective bargaining altogether.[42] It is diffi-cult to know to what extent that perception is held by the popula-tion generally. The growth of state influence in and control over the ordering of the employment relationship, however, is consis-tent with the forecasts of comparative economists and other interested scholars.[43]

The *emphasis on individualism* so characteristic of American society is the *third strand* in my inquiry. Because it is such a deeply embedded theme, it is perhaps the most abstract of the three mentioned. It is also undoubtedly the most powerful in its implications.

In his classic study, *Democracy in America,* Alexis de Toc-queville, writing in the mid-1830s, noted that the word indi-vidualism was new. "Our fathers," he wrote, "only knew about egoism," which he defined as a "passionate and exaggerated love of self" which leads persons to think about all things in terms of themselves. Individualism, on the other hand, "is a calm and considered feeling which disposes each citizen to isolate himself" from others and to leave the greater society to see to itself. Egoism, de Tocqueville states, "springs from a blind instinct," while individualism instead is rooted "in misguided judgement rather than depraved feeling," which "is due more to inadequate understanding than to perversity of heart."[44] This new feeling, de Tocqueville wrote, originated in democracy and would grow as social equality spread. Its effect, he forecast, would be to form in people the habit of "thinking of themselves in isolation"[45] and

---

[41] *Id.*

[42] *E.g., Beyond Unions,* BUS. WEEK, July 8, 1985, at 72.

[43] *See* Kerr, Dunlop, Harbison, & Myers, *supra* note 37; D. Bell, THE COMING OF POST-INDUSTRIAL SOCIETY (1973).

[44] DEMOCRACY IN AMERICA 506–507 (1968).

[45] *Id.* at 508.

imagining that the whole of their destinies rests in their hands alone, unaffected by what occurs to the community in general.

Such habits, de Tocqueville warned, threatened democracy itself. Despotism, he noted, guarantees its continuation through the isolation of its citizens. It puts barriers to their association, encourages people to mind solely their own affairs, and promotes indifference and detachment as sorts of public virtues. Though dangerous in all times, de Tocqueville stated, despotism is especially to be feared in a democracy since the "vices originated in despotism are those favored" by conditions of equality and democracy.[46]

The kind of despotism which threatens a democracy, de Tocqueville observed, is of a different character from those seen in the past. It would consist of a form of soft tyranny, whose oppression would "degrade man rather than torment them."[47] The people in this regimen exist for and in themselves, each preoccupied by his own matters, unaware and unconcerned with the fate of others, save that of his children and nearest friends. The role of government is as an "immense, protective power."[48] It works for the peoples' happiness by anticipating and providing for their needs, managing and settling their concerns, and ordering their affairs. It slowly "restricts the activity of free will within a narrower compass"[49] by continually extending the reach and scope of its decisionmaking over matters both great and slight. Its intervention in the latter, stated de Tocqueville, is even more malignant than control over the former. "Subjection in petty affairs,"[50] he explained, manifests itself daily and affects all citizens. While it "never drives men to despair,"[51] it does teach them to give up the use of their free will. Such a government, he stated, "does not break men's will, but softens, bends and guides it; it seldom enjoins, but often inhibits."[52] In this regimen, he declared, "the citizens quit their state of dependence just long enough to choose their masters, and then fall back into it."[53] The product of this system is an inert citizenry who are the objects of

---

[46] *Id.* at 509–10.
[47] *Id.* at 691.
[48] *Id.* at 692.
[49] *Id.*
[50] *Id.* at 694.
[51] *Id.*
[52] *Id.*
[53] *Id.* at 693.

administration rather than active agents determining their own course.

The pernicious effects of this individualism, de Tocqueville wrote, had been neutralized in the United States by the formation of free associations of all types.[54] Through these groups, citizens undertake to accomplish the ends of daily life, putting the control of and responsibility for these matters directly into their hands. Self-government is thereby promoted, autonomy safeguarded and increased. Such associations are thus schools for democracy, where habits of self-rule are inculcated and practiced. "The more government takes the place of associations," warned de Tocqueville, "the more will individuals lose the idea of forming associations and need the government to come to their help. That is a vicious circle of cause and effect."[55]

The narrative the law tells suggests that just such a vicious circle has been operating. As employee self-association and the practice of collective bargaining have declined, the state is increasingly coming to determine the order of the employment relationship. For the reasons delineated by de Tocqueville, I find such a trend most alarming.[56] Consequently, I am far less sanguine about the "status quo"—and the future—than is Professor Oberer.

I do not mean to be understood as suggesting that unionism be mandated or that means be found to spark what Professor Oberer termed the "sense of grievance" among employees. I do suggest, however, that this is an appropriate moment to consider and evaluate carefully our present situation. Law is a constitutive force in society and does significantly influence what we are and will become. Collective bargaining affords citizens the means to participate in the forming and administration of the law that determines the details of daily life. It thereby encourages the habits of self-governance and direct responsibility. It also affords individuals increased control over their personal circumstances. Collective bargaining then is like de Tocqueville's New England Township: as institutions they "are to liberty what primary schools are to science; they teach people to appreciate

---

[54] *Id.* at 509–17.

[55] *Id.* at 515.

[56] The existence in present American society of the sort of atomized individualism forecast by de Tocqueville as likely to develop is confirmed by R. Bellah, R. Madsen, W. Sullivan, A. Swindler, & S. Tipton in their study, HABITS OF THE HEART: INDIVIDUALISM AND COMMITMENT IN AMERICAN LIFE (1985).

its peaceful enjoyment and accustom them to make use of it."[57] A long view of the matter suggests that our best interest as a society may be best served by removing the obstructions and impediments to private ordering before that opportunity is completely foreclosed.

---

[57] *Supra* note 44, at 63.

CHAPTER 6

BOARD PROCEDURES, REMEDIES, AND THE ENFORCEMENT PROCESS

CHARLES J. MORRIS*

The 50th anniversary of the National Labor Relations Act provides one more occasion to assess the Labor Board's performance. That performance has been assessed many times before, indeed with boring regularity.[1] The resulting cries of woe and despair have been heard so often that one can only wonder whether there is anyone out there listening, and whether the appraisal on which I am about to embark will be ignored as just another cry of wolf. Perhaps. But 50 years is surely time enough for the Board to have demonstrated whether it can reasonably fulfill the primary statutory objectives with which it was invested.

This paper focuses on Board procedures, structural organization, and remedial processes. It does not directly examine substantive law. Of course changes in substantive law usually attract the most public attention. The pendulum-like swings of substantive law from administration to administration are indeed noteworthy; and whenever a major substantive law decision is

---

*Professor of Law, Southern Methodist University.

[1] *E.g.*, to note only some of the recent literature: Gould, *Some Reflections on Fifty Years of the National Labor Relations Act: The Need for Labor Board and Labor Law Reform*, 38 STAN. L. REV. 937 (1986); Mikva, *The Changing Role of the Wagner Act in the American Labor Movement*, 38 STAN. L. REV. 1123 (1986); Weiler, *Milestone or Tombstone: The Wagner Act At Fifty*, 23 HARV. J. ON LEGIS. 1 (1986); St. Antoine, *Federal Regulation of the Workplace in the Next Half Century*, 61 CHI.-KENT L. REV. 631 (1985); Gross, *Conflicting Statutory Purposes: Another Look at Fifty Years of NLRB Law Making*, 39 INDUS. & LAB. REL. REV. 7 (1985); Morris & Turk, *A Labor Board Roundup and Forecast: The Balance Continues*, 11 EMPLOYEE REL. L.J. 32 (1985); Estreicher, *Policy Oscillation at the Labor Board: A Plea for Rulemaking*, 37 AD. L. REV. 163 (1985); Dotson, *Processing Cases at the NLRB*, 34 LAB. L.J. 215 (1985); Walther, *Suggestions and Comments on the Future Direction of the NLRB*, 34 LAB. L.J. 215 (1985); Weiler, *Striking a New Balance: Freedom of Contract and the Prospects for Union Representation*, 98 HARV. L. REV. 1769 (1983); Modjeska, *In Defense of the NLRB*, 33 MERCER L. REV. 851 (1982); Irving, *Crisis at the NLRB: A Call for Reordering Priorities*, 7 EMPLOYEE REL. L.J. 47 (1981); Irving, *Do We Need a Labor Board?*, 30 LAB. L.J. 389 (1979); Fanning, *National Labor Relations Act and the Role of the NLRB*, 29 LAB. L.J. 683 (1978).

overturned one is again reminded of the doctrinal instability which characterizes the interpretation of the National Labor Relations Act. But I am of the view that such substantive law changes, whether effected by the Reagan Board, by a prior Board, or by a future Board, are of lesser importance than the slow and silent erosion of the Board's enforcement authority which has been occurring for more than two decades.

Although the pace of this deterioration has been gradual, its consequences have been devastating. This erosion of the Board's effectiveness has undermined its capacity to discharge its basic statutory duties. So much so that I am convinced that if the Board can no longer fulfill the essential objectives of the Act, then it should move over and allow some other entity to take its place. To translate a well-known expression: The time has come for the NLRB either to do what it is supposed to do or get off the vessel on which it is sitting.

If the Board as an institution is either structurally unable or politically unwilling to enforce the statute, and enforce it with stability and reasonable regard for stare decisis—assuming that we really want to enforce the statute—then perhaps we should explore some other means to accomplish that task. One such means would be an Article III labor court.[2] That alternative, however, should be viewed as a last resort. On the other hand, if the Board does have the statutory capacity to function as Congress intended—and I firmly believe that it has—and if the real problem is essentially an institutional unwillingness to utilize available statutory procedures and remedies, a reinvigorated Board determined to enforce the Act, which may be improbable but not inconceivable, would be preferable to a labor court, for the latter alternative would indeed represent a drastic and unfamiliar direction for American labor law. Although a labor court should, theoretically, function soundly and efficiently, it would still be an untried entity; therefore such an option should be pursued only after it has been demonstrated beyond a reasonable doubt that the Board is either inherently incapable of fulfilling its major statutory functions or is not likely to do so in the foreseeable future.

Although a strong case can be made for an Article III court, and I shall discuss some of the features of such a court in this

---

[2] See Morris, The Case for Unitary Enforcement of Federal Labor Law—Concerning a Specialized Article III Court and the Reorganization of Existing Agencies, 26 Sw. L.J. 471 (1972).

paper, I prefer on this occasion to stress the desirability of attempting a nonlegislative restructuring and a corresponding revitalization of the Labor Board itself. I believe such an approach is possible, though perhaps not very probable in view of the formidable political and inertial forces that such a program would have to overcome. Nevertheless, in case an institutional desire to enforce the Act effectively should unexpectedly arise in the future, it seems appropriate to explore what could be accomplished under the existing statute.

I. Statutory Objectives

I began this discussion with the assumption that the Board has not been fulfilling its basic statutory objectives. Although that conclusion has been amply documented,[3] I shall nevertheless review some of the pertinent studies and also some statistical evidence, for I want to compare such data against an available objective standard that defines what the Board's enforcement record ought to be. What standard could be more objective than the one provided by the statement of congressional intent imprinted upon the statute itself? Reexamination of that statutory intent is in order because there has been an inaccurate perception in much of the recent debate about the fundamental roles of the National Labor Relations Board. Statutory language and legislative history are clear, however, as to what those roles were intended to be.

Let me note the obvious at the outset. The original intent contained in the Wagner Act was substantially expanded by later legislative amendments, particularly by the Taft-Hartley Act. However, notwithstanding some revisionist views to the contrary, those amendments did not change the core objective of the statute. That conclusion may come as a surprise to some, but the

---

[3] *See, e.g.,* Flanagan, *NLRA Litigation and Union Representation,* 38 STAN. L. REV. 957 (1986); W. Cooke, UNION ORGANIZING AND PUBLIC POLICY: FAILURE TO SECURE FIRST CONTRACTS (1985); R. Freeman & J. Medoff, WHAT DO UNIONS DO? 228–45 (1984); Kleiner, *Unionism and Employer Discrimination: Analysis of 8(a)(3) Violations,* 23 INDUS. REL. 234 (1984); Weiler, *Promises to Keep: Securing Workers' Rights to Self-Organization Under the NLRA,* 96 HARV. L. REV. 1769 (1983); U.S. General Accounting Office, *Concerns Regarding Impact of Employee Charges Against Employers for Unfair Labor Practices* (1982); Roomkin & Block, *Case Processing Time and the Outcome of Representation Elections: Some Empirical Evidence,* U. ILL. L.F. 75 (1981); S. Catler, *Labor Union Representation Elections: What Determines Who Wins?* (unpublished thesis, 1978), summarized in R. Freeman & J. Medoff, *supra* at 235.

evidence for it is written clearly in the amended statute itself, and it was authoritatively voiced in pertinent legislative reports and debates. While it is true that the Taft-Hartley Act added two important new dimensions to the scope of the Act, the underlying statutory objective remained intact.

There are two statutory statements of policy to be examined. Section 1[4] of the original Wagner Act set out the basic statutory objective. And although the Taft-Hartley Congress added language to that section, the expression of the Act's core intent was deliberately left undisturbed. The Taft-Hartley Congress also added another declaration of intent in the overall Labor Management Relations Act, which was a separate Section 1[5] that preceded Title I, which became the amended version of the National Labor Relations Act. Both declarations require our attention.

The Wagner Act declaration opened by stating that "[t]he denial by employers of the right of employees to organize and the refusal by employers to accept the procedure of collective bargaining lead to strikes and other forms of industrial strife or unrest . . ."; the Taft-Hartley Congress changed that statement by inserting the word "some" before "employers" in both phrases. It thus removed the blanket indictment of *all* employers but still pointly accused "some employers" of denying employees the right to organize and of refusing to accept the collective bargaining process. This was taken from the Senate version of the amended Act,[6] but the House acceded to it following its adoption by Conference Committee. The original House version would have eliminated the Wagner Act declaration of policy completely.[7] The Congress thus deliberately retained the Wagner Act declaration of basic statutory policy, which included the following statements:

> Experience has proved that protection by law of the right of employees to organize and bargain collectively safeguards commerce from injury, impairment, or interruption, and promotes the flow of commerce by removing certain recognized sources of industrial strife and unrest, by encouraging practices fundamental to the

---

[4] National Labor Relations (Wagner) Act [hereinafter NLRA] §1, 29 USC §151 (1982).
[5] Labor Management Relations (Taft-Hartley) Act [hereinafter LMRA] §101 (1947), 29 USC §141 (1982).
[6] S. 1126, 80th Cong., 1st Sess. (1947).
[7] H.R. 3020, 80th Cong., 1st Sess. (1947).

friendly adjustment of industrial disputes . . . and by restoring
equality of bargaining power between employers and employees.

Whereupon it was expressly declared that the "policy of the
United States" was the

> encouraging [of] the practice and procedure of collective bargaining
> and . . . protecting the exercise by workers of full freedom of asso-
> ciation, self-organization, and designation of representatives of
> their own choosing, for the purpose of negotiating the terms and
> conditions of their employment or other mutual aid or protection.

The Taft-Hartley Act thus reaffirmed those statements as the
central policy of the statute.

That being so, has there been a misapprehension of the congressional intent behind the Taft-Hartley Act? Yes, and that
misapprehension stems from a popular failure to distinguish
between the *perception* of certain anticollective bargaining decisions of the Board and the conspicuous failure of the Board to
provide vigorous enforcement of Section 7 rights and the *reality*
of the compromise which was reached in the Taft-Hartley conference committee to reconcile differences between the House
and Senate bills. A distinction should thus be made between
what the Board has done—or failed to do—since passage of
Taft-Hartley and what the statute actually says that it should do.
Time may have changed the popular perception of the proper
role of the NLRB, but it should not have had any effect on the
determination of what the congressional intent was in 1947.
Accordingly, I cannot fully agree with James Gross' assessment
that "the Taft-Hartley Act contains conflicting statements of
purpose that open the national labor law to conflicting interpretations of congressional intent."[8] Regardless of his observation that "Smith, Hartley, and the majority of the House
certainly did not intend to promote collective bargaining as the
solution to labor problems,"[9] the fact remains that the conference committee rejected the House bill's attempted repeal of

---

[8] Gross, *supra* note 1, at 13.

[9] *Id.* Gross seems to ignore the conference committee's rejection of the House's version
and its pointed retention of the basic Wagner Act objectives, which also added the new
paragraph relative to union unfair labor practices, for he concludes that the LMRA's new
"statement of policy . . . was intended at least to weaken, and possibly to eliminate,
collective bargaining." *Id.* Such a conclusion is an unwarranted reading of legislative
history in view of the unambiguous language of the statute and the specific rejection of the
House sponsor's anticollective bargaining position.

the statutory statement that collective bargaining is the national labor policy; and there is nothing in the separate statement of "purpose and policy" contained in the new Taft-Hartley preamble which diluted or was inconsistent with that core statement of policy.

It is true that most of the new Taft-Hartley provisions could be—and they certainly were—viewed as antiunion. But those provisions, as well as the corresponding provisions declaring the legislative purpose, did not change the core objective of the statute. Primarily, the Taft-Hartley amendments added substantial union unfair labor practices and also a number of provisions which slowed down the procedures for establishing representation. These amendments did indeed provide new statutory objectives for the Board, but they were in addition to, not a replacement for, the Act's original objectives. The new provisions were reflected in a new paragraph[10] inserted within the original Wagner Act statement of policy, which noted "certain practices of some labor organizations . . . burdening or obstructing commerce . . . through strikes and other forms of industrial unrest. . . ." Additionally, as previously noted, there was a separate "Declaration of Policy" added to the all-inclusive Labor Management Relations Act which stressed the need for "employers, employees, and labor organizations each [to] recognize under law one another's legitimate rights in relations with each other. . . ." That declaration further stated that:

> It is the purpose and policy of this Act . . . to prescribe the legitimate rights of both employees and employers in their relations affecting commerce, to provide orderly and peaceful procedures for preventing the interference by either with the legitimate rights of the other, to protect the rights of individual employees in their relations with labor organizations . . ., to define and proscribe practices on the part of labor and management which . . . are inimical to the general welfare, and to protect the rights of the public in connection with labor disputes. . . .

It thus seems clear that the totality of the policy language in the Taft-Hartley Act did two things: *First,* it reaffirmed the basic objectives of the Wagner Act, which were to protect the right of employees to organize and to encourage the "practice and procedure" of collective bargaining. *Second,* it declared certain

---

[10] LMRA §101, 29 USC §141 (1982).

activities of labor organizations to be improper; but in doing so it emphasized the use of "orderly and peaceful procedures" for dispute settlement, which procedures were provided by the statute. Indeed, the statute not only provided for the National Labor Relations Board, it also provided, among other things, for the establishment of the Federal Mediation and Conciliation Service,[11] for a procedure to handle national emergency disputes,[12] and for judicial enforcement of collective bargaining agreements.[13] Nowhere did the statute provide for any dilution of Section 7[14] rights; indeed it reaffirmed and added to those rights, for it provided that employees would also have "the right to refrain" from organizational and concerted activities. And nowhere did it retreat from the guarantee of the right of employees to "form, join, or assist labor organizations" or deviate in any manner from the statutory commitment to the concept of collective bargaining as the cornerstone of national labor policy. Indeed, in commenting on the bill which he and his committee colleagues were recommending,[15] Senator Taft reaffirmed the centrality of collective bargaining. He said:

> Basically, I believe that the committee feels, almost unanimously, that the solution of our labor problems must rest on a free economy and on free collective bargaining. The bill is certainly based on that proposition.[16]

And during the Senate debate which preceded the vote to override President Truman's veto, Senator Taft emphasized that the bill "is based on *the theory of the Wagner Act. . . .* It is based on the theory that *the solution of the labor problem in the United States is free, collective bargaining. . . .*"[17]

Thus, notwithstanding some popular misconceptions, it is evident from both the language of the statute and its legislative history that the Taft-Hartley Act did not change the basic national commitment to the encouragement of collective bargaining and the protection of the rights of employees under

---

[11] LMRA §202 (1947), 29 USC §172 (1982).

[12] LMRA §§206–210, 29 USC §§176–179 (as codified (1964)).

[13] LMRA §301, 29 USC §185 (1982).

[14] LMRA §7, 29 USC §157 (1982).

[15] SENATE COMMITTEE ON LABOR AND PUBLIC WELFARE, S. REP. No. 1126, 80th Cong., 1st Sess. (1947).

[16] 2 LEGISLATIVE HISTORY OF THE LABOR MANAGEMENT RELATIONS ACT, 1947 at 1007 (1948).

[17] *Id.* at 1653 (emphasis added).

Section 7 to organize and engage in concerted activity for "the purpose of collective bargaining or other mutual aid or protection." It only added that employees also had the right to refrain from such activity.[18]

Consequently, although the 80th Congress substantially amended the Wagner Act, the nature of those amendments did not alter the basic statutory direction of national labor policy. The 80th Congress was concerned with the power of "big labor." The hearings and debates and the resulting legislation focused on curbing much of that power regarding secondary boycotts, closed- and union-shop agreements, certain strikes and picketing which on occasion had turned into violent confrontations, jurisdictional disputes, and certain features of internal union affairs. Important structural and procedural modifications, particularly the separation of the office of General Counsel from the Board proper, were also enacted. And the Supreme Court's pronouncement regarding the Constitutional right of free speech[19] was codified into Section 8(c) of the statute. But *no substantive changes were made in the text of the provisions defining employer unfair labor practices.* Nor were any such changes made by the 1959 Landrum-Griffin amendments.[20] Accordingly, the employer unfair labor practices which are contained in the statute today are basically the same as they were 50 years ago, and their accompanying declarations of congressional intent were reconfirmed by the Taft-Hartley Congress and not disturbed by the Landrum-Griffin Congress.

The objective standard by which the Board's record should be measured is therefore the declaration of policy contained in Section 1 of the NLRA. Accordingly, in assessing how well the Board has fulfilled its statutory mandate, we must look primarily to Sections 7 and 8(a), for these are the provisions which con-

---

[18] Professor Gross accurately observes that: "The 1947 Declaration of Policy, coupled with a passage added in 1947 to Section 7 that affirms workers' right to refrain from engaging in collective bargaining, has been interpreted to mean that free choice and individual rights are at least as important as the right to collective bargaining." *Id.* But the right of employees to refrain from engaging in Section 7 activity was never intended to diminish the enforcement of Section 7 rights for employees who affirmatively wish to exercise them.

[19] NLRB v. Virginia Elec. & Power Co., 314 US 469, 9 LRRM 405 (1941). *See also* NLRB v. American Tube Bending Co., 134 F2d 993, 12 LRRM 615 (CA 2), *cert. denied,* 320 US 768 (1943). See discussion in C. Morris, ed., Dev. Lab. Law 2d ed., 80–82 (BNA Books, 1983).

[20] Labor Management Reporting and Disclosure Act, 29 USC §§153, 158–160, 164, 186–187, 401–402, 411–415, 431–440, 461–466, 481–483, 501–504, 521–531 (1959).

tinue to contain the core rights and duties guaranteed by the Act. The union unfair labor practices which were written into Section 8(b) were designed to curb union power; and those provisions, especially the ones which limited the use of economic coercion against employers, have been consistently enforced with remarkable success.[21] The latter provisions, however, are ancillary to the core provisions of Sections 7 and 8(a) because, in the main, union unfair labor practices depend on the existence of established unions. In particular, the secondary boycott and jurisdictional dispute provisions in Section 8(b)(4)[22] assume the existence of unions which have bargaining rights with primary employers; and the recognitional and organizational picketing provisions of Section 8(b)(7),[23] which were added by the Landrum-Griffin Act in 1959, merely emphasize the primacy of Section 9 procedures and requirements for the establishment of union recognition.

II. The Enforcement Record

Whereas the Board's record of enforcement of Sections 8(b)(4) and 8(b)(7) indicates that it has been reasonably efficient as to those unfair labor practices directed against unions, its record of enforcement of the core employee protection sections, that is, cases which involve employer interference with organizational activity under Section 8(a)(1), discriminatory discharge cases under Section 8(a)(3), and refusal-to-bargain cases under Section 8(a)(5), has been woefully inadequate. In addition, the delay factor in both representation ("R") cases and unfair labor practice ("C") cases has severely hampered the implementation of those basic statutory rights. This record of inadequate performance is not a recent phenomenon. It is not a failing that can be charged only to the Reagan Board. Several important studies covering periods of many years have documented the Board's impotence in providing effective enforcement of the core provisions of the statute.

---

[21] *See* Morris, *The Deterrent Effect of Quick, Certain and Strong Remedies on Unfair Labor Practices Under the LMRA,* 15 INDUS. & LAB. REL. REP. 16 (1978); Flanagan, *supra* note 3, at 979–80.

[22] NLRA §8(b)(4), 29 USC §158(b)(4) (1982).

[23] NLRA §8(b)(7) (as amended (1959)), 29 USC §158(b)(7) (1982).

Harvard economists Richard Freeman and James Medoff summarized and evaluated many of those studies and also certain statistical data contained in the Board's annual reports.[24] Among their conclusions are the following:

1. Union success in achieving bargaining rights is significantly lower where there is a long delay between the filing of the petition and the holding of the election. That conclusion is also supported by the independent findings of Myron Roomkin and Richard Block;[25] their study, based on magnetic tape data supplied by the Board for fiscal years 1973–78, found that delay was indeed linked to election outcome, the implication being "that delay affects elections the most when the outcome is in doubt and this class of contests generally result in a vote against unionization."[26] They noted that "[i]f delay results in creating an employer win from what would otherwise be a union win, then the delay has resulted in a change in the substantive outcome of the process."[27]

2. Freeman and Medoff further conclude that illegal employer discrimination against union activists, particularly firing, has a substantial impact on union success in winning elections; and "[o]nly in the rare case where a fired worker is ordered reinstated by the NLRB and actually returns to his job *before* the election does breaking the law backfire."[28]

3. Analyzing Board statistics from 1960 to 1980, they observe that although the number of union elections scarcely changed during that period, the number of illegal activities committed by employers rose 400 percent; the number of charges of discharges for union activity rose 300 percent; and the number of employees awarded back pay rose 500 percent. They translate such impersonal statistics into the stark reality of what actually happens in an election campaign, demonstrating how irrelevant the Board's enforcement processes have become, for they observed that:

Despite increasingly sophisticated methods for disguising the cause of such firings, more employers were judged guilty of firing workers

[24] *Supra* note 3, at 236.
[25] *Case Processing Time and the Outcome of Representation Elections: Some Empirical Evidence*, 1981 U. Ill. L. Rev. 75 (1981).
[26] *Id.* at 90.
[27] *Id.* at 97.
[28] *Supra* note 3, at 236.

for union activity in 1980 than ever before. To obtain an indication of the risk faced by workers desiring a union, one may divide the number of persons fired for union activity in 1980 by the number of persons who voted for a union in elections. The result is remarkable: one in twenty workers who favored the union got fired. Assuming that the vast bulk of union supporters are relatively inactive, the likelihood that an outspoken worker, exercising his or her legal rights under the Taft-Hartley Act, gets fired for union activity is, by these data, extraordinarily high. Put differently, there is roughly one case of illegal discharge deemed meritorious by the NLRB for every NLRB representation election.[29]

Obviously, the Board has not succeeded in providing effective enforcement. Nor has it created a legal atmosphere conducive to the achievement of widespread voluntary compliance. In this regard, the National Labor Relations Act may be compared with Title VII of the 1964 Civil Rights Act,[30] which when enacted was no more popular than the Wagner or Taft-Hartley Acts. The remedial sections of the NLRA and Title VII have much in common. Both provide for "affirmative action" orders, indeed the NLRA was the source of the "affirmative action" language in Title VII;[31] and both statutes are designed to be remedial rather than punitive in their application. The compliance history of the two statutes, however, presents a study in contrasts. Title VII has generally been firmly enforced with meaningful remedies;[32] it has thus proved to be less costly to comply with that statute than to violate it.[33] The opposite has been true of the NLRA. As to the core portions of the latter statute, the Board has patently failed to fulfill its mandate "to prevent" persons from engaging in unfair labor practices[34]—statutory language which implicitly endorses the concept of voluntary compliance. It is an irony of the statutory scheme that Section 10, which covers enforcement, is entitled "*Prevention* of Unfair Labor Practices."[35] In the aggregate, the Board has been singularly unsuccessful in preventing

---

[29] *Id.* at 232–33.

[30] §706(g) of the Civil Rights Act of 1964, Tit. VII, 42 USC §2000e-5(g).

[31] *See* Franks v. Bowman Transp. Co., Inc., 424 US 747, 764 n.21, 12 FEP 549 (1976); Albemarle Paper Co. v. Moody, 422 US 405, 417, 10 FEP 1181 (1975).

[32] *See generally,* B. Schlei & P. Grossman, EMPLOYMENT DISCRIMINATION LAW 2d ed. (BNA Books, 1983).

[33] *See* Blumrosen, *Six Conditions for Meaningful Self-Regulation,* 69 A.B.A.J. 1264 (1983).

[34] National Labor Relations (Wagner) Act §10(a), 29 USC §160(a) (1982).

[35] *Id.* (emphasis added).

the commission of unfair labor practices under the core provisions of the Act.

Not only has the Board not prevented such practices, it has actually *encouraged* their commission by virtue of its ineffective processes. A recently published study by Morris Kleiner[36] found that employers who have been found guilty of unfair labor practices are *more* likely rather than *less* likely to commit further unfair labor practices. The study, which was based on a regression analysis of NLRB case data from 1970 to 1980,[37] determined that:

> Firms that have previously violated Section 8(a)(3) may have found that the marginal benefits outweigh the marginal costs. Firms that violate this section of the Act may find significant benefits in the chilling effect on union organization efforts and on union aggressiveness once they are organized. If this occurs, then using the same (illegal) tactic again may be cost-effective strategy, even if the firm loses the case before an administrative judge.[38]

Observing that empirical results were consistent with that theory, Kleiner noted that

> [t]he past violations variable [was] statistically significant and suggest[ed] that firms that have committed unfair labor practices in previous years are more likely to commit them in the current period. . . . [F]irms that committed past violations were over twice as likely to commit current violations. These results support the hypothesis that the law's penalties do not serve as a major barrier to employer discrimination.[39]

Thus, not only is it cost-effective for an employer to discharge union activists in breach of Section 8(a)(3), a violation which most often occurs before an election, it is apparently also cost-effective for an employer to violate the Act after the election. Evidence also indicates that it is advantageous to an employer's prospects for not reaching agreement on a collective bargaining contract if there is a delay in Board procedures, such as may occur in the processing of objections to an election. A recent

---

[36] *Supra* note 3.

[37] The study examined specific information about a random sample of firms listed on the American Stock Exchange, using Standard and Poors' COMPUSTAT as a data source.

[38] *Id.* at 237.

[39] *Id.* at 240.

investigation of first-contract negotiation outcomes conducted by William Cooke[40] found

> [e]mpirical support . . . for the hypothesis that . . . NLRB delays in the resolution of employer objections and challenges to election results, the refusal to bargain in good faith and discrimination subsequent to election victories have profound effect upon reducing the probability of agreement.[41]

Quantifying the effects of post-election unfair labor practices and delay factors, Cooke concluded that "employers who refused to bargain in good faith and/or illegally discharged union activitists . . . reduced the probability of unions successfully negotiating contracts by 32–36 percentage points;"[42] and the estimated magnitude of negative relationship between NLRB procedural delay and the securing of a contract indicated "that, on average, every one month delay between election date and close of objections and challenges to election outcomes reduces the probability of obtaining an agreement by as much as 4 percentage points."[43] That study thus revealed that even when unions win elections they often fail to achieve the statutory objective of a contractual collective bargaining relationship, for during the period 1979–80 in one of every four union certification victories the union subsequently failed to obtain a collective agreement.[44]

With such findings, it is indeed disheartening to look back upon half a century of the Board's efforts to enforce the basic provisions of the Act, particularly during the last part of that period. But one need not resort to controlled investigations or even to the abundant anecdotal evidence which every union representative can readily supply in order to learn of the Board's failures. A ready source of data, which the foregoing studies have also used, is the compilation of statistical tables in the Board's own annual reports. One could begin with any of the earlier years, and a comparison with recent years would yield the same general trend. I selected the 20-year span from 1962 to

---

[40] UNION ORGANIZING AND PUBLIC POLICY: FAILURE TO SECURE FIRST CONTRACTS (1985). The study was conducted pursuant to a grant from the W.E. Upjohn Institute for Employment Research.

[41] *Id.* at 94.

[42] *Id.* at 90.

[43] *Id.*

[44] *Id.* at 94.

1981, which reveals a twofold increase in charges of discriminatory discharges under Section 8(a)(3), a sevenfold increase in the number of employees receiving back pay for unlawful discharges, and a threefold increase in Section 8(a)(5) refusal-to-bargain charges.[45] Such drastic increases cannot be explained by increases in organizational activity, for union organizing declined during that same period. Using the number of employees eligible to vote in representation elections[46] as a barometer of organizational activity, it is noted that in 1962 there were 536,047 eligible voter employees, but in 1981 that number had declined to 449,243; thus, in relation to the volume of union activity, the increase in employer unfair labor practices is even greater than that revealed by the raw figures. Furthermore, a contrast between Section 8(a)(3) activity in 1970 and such activity in 1980–81 (the most recent years for complete available figures), demonstrates dramatically how steep the increase has been. In 1970 there were 608,558 employees eligible to vote in representation elections. The following year, 6,738 employees received back pay in employment discrimination cases. In other words, taking into consideration lag time for processing such cases, approximately one percent of all employees who were involved in election campaigns in 1970 had meritorious cases involving employment discrimination under the Act. Although such a rate of discriminatory employment activity, including discharges, may seem high, and indeed it is, it seems almost acceptable compared with the upward trend for such violations that peaked during the 1980–81 period. In 1980, 521,602 employees were involved in election campaigns, and in the following year 25,929 employees received back pay because of employment discrimination. Thus, approximately five percent of all employees in organizationally active bargaining units were

---

45 1962 NLRB ANN. REP., Table 2 (1963); 1963 NLRB ANN. REP. Table 2 (1964); 1964 NLRB ANN. REP. Table 2 (1965); 1965 NLRB ANN. REP. Table 2 (1966); 1966 NLRB ANN. REP. Table 2 (1967); 1967 NLRB ANN. REP. Table 2 (1968); 1968 NLRB ANN. REP. Table 2 (1969); 1969 NLRB ANN. REP. Table 2 (1970); 1970 NLRB ANN. REP. Table 2 (1971); 1971 NLRB ANN. REP. Table 2 (1972); 1972 NLRB ANN. REP. Table 2 (1972); 1973 NLRB ANN. REP. Table 2 (1973); 1974 NLRB ANN. REP. Table 2 (1974); 1975 NLRB ANN. REP. Table 2 (1975); 1976 NLRB ANN. REP. Table 2 (1976); 1977 NLRB ANN. REP. Table 2 (1977); 1978 NLRB ANN REP. Table 2 (1978); 1979 NLRB ANN. REP. Table 2 (1980); 1980 NLRB ANN. REP. Table 2 (1980); 1981 NLRB ANN. REP. Table 2 (1981). At the time of presentation, the 1981 ANNUAL REPORT was the latest available. Now see also 1982 NLRB ANN. REP. Table 2 (1982); 1983 NLRB ANN. REP. Table 2 (1983).
46 NLRB ANN. REP. Table 13, 1962–81.

terminated or otherwise denied compensation because of their union involvement. These figures are not unlike the findings of Freeman and Medhoff, which were arrived at using a different method of computation.[47]

The statistical tables in the Board's annual reports also reveal that union unfair labor practices directed at employers have not been increasing. Since the early 1970s the level of charges for secondary boycotts and jurisdictional disputes under Section 8(b)(4) and organizational and recognitional picketing under Section 8(b)(7) has remained relatively constant.[48] The Board has thus been reasonably successful in enforcing those provisions and in deterring the wholesale commission of union violations, albeit with the aid of Section 10(1)[49] injunctions and the presence of private damage suits under Section 303 of the Taft-Hartley Act[50] for conduct which also violates Section 8(b)(4). But such enforcement success is not sufficient to justify the Board's continuing to operate in the same old way, for as I noted earlier, Sections 8(b)(4) and 8(b)(7) are ancillary to the Act's fundamental purpose of protecting employees in regard to organizational and collective bargaining activity. It is worth noting that the Board's record of success in discouraging the commission of union unfair labor practices directed against individual employees (specifically Sections (b)(1)(A) and 8(b)(2)) is hardly better than its record against employers, although the number of such charges is relatively small in relation to the number of charges filed against employers.[51]

This appraisal of the Board's enforcement record reveals that notwithstanding the substantial number of employers against whom meritorious unfair labor practice charges have been filed in recent years, the Board has not been able to protect employees by providing effective enforcement of the core provisions of the Act. Although the statistical data do not indicate that all employers who are involved in organizational campaigns violate the Act, such evidence does suggest and tends to confirm the popular

---

[47] *Supra* note 3, at 233, 283 n.12. The exact percentage of employees among eligible voters who were discharged for union activity in any given year cannot be determined with precision from the Board's statistics, but there can be no doubt that the percentage is too high for a showing of either effective enforcement or substantial voluntary compliance.

[48] *See* NLRB ANN. REP., 1973–81, *supra* note 45.

[49] National Labor Relations Act §10(1) (as amended (1947)), 29 USC §160(1). *See* Flanagan, *supra* note 3, at 979–80.

[50] Labor Management Relations (Taft-Hartley) Act §303, 29 USC §187.

[51] *See* Morris, *supra* note 21, at 20.

belief[52] that nonunion employers are more concerned with *avoidance* of the Act's requirements than with *compliance* with the Act's objectives. In other words, the spirit of the Act is regularly violated even when no violations of specific provisions are found or even charged. The prevalence of such efforts at union avoidance, coupled with the Board's dismal record in failing to provide meaningful remedies in the cases where violations are found, support the conclusion that the Board has failed in its primary mission.

III. National Labor Policy: An Assumption

A question that needs asking is whether the basic policy of the Act still represents the nation's true industrial relations policy? If it does, then the core provisions of the statute ought to be enforced and further debate should center on the most suitable means of enforcement. On the other hand, if it does not—if it is no longer the national policy to encourage free collective bargaining and the rights of employees to organize—then we should quit pretending that such is the policy. And Congress should quit pretending. In which case Congress should reject the Wagner Act policy in unambiguous statutory language and repeal or legislatively emasculate the core provisions of the Act. But if that should happen, then, with collective bargaining on the wane, there would surely follow a marked diminution of employer incentive to avoid unionization by the current practice of duplicating or competing with union conditions.[53] The need for representation or at least protection of employee interests would remain, but other legal remedies or structures would probably evolve to fill the resulting vacuum: For example, there might be a significant expansion of common law wrongful discharge actions with accompanying development of employment-at-will case law; a series of pervasive statutory regulations of additional aspects of the employment relationship, at both the state and federal level, would possibly be enacted; and a new wave of unionism without the blessing of supporting legislation might even emerge.

It is not my purpose here to engage in a weighing of substantive industrial relations policies, for it is my assumption that the

---

[52] *See, e.g.,* F. Faulkes, PERSONNEL POLICIES IN LARGE NONUNION COMPANIES (1980).
[53] *Id.* at 154 & 341.

policy contained in the present law is both valid and desirable. Although such an assumption is a prerequisite to justifying a search for a more effective means to enforce the present policy, I have not made that assumption lightly. I have based it on the conclusion that over the years we have seen sufficient examples of healthy collective bargaining to know that the NLRA system fits comfortably within the general democratic framework of American political and economic life. Furthermore, notwithstanding the Board's bleak record in protecting employee rights, the NLRA, with its emphasis on employee self-determination, offers a suitable framework for channeling workers' participation into new decisionmaking processes concerning matters that affect their legitimate employment-related interests.[54]

Because of the far-reaching changes that have occurred in American economic life during the last decade, there is definitely a felt need to find appropriate means to organize industrial relations in a manner that will maximize productivity. The NLRA is not inappropriate for that task. The basic structure of the Act was devised with remarkable foresight. Given the proper institutional will, that statute could furnish the Board with a flexible means to provide positive responses to the demands of the industrial relations community for innovative and improved techniques for the organization of work—some of which might emphasize cooperative rather than adversarial arrangements—in order to better cope with this nation's ongoing process of either deindustrialization or reindeustrialization.

Another observation of Freeman and Medhoff is in order. After viewing the economic evidence and noting the decline of organized labor in the United States, a phenomenon which they found unique among modern democratic industrial societies, they expressed the following opinion:

> We favor legal changes that will make it easier to unionize because we believe continued decline in unionization is bad not only for unions and their members but for the entire society. Because our research shows that unions do much social good, we believe the "union free" economy desired by some business groups would be a

---

[54] That framework would be even more suitable were it not for certain Supreme Court decisions which have unnecessarily restricted the scope and subject matter of collective bargaining, particularly *NLRB v. Wooster Div. of Borg-Warner Corp.*, 356 US 342, 42 LRRM 2034 (1958); *First National Maintenance Corp. v. NLRB*, 452 US 666, 107 LRRM 2705 (1981); *NLRB v. Yeshiva Univ.*, 444 US 672, 103 LRRM 2526 (1980).

disaster for the country. . . . In a well-functioning labor market, there should be a sufficient number of union and non-union firms to offer alternative work environments to workers, innovation in workplace rules and conditions, and competition in the market. . . .[55]

The legal changes to which they referred need not be substantive changes. They need only to be changes that will make the present law work the way it was intended.

IV. Enforcement Alternatives

If one accepts the premise that the existing primary statutory mandate is healthy for the country, as I have done, then one must squarely confront the harsh evidence of the Board's enforcement record. I have done that, and I have concluded that the Board as presently structured and motivated cannot fulfill its mandate; therefore the time has come—indeed it is long overdue—for a drastic overhaul of the Act's system of enforcement. There are several different ways this might be attempted.

One approach, perhaps the most popular of all, is the one which was typified by the Labor Reform Bill that failed to pass the Congress in 1978.[56] That approach would amend the Act by conferring new powers on the Board and increasing the number of Board members. But such a palliative would simply pass the buck to Congress. Such an approach seeks a quick fix to be accomplished by beefing up the Board's remedial powers, thereby hoping to achieve essentially the same ultimate goals that the Board already has the power to accomplish with its present statutory authority. It is true that some of the proposed new remedies, for example, self-enforcing Board orders, would be useful additions to the Board's arsenal of weapons; yet there is little reason to believe that adding a package of new legislative remedies would make much of a difference, at least without a marked change in the Board' enforcement philosophy. Furthermore, in view of the Pandora's Box syndrome which usually accompanies major efforts to amend this Act,[57] any proposed congressional amendments should be looked upon with a mix-

---

[55] *Supra* note 3, at 250.

[56] Labor Law Reform Bill, H.R. 8410, 95th Cong., 1st Sess. (1977), and S. 1883, 95th Cong., 2d Sess. (1978). *See* C. Morris, *supra* note 19, at 66–67.

[57] *E.g.*, compare the original Kennedy bill of 1959, S. 505, 80th Cong., 1st Sess., with the final outcome in the 1959 Landrum-Griffin Act. *See* 1 LEGISLATIVE HISTORY OF THE LABOR-MANAGEMENT REPORTING AND DISCLOSURE ACT OF 1959, 1–79 (1959).

ture of skepticism and hesitation. This paper will therefore not discuss the various tack-on amendments which have been proposed to give the Board more clout. I prefer that the Board first use the clout it already has.

A second approach, which I shall present only in broad outline, would follow from the recognition that if the Board inherently cannot or will not make a genuine effort to use its present authority effectively, then it should be dismantled, at least as to its unfair labor practice jurisdiction; in which event a judicial solution should be given serious consideration. However, I would not suggest transfer of unfair labor practice jurisdiction to the existing federal district courts, for under that approach NLRA cases would become bogged down in clogged dockets, and uneven construction of statutory provisions, and needless unwieldiness in the enforcement process would surely follow. But what could be usefully considered is the establishment of a specialized federal labor court capable of functioning with full judicial authority under Article III of the Constitution. Such a court, with its instant process, its capacity to require effective compliance with its orders, and its ability to function as a court of equity and tailor-make orders to meet specific needs, could be a viable alternative for enforcement of the unfair labor practice provisions of the statute.

A third approach, one which should be given the most attention, is for the Board to make a determined effort to use its existing authority more efficiently. That approach, however, requires some important preconditions, which I shall discuss in due course. The Board's unused or undcrused existing authority, to which I shall refer in some detail regarding this third approach, includes the following: (1) substantive rule making (which I shall highlight); (2) streamlining of "R" case procedures; (3) making discovery available; (4) increasing the use of Section 10(j) injunctions, especially in discharge cases; (5) reorganization of administrative law judge operations; (6) ordering damage-specific final remedies; and (7) increasing the use of Sections 10(e) and 10(f) injunctions. Before examining this reform approach I shall briefly touch upon the second alternative, the labor court, for it can provide yet another standard for comparison.

V. The Labor Court Alternative

Fifty years of history has taught us that the NLRB is neither a true administrative agency nor an effective substitute for a court. Lacking a strong will to use available statutory processes more extensively and more creatively, the NLRB has become a paper tiger because its unfair labor practice jurisdiction, which is essentially a judicial function, is divorced from meaningful judicial process.

The highly politicized nature of Board appointments may be the primary reason why the Board has been either unwilling or unable to make better use of available processes to achieve effective enforcement of critical parts of the statute. The necessary institutional will may have been sapped by the political appointment process, the same process which has been responsible for the pendulum-like swings which have historically characterized NLRB decisions. I find few redeeming features in that process.

Although many employers may not be unhappy with the present position of the pendulum, they should remember that the pendulum swings both ways. As Leonard Janofsky, a respected management labor lawyer and former president of the American Bar Association once said on behalf of the United States Chamber of Commerce, "[w]hat alarms the business community is that the NLRB restructures the Federal labor law to coincide with the political and socioeconomic predilections respecting industrial relations of those individual members who happen to constitute a majority of the Board at any particular time."[58] Ironically, exactly the same thing is being said today about what alarms the labor union community. Allowing the pendulum to swing back again, and then again, ad infinitum, is obviously not the answer. But if the Board will not use its available resources to execute its authority effectively, what then is the answer? If those are the conditions, the answer may be that the time has come for labor and management, for their own good as well as the public good, to support another method to enforce the nation's labor and employment laws. Such an alternative can be found in the creation of a court under Article III of the Constitution, for that article defining the judiciary branch provides basis for the establishment of a federal court with specialized jurisdiction.[59] I shall here outline, with minor modifications, a plan which I suggested several years ago.[60]

---

[58] *Hearings on Congressional Oversight of Administrative Agencies (NLRB) Before the Subcomm. on Separation of Powers of the Senate Comm. on the Judiciary*, 90th Cong., 2d Sess., Pt. 1, at 356 (1968).

[59] *See, e.g.*, Glidden Co. v. Zdanok, 370 US 530, 50 LRRM 2693 (1962) (Court gave effect to a congressional declaration that the Court of Customs and Patent Appeals was a "court established under Article III. . . ."). *Accord* Brenner v. Mason, 383 US 519 (1966). *See* Morris, *supra* note 2, at 471, 497 n.165.

[60] *Supra* note 2.

Serious enforcement problems also exist regarding other federal labor and employment laws, though the problems under the NLRA are clearly the most acute of all these statutes. The problems applicable to such other laws mostly concern conflicting and overlapping jurisdiction and jurisdiction which is sometimes too narrow for the enforcing tribunal and sometimes too widely scattered for efficient administration. High on the list of federal laws which could be advantageously administered by a centralized labor court are two related areas of statutorily based federal common law: (1) the law which defines a union's duty of fair representation[61] and (2) the law applicable to labor arbitration and the collective bargaining contract,[62] both of which doctrines arise from general language in the Taft-Hartley and Railway Labor[63] Acts. Both of those statutes would be covered by the labor court's jurisdiction. The Railway Labor Act (RLA) certainly suffers from the absence of a centralized decisionmaking authority.[64] Although the federal district courts can and often do provide prompt judicial process when needed under that statute, the absence of RLA expertise among many hundreds of different district judges creates obvious problems, including a lack of consistency in interpretation and enforcement.[65] And the present division of jurisdiction in fair representation cases between the courts and the NLRB leaves neither

---

[61] Steele v. Louisville & Nashville R.R., 323 US 192, 15 LRRM 708 (1944); Ford Motor Co. v. Huffman, 345 US 330, 31 LRRM 2548 (1953); Vaca v. Sipes, 386 US 171, 64 LRRM 2369 (1967).

[62] §301 of the LMRA, 29 USC §185. *See* Morris, *Twenty Years of Trilogy: A Celebration,* Decisional Thinking of Arbitrators and Judges, Proceedings of 33d Annual Meeting, National Academy of Arbitrators, ed. J. Stern & B. Dennis 331 (BNA Books, 1980).

[63] The duty of fair representation arises from the statutory grant of exclusive jurisdiction to a labor union designated as bargaining representative. *See* cases cited in note 61 *supra.* The enforceability of collective bargaining agreements is defined by federal common law derived from basic language in both statutes. Textile Workers v. Lincoln Mills, 353 US 448, 40 LRRM 2113 (1957); Machinists v. Central Airlines, 372 US 682, 52 LRRM 2803 (1963).

[64] The National Mediation Board has no jurisdiction to interpret or enforce the substantive provisions of the RLA; accordingly, the federal courts have that responsibility. *See* Virginian Ry. v. System Fed'n No. 40, Ry. Employees Dep't, 300 US 515, 1 LRRM 743 (1937); Detroit & Toledo Shore Line R.R. v. Transportation Union, 396 US 142, 72 LRRM 2838 (1969).

[65] *See* Morris, *Procedural Reform in Labor Law—A Preliminary Paper,* 35 J. Air L. & Com. 537 (1969), which suggests that "[t]he absence at the trial court level of a concentration of judicial experience and specialization in the law of the Railway Labor Act impedes proper comprehension and efficient enforcement of a complex statute." *Id.* at 552.

tribunal with sufficient jurisdiction. The courts have no jurisdiction over unfair labor practice aspects of union coercion and restraint under Sections 8(b)(1)(A) and 8(b)(2), or of related Section 8(a)(3) conduct by an employer;[66] and the Board has no jurisdiction over an employer in a fair representation case arising solely under Section 8(b)(1)(A); thus it cannot adjudicate the underlying contractual dispute and order reinstatement as a remedy.[67] Similar conflict and accommodation problems arise with increasing frequency between the NLRB's unfair labor practice jurisdiction and the jurisdiction of arbitrators to resolve contractual disputes subject to federal court review under Section 301.[68] Such problems of both inadequate and overlapping jurisdiction could be substantially alleviated by a unitary system with a single judicial tribunal at its center. Thus, as is presently the practice in most other areas of federal law, all related causes of action could be joined in a single proceeding. For example, an action raising unfair labor practice questions, including the duty of fair representation,[69] but also contract enforcement issues arising under Section 301, could be treated in a single action so that deferral to arbitration,[70] when appropriate, could be pursued without sacrifice of judicial oversight; and strong judicial remedies, such as injunctions, when and where appropriate, could be imposed without unnecessary delay.

Among the other federal labor and employment statutes over which the labor court could usefully assume jurisdiction are Title VII of the Civil Rights Act,[71] the Age Discrimination in

---

[66] See supra note 2, at 485–86.

[67] Id. See, e.g., San Francisco Newspaper Printing Co. d/b/a San Francisco Newspaper Agency (Printing & Graphic Communications Local 4) 272 NLRB 899, 117 LRRM 1420 (1984); Electrical Workers (IUE) Local 485 (Automotive Plating Corp.), 183 NLRB 1286, 74 LRRM 1396 (1970), supplementing 170 NLRB 1234, 67 LRRM 1609 (1968), enforced, 454 F2d 17, 79 LRRM 2278 (CA 2, 1972).

[68] Olin Corp., 268 NLRB 573, 115 LRRM 1056 (1984). See also Ryder Truck Lines, 273 NLRB No. 98, 118 LRRM 1092 (1984), vacated and remanded sub nom. Taylor v. NLRB, 786 F2d 1516, 122 LRRM 2084 (CA 11, 1986); National Radio Co., 198 NLRB 527, 80 LRRM 1718 (1972); Collyer Insulated Wire, 192 NLRB 837, 77 LRRM 1931 (1971); Dubo Mfg. Corp., 142 NLRB 431, 53 LRRM 1070 (1963); Raytheon Co., 140 NLRB 883, 52 LRRM 1129 (1963), set aside, 326 F2d 471, 55 LRRM 2101 (CA 1, 1964); Spielberg Mfg., 112 NLRB 1080, 36 LRRM 1152 (1955).

[69] See generally, J. McKelvey, ed., THE CHANGING LAW OF FAIR REPRESENTATION (1985).

[70] See generally, Morris, NLRB Deferral to the Arbitration Process: The Arbitrator's Awesome Responsibility, 7 INDUS. REL. L.J. 290 (1985).

[71] Civil Rights Act of 1964, Tit. VII, 42 USC §2000e (1982).

Employment Act,[72] the Labor Management Reporting and Disclosure (Landrum-Griffin) Act,[73] the Occupational Safety and Health Act,[74] and the Fair Labor Standards Act.[75] This is not an all-inclusive list. A determination of which statutes should be covered would depend on many factors, particularly the extent to which a particular statute overlaps another statute over which the court would have jurisdiction, the extent to which centralized judicial administration is important or desirable, and considerations of judicial efficiency and convenience to the affected parties.

The labor court which I have in mind would be the centerpiece within an integrated system of administration and enforcement of selected federal labor and employment laws. Organized under Article III of the Constitution, the court would be a part of the judicial branch of the government. It would perhaps be called the "United States Labor Court." There would also be an administrative agency that would determine bargaining units and generally perform the other representation and election functions provided for under both the NLRA and the RLA. This agency would be empowered to engage in rule making[76] related to those functions. In addition, it would handle investigations and prosecutions concerning statutory violations under both statutes (including unfair labor practices under the NLRA). Inasmuch as this agency would have no judicial function, unlike the present NLRB, there would no longer be a need for a separate General Counsel. The agency itself would assume all of the functions of the General Counsel under the NLRA and would also perform similar functions of investigating and prosecuting under the RLA (the latter statute does not provide for a public prosecutor). This new agency, which might be called the "National Labor and Employment Board" (NLEB), would in effect represent a merger of the nonjudicial functions (and probably also the personnel) of several existing agencies, particularly the NLRB and the National Mediation Board (NMB).[77]

---

[72] Age Discrimination in Employment Act of 1967, 29 USC §§621–634 (1982).

[73] Labor-Management Reporting and Disclosure (Landrum-Griffin) Act, of 1959, 29 USC §§153, 158, 159, 160, 164, 186, 187, 401, 402, 411–415, 431–440, 461–466, 481–483, 501–504, 521–531 (1982).

[74] Occupational Safety and Health Act of 1970, 5 USC §§5108, 5314, 5315, 7902, 15 USC §§633, 636; 18 USC §1114; 29 USC §§553, 651–678; 42 USC §3142–1; 49 USC App., §1421 (1985).

[75] Fair Labor Standards Act of 1938, 29 USC §§201–219, 255, 260 (1980).

[76] *See* discussion of substantive rule making in Part VI-A, *infra*, at notes 83–157.

The NMB's mediation functions (and probably also some of its personnel) would be merged with that of the Federal Mediation and Conciliation System (FMCS).[77] The EEOC and other affected administrative agencies might also be merged into the NLEB; however, unification and merger of all the covered administrative agencies is not essential to the plan. In fact, there may be significant advantage in retaining several specialized agencies, with their separate identities, such as the EEOC and OSHA.[79]

The Labor Court should consist of a sufficient number of judges to handle its jurisdiction adequately. No significant increase in the total number of life-tenured federal judges would necessarily result from the creation of this court, however, for the regular district courts would be relieved of a substantial case load of labor and employment law actions.[80] An arbitrary number of 13 tenured (lifetime appointed) judges for the new court is here suggested. But so that no single President would make all or even most of the appointments, the initial appointments should be spread over a period of four presidential terms: four appointments to be made immediately, and three appointments to be made during each of the following three presidential terms. Until the court achieves its full number of judges, it would augment its existing complement of regular judges by following the customary practice of borrowing judges from other federal benches. Should more regular judges be required, Congress could always authorize their appointment. The political pressures at work in the appointment process, which would of course require Senatorial confirmation, would be national in scope. A bench of highly qualified judges should therefore be an attainable goal.

---

[77] Railway Labor Act, §§4 & 5, 45 USC §§154 & 155 (1982).

[78] See LMRA §§201–205, 29 USC §§171–175 (1982).

[79] Equal Employment Opportunity Commission, 42 USC §§200e–4 & 5 (1982); Occupational Safety and Health Administration, 29 USC §§651–678 (1985).

[80] See REPORTS OF THE JUDICIAL CONFERENCE & REPORT OF THE ADMIN. OFFICE 1973–1983, wherein statistical compilations for the years 1961–77 indicate that labor and employment discrimination cases approximate 12–16% of the entire federal court docket. Labor cases have increased steadily each year, from 2,484 in 1961 to 7,739 in 1977. Civil rights cases, including employment discrimination, have increased from 296 in 1961 to 13,113 in 1977. The majority of the federal court civil docket consists of contract and torts actions, including personal and marine injury cases, which combined account for approximately 40% of all federal court cases. The remainder of the docket consists of various statutory actions.

The court would also make substantial use of nontenured "labor judges" whose function would be similar to that of the present administrative law judges (ALJs) under the NLRA. The court would determine its own method of operation: Thus it could act through its nontenured labor judges,[81] through a single tenured judge, through panels of tenured judges, or *en banc*. And it would exercise its own discretion as to how, where, and when it would sit, though it would presumably be headquartered in Washington, D.C.

A key element in this unitary plan is that actions arising under the NLRA or the RLA could be filed in the Labor Court either by the NLEB after issuance of a complaint, or, should that agency refuse to issue a complaint, by the charging party acting alone; in the latter instance, the NLEB would have the right to intervene in the court proceeding. Discovery,[82] subject to appropriate limiting rules and judicial supervision, would be available to all parties and in all types of cases.

No change is contemplated in the present system of judicial review. Differences among the circuits, which provide an opportunity for cross-fertilization of interpretative and reviewing approaches, is a desirable feature which could counterbalance any tendency toward overspecialized expertise that might otherwise develop within a single court of limited jurisdiction. Final reconciliation of differences among the circuits would continue to be the responsibility of the Supreme Court. It is reasonable to expect, however, that the judicial stature of this United States Labor Court would eventually be so prestigious—in marked contrast to the manner in which the NLRB has so often been viewed by the appellate courts—that there would be greater deference to its decisions; consequently, there should be fewer appeals and fewer reversals.

In view of the judicial power of such a Constitutional court, the Labor Court would command considerable respect. It would have the power to issue temporary restraining orders or such other injunctive or other relief as may be appropriate in an

---

[81] Bankruptcy judges received a similar extension of authority in the wake of NLRB v. Bildisco & Bildisco, 465 US 513, 115 LRRM 2805 (1984). *Bildisco* held that companies could alter collective bargaining agreements amid Chapter 11 bankruptcy proceedings. That decision prompted federal lawmakers to pass the Bankruptcy Amendments and Federal Judgeship Act of 1984, Pub. L. 98-353, §541.

[82] *See* discussion of making discovery available, at Part VI-C, *infra*, at notes 159–61.

unfair labor practice or other type of case within its jurisdiction. All of its orders, whether temporary or final, would be self-enforcing and subject to contempt penalties for their violation. There is every reason to believe that the National Labor Relations Act, including its core provisions, would be effectively enforced under the foregoing plan. If the Board will not or cannot enforce the statute, this specialized federal labor court should be able to do so with efficiency and respect.

VI. Labor Board Reform Without Legislation

A labor court, however, should be viewed as a solution of last resort. The most plausible antidote for the Board's malaise is to be found in the potential of the statute itself. But achieving that potential may never be possible. Because of the political nature of Board appointments, their short five-year terms of office, and the absence of a strong institutional commitment to vigorous enforcement of the Act, I have virtually no expectation that the Board will ever reform itself. Nevertheless, if only because "hope springs eternal," it seems worthwhile to document certain specific means by which the Board's existing authority could be used to better achieve its major statutory objectives. The following discussion will examine those means, which essentially consist of the activitation of several unused or underused procedural devices, a reorganization of certain agency functions, and the employment of more effective and more injury-specific remedies.

A. Substantive Rule Making

Substantive rule making pursuant to the Administrative Procedure Act[83] (APA) and Section 6 of the NLRA is probably the most important thing the Board can do to effectuate its process, economize its time, and advise the people who need to know— most of whom are not lawyers—what the law requires. It is this last feature, the *information factor,* which I shall especially highlight. But first I shall summarize and briefly discuss the major advantages of rule making, some of which have already been

---

[83] Administrative Procedure Act, 5 USC §§551–559, 701–706, 1305, 3105, 3344, 4301, 5335, 5372, 7521 (1982).

admirably treated by other commentators.[84] I have grouped 11 features or reasons which point up various improvements in agency action that can result from regular promulgation of substantive rules through APA notice-and-comment procedures. These should be measured against the Board's heretofore exclusive practice (save for minor exceptions)[85] of using adjudicated cases for such purposes. I do not mean to suggest that APA rule making (which I shall sometime refer to simply as "rule making") should be the Board's exclusive means to effect changes and clarifications in the law. The Supreme Court in the *Bell Aerospace*[86] case confirmed that the "choice between rule making and adjudication lies within the Board's jurisdiction,"[87] but it added the caveat that "there may be situations where the Board's reliance on adjudication would amount to an abuse of discretion or a violation of the Act."[88] It is not my purpose here to define when the Board is legally required to use rule making, although some of my illustrations may suggest situations where the nature or consequence of a particular rule change may

---

[84] *See* R. Williams, NLRB REGULATION OF ELECTION CONDUCT 503–505 (1985); Estreicher, *Policy Oscillation at the Labor Board: A Plea for Rulemaking*, NYU 37TH ANNUAL CONFERENCE ON LABOR (1984), also published in 37 AD. L. REV. 163 (1985); Subrin, *Conserving Energy at the Labor Board: The Case for Making Rules on Collective Bargaining Units*, 32 LAB. L.J. 105 (1981); Kahn, *The NLRB and Higher Education: The Failure of Policymaking through Adjudication*, 21 UCLA L. REV. 63 (1975); Silverman, *The Case for the National Labor Relations Board's Use of Rulemaking in Asserting Jurisdiction*, 25 LAB. L.J. 607 (1974); Bernstein, *The NLRB's Adjudication-Rulemaking Dilemma Under the Administrative Procedure Act*, 79 YALE L.J. 571 (1970); Peck, *A Critique of the National Labor Relations Board's Performance in Policy Formation: Adjudication and Rulemaking*, 117 U. PA. L. REV. 254 (1968); Shapiro, *The Choice of Rule Making or Adjudication in the Development of Administrative Policy*, 78 HARV. L. REV. 921 (1965); Peck, *The Atrophied Rule-Making Powers of the National Labor Relations Board*, 70 YALE L.J. 729 (1961); R. Pierce, S. Shapiro, & P. Verkuil, ADMINISTRATIVE LAW & PROCESS, 281–98 (1985); H. Friendly, THE FEDERAL ADMINISTRATIVE AGENCIES 36–52, 146–47 (1962)

[85] In NLRB v. Wyman-Gordon Co., 394 US 759, 70 LRRM 3345 (1969), the Court reviewed the Board's application of the rule adopted in *Excelsior Underwear, Inc.*, 156 NLRB 1236, 61 LRRM 1217 (1966), and concluded that the Board had engaged in rule making without complying with the requirements of the APA. However, the Court later held that the NLRB is not precluded from announcing new principles in an adjudicative proceeding and that the choice is within the Board's discretion. NLRB v. Bell Aerospace Co., 416 US 267, 85 LRRM 2945 (1974). In the years between *Wyman-Gordon* and *Bell Aerospace*, the Board conducted three unprecedented rule-making proceedings. These instances included promulgation of standards for the exercise of jurisdiction over private colleges and universities and over symphony orchestras with gross annual revenues from all sources of not less than $1 million. It ruled in another proceeding that it would not assert jurisdiction over the horse-racing and dog-racing industries. *See* Morris, *supra* note 19, at 1631 n.214–16.

[86] *Supra* note 85. *See also* NLRB v. Wyman-Gordon Co., *supra* note 85.

[87] 416 US at 293.

[88] *Id.* at 294.

indeed mandate use of APA procedures. Instead, this presentation is based on the proposition that the Board itself should voluntarily choose rule making as its primary device for announcing existing legal doctrine and promulgating new doctrine. It should choose to do so because there are inherent advantages in using rule making for such purposes.

One additional disclaimer is in order. I do not suggest that the Board should suddenly attempt to convert to an exclusive rule-making system. To be administratively realistic, the conversion would have to be gradual. But a beginning should be made; and, in particular, future major doctrinal changes should receive priority treatment for promulgation in accordance with APA rule-making procedures.

The 11 reasons for the Board to convert to use of substantive rule making are the following:

1. General language in the statute. The Act is written in broad and general language, and Congress left to the Board the responsibility of defining legal detail in accordance with legislative policy. As the Supreme Court noted in *Beth Israel Hospital* v. *NLRB,*[89] "to accomplish the task which Congress set for it, [the Board] necessarily must have authority to fill the interstices of the broad statutory provisions"[90] of the Act. Rule making is ideally suited for that purpose. The Board should therefore make use of the express authority contained in Section 6 of the Act, "to make, amend, and rescind, in the manner prescribed by the Administrative Procedure Act, such rules and regulations as may be necessary to carry out the provisions of [the National Labor Relations] Act."

2. Rule making is a source of necessary data. Case-by-case adjudication does not provide the Board with the necessary factual data or the best available analyses of such data on which to premise rules of broad application. In adjudicated cases, even those in which the Board announces major policy changes, oral argument is rarely permitted and amici briefs are rarely invited. By contrast, the rule-making process invites a dialogue between the labor relations community and the Board, for the notice-and-comment procedure contemplated by the APA encourages the parties who are likely to be affected by the proposed rule to

---

[89] 437 US 483, 98 LRRM 2727 (1978).

[90] *Id.* at 501. *See also* Republic Avaiation Corp. v. NLRB, 324 US 793, 798, 16 LRRM 620 (1945).

submit relevant data and argument which the Board must consider.[91] To merit the "expert" label that Congress intended and which the courts are expected to acknowledge,[92] the Board needs an adequate research source; it is not presently available either through the adjudicative process or through the Board's limited statutory appointment authority.[93] Under rule making procedures, data which are submitted in public and by the public will tend to reflect diverse points of view, and the accuracy and objectivity of raw data can be tested and debated in the submission and consideration process. Lacking such a process, the Board often displays an "ivory tower" syndrome, which Samuel Estreicher perceptively characterizes as "typically intuitionistic and excessively doctrinal."[94] He describes the process:

> Rather than providing a basis for decisions that only a supposedly expert agency could make—by evaluating the available empirical, economic literature and systematically distilling the accumulated experience of board personnel and of the labor relations community generally—the Board acts as a kind of Article I "talmudist" court, paring precedent, divining the true meaning of some Supreme Court ruling, balancing in some mysterious fashion competing, yet absolute-sounding values.[95]

3. Adjudicative rule making emphasizes specific facts rather than broad legislative policy. Rules promulgated in litigated cases are usually contained in decisions which are long on facts of the particular case and short on facts and reasons which would justify adoption of the broad rule being promulgated. For example, in its 1958 *Mountain Pacific*[96] decision, the Board merely asserted that it was reasonable to infer that exclusive hiring-hall

---

[91] *See* Federal Comm'n v. Texaco, 377 US 33 (1964); United States v. Storer Broadcasting Co., 351 US 192 (1956). *See also* Judge Leventhal's discussion of the rule-making process in *American Airlines* v. *Civil Aeronautics Bd.*, 359 F2d 624 (CA DC, 1966), *cert. denied*, 385 US 843 (1967). As Professor Estreicher has noted, *supra* note 84, "Rulemaking ensures a level of public participation in the policymaking process not currently available. The opportunity for public participation is automatic with each notice of rulemaking, and open to all concerned. Hopefully, the various organizations representing employees, unions and management will in time develop rulemaking staff . . . who will vigilantly monitor and contribute to the rulemaking process." *Id.* at §10.03[5].

[92] *See, e.g.,* Beth Israel Hosp. v. NLRB, *supra* note 89, *and* Republic Aviation Corp., *supra* note 90.

[93] National Labor Relations (Wagner) Act §4(a), 29 USC §154(a) (1982).

[94] *Supra* note 84.

[95] *Id.* at 172.

[96] Mountain Pac. Chapter, Associated Gen. Contractors (Hod Carriers Local 242), 119 NLRB 883, 41 LRRM 1460 (1958).

authority to refer employees "enhances the union's power and control over the employment status"[97] and this results in "the inherent and unlawful encouragement of union membership;"[98] whereupon the Board promulgated a rule requiring the insertion of specific protective language which was intended to be applicable to all exclusive hiring halls. But in *Teamsters Local 357* v. *NLRB*[99] the Supreme Court reversed the Board, noting that the rule inferred the existence of discrimination under Sections 8(a)(3) and 8(b)(2) without any showing of discrimination. Query: Had the Board designed a more carefully crafted hiring-hall rule, perhaps under Section 8(b)(1)(A) alone, and based it, at least in part, on empirical data obtained in an APA rule-making proceeding, and had it provided an articulated rationale derived from such data, would the Court have invalidated it? Perhaps not.

A recent example in which the Board emphasized the facts of the particular case while virtually ignoring facts and accompanying rationale pertinent to the broad rule which was being promulgated, was the decision in *Rossmore House*.[100] That case concerned interrogation of a known union adherent. The Board used the occasion to reverse a rule which a prior Board had announced in *PPG Industries*.[101] Not surprisingly, the PPG Board had been equally guilty of failing to spell out its findings and rationale. The Board in *PPG*, relying on various prior decisions,[102] concluded that an employer's inquiries about an employee's union sentiments, regardless of the fact that the employee had been open and active in his support of the union, reasonably tends to coerce employees in the exercise of their Section 7 rights because it "conveys an employer's displeasure with an employee's union activity. . . ."[103] The Board in *Rossmore* adopted an entirely new rule to the effect that interrogation about union sentiments, whether of a known adherent or any other employee, would be unlawful only if "under all the circumstances the interrogation reasonably tends to restrain,

---

[97] *Id.*, 41 LRRM at 1461.

[98] *Id.*, 41 LRRM at 1462.

[99] 365 US 667, 47 LRRM 2906 (1961).

[100] 269 NLRB 1176, 116 LRRM 1025 (1984). The "emphasis on what may well be idiosyncratic specific facts diverts the agency's attention from the broad policy implications of the rule under consideration." Pierce, Shapiro, & Verkuil, *supra* note 84 at 283.

[101] 251 NLRB 1146, 105 LRRM 1434 (1980).

[102] *See, e.g.*, Anaconda Co., 241 NLRB 1091, 101 LRRM 1070 (1979); Paceco, Div. of Fruehauf Corp. v. NLRB, 237 NLRB 399, 99 LRRM 1544 (1978); ITT Automotive Elec. Prods. Div., 231 NLRB 878, 96 LRRM 1134 (1977).

[103] 251 NLRB at 1147.

coerce, or interfere with" Section 7 rights.[104] It also provided a footnote[105] which suggested some of the factors which may be considered in analyzing alleged interrogations; but nowhere did the Board provide an explanation of why employer interrogation about union activity would not presumptively coerce, or at the very least interfere, with employee organizational rights or why the employer would have any legitimate need or reason under ordinary circumstances[106] to make the inquiry. Whether it was a Carter Board contemplating the *PPG* rule or a Reagan Board contemplating the *Rossmore House* rule, APA rule making would have required the Board to receive and consider proffered empirical data and other input from the industrial relations community as to the effect of employer interrogation during a union organizing campaign and to explain how and why the resulting rule would implement the statutory objective.

Another prime example of the need to articulate the reasoning behind a substantive rule, and the inadequacy of the adjudicative process for that purpose, may be found in the Board's present quandry over the *Meyers*[107] rule. The single employee in the case had been discharged from his employment as a truck driver because of his safety complaints and his refusal to drive an unsafe truck after reporting its condition to a state public safety agency. Inasmuch as there was no union involved, the case raised the issue of the rule enunciated in *Allelulia Cushion Co.*, [108] which would have treated such conduct as protected constructive concerted activity under Section 7. The Reagan Board chose *Meyers* as its adjudicative vehicle to overturn the *Allelulia* rule; indeed, it went even further and announced a broad rule defining situations which were not covered by the *Meyers* facts. Oral argument and amici briefs were not invited; nor was the public informed of any proposed new rule, as would have been required under APA procedures. The new rule announced in the case was the following:

> In general, to find an employee's activity to be "concerted," we shall require that it be engaged in with or on the authority of other

---

[104] 269 NLRB at 1177–78.

[105] *Id.* at 1178 n.20.

[106] *See, e.g.,* Johnnie's Poultry Co., 146 NLRB 770, 55 LRRM 1403 (1964), *enforcement dénied,* 334 F2d 617, 59 LRRM 2117 (CA 8, 1965).

[107] Meyers Indus., 268 NLRB 493, 115 LRRM 1025, *remanded sub nom.* Prill v. NLRB, 755 F2d 941, 118 LRRM 2649 (CA DC, 1985).

[108] 221 NLRB 999, 91 LRRM 1131 (1975).

employees, and not solely by and on behalf of the employee himself. Once the activity is found to be concerted, an 8(a)(1) violation will be found if, in addition, the employer knew of the concerted nature of the employee's activity, the concerted activity was protected by the Act, and the adverse employment action at issue (e.g., discharge) was motivated by the employee's protected concerted activity.[109]

On review of the Board's decision, the D.C. Circuit remanded the case for further consideration. Judge Harry Edwards' majority opinion explained that the Board had erred in (1) holding that its construction of the rule was "mandated by the statute," (2) that the new rule imposed requirements in addition to that required for reversal of *Alleluia,* which was the only rationale the Board provided for its action, and (3) that the decision "contains not a word of justification for its new standard in terms of the policy of the statute."[110] Following remand, the Board requested the parties to provide statements of position; but it did not appeal generally for public input. Even the discharged employee's counsel, that is, the General Counsel, had now abandoned his case, for the present General Counsel takes the position that his protest was not protected concerted activity, therefore his discharge did not violate the statute.[111] The Board thus plans to issue a new rule through the adjudicative process without benefit of any empirical data and with virtually no input from the persons and parties most likely to be affected by the rule. The persons who will be most affected will be nonunion employees who may engage in conduct, knowingly or unknowingly, that may get them discharged. Those are the persons for whom the core provisions of the statute were intended.

APA rule making would provide the Board with a means to obtain data as to what really happens in the workplace—not just what happened at the one establishment involved in the case which arrives by chance when the Board chooses to write a new rule. Rule making also provides a means for the Board to receive informed and diverse opinion on the subject, after which it has an opportunity to consider relevant data and various points of

---

[109] 115 LRRM at 1029.

[110] 755 F2d at 950.

[111] *General Counsel's Statement of Position on Remand* filed by General Counsel Rosemary Collyer in Case No. 7-CA-17207 (268 NLRB No. 73), Sept. 27, 1985. *See also* 730 LAB. L. REP. (CCH), at 4, Feb. 14, 1986.

view. The end product should be a rule for which the Board is able to provide an adequate rationale, as the D.C. Circuit, based on established authority,[112] was requiring in its *Meyers* remand.

4. Rule making reduces litigation. Development of doctrine through the adjudicative process emphasizes fact-oriented decisionmaking and encourages parties to take risks and test the outer limits of the law. It provides minimal incentive for voluntary compliance and settlement. Looking back on half a century of the adjudicating process in action, it can truly be said that adjudication begets adjudication. On the other hand, rule making can provide a greater measure of stability—which this law certainly needs—and also uniformity of application. Yet rule making need not be synonymous with rigidity. As Merton Bernstein noted 16 years ago in his seminal article on NLRB rule making, "the rigors of rule making uniformity can be ameliorated by interpretation in adjudication, while the mere existence of a rule will forestall many potential cases or provide the basis for summary disposition of many others."[113]

5. Rule making uses agency resources more efficiently. With the Board's overcrowded docket and the lengthy delays which characterize most "C" cases and many "R" cases, the Board should welcome rule making as a means to expedite the case-handling process. The wheel need not be reinvented in every case. Yet the Board stands helpless while the same types of unfair labor practice situations move repetitively and slowly through the decisional process.[114] Clear substantive rules would allow many of those cases to be handled on a summary basis. And on the "R" case side, one cannot seriously dispute the fact that almost all bargaining unit determinations could be reduced to specific rules.[115] If that were to happen, the need for contested on-the-record hearings would vanish in most "R" cases. Again it should be noted, however, that in exceptional cases the Board would not be bound by the straitjacket of inflexible rules, for the agency

---

[112] Federal Communications Comm'n v. RCA Communications, Inc., 346 US 86, 94 (1953). *See discussion* in *Prill,* 755 F2d at 957.

[113] *The NLRB's Adjudication—Rule Making Dilemma Under the Administrative Procedure Act,* 79 YALE L.J. 571, 592 (1970).

[114] *See* NLRB ANN. REP., Table 2, *supra* note 45.

[115] *See Determinations of Scope of Unit,* CLASSIFIED INDEX OF DECISIONS OF THE REGIONAL DIRECTORS OF THE NATIONAL LABOR RELATIONS BOARD IN REPRESENTATION PROCEEDINGS, editions December 1976, December 1981, January 1984, and December 1984. *See also* Subrin, *supra* note 84.

is empowered both to interpret rules and to make exceptions to rules whenever warranted by significant factual differences.

6. *Effect on appellate review.* Rule making should improve the Board's appellate image. Doctrinal changes backed by adequate data derived from broad public input, accompanied by a well-reasoned statement of the basis for the rule, would provide the courts of appeal with evidence of genuine agency expertise to which they should be more likely to defer.[116] Furthermore, the existence of an APA-promulgated rule would tend to focus the reviewing process on policy and statutory interpretation rather than on the facts peculiar to individual cases. If the Board can achieve greater respect in the courts, it may also achieve greater respect in the industrial relations community which it was created to serve.

7. *The prevention factor.* Rule making would allow the Board to emphasize the prevention of unfair labor practices rather than merely the remedying of such practices after they have already occurred. For one to comply with the law voluntarily, one first needs to know what the law requires. Rule making permits the Board to react swiftly to a perceived need without having to rely on delay and haphazard chance to produce the rule-making opportunity. As Professor Bernstein observed, "[r]ule making provides the agency with the opportunity to initiate changes in its own doctrine, whereas adjudication leaves the initiative to the few private parties who have the resources, the hardheadedness, or the innocence to persevere in the litigation process."[117]

8. *Rule making provides a more suitable medium for articulation of reasons behind rules.* Reliance on rule making as the vehicle of major shifts in policy provides a more appropriate medium for the agency to justify its action. The APA specifies that the agency shall incorporate in the rule "a concise general statement of [its] basis and purpose."[118] Aside from the obvious utility of this requirement from the standpoint of the users of the rule, this "basis and purpose" statement may also be essential to the process of judicial review.[119] The D.C. Circuit noted in *Portland Cement Ass'n* v. *Ruckelshaus:* "It is not consonant with the purpose

---

[116] *See supra* note 80.

[117] *Supra* note 113, at 590–91.

[118] Administrative Procedure Act, 5 USC §533 (c) (1982).

[119] *See, e.g.,* Kennecott Copper Corp. v. Environmental Protection Agency, 462 F2d 846 (CA DC, 1972); Portland Cement Ass'n v. Ruckelshaus, 486 F2d 375, 393–94 (CA DC, 1973). *See also* B. Schwartz, ADMINISTRATIVE LAW 173–74 (2d ed., 1984).

of a rule-making proceeding to promulgate rules on the basis of inadequate data, or on data that . . . is known only to the agency."[120] It is obviously much easier to change a rule by adjudication than by notice-and-comment rule making; and it is also easier to justify the former action by a generalized public statement, such as one which says that the pendulum has swung too far in one direction and that the Board is now only returning it to the middle. But rule making would at least encourage and possibly require the Board to explain fully, with reference to the intent of the law and not merely with reference to the facts of a specific case, why a particular policy shift is needed to implement the law.

9. *Rule making assists the Congress in its oversight responsibilities.* If Congress should disagree with a substantive action of the Board, the offensive rule can be pinpointed with precision and changed by specific legislative amendment if it is deemed contrary to contemporary congressional intent. This "watchdog potential" in rule making may serve to keep an agency ever aware that Congress is watching; and the existence of specific APA rules may also make it easier to change the law without butchering the entire statute.[121]

10. *The General Counsel factor.* Two features relating to the peculiar role of the General Counsel under the Act tend to inhibit the Board's capacity for fully effective rule making through exclusive utilization of the adjudicative process: (1) Unlike other federal agencies, the Labor Board and its General Counsel are separate entities,[122] and (2) the General Counsel's discretion to refuse to issue a complaint is unreviewable.[123] These factors make it virtually impossible, or at least awkward, for the Board to initiate doctrinal changes that are likely to result in the imposition of substantial monetary liability. A good exam-

---

[120] 486 F2d at 393–94.

[121] *E.g.*, in 1974 Congress was able to pinpoint a rule with which it disagreed and thereafter repeal it without affecting the statute as a whole. *See* regulation of Department of Transportation providing for ignition interlock of automobile seatbelts, 37 FR 13265, February 24, 1972, codified at 49 CFR §571.208. It was repealed by the National Traffic and Motor Vehicle Safety Act of 1966, Amendments, Pub. L. 93-492, §109 (1974), 88 Stat 1482.

[122] §3(d). *See* Rodgers, *Later History and Development of the N.L.R.B.*, 29 GEO. WASH. L. REV. 252, 261–65 (1960). *See also* M. McClintock, NLRB GENERAL COUNSEL—UNREVIEWABLE POWER TO ISSUE AN UNFAIR LABOR PRACTICE COMPLAINT 10–19 (1980).

[123] George Banta Co. v. NLRB, 626 F.2d 354, 104 LRRM 3103 (CA 4, 1980). *See also* NLRB v. Sears, Roebuck & Co., 421 US 132, 89 LRRM 2001 (1975); Vaca v. Sipes, *supra* note 61, at 182 (1967); McClintock, *supra* note 122; C. Morris, *supra* note 19, at 1696–97.

ple of this may be seen in the recent utilization of the *Mackay*[124] "rule" by many companies as a means to replace union employees with nonunion personnel, thereby divesting the incumbent union of its bargaining rights. This well-known rule recognizes the right of an employer to make permanent replacements of striking employees during an economic strike. But unknown to many, this rule was never actually "promulgated by the Board, either in an adjudicated case or through APA rule making. It was derived from language in dictum[125] contained in the Supreme Court's 1938 decision in the *Mackay* case; the Board never enunciated a formal reason for the rule, nor did it ever explain why permanent replacements, as distinguished from temporary replacements, would be deemed essential to the employer's operation of its business during a strike. In 1967 the Supreme Court issued its decision in *NLRB* v. *Great Dane Trailers, Inc.*[126] in which it stated that "if it can reasonably be concluded that the employer's discriminatory conduct was 'inherently destructive' of important employee rights," despite evidence of legitimate business motivation and the absence of proof of anti-union motivation, the employer could be found in violation of Sections 8(a)(1) and 8(a)(3).[127] In view of the "inherently destructive" impact of permanent replacements on unionized employees and the collective bargaining process, a strong case can be made that an employer should be required to prove that it cannot operate its struck business with temporary replacements before it could legally justify the hiring of permanent replacements during a strike. The Board in fact does require that only temporary replacements be used during offensive lockouts.[128] During a period of high unemployment it is especially likely that ample numbers of job applicants would accept temporary employment. But even if the Board wanted to change the *Mackay* rule, under an adjudicative rule-making system it would be

---

[124] NLRB v. Mackay Radio & Tel. Co., 304 US 333, 2 LRRM 610 (1938).

[125] *Id*, 2 LRRM at 614.

[126] 388 US 26, 65 LRRM 2465 (1967).

[127] *Id.* at 34.

[128] *See* discussion and cases cited in C. Morris, *supra* note 19, at 195–208, and the following cases: Inland Trucking Co. v. NLRB, 440 F2d 562, 76 LRRM 2929 (CA 7), *cert. denied*, 404 US 858 (1971); Inter-Collegiate Press v. NLRB, 486 F2d 837, 84 LRRM 2562 (CA 8, 1973), *cert. denied sub nom.* Bookbinders Local 60 v. NLRB, 416 US 938 (1974). *Cf.* Johns-Manville Prods. Corp., 223 NLRB 1317, 92 LRRM 1103 (1976), *enforcement denied*, 557 F2d 1126, 96 LRRM 2010 (CA 5, 1977), *cert. denied sub nom.* Oil Workers v. NLRB, 436 US 956 (1978).

difficult if not impossible to do so. If a charge were filed alleging that an employer had violated Section 8(a)(3) by permanently replacing strikers, thereby causing permanent economic damage to the union members and destruction of the bargaining relation, the General Counsel would be expected to dismiss such a charge and the Board would not have the opportunity to rethink the rule. Indeed, even if the General Counsel should choose to seek to change the rule by issuing a complaint, the potential back-pay liability which the employer would face would be so great that the Board's retroactive imposition of the rule change would probably represent an abuse of administrative discretion and a violation of due process, such as the Supreme Court had in mind in its *Bell Aerospace* caveat.[129] But if the rule change were not made retroactively applicable in the subject case, what of the rights of the displaced employee and the union that had lost its majority? The only reasonable answer to this quandry—and the quandry could apply also to any other contemplated rule change which would impose more restrictive penalties than presently exist—is rule making in accordance with APA procedures. The proper way to change such a rule would be for the Board to announce in advance its proposed rule change, and thereafter it would receive, through notice and comment procedures, empirical data and opinion from the various constituencies who would be affected by the proposed rule.[130]

11. Information factor. This brings me to the last feature on my list. The information factor in rule making is of special importance to an agency whose primary coverage extends to millions of individual employees with levels of education and sophistication that range from illiterate, unskilled, and naive at one end of the spectrum to highly educated, professional, and astute at the other end. Adequate dissemination of substantive rules to persons whose employment can be affected by those rules is a critical but missing element in the task of the NLRB. The sampling of

---

[129] *Supra* note 88.

[130] *See supra* notes 91–95 and accompanying text. For another example of the pernicious effect of the "General Counsel factor," *see Connell Constr. Co.* v. *Plumbers Local 100,* 421 U.S. 616, 89 LRRM 2401 (1973), in which the Supreme Court in the context of an antitrust action promulgated a new rule under §8(e), the "hot-cargo" provision of the NLRA, despite the fact that the Board had not previously passed on the rule, for the General Counsel had refused to issue a complaint when the charge was filed. It was thereafter that the charging party filed his antitrust action in federal court. *See* Morris, *supra* note 19, at 1231–34.

suggested rules which follow contain many illustrations of the function and importance of rules as conveyers of essential legal information.

Here are some illustrative areas which would benefit from the promulgation of specific APA rules:

a. A rule requiring *posting of a general notice of the Act's basic requirements* (in plain English and other appropriate languages) on employee and members' bulletin boards by all employers and unions subject to the Board's jurisdiction. I have never been able to understand why the Board has avoided taking this simple but important step toward informing employees of their rights under the Act. Most employees do not know what the NLRB does or what the law requires. My own unscientific poll supports what I had suspected and what others can easily verify: which is that, except for those persons who have had personal experience with collective bargaining or have been involved in a union election campaign, the overwhelming majority of adults in the United States—and the number is even greater among employees within the statutory definition[131]—do not know what the National Labor Relations Board does or that union organizational rights can be realistically protected. A surprisingly large number have never even heard of the NLRB. Is there any wonder that Fred Faulkes' incisive study of personnel policies in large nonunion companies[132] revealed that a number of those companies maintain employee committees, plans, and/or grievance procedures which appear to qualify as labor organizations within the meaning of Section 2(5) of the Act?[133] Many of those companies may be in violation of Section 8(a)(2)'s prohibition against employer support or domination of such entities, but most of the employees involved in those plans do not know what their legal rights are; and if they did, they would not know how to enforce them.

The same lack of information, with the same corresponding need, is characteristic of employees and prospective employees at almost every company where employees are not represented by a union. To put it bluntly, most employees do not believe that they cannot be fired or adversely affected if they engage in even

---

[131] NLRA §2(3), 29 USC §152(3) (1982).
[132] *Supra* note 52.
[133] NLRA §2(5), 29 USC §152(5) (1982).

the mildest and most "protected" forms of union activity. But not only do working employees need to know their rights and how to inquire about possible statutory violations or representation procedures, prospective employees—that is, job applicants—also need to know about their rights. As Justice Frankfurter reminded us long ago in *Phelps Dodge Corp.* v. *NLRB*,[134] "discrimination in hiring is twin to discrimination in firing."[135] A general posting of NLRA rights and procedures would help provide the needed information, for it is just as unlawful for a new automotive employer in Tennessee to deny employment to an experienced laid-off auto worker from Detroit because of his union membership as it would be to fire an existing employee for the same reason. But without the benefit of a clearly posted rule to that effect to remind the job interviewer and the job applicant, the *Phelps Dodge* rule will rarely be enforced.

The notice which would be posted under this rule would be of the same nature as the notices which are already found on employee bulletin boards advising of rights under other federal laws, such as Title VII,[136] the Fair Labor Standards Act,[137] and the Occupational Safety and Health Act.[138] This general notice should also contain an "800" telephone number for hot-line information, a service which some other federal agencies presently make available to the public.[139] It should not be difficult to reach the NLRB, but it is. For example, in my own city of Dallas if an employee wanted to call the nearest NLRB regional office, a long-distance telephone call would be required. But even that would not be easy, for the telephone number would not be found in the local directory; in fact the employee would have no convenient way of knowing that the regional office is located in Fort Worth. The Board could certainly do more to advertise its services if it really wanted to.

b. Rules relating to *organizational campaigns* should be clearly spelled out and then made available to employees, to unions, and

---

[134] 313 US 177, 8 LRRM 439 (1941).

[135] *Id.* at 187.

[136] Civil Rights Act of 1964, Tit. VII, 42 USC §2000e.

[137] Fair Labor Standards Act of 1938, 29 USC §215 (1982); 29 CFR §694.2 (1985).

[138] Occupational Safety and Health Act, 29 USC §660 (1982); 29 CFR §1903.2(a)(1), (a)(2) (1985).

[139] *E.g.*, the Environmental Protection Agency maintains a "hot-line" number, 1-(800)-424-9346, for the reporting of hazardous waste.

to employer representatives, including supervisors. These rules presently exist in a plethora of decisions. Attorneys can usually find them, but not always quickly. Affected employees, however, may never learn about them until it is too late. Many of the present adjudicated rules are fact-oriented, such as the one referred to above in the *Rossmore House*[140] case, so that the rule does, not really discourage unlawful conduct. Accordingly, the Board should promulgate clearly understandable rules relating to such subjects as *campaign misrepresentation*;[141] *access to the employer's premises* by union organizers and employees (both on-duty and off-duty);[142] *solicitation* and *distribution* of union authorizations and literature;[143] *interrogation* and *polling* as to employees' union sentiments or activity;[144] permissible *activity by employers*, including supervisors;[145] and prohibitions relating to *union promises and grants of benefit.*[146]

c. Rules relating to employee rights to engage in *concerted activity for "mutual aid or protection."*[147] These rules are particularly important for employees in nonunion establishments, for such persons will not ordinarily have access to a union as a source of information. And *Weingarten*[148] rules should also be made available to employees directly, because they must be invoked by the employee involved, not by his or her union.[149]

---

[140] *Supra* note 100.

[141] Midland Nat'l Life Ins. Co., 263 NLRB 127, 110 LRRM 1489 (1982); Shopping Kart Food Mkts., Inc., 228 NLRB 1311, 94 LRRM 1705 (1977).

[142] *See, e.g.,* NLRB v. Knogo Corp., 727 F2d 55, 115 LRRM 2756 (CA 2, 1984); Harvey's Wagon Wheel, Inc., 236 NLRB 1670, 98 LRRM 1501 (1978).

[143] *See, e.g.,* Republic Aviation Corp. v. NLRB, 324 US 793, 16 LRRM 620 (1945); Our Way, Inc.; 268 NLRB 394, 115 LRRM 1009 (1983); Eastex, Inc. v. NLRB, 437 US 556, 98 LRRM 2717 (1978); Presbyterian/St. Luke's Medical Center v. NLRB, 723 F2d 1468, 115 LRRM 2306 (CA 10, 1983); NLRB v. Jack August Enters., Inc., 583 F2d 575, 99 LRRM 2582 (CA 1, 1978).

[144] *See, e.g.,* Rossmore House, *supra* note 100; Midwest Stock Exch., Inc. v. NLRB, 635 F2d 1255, 104 LRRM 2243 (CA 7, 1980); P.S.C. Resources, Inc. v. NLRB, 576 F2d 380, 98 LRRM 2432 (CA 1, 1978); NLRB v. J.P. Stevens Co., 563 F2d 8, 96 LRRM 2150 (CA 2, 1977); Fuqua Indus., Inc., 268 NLRB 860, 115 LRRM 1112 (1984); Struksnes Constr. Co., 165 NLRB 1062, 65 LRRM 1385 (1967).

[145] *See, e.g.,* M.A.N. Truck & Bus Corp., 272 NLRB 1279, 117 LRRM 1480 (1984) (additional paid holidays allowed); Pickering & Co., Inc., 254 NLRB 1060, 106 LRRM 1248 (1981) (supervisor's threat of plant closure unlawful despite repudiation by company president).

[146] NLRB v. Savair Mfg. Co., 414 US 270, 84 LRRM 2929 (1974).

[147] NLRA §7, 29 USC §157 (1982).

[148] NLRB v. J. Weingarten, Inc., 420 US 251, 88 LRRM 2689 (1975).

[149] *Id. See* Morris, *supra* note 19, at 149–56.

d. Rules *defining labor organizations* within the meaning of Section 2(5) of the Act and rules relating to *employer domination, support, and assistance to labor organizations* under Section 8(a)(2). As previously noted, these rules are especially important in nonunion establishments.[150] And the rule relating to lawful *recognition of labor organizations*, derived from the Supreme Court's decision in *Bernhard-Altmann*,[151] should also be promulgated and made widely available, thus advising employees and employers how they can lawfully achieve recognition of an employee plan, committee, or other labor organization.

e. Rules defining an employee's rights regarding union representation, including the union's *duty of fair representation*,[152] rights regarding *union security*,[153] *checkoff* of union dues,[154] *hiring halls*,[155] and rights concerning *resignations from union membership* in relation to strikes.[156] All of these rules relate to day-to-day conduct at unionized establishments and at union halls and offices. Clear notice of such rules would facilitate compliance with their requirements and thereby reduce the level of contested litigation.

f. There should also be a comprehensive set of rules defining *appropriate bargaining units*. The existence of such rules would assist in speeding up the representation and election process.[157]

The foregoing list is not intended to be complete, but it is especially illustrative of those rules for which the information factor is of importance. For the most part, these are rules which

---

[150] *See* discussion of concerted activity for mutual aid and protection at notes 131–49 *supra*.

[151] Garment Workers v. NLRB (Bernhard-Altmann Tex. Corp.) 366 US 731, 48 LRRM 2251 (1961).

[152] *See, e.g.*, Vaca v. Sipes, *supra* note 61; Steele v. Louisville & Nashville R.R., *supra* note 61; Truck Drivers Local 568 v. NLRB, 379 F2d 137, 65 LRRM 2309 (CA DC, 1967); Rubber Workers Local 12 (Goodyear Tire & Rubber Co.) v. NLRB, 368 F2d 12, 63 LRRM 2395 (CA 5, 1966).

[153] *See, e.g.*, Teamsters Local 46 (Port Distrib. Corp.), 236 NLRB 1175, 98 LRRM 1519 (1978); Plasterers Local 32 (McCrory & Co., Inc.), 223 N.LRB 486, 91 LRRM 1515 (1976).

[154] H.K. Porter Co. v. NLRB, 397 US 99, 73 LRRM 2561 (1970).

[155] Teamsters Local 357 v. NLRB, 365 US 667, 47 LRRM 2906 (1961); Asbestos Workers Local 80, 270 NLRB 1124, 116 LRRM 1304 (1984).

[156] Pattern Makers League v. NLRB (Rockford-Beloit Pattern Jobbers), 473 US ___, 119 LRRM 2928 (1985).

[157] *See* reference to rule making for unit determination in legislative history of the Labor Reform Bill of 1978, *supra* note 56, S. Rep. No. 95-628, 95th Cong., 2d Sess. 18–20 (1978). *See also* note 115 *supra* and favorable discussion in concurring opinion of Member Dennis and dissenting opinion of Member Zimmerman in *St. Francis Hosp.*, 271 NLRB 948, 954-55, 958, 116 LRRM 1465 (1984).

employees and employers need to know regardless of the availability of lawyers. In fact, the NLRA has become too much the exclusive domain of lawyers. Lawyers should and will always have an important role to play in the administration and enforcement of this Act, but they should not dominate the stage. The promulgation and dissemination of clear substantive rules would help to return the Act to the primary players, that is, employees, employers, and union representatives.

B. Streamlining of "R" Case Procedures

The representation and election process can be expedited by the use of two interrelated devices: (1) *rule making,* particularly rules defining appropriate bargaining units, which I have previously noted, and (2) *show cause* or *summary judgment* hearings. The Act does not specify the nature of the hearing required by Section 9(c)(1)(B) except that it be "appropriate." There is no requirement that a full-dress oral hearing be held regardless of the existence of bona fide contested issues. "Show cause" and "summary judgment" procedures, especially when coupled to rules relating to bargaining units, could substantially reduce the incidence of "live" on-the-record hearings. Other agencies have enjoyed outstanding success in using written submissions in routine cases;[158] the Board could use similar procedures in most "R" cases.

C. Making Discovery Available

Interrogatories, depositions, prehearing subpoenas, and other discovery devices, when used under proper supervision, could facilitate the enforcement process. The unreviewable discretion of the General Counsel to issue complaints and dismiss unfair labor practice charges can be justified from a due process standpoint[159] only if all reasonable efforts are made, or made available, for gathering evidence relating to a charge filed in good faith. It is indeed strange for a law enforcement agency to operate with a self-imposed handicap such as the Board's prohibition on compulsory discovery process. The greater the like-

---

[158] *See* P. Rothchild & C. Kotch, Jr., FUNDAMENTALS OF ADMINISTRATIVE PRACTICE AND PROCEDURE 162–69 (1981); Cooper Labs, Inc. v. Food & Drug Admin., 501 F2d 772 (CA DC, 1974).

[159] *Cf.* Mathew v. Eldridge, 424 US 319 (1976).

lihood of law violators being prosecuted (which in NLRB parlance means having a complaint issue), the less incentive there is for violations to occur. Discovery can be a means to ferret out evidence that the charging party or regional attorney has reason to believe is there but is unobtainable without compulsory process.

Discovery can also facilitate the settlement of cases. A high settlement rate is consistent with vigorous enforcement of the Act, provided the achieved settlements produce remedies and compliance consistent with the Act's objectives; but this result requires a realistic appraisal of available evidence by both sides. Discovery can lead not only to settlement but also to shorter hearings; both results are desirable.

The often expressed fear that employees will be intimidated through depositions is groundless. Discovery can be controlled and protected, and witnesses who testify in depositions are more visible and thus less likely to be targets of discrimination because of their visibility. Discovery, however, should not be granted without restrictions, for discovery can indeed be abused.[160] The process can be regulated and protected by requiring a showing of "reasonable need" for the discovery device sought, and administrative law judges are the logical persons to provide such oversight and protection.[161]

D. Increasing the Use of Section 10(j) Injunctions, Especially in Discharge Cases

The Taft-Hartley Congress was mindful of the Board's need for speedy injunctive relief for "all types of unfair labor practices,"[162] not just for secondary activity for which Section 10(1)[163] mandatory injunctions were provided. Section 10(j) was therefore written into the Act to provide

---

[160] *See Report of Federal Procedure Committee, Litigation Section, American Bar Association, 1984–85,* containing a survey which "confirms the federal courts' broad range of powers to sanction improper . . . discovery . . . and the courts' willingness to use that power to punish and deter abuses in the litigation process." *Cf.* Roadway Express, Inc. v. Piper, 447 US 752 (1980); National Hockey League v. Metropolitan Hockey Club, Inc., 427 US 639 (1976).

[161] *See* discussion of the proposed reorganization of Administrative Law Judge Operations, at Part VI-E, *infra,* at note 176.

[162] 1 NLRB LEGIS HIST. OF THE LABOR MANAGEMENT RELATIONS ACT, 1947, at 414 (1948).

[163] NLRA §10(1), 29 USC §160(1).

provisional or interim relief pending final Board action in a case. It was contained in the original Senate Committee bill[164] for which the Committee Report noted that "the Board will not wait, if the circumstances call for [injunctive] relief, until it has held a hearing [and] issued its order. . . ."[165] Nevertheless, Section 10(j) injunctions were little used during the early Taft-Hartley years. Their use gradually increased, and in recent years the record of successful use has been outstanding.[166] The Section 10(j) remedy received its strongest boost from General Counsel John Irving; his 1979 memorandum report[167] on Section 10(j) utilization still provides the basic guidelines for these actions. Irving's appraisal of the device in that memorandum is well worth quoting. He said:

> I strongly believe that Section 10(j) is an important tool for accomplishing the remedial purposes of the Act. The timely use of such injunction proceedings in appropriate circumstances permits maintenance of the status quo ante to assure that the Board's final order, when entered, will not be a nullity. It provides a means for assuring that the remedial purposes of the Act will not be frustrated by the delays inherent in the statutory framework for litigation.[168]

His report provided a statistical analysis which demonstrated how useful and successful the device could be. The report examined 175 cases in which petitions for injunctions had been filed. Of the 175 cases, the objectives of the Section 10(j) proceedings were accomplished in whole or in substantial part in 142 cases, or 81 percent. Of these 142 cases, 82 were concluded with a settlement of the Section 10(j) aspects of the case (and in the great majority of these the underlying Board case was also settled),[169] while in the other 60 cases an injunction was obtained, albeit in some instances the court did not grant the full extent of affirmative relief sought by the Board.[170]

General Counsel Irving noted that what was most striking about those statistics was "the high settlement rate,"[171] for in all

---

[164] S. 1126, 80th Cong., 1st Sess. (1947).

[165] *Supra* note 162, at 433.

[166] *See* Irving, *Report on Utilization of Section 10(j) Injunction Proceedings July 1, 1975, Through June 30, 1979*, NLRB-CC Memo. 79-77 (1979); Nash, *Report on 10(j) Proceedings August 1971–July 1, 1975*, NLRB-GC Memo., (1975).

[167] *Supra* note 166.

[168] *Id.* at 1.

[169] *Id.* at 4 n.3.

[170] *Id.* at 4.

[171] *Id.* at 5.

of those cases the respondent had previously shunned the Region's efforts to obtain a settlement.

Although the Board filed 73 Section 10(j) actions in the district courts in 1979, many more, even hundreds more, could have been filed. This is not a criticism of John Irving's Section 10(j) stewardship in any way; on the contrary, he deserves commendation because he demonstrated what could be done with this versatile remedial device. But even more can be done.

Let me be specific. Section 10(j) injunctions should be used almost routinely in discharge cases, particularly when the discharge occurs within the context of an organizational campaign. This would not flood the courts. Once it has been demonstrated that the remedy is available and likely to be used, there will be no advantage to an employer in discharging union activists; in fact, the judicially enforced return of such an employee prior to an election would be counterproductive to the employer's campaign. The Section 10(j) injunction is thus an important preventive measure. But even after the injunction complaint is filed in court, experience demonstrates that the case is as likely to settle as it is to go to trial. Experience under the Railway Labor Act, where injunctions against Section 8(a)(3) type conduct is presently available, suggests that such availability of quick judicial process[172] tends to discourage illegal discharges.

The potential of Section 10(j) has hardly been touched. It can be used against any kind of unfair labor practice, both against unions and against employers; it can be used whenever the Board's ordinary remedy is too late or otherwise inadequate. The Third Circuit in *Eisenberg* v. *Wellington Hall Nursing Home*[173] recognized the importance of this temporary injuctive remedy: "When the Board files an application for [10(j)] relief it is not acting on behalf of individual employees but in the public interest. . . . That interest is the integrity of the collective bargaining process."[174]

The statute requires that Section 10(j) injunctions be authorized by the Board. Thus, the General Counsel must first request the authorization, and if and when it is granted (and it is almost always granted) the General Counsel proceeds to file the action in court. The present loosely structured procedure is awk-

---

[172] *E.g.*, Airline Pilots v. Alaska Aeronautical Indus., 95 LRRM 2868 (D. Alaska, 1977).
[173] 651 F2d 902, 107 LRRM 2958 (CA 3, 1981).
[174] *Id.* at 907 n.4.

ward,[175] but such awkwardness is only the product of the long-time failure of the Board and General Counsel to make a combined effort to streamline the process. Section 10(j) cases could move almost as fast as Section 10(1) cases, provided the Board and the General Counsel wanted to achieve that result.

The streamlined Section 10(j) process should begin with the filing of the charge. The charge form itself should make preliminary inquiry as to the need for rapid and temporary relief. And with a quick screening process at the regional level, the General Counsel's recommendation to the Board could move rapidly. The case should also receive expedited treatment on the Board side. A rotating three-member panel could be maintained on a standby basis at all times and thus be available to authorize filing the action without delay; and one member, also designated on a rotating basis, could be primarily responsible for the Section 10(j) docket. The process could become routine and simple if the General Counsel's recommendations are prompt and adequate. These procedures would not be difficult, and they could be activated with amazing speed if the Board and General Counsel should decide to use this remedy to compensate for the sluggishness of the Board's ordinarily slow hearing and remedial processes. The benefits to the enforcement process could be phenomenal.

E. Reorganization of Administrative Law Judge Operations

In its adjudication of unfair labor practices, the Board is a court. It is as much a court as the United States Tax Court.[176] Both are Article I (legislative) courts, but the Tax Court is perceived as a court, whereas the Board is not. The long tenure of tax judges—15 years—certainly makes a difference; nevertheless, given the desire, the Board could act more like a court as to many of its functions. It was not enough to change the title of trial examiners to administrative law judges. They must also function like judges, at least to the extent allowed by the statute. Their judicial function could be improved if they were permitted to act more like court judges. Within the limits allowed by the statute, the following recommendations are designed to assist in their achieving that status.

[175.] See NLRB CASE HANDLING MANUAL, (Pt. 1), Unfair Labor Practice Proceedings, §§10310–12 (1983).

[176] Internal Revenue Code, 26 USC §7441 (1982).

1. The ALJs should be geographically decentralized, not merely located (as at present) for reasons of administrative convenience and individual ALJ choice. This decentralization should be part of an integrated scheme of enforcement. Although individual ALJs should be subject to both temporary and permanent geographical transfer to meet the needs of the agency's docket, for the most part they should be conveniently located in major metropolitan cities where the parties, that is, their attorneys, will have easy access to them, to their chambers, and to their courtrooms.

2. As soon as a complaint issues the case should be assigned to a designated ALJ. That assignment might be changed later if necessary, but to the extent possible the same ALJ should handle every motion and ruling that has to be made on his or her assigned case until that case reaches the Board.

3. Pretrial conferences, discovery motions, summary judgment motions (including partial summary judgments) should be entertained and encouraged. The parties should know they are in a "court" where there is a real, live judge available to hear their motions.

4. The ALJ should also be an additional conduit for Section 10(j) injunctive relief. Should it become apparent to the assigned ALJ, by appropriate motion, that facts exist that require temporary judicial restraint, the judge should make such recommendation to the Board, either in an interim order or as part of the ALJ decision; and the Board should give such recommendation great deference, for the recommendation comes from the very person who, at that stage of the proceeding, is in the best position to make an objective assessment of the need for extraordinary remedial action.

I believe that if the Board were to allow the ALJs to act more like judges, their enhanced role would encourage settlements, reduce hearing time, and generally project a better image for the entire agency.

F. Ordering Damage-Specific Final Remedies

Ironically, the familiar "affirmative action" concept originated with the National Labor Relations Act, which was the source of similar language in Title VII of the Civil Rights Act of 1964.[177]

---

[177] Civil Rights Act of 1964, §706(g), 42 USC §2000e-5(g) (1970). *See* Franks v. Bowman Transp. Co., *supra* note 31; Albemarle Paper Co. v. Moody, *supra* note 31; Morris, *The Role of the Courts in the Collective Bargaining Process: A Fresh Look at Conventional Wisdom and Unconventional Remedies*, 30 VAND. L. REV. 661, 676–77 (1977).

But in the hands of federal district judges, the affirmative action concept was used imaginatively and effectively to make Title VII the law of the land for which there was substantial voluntary compliance—something that has never been true of the NLRA. It is indeed late—but it will never get any earlier; so the Board should now go forward and order more effective "make-whole" remedies. As long as such remedies reasonably restore the status quo ante, they should be able to pass judicial muster and not be reversed for being either punitive or in violation of Section 8(d), which is what occurred in the *H.K. Porter*[178] case. Here are some suggested examples of damage-specific remedies:

1. *Section 8(a)(5) orders that relate to every item of unilateral activity affecting mandatory subjects of bargaining.* This remedy, to be fully effective, should be coupled with a rule which clearly puts bargaining parties on notice that once a labor organization has been established as bargaining agent, *every* action of the employer relating to mandatory subjects, including discipline, discharges, layoffs, promotions, and of course merit increases, must be negotiated to impasse with the bargaining agent. Although a union could conditionally waive its negotiation rights as to individual and ad hoc situations pending agreement on an entire collective bargaining contract, it could also withdraw that waiver whenever it felt that bargaining on the contract was not progressing satisfactorily. In the event of a finding of a Section 8(a)(5) violation, the Board, similar to its approach in *Trading Port*,[179] should seek to remedy each situation in which the employer has acted unilaterally, even if that requires nullifying some promotions, demotions, wage changes, and other actions involving conditions of employment, including layoffs and discharges where the Board can determine that they were not made for cause.[180] The Board's process should not be looked upon as a game, with certifications and cease-and-desist orders being viewed merely as separate rounds in the sport of

178 H.K. Porter Co., Inc., 153 NLRB 1370, 59 LRRM 1462 (1965), *enforced sub nom.* Steelworkers v. NLRB, 363 F2d 272, 62 LRRM 2204 (CA DC), *cert. denied,* 385 US 851 (1966), *reconsidered,* 389 F2d 295, 66 LRRM 2761 (1967), *supplemented,* 172 NLRB 966, 68 LRRM 1337 (1968), *aff'd,* 414 F2d 1123, 71 LRRM 2207 (CA DC, 1969), *rev'd,* 397 US 99, 73 LRRM 2561 (1970).

179 Seeler v. Trading Port, Inc., 517 F2d 33, 89 LRRM 2513 (CA 2, 1975).

180 *Cf.* NLRB v. Thayer Co., 213 F2d 748, 34 LRRM 2250 (CA 1), *cert. denied,* 348 US 883 (1954), *supplemented,* 115 NLRB 1591, 38 LRRM 1142 (1956).

"industrial-relations combat." The duty to bargain should be made to be what it was intended to be: a duty.

2. *Interest on back-pay awards* should be based on what it would have cost the dischargee to borrow the money of which he or she was deprived as a result of the unlawful termination—in other words, consumer-loan rates, which are rarely lower than 16 percent and often as high as 21 percent. For some employers, it might no longer be cost-effective to discharge employees to discourage pro-union sentiment.

3. *"Frivolous defense" reimbursement* for attorneys fees, organizational expenses, dues, etc.[181] should be ordered more often. This remedy should be based upon an examination of all of the respondent's defenses, and if one or only a few of a larger number of mostly frivolous defenses is debatable, the stronger reimbursement remedy should apply.[182]

4. *Other examples.* What is required for an effective remedy is a matching of the offense with the harm that it has caused. The remedy selected should be a solution consistent with the Act's objectives. One example of a missed opportunity was the Board majority's failure to adopt Member Walther's remedy in *Atlas Tack Corp.*,[183] where the employer had reduced compensated time by unilaterally changing break and lunch periods and the length of the workday. Member Walther dissented from imposition of the traditional remedy of distributing the sum among past and present employees, which did virtually nothing to restore the collective bargaining process that had been bypassed, proposing instead to treat the total amount of back pay as a fund over which the parties could negotiate at the bargaining table. He reasoned that "the highest possible priority must be given to restoring the union to its pre-unlawful conduct strength. . . . [E]very effort must be made to create an environment in which it is economically advantageous for the employer to engage in meaningful collective bargaining.[184] That kind of analysis could be used effectively in many situations, so that "make whole" would become an attainable goal.

---

[181] *E.g.*, Truck Drivers Local 705 (Gasoline Retailers Ass'n of Metropolitan Chicago), 210 NLRB 210, 86 LRRM 1011 (1974).

[182] *See* Morris, *supra* note 177, at 667–80.

[183] 226 NLRB 222, 93 LRRM 1236 (1976). *See* Morris, *supra* note 177, at 683–84.

[184] 226 NLRB at 223.

G. Section 10(e) and 10(f) injunctions

The provisions in Section 10 relating to enforcement and review of the Board's final orders in a U.S. Circuit Court of Appeals contain authority for the appellate court to issue "such temporary relief or restraining order as it deems just and proper." I recognize the reluctance of many Courts of Appeal to grant such relief, primarily due to the Board's own delayed process.[185] Nevertheless, a strong and persistent effort should be made to use this injunctive power with some frequency. This may require the Board not only to speed up its own decisional process in general, but also to establish a hearing record in specific cases showing the need for such relief. Partial remand to the ALJ who originally heard the case to make special findings of fact regarding the need for certain damage-specific remedies may be appropriate. Also special hearings on the issue of appropriate remedy, conducted by the ALJ prior to the time the case goes to the Board, may at times be justified. The latter device would be another advantage of having the same ALJ in charge of the case from the day the complaint issues to the day the case is transferred to the Board on exceptions.

VII. Where Do We Go From Here?

Where do we go from here? This last set of recommendations, which has focused on procedures and remedies already in the statute, was based on the premise that Congress intended the Act to be enforceable as to all its provisions and that the Act contains adequate means to achieve such enforcement. But how can the Board and the General Counsel be convinced to utilize those means? And how can a President (or Presidents) in the appointment process be convinced to make consistent appointments of highly qualified persons of judicial temperament, preferably nonpolitical appointments, where there will be a mutual understanding and expectation that their mandate includes an intent to exercise the full statutory powers of the position? Let me

---

[185] *E.g.*, NLRB v. Aerovox Corp. of Myrtle Beach, 389 F2d 475, 67 LRRM 2158 (CA 4, 1967). *See* Irving, *Attachment C*, LABOR RELATIONS YEARBOOK—1976, 378–81 (BNA Books, 1977), regarding Section 10(e) relief, in which the General Counsel stated: "Overcoming the reluctance of the courts to grant 10(e) relief would be a highly significant step in achieving the remedial purposes of the Act." *Id.* at 381. That memorandum also noted, "if there is to be court acceptance of the 10(e) remedy, the problem of administrative delay must be alleviated." *Id.* at 381. Unfortunately, the problem still exists.

hasten to add that over the years almost all of the appointees to the Board and to the office of General Counsel have been eminently qualified, but there was never any special expectation or implied mandate that they would enforce the Act with full vigor and imagination.

As I indicated earlier, I am pessimistic about the Board's future. But the Board is too important to the American political and economic system to be jettisoned without every reasonable effort being made to save it and use it. If a President had the desire and political courage, as well as either strong popular support or substantial consensus among leading figures in the industrial relations community, or if the majority of the Board and the General Counsel, acting with the independence which is supposed to characterize an independent federal agency, were similarly motivated to chart a new course, then perhaps—just perhaps—the Board might be steered in a new direction; and it might become sufficiently depoliticized to achieve most of its true potential, or at least to make a beginning move in that direction. But if this does not occur, then we should explore other alternatives, including a labor court.

Regardless of the direction taken, the National Labor Relations Act itself can be of inestimable value to the American industrial relations system and the economy it was intended to serve. Long-range economic objectives, particularly those relating to more equitable income distribution domestically and more successful industrial competition internationally, can benefit from a smoothly functioning industrial relations system, especially a system such as the National Labor Relations Act, which is based on principles of democracy and freedom of choice. The normative patterns which that Act was intended to foster can and should serve a vital role in moving this nation's economy toward those long-range objectives.

Responses

A VIEW FROM THE INSIDE

ROSEMARY M. COLLYER*

Virtually every participant in this symposium volume has emphasized the 50th anniversary as an occasion for evaluating

* General Counsel, National Labor Relations Board.

the successes and the failures of the National Labor Relations Act. I will be no different.

Fifty years is a long time as government policies go. When one considers that the National Labor Relations Act has been the labor policy of this nation for more than 25 percent of its Constitutional history, one realizes by just how much our national labor policy has contributed to the American way of life and thought. The Act has seen modification and expansion in the years since 1935 but, as Professor Morris has suggested, its basic principles have remained intact. Section 7, the secret ballot, and the concept of exclusive representation are but three of its fundamental principles; principles that have become almost self-evident to us 50 years later. We may debate just how these principles should apply this year and beyond. But that debate has been continuing since the first expression of national policy in the 1930s and does not affect the almost universal acceptance of the need for and the wisdom of our national labor policy.

Professor Morris argues that the Board has not done a very good job in its enforcement of the Act, and he is not without his supporters. He has suggested that there has been an erosion of the Board's enforcement authority during the past two decades and that unless the Board is willing to enforce the statute, and to do so with a reasonable regard for stare decisis, then other methods of enforcing our national labor policy, most notably, a labor court, should be sought.

I must disagree with Professor Morris. Of course, I am not going to argue and suggest that the Board and the Office of the General Counsel are perfect. I doubt that there are many people, Professor Morris included, who would argue that any judicial system is perfect, even our Article III courts. That being so, is there any reason to believe that the simple substitution of one forum for another would occasion any major improvements in how the Act is enforced? I think not. Indeed, I would argue that the substitution of a labor court for the Board would undoubtedly increase the time it takes to finally resolve unfair labor practice and representation cases.

The Labor Court proposal would exacerbate timeliness problems because it would do away with the concept—embodied in Section 3(d) of the NLRA—of a public prosecutor with final authority to determine whether unfair labor practice charges warrant prosecution. While Professor Morris' administrative agency would perform the functions of investigating unfair labor practice cases and prosecuting them before the Labor Court, he would, in cases in which the agency refuses to issue a complaint, permit the charging party acting alone to prosecute the case before the court. In my view this would sacrifice—without any corresponding gain—the expeditious procedure for the disposition of no merit charges inherent in the present structure. One example: Today, with prompt investigations, we resolve over 90 percent of the cases within 45 days, and without formal litigation. That is a fine record, and I shall come back to this a little later to show how we also assure that these resolutions are properly made.

If an outside review procedure existed, it would extend the period of uncertainty as to whether something done by an employer or a union is legal—leading to an increase in hostility, the hardening of positions, and the likelihood of a strike or lockout. Moreover, there would be no protection for labor or management from baseless prosecutions. I am sure that this reviewing authority would sustain most refusals to issue complaint, but in the meantime respondents would be required to defend themselves at yet another level, with all the additional costs that implies, both to them and to the taxpayers.

But perhaps I have jumped ahead of myself. Professor Morris has indicated that in his view, the Labor Court should be a last resort and that ideally, the restructuring he would like and the revitalization he considers necessary, can come from within the agency itself. All of that assumes the question: Is there a problem? And if there is, what exactly is it?

One particular area referenced by Professor Morris in his paper is time delay. Let's begin with a look at the Agency with the Office of the General Counsel. In my view, there is every reason to be proud of and even to celebrate the fine time record of the regional offices and the headquarters offices of the General Counsel. It is a record that has been achieved through the efforts of a dedicated career staff and a generally cooperative labor-management bar. While I am sure that much of this information is well known, some of this record is worth repeating. The regions regularly investigate and decide unfair labor practice cases within 30 days of their filing. As to meritorious cases, those worthy of prosecution, our settlement record has been above 90 percent for four years. Stated another way, we find merit or a basis for prosecution in about 35 percent of the cases and we then settle about 95 percent of those cases.

For representation cases, the statistics are equally impressive. The rate for stipulated elections is about 80 percent and for the remaining 20 percent that require a hearing, we hold that hearing, receive briefs from the parties, and then decide the case in a median of about 40 days. We regularly meet our goal of holding elections within 50 days of the filing of a petition; a goal, I should add, that is not achieved without some complaints from both labor and management that we have woodenly applied this 50-day goal.

There is always the danger that an administrative agency will become so involved with its statistics that it forgets its mission. That is a danger of which General Counsels have always been wary, and I think our wariness and that of our staffs has basically kept us from this bureaucratic trap. These time goals are management tools; they are not ends in themselves. But they are also a barometer of the kind of response that the vast majority of charging parties and petitioners receive when they seek the assistance of the Agency. Is there *really* a timeliness problem here?

There is of course that minority of cases; those that go through the entire and sometimes tortured litigation process. They take a long time—too long. But I suggest to you that as long as they can take, there is no reason to believe that their resolution would be expedited in an Article III labor court.

Time is only one element of the process. Quality is another and equally important aspect of our work. Professor Morris' suggestion of an erosion of the Board's enforcement authority over the past 20 years raises that quality issue. For a part of the answer I went back to our figures for 1958 to see just how that enforcement authority worked in those "good old days." Why 1958? Well that was the year just prior to the famous speech of then-Senator John F. Kennedy in which he decried the delays at the Board and likened a Board proceeding to Charles Dickens' *Bleak House* trial of *Jarndyce* v. *Jarndyce*. Well, in 1958 we issued unfair labor practice complaints in a median time of 116 days, not 45. While some have feared we shortcut investigations to be timely, the evidence is clearly to the contrary. In 1958 we found merit in approximately 20 percent of the charges filed. In 1984 we found, as we have for many years, merit in about 34 percent of the cases. Stated a little differently, we now find merit in over 60 percent more of our case load than we did in 1958, and we do it 150 percent more quickly than we did then. Add to that mix the settlement rate of 90–95 percent and there is nothing that even faintly resembles erosion. Indeed, it shows that we find merit in more cases, settle more of them, and do it a lot more quickly than we did before the so-called "erosion" began.

Let me turn to another area in which I think we have generally served the statutory purposes well.

Successive General Counsels and Boards have become increasingly convinced that the Board's authority under Section 10(j) to seek temporary injunctions terminating alleged unfair labor practices and restoring and maintaining the status quo pending litigation before the Board is among the most effective weapons available to the Board in its enforcement of the Act. I firmly share this conviction.

In the past few years, we have seen a substantial decrease in the number of requests for Section 10(j) relief and in our overall case load. Recently, in response to inquiries from a House Subcommittee, I noted that the decline in Section 10(j) activity may reflect the general falloff in new organizing campaigns as well as several significant changes in the law regarding employers' rights to remove or relocate bargaining-unit work. Both of those areas historically were a major source of injunction proceedings in the past. I therefore repeat what I stated to the House Subcommittee: Any decrease in Section 10(j) activity does not reflect a diminution of my or the Agency's commitment to the utilization of injunction proceedings in appropriate cases. Indeed, just the contrary is true.

In this respect, the preliminary figures for the fiscal year of 1985 ending September 30 reveal that Section 10(j) most assuredly is "alive and well." Thus, at a time when the number of requests for Section 10(j) relief has declined from the previous year by about 15 percent (from 195 to 165 requests), the number of cases in which I requested and the Board granted authorization to initiate injunction proceedings increased 27 percent (from 30 to 38). Moreover, I am taking steps to assure that this policy of aggressive and imaginative utilization of Section 10(j) proceedings will continue, and I have identified Section 10(j) as an area of focus during my term.

I am not going to suggest that there is no room for improvement at the agency. We all know that there are individual cases that take a long time. The question is whether we need a change in the very structure of the Act and its enforcement mechanisms to do better. I am certain we can do better in these individual cases, but as far as time generally is concerned, I have my doubts that the General Counsel's Office could make any major reductions in the time that cases are under our control or even if any further reductions would be advisable. Due process will simply not permit us to squeeze our time performance much more.

For the cases that go the full litigation route, improvement can be made and is on its way. The administrative law judges have done a wonderful job of digging out of the trial backlog occasioned by a shortage of judges a few years ago. And the Board is committed to reducing its backlog and the time it takes to decide cases.

Professor Morris has suggested a number of other changes that deserve some comment. First, the proposal for a change in the "R" case hearing procedures. He has proposed "orders to show cause." That will not in my view change the requirement or obviate the Board's obligation that absent an agreement, it must hold a preelection hearing. Quite simply, Section 9(c)(1)(B) mandates such hearings and the proposal in the so-called Labor Law Reform bill of a few years ago for such a change was one of its more controversial provisions.

Second, Professor Morris has proposed that the Board begin to utilize interrogatories, depositions, prehearing subpoenas, and other discovery devices as a means of facilitating the investigative and settlement processes. This is an issue which has been debated for many years. I believe that engaging in full discovery will slow down the process rather than facilitate it. Anyone who has engaged in the private practice of law knows the length of time that discovery consumes. That delay, whether before the Board or an Article III court, would operate to the detriment of that which Professor Morris hopes to achieve. There may be a number of arguments for discovery, but expedition is certainly not one of them.

Finally, Professor Morris proposes extensive APA rule making in substantive areas of labor policy. He suggests that this procedure will lead to certainty in the law, efficiency in practice, and time conservation by the agency. While I endorse those goals, I am not convinced that a sweeping adoption of rule making will produce them.

The Board in the past had been reluctant to use rule making as a substitute for adjudication. Instead, it has preferred an incremental approach to the development of labor policy, adapting the law to the specifics of each dispute and building upon the commonality of facts in actual disputes to determine the overall structure of the law. While change occurs, the changes wrought by adjudication are less dramatic than changes achieved through rule making. Adjudication permits the testing of theories in relation to the actual facts of individual disputes. This process has been successful in addressing the endless variety of facts and circumstances that must be weighed in balancing rights under the statute. In high visibility cases, the flexibility of the adjudicatory process may draw attention and provoke criticism, but, in my opinion, the answer is not usually rule making.

Rule making may result in more stability in the law, but that stability can become rigidity and can result in a law that fails to account for the variations in approaches across the spectrum of today's labor-management relations. The solution, in my view, may lie with a careful use of rule making in limited areas. It seems to me that wholesale rule making at this watershed time of changes in the industrialization of this country may be exactly the *wrong* thing to do. Rule making based on the patterns of working life over the last 50 years could well rob the agency and labor and management of the need to approach the 1990s with new understandings of labor relations in the real world.

One thing that can be done to improve effective enforcement of the Act is to ensure compliance with the Board's orders. I have identified compliance as an urgent focus during my term as General Counsel and we are and will devote increased personnel and other resources to that effort. We are also identifying new or expanded remedies to cure violations that are found. This effort will continue during my tenure. In the areas of remedies and compliance, I agree with Professor Morris' basic thesis that we can do more to enforce the Act within the existing structure.

It is not easy to find a good closing for this commentary. I certainly do not want to leave the impression that I think everything is "just fine" at the NLRB. It is not, but then again no organization is ever "just fine."

At the same time, I cannot accept what I believe is the overly broad criticism of the Agency. We are in a highly charged field of human activity, and we have a high visibility in that field. It is to be expected that in given cases and at given times parties will be very critical of decisions by regional directors, General Counsels, or Boards. That goes with the territory. But, we cannot let that criticism ignore the outstanding record this Agency has had over its first half century. Millions of working people are better off because this Agency is and has been there and because of the way that the Act has been enforced. That needs saying over and over again, because people need to know that they can have access to a truly responsive arm of government when they need help.

A SYSTEM IN DISEQUILIBRIUM

LAURENCE GOLD*

I have a few unpleasant things to say, and I shall be very brief. At the present time, I have no faith in the efficacy of procedural change as the means to revitalizing the statute. I was thinking as I read through Professor Morris' paper that the labor injunction was as superb a procedural mechanism as could be achieved. Historically, however, it was generally felt that its ends were wrong and that its social consequences were unacceptable. I now feel that if we look at the Section 8(a) part of this Act, we must come to the conclusion that the combination of the rules themselves and the interrelated development of those rules by the Board and the courts has led to a situation with regard to employee free choice that has brought us more or less back to the situation as it obtained before the Act was passed.

Congress, the Board, and the courts have enormously underestimated the extent of employer determination to maintain the status as sole master of the enterprise and as the figure who is entitled to loyalty and to punish disloyalty. The rules that govern the organizing campaign may have changed the methods of coercion that are available, but in my judgment they have done little or nothing to change the final result. There is no employer—certainly no employer who employs a lawyer of any talent—who cannot make it absolutely plain to his employees, more or less within the limits of the law as it currently stands, that the employer does not want them to organize, that their determination as to whether or not they organize will be taken heavily into account by the employer, and that the ultimate question is whether or not they are loyal to him, and the ultimate reckoning will be punishment for disloyalty. And in those terms, insofar as the Act was designed to change the brute fact of the employer's dominance in such a situation, the Act has failed. And I do not

---

* General Counsel; American Federation of Labor and Congress of Industrial Organizations.

believe that procedural niceties and questions of whether the Board's present enforcement record—much of which is made on the backs of employers who are not content with winning almost everything in the Agency and continue to fatten up their batting average by taking cases to equally friendly courts—are at all determinative as to whether this law has vitality at this point in time.

I think that this situation has come about because today there are no major shared objectives between management and labor. This Act is important to unions in the most basic terms: whether or not there will be organization, whether or not there will be collective bargaining, and in some sense whether or not there will be a labor movement of the kind we know. But despite the strong rhetoric used by the Chamber of Commerce and the National Association of Manufacturers in commenting on marginal decisions, the Act is still not of the essence to the employer community. There is no way that the Board or the courts in administering this Act can basically change the nature of American enterprise. There will be employers and there will be a free enterprise system, no matter what the Labor Board does and no matter how the Act is interpreted. And under those terms, the equation is completely one-sided, which the employers of this country recognize. This was demonstrated vividly in 1977 and 1978 by a comparison of the response, and solidity of that response, to the initiative which labor took, and the pablum that was proposed to Congress at that time. Much of that pablum—in saying this I do not denigrate either what we tried to do or Professor Morris' paper—comes back in the form of many of his recommendations: rule making on units, more use of the injunctive process in organizing campaigns, and the like. Those proposals failed in 1978 not because they were either radical or without sound objective and neutral credentials. They failed because the management view is that the less organization there is the better and the less collective bargaining there is the better.

What will eventuate from that attitude and the stalemate it produces in the political process, in the Board, and the courts, I do not know. I can only say that it will produce something extraordinarily different from what we have today; and as in any system which is in essential disequilibrium, it will produce one of two things. It will either produce a more militant, and in those terms a better labor movement—better in the sense of a movement able to push with enormous vigor to right the social wrongs that exist today, a movement that is capable of producing a more efficient and cooperative industrial relations system—or it will produce the prelude to such a labor movement, namely, a situation such as existed in the first 30 or 40 years of this century in which people who work for a living know that they are powerless, do not know what to do about it, but look for the opportunity to change.

Major Surgery Not Required

Andrea S. Christensen*

The proposals presented by Professor Charles Morris are directed toward identifying administrative or statutory solutions to the National Labor Relations Board's pernicious problem of delay. It is Professor Morris' overriding premise that justice delayed is justice denied. While this may not be a universal truth, there is no question but that delay in the administrative process is a significant problem confronting both the Board and the federal courts that are responsible for enforcing the National Labor Relations Act, as amended, and the employers and unions whose conduct is regulated by the Board.

In my view, the problem of Board delay cannot be effectively eliminated by layering the administrative process with additional procedural hurdles or discovery techniques, such as written interrogatories, oral depositions, or expanded subpoena power. I am equally unpersuaded that the creation of yet another and separate adjudicatory body, a National Labor Court, would expedite the administrative process. In the final analysis, the only effective way to expedite the administrative timetable is to find ways to encourage the participants themselves to precipitate the changes. Only if the parties who are governed by the administrative process are determined to change the current situation, will any real progress by realized.

A successful model where management and labor have voluntarily agreed to utilize a dispute resolution system that has the capacity for greater expedition is arbitration. The arbitration system can be quick and relatively inexpensive if and when the

* Partner, Kaye, Scholer, Fierman, Hays & Handler, New York, New York.

parties want it that way, but not because the system contains a mechanism that imposes expedition on the parties.

The notion that if punitive action were taken against repeat violators of the National Labor Relations Act recidivism and delay would decline is pure hypothesis. As a practical matter, an award of punitive damages would more likely produce a contrary result, by precipitating even more vigorous resistance to the underlying statutory system. If punitive remedies are imposed, the appeals to federal courts will involve the authority of the Board to impose the penalties as well as the merits of the Board's underlying order.

Professor Morris' more drastic proposals would not be an issue if labor and management representatives were willing to work together to insist that their disputes be processed under the existing administrative structure as expeditiously as possible. Indeed, it is not a universal truth, as Professor Morris has suggested, that all employers find the Board's sluggish administrative process to work in their favor. Unresolved representational questions or threatened prosecution as to ongoing conduct or programs can seriously impair an employer's ability to conduct its business. Nor do large back-pay awards that result from delayed adjudication provide the necessary incentive for employers to settle or terminate the dispute amicably. Thus, though a joint effort between management and labor to streamline the Board's handling of its case load is not likely in most cases, parties should recognize that if either party insists upon expedition, such efforts on the part of even one party can help to overcome the inertia of the Board and the resistance of the other party.

Professor Morris' paper recounts numerous statistics as to union organizational losses caused by employer resistance or Board delay. Employers confront similar problems with the Board when filing an unfair labor practice charge against a union, though not to the same degree. One reason for this is that many employers do not expect the regional director or the Board to do any of the advance work for them.

When filing an unfair labor practice charge, many employers investigate and prepare their case in advance even before going to the regional office. Such employers prepare initial affidavits and submit them to the regional office with the relevant documents that support their charge at the same time that they file the charge. Thereafter, they personally follow through on the investigation to ensure that the charge is being investigated properly and in a timely manner and to provide whatever additional information is needed by the Board to complete its investigation.

If a charging party merely files a charge and then waits for the regional director to act, delay inevitably ensues. Full cooperation on the part of the charging party in the conduct of the investigation is critical to an expeditious conclusion of the process. If witnesses or documents are not readily produced, the charging party should not fault the Board for the delay. Indeed, Professor Morris' findings as to the Board's failure to aggressively pursue complaints filed by individuals against unions is a perfect example of the type of investigation where the regional office is permitted to follow its own schedule without any pressure from the charging party, with the result that the charge is allowed to disappear into the administrative morass.

Professor Morris' suggestion that enforcement under Title VII has been more successful is simply not true. Though civil rights advocates would be heartened to learn that there have been such successes, they would not believe it. It is, in fact, the lesson of the problems with Title VII litigation that mitigates against Professor Morris' proposal for a National Labor Court and adoption of courtroom-style procedures. The interminable delay caused by the Equal Employment Opportunity Commission in its investigations, coupled with the overuse of pretrial discovery techniques have frequently resulted in the outright dismissal of a Title VII claim, not just a delay in its adjudication.[1] For this reason alone, the Title VII model should not be considered as a prototype for expediting case administration by the Board.

The proposal that a broad-gauged judicial body of 13 national judges could adjudicate all types of labor cases is not a practical one. In the first place, it would be virtually impossible for a group of national judges to develop the type of expertise in the multitude of areas covered by the existing labor laws that would be required. To enumerate a few, a national judge would have to

---

[1] EEOC v. Dresser Indus. Inc., 668 F2d 1199, 29 FEP 249 (CA 11, 1982); EEOC v. Liberty Loan Corp., 584 F2d 853, 18 FEP 303 (CA 8, 1978); EEOC v. Martin Processing, Inc., 533 F Supp 227, 28 FEP 1825 (W.D. Va., 1982); EEOC v. Kelley Mfg. Co., 20 EMPL. PRAC. DEC. (CCH) ¶30,071 (N.D. Ala., 1979); EEOC v. Bray Lumber Co., 478 F Supp 993, 21 FEP 510 (M.D. Ga., 1979); EEOC v. American Petrofina Co., 17 EMPL. PRAC. DEC. (CCH) ¶8555 (E.D. Tex., 1977).

be conversant with the statutory provisions of not only the National Labor Relations Act, but also Title VII of the Civil Rights Act of 1964, the Age Discrimination in Employment Act, the Occupational Safety and Health Act, the Fair Labor Standards Act, the Equal Pay Act, and the developing law under the duty of fair representation doctrine. Secondly, it is not at all clear how assignment of these cases to a national court would affect the existing right to a jury trial now available under several of these federal laws.

Furthermore, the exorbitant cost of litigation in a judicial arena would preclude most individuals as well as many small unions and employers from seeking redress under these statutes. For, while the Board's investigatory and adjudicatory procedures may be slow, they are available at virtually no cost to the charging party. The transfer of jurisdiction for enforcement of these various labor laws to a labor court would seriously handicap *pro se* efforts and would require charging parties to obtain legal representation in order to effectively pursue their claims.

For these reasons, it is not likely that a National Labor Court could, as a practical matter, have a beneficial effect on expediting the enforcement activity under the National Labor Relations Act. At the present time, the Title VII case load has overwhelmed the federal trial courts. It does not seem possible that a group of 13 judges could assume this case load and also adjudicate cases involving half a dozen or more additional federal laws.

In my view, contrary to Professor Morris' position, I consider that the absence of any meaningful right to review the NLRB General Counsel's refusal to issue a complaint and the restrictions that prevent a charging party from pursuing an unfair labor practice charge directly in federal court are significant strengths in the existing system. One of the reasons for the intolerable delays involving Title VII litigation is the inability of the EEOC to foreclose litigation on nonmeritorious discrimination charges. This fact alone has disenchanted many with the viability of the federal discrimination laws. The prosecution of countless nonmeritorious discrimination cases in the federal courts significantly detracts from the credibility of the statutory scheme as a whole.

Moreover, it has not been my experience that the Board's regional directors normally decide issues that involve matters of credibility. To the contrary, in most cases, it is the presence of credibility issues that result in the issuance of a complaint to initiate a hearing before an administrative law judge. If the system is to work at all we should learn from the experience under Title VII that not every claim of unlawful conduct should be entitled to a full adversary hearing.

Professor Morris has correctly pointed out that there are virtues to administrative rule making to the extent that it can reduce the volume of litigation over uncertain statutory interpretations. But, once again rule making is an effective tool only if the parties whose conduct is to be governed by the rules are predisposed to cooperate with the system.

Many of the evils attendant to case-by-case adjudication are equally applicable to administrative rule making. Thus, parties who are so inclined can seek to test the outer limits of the rule instead of the last case. Moreover, though the process is more leisurely, rules as well as administrative precedent will change as the political composition of the rule-making body is changed.

Finally, inordinate delay can be involved in the promulgation of the rule itself. Indeed, the EEOC's efforts to obtain the requisite consensus to promulgate regulations under Title VII exemplifies the problem in this area. Moreover, any administrative agency such as the NLRB whose full member complement is so rarely in place cannot realistically engage in extensive rule making.

Thus, though rule making by the NLRB would help to clarify some of the Agency's current positions on the law, the process would have no significant impact on the problem of administrative delay unless the attitude of the parties were to change. In the case of those whose mission it is to resist the statutory system, the implementation of rule making provides a further opportunity to litigate the rule-making procedure as well as the rule itself.

A recent Ninth Circuit case is an example of a form of rule making that went awry.[2] In this case, the union filed a petition for representation on November 25, 1980, and the election was scheduled for February 26, 1981. The employer disputed the Regional Director's unit determination and a request for review was filed with the Board. The day before the election the Board granted the employer's request for review, but pursuant to Chairman Murphy's Task Force recommendations and a modification in the Board's regulations, the election was held on the

---

[2] NLRB v. Lorimar Prods., Inc., 771 F2d 1294, 120 LRRM 2425 (CA 9, 1985).

scheduled date and the ballots were impounded. Seven months after the election, in September 1981, the Board ruled that 6 of the 17 employees who voted were confidential employees and should be excluded from the unit. The ballots were opened and counted. The union won the election and the unit was certified. The employer refused to bargain, and the Board ultimately found that the employer's refusal to bargain violated Section 8(a)(5) of the Act. On appeal to the Ninth Circuit and almost *five years* after the original petition was filed, the Board's order was denied enforcement. In the Ninth Circuit's view, the Board should have conducted a *Globe* election and the Board's failure to provide two different ballots for the two possible units deprived the employees of their right to vote for the unit that was ultimately certified by the Board.

Though this case did not involve actual substantive rule making, the Board's decision to impound the ballots was based on a regulation that had been adopted following extensive study and review by leading experts in the field and formally adopted by the Board. This administrative ruling did nothing to reduce the delay involved in this type of election procedure which has now been challenged by both the Ninth and Second Circuits.[3] On the contrary, this issue has been left in a state of greater confusion than if the Board had rendered its decision on a case-by-case basis.

Professor Morris' suggestion that the National Labor Relations Board should require employers and unions to post a general notice describing the Act's basic statutory provisions has merit. Any such notice would have to be a simple, noncontroversial description of the Act's basic requirements and of the rights of employees to participate or not in the activities of a union.

As a practical matter, however, one cannot expect such a notice to accomplish much more than to ensure that employees be exposed to a basic recitation of the laws that affect their working life. If such a notice can even be read on the normally cluttered company bulletin board, it does little to educate as to the actual substance of the statutory rights and obligations involved.

I would strongly oppose, however, any proposal that the NLRB adopt the pretrial discovery procedures that have so stalled the progress of Title VII litigation through the federal

---

[3] *Id.*; Hamilton Test Sys. v. NLRB, 743 F2d 136, 117 LRRM 2248 (CA 2, 1984).

district courts. Much of the delay that currently occurs in Title VII litigation before the federal courts is caused by disputes between the litigants as to the appropriate scope of written interrogatories, oral depositions, and subpoenas. At a time when the federal district courts are attempting to reduce, and in some cases even eliminate, the extent to which pretrial discovery can be utilized, it is unlikely that there would be any receptivity to a proposal that such problems be incorporated into additional statutory enforcement procedures.

Moreover, it has been my experience that pretrial discovery does not normally shorten the actual hearing. On the contrary, discovery tends to generate even more evidence, much of which is irrelevant, but all of which the discovering party must sort through and attempt to introduce into evidence. Indeed, most litigators will affirm that the mere process of determining what should be discoverable can itself consume the lion's share of the cost of litigation. Certainly—if there is a desire to cause delay—depositions and interrogatories provide a fertile field for the recalcitrant party.

Finally, the high cost of pretrial discovery, which frequently exceeds the total cost of the actual trial would preclude most individuals and many small unions from pursuing their claims under the Act. If a deposition is taken, someone has to pay for the transcript and review the deposition for accuracy and relevance.

Once pretrial discovery is made available, it is difficult if not impossible to limit its scope. Moreover, the use of pretrial discovery virtually mandates that the parties retain counsel to represent them in these prehearing procedures. It is not conceivable that this encumbrance of the process is in the best interests of those seeking to enforce their rights under the Act.

The procedural delays currently associated with enforcement of the provisions of the National Labor Relations Act are obviously not attributable to employers alone or to employer resistance to union organizational efforts. The Board is also at fault for failing to decide issues expeditiously, which is caused in part by its uncertainty as to how to interpret the Act in light of current political pressures.

On the other hand, by comparison to the Title VII experience, Board delay has not resulted in the absolute loss of the individual or group rights that the Board is purportedly seeking to protect. The Supreme Court has held that there is no statute of limitations that governs the Board's ability to enforce its orders, though the doctrine of laches can be asserted to challenge a Board complaint to enforce a Board order.[4] The applicable standard is inexcusable delay and prejudice to the moving party.[5]

Yet, no case has been found where a Board enforcement effort has been dismissed because of laches. Even where three years intervened between the Board's issuance of a bargaining order and its filing of an action to enforce the order, which delay the Board admitted was caused by "a breakdown in communication between the office that referred the case for enforcement and the office responsible for seeking enforcement,"[6] the court refused to dismiss the complaint on the grounds of laches. In the court's view, if a majority of employees are currently no longer interested in the union's representation, relief is available by conducting another election after the one-year waiting period.

By comparison, under Title VII federal courts have dismissed an EEOC complaint because of delay even where the fault is shared by the respondent employer.[7] Considering these differing judicial approaches to this issue, adoption of the Title VII pattern—with its attachment to the litigation model—could result in even more individuals losing their opportunity to enforce their rights under the Act.

Professor Morris' suggestion that the Board should make greater use of its ability to obtain injunctive relief under Section 10(j) of the Act must be evaluated in light of the legal restraints that apply to securing this type of extraordinary relief.[8] As a basic rule, federal courts do not grant injunctive relief under Section 10(j) unless the Board can show the necessity for "preserving the status quo or of preventing irreparable harm."[9] For this reason, injunctive relief has limited applicability to the arsenal of enforcement weapons under the National Labor Relations Act since reinstatement and back pay are normally available so that the element of irreparable harm is difficult to prove. More

---

[4] NLRB v. Katz, 369 US 736, 50 LRRM 2177 (1962).

[5] NLRB v. Best Glass Co., 119 LRRM 2884 (CA 9, 1985).

[6] NLRB v. Michigan Rubber Prods., Inc., 738 F2d 111, 113, 116 LRRM 2876 (CA 6, 1984).

[7] See, e.g., EEOC v. Kelly Mfg. Co., Supra note 1.

[8] Boire v. Pilot Freight Carriers, Inc., 515 F2d 1185, 89 LRRM 2908 (CA 5, 1975), cert. denied, 426 US 934 (1976).

[9] Kaynard v. Mego Corp., 633 F2d 1026, 1033, 105 LRRM 2723 (CA 2, 1980).

importantly, the legal procedures involved in an application for injunctive relief entail additional opportunities delaying adjudication of the underlying dispute.

The unfortunate lesson of the past 50 years is that delay is inherent in the administration of the National Labor Relations Act. Moreover, there will always be employers and unions who will foster delay if it works to their advantage. But, drastic changes in the basic system that will layer it with new administrative or judicial bodies or that will superimpose the judicial prototype will not have the hoped for beneficial result.

Commentary

ROBERT J. RABIN*

Professor Morris has put forward a comprehensive blueprint for change. But it does not call for radical surgery. Quite the contrary, it is a prescription for the maximum change that can be achieved within the existing statutory structure of the NLRA, given the present political climate. I want to comment about just a few aspects of his paper. These are not criticisms in the sense that I think he is wrong, but questions that need to be explored further or that give rise to some opposing points of view.

The first concerns the pervasive shadow that has been cast by most of the papers in this volume. And that is, does anybody really care about NLRA reform? Does it really matter whether the Board's processes are improved, or has the action moved elsewhere? Laurence Gold's opening comments suggested to me that "he doth protest too much." The fact that he is concerned about the Board's lack of enforcement power suggests that if the Act were given teeth, things would be better. But then he protested very, very much, to the point of despair. That may imply that no amount of minor surgery is going to do the necessary job.

To put it another way, if Morris is correct that better enforcement of the statute would mean fewer employer violations, would unions really win more elections? Or are some of the other observers, such as Walter Oberer and Timothy O'Reilly, correct in concluding that what troubles workers cannot be addressed by the union movement?

* Professor of Law, Syracuse University.

Second, Professor Morris did not address questions of substantive law but deliberately focused his attention on procedures. But we cannot ignore that some substantive doctrines affect the unions' ability to organize and to bargain effectively. To raise several examples, the Board's recent decisions concerning the scope of protected, concerted activity[1] and interrogation[2] both have an impact upon the organizing stage. And the Board's holdings on relocation of work during the contract term[3] add a new burden on what a union can do in negotiating provisions for job security.

Third, I hope Morris' suggestion about a labor court is more a straw man to set up the case for internal reform of the Board than a true brief for a labor court. The major model of administrative law in the country today involves administrative agencies. Administrative agencies reside in our constitutional scheme somewhere between courts and legislatures. They are given a broad blueprint for action; they then implement it within these general guidelines, and their work is reviewed by the courts. There are problems with that model, and much of the thinking about administrative law is in turmoil on that account.[4] But there is nothing special about the labor experience that calls for singling out its administration and giving it the status of a court.

Indeed, I think there is much to Professor Oberer's point that an administration is entitled to administer the laws to reflect the mandate of its constituency.[5] The doctrinal shifts in the Board reflect those changes, and that is proper as long as the Board stays within its statutory command and follows the kinds of procedures that Professor Morris discusses.

Fourth, as Morris points out, none of his proposals are worth much if the body politic is unable to pressure the President to appoint the kind of people with the vision that is called for. That is a practical problem for which he proposes no solution. That also is reflective of the underlying malaise that pervades the

---

[1] Meyers Indus., 268 NLRB 493, 115 LRRM 1025 (1984).

[2] Rossmore House, 269 NLRB 1176, 116 LRRM 1025 (1984).

[3] Illinois Coil Spring Co., Milwaukee Spring Div., 268 NLRB 601, 115 LRRM 1065 (1984).

[4] *See* Bazelon, *Coping with Technology Through the Legal Process*, 61 CORNELL L. Rev. 817 (1977), and compare the opinions of Judges Bazelon and Leventhal in Ethyl Corp. v. Environmental Protection Agency, 541 F2d 1 (CA DC, 1976).

[5] *See* Justice Rehnquist's dissent in Motor Vehicle Mfrs. Assn. v. State Farm Mut. Ins. Co., 463 US 29 (1983).

papers in this volume regarding the political failure of the union movement.

Fifth, turning to the particular items of reform that were discussed, we find some dispute among the participants. For example, Professor Morris made a strong suggestion for the use of discovery, one that I found myself embracing when I first read his paper. But Andrea Christenson and Rosemary Collyer argue cogently against such a device, questioning whether the benefits gained through discovery outweigh the delays that it would impose.

Morris also mentions the increased use of discretionary injunctions when charges are filed against employers. It is hard to justify the present imbalance in the issuance of Section 8(b) injunctions compared with those under Section 8(a). It is therefore heartening to note General Counsel Collyer's endorsement of the Section 10(j) injunction device and her assurance of a "policy of aggressive and imaginative utilization of Section 10(j) proceedings."

Finally we come to the heart of the Morris paper, which is a call for rule making. When I first read this suggestion in the paper, I thought of Rip Van Winkle awakening after 20 years and saying, "Hey, I have a good idea. How about rule making?" For the idea, as Professor Morris mentioned, was advocated a long time ago, perhaps for the first time in a systematic way by Merton Bernstein.[6] But it has never been tried. And perhaps the fact that it has never been used suggests that it indeed is the answer to many of the ills that face us.

Those of us who went to law school a long time ago ought to remember that labor law was once the model for all administrative law. But if you read a modern administrative law book you will find that the current labor law experience is completely "out of sync." Most agencies function through the process of rule making; it is the norm for dealing with problems under our present administrative system.

Morris presents some very compelling reasons why rule making ought to be followed. In fact two Board members—Don Zimmerman and Patricia Dennis[7]—have supported this position

---

[6] *The NLRB's Adjudication-Rule Making Dilemma Under the Administrative Procedure Act,* 79 YALE L.J. 571 (1970).

[7] Zimmerman, *Restoring Stability in the Implementation of the National Labor Relations Act,* 1 LAB. LAW 1, 6–9, (1985); Dennis, *A Principled Approach to NLRB Decisionmaking,* 1 LAB. LAW 483, 496 (1985).

in print. And the Board's present General Counsel in her comments at least suggests that it ought to be tried on some limited basis.

I want to emphasize just one of many reasons that support rule making. It is the likelihood that through this process the Board will come up with both factual and empirical support for its conclusions, and also will be able to articulate the reason for its decisions in a way that courts can understand.

I always tell my students in labor law that we read cases in pairs. First we read a judicial opinion that talks about why the court is supposed to defer to the expertise of the administrative agency. Then we read the decision of the Board and find no demonstrated expertise. Rather, we find the Board repeating time-worn slogans or conclusory statements. I think the rule-making process would enhance tremendously the Board's capability for doing this kind of thing.

Andrea Christensen suggested another argument for rule making. She referred to the fact that employers are able to better prepare their cases before the Board. That may be one reason for the union side's dissatisfaction with the Board's processes. I discovered that in my own practice. I have worked both sides of the street at different times, and I have been amazed at the vast disparity in resources that management could pour into a case compared with a union. Perhaps rule making would allow unions to pool their resources and meet management on equal terms in advocating their positions before the Board.

Epilogue

ON TIPPING THE BALANCE IN LABOR-MANAGEMENT RELATIONS

Stephen I. Schlossberg*

We are now seeing two extreme strains in this country, like two ends of a scale with wide variations in between. Pulling at one end of the scale are those who would want to continue and accelerate the same hyperadversarial relationships that have characterized American labor relations for so many years. The Wagner and Taft-Hartley Acts were premised on the existence of such a relationship. At the other end of the scale are those who are boldly experimenting with various forms of labor-management cooperation, efforts which offer the promise of a rewarding future.

The question is, which way will the scale balance, and which way will the employers and unions in the middle move? Those in the middle are the ones who have not yet decided whether they are willing to take a chance or else are afraid to take a chance until they are forced to do so. Suppose they opt for the adversial way? If that happens, if that side of the scale prevails, then we must also recognize the obvious: that this is a pendulum society. Social and economic climates change drastically from time to time, and the whole gestalt, the whole feeling and mood of the country changes. In the 1800s and in the early part of this century the most hostile relations imaginable existed between employers and workers, almost industrial warfare. We must not forget the episodes from that violent history in Pennsylvania, in Colorado, in West Virginia, in Illinois, and in Detroit. All over this country there were hostile manifestations of what was really a nonrelationship between labor and management.

Shall it be a return to open warfare, or shall it be a movement toward the goal of cooperation? Which way the labor-manage-

* Deputy Under Secretary of Labor for Labor-Management Relations and Cooperative Programs.

406

ment community moves will largely determine the kinds of labor laws that we will have in the coming years. Because it may now be too late to convert the National Labor Relations Act into an instrument of labor-management cooperation, we must begin thinking about the kind of legislation we would want to replace or supplement that statute.

Before we can consider such legislation, however, we must decide what kind of labor relations we want. John Sheridan of Sheridan Associates, a firm that counsels companies on how to remain union-free, has offered some startling advice. He said:

> My main concern is that American Business has won too much. The take backs, the recent Greyhound Strike, indeed just about everything that has happened going back to the PATCO strike, portrays a substantially weakened labor movement, and when labor truly becomes weak, management moves in like a shark. As the pendulum swings even further over to management's side, we will see abuses of employees and employee rights. We will see high-handed behavior and unlawful acts. Nevertheless, companies have flaunted the law and will continue to do so partly because they perceive unions to be weak and partly because they see the government disengaged. Over the long pull this will result in the pendulum finally beginning to swing back in labor's favor.[1]

Then he finishes with a little piece of advice. He says, "Don't resort to overkill in dealing with labor or in designing labor policy in this setting."

I think Sheridan has given us advice worth heeding. But I could be wrong. Yet, even if there is short-term advantage in continuing to overplay the adversial game, surely in the long run the pendulum is going to swing the other way. It therefore seems evident that long-range enlightened self-interest of employers and unions does not lie in warfare and polarized behavior but at the other end of the scale. The positive results we are already seeing are so compelling that one has to take leave of one's senses to opt for war when peace can produce such abundance and a promise of more.

The most impressive thing I have seen around the country is that some employers have demonstrated courage and trust in labor-management cooperation. For instance, General Motors and others, such as Ford and Xerox, have led the way in cooper-

---

[1] CCH *Human Resources Management: Ideas & Trends in Personnel,* May 4, 1984, at 67.

ative programs that are not only likely to further the self-interest of the corporation, the union, and the workers and managers who work there, but the whole economy and the whole country. This is so because in plant after plant and situation after situation these innovative programs are proving that if you convince people that they really matter and are not marginal, that they are not mere extensions of machines and tools but are human beings who are part of the team, you will get from those people the kind of commitment, the kind of urgency in the work they are doing, and the kind of pride and joy in their work, that will make them and the enterprise competitive with workers of any nation in the world. Their labor will take on new value because it is being produced by a work force that is committed, and by a work force that believes it has a real say in the running of the enterprise, which is where the workers spend most of their waking hours. The result will be increased productivity, quality, and efficiency and an almost total elimination of unnecessary absenteeism and waste. I firmly believe that the quality and value which follow from this kind of commitment can be the key to this country's success in global competition.

We cannot compete by destroying the strongest consumer market in the world and paying the wages that are paid in Korea or in China. The United States is the greatest market in the world; consequently, the competition that we are trying to engage in is a competition which recognizes both the value of this market and the American value system. That system permits Americans to hope that they can live a little better tomorrow and that their children will surely live even better. In other words, that the American people can have an ever-rising standard of living while also paying attention to some of the important things in our society other than just money. Among other things, we must pay attention to such values as equal employment opportunity and the opportunity for everyone to be employed, and we want some form of industrial democracy.

It is not just dreamers, academicians, and those who believe in tooth fairies who are pushing these notions. There are some farsighted employers who are willing to take risks to achieve these same goals because they understand that the game is worth the candle. They have made the necessary commitment. Nevertheless, some of those who embark on this course may not succeed. From time to time some will stub their toes, make mistakes, and falter because we are all human beings, not angels. There will be mistakes, and there will be occasional failures.

Nevertheless, when a company is ready to make that kind of commitment, it will be rewarded in many economic and non-economic ways. I do not believe that these companies do it just for increased productivity, just for quality, and just for the bottom line on the financial statement. There is a strong strain in the economy and society of America today that wants to do certain things because they are right and decent. I see this among some of the companies that are leading the way in cooperative work programs.

The unions are not off the hook in this matter. They are very much involved. And unions that insist on doing things the old way will have to understand that this is not the time to go to war; this is not the time for "class war" militancy. This is not the time to be insensitive about relationships. When a union representative calls the boss "a son-of-a-bitch" in the news media during a collective bargaining situation, the residue will come back to haunt that union during the next few years of ruptured relations. Workers and the public listen to the radio, view the TV news, and read the newspapers; and I hope that corporations and unions read each other's house organs. So to move in the direction of cooperation is not easy; it requires courage. It particularly requires sensitivity in order to create a constructive climate. It is easy to alienate people who are important to an operation. Thus, if you are a union, you put yourself at some risk by throwing away the old way of doing things—the hate-the-boss-and-fight syndrome. But that approach does not work anymore. And you cannot do it half way. You cannot talk about cooperation and about working together on the one hand, while calling each other names on the other hand, whether the name-calling is by the union or by management. Such epithets as "communist," "fascist," "tyrant," and "racketeer" have no place in a cooperative environment.

What does this mean in the way of legislation? How should we design a labor law bill for the future? And I mean the future, not now, for I remember the "Pandora's box" of earlier legislative efforts. But somewhere down the road the pendulum will swing, and then it may be appropriate to try to make some corrections in the legal structures that determine or influence the relationship between labor and management. And if we are determined to continue with an adversarial system, unions will then want substantial amendments to the National Labor Relations Act to make it easier to establish a union majority, such as allowing use of a card-check as is commonly the practice under Canadian statutes, and they will want to make it easier to win strikes by prohibiting the hiring of replacements for strikers. Such polarized legislation is easy to construct.

If we look at the other side of the scale, however, and if we can foresee that the economy will be weighted toward cooperation, the job of legislative drafting may be even more difficult, but not impossible. A look at the past may help put the problem in perspective. If employers decide that workers and their unions can make a meaningful contribution, and if unions begin to see what they need to do, the task is attainable. Unions should remember that they were originally organized to obtain for workers what management in a cooperative mode is now willing to give them. The 50 years of Labor Board existence have witnessed a transition from the time when unions obtained from employers restrictive work rules and high wages, which management yielded in order to keep its so-called management rights, its control over decisionmaking, and the running of the business. Employers wanted to keep the camel's nose out of the tent. But now that has changed. They have found that the camel has something to bring to the tent, that the worker on the shop floor and the union may have a good notion of what can help the enterprise succeed. There is not a single labor leader in America—whether he or she will admit it or not—who does not know that an enterprise has to make a profit to exist, so it is in the interest of the union and the employees to help provide a constructive, healthy, and profitable business. If we put this combination together we have a recipe for success.

In some of the newer programs it is difficult to tell by looking on the shop floor who is the manager and who is the local union president. They may look and dress very much alike, and they are probably good friends. For example, at General Motors' Pontiac Fiero plant the local union president sits every morning with the plant manager at the meeting of the people who operate the plant. What is his role there? He is a member of the plant manager's staff, and he makes suggestions and helps run the plant. But in the afternoon he is handling grievances and running the union's business. The distinction between labor and management has thus been blurred in many of the successful programs. It does not matter what the programs are called—quality of work life programs, employee involvement, teams, quality circles, work councils, or whatever. The form of the structure, the mechanism, is not very important. What is important are the attitudes and symbols, the sensitivity that persons and parties have for each other. Building trust is important.

Do we need to tinker with the legal system? Yes, we do need to tinker. We need to examine existing laws and see how they affect labor-management cooperation. It may be necessary to change some laws, including the NLRA. If the laws are construed solely in the context of hostile, adversarial relations, either the constructions must change or the statutory language must change. If we are to progress along this leading edge type of society, the laws should not forbid the parties from blurring distinctions between management and labor. If we move from a hostile, adversarial society to a cooperative society, all of the old rules cannot apply. So what do we do with a statute that is not adjusted to the new world? We either adjust the statute or adjust the world. We must give serious thought to how the NLRA can be adjusted, either by interpretation or by amendment, so that it will help the parties rather than impede them in working cooperatively in the labor-management relations of the future.

INDEX